THE MAGIC HAND OF SAM PRESENTING TO THE FIRST CONGRESS, THE NAME OF GEORGE WASHINGTON, AS COMMANDER-IN-CHIEF OF THE AMERICAN FORCES. (SEE CHAP. XXXV.)

UNIV.
OF
MICH.

"SAM:"

OR THE

HISTORY OF MYSTERY.

BY C. W. WEBBER.

AUTHOR OF "THE HUNTER NATURALIST," ETC.

CINCINNATI:
H. M. RULISON, QUEEN CITY PUBLISHING HOUSE, 115½ MAIN ST.
PHILADELPHIA:
QUAKER CITY PUBLISHING HOUSE, 32 SOUTH THIRD ST.
1855.

Stereotyped and Printed by
WILLIAM OVEREND & CO.,
CINCINNATI.

TABLE OF CONTENTS.

PART I.

CHAPTER I.

CHAPTER VIII.

CHAPTER IX.

CHAPTER X.

CHAPTER XI.

CHAPTER XII.

CHAPTER XIII.

CHAPTER XIV.

CHAPTER XV.

CHAPTER XVI.

PART II.

CHAPTER XVII.

CHAPTER XVIII.

CHAPTER XIX.

CHAPTER XX.

CHAPTER XXI.

CHAPTER XXII.

CHAPTER XXIII.

CHAPTER XXIV.

CHAPTER XXV.

CHAPTER XXVI.

CHAPTER XXVII.

CHAPTER XXVIII.

CHAPTER XXIX.

CHAPTER XXX.

CHAPTER XXXI.

CHAPTER XXXII.

CHAPTER XXXIII.

CHAPTER XXXIV.

CHAPTER XXXV.

CHAPTER XXXVI.

CHAPTER XXXVII.

CHAPTER XXXVIII.

CHAPTER XXXIX.

CHAPTER XL.

CHAPTER XLI.

CHAPTER XLII.

"SAM:"

OR, THE

HISTORY OF MYSTERY.

PART I.

CHAPTER I.

The Mysterious birth of "Sam"—Some of his Youthful Feats and Characteristic Eccentricities.

ONCE, when Earth, the good mother, was in grievous tribulation because of her children, and a voice of wailing was heard among the nations, a great cloud grew up suddenly in the East, and there seemed a sign of fire and tempest within its bosom.

All the peoples felt the shadow of this great cloud upon them, but they knew not what the strange portent meant, except that, to certain minds among them, it seemed that this gathering of mighty forces must be pregnant with some MYSTERY that was to step out from its bosom soon, as if the "Son of the morning" came forth from the caves of night, and that this mystery, too, was most like to stand as an embodiment, whether an incarnated embodiment or not, of some new birth of regeneration to all mankind.

Though it was thus the wise man spoke, or rather hoped, yet there was no one who knew these things to be true; therefore the people trembled, and were afraid, while the turmoil of this cloudy PRESENCE rolled with its slow shadow over them; and when they saw it take its way toward the West, over the solitary sea, they wondered greatly whither it might be speeding. Only the Viking's wandering prow had furrowed that solitary sea, as yet, when the great cloud set forth upon its face; but there were daring men who said its shadow was a protection, and that no harm could come to any bark which sailed beneath it.

And soon, from the port of Palos, in Andalusia, a fleet of little ships, like three cockleshells, went dancing forth upon the open sea, and were quickly hid from view beneath that shadow. A mighty sailor stood within these deckless hulls, whose deep-visioned eyes saw beyond all shadows. (1492, 3d August.)

And when men saw the mighty sailor forth, then from many a port went many a vessel, to sail within his wake, and all the world was filled with wonder of the golden miracles those ships brought back. And many a gay, adventuring host went shining underneath that shadow, that its slow glooms would not give up.

At length (Dec. 11th, 1620), the great cloud, which for more than a hundred years had wandered up and down, brooding upon the sea, gathered together, and amidst a mighty anthem of the waves and winds, struck upon a headland rock, at Plymouth, and its voluminous folds, wrapping the snows for a moment, shivered as in a throe, then, thin and dim, commenced to fade upon the icy air.

Now, as the shattered cloud rose up, a strange, frail ship that seemed to have been hidden within its womb of shadow, lay trembling feebly in the offing on subsiding waves. The name of the little ship was "Mayflower."

But when the cloud was all gone, there lay stretched upon the snow-covered summit of that headland rock a gigantic form, which seemed most like some helpless and misshapen Titan, which had been thus struck dumb, blind and sprawling out of the thunders of a tempest-birth, and hurled upon the desolation.

The trees yet rocked behind the passing storm when the bright sun came out, glittering keenly from the angles of the frosty rocks, upon this pale, ungainly specter, which, born thus of the thunder, seemed the incarnation of some new and powerful FORCE.

Touched by the sun, its lips moved in inarticulate sounds, that seemed in natural consonance with the groanings of the struggling forest, which bent its trees like grass-spears beneath the heavy head, thus pillowed on them all unconsciously.

The great arms of the monstrous Youngling, cast wildly out in spasms of a troubled awakening, in the involuntary clasp of drowsy fingers, tore the old oaks from rocky fissures, and the mighty stretching of its restless feet made maelstroms with the cliff-fronts, which they tumbled into the sea.

Far away upon the crest of hills, and upon the promontories of that broken shore, the tufted red men gathered, warned by the sounding tremors in the earth and air of some strange advent. And now they thronged and gazed upon this majestic wonder, which seemed to have lain down, as if upon its own couch, within the House-of-Sky, covering with its giant limbs the land of which the pestilence had made them but of late afraid.*

Now, with a slow, upward heave, the shoulders of the Youngling arise beneath the sun, and as he sits erect with mute, upturned face and unsealed eyes, the bowed forest trees swing up again with a clangor that would have scared Behemoth, stepping on the mountains.

He spreads with lazy stretch his arms abroad, feeling among the hills—and now, with quick sense, his unused fingers clutch upon the groups of shrinking red men, and thrilled by the touch of struggling life, he lifts them, fumbling, as if with baubles, toward his mouth.

The dangling stoics howl their death-whoop while they swing through mid-air by their scalp-locks, and at the strange sound the Mighty Infant, with loosened grasp, throws up its hands in awe, for now, through eyes dim-opened in the startle,

---

* On the 16th of March, 1620, the English received a visit from one of the natives, who came boldly into Plymouth, calling out *Welcome Englishmen!* His name was Samoset, a Sagamore, who had learned a little English from the fishing vessels that had been on the coast. He informed the adventurers that the place they occupied, was called by the Indians Patuxet, and that all the people formerly inhabiting the place, died of an extraordinary sickness about four years since.—*Antiquarian Researches—E. Hoyt.*

The spot to which Providence had directed the planters had, a few years before, been rendered entirely a desert by a pestilence, which had likewise swept over the neighboring tribes, and desolated almost the whole sea-board of New England. When the Pilgrims landed, there were the traces of a previous population but not one living inhabitant. Smoke from fires in the remote distance alone indicated the vicinity of natives. Miles Standish, " the best linguist" among the Pilgrims, as well as the best soldier, with an exploring party, was able to discover wigwams, but no tenants. Yet a body of Indians from abroad was soon discovered hovering near the settlements though disappearing when pursued.—*Bancroft's United States.*

the power of the sun has overcome him. Reaching, as if to pluck the glittering toy, his upright form has straightway chinned the hills, and with folded arms, now leaning idly on their barriers, he gazes out upon the spreading space.

Some moving specs upon a far-off lake have caught his vacant eye—his outstretched grasp has reached them—and, gathering an Algonquin fleet within his fingers, he eyes, with unmoved stare, the frail canoes of bark that are crushed within unconscious pressure, then snapping the huge pines that grew along the steppes, he piled a mighty ark in play, that launched with a toss on the same waves, displaced in overflow the pent-up waters with its swing.

As children pick in idleness at any dot upon the sheet, he plucked a wigwam village by the roots, and with a stare and stride, as if their funnel-tops had proved offensive, he tore the idle bowlders from the valleys and built a towering House that would not smoke.

Now, as the sun went up and the awed savages kneeled to him, the giant Infant took a new mood. While he gazed steadfast on the blazing orb, there seemed a gnat, or some ambitious thing, that flitted before his sight. He swept his great hand down and brought the struggler to his face. It pecked and clawed him with a vicious tare, that first aroused him to the sense of pain, and tossing the warlike insect from him, he watched it cleave with unrumpled plumes, the sunward air again. He took the tameless creature down from the skies, and made its eyrie on the House he built!

INFANT SAM LEAPS UPON HIS IMAGINARY BED OF DOWN, HIS HEAD RESTING ON THE ROCKY MOUNTAINS, AND HIS FEET ON PLYMOUTH ROCK — PICKS UP SOME OF HIS BEDFELLOWS, THE ABORIGINES, AND VIEWS THEM WITH A PLAYFUL SMILE; BUT SOON FINDS THEM TO BE THORNY PLAYTHINGS.

CHAPTER II.

The young "Sam" proves a shrewd Citizen—His first Hanging Feat—The early Navigators.

THE young Sam, though born out of a cloud, proved to be rather a sharp-sighted individual. One of the first evidences of this, it will be seen, he gave in a familiar way, when he hung half-a-dozen Quakers on Boston Common, and gave as a reason for it, that "we desire their lives absent, rather than their deaths present."

It is to be supposed that this mythical personage fled from persecution; but then there was a hearty savor in the way in which he attempted to annihilate the Anabaptists, and ruled the distempered Quakers up to Haman's lodgings, which showed he had a genuine relish for persecution, *per se*.

Perhaps it was that Sam thought persecution caused mankind to thrive, for the same reason that we tell our babies, when they are caught out of doors in the summer rain, that the pelting makes them grow. At anyrate Sam took a very original view of matters and things when he found himself suddenly awake upon a new Continent. He had a dim reminiscence of having been badly treated somewhere else, and therefore concluded that it must be best, in his new condition, to treat every one else shrewdly, at least, if not badly—the Quakers and Miantonomah can tell you why! So can Butler, in his Hudibras, who seems to have known something about Sam in his earliest dealings with the simple Narragansetts:

"Our brethren of New England use
Choice malefactors to excuse,
And hang the guiltless in their stead
Of whom the churches have less need;
As lately happened. In a town
There lived a cobbler, and but one,
That out of doctrine could cut use,
And cut men's lives as well as shoes.
This precious brother having slain,
In times of peace, an Indian,
(Not out of malice, but mere zeal,
Because he was an Infidel),
The mighty Tottipottymoy
Sent to our elders an envoy,
Complaining sorely of the breach
Of league held forth by brother patch,
Against the articles in force
Between both churches, his and ours,
For which he prayed the Saints to render
Into his hand or hang the offender.
But they naturally having weighed,
They had no man for him o' the trade.
(A man that serv'd them in a double
Capacity, to teach and cobble),
Resolved to spare him, yet to do
The Indian Hoghgan, Moghgan too,
Impartial justice, in his stead did
Hang an old weaver that was bed-rid.

There had been many adventurings toward the South, before Sam came to raise a nasal hymn within the rocky wilderness, that shook a continent with long reverberations. The Cabots had surveyed the North, Verrazzani, Cartier, Roberval, De la Roche, and noble old Champlain, had named the St. Lawrence, surveyed the Arcadia of the French, and settled Quebec. Ponce de Leon, seeking for the fountain of eternal youth, remained yet an old man, though Spanish commerce, through his superstitious yet chavalric enterprise, won a new passage through the Caribbean Sea and Gulf of Mexico.

Then had come the stubborn Cortez, and many a gallant Knight went down in his miraculous conquest. But Sam, even from the embryo of his cloudy birth, has always thought the proudest thing this Cortez ever did was when he took Pamphilo de Narvaez prisoner.

This is the same person who had been sent by the jealous governor to Cuba to take Cortez prisoner, who, after having declared him an outlaw, was himself easily defeated. He lost an eye in the affray, and his own troops deserted him. When brought into the presence of the man whom he had promised to arrest, he said to him, "Esteem it great good fortune that you have taken me captive." Cortez replied, and with truth, "It is the least of the things I have done in Mexico.

But with all the cark and cant which entered into the composition of his nature, our northern Sam, nevertheless, proves himself, in a general way, to be a right loyal gentleman, that is, not particularly loyal to his king, but a most worshipful servitor of that hard-handed despot who prorogued the Long Parliament. We may as well say, *en passant*, that there seemed to have been a contest between the old Continent and the new, when they managed almost simultaneously to produce Oliver Cromwell and Sam, for they both whined at first and proved themselves reverentially absurd, yet always were victorious. Cromwell conquered an empire, and Sam, a New World.

Being both tyrants, they could not well be contrasted, but the motto of them both seems to have equally been, "Pray to God and keep your powder dry."

Raleigh, the loftiest cavalier the world has ever seen, and Smith — the veritable John Smith — the noblest of adventurers, had long ago formed colonies in Virginia, but not even the dauntless energies of Smith could make them stay colonized respectably, and San Augustine and Jamestown, and the settlements in North Carolina, and on the Chesapeake, had all proved partial failures, since the thirst for gold and wild adventure had mostly led them, rather than what he loves to call the solemn purpose to found an empire, when Sam really came, as we have seen.

CHAPTER III.

First act of Diplomacy on the part of "Sam"—His tender mercies toward the heathen King Philip, and other merciful attributes.

Though the Sam, whose birth and advent we have described, may be considered by the unbelievers as more or less of a myth, because he is not always visible to the naked eye, yet this is no sign — for it is to be remembered that his proportions are too great to be taken in by the gaze of common mortals — and for the same reason that the roar of Niagara makes a silence, thus confounding one sense — that of hearing — with the voice of nature, his great dimensions may confound another — that of sight — seeming to it only a continuation of space.

We shall perceive, however, before this legend is through, that his existence is yet a veritable one, and if we can neither see nor hear him, we can feel him, and that the grip of his giant hand is now, and has been, as unmistakable throughout the land as the shaking of his mighty feet.

Now, as a conscientious historian, we have not set out to prove Sam to have been a saint from the origin, though he may have been a very large baby. On account of his size, his wants were, of course, enormous. A childling of the elements, he could not be expected to have learned much of such unruly parentage, concerning the differences between right and wrong.

Therefore it is not to be considered particularly surprising that "the oldest act of diplomacy recorded in New England" should have been when, in their first parley with Massasoit, the chief of the Wampanoags, one of Sam's people, Mr. Winslow, was dispatched with some handsome presents and a pot of "strong water," to open a negotiation with the shy and simple savage, and that he, tempted by the novel sensations produced by the unknown drink thus offered to him, as a pledge of amity, agreed to "come in" and discuss, with Governor Carver, the terms of a treaty. Then it followed of necessity that "after an exchange of salutations, *refreshments* were placed before the chief, of which he and his people *freely* partook." That "a league of friendship was then agreed on," and that "the Indians departed well pleased with their interview," as says the impartial narrator *— can not reasonably be doubted.

Who can doubt, also, that Sam must have got greatly the better of his ally through the potency of his "refreshments?" Is it not pretty clearly shown in the fact that he actually kept faith with these poor Wampanoags, for about fifty years? But then, having nearly "pushed" King Philip, the haughty successor and grandson of this same Massasoit, "off the end of the log," upon which that good-natured old chief, as the ancient tradition goes, "had welcomed his tired limbs to sit down and rest," he made a characteristic conclusion of a long and terrible war, when, having hunted the unfortunate King through the swamps of New England, like a wolf, for having objected to being pushed off into the mud, he first shot him through the heart, in order to be sure he was dead, and then had him beheaded and quartered, by a man whom he had, as may be supposed, spiritually admonished from his birth to be named "Captain Church," for the express purpose of sanctifying this deed — we mean, of course, as a veracious narrator, that it only sounded better to Sam that such a deed should have been done by something or somebody who bore such a name.

We should not blame him if this were really true, for predilections like this were strictly, peculiarly his own; and, as he first claimed their assertion in his own immense and manly way, we can begin to understand how it was that Sam proved afterward to be such a pet of Oliver Cromwell.

It seems, altogether, a supererogation of pale-gilled Puritanism, that local historians, who presume to write a history of Sam, should so modestly pass over this most characteristic opening incident of his history, for there is quite sufficient grandeur in his nature and his plain-told acts to relieve

* Hoyt's Antiquarian Researches, page 21.

them of any necessary defense of prevaricating cant. The same story, of the first interview with Massasoit, is thus, in other words, narrated by one who seems to have felt himself "spiritually admonished," very much as we have related above concerning Captain Church, to become "the defender of the faith," instead of the historian of Sam.

"The chieftain of a race as yet so new to the Pilgrims, was received with all *the ceremonies* which the condition of the colony permitted. A treaty of friendship was soon completed in few and unequivocal terms. The parties promised to abstain from mutual injuries, and to deliver up offenders. The colonists were to receive assistance if attacked—to render it if Massasoit should be attacked unjustly. The treaty included the confederates of the sachem; it is the oldest act of diplomacy recorded in New England; it was concluded in a day, and, being founded on reciprocal interests, was sacredly kept for more than half a century. Massasoit desired the alliance, for the powerful Narragansetts were his enemies; his tribe, moreover, having become *habituated* to some English luxuries, were willing to establish a traffic, while the emigrants obtained peace, security, and the opportunities of a lucrative commerce."*

The dainty form of speech which, here including everything in the phrases "all the ceremonies which the condition of the colony permitted" skims over the "pot of strong water to the chief," and concludes that Massasoit "having become habituated to some *English* luxuries, was willing to establish a traffic," is too transcendentally rich not to be twenty-seven years in advance—as the Dial has since been published—of the first modest insinuation from the same meridian, that Massasoit, having "left Mr. Winslow in the custody of his men, as a hostage, ventured to the English, by whom he was *hospitably* entertained, and with whom he concluded the treaty, already noticed."†

The voice of Sam, himself, it is said, can yet be heard on any still day, reverberating among the Green Mountains.

---

* Bancroft's United States, vol. 1st, page 317.

† History of the United States of America, by the Rev. Charles A. Goodrich, 23d edition.

"It is all a lie, I gave Massasoit rum!" And that he made a drunken treaty, and that Sam must have held him with his lordly nation by an ascendency of fifty years, in growling, half-subjection, can only be accounted for by the enslaving habits of the "English luxuries" to which the Wampanoags had been introduced.

When the stern, heroic Philip, whose first overt act of war was caused by Sam's characteristic murder of three Indians, whom Philip was accused of having excited to the slaying of one Sansamon, a renegade Indian Missionary—which saintly personage, it seems, Philip thought had been inflicting too much piety and rum upon his nation! Sam now lifted himself up in wrath, striking with his heavy hand at the rebellious chieftain, for rum and piety, at the one blow.

Here are some of the scenes which occurred about these times, and which go to show the comparative metal of these two foes.

The English forces at Hadley, on the Connecticut, had become pressed for provisions and forage, and it was known that a large deposit of wheat, at Deerfield, fifteen miles up the river, was exposed in the stack to easy destruction by the Indians.

Captain Lathrop, with his company of eighty men, with a number of teams and drivers, was accordingly detached by the commander at Hadley, to thrash out the grain and transport it to head-quarters.

"In obedience to his orders, Lathrop proceeded to Deerfield, where Captain Mosely was then posted with a company of colony troops, and having thrashed the grain and loaded his teams, he commenced his march for Hadley, on the 18th of September, 1675. No discovery had been made of the enemy in the vicinity, and probably Lathrop did not apprehend that they were watching his movements; but it seems they were too vigilant to let slip so favorable an opportunity of depriving the English of such a valuable acquisition of stores.

"For the distance of about three miles after leaving Deerfield meadow, Lathrop's march lay through a very level country, closely wooded, where he was every moment exposed to an attack on either flank; at the termination of this distance, near the south point of *Sugar-loaf Hill*, the road approximated Connecticut river, and the left was in some measure protected. At the village now called *Muddy Brook*, in the southernly part of Deerfield, the road crossed a small stream, bordered by a narrow morass, from which the village has its name; though more appropriately it should be denominated *Bloody Brook*, by which it was for some time known.

"Before arriving at the point of intersection with the brook, the road for about half a mile ran parallel to the morass, then crossing, it continued to the south point of Sugar-loaf Hill, traversing what is now the home-lots, on the east side of the village. As the morass was thickly covered with brush, the place of crossing afforded a favorable point for surprise.

"On discovering Lathrop's march, a body of upward of seven hundred Indians planted themselves in ambuscade at this point, and lay eagerly waiting to pounce upon him while passing the morass. Without scanning the woods in his front and flanks, or suspecting the snare laid for him, Lathrop arrived at the fatal spot, crossed the morass with the principal part of his force, and halted to allow time for his teams to drag through their loads. The critical moment had arrived — the Indians instantly poured a heavy and destructive fire upon the column, and rushed furiously to close attack. Confusion and dismay succeeded. The troops broke and scattered, fiercely pursued by the Indians, whose great superiority enabled them to attack at all points. Hopeless was the situation of the scattered troops, and they resolved to sell their lives in a vigorous struggle.

"Covering themselves with trees, the bloody conflict now became a severe trial of skill in sharp shooting, in which life was the stake. Difficult would it be to describe the havoc, barbarity and misery that ensued. 'Fury raged, and shuddering pity quit the sanguine field,' while desperation stood pitted at 'fearful odds,' to unrelenting ferocity.

"The dead, the dying, the wounded, strewed the ground in all directions, and Lathrop's devoted force was soon reduced to a small number, and resistance became faint. At length the unequal struggle terminated in the annihilation of nearly the whole of the English; only seven or

BLOODY MASSACRE OF THE WHITES NEAR DEERFIELD. (CHAP. III.)

eight escaped from the bloody scene to relate the dismal tale, and the wounded were indiscriminately butchered.

"Captain Lathrop fell in the early part of the action; the whole loss, including teamsters, amounted to ninety. The company was a choice corps of young men, from the county of Essex, in Massachusetts — many from the most respectable families. Hubbard says, 'they were the flower of the country, none of whom were ashamed to speak with the enemy in the gate.' Captain Lathrop was from Salem, Massachusetts.

"Captain Mosely, at Deerfield, between four and five miles distant, hearing the musketry, made a rapid march for the relief of Lathrop, and arriving at the close of the struggle, found the Indians stripping and mangling the dead. Promptly rushing on, in compact order, he broke through the enemy, and charging back cut down all within the range of his shot, and at length drove the remainder through the adjacent swamp and further west, and after several hours of gallant fighting, compelled them to seek safety in the more distant forest. His lieutenants, Savage and Pickering, often led the troops, and distinguished themselves in a particular manner by their skill and persevering resolution.

"Just at the close of the action Major Treat, who, on the morning of the day, had marched toward Northfield, arrived on the ground with one hundred men, consisting of English, Pequot and Mohegan Indians, and shared in the final pursuit of the enemy. The gallant Mosely lost but two men in the various attacks, and seven or eight only were wounded. Probably the Indians had expended most of their ammunition in the action with Lathrop, and occasionally fought with bows and spears."

CHAPTER IV.

Specimens of "Sam's" savage battles with the Indian Tribes—The character of his Retribution.

THIS sanguinary battle, only proved that the young Sam was, as yet, too indifferent to danger to be sufficiently cautious in his military movements, because having let his people loose, to go eating wild grapes, just before the fatal attack commenced, and while he might have reasonably expected something of the sort, he succeeded in getting himself soundly drubbed. But it affords a good foil to his next act of important retribution, in which he thoroughly avenged this earliest and most serious error of his adolescence.

It is something after this fashion that the story runs. It seems that the commissioners of the colonies, who, as their representatives had by this time gotten so far along in the game of "marbles" as "plump-keeps" with the rifle, and then, from this striking stand-point of individuality, to playing partners at "long-taw" in the ring, had necessarily entered into solemn articles of confederation.

Having assembled in the name of the "United Colonies," they declared that the Narragansetts "had been deeply accessory in the present outrages," (which meant, of course, in the singular number, the late defeat of Lathrop, etc., etc., understood,) and determined that an expedition should be carried into their country; and so follows the account of this famous expedition, which resulted in one of the most savagely desperate battles ever fought in any country.

On the 9th of December, the Massachusetts and Plymouth troops, assembled at Dedham and marched about twenty-seven miles, to Woodcock's plantation; thence continuing their march through Seconek, Providence, and over Patuxet river, they arrived at Wickford, the place intended for head-quarters. On the route, Captain Mosely surprised and captured thirty-six of the enemy, and parties detached from Wickford, traversed the country in various directions; one of which burned one hundred and fifty cabins, and killed and captured several Indians. Prentice's dragoons penetrated the country as far as Pettyquamscott, which they found the enemy had burned, after killing fifteen of the inhabitants. The next day, the 18th, the whole army advanced to that place, and were joined by the Connecticut forces under Major Treat, who on his march had killed and taken a number of the enemy.

The Indians had been apprised of the designs of the English against the country, in time to prepare for their reception. Their best warriors had collected and chosen a position in a large swamp, in the center of which, on an elevation containing five or six acres, they had constructed a work of palisades, and encompassed it with a sort of hedge, or rude abattis, through which was only one principal passage into the work, and this over a long log stretching across a brook, defended by suitable flanks; and at one angle of the place, was a low gap, covered by a log four or five feet high, which might be scaled; but near this was a sort of block-house so placed as to enfilade this weak point. The fortification in every part presented a formidable defense against musketry; and from the nature of the surrounding swamp, the approach was difficult.*

The destruction of Pettyquamscott, was unfortunate for Winslow's army; for here they expected to find a cover from the inclemency of the weather; and *Bull's garrison* at this place, which had also been destroyed, would have furnished

* The site of this place is in the town of South Kingston, Rhode Island, seven or eight miles west of the south ferry to Newport.

a place of defense in case of misfortune. Deprived of shelter, the troops were compelled to remain through a stormy night, with no cover but the heavens, and as the weather was extremely cold they suffered severely. Early in the morning of the 19th, Winslow put the army in motion, to attack the enemy. The distance was about sixteen miles — the snow deep—and the provisions were carried on the backs of the men. At one o'clock in the afternoon, guided by an Indian, the army reached the skirts of the swamp, where a party of the enemy had taken post. This was instantly attacked, and the Indians driven into their works. Four companies of the van troops immediately rushed through the swamp, and accidentally arriving at the log gap, mounted that angle of the fort, but were soon compelled to fall back to avoid the destructive fire of the enemy, poured from the block-house. Reinforced by two other companies another attempt was made on the same point, and, by a most gallant charge over the log, the troops entered the fort and beat the enemy from a flanker, and notwithstanding the severity of the fire from other points, maintained it; but the enemy continuing their resistance, with great obstinacy—victory hung in doubtful suspense. The remainder of the army now pressing through the swamp, entered the fort at the point that had been carried, and the contest continued about three hours, but still with doubtful success. The enemy, driven from one covert to another, poured the English a fatal fire, reluctantly giving up their ground, and some were driven out of the fort. Captain Church, who was acting as aid to General Winslow, at the head of a volunteer party, about this time dashed through the fort, and got into the swamp in the rear, where he made a destructive fire in the rear, of a party of the enemy, who had there taken post, and were pouring in their fire upon the English; and charging with his usual gallantry, again entered the place, driving the Indians before him. But this exploit was not achieved without a severe wound. Thus attacked in different directions—forced from their covert places, and fast falling by the fire of the English the warriors gave up the contest, and fled into the wilderness.

The Indian cabins, amounting to about six hundred, were now set on fire, and in a few moments everything in the interior of the fort was involved in a blaze, and a scene of horror was now exhibited. Several hundred of the Indians strewed the ground on all sides; about three hundred miserable women and children, with lamentable shrieks, were running in every direction to escape the flames, in which many of the wounded, as well as the helpless old men, were seen broiling and roasting, and adding to the terrors of the scene by their agonizing yells. The most callous heart must have been melted to pity at so awful a spectacle.

The Indians who escaped fled to a cedar swamp not far distant, and passed the night without fire, or food, or covering, but that afforded by the boughs of trees. By information afterward obtained from a Narragansett chief, it was ascertained that they lost about seven hundred warriors at the fort, and three hundred who died of their wounds; the whole number in the place, at the commencement of the attack, was reckoned at about four thousand.

After the destruction of the place, Winslow, about sunset, commenced his march for Pettyquamscott, in a snow-storm, carrying most of his dead and wounded, where he arrived a little after midnight, with his worn-down troops. Several whose wounds probably were not mortal, overcome with cold, died on the march, and the next day thirty-four were buried in one grave. Many were severely frozen, and about four hundred so disabled that they were unfit for duty. The whole number killed and wounded was about two hundred; among the former were Captains Davenport, Gardner and Johnson, of Massachusetts, and Captains Gallup, Seely, and Marshall, of Connecticut; and Captain Mason, of the latter province, and Lieutenant Upham, of the former, afterward died of their wounds.

This expedition against the Narragansetts was conducted with spirit, and the attack on the fort exhibited the most obstinate valor on the part of the English. Much, no doubt, was due to the officers who led the troops to the assault, who were men of no common stamp. Though some had been in the service the preceding summer, and had seen hard fighting, they were little acquainted with systematic war.* To

* Captain Mosely had been an old privateer at Jamaica, and probably one of the buccaneers.—*Hutchinson*, vol. i, p. 262.

their bone and nerve, and not to skill were they indebted for their success, and the soldiers were of the same character. But, with more art and prudence, they would have achieved a victory with less expense of lives. As the assault was not made by surprise, it is obvious it was too precipitate. Had the fort been reconnoitered, and the attack made simultaneously on several points, according to a preconcerted plan, it might have been carried with a comparatively small loss on the part of the assailants. The conflagration of the cabins, *after the enemy had left the place*, was an injudicious step. Had they been saved, a comfortable lodging would have been afforded for the English, the succeeding night, the dangerous march through the snow, incumbered with the wounded, avoided, and probably many lives been saved. Captain Church readily perceived the consequences of destroying the cabins, and when he saw they were to be fired, he remonstrated against it, and persuaded the commander to put a stop to the measure; but, being then out of the fort, the conflagration became general, before the orders could be transmitted to the officers within.

We believe it was a sort of Reign-of-Terror successor of Sam, who succeeded in describing his own face by the happy phrase, "Imagine a tiger pitted with the small-pox," which disease was one of the blessings benevolently bequeathed by Sam, along with his "first best gift," the "strong water," to the Indians.

Well, if you can imagine this New-World personage, who instead of handling these Indians like baubles by their scalp-locks any longer, had now his marred features seamed with the clefts of tomahawk, and spear, and arrow, while his fair skin was all bruised, like shattered glass, with the pale scars where bullets stunned him, you will see that the Young Sam, as well as Mirabeau, had suffered a sort of small-pox in his heroic vindication of what he called the Rights of Humanity!

It will be perceived from the venerable historian's account, that Sam, like other babies, made some stupid mistakes in this plucky affair, but it must be confessed that he could very well afford to make such.

CHAPTER V.

Capture of Conanchet and of Miantonomah—Annawan, the last captain of Philip—Characteristic end of the War.

But the combat thickens in this war with Philip, who seems to have been for "Sam" a foeman well worthy of his steel. Some of the most picturesque incidents in modern history are to be found in the accounts of this first struggle. What can be finer than this simple story of the capture of Conanchet, the principal chief of the hostile Narragansetts? He was flying from a surprise by a superior force, when, accidentally plunging into the water, he wet his gun. A swift-footed Pequot (a nation friendly with Sam, because one of his first acts had been nearly to exterminate them), soon overtook the gallant chief, who, rendered *hors du combat* by the accident, surrendered to him without hesitation. Robert Hamton, a young man—a young 'Sam' of twenty-two years, coming up, began to question the chief on various subjects, to which the indignant captive with a look of contempt, replied:

"You much child—no understand matters of war—let your captain come—him I will answer!"

He was delivered to the English—conveyed to Stonnington, and, after a sort of trial, condemned to be shot by the Mohegan and Pequot sachems. On being offered his life, provided he would make peace with the English, he rejected the proffer. When told of his fate, he complacently replied, that he "liked it well—that he should die before his heart was soft, or he had said anything unworthy of himself." This haughty chief was a son of the famous Miantonomah, who was put to death by Uncas, at Sachem's Plain, and he appeared to have possessed, in a high degree, the proud spirit of his father. Though treated with such scorn by the old sachem, "the young Sam" seemed to have been close on his heels.

The murder of Miantonomah, by his obdurate foe, who was Sam's fast ally, furnishes, also, a striking illustration of the character of the enemy with whom Sam, with all his strength, had first to struggle. A narrative of this, although slightly a preceding incident, is sufficiently characteristic to make it worthy to be given here.

In 1664 a misunderstanding occurred between Uncas, the sachem of the Mohegans, with whom Sam had been in close alliance, and Miantonomah, the sachem of the Narragansetts; and a war broke out between them, into which Sam was likely to be drawn. But the rival tribes, being not yet possessed of fire-arms, and holding in wholesome recollection the first ebullition (namely, the massacre of the Pequods), of the wrath of Sam, to which we have referred, and which resulted in the almost entire extermination of this the first savage tribe which had offended him, they came to the wise conclusion that it was best to make peace with him, and fight out their private quarrel between themselves.

Miantonomah invaded the Mohegans with nine hundred of his warriors. Uncas met him at the head of four hundred of his men, on a large plain; both prepared for action, and advanced within gunshot. Before the conflict commenced Uncas advanced singly, and thus addressed his antagonist: "You have a number of men with you, and so have I with me; it is a great pity that such brave warriors should be killed in a private quarrel between us. Come, like a man, as you profess to be, and let us fight it out. If you kill me, my men shall be yours, but if I kill you your men shall be mine." Miantonomah replied, "My men came to fight, and they shall fight!" Uncas instantly fell upon the ground, and his men poured a shower of arrows upon the

Narragansetts, and with a horrible yell advanced rapidly upon them and put them to flight.

Uncas and his men pressed on and drove them down a precipice, scattering them in all directions. Miantonimoh was overtaken and seized by Uncas, who, by a shout, recalled his furious warriors. About thirty Narragansetts were slain and many wounded, among whom were many noted chiefs.

Finding himself in the hands of his implacable enemy, Miantonimoh remained silent, nor could Uncas, by any art, force him to break his sullen mood. "Had you taken me," said he to his conqueror, "I should have asked you for my life." No reply was made by the indignant chief, and he submitted, without a murmur, to his humiliating condition. He was afterward conducted to Hartford by his conqueror and delivered to the English, by whom he was held in duress until his fate should be determined by the commissioners of the colonies.

After an examination of his case, the commissioners resolved, "That as it was evident that Uncas could not be safe while Miantonimoh lived, but, either by secret treachery or open force, his life would be constantly in danger, he might justly put such a false and blood-thirsty enemy to death; but this was to be done out of the English jurisdiction, and without cruelty or torture.

Miantonimoh was delivered to Uncas, and by a number of his trusty men marched to the spot where he was captured, attended by two Englishmen, to see that no torture was inflicted; and the moment he arrived at the fatal spot, one of Uncas's men came up behind, and with his hatchet split the skull of the unfortunate chief. It is stated that the savage Uncas then cut out a piece of the shoulder of the dead body and ate it with triumph, exclaiming:

"It is the sweetest meat I ever ate! it makes my heart strong!" The body was buried on the spot and a heap of stones piled upon the grave. The place, since that time, has been known by the name of Sachem's Plain, and is situated in the town of Norwich, Connecticut.

It was most probable, from witnessing and participating in, (with the exception of the Cannibalism, of course,) such scenes as these we are relating, that the "heart" of our Infant Prodigy was rapidly made "strong," too — for it certainly must have required considerable strength of heart, or of something else, perhaps more dubious in its significancy, to have enabled the big-fisted innocent to perpetrate the fate with which he visited the heroic Annawan, the wisest and noblest captain of the murdered Philip.

This was an achievement of the veritable Captain Church, whom we have noticed for his orthodox name, and which occurred in this wise.

Annawan, Philips' chief captain and counselor, was now at the head of the hostile Indians. He was an artful and long experienced warrior, and had often declared that the English should not take him while alive. After the defeat at the swamp, where his comrades were killed, he, with fifty or sixty of his best men, took post in Squanaconk Swamp, in the southeast part of Rehoboth. Several Indians, from his camp, were soon after captured, among whom was an Indian with his daughter.

By these Church was informed of the situation of Annawan's camp, and by a stratagem which none but the most daring would have adopted, succeeded in capturing the whole without resistance. At the head of a small party, conducted by the captured Indian and his daughter, who, it appears, readily engaged in the attempt, Church, by a cautious approach in the evening, reached the edge of a rocky precipice, under which Annawan was encamped, and made a critical examination of the position.

A tree had been felled close under the precipice and boughs placed against it to form a sort of hut; fires were burning near, pots and kettles boiling, and spits turning, loaded with meat, the fire-arms stood near the foot of the rock, resting upon a pole supported by crotches and covered with a mat, to keep them dry; the Indians were separated into three parties at small distances, surrounded by a rude abattis, and Annawan, with his son, lay reposing very near the arms.

Having viewed the camp sufficiently, Church and his party withdrew and formed his plan for the surprise. Informed by his guide that no one was allowed to go out or enter the camp except by the precipice, he determined to make his effort in that direction. The guide and his daughter, with baskets upon their backs, as if bringing in provisions, were directed to precede Church and his men, while the latter, close in the rear and covered by the shadows of the guides, were to descend the rocks. The descent was found to be difficult, but by letting themselves down by the bushes growing in the fissures of the rocks, the party reached the bottom without alarming the Indians.

Church, with a hatchet in his hand, seized the arms at the feet of Annawan, who, starting up on end, cried out "Howah!" and despairing of an escape, fell back in his couch. After the arms were secured parties went to the other Indians, informing them their chief was a prisoner, and that if they would submit their lives would be spared. The whole readily complied with the terms, and all appeared cheerful.

Church now inquired of Annawan what he had for supper, "for," said he, "I have come to sup with you." The chief, in a loud voice, ordered his women to prepare one, and inquired of his conqueror whether he would choose cow or horse beef. Church replied cow beef, and the supper was soon prepared, and all ate heartily. After suitable guards were posted the Indians lay down, and Church attempted a short repose near his captured chief; but neither slept. Some time had elapsed in silence, when Annawan arose from his couch and slowly retired into the wood. Church, apprehensive of some hostile design, drew near to Annawan's son and prepared for the worst.

At length, the chief returned with a pack, placed it on the ground, and falling on his knees before it, said:

"Great Captain, you have killed Philip and conquered his country—I believe that I and my company are the last who war against the English—I suppose the war is ended by your means." Then, opening the pack, he drew out a belt curiously wrought with wampum in various figures of flowers, birds and beasts, which, when hung upon the Captain's shoulders, reached to his feet. Another belt of wampum was next taken out, wrought in the same manner, which was worn on the head of the warrior, hanging down the back, to which two flags appended, waving behind. A third, with a star, and edged with red hair, was taken out, which, when hung upon the neck, descended to the breast.

These, with two horns of glazed powder, and a red cloth blanket, constituting the royal dress of Philip, were presented to Captain Church, who, Annawan said, had "won them, and he was happy in having an opportunity of delivering."

The remainder of the night was spent in free conversation, in which the captured chief recounted his various exploits in the present, as well as former wars under Philip's father. The next day, Church marched his prisoners to Taunton, where he joined those that had been captured when Philip was killed, and had been ordered to that town. Annawan, with another chief, was perfidiously put to death at Boston, not long after. A few more exploits of Captain Church, in which a number of the Indians were captured and the few remaining tribes submitted, ended the war in this quarter.

"A few more exploits" of this sort, with a vengeance, and "Church," as well as State were likely to become quite as indivisible as Sam had heretofore consistently aspired to make them. It was, of course, only because unpleasant to "Captain Church," that when "a young minister, godly and zealous, having precious gifts," came among them, who dared to assert that "the doctrine of persecution for cause of conscience is most evidently and lamentably contrary to the doctrine of Christ Jesus," they should have banished him, in the superflux of christian charity, to wander through the dangers of a remote, unknown and savage wilderness. Yes, this same Sam, concerning whom his locally-canonized historian* asserts with iteration, *passim*, that "the purity of religion and civil liberty were the objects nearest the wishes of the emigrants," turned forth into the howling wilderness, the valiant Roger Williams, because he had spoken one of the freest and most pregnant truths that ever fell from mortal lips.

There was a charming consistency in this course, for, having set Hooker, their controversial champion, forth to meet the startling proposition of "liberty of conscience," and having found him, in their own convictions, foiled by the clear, serene intellect of his interlocutor, they concluded it was best, for the interests of "Church" and State, to extend the grace of starvation on the bleak and forlorn steps of the untracked southwest to the man who stood ready to die by the assertion that "the civil magistrate might not intermeddle, even to stop a 'Church' from infidelity and heresy." Thus

* Bancroft, page 359.

was dismissed the mild and valiant founder of Rhode Island, the chivalric State, which, though small in its area, has, in the sentiment from which it sprung, widened its limits to the circumference of the world! that is, a world of recognition and of yearning! For, unfortunately, Earth is not yet free.

How far our friend Sam was disposed to recognize this liberty, is admirably displayed in the tone of the following harangue, delivered by the amiably belligerent saint, Mr. Hooker, that man of "vast attainments," to whom we have referred as the special champion pitted against freedom of thought and Roger Williams.

When the ninety men had assembled to go and roast the feeble Pequods, which, it will be remembered, they did most effectually, exterminating, with fire and sword, an entire nation, this mouthpiece of christian charity thus addressed them:

"Fellow soldiers, countrymen and companions, you are this day assembled by the special providence of God; you are not collected by wild fancy, nor ferocious passions. It is not a tumultous assembly, whose actions are abortive, or if successful, produce only theft, rapine, rape and murder; crimes inconsistent with nature's light, inconsistent with a soldier's valor. You, my dear hearts, were selected from your neighbors, by the godly fathers of the land, for your known courage, to execute such a work.

"Your cause is the cause of heaven; the enemy have blasphemed your God, and slain his servants; you are only the ministers of his justice. I do not pretend that your enemies are careless or indifferent: no, their hatred is inflamed, their lips thirst for blood; they would devour you, and all the people of God; but, my brave soldiers, their guilt has reached the clouds; they are ripe for destruction; their cruelty is notorious; and cruelty and cowardice are always united.

"There is nothing, therefore, to prevent your certain victory but their nimble feet, their impenetrable swamps and woods; from these your small numbers will entice them, or your courage drive them. I now put the question—Who would not fight in such a cause? fight with undaunted boldness? Do you wish for more encouragement? More I give you. Riches waken the soldier's sword; and though you will not obtain silver and gold, on the field of victory, you will secure what is infinitely more precious; you will secure the *liberties, the privileges, and the lives of Christ's Church, in this New World.*

"You will procure safety for your affectionate wives, safety for your prattling, harmless, smiling babes; you will secure all the blessings enjoyed by the people of God in the ordinances of the gospel. Distinguished was the honor conferred upon David, for fighting the battles of the Lord; this honor, O! ye courageous soldiers of God, is now prepared for you! You will now execute his vengeance on the heathen; you will bind their kings in chains and their nobles in fetters of iron. But perhaps some one may fear that a fatal arrow may deprive him of his honor.

"Let every faithful soldier of Jesus Christ be assured, that if any servant be taken away, it is merely because the honors of this world are too narrow for his reward; an everlasting crown is set upon his head; because the rewards of this life are insufficient. March then with Christian courage, in the strength of the Lord; march with faith in his divine promises, and soon your swords shall find your enemies; soon they shall fall like leaves of the forest under your feet."

Cromwell's troops always went into battle prayerfully, but we think this rather peculiar specimen of saintly eloquence, would have astonished any Barebones of them all, and yet this earliest counselor of Sam, would appear to have been, according to his historian, a man of "vast endowments, strong will and energetic mind."

CHAPTER VI.

The humorous Nathaniel Word—Sam's theory of Government through his assistance—Blue Laws.

AFTER this, we think we can afford to quote some account of the theory of government promulgated by one of the co-temporaries — and we may as well suppose — friends of this grave didactic teacher, the humorous Nathaniel Word, as he is called:

"Poley-piety," says he, "is the greatest piety in the world. To authorize an untruth, by toleration of the State, is to build a sconce against the walls of Heaven, to batter God out of his chair. Persecution of true Religion and toleration of false, are the Jannes and Jambres to the Kingdom of Christ, whereof the last is by far the worst. He that is willing to tolerate an unsound opinion, that his own may be tolerated, though never so sound, will, for a creed, hang God's Bible at the devil's girdle. It is said that men ought to have liberty of Conscience, and that it is persecution to debar them of it. I can the rather stand amazed than reply to this; it is an astonishment that the brains of men should be parboiled in such impious ignorance."

This is the same facetious gentleman who, about this time, in conjunction with other and worthy collaborateurs, drew up a code of laws for Sam, which he, or rather they, designated as the "Body of Liberties," which, it seems, was compiled chiefly from the code of Moses, and, though the date of their being commended to the general court, was as early as the year 1639, let it be mentioned to the everlasting credit of Sam, that they were not accepted, even by his unwilling innocence, until 1641, and that even then, the whole proposed by the amiable originators was not adopted by him without some little variation.

The following extracts from the laws, will show the peculiar spirit of Sam's Puritan fathers:

"Blasphemy, which is the cursing of God by atheism or the like, to be punished with death.

Idolatry to be punished with death.

Witchcraft, which is fellowship by covenant with a familiar spirit, to be punished with death.

Consulters with witches not to be tolerated, but either to be cut off by death or banishment.

Heresy, which is the maintenance of some wicked errors, overthrowing the foundation of the Christian religion; which obstinacy, if it be joined with endeavor to seduce others thereunto, to be punished with death; because such a heretic, no less than an idolater, seeketh to thrust the souls of men from the Lord their God.

To worship God in a molten or graven image, to be punished with death.

Such members of the church as do willfully reject to walk, after due admonition and conviction, in *the Church's establishment*, and their Christian admonitions and censures, shall be cut off by banishment.

Whoever shall revile the religion and worship of God, and the government of the church, as it is now established, to be cut off by banishment.—*Cor.* v, 5.

Willful perjury, whether before the judgment-seat, or in private conference, to be punished with death.

Profaning the Lord's day, in a careless and scornful neglect, or contempt thereof, to be punished with death.

Reviling the magistrates in highest rank among us, to wit: the governors and council, to be punished with death.—1 *Kings* ii, 8, 9 and 46.

Rebellious children, whether they continue in riot or drunkenness, after due correction from their parents, or whether they curse or smite their parents, to be put to death.—*Ex.* xxi, 15, 17; *Lev.* xx, 9.

Adultery, which is the defiling of the marriage bed, to be punished with death. Defiling a woman espoused, is a kind of adultery, and punishable by death of both parties, but if a woman be forced, then by the death of the man only.—*Lev.* xx, 10; *Deut.* xxii, 22–27.

Incest, which is the defiling of any near of akin, within

the degrees prohibited in Leviticus, to be punished with death.

Whoredom of a maiden in her father's house, kept secret till after her marriage with another, to be punished with death.—*Deut.* xxii, 20, 21.

Man stealing to be punished with death.—*Ex.* xxi, 16.

False-witness-bearing to be punished with death."

Concerning the *Rights of Inheritance*, the following, among others, were the laws:

"That no free burgess, or free inhabitant of any town, shall sell land allotted to him in the town (unless the free burgesses of the town give consent unto such sale, or refuse to give due price, answerable to what others offer, without fraud,) but to some one or other of the free burgesses or free inhabitants of the same town.

That if such lands be sold by any others, the sale shall be made with reservation of such rent-charge, to be paid to the town stock or treasury of the town, as either the former occupiers of the land were wont to pay toward all the public charges thereof, whether in church or town; or at least after the rate of three shillings per acre, or some such like proportion, more or less, as shall be thought fit.

For the supporting of the worship of God in church fellowship, it was ordered: 'That wheresoever the lands of any man's inheritance shall fall, yet no man shall set his dwelling-house above the distance of half a mile, or a mile at the farthest, from the meeting of the congregation, where the church doth usually assemble for the worship of God.'

If a man have more sons than one, then a double proportion to be assigned and bequeathed to the eldest son, according to the law of nature; unless his own demerit deprive him of the dignity of his birth.

Under the head of *Trespasses*, the following is found: 'If a man's ox, or other beast, gore or bite, and kill a man or woman, whether child or riper age, the beast shall be killed, and no benefit of the dead beast reserved to the owner. But if the ox, or beast were wont to push or bite in time past, and the owner hath been told of it, and hath not kept him in, then both the ox, or beast, shall be forfeited, and the owner also put to death, or fined to pay what the judges and persons damnified, shall lay upon him.'"

LESS HEINOUS CRIMES.

"Forcing a maid (or rape), was not to be punished with death by God's law, but with fine or penalty to the father of the maid—by marriage of the maid defiled, if she and her father consent; or with corporeal punishment of stripes for his wrong, as a slander.

Fornication to be punished with the marriage of the maid, giving her a sufficient dowry; or with stripes, though fewer from the equity of the former case.

In time of war, 'men betrothed and not married, or newly married, or such as have newly built or planted, and not received the fruits of their labor, and such as are faint-hearted men not to be pressed or forced against their wills, to go forth to wars.—*Deut.* xx, 5–8, and xxiv, 5. All wickedness to be removed out of the camp, by severe discipline.—*Deut.* xxiii, 9, 14. And in war, men of a corrupt and false religion are not to be accepted, much less sought for.—2 *Chron.* xxv, 7, 8. Women, especially such as have lain by man—little children and cattle, are to be spared and reserved from spoil.—*Deut.* xx, 14. Some minister to be sent forth to go with the army, for their instruction and encouragement.'—*Deut.* xx, 2, 3, 4.

Every town was to have judges within themselves, who were empowered, once in each month, or in three months at the farthest, to hear and determine civil as well as criminal causes, which were not capital; reserving liberty of appeal to the court of governor and assistants.—*Deut.* xvi, 18. In defect of a law in any case, the decision was to be by the word of God.

An abstract of the laws was published in London, by William Aspinwall, in 1641. 'Wherein,' says he, 'as in a mirror, may be seen the wisdom and perfection of Christ's kingdom, accommodable to any state or form of government in the world, that it is not *antichristian and tyrannical.*' In an address to the reader, he says: 'Concerning which model, I dare not pronounce that it is without imperfection in every particular; yet, this I dare be bold to say, that it far surpasseth all the municipal laws and statutes of any of the Gentile nations and corporations under the code of Heaven.'"

CHAPTER VII.

Commencement of the Witch-burning Comedy—Exemplary Mr. Philip Smith, and the Valdemar Case.

IT must be confessed, after Sam's first "Body of Rights," that we can not well be surprised at any reasonable amount of fantastic bigotry originating about these times. The famous code of "Blue Laws," of which this bill was the foundation, seems so much a matter of course, as to have no room for comment—while even the "Witch burning" of 1692, appears only a consequential ebullition of the same grim juvenility; as for the "Slave-trade,"* to which Sam is now accused of being somewhat opposed, how else could it have originated in a New World, but in this same spirit of youthful indiscretion? As for selling the miserable remnants of the gallant tribes, whom his wholesale massacre nearly extirpated into foreign bondage, it was, confessedly practical by Sam for two hundred years, and justified by "the sternest morality!"†

But as the hanging of the Quakers was the coolest, so the hanging of the witches was the most ludicrous feat of the young Sam. The stories which the chronicles of that period tell of his facetious freaks under the influence of this new pietistic whim, are truly refreshing and worthy of our recurrence.

It may be supposed that, having been signally defeated in all his attempts at retaliation against the French and Indians in "King William's war," which broke out in 1690, and finding little consolation in the easy capture of the insignificant fortress of "Port Royal," for the tremendous rebuff of his boastful expedition against Quebec, Sam grew sulky in his misfortune, and, like other pious souls at such times, began to see sights and dream dreams.

---

* Bancroft, p. 173, 4.

† Idem, p. 163.

It seems, that as early as 1645, he had been spiritually exercised upon the grave subject of "prestigious agency," and that divers and sundry bedridden dames, and dim old specimens of the "burning and shining lights of Israel" had been put to death for the above awfully named crime, for Hudibras' ingenious reason, that they were men and women who could be better spared to the State.

But Sam surely outdid himself in Hadley, Connecticut, in 1684. One of his pet saints, Cotton Mather, tells this story—Magnalia, vol. 2, book 6—and it will be read with not the less interest, since all the modern children of Sam will recognize in it the original and perfect skeleton of the celebrated "Valdemar case" of Edgar A. Poe exhumed.

It is given in the exact language of Cotton, which must be the excuse for any indelicacies of phraseology peculiar to the rugged earnestness of the writer and his times:

"Mr. Philip Smith, aged about fifty years, a son of eminently virtuous parents, a deacon of a church in Hadley, a member of the General Court, a justice in the country court, a selectman for the affairs of the town, a lieutenant of the troop, and which crowns all, a man for devotion, sanctity, gravity, and all that was honest exceeding exemplary, such a man was, in the year 1684, murdered with a hideous witchcraft, that filled all those parts of New England with astonishment. He was, by his office, concerned about relieving the indigence of a wretched woman in the town, who being dissatisfied at some of his just cares about her, expressed herself unto him in such a manner, that he declared himself, thenceforward, apprehensive of receiving mischief at her hands.

"About the beginning of January, he began to be very valetudinarious, laboring under pains that seemed ischiatic. The by-standers could now see in him one ripening apace for another world, and filled with grace and joy to a high degree. He showed such weanedness from, and weariness of the world, that he knew not (he said), whether he might pray for his continuance here; and such assurance he had of the Divine love unto him, that in raptures he would cry out, *Lord, stay thy hand, it is enough, it is more than thy frail servant can bear.* But in the midst of these things he still uttered a hard suspicion that the ill-woman who had threatened him, had made impressions with enchantments upon him. While he remained yet of a sound mind, he very sedately, but very solemnly charged his brother to look well after him. Though he said he now understood himself, yet he knew not how he might be. But be sure (said he) to have a care of me; for you shall see strange things. There shall be a wonder in Hadley! I shall not be dead, when 'tis thought I am! He pressed this charge over and over, and afterward became delirious; upon which he had a speech incessant and voluble, and (as was judged) in various languages. He cried out not only of pains, but also of pins tormenting him in several parts of his body; and the attendants found one of them.

"In his distress, he exclaimed much upon the woman aforesaid and others, as being seen by him in the room; and there was, divers times, both in that room and over the whole house, a strong smell, something like musk, which once particularly so scented an apple roasting at the fire, that it forced them to throw it away. Some of the young men in the town being out of their wits at the strange calamities thus visited upon one of their most beloved neighbors, went three or four times to give disturbance unto the woman thus complained of; and all the while they were disturbing her, he was at ease, and slept as a weary man; yea, these were the only times that they perceived him take any sleep, in all his illness.* Gallipots of medicines, provided for the sick man, were unaccountably emptied; and audible scratchings were made about the bed, when his hands and feet lay wholly still and were held by others. They beheld fire sometimes on the bed, and when the beholders began to discourse of it, it vanished away. Divers people actually felt something often stir in the bed, at a considerable distance from the man; it seemed as big as a cat, but they could never grasp it; several trying to lean on the bed's head, though the sick man lay wholly still, the bed would shake so as to knock their heads uncomfortably. A very strong man could not lift the sick man to make him lie more easily, though he applied his utmost strength unto

* Hutchinson says they dragged the woman out of her house—hung her up till she was nearly dead, then let her down—rolled her sometime in the snow, and at last buried her in it, and there left her; but it happened she revived, and the melancholy man died.—History of Massachusetts, vol. 2, p. 24.

it; and yet he could go presently and lift a bedstead and bed, and a man lying on it, without any strain to himself at all. Mr. Smith dies; the jury that viewed his corpse, found a swelling on one breast, his privates wounded or burned, his back full of bruises, and several holes that seemed made with awls. After the opinion of all had pronounced him dead, his countenance continued as lively as if he had been alive; his eyes closed as in a slumber, and his nether jaw not falling down.

"Thus he remained from Saturday morning about sunrise, till Sunday in the afternoon, when those who took him out of bed found him still warm, though the season was as cold as had almost been known in any age; and a New England winter does not want for cold. On the night following, his countenance was yet fresh as before; but on Monday morning they found the face extremely tumefied and discolored. It was black and blue, and fresh blood seemed running down his cheek upon the hairs. Divers noises were also heard in the room where the corpse lay; as the clattering of chairs and stools, whereof no account could be given. This was the end of so good a man!"

CHAPTER VIII.

The Origin of the Witch Persecutions—Character of Cotton Mather—Cotton Mather and his Invisibles—Parris his associate and conspirator—Hanging of George Burroughs—Decline of the delusion and Mather's despair—Quaint specimens from Mather's Works—White Slavery.

SUCH is the sententious conclusion of this marvelous tale. We would suppose that Sam would always step behind the Alleghanies to grin, when he heard this story now-a-days; but such is by no manner of means the express fact, for, as we hear, spirit rappings, table knockings, dancing chairs, etc., seem to constitute quite as real a portion of his pet superstitions, in these modern times, as ever, and a Judge Edmonds appears only to have stepped into the shoes of that quaint ancient, Cotton Mather, who, by the way, concludes a philippic against those who ventured to doubt concerning the doings of his pet "Invisibles" and to deny the prestige of his "wandering demons" in the following words:

"Flashy people may burlesque these things; but when hundreds of the most sober people in a country where they have as much mother wit, certainly, as the rest of mankind, *know them to be true;* nothing but the absurd and froward spirit of sadducism can question them.

"I have not mentioned so much as one thing that will not be justified, if it be required, by the oaths of more consistent persons than any that can rule these odd phenomena—nor are these a tenth part of the prodigies that fell out among the prodigies of New England."

The reverend old sinner who talks thus has already been accessory to the fact—a chief accessory at that—of the burning, pressing and hanging of nineteen, beside the arrest and imprisonment, with intent to hang, of hundreds more of human trophies to his fantastic passion for these "Invisibles;"

yet so strong is his belief in spirits, that he coolly condemns all unbelievers, as possessed of one of his "wandering demons," we suppose, under the cabalistic title of the "spirit of sadducism."

Fie! for shame, Sam, it was bad enough to deal in the black art yourself with your pet saints, without condemning in this wise, all the world and the rest of mankind to the fate of the herd of swine.

Yes, the darling exploit of himself and his crony Cotton, referred to above, was the famous Salem witch burning of 1692, and it is quite an illustration of the progressive spirit of the modern Sam, to observe how interestingly candid this same historian, the same who tells us about his first treaty with the Indians and its "ceremonies!" has suddenly become in speaking of this achievement. Hear first how Cotton Mather was characterized:

"Was Cotton Mather honestly credulous? Ever ready to dupe himself, he limited his credulity only by the probable credulity of others. He changes or omits to repeat his statements without acknowledging error, and with a clear intention of conveying false impressions. He is an example how far selfishness, under the form of vanity and ambition, can blind the higher faculties, stupefy the judgment, and dupe consciousness itself. His self-righteousness was complete till he was resisted."*

But hear, in the same connection, some titbits of description from the same source, of one Samuel Parris, of Salem, with whom this pleasant business seems to have originated in that town. He was, it seems, the minister, and there had been between him and a part of his people a strife so bitter that it had even attracted the attention of the General Court.

"The delusion of witchcraft would give the opportunities of terrible vengeance. The family of Samuel Parris, his daughter, a child of nine years, and his niece, a girl of less than twelve, began to have strange caprices. He that will read Cotton Mather's Book of General Providences, may read of what these children suffered; and Tituba, an Indian female servant, who had practiced some wild incantations, being betrayed by her husband, was scourged by Parris, her master,

---

* Bancroft, vol 3, page 97.

WITCH-BURNING, BY COTTON MATHER—SAM BLOWING THE FLAMES. (SEE CHAP. VIII.)

into confessing herself a witch." "There was no motive, it seems, to hang this Tituba"—not at all; "she was saved as a living witness to the reality of witchcraft." As the affair proceeded, our friend Parris, backed by "Cotton Mather, who had staked his own reputation for veracity on the reality of witchcraft, first prayed for a good issue; and then Brother Parris proceeded to demand of his niece, the girl of twelve years of age, the names of the devil's instruments who bewitched the band of the afflicted; and then became at once informer and witness."

In those days there was no prosecuting officer, and Parris was at hand to question his Indian servants and others, himself prompting the answers and acting as recorder to magistrates.

The recollection of the old controversy in the parish could not be forgotten, and Parris, moved by personal malice as well as by blind zeal, stifled the accusations of some—such is the testimony of the people of his own village—and at the same time, vigilantly promoting the accusations of others, was the beginner and procurer of the sore afflictions to Salem and the country. Women, the older, the more harmless and unprotected the better, seem first to have been the helpless objects of his ecclesiastical solicitude, and having hung a score or two of them, and one very decrepid old woman of fourscore, he gained, at length, through impunity, the spiritual courage to do that which he had long wished, through such bloody inspiration to do, namely: attack a live man—one George Burroughs, who had been his rival.

Burroughs, it seems, had preached with great unction in Salem, and had friends "who desired he should be there." He, too, was a skeptic in witchcraft, and "the gallows was to be set up, not for those who professed themselves witches, for they were carefully protected as the seed of the faith, "but for those who rebuked the delusion." So George Burroughs, who seems to have been a very fine specimen of a young Sam, as one of the chief accusations against him was that he was possessed of incredible strength, was condemned to be hanged by the evidence of dumb witnesses, and our favorite Cotton Mather pronounces the facts of this dumbness and of the incorrigible having given evidence of preternatural muscular strength, "enough!"

If his spiritual friends of New England had happened to have caught Sam himself, in the body, asleep, with his head pillowed on the hills, they would have been sure to have built a fire in the valleys under him, in the hope to set the pines in a blaze and roast him—ungrateful friends!

But the execution of the doughty George Burroughs was likely to be stayed—first, because it was a novelty to hang a minister, and next, because he repeated the Lord's Prayer with great clearness on the scaffold. To be sure, he also made an eloquent plea against witchcraft and in defense of his innocence, but that went as for nothing until his repetition of the prayer, which, it was believed, those possessed of the devil were unable to do, touched at last upon their convictions, and "the spectators were like to hinder the execution," when the amiable Cotton Mather, whose self-love was touched by Burroughs' absolute denial that there was or could be any such thing as witchcraft, appeared on horseback among the crowd, and addressed the people, caviling at the ordinance of Burroughs as though he had been no true minister, insisting on his guilt, and hinting that the devil could sometimes assume the appearance of an angel of light, thus pleading might and main for the hanging, "and the hanging proceeded!"

Thus this loving couple, Parris and Mather, were sustained, and their pet "invisibles" vindicated! But this amusement had to stop somewhere, of course, and poor Cotton Mather, in his despair at the loss thereof, "had temptations to atheism and to the abandonment of all religion," as he relates himself in his diary. What is styled "the inexorable indignation" of the awakened people, only drove the cunning sportsman, Parris, from the village. Terrible punishment this, compared with the deeds of the man; but Sam, about these parts, was always "inexorable," according to his pet historians, especially when engaged in stringing up old men and women to please the whims of two of his parsons, we would suggest. Amiable Sam!

But let us take a farewell glance at this delectable Reverend Cotton Mather, D. D., F. R. S. A few extracts from his master work, entitled "Magnalia Christi Americana," will shed a flood of light upon his peculiarly amiable character.

"'Tis very likely that the *evil angels* may have a particular

energy and employment, oftentimes in mischiefs done by thunder. There (in the air) Satan can do mighty things—command much of the magazine of Heaven. Satan let loose by God can do wonders in the air. He can raise storms, he can discharge the great ordinance of Heaven, thunders and lightning; and by his art can make them more terrible and dreadful than they are in their own nature. 'Tis no heresy or blasphemy to think that the prince of the power of the air hath as good share in Chemistry as goes to the making of *Aurum fulminans.*

"The devil is the prince of the power of the air, and when God gives him leave, he has vast power in the air, and armies that can make thunder in the air. A great man has, therefore, noted it, 'that thunders break oftener on churches than any other houses, because the demons have a peculiar spite at houses that are set apart for the peculiar service of God.'"

Quitting the direct agency of the devil, the doctor details many other prodigies, which he supposes ominous of great events, and which he probably imputed to the *good angels,* one or more of whom he believed presided *in the air,* over every town and village. A short time prior to Philip's war he relates, in a grave and serious manner, that noises were heard in the air, similar to the discharge of artillery and small arms, accompanied with the beating of drums as in a battle. In several places invisible troops of horse are said to have been heard, riding through the air. His *naval apparition* must not be omitted. A ship sailed from a port in New England for Europe, with many passengers, and was supposed to be foundered at sea; but as the event was doubtful, the people remained in suspense. At length, behold! a ship rigged out in every part similar to the one that had been lost, entered the harbor of New Haven, and winged its way through the air, directly in the face of the wind, until it arrived near the wharf, when its masts and rigging went overboard, and many signals of distress were displayed; but soon the whole vanished from the sight. "Now," adds the sage, "prepare for the event of those prodigies; but count me not struck with a Livian superstition in reporting prodigies, for which I have such incontestable proofs." Many other extraordinary and unaccountable phenomena are also detailed with great minuteness by the doctor; but it is believed the reader will be satisfied with those already given.

"In the days of Moses, it seems the deserts were counted very much the habitation of devils. Who can tell whether the envy of the devils at the favor of God unto men, may not provoke them to affect retirement from the sight of populous and prosperous regions, except so far as they reckon their work of tempting mankind, necessary to be carried on?

"Whatever becomes of the observations which we have hitherto been making, there has been too much cause to observe that the Christians who were driven into the American desert, which is now called New England, have, to their sorrow, seen Azazel dwelling and raging in very tragical instances. The devils have doubtless felt a more than ordinary vexation, from the arrival of these Christians, with their sacred exercises of Christianity in this wilderness. But the sovereignty of heaven has permitted them still to remain in the wilderness for our vexation as well as their own."

Saintly Cotton in this manner is dismissed.

But it seems this was not the only instance in which Sam dealt in the black arts; we have insinuated that in the temper of his Body of Rights originated the slave trade. Here is the direct statement: "A ship of one Thomas Keyser, or one James Smith, the latter a member of the church of Boston, first brought upon the colonies the guilt of participating in the traffic in African slaves.* They openly sailed for Guinea to trade for negroes;" but here follows the amusing justification of Puritanism: "But throughout Massachusetts the cry of justice was raised against them as malefactors and murderers, the guilty men were committed for the offense, and after advice with the elders the representatives of the people bearing witness against the heinous crime of man-stealing, ordered the negroes to be restored, at the public charge, to their native country, with a letter expressing the indignation of the General Court of their wrongs."†

We can hear the stentorian mirth of Sam on hearing this ingenious story, shaking the hills far away to the nethermost ocean. Ho! "a letter expressing the indignation of the General Court!" Ha! ha! who was there to read the letter in Guinea?

* Bancroft, page 173—volume 1st. † Idem, page 173—vol. 1st.

But to show that this "bearing witness against the heinous crime of man-stealing" was in reality something of a joke, let us read the following:

"The practice of selling the natives of North America into foreign bondage, continued for nearly two centuries; and even the sternest morality pronounced the sentence of slavery and exile on the captives whom the field of battle spared. The excellent Winthrop enumerates Indians among his behests. The articles of the early New England confederacy class persons among the spoils of war. A scanty remnant of the Pequod tribe in Connecticut, the captives treacherously made by Waldron in New Hampshire, the harmless fragments of the tribe of Annawan, the orphan offspring of King Philip himself, were all doomed to the same hard destiny of perpetual bondage. The clans of Virginia and Carolina, for more than a hundred years, were hardly safe against the kidnappers. The universal public mind was long and deeply vitiated."

But how does it happen that while the clans of Virginia and Carolina were comparatively safe against the kidnappers—these "profligate and luxurious populations" as they are uniformly termed by these apologetic scriveners—that the saints of the northern plantations of Sam had been recognizing Indian, as well as Negro slavery for nearly two centuries? It is time this question were looked into, and in our next we shall endeavor, as the impartial legendary of Sam, to ascertain if the "mild and saintly Winthrop," as he is elsewhere named, was the only one of the "elect" who even enumerated Indians among his bequests.

CHAPTER IX.

Slavery White, Black, Red and Yellow—Impudence of the clamor about Slavery, raised by those with whom it originated—Slavery old as time—Historical, of the different forms of Slavery.

WE promised to take up the subject of slavery, white, black, red and yellow, in our last chapter of these antiquities of Sam—we accordingly invoke these "white spirits and black, blue spirits and gray," and here they are upon the block in form. "What! what! what!" as George III used to say.

Well, Sam, who is much the most powerful despot of the two, and a very long way from being "a royal idiot" at that, says that this whole subject of Slavery is a mere mess of twattle; that those sleek-haired, round-headed would-be-sons of his, who are making such a fuss about it, are but sniveling cubs at the best—and that he does not intend they shall continue to worry his curly-haired children of the South about this slavery business, without his understanding why.

He exclaims with a far-reverberating jeer—Whoo-oop! fiddle-faddle, what are you making all this wide-mouthed hullabaloo about, you noisy boobies?

You are the very scamps who commenced the slave trade, and who are first responsible for all its villainies—are you not? You have trafficked in black flesh, in yellow flesh, in red flesh, and worst of all, in white flesh—your own flesh and blood!

You put up a "poor mouth" about slavery, whining saintly-like, about the rights of man! *You,* who have been from the beginning the most ruthless, the most unscrupulous traffickers in "God's image," the least magnanimous, the most mercenary, the most savage of all kidnappers,—you, who could write an apologetic letter to the chiefs of Congo, for stealing their people, to curse a New World with the damning incubus of slavery, and then send a man-thief in a slave-ship to be the translator of your pious and penitent epistle!

You impudent fellows, you deserve to be spanked all round! and, if I, Sam, should chance to bring down my heavy hand upon you, you will be resolved into cherry-bums (cherubims)—that is, you shall have nothing left to sit down upon, henceforth and forever!

Sam thrusts the keen blade of wit into the bladder of slavery, when he says in the spirit of learned intelligence: Slavery and the slave-trade are older than the records of human society; they are found to have existed wherever the savage hunter began to assume the habits of pastoral or agricultural life, and, with the exception of Australasia, they have extended to every portion of the globe; they pervaded every portion and every nation of civilized antiquity. The earliest glimpses of Egyptian history exhibit pictures of bondage; the oldest monuments of human labor on the Egyptian soil are evidently the results of slave labor. The founder of the Jewish nation was a slaveholder and a purchaser of slaves. Every patriarch was lord in his own household.

The Hebrews, when they burst the bands of their thraldom, carried with them beyond the desert, the institution of slavery. The light that broke from Sinai scattered the corrupting illusions of polytheism; but slavery planted itself even in the promised land, on the banks of Siloa, near the oracles of God. The Hebrew father might doom his daughter to bondage; the wife and children, and posterity of the emancipated slave remained the property of the master and his heirs; and if a slave, though mortally wounded by his master, did but languish of his wounds for a day, the owner escaped with impunity, for the slave was his master's money. It is even probable that, at a later period, a man's family might be sold for the payment of debts.

The countries that bordered on Palestine were familiar with domestic servitude; and, like Babylon, Tyre also, the oldest and most famous commercial city of Phenicia, was a market "for the persons of men." The Scythians of the desert had already established slavery throughout the plains and forests of the unknown north.

Old as are the traditions of Greece, the existence of slavery is older. The wrath of Achilles grew out of a quarrel for a slave; the Grecian dames had crowds of servile attendants; the heroes before Troy made excursions into the neighboring villages and towns to enslave the inhabitants. Greek pirates, roving like the Corsairs of Barbary, in quest of men, laid the foundation of Greek commerce; each commercial town was a slave-mart, and every cottage near the sea-side was in danger from the kidnapper. Greeks enslaved each other. The language of Homer was the mother-tongue of the Helots; the Grecian city that made war on its neighbor city exulted in its capture as a source of profit; the hero of Macedon sold men of his own kindred and language into hopeless slavery. The idea of universal free labor had not been generated. Aristotle had written that all mankind are brothers; yet the thought of equal enfranchisement never presented itself to his sagacious understanding. In every Grecian Republic slavery was an indispensable element.*

Though slavery may have been an indispensable element in every republic of Greece, Sam does not consider it indispensable that it should lard the machinery of every republic which constitutes a portion of his confederacy.

After his primitive settlements at Providence and Boston had made their fortunes out of the original importations, it seemed to be most respectable that they should retire from the slave-trade—ignore it—and, hugging their dollars, turn about and denounce the South, who has been their chief purchasers, and who alone could make it pay.

This was very nice, indeed, and so particularly conscientious, when we remember that the maritime adventurers of those days, joining the principles of bigots with the bold designs of pirates and heroes, esteemed the wealth of the countries which they might discover, as their rightful plunder, and the inhabitants, if Christians, as their subjects; if

---

* For the collocation of the above facts, the author is indebted to the historian, Bancroft.

infidels, as their slaves. Even Indians of Hispaniola were imported into Spain. Cargoes of the natives of the North were early and repeatedly kidnapped.

The coasts of America, like the coasts of Africa, were visited by ships in search of laborers, and there was hardly a convenient harbor on the whole Atlantic frontier of the United States, which was not entered by slavers. The native Indians themselves, were ever ready to resist the treacherous merchants; the freemen of the wilderness, unlike the Africans, among whom slavery had existed from immemorial time, would never abet the foreign merchant, or become his factors in the nefarious traffic. Fraud and force remained, therefore, the means by which, near Newfoundland or Florida, on the shores of the Atlantic, or among the Indians of the Mississippi valley, Cortereal and Vasquez de Ayllon, Porcallo and Soto, with private adventurers, whose names and whose crimes may be left unrecorded, transported the natives of North America into slavery in Europe and the Spanish West Indies.

The glory of Columbus himself, did not escape the stain; enslaving five hundred native Americans, he sent them to Spain, that they might be publicly sold at Seville.*

It seems that to Sir John Hawkins, a precursory peer of that distinguished lady-philanthropist, the Countess of Sutherland, belongs "the odious distinction of having first interested England in the slave-trade." Pious Old England, who is now so horrified by the enormities of the traffic, did also, it seems, her chivalric devoir in planting the curse upon a New World.

What wonder that she should be so dramatically and disinterestedly moved now, about exorcising the curse which she has entailed upon the juvenile Sam, along with that of annihilation upon the Hindoos, opium upon the Chinese, imposts upon Australia, cockneyism upon Canada, and friendship upon France, not to speak of the taxation, and so forth, of '76?

But just hear what this godly Old England did, and you will find that the puritanical children of Sam have been the fit collaborateurs of that most reverend and holy dame, who

---

* **Bancroft, page 159, Vol. 1.**

5

has historically, and according to a fixed system, coined her own, as well as the heart's blood of others, into gold.

Conditional servitude under indentures or covenants, had from the first, existed in Virginia. The servant stood to his master in the relation of a debtor, bound to discharge the costs of emigration, by the entire employment of his powers for the benefit of his creditor. Oppression early ensued; men who had been transported into Virginia, at an expense of eight or ten pounds, were sold sometimes for forty, fifty or even threescore pounds.

The supply of white servants became a regular business, and a class of men, nicknamed Spirits, used to delude young persons, servants, and idlers, into embarking for America, as to a land of spontaneous plenty. White servants came to be a usual article of traffic. They were sold in England to be transported, and in Virginia were resold to the highest bidder, like they were purchased on shipboard, as men buy horses at a fair. In 1672, the average price in the colonies, where five years of service were due, was about ten pounds, while a negro was worth twenty or twenty-five pounds. So usual was this manner of dealing in Englishmen, that not the Scots only, who were taken in the field of Quebec, were sent into involuntary servitude in New England, but the Royalists, prisoners of the battle of Worcester, and the leaders in the insurrection of Penruddoc, in spite of the remonstrance of Haselrig and Henry Vane, were shipped to America.

At the corresponding period, in Ireland, the crowded exportation of Irish Catholics was a frequent event, and was attended by aggravations, hardly inferior to the usual atrocities of the African slave-trade. In 1685, when nearly a thousand of the prisoners condemned for participating in the insurrection of Monmouth, were sentenced to transportation, men of influence at court, with rival importunity, scrambled for the convicted insurgents as a merchantable commodity!

CHAPTER X.

Slavery brought home to the Children of "Sam"—Pure Domestic Aspect—Original existence in all the Colonies—Sam's Slave Panic in New York.

"SAM" says, with a dry laugh, "Ha! ha! my Bigots of the North!—you see by this time, that Slavery has not been the peculiar crime of my southern children! Jew and Gentile, Greek, Heathen, Infidel, and all have alike been participators in this world-entailed crime—if you must have it such—and that, therefore, to say the most of it, you can not make it appear to have *originated* with what you self-righteously term the God-forsaken adventurers of the South. Why, as for that, the first one of the colonies which made the prohibition of your own first pet staples, Rum and Slaves, a fundamental law of its original organization, happens to have been a southern colony—Georgia.

Yes, the mild and amiable Oglethorpe, who, in England had been a prominent champion of the repeal of the law of imprisonment for debt, and who was the founder of Georgia, obtained, by his influence with the trustees of the company, not only the prohibition of Rum and Slaves, but also a recognition of religious toleration for his colony—that same religious toleration which you had banished the great and good Roger Williams for even advocating! Among the first emigrants sent over to Savannah were forty Jews, whom you would no doubt have drawn and quartered had they attempted to effect a lodgment in your godly Plymouth! To be sure, they excluded Catholics at the same time, as was very natural, because it was from their savage persecutions that the Lutherans and Moravians—who constituted the bulk of the earliest emigrations—had fled for refuge in the wilds of the savannah.

But, as you Round Heads seem to have entirely forgotten the facts of your own early history in relation to this same subject of Slavery, it is time you were reminded of it, once for all, and you shall have the details in full, from the pen of your own peculiar historian, Hildreth—who, whatever may be his occasional brusqueries of manner when speaking of men peculiarly obnoxious for their Southernisms, is the only really competent national Historian you have ever produced. He opens this subject—which he has so ably treated—with a snarl very characteristic of the latitude of Boston, by pleasantly remarking that the results of their own idleness, inexperience, and incapacity, joined to the inevitable obstacles which every new settlement must encounter, were obstinately ascribed by the inhabitants of Georgia to that wise but ineffectual prohibition of slavery, one of the fundamental laws of the province. The convenience of the moment caused future consequences to be wholly overlooked. Every means was made use of to get rid of this prohibition. Even Whitfield and Habersham, forgetful of their former scruples, strenuously pleaded with the trustees in favor of slavery, under the old pretense of propagating in that way the Christian religion. "Many of the poor slaves in America," wrote Habersham, "have already been made freemen of the heavenly Jerusalem." The Salzburgers for a long time had scruples, but were reassured by advice from Germany: "If you take slaves in faith, and with intent of conducting them to Christ, the action will not be a sin, but may prove a benediction." Thus, as usual, the religious sentiment and its most disinterested votaries were made tools of by avarice for the enslavement of mankind. Habersham, however, could hardly be included in this class. Having thrown off the missionary, and established a mercantile house at Savannah, the first, and for a long time the only one there, he was very anxious for exportable produce. The counselors of Georgia, for the president was now so old as to be quite incapacitated for business, winked at violatious of the law, and a considerable number of negroes had been already introduced from Carolina as hired servants, under indentures for life or a hundred years. The constant toast at Savannah was "The one thing needful," by which was meant negroes. The leading men, both at

Inverness and Ebenezer, who opposed the introduction of slavery, were traduced, threatened and persecuted. (1749.)

Thus beset, the trustees yielded at last, on condition that all masters, under 'a mulct of £5,' should be obliged to compel their negroes 'to attend at some time on the Lord's day for instruction in the Christian religion'—the origin, doubtless, of the peculiarly religious character of the negroes in and about Savannah. The trustees also abolished the restrictions hitherto existing on the tenure and transfer of lands. The aged Stevens having given up his office to Henry Parker, a colonial Assembly was called, not to legislate, for that power belonged solely to the trustees, but to advise and consult. Parker was presently succeeded by Patrick Graham.

By custom or by statute, whether legal or illegal, slavery existed as a fact in every one of the Anglo-American colonies. The soil and climate of New England, made slaves of little value there, except as domestic servants. In 1701, the town of Boston had instructed its representatives in the General Court, to propose 'putting a period to negroes being slaves.' About the same time, Sewall, a judge of the Superior Court, afterward chief justice of Massachusetts, published 'The Selling of Joseph,' a pamphlet tending to a similar end. But these scruples seem to have been short-lived. With the increase of wealth and luxury, the number of slaves increased also. There were in Massachusetts, in 1754, as appears by an official census, twenty-four hundred and forty-eight negro slaves over sixteen years of age, about a thousand of them in Boston—a greater proportion to the free inhabitants than is to be found at present in the city of Baltimore. Connecticut exceeded Massachusetts in the ratio of its slave population, and Rhode Island exceeded Connecticut. Newport, grown to be the second commercial town in New England, had a proportion of slaves larger than Boston. The harsh slave laws in force in the more southern colonies, were unknown, however, in New England. Slaves were regarded as possessing the same legal rights as apprentices; and masters, for abuse of their authority, were liable to indictment. Manumissions, however, were not allowed, except upon security, that the freed slaves should not become a burden to the parish. (1750).

In the provinces of New York and New Jersey, negro slaves were employed, to a certain extent, not only as domestic servants, but as agricultural laborers. In the city of New York, they constituted a sixth part of the population. The slave code of that province was hardly less harsh than that of Virginia.

In Pennsylvania the number of slaves was small, partly owing to the ample supply of indented white servants, but partly, also, to scruples of conscience on the part of the Quakers. In the early days of the province, in 1688, some German Quakers, shortly after their arrival, had expressed the opinion that slavery was not morally lawful. George Keith had borne a similar testimony; but he was disowned as schismatic, and presently abandoning the society, was denounced as a renegade. When Penn, in 1699, had proposed to provide by law for the marriage, religious instruction, and kind treatment of slaves, he met with no response from the Quaker Legislature. In 1712, to a petition in favor of emancipating the negroes, the Assembly replied, 'that it was neither just nor convenient to set them at liberty.' They imposed, however, a heavy duty, in effect prohibitory, and intended to be so, on the importation of negroes. This act, as we have seen, was negatived by the crown. The policy, however, was persevered in. New acts, passed from time to time, restricted importations by a duty first of five, but lately reduced to two pounds per head. The Quaker testimony against slavery, was renewed by Sandiford and Lay, who brought with them to Pennsylvania, a strong detestation of the system of servitude which they had seen in Barbadoes in all its rigors. The same views began presently to be perseveringly advocated by Woolman and Benezet, whose labors were not without effect upon the Quakers, some of whom set the example of emancipating their slaves. Franklin was also distinguished as an early and decided advocate for emancipation. The greater part of the slaves of Pennsylvania were to be found in Philadelphia. A fourth part of the inhabitants of that city were persons of African descent, including many, however, who had obtained their freedom. (1750).

In the tobacco growing colonies, Maryland, Virginia, and

North Carolina, slaves constituted a third part or more of the population. In South Carolina, where rice was the principal produce, they were still more numerous, decidedly outnumbering the free inhabitants. (1750.)

The slave code of South Carolina, as revised and re-enacted in a statute still regarded as having the force of law, had dropped from its phraseology something of the extreme harshness of the former act. It contained, also, some provisions for the benefit of the slaves, but, on the whole, was harder than before. 'Whereas,' says the preamble to this act, (1740), 'in his majesty's plantations in America, slavery has been introduced and allowed, and the people commonly called negroes, Indians, mulattoes, and mestizoes have been deemed absolute slaves, and the subjects of property in the hands of particular persons, the extent of whose power over such slaves, ought to be settled and limited by positive laws, so that the slaves may be kept in due subjection and obedience, and the owners and other persons having the care and government of slaves, may be restrained from exercising too great rigor and cruelty over them, and that the public peace and order of this province may be preserved,' it is therefore enacted that 'all negroes, Indians mulattoes and mestizoes (free Indians in amity with this government, and negroes, mulattoes, and mestizoes who are now free, excepted), who now are, or shall hereafter be in this province, and all their issue and offspring born and to be born, shall be, and they are hereby declared to be and remain forever hereafter absolute slaves, and shall follow the condition of the mother, and shall be claimed, held, taken, reputed, and adjudged in law to be chattels personal.' This provision, which deprives the master of the power of manumission, and subjects to slavery the descendant of every slave woman, no matter how many degrees removed, nor who may have been the male ancestor, nor what color, was subsequently adopted in the same terms, by the Georgia Legislature, as the law of that province. A suit for freedom might be brought by any white man who chose to volunteer for that purpose on behalf of any person claimed as a slave. But, in all such suits, 'the burden of proof shall lie upon the plaintiff, and it shall always be presumed that every negro, Indian, mulatto, and mestizo is a slave unless the contrary can be made to appear, the Indians in amity with this government excepted, in which case the burden of proof shall lie on the defendant.' Masters were forbidden to allow their slaves to hire their own time; to let or hire any plantation; to possess any vessel or boat; to keep or raise any horses, cattle, or hogs; to engage in any sort of trade on their own account; to be taught to write; or to have or wear any apparel (except livery servants) 'finer than negro cloth, duffils, kerseys, osnabergs, blue linen, check linen, or coarse garlix or calicoes, checked cotton or Scotch plaid;' and any constable seeing any negro better clad, might seize the clothes and appropriate them to his own use. It was forbidden to work slaves on Sundays, under a penalty of five pounds; for working them more than fifteen hours daily in summer, and fourteen in winter, a like penalty was imposed. Upon complaint to any justice that any master does not provide his slaves with sufficient 'clothing, covering, or food,' the justice might make such order in the premises as he saw fit, and fine the master not exceeding twenty pounds. 'And whereas cruelty is not only highly unbecoming those who profess themselves Christians, but odious in the eyes of all men who have any sense of virtue and humanity,' the fine for the willful murder of a slave was increased to £700 currency, with incapacity to hold any office, civil or military, and in case of inability to pay the fine, seven years' labor in a frontier garrison or the Charleston workhouse. For killing a slave in the heat of passion, for maiming, or inflicting any other cruel punishment 'other than by whipping or beating with a horsewhip, cowskin, switch, or small stick, or by putting in irons or imprisonment,' a fine of £320 was imposed; and in case of slaves found dead, maimed, or otherwise cruelly punished, the masters were to be held guilty of the act unless they make the contrary appear. (1750.)

No statute of North Carolina seems ever to have been declared who were or might be held as slaves in that province, the whole system being left to rest on usage, or the supposed law of England. But police laws for the regulation of slaves were enacted similar to those of Virginia, and the Virginia prohibition was also adopted of manumissions, except for meritorious services, to be adjudged by the governor and council. (1741.)

Among the ten acts of the late Virginia revision rejected by the king, was one (1751) 'concerning servants and slaves,' a consolidation and re-enactment of all the old statutes on that subject, the substance of which has been given in former chapters. It appears from the address, already quoted, of the Assembly to the king (1752) on the subject of this veto, to have been a standing instruction to the governor not to consent to the re-enactment of any law once rejected by the king, without express leave first obtained upon representation of the reasons and necessity for it. Such a representation was accordingly made by the Assembly as to eight of the ten rejected laws. The act concerning servants and slaves was not of this number (1753), yet we find it re-enacted, within a year after, in the very same words. Why the royal assent had been refused does not appear. It could hardly have been from any scruples on the subject of slavery (1750); for among the acts expressly approved was one 'for the better government of Indians, negroes and mulattoes,' which provided that the death of a slave under extremity of correction should not be esteemed murder, unless it were proved by the oath of at least one 'lawful and credible witness' that the slave was willfully and maliciously killed; persons indicted for the murder of a slave, and found guilty of manslaughter only, to 'incur no forfeiture or punishment.' Slaves set free without leave from the governor and council, might be sold at public auction by the churchwardens of any parish in which such freed slave might reside for the space of a month. The same statute also continued the authority formerly given to the county courts to 'dismember' disorderly slaves 'notoriously guilty of going abroad in the night, or running away and lying out,' and not to be reclaimed by the common methods—an authority very much abused, if we may judge by a subsequent statute, which declares this dismembering 'to be often disproportioned to the offense, and contrary to the principles of humanity,' and prohibits the castration of slaves except on conviction of an attempt to ravish a white woman. (1769.)

The negroes imported from the African coast, whose descendants now constitute a sixth part of the population of the United States, were not by any means of one nation, language, or race. A single slave ship often brought to America a great variety of languages and customs, a collection of unfortunate strangers to each other, or perhaps of hereditary enemies, with no common bond except that of servitude. Hence a want of union and sympathy among the slaves, which, joined to their extreme ignorance and simplicity, prevented co-operation, and rendered it easy to suppress such outbreaks as occasionally occurred. (1750.) Even in complexion and physiognomy, the most obvious characteristic of the negroes, there were great differences. Some were of a jet black, often with features approaching the European standard; others of a mahogany or reddish black, with features less shapely and regular; and others yet of a tawny yellow, with flat noses and projecting jaws—an ugliness often, but erroneously, esteemed characteristic of all the African races, but which seems to have been principally confined to the low and swampy grounds about the Delta of the Niger. The negroes marked by these shapeless features were noted also for indomitable capacity of endurance, and were esteemed, therefore, the best slaves. Intermixture among themselves, and a large infusion of European blood, have gradually obliterated these differences, or made them less noticeable.

Contrary to what happened in the West Indies, in the Anglo-North American provinces the natural increase of the slave population was rapid. The women were seldom put to the severer labors of the field. The long winter secured to both sexes a season of comparative rest. Such was the abundance of provisions, that it was cheaper to breed than to buy slaves. Those born in America, and reared up on the plantations, evidently surpassed the imported Africans both physically and intellectually. Of the imported slaves a few were Mohammedans, among whom were occasionally found persons of some education, who knew Arabic, and could read the Koran. But the great mass were pagans, in a condition of gross barbarism. They brought with them from Africa many superstitions, but these, for the most part, as well as the negro languages, very soon died out.

Zealous for religion as the colonists were, very little effort was made to convert the negroes, owing partly, at least, to a prevalent opinion that neither Christian brotherhood nor the law of England would justify the holding Christians as slaves. Nor could repeated colonial enactments to the contrary entirely root out this idea, for it was not supposed that a colonial statute could set aside the law of England. What, precisely, the English law might be on the subject of slavery, still remained a matter of doubt. Lord Holt had expressed the opinion, as quoted in a previous chapter, that slavery was a condition unknown to English law, and that every person setting foot in England thereby became free. American planters, on their visits to England, accompanied by their slaves, seem to have been annoyed by claims of freedom set up on this ground, and that, also, of baptism. To relieve their embarrassments, the merchants concerned in the American trade had obtained a written opinion from Yorke and Talbot, the attorney and solicitor-general of that day. (1729.) According to this opinion, which passed for more than forty years as good law, not only was baptism no bar to slavery. but negro slaves might be held in England just as well as in the colonies. The two lawyers by whom this opinion was given, rose afterward, one of them to be chief justice of England, and both to be chancellors. Yorke, sitting in the latter capacity with the title of Lord Hardwicke (1749), had recently recognized the doctrine of that opinion as sound law. (Pearce *vs.* Lisle, Ambler, 76.) He objects to Lord Holt's doctrine of freedom, secured by setting foot on English soil, that no reason could be found 'why slaves should not be equally free when they set foot in Jamaica or any other English plantation.' 'All our colonies are subject to the laws of England, although, as to some purposes, they have laws of their own.' His argument is, that if slavery be contrary to English law, no local enactments in the colonies could give it any validity. To avoid overturning slavery in the colonies, it was absolutely necessary to uphold it in England. At a subsequent period, as we shall presently see, the law of England was definitively settled in favor of liberty, the extra-judicial opinion of Talbot and Hardwicke being set aside by a solemn decision of the King's Bench. (1750.)

The remaining exclusive privileges of the Royal African Company having expired, the English government undertook to maintain, at their own expense, the forts and factories on the African coast; and thus the slave trade was thrown open to free competition. The recent introduction of the cultivation of coffee into the West Indies, and the increasing consumption in Europe of colonial produce, gave fresh impulse to this detestable traffic, and it now began to be carried on to an extent which soon roused against it the indignant humanity of an enlightened age. The West Indies were the chief market; but the imports to Virginia and the Carolinas were largely increased. New England rum, manufactured at Newport, was profitably exchanged on the coast of Africa for negroes, to be sold in the southern colonies; and vessels sailed on the same business from Boston and New York. The trade, however, was principally carried on by English merchants of Bristol and Liverpool. Except in Pennsylvania, the colonial duties levied on the import of slaves were intended chiefly for revenue. They were classed in the instructions to the royal governors with duties on British goods, as impediments to British commerce not to be favored. On this ground several of these acts received the royal veto. Yet Virginia, as we have seen, was allowed to impose such duties as she pleased, on the sole condition of making them payable by the buyer. (1750.)

The importation of indented white persons, called 'servants,' or sometimes 'redemptioners,' in distinction from negroes, who were known as slaves, was still extensively carried on, especially in the middle colonies. The colonial enactments for keeping these servants in order, and especially for preventing them from running away, were often very harsh and severe. They were put, for the most part, in these statutes, on the same level with the slaves, but their case in other respects was very different. In all the colonies, the term of indented service, even where no express contract had been entered into, was strictly limited by law, and, except in the case of very young persons, it seldom or never exceeded seven years. On the expiration of that term, these freed servants were absorbed into the mass of white inhabitants, and the way lay open before them and their children to wealth and social distinction. One of the future signers of the Declaration of Independence was brought to Pennsylvania as a redemptioner. In Virginia, at the expiration of his term of service, every redemptioner, in common with other immigrants to the colony, was entitled to a free grant of fifty acres of land, and in all the colonies certain allowances of clothing were required to be made by the late masters. Poverty, however, and want of education on the part of the mass of these freed men, kept them too often in a subservient condition, and created in the middle as well as in the southern colonies, an inferior order of poor whites, a distinction of classes, and an inequality in society almost unknown in republican New England.

The position of the Africans was much more disastrous. Not only were they servants for life, which possibly the law of England might have countenanced, but by colonial statute and usage this servitude descended to their children also. The few set free by the good-will or the scruples of their masters seemed a standing reproach to slavery, and an evil example in the eyes of the rest. They became the objects of a suspicious legislation, which deprived them of most of the rights of freemen, and reduced them to a social position very similar, in many respects, to that which inveterate prejudice in many parts of Europe has fixed upon the Jews. Hence, too, legislative restraints on the bounty or justice of the master in manumitting his slave.

Intermarriage with the inferior race, whether bond or free, was prohibited by religion as a sin, by public opinion as a shame, and by law as a crime. But neither law, Gospel, nor public opinion could prevent that amalgamation which, according to all experience, inevitably and extensively takes place whenever two races come into that close juxtaposition which domestic slavery of necessity implies. Falsehood and hypocrisy took the place of restraint and self-denial. The Dutch, French, Spanish, and Portuguese colonists, less filled with pride of race, and less austere and pretending in their religious morality, esteemed that white man mean and cruel, who did not, so far as his ability permitted, secure for his colored children emancipation and some pecuniary provision. Laws were even found necessary, in some of those colonies, to limit what was esteemed a superfluity of parental tenderness. In the Anglo-American colonies, colored children were hardly less numerous. But conventional decorum, more potent than law, forbade any recognition by the father. They followed the condition of the mother. They were born, and they remained slaves. European blood was thus constantly transferred into servile veins; and hence, among the slaves sold and bought to-day in our American markets, may be found the descendants of men distinguished in colonial and national annals.'

In 1741, says Hildreth, the city of New York became the scene of a cruel and bloody delusion, less notorious, but not less lamentable than the Salem witchcraft. That city now contained some seven or eight thousand inhabitants, of whom twelve or fifteen hundred were slaves. Nine fires in rapid succession, most of them, however, merely the burning of chimneys, produced a perfect insanity of terror. An indented servant woman purchased her liberty and secured a reward of £100, by pretending to give information of a plot formed by a low tavern-keeper, her master, and three negroes to burn the city and murder the whites. This story was confirmed and amplified by an Irish prostitute convicted of a robbery, who, to recommend herself to mercy, reluctantly turned informer. Numerous arrests had been already made among the slaves and free blacks. Many others followed. The eight lawyers who then composed the bar of New York, all assisted by turns on behalf of the prosecution. The prisoners, who had no counsel, were tried and convicted upon most insufficient evidence. The lawyers vied with each other in heaping all sorts of abuse on their heads, and chief justice Delancey, in passing sentence, vied with the lawyers. Many confessed, to save their lives, and then accused others. Thirteen unhappy convicts were burned at the stake, eighteen were hanged, and seventy-one transported. (1741.)

The war and the religious excitement then prevailing, tended to inflame the yet hot prejudices against Catholics. A non-juring schoolmaster, accused of being a Catholic priest in disguise, and of stimulating the negroes to burn the city by promises of absolution, was condemned and executed. Glutted with blood, and their fright appeased, the citizens began at last to recover their senses. The informers lost their credit, and a stop was put to these judicial murders.

One of your periodical frights! says Sam. Now will you hush about slavery, once and forever? You deserve to be spanked and put to bed—the whole of you!

CHAPTER XI.

Puritan Sam and Individuality—"Day" first Printer—abuse of the Virginia Settlers in the "Yellow covered Literature" of History—Who were the true Discoverers and Settlers of America?

BUT enough of Puritanical Sam for the present. We have seen him to be a strange compound of manhood and cant, a bigot, a bully, a hero and a savage, as well as the proud originator of the grave problem of "individuality," or "the one man development," which made him with so much emphasis, "Soldier, Slaver, Psalmist, Cobler, Farmer, Persecutor, Parson, Legislator and good Citizen alike." This idea, which however little understood in Europe, and especially in France, constitutes the basis of the much abused idea of "Liberty and Equality." But the Plymouth Sam was not the only hero of progressive humanity, although he has managed, from the fact of having had the earliest printing-press, to have been systematically and pertinaciously his own glorificator, in asserting what amounts to as much.

The first printing in America was done in New England, in 1639, by one "Day," who was very properly named as the originator of Light. The proprietor of this first press, was characteristically a clergyman, who was quite as characteristically named "Glover;" but unluckily, he died on the passage. It seems somewhat significant, that the first thing printed should have been the "Freeman's Oath;" the second an almanac; the third, an edition of the Psalms. Since this important event, it is quite natural that most of the Psalmody of Puritanical Sam, should have been in and for his own honor.

Having, for a long time, the exclusive control of the "Day," of the printing-press, he has managed to make, as much as possible, a dark lantern of it, casting its light only where it best suited his interest and bigotries.

This may be well enough says Sam, but while he has been thus assiduously staining paper in his own glorification, my Southern children have been producing the material out of which this same paper is manufactured; and, watching his round-headed brother manufacture a "character" for himself, has been content with producing orators, statesmen, generals, and presidents for him.

The first adventurers who settled St. Augustine in Florida, and Jamestown in Virginia, Sam continues, have been methodically characterized by my Quaker-hanging descendants, as "dissolute and 'sensual' vagabonds, who left their respective countries 'for their country's good.'" But *we, Sam,* have never been able to discover, why the adventurers who dared the perils of storm, and sea, and wilderness in the South, were not as good and true men—the nasal twang left out—as those who presume they have performed the same feats at the North.

Sam thinks it is about time that this ridiculous cant should be rebuked. There is an old fable which tells us that, once upon a time, there came a question between the lion and a man, as to which should rank superior. The man, in proof of his argument, made a sculpture of a human figure astride of a lion; the lion's answer was: "Make me the sculptor, and then you would be underneath my paws."

Thus it is the Southern Sam has never been an illustrator of himself in idle words, but an actor, a power, and a governing presence; and therefore it is, that Puritanical Sam makes a harmonican of his nose, in speaking of his "dissolute" Southern brother. We say harmonican, because it is an instrument invented since the "Blue Laws," or else he would not dare to play upon that even—if it had been a harp now, it would have been all legitimate.

The best of the joke is, says Sam, that these patronizing inventors of the "yellow-covered Literature" of History, who have thus systematically stigmatized a portion of my Family, seem to be utterly oblivious of the fact, that the Southern races are most intimately connected with the primitive history of my small plantation, and to them belong the undivided honor, not only of discovering a New World, but of settling it with a people who had something else in their brains beside the menial obscurities of bigotry.

Did Columbus affect codfish and psalmody when he discovered a New World? No! Sam says that "Columbus, in a rich dress, and with a drawn sword, soon after landed with his men, with whom having kneeled and kissed the ground with tears of joy, he took formal possession of the island, in the name of Queen Isabella, his patroness."

Yes! the discoverer of a New World, first kneeled to his God, then kissed the face of his mother earth, as all her truest, proudest children would have done in such conditions. He had no voice just then—the mighty minstrelsy of winds and waves filled all the air, and he who could invent a world before Yankeedom had been invented, was mute.

But to Sam, it has always seemed that one of the important institutions of Puritanism, has been a "clamor." He will not undertake to say "sound for fury," but its significant opposite.

The peerless Knight, Sir Walter Raleigh, was properly the founder of North Carolina and Virginia; he, the most chivalrous, the most learned of adventurers, the genial and accomplished historian of the old world, was naturally among the chief architects of a New.

Raleigh, whose ample means and unconquerable energy, were lavished upon the sublimest idea which ever possessed the minds of men—the occupation of a New World—Raleigh, the lover of "the great Queen," the "Gloriana" of Spencer—the master intellect of the greatest period of English history—the Shakspearian of deeds—may assuredly be with justice, characterized as the chief promoter of "sensual and dissolute vagabondism" in the settlement of a region, which has since been so unfortunate as to have produced a Washington, a Patrick Henry, a Jefferson, a Madison, a Monroe, *et ii omnes*—not to speak of Randolph, Old Rough and Ready, etc.

Unlucky Raleigh! were your cavaliers all actually released from the galleys and prisons of Europe? Let us hear the story of the chiefest ignoble among them. We give the simple narrative, and leave cant to gasp over it.

CHAPTER XII.

Formation of the London Company for the Settlement of Virginia—Birthplace of Capt. John Smith, and early crosses—Enters the service of Austria—Single combats in presence of both armies—Prisoner among the Tartars—Romantic adventures and escape—Joins the London Company—Prisoner among the Indians—Saved from death by the youthful Pocahontas—Other achievements in America.

PRIOR to the year 1607, a period of one hundred and fifteen years from the discovery of San Salvador, by Columbus, attempts had been made to effect settlements in various parts of North America; but no one proved successful until the settlement at Jamestown.

In 1606, King James I, of England, granted letters patent, an exclusive right or privilege, to two companies, called the London and Plymouth Companies, by which they were authorized to possess the lands in America, lying between the 34th and 45th degrees of north latitude; the southern part called South Virginia, to the London, and the northern, called North Virginia, to the Plymouth Company.

Under this patent the London Company sent Capt. Christopher Newport to Virginia, December 20, 1606, with a colony of one hundred and five persons to commence a settlement on the island Roanoke, now in North Carolina. After a tedious voyage of four months, by the circuitous route of the West Indies, he entered Chesapeake Bay, having been driven north of the place of his destination.

Here it was concluded to land; and proceeding up a river, called by the Indians Powhattan, but by the colony, James river, on a beautiful peninsula, in May, 1607, they began the first permanent settlement in North America, and called it Jamestown.

The government of this colony was formed in England by the London Company. It consisted of a council of seven persons, appointed by the Company, with a president chosen by the council from their number, who had two votes. All matters of moment were examined by this council, and determined by a majority. Capt. Newport brought over the names of this council, carefully sealed in a box, which was opened after their arrival.

Among the most enterprising and useful members of this colony, and one of its magistrates, was Captain John Smith. As he acted a distinguished part in the early history of the colony of Virginia, a brief sketch of his life will be interesting.

He was born in Willoughby, in Lincolnshire, England, in 1579. From his earliest youth, he discovered a roving and romantic genius, and appeared irresistibly bent on extravagant and daring enterprises. At the age of thirteen, becoming tired of study, he disposed of his satchel and books, with the intention of escaping to sea; but the death of his father just at that time, frustrated his plans for the present, and threw him upon guardians, who, to repress the waywardness of his genius, confined him to a counting-room. From a confinement so irksome, however, he contrived to escape not long after, and with ten shillings in his pocket, entered the train of a young nobleman traveling to France.

On their arrival at Orleans, he received a discharge from further attendance upon Lord Bertie, who advanced him money to return to England.

Smith had no wish, however, to return. With the money he had received he visited Paris, from which he proceeded to the low countries, where he enlisted into the service as a soldier. Having continued some time in this capacity, he was induced to accompany a gentleman to Scotland, who promised to recommend him to the notice of King James. Being disappointed, however, in this, he returned to England and visited the place of his birth. Not finding the company there that suited his romantic turn, he erected a booth in some wood, and in the manner of a recluse, retired from society, devoting himself to the study of military history and tactics, diverting himself at intervals with his horse and lance.

Recovering, about this time, a part of his father's estate,

which had been in dispute, in 1596 he again commenced his travels, being then only seventeen years of age. His first stage was Flanders, where, meeting with a Frenchman who pretended to be heir to a noble family, he was prevailed upon to accompany him to France. On their arrival at St. Valory, in Picardy, by the connivance of the shipmaster, the Frenchman and attendants robbed him of his effects, and succeeded in making their escape.

Eager to pursue his travels, he endeavored to procure a place on board a man-of-war. In one of his rambles, searching for a ship that would receive him, he accidentally met one of the villains concerned in robbing him. Without exchanging a word, they both instantly drew their swords. The contest was severe, but Smith succeeded in wounding and disarming his antagonist, and obliged him to confess his guilt. After this rencounter, having received pecuniary assistance from an acquaintance, the Earl of Ployer, he traveled along the French coast to Bayonne, and then crossed to Marseilles, visiting and observing everything in his course which had reference to naval or military architecture.

At Marseilles he embarked for Italy in company with a number of pilgrims. But here, also, new troubles awaited him. During the voyage, a tempest arising, the ship was forced into Toulon, after leaving which contrary winds so impeded their progress that, in a fit of rage, the pilgrims imputing their ill fortune to the presence of a heretic, threw him into the sea.

Being a good swimmer, he was enabled to reach the island of St. Mary, off Nice, at no great distance, where he was taken on board a ship, in which, altering his course, he sailed to Alexandria in Egypt, and thence coasted the Levant. Having spent some time in this region, he sailed on his return, and on leaving the ship, received about two thousand dollars, as his portion of a rich prize, which they had taken during the voyage.

Smith landed at Antibes. He now traveled through Italy, crossed the Adriatic, and passed into Styria, to the seat of Ferdinand, Archduke of Austria. The Emperor being at that time at war with the Turks, he entered his army as a volunteer.

By means of his valor and ingenuity, aided by his military

knowledge and experience, he soon distinguished himself, and was advanced to the command of a company, consisting of two hundred and fifty horsemen, in the regiment of Count Meldrick, a nobleman of Transylvania.

The regiment in which he served was engaged in several hazardous enterprises, in which Smith exhibited a bravery admired by all the army, and when Meldrick left the Imperial service for that of his native prince, Smith followed.

At the siege of Regal he was destined to new adventures. The Ottomans deriding the slow advance of the Transylvania army, the Lord Turbisha dispatched a messenger with a challenge, that for the diversion of the ladies of the place, he would fight any captain of the Christian troops.

The honor of accepting this challenge was determined by lot, and fell on Smith. At the time appointed, the two champions appeared in the field on horseback, and in the presence of the armies, and of the ladies of the insulting Ottoman, rushed impetuously to the attack. A short but desperate conflict ensued, at the end of which Smith was seen bearing the head of the lifeless Turbisha in triumph to his general.

The fall of the chief filled his friend Crualgo with indignation, and roused him to avenge his death. Smith accordingly soon after received a challenge from him, which he did not hesitate to accept, and the two exasperated combatants, upon their chargers, fell with desperate fury upon each other. Victory again followed the falchion of Smith, who sent the Turk headlong to the ground.

It was now the turn of Smith to make the advance. He dispatched a messenger therefore to the Turkish ladies, that if they were desirous of more diversion of a similar kind, they should be welcome to his head, in case their third champion could take it.

Bonamalgro tendered his services, and haughtily accepted the Christian's challenge. When the day arrived the spectators assembled, and the combatants entered the field. It was an hour of deep anxiety to all; as the horsemen approached a deathlike silence pervaded the multitude. A blow from the saber of the Turk brought Smith to the ground, and for a moment it seemed as if the deed of death was done. Smith, however, was only stunned. He rose like a lion, when he shakes the dew from his mane for the fight, and vaulting into the saddle, made his falchion "shed fast atonement for its first delay." It is hardly necessary to add that the head of Bonamalgro was added to the number.

Smith was received with transports of joy by the prince of Transylvania, who, after the capture of the place, presented him with his picture set in gold, granted him a pension of three hundred ducats a year, and conferred on him a coat of arms, bearing three Turks' heads in a shield.

In a subsequent battle between the Transylvanian army and a body of Turks and Tartars, the former was defeated, with a loss of many killed and wounded. Among the wounded was the gallant Smith. His dress bespoke his consequence, and he was treated kindly. On his recovery from his wounds, he was sold to the Bashaw Bogul, who sent him as a present to his mistress at Constantinople, assuring her that he was a Bohemian nobleman whom he had conquered, and whom he now presented to her as her slave.

The present proved more acceptable to the lady than her lord intended. As she understood Italian, in that language Smith informed her of his country and quality, and by his singular address and engaging manners, won the affection of her heart.

Designing to secure him to herself, but fearing lest some misfortune should befall him, she sent him to her brother, a Bashaw, on the borders of the sea of Asoph, with a direction that he should be initiated into the manners and language, as well as the religion of the Tartars. From the terms of her letter, her brother suspected her design, and resolved to disappoint her. Immediately after Smith's arrival, therefore, he ordered him to be stripped, his head and beard to be shaven, and with an iron collar about his neck, and a dress of hair-cloth, he was driven forth to labor among some Christian slaves.

The circumstances of Smith were peculiarly afflicting. He could indulge no hope, except from the attachment of his mistress, but as her distance was great, it was improbable that she would soon become acquainted with the story of his misfortunes.

In the midst of his distress, an opportunity to escape presented itself, but under circumstances, which, to a person of a less adventurous spirit, would have served only to highten his distress. His employment was thrashing, at the distance of a league from the residence of the Bashaw, who daily visited him, but treated him with rigorous severity, and in a fit of anger, even abused him with blows. This last, was treatment to which the independent spirit of Smith could not submit. Watching a favorable opportunity, on an occasion of the tyrant's visit, and when his attendants were absent, he leveled his thrashing instrument at him and laid him in the dust.

He then hastily filled a bag with grain, and mounted the Bashaw's horse, put himself upon fortune. Directing his course toward a desert, he entered its recesses, and continuing to conceal himself in its obscurities for several days, at length made his escape. In sixteen days he arrived at Exapolis, on the river Don, where meeting with the Russian garrison, the commander treated him kindly, and gave him letters of recommendation to other commanders in that region.

He now traveled through a part of Russia and Poland, and at length reached his friends in Transylvania. At Leipsic he enjoyed the pleasure of meeting his Colonel, Count Meldrick, and Sigismund, Prince of Transylvania, who presented him with fifteen hundred ducats. His fortune being thus in a measure repaired, he traveled through Germany, France, and Spain, and having visited the kingdom of Morocco, returned once more to England.

Such is a rapid view of the life of this interesting adventurer, down to his arrival in his native land. At this time, the settlement of America was occupying the attention of many distinguished men in England. The life of Smith, united to his fondness for enterprises of danger and difficulty, had prepared him to embark with zeal, in a project so novel and sublime as that of exploring the wilds of a newly discovered continent.

He was soon attached to the expedition, about to sail under Newport, and was appointed one of the magistrates of the colony sent over at that time. Before the arrival of the colony, his colleagues in office becoming jealous of his influence, arrested him on the absurd charge that he designed to murder the council, usurp the government, and make himself king of Virginia. He was, therefore, rigorously confined during the remainder of the voyage.

On their arrival in the country he was liberated, but could not obtain a trial, although in the tone of conscious integrity, he repeatedly demanded it. The infant colony was soon involved in perplexity and danger. Notwithstanding Smith had been calumniated, and his honor deeply wounded, his was not the spirit to remain idle when his services were needed. Nobly disdaining revenge, he offered his assistance, and by his talents, experience, and indefatigable zeal, furnished important aid to the infant colony.

Continuing to assert his innocence, and to demand a trial, the time at length arrived when his enemies could postpone it no longer. After a fair hearing of the case, he was honorably acquitted of the charges alleged against him, and soon after took his seat in the council.

The affairs of the colony becoming more settled, the active spirit of Smith prompted him to explore the neighboring country. In an attempt to ascertain the source of Chickahoming river, he ascended in a barge as far as the stream was uninterrupted. Designing to proceed still further, he left the barge in the keeping of the crew, with strict injunctions on no account to leave her, and with two Englishmen and two Indians left the party. But no sooner was he out of view, than the crew, impatient of restraint, repaired on board the barge, and proceeding some distance down the stream, landed at a place where a body of Indians lay in ambush, by whom they were seized.

By means of the crew, the route of Smith was ascertained, and a party of Indians were immediately dispatched to take him. On coming up with him, they fired, killed the Englishmen, and wounded himself. With great presence of mind, he now tied his Indian guide to his left arm, as a shield from the enemies' arrow, while with his musket he dispatched three of the most forward of the assailants.

In this manner he continued to retreat toward his canoe, while the Indians, struck with admiration of his bravery, followed with respectful caution. Unfortunately, coming to a sunken spot filled with mire, while engrossed with eyeing his pursuers, he sunk so deep, as to be unable to extricate himself, and was forced to surrender.

Fruitful in expedients to avert immediate death, he presented an ivory compass to the chief, whose attention was arrested by the vibrations of the needle. Taking advantage of the impression which he had thus made, partly by signs, and partly by language, he excited their wonder still more by telling them of its singular powers.

Their wonder, however, seemed soon to abate, and their attention returned to their prisoner. He was now bound and tied to a tree, and the savages were preparing to direct their arrows at his breast. At this instant the chief holding up the compass, they laid down their arms, and led him in triumph to Powhattan, their king.

Powhattan and his council doomed him to death, as a man whose courage and genius were peculiarly dangerous to the Indians. Preparations were accordingly made, and when the time arrived, Smith was led out to execution. His head was laid upon a stone, and a club presented to Powhattan, who, himself claimed the honor of becoming the executioner. The savages in silence were circling round, and the giant arm of Powhattan had already raised the club to strike the fatal blow, when, to his astonishment, the young and beautiful Pocahontas, his daughter, with a shriek of terror, rushed from the throng, and threw herself upon the body of Smith. At the same time she cast an imploring look toward her furious but astonished father, and in all the eloquence of mute, but impassioned sorrow, besought his life.

The remainder of the scene was honorable to Powhattan. The club of the chief was still uplifted, but a father's pity had touched his heart, and the eye that had first kindled with wrath, was now fast losing its fiercenesss. He looked round as if to collect his fortitude, or perhaps, to find an excuse for his weakness, in the pity of the attendants. A similar sympathy had melted the savage throng, and seemed to join in the petition, which the weeping Pocahontas felt, but durst not utter: "My father! let the prisoner live." Powhattan raised his daughter, and the captive, scarcely yet assured of safety, from the earth.

Shortly after, Powhattan dismissed Captain Smith with assurances of friendship, and the next morning, accompanied with a guard of twelve men, he arrived safely at Jamestown, after a captivity of seven weeks.*

* Burk's Virginia.

CHAPTER XIII.

Historical depreciation of Sam's Southern children—Abusive epithets current—Contrast with the first Northern Settlements—Who, apparently, under the ban of Providence?—Who were the Discoverers and Explorers of the New World?

So much for the peerless chevalier—the Father of Virginia, and Explorer of the North,*—illustrious John Smith! Nor is this all of his career. It had been chiefly through his influence, that James I was induced to grant the "first colonial charter" under which the English were planted in America; although the great majority of Sam's children have never to this day, heard that there was any other place settled in "the beginning," but Plymouth, or any code of laws instituted than the precious "Body" of Rights, with its "Blue" Lights, or Laws, to which we have referred; yet not only is it true, that to John Smith and Virginia we owe the "first colonial charter" in 1606, but to John Smith and Virginia do we owe, in June, 1619, the "first colonial assembly" that ever met in America, and which was convened at Jamestown.

While John Carver, Cotton Mather, and the "Saintly Winthrop," are names canonized throughout the land as the select forerunners of Freedom—so many "Baptists" proclaiming in the wilderness the "good news" of the approaching regeneration of humanity—John Smith remains plain "John Smith," who was "saved by Pocahontas."

---

*In 1614, Captain John Smith sailed from England, with two ships, to America. He ranged the coast from Penobscot to Cape Cod. On his return to England, he presented a map of the country to Prince Charles, who named it New England. Thus was the first survey of her own coast, and which resulted in giving her a name, made by the founder of these Southern institutions now so villified by New England.

Sam says fiddle-faddle! the "brazen tongue" wagged by these clerkly fellows is tiresome; they have kept up one eternal too-oo! too-oo! too-oot! in defense of the saintly villains and villainies of their early times when nobody was attacking them. For who troubled themselves about it, since vices and cruelties were, as everybody knew, to be expected in the settlement of all new countries? But not content with taking their chances in the impartial recognition of mankind, and confining themselves to the plain narrative of facts, they have exhibited a systematic effort to forestall what might be expected to become the natural sentiment—a conscious, nervous special pleading in advance, has betrayed the apprehension of justifiable attack. The purpose to "make a character" where they could lay claim to none. Demanding of the credulity of mankind for the Puritan, the united attributes of apostle, saint, lawgiver, statesman, warrior, and psalmodist, they dismiss the renowned and noble founder of Virginia with the contemptuous implication of petty adventure—his illustrious name coupled with a silly story of rescue by a forlorn Indian maiden, (who was in fact, a little child)—as though this "lovely Indian princess" were indeed the heroic actor in the only scene in his career worth recording, while the poor John Smith was merely a passive instrument.

Nor is this all, saith Sam. While, although with pretentious humility, they have very properly, never emulated the "gallant spirit" of the cavaliers, yet, as a saving clause for their self-righteousness, they have stigmatized them as "dissolute gallants, packed off to escape worse destinies at home, broken tradesmen, gentlemen impoverished in spirit and fortune, rakes and libertines; men more fitted to corrupt than to found a commonwealth,"* winding up this delectable catalogue with the pious exclamation: "It was not the will of God that the new State should be formed of these materials—that such men were to be the fathers of a progeny born on the American soil, who were one day to assert American liberty by their eloquence, and defend it by their valor."†

Then as cumulative evidence that the hand of Providence had clearly interposed to prevent such prayerless "vaga-

* Bancroft, page 138, 1st. vol. † Idem, page 138.

bonds" from becoming fathers of a State, they say in the next breath: "John Smith, being wounded and compelled to return to Europe, at his departure, he had left more than four hundred and ninety persons in the colony; in six months, indolence, vice, and famine reduced the number to sixty, and these were so feeble and dejected, that if relief had been delayed but ten days longer, they must have utterly perished."*

Away with such driveling cant, says Sam. If suffering from famine and other necessary and usually attendant dangers of settlement in a new country, be any evidence that God has willed that a set of "vagabonds" should not be permitted to perpetuate their spawn upon the face of a new country, destined to be the home of a free people, what becomes of your own story of the sufferings of the "Pilgrim Fathers?" "After some days they began to build—a difficult task for men of whom one-half were wasting away with consumptions and lung fevers." †

This only a few days after landing, too, quoth Sam; pretty recreations these ascetic self-denying Puritans must have indulged in on board that same immaculate May-Flower! Ask any of my physicians out of New England what habits are most likely to engender consumption, under such circumstances, thunders he in wrath, ask them too if *men* usually "waste away with consumptions and lung fevers" in three or four days!—and you will be apt to find why it is that these fellows did not emulate the "gallant spirit" of the cavaliers.

But this is not all, continues the inexorable Sam, whose pluck is up at hearing his southern children thus gratuitously made the sole plenary examples of the results of vice, indolence and crime.

Was the hand of Providence in it for the extermination of the embryo of a race of hypocritical blue-law enactors, persecuting witch-burners and savage kidnappers, when "a shelter not less than comfort, had been wanting, the living being scarcely able to bury the dead, the well not sufficient to take care of the sick? At the season of distress, there were but seven able to render assistance. The benevolent

* Bancroft, page 140, vol. 1. † Idem, page 313, vol. 1.

Carver had been appointed Governor; at his first landing he had lost a son; soon after the departure of the May-Flower for England his health sunk under a sudden attack, and his wife, broken-hearted, followed him in death. William Bradford, the historian of the colony, was soon chosen his successor. The record of misery was kept by the graves of the governor and half his company." Was this the hand of Providence? But let us hear more. "But if sickness ceased to prevail, the hardships of privation and want remained to be encountered. In the autumn an arrival of new emigrants, who came unprovided with food, compelled the whole colony, for six months in succession, to subsist on half allowance only." "I have seen men," says Winslow, "stagger by reason of faintness for want of food." They were once saved from famishing by the benevolence of fishermen off the coast. Sometimes they suffered from oppressive exaction on the part of ships that sold them provisions at the most exorbitant prices. Nor did their miseries soon terminate. Even in the *third year* of the settlement the victuals were so entirely spent, that "they knew not at night where to have a bit in the morning." Tradition declares that, "at one time, the colonists were reduced to a pint of corn, which being parched and distributed, gave to each individnal only five kernels; but rumor falls short of reality; for three or four months together they had no corn whatever. When a few of their old friends arrived to join them, a lobster or a piece of fish, without bread or anything else but a cup of fair spring water, was the best dish which the hospitality of the whole colony could offer. Neat cattle were not introduced till the fourth year of the settlement. Yet during all this season of self-denial and suffering, the cheerful confidence of the Pilgrims in the mercies of Providence remained unshaken."

Ho! ho! says Sam, with a laugh that makes the very codfish stand upon their tails in wonder. "The living scarce able to bury the dead! the well not able to take care of the sick!" but seven were "able to render assistance." "Colonists reduced to five grains of corn apiece!" this seems a bad business! What was the hand of Providence—of which they are so fond of speaking familiarly—doing with these saints about these times? Not exterminating them as unfit to become the "progenitors of freemen!" oh, no! "Chastening *us;* but as for those blackguard cavaliers down yonder at Jamestown, he is exterminating them!" Hoo! ho! yet you were the nearest exterminated of the two! But as "the cheerful confidence of the Pilgrims in the mercies of Providence remained unshaken," we must take it for granted that the Providence of the Pilgrims and the Providence of the cavaliers were two different powers in the "State"—In no event does this seem more apparent than in the fact that this doleful sixty,—the remnant of the doomed four hundred and ninety—even after having been joined by a destitute reinforcement,—which had been wrecked on the way to join them with supplies, thus rendering their desperation even more forlorn—having embarked with the mad hope of returning across the sea in ships built of cedar logs, without provisions, met at the mouth of the river the long boat of Lord Delaware, who had just arrived on the coast with new emigrants and abundant supplies.

Now, if Providence be the benign and solemn source of a great and unexpected good to mankind for wise purposes, beyond its ken, which is the aspect of that majestic power, in which wise and good men love best to regard its mysterious doings, then does Sam look upon *this* as one of those events which might justly be styled providential! That thus these "dissolute" and "vagabond" sons of Sam did so regard it, let this same narrator from whom we have been quoting show. In the intellectual zeal of natural justice, he sometimes manages to forget his cue of Puritan, and burst forth into an involuntary apotheosis of truth without regard to locality.

It was on the tenth day of June that the restoration of the colony was solemnly begun by supplications to God. A deep sense of the infinite mercies of his providence overawed the colonists who had been spared by famine, the emigrants who had been shipwrecked and yet preserved, and the new comers who found wretchedness and want when they had expected the contentment of abundance. The firmness of their resolution repelled despair.

"It is," said they, "the arm of the Lord of Hosts who would have his people pass the Red Sea and the wilderness, and then possess the land of Canaan." Dangers avoided inspire trust in providence. "Doubt not," said the emigrants to the people of England, "'God will raise one State and build his church in this excellent clime.' After solemn exercises of religion, Lord Delaware caused his commission to be read; a consultation was immediately held on the good of the colony, and its government was organized with mildness but decision. The evils of faction were healed by the unity of the administration and the dignity and virtues of the governor, and the colonists, excited by mutual emulation, performed their tasks with alacrity. At the beginning of the day they assembled in the little church, which was kept neatly trimmed with the wild flowers of the country; next they returned to their houses to receive their allowance of food. The settled hours of labor were from six in the morning till ten, and from two in the afternoon till four. The house was warm and secure, covered above with strong boards, and matted on the inside after the fashion of the Indian wigwams. Security and affluence were returning."

Sam thinks that this can hardly be said to describe a doomed and God-forsaken crew of "profligate vagabonds," nor can he conceive from whence on the face of the story the "licentiousness" so grievously complained of can proceed, unless it be in the contrast which the "little church kept neatly trimmed with the wild flowers of the country" offered to the sulky smoke-dens in which the Pilgrims offered up their morose and vindictive oblations to the God of Light and Peace.

"Security and affluence were returning," yet Sam insists that the unfortunate "sixty" dedicated by Providence to annihilation were still left to multiply and replenish beneath the protecting arm of the "Lord of Hosts" whom they so devoutly adored for his mercies, and that, too, in spite of the "particular Providence" of their more unfortunate northern brothers.

But, forsooth, what seems to have constituted the knights and gentlemen, the peers and followers of Columbus, the Cabots, Cortes, De Soto, Raleigh, and John Smith—"dissolute vagabonds" and "mere adventurers?" "They came to search for gold," snuffle my puritanical boobies; says Sam, and what of it? To what other instincts than the love of gold and glory do we owe the commerce and expanding civilization of the old world, as well as the discovery, conquests, and civilization of the New? America was then the California of Europe; your disinterested sons have only crowded into California "for liberty to worship God" of course—or "to found an empire," no doubt.

When your fractious, meddlesome and noisy progenitors, were driven out of England for England's good, and could not stay even in fat, frouzy and most patient Holland, when the fatigued toleration of Europe would no longer permit you a spot whereon to rest the soles of your feet; then, of course, as "America was the region of romance, where the heated imagination could indulge in the boldest delusions, where the simple natives wore the most precious ornaments, and by the side of the clear runs of water the sands sparkled with gold;"* thither, your eyes, in common with those of all the world, were turned, and the spirit moved you to "found an empire" based upon "the right to worship God."

Not by any manner of means that you were moved thereto by any lust for gold or base carnal desire whatever!—although, at that time, gold was being sought with equal eagerness along the whole Atlantic border—from the voyagers in search of a northwest passage among the arctic ice and snow, who took home the holds of their vessels filled with what they thought to be golden earth—to the ungodly adventurers at Jamestown in the South!

But "who would have expected to find gold on the bleak rocks of Plymouth?" and beside, their historian says, "They knew they were pilgrims, and looked not much on these things, but lifted up their eyes to heaven, their dearest country, and quieted their spirits."†

Very well—it would seem then that they had indeed no other country to lift their eyes to, for the same historian says, "they had no homes to go to—so that at last the magistrates were glad to be rid of them on any terms." It would not do to call these people "vagabonds," of course, because, with a sanctimonious upturning of the eyes they had said "they looked not much on these things!" But as with an impious familiarity which has always characterized their modes of speech, they "found God going along with them," and turned their eyes upon North Virginia, applying to the Virginia Company for a patent.

* Bancroft. † Bradford.

Now Virginia was understood to be the *safest* place around which the aroma of hidden wealth in treasure clung, and *thither* they set out to go in the Speedwell and the Mayflower. They were driven off their course by storms, and landed at Plymouth "on compulsion!"

But Sam would remind them that "the beauty and immeasurable wealth of Guiana had been painted in dazzling colors by the brilliant eloquence of Raleigh; but the *terrors* of the tropical climate, the wavering pretensions of England to the soil, and the proximity of bigoted Catholics led them rather to look toward the most northern parts of Virginia."*

We can very well comprehend now, quoth Sam, how, in their humility, they have never emulated the "gallant spirit" of the "vagabond" cavaliers!

How many new worlds would have been discovered? How many Perus and Mexicos conquered? How many Mississippis found and Virginias built up, had these stigmatized cavaliers been turned aside by the "terrors" of tropical climates, wavering pretensions of kings, or proximity of adverse creeds?

---

* Bancroft.

CHAPTER XIV.

Prosperity of the Colony of Jamestown under the rule of Captain Smith—Sudden Treachery of the Indians and great Massacre of the Settlers.

BUT enough of this. It would seem that under the tutelary guardianship of Smith, the colonies were now prospering greatly. The first cotton grown in the United States had now been planted under his auspices (1621); and its "plentiful coming up" had been a subject of interest in America and England. "Yes," says Sam, "these libertine vagabonds seem likely to prove themselves first in everything."

The relations with the natives had been, as yet, comparatively pleasant. There had been quarrels, but no wars. From the first landing of colonists in Virginia, the power of the natives was despised. Their strongest weapons were such arrows as they could shape without the use of iron—such hatchets as could be made from stone, and an English mastiff seemed to them a terrible adversary.

Within sixty miles of Jamestown, it is computed, there were no more than five thousand souls, or about fifteen hundred warriors. The natives, naked and feeble compared with the Europeans, were nowhere concentrated in considerable villages, but dwelt dispersed in hamlets, with from forty to sixty in each company. Few places had more than two hundred, and many had less. It was also unusual for any large portion of the tribes to assemble together.

Smith once met a party that seemed to amount to seven hundred, and so complete was the superiority conferred by the use of fire-arms, that with fifteen men he was able to withstand them all. No uniform care had been taken to conciliate their good-will, although their condition had been improved by some of the arts of civilized life. A house having been built for Opechancanough, after the English fashion, he took such delight in the lock and key that he would lock and unlock the door a hundred times a day, and thought the device incomparable.

When Wyatt arrived, the natives expressed fear lest his intentions should be hostile. He assured them of his wish to preserve inviolable peace, and the emigrants had no use for fire-arms except against a deer or fowl. The penalty of death for teaching an Indian to use a musket was forgotten; and they were now employed as fowlers and huntsmen. The plantations of the English were widely extended in unsuspecting confidence wherever rich land invited to the culture of tobacco; nor were solitary places avoided, since there would be less competition for the ownership of the soil.

Powhattan, the father of Pocahontas, remained, after the marriage of his daughter, the firm friend of the English. He died in 1618, and his younger brother was now the sole heir to his influence. Should the native occupants of the soil consent to be driven from their ancient patrimony? Should their feebleness submit to contempt, injury, and the loss of their lands? The desire of self-preservation, the necessity of self-defense seemed to demand an active resistance. To preserve their dwellings, the English must be exterminated. In open battle the Indians would be powerless.

Conscious of their weakness, they could not hope to accomplish their end, except by a preconcerted surprise. The crime was one of savage ferocity. They were timorous and quick of apprehension, and consequently treacherous. The attack was concocted with impenetrable secrecy. To the very last hour the Indians preserved the language of friendship; they borrowed the boats of the English to attend their own assemblies; on the very morning of the massacre they were in the houses and at the tables of those whose death they were plotting. "Sooner," said they, "shall the sky fall than peace be violated on our part."

At length, on the 22d of March, at one and at the same instant of time, the Indians fell upon an unsuspecting population, which was scattered through distant villages extending one hundred and forty miles on both sides of the river. The onset was so sudden that the blow was not discerned until it fell. None were spared—children and women as well as men; missionaries, who had cherished the natives with untiring gentleness; the liberal benefactors from whom they had received daily kindnesses; all were murdered with indiscriminate barbarity and every aggravation of cruelty. The savages fell upon the dead bodies, as if it had been possible to commit on them fresh murder.

In one hour three hundred and forty-seven persons were cut off, yet the carnage was not universal, and Virginia was saved from so disastrous a grave. The night before the execution of the conspiracy, it was revealed by a converted Indian to an Englishman whom he wished to rescue. Jamestown and the nearest settlements were well prepared against an attack, and the savages, as timid as they were ferocious, fled with precipitation from the apparent wakeful resistance. Thus the larger part of the colony was saved.

A year after the massacre, there still remained two thousand five hundred men. The total number of the emigrants had exceeded four thousand.*

Thus it seems that these "dissolute adventurers" had, up to this time, cultivated the most amicable relations with their savage neighbors, and that it was not until this horrible massacre of the trusting colonists, that "plans of industry were entirely succeeded by schemes of revenge," and a war of extermination ensued. These conditions, Sam thinks, as something unlike those which preceded the ruthless slaughter of the miserable and defenseless Pequods by his sanctimonious sons! Nor does Sam hear anything of "Rum" as a contracting party in the peace which was made with Powhattan.

---

* This account we epitomize from Bancroft.

CHAPTER XV.

Origin of "First Families" in Virginia—Auction of wives to the Virginians—Sam's idea of Aristocracy—Virginians obtain the right of trial by Jury—of Representative Government also—Religious toleration first granted them, repealed.

BUT Sam turns now suddenly toward the South, and a humorous twinkle broadens on his wide countenance, as he regards for a moment the lordly airs of "some of our First Families"—then planting his huge finger upon the page of History which follows—he bursts into a great guffaw.

"'The people of Virginia had not been settled in their minds,' and, as before the recent changes, they had gone there with the design of ultimately returning to England, it was necessary to multiply attachments to the soil. Few women had as yet dared to cross the Atlantic; but now, the promise of prosperity, induced ninety agreeable persons, young and incorrupt, to listen to the wishes of the company, and the benevolent advice of Sandys, and to embark for the colony, where they were assured of a welcome. They were transported at the expense of the corporation, and were married to the tenants of the company, or to men who were able to support them, and who willingly defrayed the cost of their passage, which was rigorously demanded. The adventure, which had been in part a mercantile speculation, succeeded so well, that it was designed to send, the next year, another consignment of one hundred; but before these could be collected, the company found itself so poor, that its design could be accomplished only by a subscription. After some delays, sixty were actually dispatched—maids of virtuous education, young, handsome, and well recommended. The price rose from one hundred and twenty to one hundred and fifty pounds of tobacco, or even more; so that all the original charges might be repaid. The debt for a wife was a debt of honor, and took precedence of any other; and the company in conferring employments, gave preference to the married men. Domestic ties were formed; virtuous sentiments and habits of thrift ensued; the tide of emigration swelled; within three years, fifty patents for land were granted, and three thousand, five hundred persons found their way to Virginia, which was a refuge even for 'Puritans.'"

"Hoo, hoo, hoo!"—"first families" indeed! when your great, great grandmothers, were bought off of transport ships for a hundred and twenty to a hundred and fifty pounds of tobacco each. "Here is the aristocratic for you!" he shouts hoarsely, clutching with outstretched arm the tufted crest of an Alleghany summit, which he rocks and heaves as if to tear it by its roots from out his path, and thereby shaking the chain along its whole length into a shiver. "The power and will to do—to move—to overcome—this is my aristocracy."

The indignation of Sam was only transient, for as he saw the startled mountains cradled back to sleep again in shortened vibrations, he smiled complacently, and said, with a slow speech and humorous twinkle: "Why, that youngster of mine, California, will, at this rate, soon be pluming himself upon a special aristocratic caste, sprung from the loins of those innocent maidens captivated and bewitched into his embraces by that enterprising admirer of the multiplication and replenishing of the earth system—Mrs. Farnham!" But then, he adds thoughtfully, with his foot in a notch, and leaning his elbow upon the now quiet summit of the mountains—as he looks out on the West—"this young fellow is rather knowing of his age; he was born with a pickaxe in his hand; and understands that honor is alone to be won by labor—he'll do."

But the mood of Sam has suddenly changed; and so ye slavish "Howlers of the East," it has never got into your "round heads," that after the formal concession of "legislative liberties," the next charter of rights obtained for the "liberty of which ye cant so much, was that of the right of trial by jury of peers" in this profligate and ungodly colony of Virginia! and furthermore, that this right was obtained in defiance of the interference of King James, by the London Company, who elected as Treasurer, the Earl of Southampton, the early friend of Shakspeare!

Under this organization, the Treasurer was in reality the most important officer. Indeed nothing could move without his co-operation, and "it is natural," says Sam, "that the early friend of Shakespeare—who was so far before the old world in reach of freedom of thought—should have been the earliest promoter of the right of trial by jury in the New World."

Sam disdains to call himself the "child of Shakespeare," or anybody else, because he is alone the child of the elements, and his children the sons of Sam; yet it rather pleases the stalwart gentleman that his children down South obtained the "right of trial by jury" first through an early friend of Shakespeare, and perpetuated it, together with the novelty of "legislative liberties" to all the other colonies.

The system of representative government and trial by jury was thus (1621) established in the new hemisphere as an acknowledged right. The colonists ceasing to depend as servants on a commercial company, now became enfranchised citizens. Henceforward the supreme power was held to reside in the hands of the colonial parliament and of the King, as King of Virginia. The ordinance was the basis on which Virginia erected the superstructure of its liberties. Its influences were wide and enduring, and can be traced through all following years of the history of the colony. It constituted the plantation in its infancy a nursery of freemen, and succeeding generations learned to cherish institutions which were as old as the first period of the prosperity of their fathers.

The privileges which were now conceded could never be wrested from the Virginians; and as new colonies arose at the South, their proprietaries could hope to win emigrants only by bestowing franchises as large as those enjoyed by their elder rival. The London company merits the fame of having acted as the successful friend of liberty in America. It may be doubted whether any public act during the reign of King James was of more permanent or pervading influence; and it reflects glory on the Earl of Southampton, Sir Edwin Sandys, and the patriot party of England, who, unable to

establish guarantees of a liberal administration at home, were careful to connect popular freedom so intimately with the life, prosperity and state of society of Virginia, that they never could be separated.

Thus it would appear, says Sam, that my dissolute vagabonds of Virginia managed to thrive in one way and another amazingly. Not only did they contrive to obtain first from the Crown those concessions which constitute in themselves the magna charta of American freedom, and were afterward emulated and imitated in the constitutions of other colonies, but they likewise set the noble example of religious toleration, and while their bigoted and canting brothers of Plymouth were banishing a Roger Williams and the Anabaptists, hanging the inoffensive Quakers, burning, pressing, and drawing and quartering miserable old women, under the name of witches; these profligate colonists, although firm believers in the union of church and state, were inviting these very Puritans to come among them and settle in peace.

The condition of contending parties in England had now given to Virginia an opportunity of legislation independent of European control; and the voluntary act of the assembly restraining religious liberty, adopted from hostility to political innovation, rather than a spirit of fanaticism, or respect to instructions, proves conclusively the attachment of the representatives of Virginia to the Episcopal church and the cause of royalty. Yet there had been Puritans in the colony almost from the beginning; even the Brownists were freely offered a serene asylum. "Here," said the tolerant Whitaker, "neither surplice nor subscription is spoken of," and several Puritan clergy emigrated to Virginia. They were so contented with their reception, that large numbers were preparing to follow, and were restrained only by the forethought of English intolerance. We have seen that the Pilgrims at Plymouth were invited to remove within the jurisdiction of Virginia; Puritan merchants planted themselves at James river without fear, and emigrants from Massachusetts had recently established themselves in the colony. The honor of Land had been vindicated by a judicial sentence, and south of the Potomac the decrees of the court of high commission were allowed to be valid, but I find no traces of persecution in the earliest history of Virginia.

ARRIVAL OF SHIP FROM ENGLAND LADEN WITH FEMALES TO BE SOLD TO THE VIRGINIANS FOR WIVES, IN EXCHANGE FOR

This is the self same historian who calls the early settlers of Virginia by such terrible hard names and denounces them as under the ban of Providence, because of their unworthiness to become the perpetuators of a race of freemen. "Strange," says Sam, "that a people accursed of God should have been the very originators of the fundamental ideas of freedom."

Although this gracious invitation had, by a special mission sent to Boston for the purpose, been extended in form to the ministers of Puritanism to come and settle in Virginia, yet the breaking out of the democratic revolution in England alarmed the loyalty of the colonists, who now dreaded the well-known meddlesome, prying, mischief-making proclivities of the malignant Calvinists which had procured their extirpation from the old world, and the invitation was withdrawn and such non-conformists with Episcopacy were very properly banished from the colony.

Sam says they did perfectly right in this, for from all the facts of their old world career, the Virginians had the very best reasons for expecting nothing but incendiary agitation at such a crisis, and were justly indisposed to warm a viper in their own bosoms.

The historians of Puritanism are compelled to speak of this justifiable act of self-defense only in such modified terms as the following: "Virginia thus displayed, though with comparatively little bitterness, the intolerance which for centuries had almost universally prevailed throughout the Christian world."

CHAPTER XVI.

Repeal of Charter of London Company—The Bacon Rebellion—Death of Bacon and character of same.

BUT the great event of Virginia history was the repeal of the Charter of the London Company about this period, (June, 1624,) and the colony now became dependent upon herself—her own legislative assembly and the king directly. They purchased a confirmation of all those franchises which the liberal prepossessions of the London Company had gradually conceded by the struggle for the surrender of the monopoly of tobacco to the spendthrift monarch Charles I. "The first recognition on the part of a Stuart of a representative assembly in America" was of that called by Charles to consider his offer of a contract for the whole crop of tobacco.

The erring monarch, to obtain the monopoly, carelessly overlooked the dangers of this elective legislature. Fortunate recklessness! though the firmness of the Virginia Assembly defeated him.

Yet this auspicious event has its drawbacks, which proved sufficiently formidable, beyond a doubt. This first attachment of the crown was rapidly followed by other interferences with, and encroachments upon, the liberty of trade, until at last, in 1641, "England claimed that monopoly of colonial commerce which was ultimately enforced by the navigation act of Charles II."

Charles I, although he had pertinaciously expressed his "will and pleasure to have the sole pre-emption of all tobacco," had as yet failed of accomplishing his object. He, however, by a cunning indirection, finally succeeded in achieving what amounted to the same end.

No vessel laden with colonial commodities might sail from the harbors of Virginia for any ports but those of England, that the staple of those commodities might be made in the mother country; and all trade with foreign vessels, except in case of necessity, was forbidden. This ordinance, which constituted the original of the oppressive "Navigation Act," was the cause of infinite and grievous troubles to the Virginia colony.

In 1676, while the Indian war was still going on, complaints were made in England against the colonies for violating the acts of trade. These acts imposed oppressive customs upon certain commodities, if imported from any country beside England, or if transported from one colony to another. The acts were considered by the colonies as unjust, impolitic and cruel. For several years they paid little attention to them, and his majesty at length required that agents should be sent to England to answer in behalf of the colonies for these violations.

By the acts of trade none of the colonies suffered more than Virginia and Maryland, their operation being greatly to lessen the profits on their tobacco trade, from which a great portion of their wealth was derived. In addition to these sufferings, the colony of Virginia, in violation of chartered rights, was divided and conveyed away in proprietary grants. Not only uncultivated woodlands were thus conveyed, but also plantations which had long been possessed, and improved according to law and charter.

The Virginians complained, petitioned, remonstrated, but without effect. Agents were sent to England to lay their grievances at the foot of the throne, but were unsuccessful. At length their oppression became insupportable, and the discontent of the people broke out into open insurrection.

At the head of this insurrection was placed one Nathaniel Bacon, an Englishman, who, soon after his arrival had been appointed a member of the council. He was a young man of commanding person, and great energy and enterprise.

The colony at this time was engaged in war with the Susquehanna Indians. Bacon dispatched a messenger to Governor Berkley, requesting a commission to go against the Indians. This commission the governor refused, and, at the same time, ordered Bacon to dismiss his men, and on penalty of being declared a rebel, to appear before himself and the council. Exasperated by such treatment, Bacon, without disbanding the rest of his men, proceeded in a sloop with forty of them, to Jamestown. Here a quarrel ensued, and Berkley illegally suspended him from the council. Bacon departed in a rage with his sloop and men, but the governor pursued him, and adopted such measures that he was taken, and brought to Jamestown.

Finding that he had dismissed Bacon from the council illegally, he now admitted him again, and treated him kindly. Soon after, Bacon renewed his importunity for a commission against the Indians. Being unable to effect his purpose, he left Jamestown privately, but soon again appeared with six hundred volunteers, and demanded of the assembly then sitting, the required commission. Being overawed, the assembly advised the governor to grant it. But soon after Bacon had departed, the governor, by the same advice, issued a proclamation, denouncing him as a rebel.

Hearing what the governor had done, Bacon, instead of marching against the Indians, returned to Jamestown, wreaking his vengeance upon all who opposed him. Governor Berkley fled across the bay to Accomac, but the spirit of rebellion had gone before him. He therefore found himself unable to resist Bacon, who now ranged the country at pleasure.

At length, the governor, with a small force under command of major Robert Beverly, crossed the bay to oppose the malcontents. Civil war had now commenced. Jamestown was burnt by Bacon's followers; various parts of the colony were pillaged, and the wives of those that adhered to the governor's party were carried to the camp of the insurgents.

In the midst of these commotions, it pleased the Supreme Ruler to withdraw Bacon by a natural death. The malcontents, thus left to recover their reason, now began to disperse. Two of Bacon's generals surrendered and were pardoned, and the people quietly returned to their homes.

Upon this Berkley resumed the government, and peace was restored. This rebellion formed an era of some note in the history of Virginia, and its unhappy effects were felt for thirty years. During its continuance, husbandry was almost wholly neglected, and such havoc was made among all kinds of cattle that the people were threatened with distressing famine. Sir William Berkley, after having been forty years governor of Virginia, returned to England, where he soon after died.

Three years afterward, 1679, lord Culpepper was sent over as governor, with certain laws prepared in conformity to the wishes of the ministry of England, and designed to be enacted by the assembly in Virginia. One of those laws provided for raising a revenue for the support of the government. It made the duties perpetual, and placed them under the direction of his majesty.

On presenting these laws to the Assembly, Culpepper informed them that in case they were passed, he had instructions to offer pardon to all who had been concerned in Bacon's rebellion, but if not, he had commissions to try and hang them as rebels, and a regiment of soldiers on the spot to support him. The Assembly, thus threatened, passed the laws.

Berkley resumed the government indeed, but it seems to have been a bloody peace which he restored. After the death of Bacon, the mortified vanity of the irascible old cavalier raged against his broken and disbanded followers and abettors, until twenty-two had been hanged. It will be recollected, however, that he was a royalist governor, appointed by the king, and that his victims were the first martyrs to freedom on the American soil. Even the king disapproved of his ferocity. "The old fool," said the kind-hearted Charles II, "has taken away more lives in that naked country, than I for the murder of my father."

"He would have hanged half the country had we let him alone," said the colonial member from Northampton to his colleague from Stafford.

The Nathaniel Bacon who headed this unfortunate (in one sense only—that he died so early,) rebellion, appears to have been from the first distrusted by Berkley. A native of England, born during the contests between parliament and the king, his active mind had been awakened to a consciousness of popular rights and popular power, he had not, therefore, yielded the love of freedom to the enthusiasm of royalty. "Possessed of a pleasant address and powerful elocution," he had rapidly risen to distinction in Virginia. Quick of apprehension, brave, choleric, yet discreet in action, the young and wealthy planter carried to the banks of James river, the liberal principles which he had gathered from "English experience;" no wonder, then, that groaning under the grievous imposition of the "navigation acts," under the arbitrary distribution of their lands—many of which were old, settled and improved plantations—given away without any regard to the rights of the settlers, by the careless prodigality of Charles II, to such men as Lord Culpepper, one of the most covetous in England, and Henry, Earl of Arlington, the dissolute, but accomplished father-in-law to the king's son by lady Castlemain, who, in a word, became jointly, factors of the King as joint owners of Virginia—together with the immediate pressure of a fierce war with the Susquehannas and Seneca Indians, retaliations for which the royalist, Governor Berkley, refused to sanction with his commission to Bacon; no wonder then, we say, that the people were "much infected" with the principles of this gallant planter, and of the Speaker of their assembly, Thomas Godwin, "notoriously a friend to all the rebellion and treason which distracted Virginia;" no wonder, too, that the gallant Bacon was hailed as the "darling of their hopes, the appointed defender of Virginia," when, having been elected by the Assembly, commander-in-chief, he took charge of the "grand rebellion in Virginia!"

The rebels under his command, both in the field and as a leading burgess in the Assembly, having compelled the unwilling Berkley to concede many important demands for amelioration, and this grateful feature of the legislation of the Assembly having been ratified, "that better legislation" was completed, according to the new style of computation, on the fourth day of July, 1676, just one hundred years to a day, before the Congress of the United States adopting the declaration which had been framed by a statesman of Virginia, who, like Bacon, was "popularly inclined," began a new era in the history of man. The eighteenth century in Virginia was the child of the seventeenth; and Bacon's rebellion, with the corresponding scenes in Maryland, Carolina, and New England, was the early harbinger of American independence and American nationality.

"Pretty good," says Sam, "for my Southern vagabonds!"

PART II.

CHAPTER XVII.

A new mystery—The rise of Luther and Protestant wars—Advent of the mystery of Jesuitism.

THOUGH Sam was in himself a mystery of the New World, yet was he not the only clouded Force to which these portentous times gave birth, and which was to become alike his foe and the terror of the old world as well as the New.

A mysterious Force! yes, a terrible mystery!—the mystery of spiritual annihilation!—the mystery of "walking corpses"* of humanity demonized to the greater glory of God!

Momentous years were those (1537 and 1620) which gave birth to the order of Jesuits and to Sam. Memorable forever will they be in the record of human struggle. Strange that out of the mighty travail of the Protestant Revolution of the sixteenth century in Europe should have sprung these two births, the one so eventful to the death, the other to the life of hope for humanity! that to the smiting of the powerful wands of Luther and Calvin, upon the shadowy turmoil these giant foes stepped forth, the one beneath the sun of day, the other beneath the umbrage of deep night.

But as we have looked upon the birth of Sam, seen something of the stormy contrasts and opposing traits which constituted the majestic elements of the formative period of his career; have, in a word, regarded his prodigious infancy at

* *Perinde ac cadaver*—The last words of the founder of the order of Jesuits.

the North and at the South, in the early Puritan and Cavalier, we may now turn our eyes on the same period in the coming of his arch and most deadly enemy.

The sixteenth century was, indeed, a period of ferment in the world's history! Absolutism had attained the climax of prerogative throughout the christian world. Europe was divided between three masters, Henry VIII, of England, Francis I, of France, and Charles V, of Spain, who held it in as many fields, and were fighting a triangular battle for the possession of the whole, with the aid of mercenary armies; for the feudal system, trampled in the dust, was no longer rampant to the setting up and pulling down of kings.

The gold of the newly-discovered Western World of Sam had now become a puissant arbitrator in these kingly quarrels, and soon the old time chimera of the "balance of power" seemed likely to come home to roost beneath the roof-tree of Charles V, of Spain.

Henry VIII, who, between the divorcing and beheading his wives, plundering the monasteries and keeping in check beneath his heel the dying throes of the "king-making" turbulence—the "Warwick" blood of his nobility—found sufficient employment at home, after the issue of the electoral Congress of Frankfort, to retire upon from this contest and leave France and Spain to fight it out. Their wars continued to redden the fields of Europe with but little avail.

Meanwhile, as a compensation for these evils, the human mind, casting off the prejudices and ignoranoe of the middle ages, marches to regeneration. Italy becomes for the second time the center from whence the light of genius and learning shines forth over Europe. Leonardo da Vinci, Tiziano, Michael Angelo, are the sublime, the most divine interpreters of art. Pulci, Ariosto Poliziano, give a new and creative impulse to literature, and are the worthy descendants of Dante. Scholasticism, with its subtle argumentatious, vague reasonings, and illogical deductions, is superseded by the practical philosophy of Lorenzo and Machiavelli, and by the irresistible and eloquent logic of the virtuous but unfortunate Savonarola. Men who, for the last three centuries, had been satisfied with what had been taught and said by Aristotle and his followers—who, as the last and incontrovertible argument, had been accustomed to exclaim, *ipse dixit*, now

IGNATIUS LOYOLA FOUNDER OF THE ORDER OF JESUITS — HIS MOTTO TO THE WORLD, BEING "AD MAJOREM DEI GLORIAM;" WHICH IS TO SAY — TO THE GREATER GLORY OF GOD; WHILE HIS SPIRITUAL ADVISER WHISPERS — TO THE GREATER GLORY OF LOYOLA AND I. (PART II, CHAP. XVII.)

begin to think for themselves, and dare to doubt and discuss what had hitherto been considered sacred and unassailable truths. The newly-awakened human intellect eagerly enters upon the new path, and becomes argumentative and inquiring, to the great dismay of those who deprecated diversity of faith; and the Court of Rome, depending on the blind obedience of the credulous, anathematizing every disputer of the Papal infallibility, views with especial concern this rising spirit of inquiry, and has to tremble for its usurped power.

Luther, the dogged monk, with the yearnings of an enslaved and trampled world, writhing like vexed serpents in his brawny breast, having been treated with contumely in his first humble appeal to his spiritual father, the Pope, for the solution of the conscientious doubts which had overtaken him in his too earnest study of the "Holy Book," threw himself suddenly upon his own obdurate and self-reliant will, and hurling his defiance back against his late master, in answer to the Bull of Excommunication with which he had been favored, stood *cap-a-pie,* in the breach which he had already made, to battle to the death for his doctrines.

The art of printing came opportunely to his aid, and wielding its magic, marvelous to tell, this burly champion proved meet to encounter, visor up and single hand, the serried chivalry of Europe and the wrong.

The German princes, partly persuaded of the truth of Luthers' doctrines, partly desirous to escape the exacting tyranny of Rome which drained their subjects' pockets, supported the Reformer. They protested at Spires, and at Smalkaden made preparations to maintain their protest by arms. In a few years, without armed violence, but simply by the persuasive force of truth, the greater part of Germany became converted to the Reformed faith. The honest indignation of Zuinglius in Switzerland, and, conspiring with the diffusion of the truth, the unbridled passions of Henry VIII in England, alike rescued a considerable portion of their respective countries from the Romish yoke. In France and in Navarre the new doctrines found many warm adherents; while in Italy itself, at Brescia, Pisa, Florence, nay even at Rome and at Faenza, there were many who more or less openly embraced the principles of the Reformation. Thus, in a short time, the Roman religion, founded in ancient and deep-rooted prejudices, supported by the two greatest powers in the world, the Pope and the Emperor, defended by all the bishops and priests who lived luxuriously by it, was overturned throughout a great part of Europe.

Now was the time, when gloom had settled upon the cupola of St. Peter's, when the thunders of the Vatican were tamed, and the debauched and hoary despotism of Rome tottered on a throne of straw—now was the time which was to add terror to terror, crime to crime, which, in a new birth of darkness, was to people earth with incarnate ghosts more drear and powerful of evil than the creatures of a supernal hell.

The period had come when, in the dulcet language of the Fathers of the Church, it was declared " that, as from time to time new heresies have inflicted the Church of God, so He has raised up holy men to combat them; and as he had raised up St. Dominic against the Albigenses and Vaudois, so *He* sent Loyola and his disciples against the Lutherans and Calvinists."*

It is of this new mystery, according to such authority, "raised up by God," to resist those elements out of which the birth of Sam came, that we would now proceed to narrate.

---

* Helyot, Histoire des Ordres Monastiques, Religieux et Militaires, tome vii, p. 452. When we have modern authors we quote from Sacchinus Orlandinus, etc., we shall quote them, as books are easily to be had.

CHAPTER XVIII.

Life of Ignatius Loyola, founder of the Order—Spiritual exercises—The Weeks—The Contemplations—Loyola a Pilgrim to the Holy Places—His persecutions—His first disciples, Xavier, Le Fevre—Lainez and Rodrigues vow to go to the Holy Land and convert Infidels—Vow of perpetual chastity and poverty—The vow of unquestioning obedience—Refusal of the Holy See to recognize the Order—Cunning vow of obedience to the Pope—Obtains his recognition—Bull of recognition.

INIGO, or, as commonly called, Ignatius Loyola, the youngest of eleven children, of a noble and ancient family, was born in the year 1491, in his father's castle of Loyola at Guipuscoa in Spain. He was of middle stature and rather dark complexion; had deep-set, piercing eyes, and a handsome and noble countenance. While yet young he had become bald, which gave him an expression of dignity, that was not impaired by a lameness arising from a severe wound. His father, a worldly man, as his biographer says, instead of sending him to some holy community to be instructed in religion and piety, placed him as a page at the court of Ferdinand V. But Ignatius, naturally of a bold and aspiring disposition, soon found that no glory was to be reaped in the antechambers of the Catholic King; and delighting in military exercises, he became a soldier—and a brave one he proved. His historians, to make his subsequent conversion appear more wonderful and miraculous, have represented him as a perfect monster of iniquity; but, in truth, he was merely a gay soldier, fond of pleasure, no doubt, yet not more debauched than the generality of his brother officers. His profligacy, whatever it was, did not prevent him from being a man of strict honor, never backward in time of danger.

At the defense of Pampeluna against the French, in 1521, Ignatius, while bravely performing his duty on the walls, was struck down by a ball, which disabled both his legs.

With him fell the courage of the besieged. They yielded, and the victors entering the town, found the wounded officer, and kindly sent him to his father's castle, which was not far distant. Here he endured all the agonies which generally attend gunshot wounds, and an inflammatory fever which supervened, brought him to the verge of the grave—when, "O! miracle!" exclaims his biographer, "it being the eve of the feast of the glorious saints Peter and Paul, the prince of the apostles appeared to him in a vision, and touched him, whereby he was, if not immediately restored to health, at least put in a fair way of recovery." Now the fact is, that the patient uttered not a syllable regarding his vision *at the time;* nevertheless, we are gravely assured that the miracle was not the less a fact. Be this, however, as it may, Ignatius undoubtedly recovered, though slowly.

During his long convalescence, he sought to beguile the tedious hours of irksome inactivity passed in the sick chamber by reading all the books of knight-errantry which could be procured. The chivalrous exploits of the Rolands and Amadises made a deep impression upon his imagination, which, rendered morbidly sensitive by a long illness, may well be supposed to have been by no means improved by such a course of study. When these books were exhausted, some pious friend brought him the Lives of the Saints. This work, however, not suiting his taste, Ignatius at first flung it aside in disgust, but afterward, from sheer lack of better amusement, he began to read it. It presented to him a new phase of the romantic and marvelous, in which he so much delighted. He soon became deeply interested, and read it over and over again. The strange adventures of these saints—the praise, the adoration, the glorious renown which they acquired, so fired his mind, that he almost forgot his favorite Paladins. His ardent ambition saw here a new career opened up to it. He longed to become a saint.

Yet the military life had not lost its attractions for him. It did not require the painful preparations necessary to earn a saintly reputation, and was, moreover, more in accordance with his education and tastes. He long hesitated which course to adopt—whether he should win the laurels of a hero, or earn the crown of a saint. Had he perfectly recovered from the effects of his wound, there is little doubt but that he would have chosen the laurels. But this was not to be. Although he was restored to health, his leg remained hopelessly deformed—he was a cripple for life.

It appeared that his restorer, St. Peter, although upon the whole a tolerably good physician, was by no means an expert surgeon. The broken bone of his leg had not been properly set; part of it protruded through the skin below the knee, and the limb was short. Sorely, but vainly, did Ignatius strive to remove these impediments to a military career, which his unskillful though saintly surgeon had permitted to remain. He had the projecting piece of bone sawn off, and his shortened leg painfully extended by mechanical appliances, in the hope of restoring it to its original fine proportions. The attempt failed; so he found himself, at the age of thirty-two, with a shrunken limb, with little or no renown, and by his incurable lameness, rendered but slightly capable of acquiring military glory. Nothing then remained for him but to become a saint.

Saintship being thus, as it were, forced upon him, he at once set about the task of achieving it, with all that ardor which he brought to bear upon every pursuit. He became daily absorbed in the most profound meditations, and made a full confession of all his past sins, which was so often interrupted by his passionate outbursts of penitent weeping, that it lasted three days.* To stimulate his devotion, he lacerated his flesh with the scourge, and abjuring his past life, he hung up his sword beside the altar in the church of the convent of Montserrat. Meeting a beggar on the public road, he exchanged clothes with him, and thus habited in the loathsome rags of the mendicant, he retired to a cave near Menreze, where he nearly starved himself.

When he next reappeared in public, he found his hopes almost realized. His fame had spread far and wide; the people flocked from all quarters to see him—visited his cave with feelings of reverend curiosity—and nothing was thought of but the holy man and his severe penances. But now the Evil Spirit began to assail him. The tender conscience of Ignatius began to torment him with the fear that all this public notice had made him proud; that, while he had

* Helyot, Hist. des Ord. Mon., Rel. et Mil., tome vii, page 456.

almost begun to consider himself a saint, he was, in reality, by reason of that belief itself, the most heinous of sinners. So imbittered did his life become in consequence of these thoughts, that he went well nigh distracted.

But God supported him; and the Tempter, baffled in his attempts, fled. Ignatius fasted for seven days, neither eating nor drinking; went again to the confessional, and, receiving absolution, was not only delivered from the stings of his own conscience, but *obtained the gift of healing the troubled consciences of others.*[*] This miraculous gift Ignatius is believed to have transmitted to his successors, and it is in a great measure to this belief, that the enormous influence of the Company of Jesus is to be attributed, as we shall see hereafter.

Now that Ignatius could endure his saintship, without being overwhelmed by a feeling of sinfulness, he pursued his course with renewed alacrity. Yet it was in itself by no means an attractive one. In order to be a perfect Catholic saint, a man must become a sort of misanthrope—cast aside wholesome and cleanly apparel, go about clothed in filthy rags, wearing haircloth next his skin, and, renouncing the world and its inhabitants, must retire to some noisome den, there to live in solitary meditation, with wild roots and water for food, daily applying the scourge to expiate his sins—of which, according to one of the disheartening doctrines of the Catholic Church, *even* the just commit at least *seven a day*. The saint must enter into open rebellion against the laws and instincts of human nature, and consequently, against the will of the Creator. And although it can not be denied that some of the founders of monastic orders conscientiously believed that their rules were conducive to holiness and eternal beatitude, nevertheless, we may with justice, charge them with overlooking the fact that, as the transgression of the laws of nature invariably brings along with it its own punishment—a certain evidence of the Divine displeasure—true holiness can not consist in disregarding and opposing them.

Ignatius, however, continued his life of penance, made to the Virgin Mary a solemn vow of perpetual chastity,

---

[*] Helyot, Hist. des Ord. Mon., Rel. et Mil., tome vii, page 456.

begged for bread, often scourged himself, and spent many hours a day in prayer and meditation. What he meditated upon, God only knows. After a few months of this ascetic life, he published a little book, which much increased his fame for sanctity. It is a small octavo volume, and bears the title of *Spiritual Exercises*.* As this work, the only one he has left, is the acknowledged standard of the Jesuits' religious practice, and is by them extolled to the skies, we must say some few words about it.

First of all we shall relate the supernatural origin assigned to it by the disciples and panegyrists of its author.

He (Ignatius) had already done much for God's sake, and God now rendered it back to him with usury. A courtier, a man of pleasure, and a soldier, he had neither the time nor the will to gather knowledge from books. But the knowledge of man, the most difficult of all, was divinely revealed to him. The master who was to form so many masters, was himself formed by divine illumination. He composed the Spiritual Exercises, a work which had a most important place in his life, and is powerfully reflected in the history of his disciples.

This quotation is from Cretineau Joly, (vol. i, p. 18,) an author who professes not to belong to the society but whose book was published under the patronage of the Jesuits, who, he says, opened to him all the depositories of unpublished letters and manuscripts in their principal convent, the Gesu at Rome; he wrote also a virulent pamphlet against the great Pontiff Clement XIV, the suppressor of the Jesuits. Hence we consider ourselves fairly entitled to rank the few quotations we shall make from him as among those emanating from the writers that belong to the Order; and we are confident that no Jesuit would ever think of repudiating Cretineau Joly. This author proceeds to state that in the manuscript in which Father Jouvency narrates in elegant

---

* By the term Spiritual Exercises, Catholics understand that course of solitary prayer and religious meditation, generally extended over many days, which candidates for holy orders have to perform in the seclusion of a convent, previous to being consecrated. Again, when a priest incurs the displeasure of his Superior, he is sent as a sort of prisoner to some convent, there to perform certain prescribed spiritual exercises, which, in this case, may last from one to three weeks.

Latin those strange events, it is said—this light shed by the divine will upon Ignatius showed him openly and without vail the mystery of the adorable Trinty and other arcana of religion. He remained for eight days as if deprived of life. What he witnessed during this ecstatic trance, as well as in many other visions which he had during life, no one knows. He had indeed committed these celestial visions to paper, but shortly before his death he burned the book containing them, lest it should fall into unworthy hands. A few pages, however, escaped his precautions, and from them one can easily conjecture that he must have been from day to day loaded with still greater favors. Chiefly was he sweetly ravished in contemplating the dignity of Christ the Lord, and his inconceivable charity toward the human race. As the mind of Ignatius was filled with military ideas, he figured to himself Christ as a general fighting for the divine glory, and calling on all men to gather under his standard. Hence sprang his desire to form an army of which Jesus should be the chief and commander, the standard inscribed — "*Ad majorem Dei Gloriam.*"

With deference to M. Joly, we think that a more mundane origin may be found for the "Exercises," in the feverish dreams of a heated imagination. Be this as it may, however, we shall proceed to lay before our readers a short analysis of it, extracted from Cardinal Wiseman's preface to the last edition. He says: "This is a practical, not a theoretical work. It is not a treatise on sin or on virtue; it is not a method of Christian perfection, but it contains the entire practice of perfection, by making us at once conquer sin and acquire the highest virtue. The person who goes through the Exercises is not instructed, but is made to act; and this book will not be intelligible apart from this view."

The reader will observe that it is divided into four *weeks;* and each of these has a specific object, to advance the exercitant an additional step toward perfect virtue. If the work of each week be thoroughly done, *this is actually accomplished.**

"The first week has for its aim the cleansing of the conscience from past sin, and of the affections from their future dangers. For this purpose, the soul is made to convince

* The italics here are our own.

itself deeply of the true end of its being—to serve God and be saved, and of the real inutility of all else. This consideration has been justly called by St. Ignatius, the *principle* or *foundation* of the entire system." The Cardinal assures us that the certain result of this first week's exercises is, that "sin is abandoned, hated, loathed."

"In the second, the life of Christ is made our model; by a series of contemplations of it, we become familiar with its virtues, enamored of his perfections; we learn, by copying him, to be obedient to God and man; meek, humble, affectionate; zealous, charitable, and forgiving; men of only one wish and one thought—that of doing ever God's holy will alone; discreet, devout, observant of every law, scrupulous performers of every duty. Every meditation on these subjects shows us how to do all this; in fact, makes us really do it.* The third week brings us to this. Having desired and tried to be like Christ in action, we are brought to wish and to endeavor to be like unto him in suffering. For this purpose his sacred passion becomes the engrossing subject of the Exercises. But she (the soul) must be convinced and feel, that if she suffers, she also shall be glorified with him; and hence the fourth and concluding week raises the soul to the consideration of those glories which crowned the humiliations and suffering of our Lord." Then after a highly figurative eulogium upon the efficacy of the Exercises "duly performed," the reverend prelate proceeds to show that the one "essential element of a spiritual retreat," (for so the Exercises reduced to action are properly called,) "is *direction.*" In the Catholic church no one is ever allowed to trust himself in spiritual matters. The sovereign pontiff is obliged to submit himself to the direction of another in whatever concerns his own soul. The life of a good retreat is a good director of it. This director modifies, (according to certain written rules,) the order of the Exercises, to adapt them to the peculiar character of the exercitant; regulates the time employed in them, watches their effects, and like a physician prescribing for a patient, varies the treatment according to the symptoms exhibited, encouraging those which seem favorable, and suppressing those which are detrimental to the

---

* Stephens.

desired result. "Let no one," says the Cardinal, "think of undertaking these holy Exercises without the guidance of a prudent and experienced director."

It will be seen that the *weeks* of the Exercises do not mean necessarily a period of seven days. The original period of their performance was certainly a month; but even so, more or less time was allotted to each week's work according to the discretion of the director. Now, except in very particular circumstances, the entire period is abridged to ten days; sometimes it is still further reduced,

It will be observed from the above extracts that the Cardinal, ignoring the fact that the sinner's conversion must be effected entirely by the operation of the Holy Spirit, seems to regard the unregenerate human soul merely as a piece of raw material, which the "director" may, as it were, *manufacture* into a saint, simply by subjecting it to the process prescribed in the Exercises.

In regard to the merits of the book, I cannot agree either with Wiseman or a very brilliant Protestant writer,* who, speaking of the approbation bestowed on it by Pope Paul III, says—"Yet on this subject the chair of Knox, if now filled by himself, would not be very widely at variance with the throne of St. Peter." The book certainly does not deserve this high eulogium. However, it cannot be denied that, amidst many recommendations of many absurd and superstitious practices proper to the Popish religion, the little volume does contain some very good maxims and precepts. For instance, here are two passages to which I am sure that not even the most anti-Catholic Protestant could reasonably object. At page 16 it is said:

"Man was created for this end, that he might praise and reverence the Lord his God, and, serving him, at length be saved.† But the other things which are placed on the earth were created for man's sake, that they might assist him in pursuing the end of creation, whence it follows, that they are to be used or abstained from in proportion as they benefit or hinder him in pursuing that end. Wherefore we ought to be indifferent toward all created things (in so far as they are subject to the liberty of our will, and not prohibited), so

* Stephens. † See the Shorter Catechism, Qu. 1.

that (to the best of our power) we seek not health more than sickness, nor prefer riches to poverty, honor to contempt, a long life to a short one. But it is fitting, out of all, to choose and desire those things only which lead to the end." And again, at page 33, "the third (article for meditation) is, to consider myself; who or what kind I am, adding comparisons which may bring me to a greater contempt of myself; as if I reflect how little I am when compared with all men, then what the whole multitnde of mortals is, as compared with the angels and all the blessed: after these things I must consider what, in fact, all the creation is in comparison with God, the Creator, himself; what now can I, one mere human being, be! Lastly, let me look at the corruption of my whole self, the wickedness of my soul, and the pollution of my body, and account myself to be a kind of ulcer or boil, from which so great and foul a flood of sins, so great a pestilence of vices has flown down.

"The fourth is to consider what God is, whom I have thus offended, collecting the perfections which are God's peculiar attributes and comparing them with my opposite vices and defects; comparing, that is to say, his supreme power, wisdom, goodness, and justice, with my extreme weakness, ignorance, wickedness, and iniquity."

But then the above Exercises are followed by certain Additions, which are recommended as conducing to their better performance. Some of these are very strange; for instance, the fourth is, "to set about the Contemplation itself, now kneeling on the ground, now lying on my face or on my back, now sitting or standing, and composing myself, in the way in which I may hope the more easily to attain what I desire. In which matter, these two things must be attended to; the first that if, on my knees or in any other posture, I obtain what I wish, I seek nothing further. The second, that on the point in which I shall have attained the devotion I seek, I ought to rest, without being anxious about pressing on until I shall have satisfied myself. The sixth, that I avoid those thoughts which bring joy, as that of the glorious resurrection of Christ; since any such thought hinders the tears and grief for my sins, which must then be sought by calling in mind rather death or judgment. The seventh, that, for the same reason, I deprive myself of all the brightness of the light, shutting the doors and windows so long as I remain there (in my chamber), except while I have to read, or take my food." At page 55 we find, in the second Week: "The Fifth Contemplation is the application of the senses to those (contemplations) mentioned above. After the preparatory prayer, with the three already mentioned preludes, it is eminently useful to exercise the five imaginary senses concerning the first and second contemplations in the following way, according as the subject shall bear:

'The first point will be, to see in imagination all the persons, and, noting the circumstances which shall occur concerning them, to draw out what may be profitable to ourselves.

'The second, by hearing as it were, what they are saying, or what it may be natural for them to say, to turn all to our own advantage.

'The third, to perceive, by a certain inward taste and smell, how great is the sweetness and delightfulness of the soul imbued with divine gifts and virtues, according to the nature of the person we are considering, adapting to ourselves those things which may bring us some fruit.

'The fourth, by an inward touch, to handle and kiss the garments, places, footsteps, and other things connected with such persons; whence we may derive a greater increase of devotion, or of any spiritual good.

'This contemplation will be terminated, like the former ones, by adding in like manner, *Pater noster.*'"

At page 52, among other things "to be noted," is:

"The second, that the first exercise concerning the Incarnation of Christ is performed at midnight; the next at dawn; the third about the hour of mass; the fourth about the time of vespers; the fifth a little before supper, and on each of them will be spent the space of one hour; which same thing has to be observed henceforward, everywhere."

CHAPTER XIX.

Loyola's early tribulations — His inflexible Will—Obtains the critical Pledge of implicit obedience from his disciples—Bull of final recognition from the Pope.

LOYOLA'S next step toward holiness was a pilgrimage to Palestine to convert the infidels. What he did in the Holy Land we do not know; his biographer tells us only that he was sent back by the Franciscan friar who exercised there the Papal authority.*

On his homeward voyage, Ignatius conceived that a little learning would perhaps help him in the task of converting heretics, and thus furnish him with an additional chance of rendering himself famous; so after his return, he attended a school at Barcelona, for two years, where, a full-grown man of thirty-four, he learned the rudiments of the Latin language, sitting upon the same bench with little boys.

Having failed to make any proselytes to his extravagances at Barcelona, he went to Alcala, and studied in the university newly erected there by Cardinal Ximenes. Here he attracted much public notice by the eccentricities of his fanatical piety. He wore a peculiar dress of coarse material, and by his fervid discourse, contrived to win over to his mode of life, four or five young men, whom he called his disciples. But he was regarded with suspicion by the authorities, who twice imprisoned him. He and his converts were ordered to resume the common garb, and to cease to expound to the people the mysteries of religion.† Indignant at this, Ignatius

* Hel., Hist. Des Ord. Mon., Rel. et Mil., tome vii, p. 461.

† Ibid, tome vii, page 64.

immediately set out for Paris, where, in the beginning of 1528, he arrived alone, his companions having deserted him.

His persecutions at Alcala had taught him prudence; so that, although his attempts at notoriety in Paris, in the way of dress, manners and language, brought him before the tribunal of the Inquisition,* he nevertheless had managed matters so cautiously, as to escape all punishment. Here, while contending with the difficulties of the Latin grammar,† he was ever revolving in his vast and capacious mind, some new scheme for fulfilling his desires and gratifying his passion for renown. But as yet he knew not what he was destined to accomplish. There seems no ground for supposing that he could already have formed the gigantic and comprehensive project of establishing, on the basis on which it now stands, his wonderful and powerful society. No; he only contrived, as he had done in Spain, to enlist some followers, over whom he could exercise an absolute control, for the furtherance of any future project. In this, his success had far exceeded his expectations. The magnanimous and heroic Xavier, the intelligent and interesting Le Fevre, the learned Lainez, the noble and daring Rodrigues, and some three or four others, acknowledged him as their chief and master.

It may at first sight, appear strange that such privileged intelligences should have submitted themselves to a comparatively ignorant ex-officer. But when it is borne in mind, that Ignatius had a definite end, toward which he advanced with steady and unhesitating steps, while his companions had no fixed plan—that he was endowed with an iron will, which

* Hel., Hist. Des Ord. Mon., Rel. et Mil., tome vii, page 464.

† Once for all, I promise my readers that I am not going to trouble them with the narrative of all the miraculous legends related concerning Loyola. They are, in most instances, so absurd, as to be beneath the dignity of history. Let the two following suffice as specimens. It is said that the devil, determined to prevent his learning Latin, so confused his intellect, that he found it impossible to remember the conjugation of the verb *amo;* whereupon he scourged himself unmercifully every day, until by that means the evil spirit was overcome; after which, the saint was soon able to repeat *amo* in all its tenses. Again, when Ignatius was in Venice, on his way to the Holy Land, it is said that a wealthy senator of that city, Travisini by name, while luxuriously reclining on his bed of down, was informed by an angel that the servant of God was lying upon the hard stones under the portico of his palace. Whereupon the senator immediately arose and went to the door, where he found Ignatius.

neither poverty nor imprisonment, nor even the world's contempt, could overcome—that, above all, he had the art to flatter their respective passions, and to win their affections by using all his influence to promote their interests, it is less surprising that he should have gained an immense influence over those inexperienced and ingenuous young men, on whose generous natures, the idea of devoting their lives to the welfare of mankind, had already made a deep impression. Loyola's courage and ambition were strongly stimulated by the acquisition of disciples so willing and devoted—so efficient for his purpose, so attached to his person; and he began to consider how he might turn their devotion to the best account.

After some conferences with his companions, he assembled them all on the day of the Assumption, 16th August, 1534, in the church of the Abbey of Montmartre, where, after Peter Le Fevre had celebrated mass, they each took a solemn vow to go to the Holy Land and preach the gospel to the Infidels. Ignatius, satisfied for the present with these pledges, left Paris, in order, as he asserted, to recruit his health by breathing his native air at Loyola before setting out on his arduous mission, and doubtless also to find solitude and leisure in which to meditate and devise means for realizing his ambitious hopes. His disciples remained in Paris to terminate their theological studies, and he commanded them to meet him again at Venice, in the beginning of 1537, enjoining them, meanwhile, if any one should ask them what religion they professed, to answer that they belonged to the Society of Jesus, since they were Christ's soldiers.*

Our saint preceded them to Venice, where he again encountered some difficulties and a little persecution; but he endured all with unflinching patience. He became acquainted with Pierra Caraffa, (afterward Pope Paul IV). This harsh and remarkable man had renounced the bishopric of Theata, to become the companion of the meek and gentle Saint Gajetan of Tyenne, and with his assistance had founded the religious order of the Theatines. The members of this fraternity endeavored by exemplary living, devotion to their clerical

* Negroni expounds the word *societas* "quasi dicas cohortem aut centuriam que ad pugnam cum hostibus spiritualibus conserendam conscripta est."

duties of preaching and administering the sacraments, and ministering to the sick, to correct the evils produced throughout all Christendom by the scandalous and immoral conduct of the regular and secular clergy. To Caraffa, who had already acquired great influence, Ignatius attached himself, became an inmate of the convent he had founded, served patiently and devotedly in the hospital which he directed, and shortly became Caraffa's intimate friend. This fixed at once the hitherto aimless ambition of Loyola. He conceived the idea of achieving power and fame, if not as the founder of a new order, at least as the remodeler of one already existing. With this design he submitted to Caraffa a plan of reform for his Order, and strongly urged its adoption. But Caraffa, who perhaps suspected his motive, rejected his proposal, and offered to admit him as a brother of the order as it stood. This, however, did not suit Ignatius, whose proud nature could never have submitted to play even the second part, much less that of an insignificant member in a society over which another had all power and authority. He therefore declined the honor, and at once determined to found a new religious community of his own. Aware, however, of the difficulties he might have to overcome, he resolved to proceed with the utmost caution.

Being under a vow to go to convert the Infidels in the Holy Land, he gave out that to this work alone were the lives of himself and his companions to be devoted. Accordingly as soon as they arrived in Venice he sent them to Rome to beg the Pope's blessing on their enterprise, as he said; and also, no doubt, to exhibit them to the Roman court as the embryo of a new religious order. The reason assigned by his historians for his not going to Rome along with them is, that he feared that his presence there might be prejudicial to them. It is just as likely that he was afraid, lest beneath his cloak of ostentatious humility, the discerning eye of Pope Paul might detect his unbounded ambition.

At Rome his disciples were favorably received, the Pontiff bestowed the desired benediction, and they returned to Venice, whence they were to sail for Palestine.

Here Ignatius prevailed upon them to take vows of perpetual chastity and poverty, and then, under pretext of the war which was raging at the time between the Emperor and the Turks, they abandoned their mission altogether. So ended their pious pilgrimage.

Taking with him Lainez and Le Fevre, Loyola then proceeded to Rome, and craved audience of the Pope.

The chair of St. Peter was at this time occupied by Paul Farnese, that same Pope who opened and in part conducted the Council of Trent; who instigated the emperor to the war against the Protestants; who sent, under his grandson's command, 12,000 of his own troops into Germany to assist in that war; and who lifted up his sacrilegious hand to bless whoever would shed Protestant blood. He had been scandalously incontinent; and if he did not, like Alexander VI, entirely sacrifice the interests of the church and of humanity to the aggrandizement of his own family, nevertheless, his son received the dukedom of Placentia, and his grandsons were created cardinals at the age of fourteen, and one of them was intended to be duke of Milan. However, Paul had some grandeur in his nature. He was generous, and therefore popular, and his activity was indefatigable. But Sarpi says of him, that of all his own qualities, he *did not appreciate any nearly so much as his dissimulation.*[*]

By this amiable pontiff Ignatius and his companions were kindly received. He praised their exemplary and religious life, questioned them concerning their projects, but took no notice of the plan they hinted at of originating a new religious order.

But Loyola was not thus to be discouraged. He summoned to Rome all his followers (who had remained in Lombardy, preaching with a bigoted fanaticism, and calling the citizens to repentance) and gave them a clearer outline than he had hitherto done of the Society he proposed to establish. This they entirely approved of, and took another vow (the most essential for Loyola's purpose) of *implicit and unquestioning obedience to their superior.* Admire here the cautious and consummate art by which Ignatius, step by step, brought his associates to the desired point.

Notwithstanding the repeated refusals of the Court of Rome to accede to his wishes, neither the courage nor the perseverance of Ignatius failed him. After much reflection,

---

[*] Fra Paoli Sarpi, *Hist. of the Council of Trent*, p. 118.

he at last thought he had discovered a way to overcome the Pope's unwillingness. Consulting with his companions, he persuaded them to take a fourth vow, viz: one of obedience to the Holy See and to the Pope *pro tempore,* with the express obligation of going, without remuneration, to whatever part of the world it should please the Pope to send them. He then drew up a petition, in which were stated some of the principles and rules of the order he desired to establish, and sent it to the Pope by Cardinal Contarini.

This fourth vow made a great impression on the wily pontiff; yet so great was his aversion to religious communities, some of which were just then the objects of popular hatred and the plague of the Roman Court, that he refused to approve of this new one until he had the advice of three cardinals, to whom he referred the matter. Guidiccioni, the most talented of the three, strenuously opposed it; but Paul, who perhaps had by this time penetrated the designs of Loyola, and perceived that the proposed society could not prosper unless by contending for and maintaining the supremacy of the Holy See, thought it would be the best policy to accept the services of these volunteers, especially as it was a time when he much needed them. Consequently, on the 27th September, 1540, he issued the famous bull, *Regimini militantis Ecclesiæ*, approving of the new Order under the name of "The Society of Jesus." We consider it indispensable to give some extracts from this bull.

"Paul, Bishop, Servant of the Servants of God, for a perpetual record. Presiding by God's will over the government of the Church, etc.* * * * * * Whereas, we have lately learned that our beloved son Ignatius de Loyola, and Peter Le Fevre, and James Lainez, and also Claudius Le Jay, and Paschasius Brouet, and Francis Xavier; and also, Alphonso Salmeron and Simon Rodrigues, and John Coduri, and Nicholas de Bobadilla, priests of the cities, etc.,* * * * * inspired, as is piously believed, by the Holy Ghost, coming from various regions of the globe, are met together and become associates, and renouncing the seductions of this world, have dedicated their lives to the perpetual service of our Lord Jesus Christ, *and of us, and of other our successors, Roman Pontiffs;* and expressly for *the instruction of boys* and other ignorant people in Christianity; and above all, for the spiritual consolation of the faithful in Christ, by hearing confessions.* * * * * * We receive the associates under our protection and that of the Apostolic See; conceding to them, moreover, that some among them may freely and lawfully draw up such Constitutions as they shall judge to be conformable to, etc. * * * * * We will, moreover, that into this Society there be admitted to the number of sixty persons only, desirous of embracing this rule of living, and no more, and to be incorporated into the Society aforesaid."

The above-named ten persons were the first companions of Loyola, and, with him, the founders of the Society. But the merit of framing the Constitution which was to govern it belongs solely to Ignatius himself. He alone, among them all, was capable of such a conception. He alone could have devised a scheme by which one free rational being is converted into a mere automaton — acting, speaking, even thinking, according to the expressed will of another. There is no record in history of any man, be he king, emperor, or pope, exercising such absolute and irresponsible power over his fellow-men as does the General of the Jesuits over his disciples. In *Spiritual Exercises* Loyola appears to be merely an ascetic enthusiast; in the *Constitution* he shows himself a high genius, with a perfect and profound knowledge of human nature and of the natural sequence of events. Never was there put together a plan so admirably harmonious in all its parts, so wonderfully suited to its ends, or which has ever met with such prodigious success.

Prompt, unhesitating obedience to the commands of the General, and (for the benefit of the Society, and *ad majoram Dei gloriam*) great elasticity in all other rules, according to the General's good-will, are the chief features of this famous Constitution, which, as it constitutes the Jesuit's code of morality, we shall now proceed to examine, doing our best to show the spirit in which it was dictated.*

* The historian of Sam is indebted for this elegant sketch of the life of Loyola, and progress of the "Order of Jesus," thus far, principally to the learned investigations of the accomplished M. Nicolini, the most magnanimous but indefatigable of the modern foes of Jesuitism.

CHAPTER XX.

Was Ignatius Loyola a Bigot?—other Bigots of the same stamp—Sam's indignation aroused—Hideous sacrilege and spiritual tyranny—*Perinde ac si cadaver.*

"BUT Ignatius Loyola was a bigot," say the more mild extenuators of his system, and much is to be forgiven the devotee of an idea so holy as that embodied in the motto of the Society founded by him. "*Ad majoram dei gloriam,*" should cover a multitude of sins!

"Pah!" says Sam, "and so your mild philosophy might prate concerning Mohammed, who, with fire and sword to the cleaving asunder of the joints and marrow of nations, carried that other idea, 'God is great and Mohammed is his Prophet,' throughout the eastern world, and with his foot upon the neck of the subjugated peoples, compelled them to call aloud that charmed phrase. So the drunken Nero burns a city, the huge oblation to his fiddle, which happened to be just then his supreme fantasy—his God! And it is such hideous and savage selfists as Loyola, Mohammed, and Nero, that you, daintily, in set form of speech, name *bigots*, forsooth!"

Bigoted, unreasonably devoted to what? to an inspiration, to an idea or a whim? These have led alike to carnage, crime and horror; alike, they have rendered names illustriously, infamously notorious; alike they have caused men to be worshiped in the place of God; alike in each, hideous, cunning egotism has taken shelter behind a phrase. God! Prophecy! and Music! the most beautiful and exalting of all words which constitute, in the ideas they represent, the triune hope of humanity, have been respectively, used and appropriated as "magic shields" for the protection of the arch evil doers against our race.

"And, yes," continues Sam, indignantly, "another sacred word has been as foully misapplied. It was the 'destiny' of the mathematical monster, Napoleon I, to tear the tinseled royalties of Europe into shreds, to form the emblazoned robe of patchwork which was to wrap the imperial pigmy for awhile.

"It was the 'destiny' of Napoleon II, to die early of the precocious development of this selfsame faculty of mathematics with which he was blessed, along with Zera Colburn—the 'Nigger Calculator'—and sundry other semi-idiotic innocents of the same order. It was 'destiny' which led the 'kite's egg hatched in the eagle's nest'—Napoleon III, of France—through the gloomy mists of massacre and perjury, to a gilded stall which he has dared to 'name a throne.'

"Ay, these are '*bigots*' for you," roars Sam; "yes, bigots—bigots of the old sort, cold, crafty, coward monsters, who have stolen the watchwords of instinct and of freedom for their impious exaltation.

"They must be God's 'i' faith;'—'the butcher shall be butchered in his own stall, and a sea of blood shall hold his soul among its monsters!'"

The Titan shakes his finger at the East, and smiling, calmly says: "Thy day is past, thou storied, gorgeous East! Thine unnatural crimes, in name of every sacredness, shall no longer pass unchallenged!

"How darest thou crush the life and heart out of 'him' who walks with upright countenance before the Lord, when each several man is monarch, as old Adam was? How darest thou, hemispherical and hoary 'bigot,' claim to be what thou art not—*infallible?* My people know me—the spirit, the will, the power of a New World—the luminous presence in the realm of thought! Ay, I, Sam, shall yet relieve you, as I shall relieve my own children, from the pestilent absurdities of 'bigotry!' What am I but the gigantic individual, the sovereign man, the future Emperor of sky-rimmed Space?

"Thou must go back to first principles in me, thou dim and colorless Orient! Man is of the earth, earthly; therefore, as its superior *Form*, you must accept me; you can not get away in time from the condition. It is the law of my being. I must yet assert for my children—for the Brotherhood of mankind—not a God, not a prophecy, not a butcher's stall, not destiny, but a calm truth, and powerful edict—be yourselves—(tremendous phrase!)—'be yourselves!' be, *first* of all, *Men!* second, Warriors! third, Lovers! with a sublime justice, lovers alike of those who struggle and of those who win; and *then* away with hounding bigotries!"

Could he have been the lover of mankind who framed the "Constitutions of the Society" of Jesus? We shall see whether he was not rather the satanic foe of that instinct of "individuality" which underlies all just ideas of freedom, and which has been the immemorial antipode of despotism. Who could have based an association of men, for whatever purpose, upon the utter abnegation of this cardinal principle, but one who, isolated in selfism, ignored in hideous fantasy, the rights of others to live, and move, and have a being, spiritually. Let us give some idea of these monstrous "Constitutions."

Huge corruptions and great confusions had crept into the Roman Catholic world. The different monastic orders were at war with one another. The bishops accused the Pope of tyranny; the Pope denounced the bishops as disobedient. The mass of the people were deplorably ignorant, and general disorder prevailed.

Now mark with what admirable art, what profound sagacity Ignatius modeled a society, which, by displaying the virtues directly opposed to the then prevailing vices, should captivate the affections and secure the support of the good and the pious, while, by underhand practices, and above all, by showing unusual indulgence in the confessional, it should obtain an influence over the minds of the more worldly believers.

In order that diversity of opinion and the free exercise of individual will should not produce division and confusion within this new Christian community, Loyola enacted that in the whole society, there should be no will, no opinion, but the General's. But, in order that the General might be enabled profitably to employ each individual member, as well as the collective energy and intelligence of the whole society, it was necessary that he should be thoroughly acquainted with his character, even to its smallest peculiarities. To insure this, Ignatius established special rules. Thus, regarding the admission of postulants, he says:

"Because it greatly concerns God's service to make a good selection, diligence must be used to ascertain the particulars of their person and calling; and if the Superior who is to admit him into probation cannot make the inquiry, let him employ from among those who are constantly about his person some one whose assistance he may use, to become acquainted with the probationer, to live with him and examine him; some one endowed with prudence, and not unskilled in the manner which should be observed with so many various kinds and conditions of persons." * In other words, set a skillful and prudent spy over him, to surprise him into the betrayal of his most secret thoughts. Yet, even when this spy has given a tolerably favorable report, the candidate is not yet admitted —he is sent to live in another house, in order that he may be more thoroughly scrutinized, to know whether he is fitted to be admitted to probation. † When he is thought suited for the Society, he is received into the "house of first probation;" and, after a day or two, "he must open his conscience to the Superior, and afterward make a general confession to the confessor who shall be designed by the Superior. ‡ But this is not all, for "in every house of probation there will be a skillful man to whom the candidate shall disclose all his concerns with confidence; and let him be admonished to hide no temptation, but to disclose it to him, or to his confessor, or to the Superior; nay, to take a pleasure in thoroughly manifesting his whole soul to them, not only disclosing his defects, but even his penances, mortifications and 'virtues.' § When the candidate is admitted into any of their colleges, he must again "open his conscience to the rector of the college, whom he should greatly revere and venerate, as one who holds the place of Christ our Lord, keeping nothing concealed from him, not even his conscience, which he should disclose to him, (as it is set forth in the Examen,) at the appointed season, and oftener, if any cause require it; not opposing, not contradicting, nor showing an opinion, in any case opposed to his opinion."

The information thus collected regarding the tastes, habits,

* Const. Socie. Jesu. pars 1, cap i, § 3.

† Const. pars 1, cap ii, § 1.

‡ Const. pars i, cap. iv, § 6.

§ Const. pars vi, cap. i, § 1.

and inclinations of every member, is communicated to the General, who notes it down in a book, alphabetically arranged, and kept for the purpose, in which also he receives twice a year a detailed report upon every member of the Society, he from time to time adds whatever seems necessary to complete each delineation of character, or to indicate the slightest change. Thus, the General knowing the past and the present life, the thoughts, the desires of every one belonging to the Society, it is easy to understand how he is enabled always to select the fittest person for every special service.

But this perfect knowledge of his subordinates' natures would be of but little use to the General, had he not also an absolute and uncontrolled authority over them. The Constitution has a provision for insuring this likewise. It declares that the candidate "must regard the Superior as Christ the Lord, and must strive to acquire perfection in every point, in execution, in will, in intellect; doing what is enjoined with all celerity, spiritual joy and perseverance; persuading ourselves that everything is just; suppressing every repugnant thought and judgment of one's own, in a certain obedience; * * * * * * and let every one persuade himself that he who lives under obedience should be moved and directed, under Divine Providence, by his Superior, just as if he were a corpse, (*perinde ac si cadaver esset,*) which allows itself to be moved and led in any direction. And so absolutely is this rule of submissive obedience enforced, that the Jesuit, in order to obey his General, must not scruple to disobey God. The warnings of conscience are to be suppressed as culpable weaknesses; the fears of eternal punishment banished from the thoughts as superstitious fancies; and the most heinous crimes, when committed by command of the General, are to be regarded as promoting the glory and praise of God.

Sam is, to be sure, no lover of Jack-Cadeism in any of its forms, and regards the Revolutionary spirit as an instinct to be carefully watched, lest it should fall into dangerous extremes; but there never has been the time yet—even since he dangled the Red men by their scalp-locks before his eyes—when he did not feel moved unto wrath at the hearing of such frightful lies as this against God and his children; and so have such lies thriven in his hand, that in these latter days, his fingers verily tingle to grip, sponsors and all, in the heavy clutch of his annihilating anger!

What a mockery! "The Jesuit, in order to obey his General, must not scruple to disobey God." "Crimes, when committed by the command of the General, are to be regarded as promoting the glory and praise of God." Hideous mockery! While Sam stands still to think—to realize—the throes of agonized earth beneath his feet rock him as if the Great Mother were convulsed with sobbing! A terrible story—that thus man should be unto his brother! A more hideous Cain hath arisen—for while that first Cain slew the body, this one hath slain the soul—soul, sense and conscience!

Ah! that Reverence—that sublimest instinct, should be thus abused!—that the cold and cunning devices of this Loyola Fratricide, should, by artfully shading off this noble fatuity into forms, each seemingly more crystallized and perfect than the last, lead soul, mind and will at last, into the dizzying labyrinth of Fanaticism, from whence, the "individual" never escapes, and where the whole man is murdered!

"No constitution, declaration, or any order of living, can involve an obligation to commit sin, mortal or venial, *unless the spirit command it* in the name of our Lord Jesus Christ, or in virtue of holy obedience; which shall be done in those cases or persons wherein it shall be judged that it will greatly conduce to the particular good of each, or to the general advantage; and, instead of the fear of offense, let the love and desire of all perfection succeed, that the greater glory and praise of Christ, our Creator and Lord, may follow."

Sam is no egoist; he believes profoundly in the sentiment of modern "Protestant" Christianity; but how can that faith which took for its apostles, "men of no account," to be the mythical representatives of Freedom, submit to be the slaves of those who commit sin, mortal or venial, "in the name of our Lord Jesus Christ," or "in virtue of holy obedience!" Obedience! to what? The command of the Superior—the General—the Emperor—the Czar—the Tyrant over soul as well as body; over mind as well as will; the despot, before the face of whom, the swollen head of Caligula diminishes to a very point of infamy, in the story of old Time. What a thought for the proud and self-poised sons of freedom to

11

dwell upon, "just as if it were a *corpse* which allows itself to be moved and led in any direction, by a single man! Imbecile fatuity! and dost thou dare to hope to wreak upon the children of Sam, the overgrown curse—the malignities of which the electric thunders of modern progress, under his lead, shall overcome!

It can not be that it is a comfortable creed for Calvinistic Protestantism, this—that a mortal man is to recognized as God! Yet it is thus that the Jesuit must believe, and in conformity with this must act. We shudder at the thought of all the atrocities which had been perpetrated at the order of this other old man of the mountain, who presents to his agents the prospects of eternal bliss as the reward of their obedience.

But this is not enough. Not content with having thus transferred the allegiance of the Jesuit from his God to his General, the Constitution proceeds to secure that allegiance from all conflict with the natural affections or worldly interests. The Jesuit must concentrate all his desires and affections upon the Society. He must renounce all that is dear to him in this life. The ties of family, the bonds of friendship, must be broken. His property must, within a year after his entrance into the Society, be disposed of at the bidding of the General; and he will accomplish a work of greater perfection if he dispose of it in benefit of the Society. And that his better example may shine before men, he must put away all strong affections for his parents, and refrain from the unsuitable desire of a bountiful distribution, arising from such disadvantageous affections.*

He must, beside, forego all intercourse with his fellow-men, either by word of mouth or by writing,† except such as his Superior shall permit. He shall not leave the house, except at such times and with such companions as the Superior shall allow. Nor within the house shall he converse, without restraint, with any one at his own pleasure, but with such only as shall be appointed by the Superior.‡ Such was the

* Examen, iv, § 11; and Const. pars iii, cap. i, § 7–9.

† After his entrance into the house of first probation, the Jesuit is not allowed either to receive or send away any letter which has not been previously read by his Superior.

‡ Const. pars iii, cap. i, § 2, 3.

strictness with which these rules were enforced, that Francis Borgia, Duke of Candia, afterward one of the saints of the Society, was at first refused admittance into it, because he delayed the settlement of the affairs of his dukedom, and refused to renounce all intercourse with his family; and although, by a special rescript from the Pope, he was enrolled as a member, Ignatius, for three years, sternly denied him access to the house of the community, where he was not admitted, till he had renounced all intercourse with the external world.

But not only is all friendly communication forbidden to the Jesuit, but he is also placed under constant espionage. He is never permitted to walk about alone, but, whether in the house or out of doors, is always accompanied by two of his brothers.* Each one of this party of three acts, in fact, as a spy upon his two companions. Not, indeed, that he has special instruction from his Superior to do so, but knowing that they, as well as himself, have been taught that it is their duty to inform the General of every suspicious or peculiar expression uttered in their hearing, he is under constant fear of punishment, should either of them report anything regarding the other which he omits to report likewise. Hence it is very seldom that a Jesuit refrains from denouncing his companion. If he does not do so at once, his sinful neglect becomes revealed in the confessional, to the special confessor appointed by the Superior.

Then, in order that these members, so submissive in action to their General, should not differ in opinion among themselves, and so occasion scandal in the Catholic world, and to oppose a uniformity of doctrine to that of the free examen of the Protestants, the Constitution decrees as follows: "Let all think, let all speak, as far as possible, the same thing,

* Let not any reader accuse me of inaccuracy on this point upon the ground that Jesuits actually walk about the streets in this country single, or even in disguise. They must take notice that every rule of the Constitution is this clause—"Except the General order otherwise, for the greater glory of God, and the benefit of the Society." It is not "for the greater glory of God, and the benefit of the Society," that the Jesuit, to escape suspicion, should go alone?—that he should be introduced into your family circle as a Protestant gentleman?—that he should, to gain our unsuspecting confidence, enact the part of your gay companion at theaters, concerts and balls?—that he should converse with you upon religious ma ters, beginning always by cursing the Pope, etc.?

according to the apostle. Let no contradictory doctrines, therefore, be allowed, either by word of mouth or public sermons, or in written book, which last shall not be published without the approbation and the consent of the General; and indeed, all difference of opinion regarding practical matters should be avoided."* Thus, no one but the General can exercise the right of uttering a single original thought or opinion. It is almost impossible to conceive the power, especially in former times, of a General having at his absolute disposal such an amount of intelligences, will and energies.

At a glance how terrible seems this postulate. "No one but the General can exercise the right of uttering a single original thought or opinion." How ludicrous! a man-God! the infallible mated with the fallible!

The physical bonds of feudalism, of absolute slavery, repulsive as they are, seem the merest silken ties, compared to this monstrous despotism, this double tyranny! What then is left of the man?—surely not the soul! It must then, indeed, be a corpse—"*cadaver*"—with a fearful realization.

---

*Const. pars iii, cap. i § 18.

CHAPTER XXI.

Insidious cunning of the Jesuits—Death extortions—Robbery and Ruin of their Devotees—Scandalous scenes in the interior—Life of Jesuitism—Loyola entangled with the "Sisters"—Secret Jesuits.

But in no part of the Constitution is the diabolical cunning of the insidious spirit of Loyola more conspicuously exhibited than in the rules he has established concerning what he calls the *vow of poverty* and gratuitous performance of the duties of the sacred ministry.

The discredit and hatred which weighed upon the clergy and the monastic orders was in great part due to the ostentatious display of their accumulated wealth and to the venality of their sacred ministry. To guard against this evil, Ignatius ordained that "poverty should be loved and maintained as the firmest bulwark of religion." The Jesuit was forbidden to possess any property, either by inheritance or otherwise. He was required to live in an inexpensive house, to dress plainly, and avoid all appearance of being wealthy. The churches and religious houses of the order were to be without endowments. The colleges alone were permitted to accept legacies or donations for the maintenance of students and professors. No limit was assigned to these gifts, the management of which was intrusted entirely to the General, with power to appoint rectors and administrators under him. These functionaries, generally chosen from among the coadjutors, and very rarely from the professed Society, although debarred by their vow of perpetual poverty from the possession of the smallest amount of property, are yet, by this ingenious trick, enabled to hold and administer the entire wealth of the Society. We shall afterward see, and especially in the famous process of Lavallette, in what a large sense they understood the word *administer*. So much for the display of wealth. With respect to the venality of the sacred ministry, they declared that "no Jesuit shall demand or receive pay, or alms, or remuneration for mass, confessions, sermons, lessons, visitations, or any other duty which the Society is obliged to render, and to avoid even the appearance of covetousness, especially in offices of piety which the Society discharges for the succour of souls, let there be *no box* in the church, into which alms are generally put by those who go thither to mass, sermon, confession, etc.* Thus the Jesuit refuses to accept a few paltry sixpences for performing mass, or a fee of some shillings per quarter for teaching boys. He disdains to appear mercenary. He would much rather be *poor*. He looks for no reward. Yet those little boys whom he instructs gratuitously and with such affectionate tenderness that he cannot bring himself to chastise them, but must have the painful though necessary duty performed by some one not belonging to the Society; these boys, I say, will become men, many of them religious bigots, strongly attached to their kind preceptors, to whom they will then pay the debt of gratitude incurred in their youth.

Alas for such gratitude! How many families have had cause to deplore it! How many children have been reduced to beggary by it! How many ancient and noble houses has it precipitated from the hight of affluence and splendor into the depth of poverty and wretchedness! Who can number the crimes committed in the madness of despair occasioned by the loss of the family inheritance! That the parent may suffer a few years less of purgatory, the child has been too often condemned to misery in this life, and perhaps to eternal punishment in the next. But all this is of no consequence. The man who has been led thus to disregard one of his most sacred parental duties, in order to found a Jesuits' College or endow a professorship, will be saved, because they promise him: "In every college of our Society let masses be celebrated once a week *forever*, for its founder and benefactor, whether dead or alive. At the beginning of every month, all the priests who are in the college, ought to offer the same sacri-

* Const. pars iv, cap. 1, § 1, 6.

fice for them; and a solemn mass, with a commemorative feast, shall be celebrated on the anniversary of the donation, and a wax candle offered to the donor or his descendants." Beside this, "the donor shall have three masses while alive, and three masses after his death, by all the priests of the Society, with the prayers of all its members; so that he is made partaker of all the good works which are done, by the grace of God, not only in the college which he has endowed, but in the whole Society."*

By such allurements do these crafty priests, with diabolical cunning, snatch princely fortunes from the credulous and superstitious believers. And so assiduous and successful were they, even at the very beginning, that, only thirteen years after the establishment of the Order, during Loyola's lifetime, they already possessed upward of a hundred colleges, very largely and richly endowed.

Now, let not my Protestant readers wonder how sensible men can be induced, by such ephemeral and ill-founded hopes, to disinherit their families to enrich these hypocritical monks. They must remember that the Romish believer views these matters in quite a different light from that in which they see them. Masses and prayers are, in his belief, not only useful, but indispensable. For lack of them he would writhe for centuries amid the tormenting fires of purgatory, the purifying pains of which are described by his priest, with appalling eloquence, as being far more excruciating than those of hell. According to the doctrine of his Church, every soul (one in a million only excepted) who is not eternally damned, must, ere it enter heaven, pass a certain time in this abode of torture for the expiation of its sins. And let him not take comfort from the fact that his conscience does not reproach him with the commission of any heinous crime. The catalogue of sins by which he may be shut out from eternal blessedness is made fearfully long, and detailed with great minuteness. The most upright and pious of men must condemn himself as a presumptuous sinner, if he for an instant harbors the hope of escaping the purifying fire. So he becomes quite resigned to his fate, and all his care in this life is, how to appease the Divine anger and shorten the period of

* Const. pars iv, cap. 16, § 3.

his exclusion from heaven. This he is taught to do—not by trusting to the righteousness of Jesus Christ, with the true repentance which manifests itself through a holy life, but by accumulating on his head hundreds of masses and millions of days of indulgence. Hence the innumerable masses and prayers which he sends before him during his life, as if to forestall his future punishment and bribe the Divine justice. And when the terrible moment arrives—that moment in which he is about to appear before the awful Judge, beneath whose searching eye his most secret thoughts lie bare—when trembling at the strict account that is about to be demanded of him, his fears represent to his excited imagination the most trifling shortcomings as mortal sins—when, with the decline of bodily strength, his enfeebled mind becomes more easily worked upon—then does his Jesuit confessor, his generous master, his kind, disinterested friend, come to give him the last proof of his ever-growing affection! He seats himself at the bedside, and, serpent-like, under pretense of inducing him to repent of his sins, he draws him a fearful and impressive picture of the torments which await the damned. He descants to him with oily sanctity upon the enormity of offending the Divine Savior, who shed his precious blood to redeem us. He terrifies him with the Almighty's implacable vengeance; and when his victim, choked with heart-rending agony, distracted, despairing of his ultimate salvation, is ready to curse God and set his power and anger at defiance—then, and not till then, does the Jesuit relent. Now he raises in the sufferer's heart the faintest hope that the Divine justice may possibly be disarmed, and mercy obtained by means of masses and indulgences. The exhausted man, who feels as if he were already plunged amid the boiling sulphur and devouring flames, grasps with a frantic eagerness at this anchor of salvation; and, did he possess tenfold more wealth than he does, he would willingly give it all up to save his soul. It may be that his heart, yearning with paternal affection, shrinks at the thought of condemning his helpless ones to beggary; but nevertheless, as if the welfare of his family was necessarily connected with his own perdition, and that of the Jesuits with eternal beatitude, the family are invariably sacrificed to the Jesuits.

It is notorious, that the most diabolical tricks have been resorted to in the case of dying men whose better judgment and natural sense of duty have withstood such perfidious wiles.

Alas! the punishment of such criminal obstinacy was always near at hand; the sick-chamber has been suddenly filled with flames and sulphurous vapor, as a warning to the impenitent sinner. And if he still resisted, the Evil Spirit himself, in his most frightful shape, has appeared to the dying man, as if waiting for his soul. Ah! one's hair stands on end while listening to such sacrilegious maneuvers. The immense wealth of the Jesuits has been bequeathed to them by wills made at the last hour!

Niocolini, in a note, gives us an ingenuous glimpse into the interior life of certain of these monastic traders in the ignorances and superstitions of mankind, which seems to indicate them as admirably inclined toward certain recumbent, if not death-bed, experiences themselves:

"In most monasteries, and more particularly in those of the Capuchins and Reformed, (Reformati,) there begins at Christmas a series of feasts, which continue till Lent. All sorts of games are played, the most splendid banquets are given, and in the small towns, above all, the refectory of the convent is the best place of amusement for the greater number of the inhabitants. At carnivals, two or three very magnificent entertainments take place, the board so profusely spread that one might imagine that Copia had here poured forth the whole contents of her horn. It must be remembered that these two orders live by alms. The somber silence of the cloister is replaced by a confused sound of merry-making, and its gloomy vaults now echo with other songs than those of the Psalmist. A ball enlivens and terminates the feast; and, to render it still more animated, and perhaps to show how completely their vow of chastity has eradicated all their carnal appetite, some of the young monks appear coquettishly dressed in the garb of the fair sex, and begin the dance along with others transformed into gay cavaliers. To describe the scandalous scene which ensues, would be but to disgust my readers. I will only say, that I have myself often been a spectator at such saturnalia."

When Ignatius was living at Barcelona, he received many kindnesses and favors at the hand of a lady called Rosello. But after he had left this place, his mind was so absorbed in devising so many and lofty projects, that he entirely forgot her. She did not, however, forget Ignatius. Hearing of his increasing sanctity, of his having become the founder and general of a new Order, and "being then a widow, she resolved to abandon the world, and live in accordance with his evangelical counsels, and under the authority of the Society. With this pious resolution, and being joined in her holy enterprise by two virtuous and noble Roman ladies, she asked and received from Paul, permission to embrace this kind of life."* Ignatius had the perception to see that these ladies would be an incumbrance to him and his Order. "Yet the gratitude which he owed to his kind benefactress weighed so much upon his heart, that he consented to receive them under his protection." But he soon had reason to repent of this act of condescension; the annoyance was so great, that he confessed himself that they gave him more trouble than the whole community, because he could never get done with them. At every moment he was obliged to resolve their strange questions, to allay their scruples, to hear their complaints, or settle their differences;† and as, notwithstanding all his sagacity, Ignatius did not foresee of what advantage women could one day be to the Order, he applied to the Pope to be relieved of this charge, writing, at the same time, the following letter to Rosello:

"VENERABLE DAME ISABELLA ROSELLO—My Mother and my Sister in Jesus Christ.—In truth, I would wish, for the greater glory of God, to satisfy your good desires, and procure your spiritual progress by keeping you under my obedience, as you have been for some time past; but the continual ailments to which I am subject, and all my occupations which concern the service of our Lord, or his vicar on earth, permit me to do so no longer. Moreover, being persuaded, according to the light of my conscience, that this little Society ought not to take upon itself, in particular, the

---

* Helyot, vol. vii, p. 491. † Idem.

direction of any woman who may be engaged to us by vows of obedience; as I have fully declared to our Holy Father, the Pope, it has seemed to me for the greater glory of God, that I ought no longer to look upon you as my spiritual daughter, and only as my godmother, as you have been for many years, to the greater glory of God. Consequently, for the greater service, and the greater honor of the everlasting Goodness, I give you, as much as I can, into the hands of the sovereign Pontiff, in order that, taking his judgment and will as a rule, you may find rest and consolation for the greater glory of the Divine Majesty.—At Rome, the first of October, 1549."

The Pope complied with the request, and exempted the order from the superintendence of women; and Ignatius enacted in the Constitutions, "that no member of the Society should undertake the care of souls, nor of religious, or of any other women whatever," [Loyola's disciples thought proper to differ from him,] "so as frequently to hear their confessions, or give them directions, although there is no objection to their receiving the confession of a monastery once, and for a special reason."*

Dame Rosello and her two companions, being deprived of their spiritual father—not wishing to change him for another, so faithful were they—desisted at once from their pious undertaking, and for a time, nothing more was heard of female Jesuits; but about the year 1622, some females, more meddling than devoted, took upon themselves the task of reviving the Institution, although they were not authorized to do so. Nevertheless, they united into different communities, established houses for novitiates and colleges, chose a General

* Const, pars vi, cap. iii, § 7. To be a nun's confessor was, and is still, deemed a high privilege. Before the Council of Trent, this privilege belonged to the order of St. Francis, under whose rules most of the nuns also live. The conduct of those brothers and sisters was in the highest degree improper and scandalous. Although the Franciscans are now no longer the titular confessors of these nuns, nevertheless they are on the most friendly terms with one another; upon which friendship the Italians exercise their satirical and sarcastic wit. The confessors are now chosen by the respective bishops, who confer the honor upon their most faithful adherents, as a reward for their services. The rivalries of those sainted women, and their ingenious contrivances to engage the smile of their holy father, are notorious to every one who lives near a convent.

under the name of Proposta, and made vows into her hands of perpetual chastity, poverty and obedience. Not being restrained by any law of seclusion, they went from place to place, bustling with gossip, and causing confusion and scandal throughout the Catholic camp. The community soon spread over a great part of lower Germany, France, Spain, and was especially numerous in Italy, where it originated.

Urban VIII, after vainly endeavoring to impose upon them some rules of discipline, by a brief of the 21st of May, 1631, suppressed them.*

Thus ended the society of Female Jesuits under this name and form. But another afterward sprung up in its place, under the appellation of *Religieuse du Sacre Cœur*, having special rules very like those of the Jesuits, under whose absolute directions they now are.

In Catholic countries, above all, in France, and, we are sorry to say, in Piedmont also, very many of the highest rank in society, send their daughters to be educated in these monasteries. Had Ignatius known what powerful auxiliaries these *worthy* nuns were likely to prove to his Order, he would, in all likelihood, have borne with those petty annoyances caused to him by good dame Rosello. Ladies educated by these nuns, bring into their homes all those dissensions and cause all those evils which are so ably described by the French professor, Michelet, who lost his chair the other day, for daring to attack these all-powerful auxiliaries of Napoleon—the Jesuits.

The members of the Society are divided into four classes: the professed, coadjutors, scholars, and novices. There is also a secret fifth class, known only to the General and a few faithful Jesuits, which, perhaps more than any other, contributes to the dreaded and mysterious power of the Order. It is composed of laymen of all ranks, from the minister to the humble shoe-boy. Among the individuals composing this class are to be found many ladies, who, unknown and unsuspected, are more dangerous in themselves, and more accurate spies to the Company. These are affiliated to the Society, but not bound by any vows. The Society, as a noble and avowed reward, promises to them forgiveness for all

* Helyot, vol. iii, p. 492.

their sins, and eternal blessedness; and as a more palpable mark of gratitude, protects them, patronizes them, and, in countries where the Jesuits are powerful, procures for them comfortable and lucrative places under government, or elsewhere. If this is not sufficient, they are paid for their services in hard cash, according to an article of the Constitution, which empowers the General to spend money on *persons who will make themselves useful.* In return for these favors, they act as the spies of the Order, the reporters of what goes on in those classes of society with which the Jesuit can not mix, and serve, often unwillingly, as the tools and accomplices in dark and mysterious crimes. Father Francis Pellio, brother to the famous Silvio, in his recent quarrel with the celebrated Gioberti, to prove that the Order is not very deficient of supporters, as his opponent asserts, candidly confesses that, "the many illustrious friends of the Society, prelates, orators, learned and distinguished men of every description, the supporters of the Society, remain *occult, and obliged to be silent.*"*

Here is the formula of the vow taken by the coadjutors:—

"I. N., promise Almighty God, before his Virgin Mother, and before all the heavenly host, and you, reverend father, General of the Society of Jesus, *holding the place of God,* and of your successors; or you, reverend father, Vice-General of the Society of Jesus, and of his successors, *holding the place of God,* perpetual poverty, chastity and obedience, and therein, *peculiar care in the education of boys,* according to the manner expressed in the apostolic letters, and in the Constitution of the said Society. At Rome, or elsewhere, in such a place, day, month and year."

---

* A. Vincenzo Gioberti Fra Pellico della Campagnia di Gesu, pp. 35, 36.

CHAPTER XXII.

Monstrous Doctrine of Probableism—Doctrine of Equivocation—Terrible Corruption of the Confessional.

HAVING examined the process by which a man is annihilated and a Jesuit manufactured, it only remains for us to glance at the "moral code" of this holy company. This becomes the more necessary that, even taking into consideration all the probabilities of corruption to be anticipated as growing out of the irresponsible control of many minds and bodies by the single will of one man—the General—who alone retains the right of willing—it yet becomes impossible for any human imagination to at once realize and compass the enormities to which this flagitious despotism led. Enormities that were not merely consequential upon gradual abuse, but were cotemporaneous with the "Constitutions," *ab origine* a part and essential element of the system of Loyola.

As the Order of Jesus had been especially "raised up by God" to battle with the austere doctrines of Luther and the spiritual asceticism of the vigilant Calvin, so it became necessary that, by what one of their authorities calls "an obliging and accommodating conduct" in the confessional, they should court popularity in opposition to these strict tenets.

The great contest with the Protestants had left among the Roman Catholics a tendency, a wish, we do not say to become the better Christians, but to make a greater display of their religion. All the external practices of devotion which, in their eyes, constituted the true believer, were more eagerly resorted to, and, above all, the confessional was frequented with unprecedented assiduity. To have a confessor exclusively for one's self, was the surest sign of orthodoxy, and became as fashionable as it is now to have a box at the opera. Sovereigns, ministers, courtiers, noblemen—every man, in short, who had a certain position in society, had his own acknowledged confessor. Even the mistresses of princes pretended to the privilege, and Madame de Pompadour will prove to her spiritual guide that it is dangerous to oppose the caprices of a favorite. The Jesuits saw at once the immense advantage they would derive if they could enlarge the number of their clients, especially among the higher classes. They were already, in this particular, far advanced in the public favor; they were known to be very indulgent; had long since obtained the privilege of absolving from those sins which only the Pope himself could pardon; and Suarez, their great theologian, had even attempted to introduce confession by letter, as a more easy and expeditious way of reaching all penitents.*

But, by this time, they had made fearful progress in the art of flattering the bad passions, and winking at the vices of those who had recourse to their ministry, in order to make, as they believed, their peace with God.

So, for example, if the Jesuit confessor perceives that a penitent feels inclined to make restitution of ill-gotten money, he will certainly encourage him to do so, praise him for his holy resolution, insist to be himself the instrument of the restitution, taking care, however, that it should be known again. But if another person accuse himself of theft, but show no disposition to make restitution, be sure that the Jesuit confessor will find in some book or other of his brother Jesuits, some sophistry to set his conscience at rest, and persuade him that he may safely retain what he has stolen from his neighbor.

The existence of books to which those pernicious maxims have been consigned, having put it out of the power of the Jesuits to impugn their genuineness in order to exculpate their Society, they have cast a reproach upon the teachers of their own Church, and even blasphemed Christianity. "The probableism," says their historian, "was not born with the Jesuits; at the moment of their establishment, probableism reigned in the schools."† And again; "Ever since the origin of Christianity, the world had complained of the

* Cret. vol. ii, page 176.

† Cret. vol. iv, page 58.

austerity of certain precepts; the Jesuits came to bring relief from these grievances." *

But, that our readers may judge for themselves of the character of Jesuitical morality, we shall lay before them some of their doctrines; and in doing so, (be it observed,) we shall quote as our authorities none but Jesuit authors, and such as have been approved and are held in veneration by the Society.

It is evident that, in the confessional, everything depends upon the conception formed of transgression and sin. Now, according to the Jesuitical doctrines, we do not sin, unless we have a clear perception and understanding of the sin as sin, and unless our will freely consent to it. † The following are the consequences which the Jesuit casuists have deduced from that principle:

"A confessor perceives that his penitent is in invincible ignorance, or at least innocent ignorance, and he does not hope that any benefit will be derived from his advice, but rather anxiety of mind, strife or scandal." Should he dissemble? Suarez affirms that he ought; because, since his admonition will be fruitless, ignorance will excuse his penitent from sin. ‡

Although he who, through inveterate habit, inadvertently swears a falsehood, may seem bound to confess the propensity, yet he is commonly excused. The reason is, that no one commonly reflects upon the obligation by which he is bound to extirpate the habit; * * * and, therefore, since he is excused from the sin, he will also be excused from confession. Some maintain that the same may be said of blasphemy, heresy, and of the aforesaid oath, * * * and, consequently, that such things, committed inadvertently, are neither sins in themselves, nor the cause of sins, and therefore need not necessarily be confessed. §

---

* Le monde s'tait plaint depuis l'origine du Christianisme de l'austérité de certains precepts; les Jesuites venaient au secour de ces doleances, etc. —Cret. vol. iv, page 50.

† Busembaum, apud Ranke, vol. ii, page 394.

‡ Antony Escobar. L. Theol. morallis vigenti-quatvor Societatis Jesu Doctoribus reseratus.—Ex. de pænitentia ch. vii, N. 155. (Lugduni, 1656. Ed. Mvs. Brit.)

§ Thomas Tambourin. Methodus Expeditæ Confessionis, L. ii, ch. iii, § 3, N. 23. (Lugduni, 1659. Antverpiae, 1656. Ed. Coll. Sion.)

Wherever there is no knowledge of wickedness, there is, also, of necessity, no sin. It is sufficient to have at least a confused notion of the heinousness of a sin; without which knowledge, there would never be a flagrant crime. For instance, one man kills another, believing it indeed to be wrong, but conceiving it to be nothing more than a trifling fault. Such a man does not greatly sin, because it is knowledge only which points out the wickedness or the grossness of it to the will. Therefore, criminality is only imputed according to the measure of knowledge.

If a man commit adultery or suicide, reflecting, indeed, but still very imperfectly and superficially, upon the wickedness and great sinfulness of those crimes, however heinous may be the matter, he still sins but slightly. The reason is, that as a knowledge of the wickedness is necessary to constitute the sin, so is a full clear knowledge and reflection necessary to constitute a heinous sin. And thus I reason with Vasquez: In order that a man may freely sin, it is necessary to deliberate whether he sins or not. But he fails to deliberate upon the moral wickedness of it, if he does not reflect, at least by doubting, upon it during the act; therefore, he does not sin, unless he reflects upon the wickedness of it. It is also certain that a full knowledge of such wickedness is required to constitute a mortal sin. For it would be unworthy the goodness of God to exclude a man from glory, and to reject him forever, for a sin on which he had not fully deliberated; but if reflection upon the wickedness of it has only been partial, deliberation has not been complete; and therefore the sin is not a mortal sin.*

The practical consequences of this doctrine have been admirably represented by Pascal, in his happiest vein of irony. "Oh, my dear sir," says he to the Jesuit, who had exposed to him the aforementioned doctrine, "what a blessing this will be to some persons of my acquaintance! I must positively introduce them to you. You have never, perhaps, in all your life, met with people who had fewer sins to account for. In the first place, they never think of God at all; their vices have got the better of their reason; they have never known either their weakness or the physician who can cure

* George de Rhodes. Disput. Theologiæ Scholasticæ, tom. i. Dis. xi, quaes. xi, sec. 1 and 2, and Dis. i, q. iii, sec. 2, § 3. (Lugduni, 1671.)

it; they have never thought of 'desiring the health of their soul,' and still less, of 'praying to God to bestow it,' so that, according to M. Lemoine, they are still in the state of baptismal innocence. They have 'never had a thought of loving God, or of being contrite for their sins;' so that, according to Father Annat, they have never committed sin through the want of charity and penitence. Their life is spent in a perpetual round of all sorts of pleasures, in the course of which they have not been interrupted by the slightest remorse. These excesses had led me to imagine that their perdition was inevitable; but you, father, inform me that these same excesses secure their salvation. Blessings on you, my good father, for this new way of justifying people! Others prescribe painful austerities for healing the soul, but you show that souls which may be thought desperately diseased, are in quite good health. What an excellent device for being happy, both in this world and the next! I had always supposed that the less a man thought of God, the more he sinned; but from what I see now, if one could only succeed in bringing himself not to think of God at all, everything would be pure with him in all time coming. Away with your half-and-half sinners, who retain some sneaking affection for virtue! They will be damned, every soul of them. But commend me to your arrant sinners—hardened, unalloyed, out-and-out, thorough-bred sinners. Hell is no place for them; they have cheated the devil, by sheer devotion to his service.*"

But if you are not such an arrant, hardened sinner but that your conscience warns you of your guilt, then come to the doctrine of probability, the A B C of the Jesuitical code of morality, which will set your troublesome conscience at rest. Listen!

"The true opinion is, that it is not only lawful to follow the more probable but less safe opinion, * * * but also that the less safe may be followed, when there is an equality of probability.

"I agree in the opinion of Henriquez, Vasquez, and Perez, who maintain that it is sufficient for an inexperienced and unlearned man to follow the opinion which he thinks to be

*In quoting Pascal, we make use of the translation of Dr. M'Crie, to render the author's meaning better than we could do. P. 107.

probable, because it is maintained by good men who are versed in the art; although that opinion may be neither the more safe, nor the more common, nor the more probable.

"Sotus thinks that it would be very troublesome to a penitent, if the priest, after having heard his confession, should send him back without absolution, to confess himself again to another priest, if he could absolve him with a safe conscience against his own (the priest's) opinion; especially when another priest might not, perhaps, be readily found who would believe the opinion of the penitent to be probable.

"It may be asked whether a confessor may give advice to a penitent in opposition to his own opinion; or, if he should think in any case that restitution ought to be made, whether he may advise that the opinion of others may be followed, who maintain that it need not be made? I answer that he lawfully may * * * * * * because we may follow the opinion of another in his own practice, and therefore he may advise another person to follow it. Still it is better in giving advice always to follow the more probable opinion to which a man is ever accustomed to adhere, especially when the advice is given in writing, lest contradiction be discovered. It is also sometimes expedient to send the consulting person to another doctor or confessor who is known to hold an opinion favorable to the inquirer, provided it be probable.*

"Without respect of persons, may a judge, in order to favor his friend, decide according to any probable opinion, while the question of right remains undecided?

"If the judge should think each opinion equally probable, for the sake of his friend, he may lawfully pronounce sentence according to the opinion which is more favorable to the interests of that friend. He may, moreover, with the intent to serve his friend, at one time judge according to one opinion, and at another time according to the contrary opinion, provided, only, that no scandal result from the decision.†

"An unbeliever who is persuaded that his sect is probable, although the opposite sect may be more probable, would

---

* John of Salas. Disputationum R. P. Joannis de Salas, e Soc. Jesu. in primam secundæ D. Thomæ, tom 1, tr. 8, sec. 7, 9, N. 74, 83. (Barcinone, 1607. Ed. Bibl. Arch. Cant. Lamb.)

† Gregory of Valentia. Commentariorum Theologicorum, tom iii, dis v, quæs 7, punct iv. (Lutetiæ Parisiorum, 1609. Ed. Coll. Sion.)

certainly be obliged, at the point of death, to embrace the true faith, which he thinks to be the more probable * * * * * But, except under such circumstances, he would not * * * * * * Add to this, that the mysteries of faith are so sublime, and the Christian morals so repugnant to the laws of flesh and blood that no greater probability whatever may be accounted sufficient to enforce the obligation of believing.*

"Indeed, while I perceive so many different opinions maintained upon points connected with morality, I think that the Divine Providence is apparent; for in diversity of opinions, the yoke of Christ is easily borne.†

"A confessor may absolve penitents, according to the probable opinion of the penitent, in opposition to his own, and is even bound to do so.

"Again, it is probable that pecuniary compensation may be made for defamation; it is also probable that it can not be made. May I, the defamed, exact to-day pecuniary compensation from my defamer, and to-morrow, and even on the same day, may I, the defamer of another, refuse to compensate with money for the reputation of which I have deprived him? * * * * * I affirm that it is lawful to do at pleasure sometimes the one and sometimes the other.

"Those ignorant confessors are to be blamed who always think that they will do well in obliging their penitents to make restitution, because it is at all times more safe."‡

By this abominable doctrine the confessors were made to answer yes or no, as might be most agreeable to their penitents; and these might oblige the confessor to absolve them of their sins if they only themselves believed that they were not sins. Imagine what an arrant knave the person inclined to do evil must have become, when to the firm belief that the absolution of the confessor cleanses from all crimes, was superadded the certainty that this confessor must absolve him almost according to his own wishes. We shudder to think of it.

---

* Thomas Sanches. Opus Morale in Præcepta Decalogi. L. ii, c. i, N. 6. (Venetisif, 1614. Antuerpiæ, 1624. Ed. Coll. Sion.)

† Antony Escobar. Universæ Theologæ Moralis Receptiores absque lite Sententi, necnon Problematicæ Disquisitiones, tom. i L. sect. i, de consc. c. 2, N. 18. (Lugduni, 1652. Ed. Bibl. Acad. Cant.)

‡ Simon de Lassac. Propositions dictées dans le collège des Jésuites d' Amiens. De præcept. Decal. c. i, art. 4.

The doctrine of equivocation came in aid of that of probableism. By the former, according to Sanchez, "it is permitted to use ambiguous terms, leading people to understand them in a different sense from that in which we understand them."* "A man may swear," according to the same author, "that he never did such a thing (though he actually did it), meaning within himself that he did not do so on such a day or before he was born, or understanding any other such circumstances, while the words which he employs have no such sense as would discover his meaning."† And Filiutius proves that in so speaking one does not even lie, because, says he, it is the intention that determines the quality of the action; and one may avoid falsehood, if, after saying aloud, I swear that I have not done that, he add in a low voice, to-day; or, after saying aloud, I swear, he interposes in a whisper, that I say, and then continue aloud, that I have done that, and this is telling the truth."

With mental reservation and probableism, they have sanctioned all sorts of crimes. The varlet might help his master to commit rape or adultery, provided he do not think of the sin, but of the profit he may reap from it—so says father Bauny. If a servant think his salary is not an adequate compensation for services, he may help himself to some of his master's property to make it equal to his pretensions—so teaches the same father. You may kill your enemy for a box on the ear, as Escobar asserts in the following words: "It is perfectly right to kill a person who has given us a box on the ear, although he should run away, provided it is not done through hatred or revenge, and there is no danger of giving occasion to murders of a gross kind and hurtful to society. And the reason is, that it is as lawful to pursue the thief that has stolen our honor, as him that has run away with our property. For, although your honor can not be said to be in the hands of your enemy in the same sense as your goods and chattels are in the hands of the thief, still it may be recovered in the same way—by showing proofs of greatness and authority, and thus acquiring the esteem of men. And, in point of fact, is it not certain that

* Thomas Tamburin. Explicatio Decalogi, L. 1, c. iii, § 4, N. 15. (Lugduni, 1659. Lugduni, 1665. Ed. Coll. Sion.)

† Op. Mor. p. 2.

the man who has received a buffet on the ear is held to be under disgrace until he has wiped off the insult with the blood of his enemy?"

In short, you may be a fraudulent bankrupt, thief, assassin, profligate, impious atheist even, with a safe conscience, provided always you confess to a Jesuit confessor. It is doubtless, in this, that we are to see the efficacy of that miraculous gift, which we read at page 13, Loyola had received from heaven, and transmitted to his successors—the gift of healing troubled consciences; and this is even boldly asserted by themselves. In the *Imago primi Sæculi*, S. iii, ch. 8, are words to this effect: "With the aid of pious *finesse*, and holy artifice of devotion, crimes may be expiated now-a-days, *alacrius*, with more joy and alacrity than they were committed in former days; and a great many people may be washed from their stains almost as cleverly as they contracted them." After this quotation, we need not trouble the reader with any more regarding the doctrine of the Jesuits on social duties. We only beg of him, in order that he may well understand all the enormity of these doctrines, to look at them from the point of view of the Papists, who consider the confessional as the only way of salvation, and who blindly obey their spiritual fathers, especially if they flatter their passions, and promise them paradise as the reward of their vices.

CHAPTER XXIII.

The internal Jesuit—Sam's private opinion of the historical Jesuit, inside and out—Corruptions of the Missions—Heathenism out-heathened in India.

But we have seen enough of the internal Jesuit; the entire structure of the incarnated machine, with all its hideous enginery of evil, has been revealed to us; let us now regard him as the external man, historically as holding his place among the brotherhood of mankind.

That brotherhood to which he alone has proven himself the monstrous recreant; that brotherhood against which his fratricidal malice has perpetually wielded the assassin's weapon beneath the assassin's cloak; that brotherhood against which this Jesuit Judas has betrayed with the kiss, and for the thirty pieces of silver, too; that brotherhood, unto the grievous oppressing of which, he, with the accursed mark of Cain, beneath the whitewash on his brow, has ever abetted the tyrant and oppressor, upholding with a sanctimonious unction, the bloated arm of massacre, whose carnivals have been St. Bartholomew's days; whose spiritual ecstaticisms have been in the debauchment of the consciences of kings and queens, and the ravishment of provinces and of nations; whose darling pieties have been death-bed triumphs over dotard superstition; whose chiefest glory is in having been extirpated, as a slow and silent fungus from the bosom of every nation of Europe, at one time or another; and then with the indestructible vitality of evil, to have forced its cancerous roots to sprout again through the old cicatrice; whose greatest honor is to have grown fat, and flourished apace, battening upon the juices of that offal of ignorance, upon which it has nourished mankind, as the ant feeds its aphide, that it may live upon its milk.

To be sure, the ant drinks the milk of another insect, yet it is of a different race; but you, amiable Jesuit, have indulged a cannibal proclivity for the milk of your own. Outheroding Herod, out-vulturing the vulture, ye have preyed upon the minds and souls of men. The spiritual carrion on which ye gloat, has been a decay within the moral atmosphere which the exhausting suction of your vampire presence has produced; and ye have gone about among the nations, rejoicing in your rags, your lank, cadaverous fingers, with their filthy nails resembling most the ghoul that digs at charnels.

And yet, ye, the assassins of kings, the conspirators against the peace of nations, familiars of poison, of the "dagger and the rope," ye have set up to have been, forsooth, the mild conservators of learning, the intelligent disseminators of its luminous rays to the benighted regions of paganism. Your boast, your vaunt has been, that ye alone have carried light into the dark places; that, under the inspiration of your diabolical motto, *ad majoram dei gloriam*, the arts have been protected, letters encouraged, and all the subordinate conditions of civilization advanced. "*Ad majoram gloriam*" Loyola! and the "Company of Jesus" is the true interpretation.

That this is the true meaning of this hideous myth, we will take their own authorities, quoting from the origin of Jesuit Missions. After the death of Xavier, who was their first missionary to India, and who also appears to have been the first self-deluded "Knight-errant of an idea," plausible and imposing enough in itself, we find that the society reasserts its legitimacy in his successor.

The man who, after Xavier, had the greatest success in India, but who also perverted the character of the mission, and introduced the most abominable idolatry, was Father Francis Nobili. He arrived in Madura in 1606, and was surprised that Christianity had made so little progress in so long a time, which he attributed to the strong aversion which the Indian had for the European, and to the fact that the Jesuits, having addressed themselves more especially to the Pariahs, had caused Christ to be considered as the Pariah's

God.* He therefore resolved to play the part of a Hindoo and a Brahmin. After having learned, with wonderful facility, their rites, their manners, and their language,† he gave himself out as a Saniassi, a Brahmin of the fourth and most perfect class; and with imperturbable impudence, he asserted that he had come to restore to them the fourth road to truth, which was supposed to have been lost many thousands of years before. He submitted to their penances and observances, which were very painful; abstained from everything that had life, such as fish, flesh, eggs;‡ respected their prejudices, and, above all, the maintenance of the distinction of classes. It was forbidden the catechumen Pariah to enter the same church with the Sudra or Brahmin converts. All this was the beginning of those heathen ceremonies and superstitions with which the Christian religion was contaminated.

Great care was taken by these Roman Saniassi that they might not be taken for Feringees,§ and still greater care not to hurt the prejudices of the Hindoos. We might multiply quotations *ad infinitum*, to prove our assertions, but we shall content ourselves with two. "Our whole attention," writes Father de Bourges, "is taken up in our endeavor to conceal from the people that we are what they call Feringees; the slightest suspicion of this would prove an insurmountable obstacle to our success."‖ And Father Mauduit writes: "The catechist of a low caste can never be employed to teach Hindoos of a caste more elevated. The Brahmins and the Sudras, who form the principal and most numerous castes, have a far greater contempt for the Pariahs, who are beneath them, than princes in Europe can feel for the scum of the people. They would be dishonored in their own country, and deprived of the privileges of the caste, if ever they listened to the instructions of one whom they look upon as infamous. We must, therefore, have Pariah catechists for the Pariahs, and Brahminical catechists for the Brahmins, which causes us a great deal of difficulty. Some time ago,

* Ranke's Hist. of the Popes, vol. ii, p. 231. English translation.

† Juvencius' Hist. Soc. Jesu, pars v. tome ii, lib. xviii.

‡ Lettres Edif., tome x, p, 324.

§ Feringe was the name given by the Hindoos to the Portuguese.

‖ Lettres Edif., tome xxi, p. 77.

a catechist from the Madura mission begged me to go to Pouleour, there to baptize some Pariah catechumens, and to confess certain neophytes of that caste. The fear that the Brahmins and Sudras might come to learn the step I had taken, and thence look upon me as infamous, and unworthy ever of holding any intercourse with them, hindered me from going. The words of the holy apostle Paul, which I had read that morning at mass, determined me to take this resolution—'Giving no offense to any one, that your ministry might not be blamed.' (2 Cor. vi, 3.) I therefore made these poor people go to a retired place, about three leagues from here, where I myself joined them during the night, and with the most careful precautions, and there I baptized nine."*

* Lettres Edif., tom. x, pp. 243–245.

CHAPTER XXIV.

Jesuit Oppression—Their Policy in Foreign Missions—Their Beneficence toward the primitive Races of America—Death of the Incendiary, Wolf, the Jesuit Priest.

WE have here a fair specimen, given in the last chapter, of the manner in which the Jesuit missionary has conserved and enlightened the barbarous nations of the old world; we will now furnish some few examples of his enlightening processes in the New World. It seems that unlucky Paraguay was the first country set apart for the special ministrations of this most holy Order. It was deliberately designed by their crafty and politic General, Acquiviva, to erect this noble country into a Jesuit principality, which was to be a sort of penal colony, to which the more worthless lazaroni of the Order might be consigned in a kind of "honorable exile," as we suppose, as the monks of other orders who had accompanied the Conquestadors under the Pizarros, had openly instigated them to the perpetration of every conceivable outrage and cruelty upon the helpless nations, it became the policy of the cunning Jesuits, in conformity with their unvarying course, to compel as strong a contrast as possible with their brother monks, by their own conduct toward these people; they therefore became marvelously god-like and beneficent in their relations to them, showering them with blessings, and with presents on all occasions, until the hearts of a simple people were won; as to the use they made of them when won, we shall proceed to relate historically concerning the "reductions," as they were called in Paraguay, and "Missions," as they were known further north.

To keep these people in a state of dependence and submission, the Jesuits had secluded them from the rest of the world. No individual could leave the Reduction without permission, and no European was allowed to visit these Reductions unaccompanied, or to have free intercourse with the inhabitants. The knowledge of any other than the native language was altogether banished, and aversion and prejudices against the Europeans as carefully cherished as in ancient Egypt.

"Nor were the Reductions left unprotected against the possible attacks of foreign enemies. All able-bodied men were drilled to arms, and formed into a militia, having its regulations, its officers, its arsenal, its artillery, its ammunition. The officers were chosen by the soldiers; the arms and ammunition, not excepting the cannon, were manufactured in the Reduction, always by and under the direction of the Jesuits. On the afternoon of every Sunday, and other holidays, the militia assembled and executed military exercises and evolutions. When that militia was called forth for the service of the Spanish king, they had always at their head, and among their ranks, Jesuits, who prevented all contact with other Indians, or with Europeans, and who answered for their virtue before God, as the Indians answered for their courage before men."* Nor, indeed, did they fail in their duty when an occasion presented itself. Tribes of savages often attacked the Reductions, but were met with undoubted courage, and, generally speaking, were repulsed after sustaining severe loss.

But if, on the one hand, the Jesuits cherished among the people distrust and aversion toward strangers, they, on the other hand, diligently inculcated the exercise of hospitality and friendship among the different Reductions. On the great festival days, and especially on the day of the patron saint of any Reduction, the neighboring ones went thither in solemn procession, and were received with all possible marks of love and friendship.

Such is a sketch of the civil government of the Reductions, and of the kind of life led by the inhabitants. Objections and reproaches, and perhaps not always unfounded, have been raised against such a system. It has been said that the inhabitants of the Reductions were low and abject

* Cret., vol. iii, p. 312.

slaves, led on by the scourge, deprived even of the faculty of thinking, and confined in a perpetual imprisonment, though within a large space. Quinet, with perhaps more eloquence than reason, exclaims, "Are we sure that it (Paraguay) contains the germ of a great empire? Where is the sign of life? Everywhere else, indeed, one hears at least the squalling of the child in the cradle; here, I fear, I confess, that so much silence prevailing in the same place for three ages, is but a bad sign, and that the regime which can so quietly enervate virgin nature, can not be any other than that which develops Guatemozin and Montezuma." All this is very well said, and may be in part true. Doubtless these people were kept in perpetual infancy. Doubtless nothing great, nothing of a creating stamp, must be expected from them. Doubtless they did not develop and expand the new element of life imparted to them, as other nations have done who were more left to themselves; nor did they exercise the noblest part of their nature—the intelligence—in that pursuit for which we think man was created—the search after truth. But surely there are nations who have been placed in worse circumstances, and subjected to more disastrous influences, and more deserving our pity and commiseration. Thus, if a nation that has, through the free exercise of all its faculties and activities, arrived at a high state of civilization and refinement, should be at once crushed, as France is at the present moment, under the iron hand of despotism, that people would be really miserable, and such doleful lamentations as those of the eloquent ex-professor of the College of France would not in this case be misplaced. But these Americans, who knew nothing of the pleasures of moral and intellectual refinement but what was presented to them by their instructors, and found therein contentment, we do not know how far they deserve to be pitied. Were these people, we ask in our turn, less happy or more miserable than those tens of thousands who wallow in vices of all sorts, in the free and civilized towns of Paris and London? Are, then, squalid poverty, the groans of the oppressed and reckless sensuality, necessary elements of national happiness? These are questions which, in our opinion, deserve some consideration; and although we think the human race has been destined by the Creator to greater and nobler purposes than the mere enjoyment of a material life, and although we know that humanity must progress in its career, and that this progress can not be attained without great commotion and great evil, nevertheless, when we contemplate all the miseries which surround our state of civilization, we freely forgive the Jesuits for having, in one part of the globe, let civilization and progress sleep awhile, to render these poor Indians happy. But with all this merciful ratiocination, civilization *did* sleep in Paraguay as well as all other countries into which the benignities of Jesuitism have extended.

Better founded are the charges brought by the pious and zealous against the Jesuits, with respect to the kind of religion they taught to their neophytes. In fact, though we can not trace any such permanent system of gross idolatry as was practiced by the order in the East Indies, nevertheless, it is an undeniable fact, that what was taught by them under the name of the pure religion of Christ, was little else than a series of empty forms and superstitious observances, and that the worship which was rendered to God, was little better than a continual and motley masquerade, if we may be allowed the expression. We shall not enter into details; the following passage from Cretineau, sufficiently showing what sort of Christians, if they can be called so at all, were those converted by the Jesuits. "Those Indians had a very limited intelligence; they only understood what fell under their senses, and the missionaries were so alarmed at their stupidity, that they asked themselves whether it was possible to admit them to the participation of the sacraments. They consulted upon this point the bishops of Peru, assembled at Lima, who came to the decision that, baptism excepted, no act of Christian devotion should be imposed upon them, without infinite precautions."* It is true, that the panegyrist of the Order adds, "that the patience of the Jesuits was not discouraged for all this, and that they endeavored to render them better Christians, and, we even believe, if the man who fulfilled all the imposed external ceremonies may be called a Christian, that they succeeded in their attempt."

However, it seems that the Jesuits had so completely perverted the true spirit of the Christian religion, that even Roman Catholic bishops, who, as every one knows, are not very

* Cret., vol. iii, p. 502.

scrupulous in these matters, were shocked and indignant at their conduct, and made an attempt to put a stop to it. Bernardin of Cardenas, Bishop of Paraguay, and John Palafox, Bishop of Angelopolis, were the most prominent in their efforts to put a stop to the Jesuitical superstitions, but both were unsuccessful; both were worsted in the contest; both were obliged to wander as poor exiles out of their dioceses; and both were at last compelled to give up their bishoprics.

This is the extenuating story of him whom we have characterized as the most "magnanimous" of the foes of Jesuitism—M. Nicolini; but, although *he*, as the historian of the Order, may feel himself called upon to express, in formal terms, every conceivable palliation of a story where all seems mortally oblique, yet we, the historian of Sam, do not feel ourself under any such "Knightly ban;" because, in the first place, the foe is not a knightly one—dirty finger-nails and carcasses not constituting honorable rivals in any intellectual contest.

But, says this historian, hear what others, who are no controversialists, who have no other interest in the subject than to relate plain incidents; and it is thus we begin to hear the Hebraic motto: "By their fruits shall ye know them!" We quote first from Commissioner Bartlett's Personal Narrative.

"Although San Franciscos are as common in Mexico as Washingtons, Jeffersons, and Franklins are with us, and churches dedicated to that Saint are to be found all over the country, yet this of La Magdalena is the most celebrated and potent of all, inasmuch as it contains a celebrated figure of San Francisco, which, among other miracles, performed that of selecting the place of its abode. A party of San Franciscans, as the legend goes, were traveling in search of a proper spot to found an establishment, and had among their other effects, this sainted figure packed upon a mule. On arriving at this place, the animal carrying the precious burden became obstinate, and refused to budge. This, the worthy fathers interpreted as indicating the Saint's pleasure to stop here; so here they built the church. The original building, with the exception of the tower, is in ruins; but a new one has been erected within a few years, which is quite an imposing edifice, with two fine towers and a large dome, beneath which the Saint reposes.

"For several days previous to the 4th of October, which is the Saint's day, preparations for its celebration begin, so that the devotions and offerings, with their accompanying festivities, are in full blast a day or two in advance. La Magdalena and the church of San Francisco are the Mecca of devout Mexican Catholics.

"From the borders of Sinalao on the South, to the furthest outpost near the Gila, and from the Gulf of California to the Sierra Madre, they flock in by thousands to offer their devotions at this shrine. It is not unusual for very great sinners to bring their burden of guilt a distance of four or five hundred miles; a journey, in this country, of greater difficulty and requiring more time than one from New Orleans to Quebec. The poorer classes often come a hundred miles on foot, begging by the way. The more penitent, like the idolaters before the temple of Juggernaut, or the devout Mohammedan at the shrine of his prophet, prostrate themselves, and with their hands crossed on their breasts, advance on their knees a hundred feet or more to the church. Both men and women are thus seen toiling over the dusty street and brick pavement of the church to the presence of the Saint, who is laid out beneath the dome and in front of the altar. When the votaries reach the bier they cross themselves, and with outstretched arms repeat their prayers; they then rise to their feet, and, drawing nearer, present their offerings.

"The body of San Francisco, or rather its image, lies upon a platform or bier, clothed in rich vestments, and covered with a piece of damask of the most gorgeous colors. The head, hands and feet are alone exposed. These are made of wood, colored to represent flesh; and I was informed by a Mexican gentleman that these constituted the whole statue. The body, he told me, was merely a frame-work, stuffed with rags and cloths, to give it a form, over which the drapery was disposed. The offerings consist of money and candles; and as wax is quite expensive here, the poorer classes present candles of tallow. There was a continual jingling of money; in-fact, so constant was the dropping of silver dollars into the receptacle placed for them, that no other sound was heard. What was singular in all this mummery was, that no priest was present. The men who took the money were ordinarily dressed, having on nothing to distinguish them from the crowd around. There may have been a priest behind the altar, or somewhere not visible to the devotees; but while I stood by the side of the image and witnessed the proceeding on two occasions, I could perceive none. An estimate may be formed of the crowds here present, when I state that the receipts this year, although the attendance was less than usual, were about twelve thousand dollars, while on some former occasions, the amount of money voluntarily given had reached the sum of eighteen thousand. To the question what became of all this money, I received the usual reply of '*Quien sabe!*' A gentleman, however, told me that it went to the City of Mexico, and that neither the poor of Magdalena nor the church there derived any benefit from it."

The fat priests of Mexico can tell you what becomes of the proceeds of these rich plantations—into the coffers of the Vatican every copper of this plunder, wrung from ignorance and ignominy, goes—on it, the tonsiled leeches of the church which preaches ignorance to the masses, prey.

"In the evening I visited the church again, when I witnessed the ceremony of consecrating ribbons. The space around the image was crowded, as in the morning, with devotees, each provided with a piece of ribbon. The mode of consecrating it depended upon the ailment of the applicant. If he or she had a pain in the head, the ribbon was passed several times across the forehead of the figure by the officiating Franciscans. If blind, the ribbon was passed across the eyes; if lame, or afflicted with rheumatism, it was passed across the arms or legs; and in many instances I saw it drawn between the toes of the saint. Had some of our turtle-fed aldermen been the applicants for the latter process, one might have believed it to have been for the gout; but I fancy that a diet of frijoles and tortillas does not often engender that disease in Mexico. Some of the worshipers were provided with long pieces of ribbon, which they applied in turn to every part, a knot being tied after each application, making, probably, as one of the gentlemen observed, 'a sort of family medicine chest.' The faith of the people in this thing of wood and paint is astonishing. An old man told us with the utmost seriousness, that last May, when the cholera visited the place, and was cutting off twenty a day, they had only to bring the image into the street, and the disease at once disappeared. He was asked what he would have thought if the disease had continued. He replied that 'it was the will of the saint, and we must submit.'

"In our rambles, we dropped into an attractive-looking shop, to make inquiries about such provisions as we required. The proprietor, Señor Gonzales, was a native Castilian, which we soon perceived by the purity of his language. He at once recognized us as Americans, and after answering our inquiries, invited us into an inner apartment, furnished very handsomely, and in good taste. One of the first things I noticed here, was an American rocking-chair—an article of luxury better adapted, one would suppose, to the quiet habits of the Mexicans, with their fondness for a siesta during the heat of the day, than to those of restless Yankees. Wine and other refreshments were offered us, and an hour was agreeably spent in conversation with our new acquaintance. He gave us much information about the country, and the ceremonies we had just witnessed. While there, several strangers, also gentlemen of education and respectability, came in; and finding who we were, and of what we were in pursuit, they gave us such information as we required, and tendered us their services.

"I regretted to learn we could not procure the provisions we needed, but it was expected that the fair would bring many mules into market, so that in a few days we could obtain all that we wanted.

"In the evening we walked about the town and among the booths, which were arranged on every side of the plaza and along the principal streets. They seemed much like those which it was customary to erect in New York on the fourth of July. Cakes of various kinds, tortillas, fruits, and aguardiente, were the staple articles; but while there were booths entirely appropriated to the sale of this intoxicating liquor, I do not remember to have seen a single drunken man. In the midst of these booths was a large inclosure, covered with the boughs of trees, beneath which some hundreds were assembled, and engaged in dancing. An enormous bass drum, which was heard above all other sounds, a couple of violins, and a clarionet, ground out waltzes and polkas, while the beaux were swinging round the senoritas in a manner that would astonish our dancing community. Notwithstanding the crowd here assembled, most of whom were strangers to each other, the most perfect order was kept. The Mexican people are ardently devoted to dancing; and when they once enter into it, they do not cease until the sun appears the following day. Some of our party who were given to this amusement, thought they would like to take a few turns, so casting a glance along the line of dark-eyed damsels who occupied the benches, and selecting the most attractive, they advanced without any introduction, led them into the arena, and at once joined in the merry whirl. A perpetual fandango was thus kept up day and night, where people of all sorts, sizes, and conditions might be seen twirling to the slow measure of the Spanish reel, or the more active waltz and polka. But gambling, after all, seemed to predominate. Whole ranges of booths were devoted to this exciting amusement; and crowds of every age, sex, and class were assembled about them. Boys and girls of six and eight years of age laid down their coppers, and men their reals and dollars, while at other tables the more wealthy and aristocratic ventured their ounces. Some of the tables were attended by women, selected, not on account of their personal beauty, but for their expertness in shuffling the cards.

"We accompanied Mr. Pratt to the hills opposite our camp to take some sketches. The hills were separated from the camp by the river, on the banks of which were some hundreds of men and women bathing or washing. A few cottonwood trees grew along the valley, and the margin of the stream was lined with willow bushes. The hills here are about five hundred feet high, and from them we had a fine view of the town and the adjacent plain, which was inclosed, toward the south, by a high range of mountains. The hill was literally covered with cacti of every variety that we had seen, from tiny plants not longer than one's thumb, just projecting from some crevice, to the giant cereus, that shot up to the hight of fifty feet. The agave, yucca, fouquiera, Spanish bayonet, mezquit, and other plants, alike grew in profusion around us.

"In the evening we again visited the church, where the same scenes were going on as before described. It was now brilliantly illuminated, and a procession was marching through the crowd, each individual in it holding a lighted candle in his hand. The music was performed by a circus band from Hermosilla, which played the same pieces for the interludes of the service as it did for the performances of the evening. Some of our popular Ethiopian melodies occasionally greeted the ear."

These precious scenes are not merely characteristic of a locality; they constitute the *rule*, without exception, of Jesuit ascendency in the New World. The thousand hoary ruins of their Missions, from Cape Horn to the Sabine, tell the same story of sneaking oppression.

Hear again another story, from the same source, of the fate of a Mission.

"Situated in the midst of a fertile valley, surrounded with abundant timber and supplied by a thousand springs, with an inexhaustible flow of water, the Mission of San Gabriel flourished and became exceedingly rich. Authentic records are said to exist, which show that at one time the Mission branded fifty thousand calves, manufactured three thousand barrels of wine, and harvested one hundred thousand fanegas (two hundred and sixty-two thousand bushels) of grain a year. The timber for a brigantine was cut, sawed, and fitted at the Mission, and then transported to and launched at San Pedro. Five thousand Indians were at one time collected and attached to the Mission. They are represented to have been sober and industrious, well clothed and fed, and seem to have experienced as high a state of happiness as they are adapted by nature to receive."

But what, in the meantime, has become of those "two hundred and sixty-two thousand bushels" of grain a year? Of course they went into the treasury of the "Society," which thus fanned its loafers upon the credulity of primitive races.

But, with all the cloud of worldly cant with which the historians of New England love to involve this question of tolerance, the following story furnishes the most apt commentary upon the beneficent influence of the Jesuits upon our early history:

"Finding the incursions of the Indians likely to continue, through the machinations of the Jesuit Rolle, the government of Massachusetts resolved to carry an expedition to Norridgewock, for the purpose of destroying the place and seizing the instigator of the war. Two hundred and eight men were put under the command of Captains Harman and Moulton, and provided with whale-boats to proceed up the Kennebeck. Leaving Fort Richmond the eighth of August, they arrived at Taconick, the next day, where they left their boats under a guard of a lieutenant and forty men; the next day they commenced their march for Norridgewock, and in the evening captured the wife and daughter of Bomazeen, a well known chief, from whom they obtained exact knowledge of the state and position of the village. On the twelfth they approached the place; Harman, with a part of the force, took a route by the Indian *cornfields*, where it was supposed a part of the enemy would be found, while Moulton, with the remainder, continued on the direct route. About three o'clock in the afternoon, the latter came suddenly in view of the village, and found the Indians quiet in their cabins. Moulton then ordered his men to approach, as silently as possible, and make a close attack. An Indian, at this time, coming out of his cabin, discovered the English and gave the alarm, on which sixty warriors instantly turned out, and advanced to the attack, while the old men, women and children fled. Moulton reserved his fire until the Indians gave theirs, which proved harmless, most of the shot passing over the heads of the English; he then poured in his fire, which made unusual slaughter. The enemy then gave a second shot, and many fled toward the river, closely pursued by the English; some leaping into canoes without paddles, others took to the water and attempted to swim or wade over. As the river was narrow and of little depth, some effected their escape into the woods on the opposite side; but the greatest proportion were cut down by the English fire. Moulton then returned to the village, where the Jesuit Rolle was firing from his cabin upon a party of his men, who had previously arrived. Orders were given to seize Rolle, if possible, alive, but his resistance rendered this difficult. Lieutenant Jaques stove in the door, and finding him resolutely re-charging his gun for another shot and refusing to ask for quarter, sent a ball through his head. The old veteran Mog, attempting to defend himself in another cabin, was shot down with several others, and some were made prisoners. Having cleared the village of the enemy, it was plundered of all that was valuable, the plate, furniture of the chapel, and the devotional flag hoisted over it, not excepted. At night Moulton encamped in the place, and Harman, having completed his détour without meeting the enemy, joined him.

The next morning twenty-six dead bodies of the enemy, beside that of Rolle, were found; among which were Bomazeen, Mog, Job, Carabesset, Wisememet, and Bomazeen's son-in-law, all noted warriors; in the whole, eighty are said to have fallen. The village was set on fire, and the English returned to Taconick, and joined the guard left at that place; and proceeding down the river, they arrived at Richmond fort on the sixteenth of August, with a small loss. The scalps taken from the dead were conveyed to Boston. This severe blow proved the ruin of the Norridgewock tribe, and very much disheartened the remaining hostile Indians.

"The Jesuit Rolle had been a very active agent in, if not the principal cause of the war, and his death was considered as a very auspicious event by the English; it must be acknowledged, however, that he was a loss to the literary world. Previous to his residence at Norridgewock, he had spent six years in traveling among the various tribes in the interior of America, and he had learned most of their languages. He was nearly forty years a missionary, twenty-six of which he had spent at Norridgewock among the Indians; and with their manners and customs he had become intimately acquainted. His letters on various subjects evince that he was a man of superior natural powers, which had been improved by an education in a college of Jesuits in Europe. With the learned languages he was thoroughly acquainted, and by his assiduity he had taught many of his converts to write and read, and to correspond with him in their own language. With the principal clergymen of Boston he held a correspondence in Latin, possessed great skill in controversy, and made some attempts at Indian poetry. Pride was his foible; he took great pleasure in raillery, made the offices of devotion incentives to Indian ferocity, and even kept a flag on which was depicted a cross, surrounded by bows and arrows, which he used to hoist on a pole at the door of his church, when he gave the Indians absolution, previous to their engaging in any enterprise. A dictionary of the Norridgewock language, composed by him, was found among his papers, which is now deposited in the library of Harvard College. It is a quarto volume of about five hundred pages. Rolle was in the 67th year of his age when he was killed." *

* Hutchinson's Massachusetts, vol. ii.—Holmes' Annals, vol. ii.

CHAPTER XXV.

The deadly war of the Jesuits against Protestantism continued in the New World—Cant of Bancroft the Historian—Illustrations—Martyrdom?—Facts and Motives of Jesuit Missions—League of the Iroquois—Intrigues of the Jesuits—First Intercolonial War—Predominance of Jesuit Instigation.

BUT the Jesuit Wölf was not the only arch instigator of the Border Wars and their attendant massacres and burnings belonging to his Order. These indefatigable and bloody foes of Protestantism in all its shades and forms—not content with the slaughter of the Albigenses and Waldenses—the St. Bartholomew days — the reeking battlefields, the plundered provinces and sacked cities, with which their ferocious councils and insidious intrigues had devastated the old world—no sooner learn that some feeble remnants of their purposed victims have fled for refuge to the savage wilderness of the New World than, in pursuance of that deadly vow of extermination which was the basis of Jesuit organization, they follow them hither, and at once renew the fatal strife.

With the crafty humility which has ever characterized their initial proceedings, they came at first the single, lowly enthusiast of the cross, and then in little squads of twos and threes, with scrip and staff—the mock heralds of the Prince of Peace—the mild and patient bearers of "glad tidings" to the benighted red-man. But it is impossible for the feeble pen of the historian of "Sam" to do justice to the immaculate virtues of this heroic and self-denying Order. Hear, rather, the words of one whose lips have evidently been touched with "Holy fire," and flame forth in words meet to celebrate such transfigurations of the Divine in the human, as these Jesuit missionaries appear to him—even the Nestor of Yankee historians, George Bancroft! He alone may speak fittingly of such a theme, with that poetical effulgence of diction which, in its resonant raptures, has fairly cowed the

SAM STRETCHES FORTH HIS ARM, AND THE CATHOLIC STEEPLES OF MEXICO FALL. (SEE CHAP. XXVII.)

sober seeming of the grave historic muse with the stately tum tum of *Homeric* measures wherever he touches this topic.

Behold, then, the Jesuits Brebeuf and Daniel, soon to be followed by the gentler Lallemand, and many others of their order, bowing meekly in obedience to their vows, and joining a party of barefoot Hurons, who were returning from Quebec to their country. The journey, by way of the Ottawa and the rivers that interlock with it, was one of more than three hundred leagues, through a region horrible with forests. All day long, the missionaries must wade, or handle the oar. At night, there is no food for them but a scanty measure of Indian corn mixed with water; their couch is the earth or the rocks. At five and thirty waterfalls, the canoe is to be carried on the shoulders for leagues through thickest woods, or over roughest regions; fifty times it was dragged by hand through shallows and rapids, over sharpest stones; and thus, swimming, wading, paddling, or bearing the canoe across the portages, with garments torn, with feet mangled, yet with the breviary safely hung round the neck, and vows, as they advanced, to meet death twenty times over, if it were possible, for the honor of St. Joseph, the consecrated envoys made their way, by rivers, lakes and forests, from Quebec to the heart of the Huron wilderness. There, to the north-west of Lake Toronto, near the shore of Lake Iroquois, which is but a bay of Lake Huron, they raised the first humble house of the Society of Jesus among the Hurons—the cradle, it was said, of his church who dwelt at Bethlehem in a cottage. (1634.) The little chapel, built by the aid of the ax, and consecrated to St. Joseph, where, in the gaze of thronging crowds, vespers and matins began to be chanted, and the sacred bread was consecrated by solemn mass, amazed the hereditary guardians of the council-fires of the Huron tribes. Beautiful testimony to the equality of the human race! the sacred wafer, emblem of the divinity in man, all that the church offered to the princes and nobles of the European world, was shared with the humblest of the savage neophytes. The hunter, as he returned from his wide roamings, was taught to hope for eternal rest; the braves, as they came from war, were warned of the wrath which kindles against sinners a never-dying fire, fiercer far than the fires of the Mohawks; the idlers of the Indian villages were told the exciting tale of the Savior's death for their redemption. Two new Christian villages, St. Louis and St. Ignatius, bloomed among the Huron forests. The dormant sentiment of pious veneration was awakened in many breasts, and there came to be even earnest and ascetic devotees uttering prayers and vows in the Huron tongue—while tawny skeptics inquired, if there were indeed, in the center of the earth, eternal flames for the unbelieving.

The missionaries themselves possessed the weaknesses and the virtues of their Order. For fifteen years enduring the infinite labors and perils of the Huron mission, and exhibiting, as it was said, "an absolute pattern of every religious virtue," Jean de Brebeuf, respecting even the nod of his distant Superiors, bowed his mind and his judgment to obedience. Beside the assiduous fatigues of his office, each day, and sometimes twice in the day, he applied to himself the lash; beneath a bristling hair shirt he wore an iron girdle, armed on all sides with projecting points; his fasts were frequent; almost always his pious vigils continued deep into the night. In vain did Asmodeus assume for him the forms of earthly beauty; his eye rested benignantly on visions of divine things. Once, imparadised in a trance, he beheld the Mother of Him whose cross he bore, surrounded by a crowd of virgins, in the beatitudes of heaven. (1640.) Once, as he himself has recorded, while engaged in penance, he saw Christ unfold his arms to embrace him with the utmost love, promising oblivion of his sins. Once, late at night, while praying in the silence, he had a vision of an infinite number of crosses, and, with mighty heart, he strove, again and again, to grasp them all. Often he saw the shapes of foul fiends, now appearing as madmen, now as raging beasts; and often he beheld the image of death, a bloodless form, by the side of the stake, struggling with bonds, and, at last, falling, as a harmless specter, at his feet. Having vowed to seek out suffering for the greater glory of God, he renewed that vow every day, at the moment of tasting the sacred wafer; and, as his cupidity for martyrdom grew into a passion, he exclaimed, "What shall I render to thee, Jesus, my Lord, for all thy benefits? I will accept thy cup, and invoke thy name;" and, in sight of the Eternal Father and the Holy Spirit, of the most holy Mother of Christ, and St. Joseph, before angels, apostles, and martyrs, before St. Ignatius and Francis Xavier, he made a vow never to decline the opportunity of martyrdom, and never to receive the death-blow but with joy. (1638.)

The life of a missionary on Lake Huron was simple and uniform. The earliest hours, from four to eight were absorbed in private prayer ; the day was given to schools, visits, instruction in the catechism, and a service for proselytes. Sometimes, after the manner of St. Francis Xavier, Brebeuf would walk through the village and its environs, ringing a little bell, and inviting the Huron braves and counselors to a conference. There, under the shady forest, the most solemn mysteries of the Catholic faith were subjected to discussion. It was by such means that the sentiment of piety was unfolded in the breast of the great warrior Ahasistari. Nature had planted in his mind the seeds of religious faith : " Before you came to this country," he would say, " when I have incurred the greatest perils, and have alone escaped, I have said to myself, ' Some powerful spirit has the guardianship of my days ;' " and he professed his belief in Jesus, as the good genius and protector, whom he had before unconsciously adored. After trials of his sincerity, he was baptized ; and, enlisting a troop of converts, savages like himself, "Let us strive," he exclaimed, "to make the whole world embrace the faith in Jesus."

But this is too good to be all. Our quondam historian who, as may be seen from his account of Jean de Brebeuf, has studied the ecstaticism of Jesuit narrative with an earnestness strongly savoring of a conviction in faith, gives us another precious morceau from the same reliable source, which exhibits his huge relish for such spicy viands.

The Jesuits are determined to push a Mission into the country of the unwilling Mohawk.

" Each sedentary Mission was a special point of attraction to the invader, and each, therefore, was liable to the horrors of an Indian massacre. Such was the fate of the village of St. Joseph. On the morning of July 4, 1648, when the braves were absent on the chase, and none but women, children, and old men, remained at home, Father Anthony Daniel hears the cry of danger and confusion. He flies to the scene to behold his converts, in the apathy of terror, falling victims to the fury of Mohawks. No age, however tender, excites mercy; no feebleness of sex wins compassion. A group of women and children fly to him to escape the tomahawk—as if his lips, uttering messages of love, could pronounce a spell that would curb the madness of destruction. Those who had formerly scoffed his mission, implore the benefit of baptism. He bids them ask forgiveness of God, and, dipping his handkerchief in water, baptizes the crowd of suppliants by aspersion. Just then, the palisades are forced. Should he fly? He first ran to the wigwams to baptize the sick; he next pronounced a general absolution on all who sought it, and then prepared to resign his life as a sacrifice to his vows. (1648.) The wigwams are set on fire; the Mohawks approach the chapel, and the consecrated envoy serenely advances to meet them. Astonishment seized the barbarians. At length, drawing near, they discharge at him a flight of arrows. All gashed and rent by wounds, he still continued to speak with surprising energy—now inspiring fear of the divine anger, and again, in gentle tones, yet of more piercing power than the whoops of the savages, breathing the affectionate messages of mercy and grace. Such were his actions till he received a death-blow from a halbert. The victim to the heroism of charity died, the name of Jesus on his lips; the wilderness gave him a grave; the Huron nation were his mourners. By his religious associates it was believed that he appeared twice after his death, youthfully radiant in the sweetest form of celestial glory; that, as the reward for his torments, a crowd of souls, redeemed from purgatory, were his honoring escort into heaven."

One more glimpse of these poetic pictures, and we shall turn to common sense. The prevalence of peace now favored the advance of the French, or rather Jesuit, dominion.

"For the succeeding years, the illustrious triumvirate, Alloüez, Dablon, and Marquette, were employed in confirming the influence of France in the vast regions that extend from Green Bay to the head of Lake Superior—mingling happiness with suffering, and winning enduring glory by their fearless perseverance. For to what inclemencies, from nature and from man, was each missionary among the barbarians exposed! He defies the severity of climate, wading through water or through snows, without the comfort of fire; having no bread but pounded maize, and often no food but the unwholesome moss from the rocks; laboring incessantly; exposed to live, as it were, without nourishment, to sleep without a resting-place, to travel far, and always incurring perils—to carry his life in his hand, or rather daily, and oftener than every day, to hold it up as a target, expecting captivity, death from the tomahawk, tortures, fire. And yet the simplicity and the freedom of life in the wilderness had their charms. The heart of the missionary would swell with delight, as, under a serene sky, and with a mild temperature, and breathing a pure air, he moved over waters as transparent as the most limpid fountain. Every encampment offered his attendants the pleasures of the chase. Like a patriarch, he dwelt beneath a tent; and of the land through which he walked, he was its master, in the length of it and in the breadth of it, profiting by its productions, without the embarrassment of ownership. How often was the pillow of stones like that where Jacob felt the presence of God! How often did the ancient oak, of which the centuries were untold, seem like the tree of Mamre, beneath which Abraham broke bread with angels! Each day gave the pilgrim a new site for his dwelling, which the industry of a few moments would erect, and for which nature provided a floor of green, inlaid with flowers. On every side clustered beauties, which art had not spoiled, and could not imitate."

Now, apart from all this sky-rocketing of words, the plain historical truth concerning these so much vaunted missionary movements of the Jesuits, is clearly about this. Their sleuth-hound vengeance crossed the sea upon the track of that Protestantism which they had, as an Order, sworn to exterminate. Next to this vow, the aggrandizement of the Order, "to the greater glory of"—Loyola, was the next most vital consideration, and, in America, they only pursued the same policy in reference to this particular end which had characterized their operations in India, China, Japan, Paraguay, California, and elsewhere; their object being, clearly, in the formation of Missions, to create so many fiefs of the Order, the revenues of which would enure to the swelling its treasury.

In North America, beside the tithes, which being paid in

the rich furs of the country, were by no means inconsiderable, the Missions established would answer the double purpose of revenue and revenge; since uniformly cultivating in the hearts of their converts the most implacable enmity againt Protestantism, the Order were enabled at any time, to harass and devastate the hated settlements. And, again, having as an Order been several times banished from France, as well as from every other government of Europe as enemies to internal peace, they felt it necessary to purchase toleration by the splendor of their discoveries in pushing exploration so far ahead of settlement. Nor did all these combined, constitute the yet most important consideration to the ambitious Jesuit.

They early perceived, with that sure intelligence of foresight which has uniformly marked their operations, the future glory and grandeur of this New World, and they determined to establish for themselves here, a Theocratic empire, which would be to the Order—amidst the convulsions which their intrigues continued to cause in Europe—as a House of Refuge to which they might, as a last resort, fly for safety, and hold as a *point d'appui*, from which they might renew the contest.

See how clearly they have apprehended the importance of the New Hemisphere in this light. Paraguay, indeed the whole of South America, and Mexico on the south, California on the west, New France, or Canada on the north, all occupied by the proposed Theocracy—thus hemming in the beleaguered Protestants on three sides. What South America, Mexico and California have been—and the two first yet remaining so—virtual Theocracies—that is, governments in which the priesthood standing as the representatives of God, are alone accountable to Him for both the spiritual and temporal of their subject—or in other words, constitute the supreme governing power in the State—no one will at this day pretend to deny. That New France or Canada, was also ruled into a strict Theocracy by the Jesuits, is clearly susceptible of proof, throughout the entire cotemporary history of that period. La Hontan, an intelligent traveler, naturalist and cosmopolite—twenty years after New France had been established a bishopric through the enterprise of the

Jesuits—complains grievously of this priestly despotism, and after the remark, "that at Montreal it was a perpetual Lent," continues:

We have here a misanthropical bigot of a curé, under whose spiritual despotism, play and visiting the ladies are reckoned among the mortal sins. If you have the misfortune to be on his black list, he launches at you publicly, from the pulpit, a bloody censure. As Messieurs, the priests of St. Sulpice, are our temporal lords, they take the greater liberty to tyrannize over us. To keep well with them, it is necessary to communicate once a month. These Arguses have their eyes constantly on the conduct of the women and the girls. Fathers and husbands may sleep in all assurance, unless they have some suspicions as to these vigilant sentinels themselves. Of all the vexation of these disturbers, I found none so intolerable as their war upon books. None are to be found here but books of devotion. All others are prohibited and condemned to the flames. Our author winds up with a ludicrous account how his Petronius, left by accident on his table, was mutilated by a devout priest, who took it upon himself to tear out all the best leaves, under pretense that they were scandalous. "No one dare to be absent from great masses and sermons without special excuse. These are the times, however, at which the women take a little liberty, being sure that their husbands and mothers are at church."

Such is the concurrent testimony of all cotemporary writers—amply sustained as it is by the invariable usage and determination of Catholic—but more especially Jesuit institutions. But were such cotemporary evidence wanting at a time when the learning of the world was principally in the keeping of the catholic priesthood, there yet remains the broad and well-established historical fact, that the intercolonial wars between the English and other Protestant colonies on the north, and the Indians and Canadian French, were instigated personally by these saintly Jesuit missionaries themselves, and that the murderous forays of the Indians upon these settlements, were even led by these meek missionaries of peace. Indeed, all that saved these northern colonies from absolute extermination, was the success of that sagacious policy of the early Dutch governors of New Amsterdam, in securing the friendship and allegiance of the powerful and warlike Iroquois or Five Nations, established in the north of New York. This alliance also, politically courted and nourished by the New England colonies, was for a long period successfully maintained; opposing this formidable Indian confederacy as a barrier between their weak but growing settlements and the exterminating hate of the Jesuits. It was during the desperate efforts of these priests to gain a foothold among the Iroquois for their Missions, with a view to breaking up this—for them—unlucky league, by their intrigues, that all those bloody scenes occurred, which we have seen so elaborately celebrated in the Elegiac prose of the sympathizing historian, Bancroft. A choice subject for the lugubrious monodies of an American historian surely! Had the Jesuits, whose fate is thus deplored, succeeded earlier—as they did finally to some extent—in their scheme of disrupturing this alliance, and turned loose upon the weak settlements of the Protestant colonies, the fierce warrior hordes of the Five Nations, in addition to those formidable tribes which already yielded to their supremacy, no doubt our tender-hearted historian would have had ample inspiration for the change of his Elegiacs into Idyls, or found full employment in sounding the *Te Deum* to Loyola! Terribly as the colonies suffered as it was—with the Iroquois sometimes allies but most frequently neutral—there can be no question of the entire subjugation, if not annihilation of the Protestant colonies of the north, had such an event as this disruption taken place. Hildreth says:

Whatever the success of the French missionaries among the more northern and western tribes, they encountered in the Iroquois, or Five Nations, firm and formidable opponents. That celebrated confederacy, beside subject tribes, included five allied communities: the Senecas, the Cayugas, the Onondagas, the Oneidas, and the Mohawks; which last, as being nearest to their settlements, often gave, among the English, a name to the whole. Each of these five nations was divided into three clans, distinguished as the Bear, the Tortoise, and the Wolf. Their castles, rude forts, places of protection for the women, children, and old men, surrounded by fields of corn, beans, and squashes, the head-quarters of the several tribes, were situated on those waters of central New York, of which the names serve as memorials, and now almost the only ones, of their ancient possessors. Some slender remnants of this once-powerful confederacy still linger, however, on small reservations of their ancient territory. It was in courage, ferocity, and warlike enterprise, far more than in social institutions or the arts of peace, that the Iroquois surpassed the tribes of Algonquin descent on their eastern, southern, and western borders. It was not against those tribes as Algonquin, that the Five Nations carried on war, for their hostility was directed with even greater fury against the Hurons and Wyandots, who dwelt along the St. Lawrence and north of Lake Ontario, and who spoke dialects of the same language with themselves. The early alliance of French with those tribes, had rendered the French colonists objects of implacable hate to the Five Nations.

In vain, during a short interval of peace, strenuous efforts were made to establish a spiritual influence over these fierce warriors. Father Jogues, whose captivity had made him acquainted with the chiefs, having returned again to Canada, was sent among them as embassador and missionary—a dangerous service, in which he met the death he had formerly escaped.

Supplied with fire-arms by the Dutch, and rendered thus more formidable than ever, the Iroquois renewed a war by which the missionaries and their converts were equally endangered. Daniel, the venerable father of the Huron mission, perished in the midst of his flock, surprised and massacred by a Mohawk war-party. Brebeuf and Lallemand, taken prisoners, were burned at the stake; Gardier perished by the hatchets of the Iroquois; Chabanel was lost in the woods. The Huron missions, by these renewed onslaughts, were completely broken up. The Hurons, Wyandots, and Ottawas, greatly reduced in numbers, were driven from their country, which became a hunting-ground for the Iroquois. Subsequently the Hurons and Ottawas established themselves in the neighborhood of Mackinaw. Mohawk war-parties harassed the banks of the St. Lawrence. The unhappy colonists lived in daily dread of massacre. Quebec itself was not safe. This emergency caused a message to ask aid of New England, as mentioned in a former chapter, or, at least, a free passage for war-parties of the Eastern tribes under French influence in their march against the Mohawks—a message borne by John Godefroy, one of the council of New France, and Dreuillettes, former explorer of the passage from Quebec to the eastern coast, described in his commission as 'preacher of the Gospel to savage nations.' But the Commissioners for the United Colonies of New England listened with but a cold ear to the story of the martyrdom of the French missionaries and the sufferings of their Indian converts. No aid could be obtained in that quarter; but, after two or three years of perpetual alarm, the Iroquois consented at last to a peace.

From the earliest foothold obtained by the Jesuits among the French colonies on the north, they had been known as the instigators and fermenters of jealousies between their converts and the Puritan settlements of New England and New York. With the exception of their unvarying system of 'Reductions' —as they are best termed in all countries, and meaning nothing more than absolute slavery, spiritually and financially, by which the rich proceeds of the free-trade were, in this case, to be monopolized into the treasury of the Order—there were no purposes in which these missionaries proved themselves so indefatigably consistent, as this of mortal enmity to the Protestants wherever they appeared. Not only was this perpetual cause of irritation felt in the savage carnage of the earlier partisan or guerrilla struggles of the weak colonies with the more northern Indian tribes, and recognized as the incessant source of mortal peril beside their hard-earned firesides—although their own agency had been denied by the Jesuits—yet when the first intercolonial war (known as King William's war,) broke out, the colonists were at no loss to know who had been, and would continue to be, their most arch and deadly foes. They not only knew these crafty missionaries to be such enemies, but struck at them now as such, in spite of the pretended sanctities of their calling and garb; and that too, with the merciless and exterminating violence of a spirit of retribution fired by the memory of the thousand sneaking and incendiary wrongs which had been accumulating to their account, through so many years. Hildreth's straightforward account of the progress of this war, best illustrates the development so far.

So soon as the declaration of war between France and England became known in America, the Baron Castin easily excited the Eastern Indians to renew their depredations. In these hostilities the tribes of New Hampshire were induced also to join. Those tribes had neither forgotten nor forgiven the treachery of Waldron, at the conclusion of Philip's war, thirteen years before. Two Indian women, apparently friendly, sought and obtained a night's lodging at Waldron's garrison or fortified house at Dover. They rose at midnight, opened the doors, and admitted a party lying in wait for the purpose. Waldron, an old-man of eighty, after a stout resistance, was made prisoner. Placed by his captors in an elbow-chair at the head of a table in the hall, he was taunted with the exclamation, 'Judge Indians now!' after which he was put to death with tortures. Twenty others were killed. Twenty-nine were carried off as prisoners. The village was burned. The fort at Pemaquid, the extreme eastern frontier, was soon after attacked by a party of Penobscots, resident in the neighborhood, instigated by the Jesuit Thury, who lived among them as a missionary. The garrison, obliged to surrender, was dismissed by the Indians, but the fort, which Andros had built, was destroyed. An attack upon Casco was repulsed by Churth, the famous partisan of Philip's war, sent from Massachusetts with two hundred and fifty men. But all the settlements further east were ravaged and broken up. In hopes to engage the formidable Mohawks as auxiliaries against these eastern tribes, commissioners from Boston proceeded to Albany, then held by the members of the New York council opposed to Leisler. In a conference had there with some chiefs of the Five Nations, they expressed their determination to continue the war against Canada, but they could not be prevailed upon to lift the hatchet against their Indian brethren of the East.

Reduced to extreme distress by the late successful inroads of the Iroquois, Canada had just received relief by the arrival from France of Count Frontenac, re-commissioned as governor, and bringing with him such of the Indian prisoners sent to France as had survived the galleys, troops, supplies, and a scheme for the conquest and occupation of New York. As a part of this scheme, the Chevalier de la Coffiniere, who had accompanied Frontenac to the mouth of the St. Lawrence, proceeded to cruise off the coast of New England, making many prizes, and designing to attack New York by sea, while Frontenac assailed it on the land side. Frontenac, though sixty-eight years of age, had all the buoyancy and vigor of youth. He was a man of great energy and determination, and his former administration of the colony made him aware of the measures which the exigency demanded. The Iroquois had already retired from Montreal, and preparations were immediately made for relieving Fort Frontenac. These preparations, however, were too late, for the garrison had already set fire to the fort, and retired down the river. Means were still found, however, to keep up the communication with Mackinaw. Not able to prosecute this scheme of conquest, Frontenac presently detached three war-parties, to visit on the English frontier those same miseries which Canada had so recently experienced at the hands of the Five Nations.

In the course of the last twenty years, a number of converted Mohawks, induced to retire from among their heathen brethren, had established themselves at the rapids of St. Louis, in a village known also as Cagnawaga, on the south bank of the St. Lawrence, nearly opposite Montreal. It was chiefly these converted Mohawks, well acquainted with the settlements about Albany, who composed, with a number of Frenchmen, the first of Frontenac's war parties, amounting in the whole to a hundred and ten persons. Guided by the watercourses, whose frozen surface furnished them a path, they traversed a wooded wilderness covered with deep snows. (Jan. 1690,) Pressing stealthily forward in a single file, the foremost wore snow-shoes, and so beat a track for the rest. At night the snow was thrown up toward the side whence the wind came, and in the hollow thus scooped out the party slept on branches of pine, round a fire in the midst. A little parched corn served them for provisions, eked out by such game as they killed. After a twenty-two days' march, intent on their bloody purpose, they approached Schenectady, the object of their toil. This was a Dutch village on the Mohawk, then the outpost of the settlements about Albany. The cluster of some forty houses was protected by a palisade, but the gates were open and unguarded, and at midnight the inhabitants slept profoundly. The assailants entered in silence, divided themselves into several parties, and, giving the signal by the terrible war-whoop, commenced the attack. Shrieks of women and children answered. Doors were broken open; houses set on fire; blood flowed. Sixty were slain on the spot; twenty-seven were taken prisoners; the rest fled, half naked, along the road to Albany through a driving snow-storm, a deep snow, and cold so bitter that many lost their limbs by frost. The assailants set off for Canada with their prisoners and their plunder, and effected their escape, though not without serious loss inflicted by some Mohawk warriors, who hastened to pursue them. The terror inspired by this attack was so great, that, for the sake of aid and support, the malcontents who held Albany, submitted to the hated Leisler. But nothing could prevail on that rash and passionate chief to use his authority with moderation. He confiscated the property of his principal opponents. Bayard and Nichols were held in confinement; and for the arrest of Livingston, warrants were sent to Boston and Hartford, whither he had fled for safety.

Frontenac's second war party, composed of only fifty-two persons, departing from Three Rivers, a village half way from Montreal to Quebec, ascended the St. Francis, entered the valley of the Upper Connecticut, and thence made their way across the mountains and forests of New Hampshire. Presently they descended on Salmon Falls, a frontier village on the chief branch of the Piscataqua. (March 27, 1690.) They attacked it by surprise, killed most of the male inhabitants, plundered and burned the houses, and carried off fifty-four prisoners, chiefly women and children, whom they drove before them, laden with the spoils. While thus returning, they fell in with the third war-party from Quebec, and, joining forces, proceeded to attack Casco. A part of the garrison was lured into an ambuscade and destroyed. The rest, seeing their palisades about to be set on fire, surrendered on terms as prisoners of war. (May.)

Such was the new and frightful sort of warfare to which the English colonists were exposed. The savage ferocity of the Indians, guided by the sagacity and civilized skill and enterprise of French officers, became ten times more terrible. The influence which the French missionaries had acquired by persevering self-sacrifice and the highest efforts of Christian devotedness was now availed of, as too often happens, by mere worldly policy, to stimulate their converts to hostile inroads and midnight murders. Religious zeal sharpened the edge of savage hate. The English were held up to the Indians not merely as enemies, but as heretics, upon whom it was a Christian duty to make war. If the chaplet of victory were missed, at least the crown of martyrdom was sure.

These cruel Indian inroads seemed to the sufferers abundant confirmation of the tales of the Huguenots scattered through the colonies as the bloody and implacable spirit of the Catholic faith. These religious refugees were so numerous in Boston and New York, as to have in each of those towns a church of their own. Hatred of popery received a new impetus. It is hardly to be wondered at that the few Catholics of Maryland, though their fathers had been the founders of that colony, were disfranchised, and subjected to all the disabilities by which, in Britain and Ireland, the suppression of Catholicism was vainly attempted. Probably also to this period we may refer the act of Rhode Island, of unknown date, which excluded Catholics from becoming freemen of that colony.

CHAPTER XXVI.

The Queen Ann's, or "Second Intercolonial War" between "Sam" and the Order of Jesuits—The Order not quite ready for formidable operations in the South—Retrospective glance at acts and influences of the Catholic Priesthood in Mexico from the Conquest—Evidence of Clavigero the Catholic Historian of Mexico—The monstrous destruction of the archives of Historical Pictures in Yucatan by an "Ecclesiastic"—Destruction of the most precious Arts, which was common throughout Mexico.

THE last chapter may be well considered as settling the question of the participation and predominating influence of the Jesuit missionaries in the first intercolonial war, and as against the sorely beleaguered Protestant colonies of the north. As yet, their schemes of southern acquisition and supremacy in the South had not been consummated—their cordon of "Reductions" not sufficiently completed to make their active demonstrations in that quarter so formidable, as to render more detail on our own part necessary. The purpose of this history being rather to render clear the historical relations of "Sam" to his internal foes, than to enter systematically into more than the outline of others, which illustrate rather the minuter phases of his own huge development, and his relations to avowed and outward enemies. It now becomes necessary that we should look somewhat to those Jesuit antecedents which led immediately to the next even more extended and exterminating war—the Queen Ann's, or "Second Intercolonial war"—between "Sam" and his desperate foe—the Order of Jesus!

The moment the Jesuits found themselves comparatively secure of their foothold in Acadia, which might form for them a rallying point upon the continent, then, with that skillful mixture of military law and spiritual despotism which has always constituted the phenomenon of their ascendency in the Christian world, they pushed forward their corpse-like trainbands of helpless devotees, in eager emulation for more extended explorations and "Reductions," upon the wilderness fastnesses of the north-west, in search of the sources of certain great traditionary outlets of the then boundless limits of the New World, which they meant to claim and assert as their own, since the old seemed passing so rapidly from their grasp. Gold as well as souls seemed always to have been most discreetly mingled with their aspirations for conquest in America; and the earliest delusions of gold in Acadia, which so rapidly gave way before the sterner facts of a bleak and inhospitable reality, had been kept alive by vague rumors of a mighty empire, drained by endless rivers flowing through sands of gold, which held their sources far in a mysterious interior, and had fired anew immaculate ecstaticisms which look to their final realization in a "golden city," which, either in heaven or on earth was to constitute their reward. The prodigious results of the conquests of Cortez and the Pizarros had not wanted of circulation through the right hands—but then, although the holy Order of Jesus had not been organized, its founders had not failed to participate in, and comprehend the benefits of, such acquisitions—indeed, it had been during the immediate ferment of European mind, caused by the introduction of this new and mighty element, that the crafty and sagacious intellect of Loyola projected this late and most fatal organization on this the sole predominating idea of Jesuitism—though the enmity to Protestantism was the next of course, as he saw in it the mortal antagonism of spiritual despotism!

That these apparently unselfish enterprises of the early Jesuits should have proceeded from such causes, why need we stop to argue? But it may be well that we should give a few preliminary facts as illustrating, here and there, the condition in which the early catholic conquest left Old and New Mexico. First, as showing in how much the Catholic Church proper has *conserved* to the preservation of the ancient literature and arts of all countries which have been conquered by Catholic arms. This event we now quote, occurred during the reign of Charles V, of Spain, when as the dominant power of Europe, he could afford to wage single-handed war against the rest of the world—when Cortez was sending him the ravished treasures of the New World, and completing the conquest of the whole Mexican empire—when his steel-clad cohorts were led by tonsiled priests bearing the holy cross and every new scene of rapine and massacre was only consecrated by the Catholic Priests. One of their own number, Clavigero, in a formal history of the early Mexican Empire and conquest by his own friends, is compelled to relate as follows, in his zeal as an antiquarian, concerning one incident of the conquest of Yucatan:

Though games, dances, and music, conduced less to utility than pleasure, this was not the case with History and Painting; two arts which ought not to be separated in the history of Mexico, as they had no other historians than their painters, nor any other writings than their paintings to commemorate the events of the nation.

The Toltecas were the first people of the New World who employed the art of painting for the ends of history; at least we know of no other nation which did so before them. The same practice prevailed, from time immemorial, among the Acolhuas, the seven Aztecan tribes, and among all the polished nations of Anahuac. The Chechemecas and the Otomies were taught it by the Acolhuas and the Toltecas, when they deserted their savage life.

Among the paintings of the Mexicans, and all those nations, there were many which were mere portraits or images of their gods, their kings, their heroes, their animals, and their plants. With these the royal palaces of Mexico and Tezcuco both abounded. Others were historical, containing an account of particular events, such as are the first thirteen paintings of the collection of Mendoza, and that of the journey of the Aztecas, which appears in the work of the traveler Gemelli. Others were mythological, containing the mysteries of their religion. Of this kind is the volume which is preserved in the great library of the Order of Bologna. Others were codes, in which were compiled their laws, their rites, their customs, their taxes, or tributes; and such are all those of the above mentioned collection of Mendoza, from the fourteenth to the sixty-third. Others were chronological, astronomical, or astrological, in which was represented their calendar, the position of the stars, the changes of the moon, eclipses, and prognostications of the variations of the weather. This kind of painting was called by them *Tonalamatl.* Siguenza makes mention* of a painting representing such like prognostications which he inserted in his Ciclographia Mexicana. Acosta relates 'that in the province of Yucatan, there were certain volumes, bound up according to their manner, in which the wise Indians had marked the distribution of their seasons, the knowledge of the planets, of animals, and other natural productions, and also their antiquity; things all highly curious and minutely described;' which, as the same author says, were lost by the indiscreet zeal of an ecclesiastic, who, imagining them to be full of superstitious meanings, burned them, to the great grief of the Indians, and the utmost regret of the curious among the Spaniards. Other paintings were topographical, or chorographical, which served not only to show the extent and boundaries of possessions, but likewise the situation of places, the direction of the coasts, and the course of rivers. Cortez says, in his first letter to Charles V, that having made inquiries to know if there was any secure harbor for vessels in the Mexican gulf, Montezuma presented him a painting of the whole coast, from the port of *Chalchiuhcuecan,* where at present Vera Cruz lies, to the river Coatzacualco. Bernal Diaz relates that Cortez also, in a long and difficult voyage which he made to the Bay of Honduras, made use of a chart which was presented to him by the lords of Coatzacualco, in which all the places and rivers were marked from the coast of Coatzacualco to Huejacallan.

The Mexican empire abounded with all those kinds of paintings; for their painters were innumerable, and there was hardly anything left unpainted. If those had been preserved, there would have been nothing wanting to the history of Mexico; but the first preachers of the gospel, suspicious that superstition was mixed with all their paintings, made a furious destruction of them. Of all those which were to be found in Tezcuco, where the chief school of painting was, they

---

* In his work entitled, Libra Astronomica, printed in Mexico.

collected such a mass, in the square of the market, it appeared like a little mountain; to this they set fire and buried in the ashes the memory of many most interesting and curious events. The loss of those monuments of antiquity was inexpressibly afflicting to the Indians, and regretted sufficiently afterward by the authors of it, when they became sensible of their error; for they were compelled to endeavor to remedy the evil, in the first place, by obtaining information from the mouths of the Indians; secondly, by collecting all the paintings which had escaped their fury, to illustrate the history of the nation; but although they recovered many, these were not sufficient; for from that time forward, the possessors of paintings became so jealous of their preservation and concealment from the Spaniards, it has proved difficult, if not impossible to make them part with one of them.*

* The History of Mexico; Collected from Spanish and Mexican Historians, from Manuscripts and ancient Paintings of the Indians, together with the Conquest of Mexico by the Spaniards; Illustrated by Engravings, with Critical Dissertations on the Land, Animals, and Inhabitants of Mexico. By Abbé D. Francesco Saverio Clavigero. Translated from the original Italian, by Charles Cullen, Esq. In three volumes. Vol. ii.

CHAPTER XXVII.

Vandalism of the Catholic Priesthood continued in New Mexico—Antiquarian researches concerning the first Missions to New Mexico—Conquest of California—Various efforts to penetrate the mysterious gold region by the Catholic governors of California—Extermination of the Catholic Spaniards of the Conquestador-Occupation—Hidden ruins and strange Traditions—Ruins of magnificent Catholic Cities—Marvelous treasures won by Cortez from Montezuma.

CLAVIGERO'S account of the destructive proclivities of the Catholic priests who accompanied the Conquestadors under Cortez, to the dismemberment and annihilation of the nationalities of the Mexican empire, does not cover the whole ground of complaint with which universal history teems against these rare conservators of the literature and science of the world. Nor was it to Old Mexico proper, that these vandalish ravages of savage intolerance were confined. We shall turn to New Mexico, which is nearer home, for the examples of exterminating bigotry, which surpass in enormity the wrongs of even the old empire.

The gold-craving white man seems to have been destined, according to the ancient faith of the natives of Mexico, to be its scourge and conqueror.*

Cortez found Mexico half conquered for him by an old tradition. It was taught in their temples, and believed by the whole Indian population, that a race of white men was to come from the east to rule the natives of the land. The apparition of a band of fair-complexioned men clothed in arrow-proof garments of steel, and armed with the death-dealing firebolts of heaven, sealed the truth of this immemorial prediction to the awe-struck Mexicans, and they bowed in the helpless submission of their superstitious fears, to the wonderful strangers. However this belief originated, it is

* See Appendix, for curious note.

singular that it should have preceded the approach of the white man on every part of America, and that its active effect should to this day, fortify the unexplored gold region against his advance within its limits.

Perhaps this land, in which are, unquestionably, existent edifices of Aztec construction, and which still hears the name of Montezuma pronounced with reverence, may have been the cradle of the proud conquerors who swept the Mexican plateau, and planted there the golden empire which Cortez overthrew. If so, in this, their last unsubdued stronghold, the light and liberality of American enterprise may yet discover the final dwelling-place of their history and religion, and that will be of more worth than their glittering ores.

There is a curious Indian superstition, familiar to most of the early Texan borderers, often told in connection with the sad prophecy of the extinction of the red race under the breath of white civilization. The Indians affirm that the honey-bee always goes before the white settler to warn the red-man to retire and yield up his hunting-grounds to the dominion of the ax and plow. In 1820, the Indians say, the first bees made their appearance on the Brazos and Colorado rivers, in Texas, and five years after, Austin's settlement arose on their banks and rendered the Indians thenceforth, aliens and intruders on their native soil.

Before the invasion of Mexico by the Spaniards, there was no mining science in the country, and the gold, which greatly outbalanced the silver in quantity, was simply gathered from or near the surface of the ground, and mostly brought by porters from great distances in the interior of the country. The preponderance of gold before, and of silver since the Conquest, is readily explained by the introduction of a more elaborate and thorough mining system. Silver is rarely found in a pure, unmixed state on the surface, and could only be produced, in large quantities, by the cruel and scientific despotism of Spain. The skill, implements, and experience of European art, and the human force of thousands upon thousands of the native population, were turned into the mines, and then the ore was pursued into the bowels of the earth by the conquerors; and numberless silver-mines, that lay untouched and useless under the simple Aztec rule, became immensely productive under the Spaniards. Gold mines were seldom worked when found; and those distant ones, from which the native princes gathered a ready harvest, independent of science, and without penetrating the earth, are now lost in obscurity. In the reckless annihilation of the native priesthood, and the sweeping destruction of their records, the Catholics buried much valuable lore. As if their murdered faith had, in its last death-agony, pressed the signet of forgetfulness on the lips of its desolate and abandoned children, the most beautiful of their arts, and the most coveted of their gifts passed away from the native Mexicans in a single generation. It seemed to be with them a religious and patriotic duty to extinguish every light that could serve their hard taskmasters. Art has lost their exquisite colors for painting, their gorgeous feather-work, their adamantine-tempered copper; and science misses their historic records and their astronomical calculations, while avarice mourns the lost secret of their mines of emeralds, amethysts, and rich beds of gold.

For the first two centuries after the conquest by Cortez, the Indian population maintained a stern and desperate silence on the subject of gold. It was rare that either bribes or tortures could induce an Indian to admit that he knew where any could be found, and thus those mines in the more remote provinces fell into immediate oblivion. The vague and traditionary evidences of their existence, were not incentives enough to warrant the toil and danger of exploration and conquest, while those at home, in the midst of a subdued serf-population, gave such prompt and liberal returns.

Some may suppose that the chaos and oppression of the Spanish Conquest could not so utterly extinguish the knowledge of excessively rich mines, as to prevent their avaricious conquerors from bringing them to use, however remote their situation; but to this may be opposed the undeniable fact, that the locality of the emerald mines is absolutely lost, though their existence *somewhere* is as positively a matter of record as any event of the Conquest. The same destroying power that swept away the temples, the religion, the social customs, the national records, and even the language and history of the conquered race in one overwhelming wave, annihilated, also, much knowledge that would have been acceptable from its own interest.

Light enough, and temptation enough, remained however, to urge the Spaniards to attempt the subjugation of the California basin; but all that we know certainly of their expedition is, their unsatisfactory results, and the shadowy reports brought back by the survivors, of well-built cities in the interior, and treasures of gold in the encircling mountains of the unconquerable country. On the San Saba, as well as on the Pecos, there is unquestionably, vast mineral wealth, formerly not unknown to the Mexicans, but which nothing but the firm, stable protection of our government, and the enterprising audacity of our citizens, can hope to wrest from the superstitious control of the Indians.

The wide expanse of country above the Rio Gila, and between that river and the Rio Colorado, as also the territory next beyond the mountains to the eastward, embracing the valley of the Rio Grande, and that of the Pecos, early attracted the attention of the Spaniards. No sooner had they subdued the Aztecs and their dependencies, than they turned their armed enterprises northward, toward the regions just indicated, and concerning the mineral riches of which, they had received, from their first landing in Mexico, many vague but glowing accounts. The history and results of their enterprises may be thus rapidly summed up.

No sooner had the general subjugation of Mexico and its immediate dependencies been completed, and its provinces partitioned among the Spanish leaders, than the attention of the latter was directed to the unknown region beyond them, and of the relics and magnificence of which they often received the most exaggerated accounts. Nuno de Guzman, to whom had been assigned the governorship of New Gallicia, comprising the northern division of Mexico, heard many of their accounts, relating to the countries northward of his jurisdiction, which excited his curiosity and influenced his avarice. He had in his service a Tejos (Taos?) Indian, who told him of a vast northern country, abounding in gold and silver. Confiding in his accounts, Guzman collected an army, and in 1530, in less than ten years after Cortez entered the valley of Anahuac, started for this unknown region. Difficulties intervened, and the death of his Indian guide induced him to abandon his enterprise, although entertaining implicit faith in the reports that had reached him.

The accounts of Cabeca de Vaca, who penetrated from the coast of Florida to the Pacific, and who, six years after the abandonment of Guzman's expedition, succeeded in reaching the city of Mexico, revived the waning excitement in respect to the rich mineral region of the north. Although he could convey no personal information on the subject, he had satisfied himself of the existence of a semi-civilized people in that direction, and had received from the Indians accounts of its riches, coinciding with those of the Taos Indian already named.

Vasquez Coronado, who had succeeded Guzman in the governorship of New Gallicia, immediately took measures to ascertain the truth of these reports. He dispatched northward, with instructions to penetrate to these regions, a monk named Niza, who penetrated as far as the Gila, when, frightened by the prospect before him, he returned to Coronado, bringing him a long account of his adventures, partly true, but for the most part, as was afterward discovered, fabulous. He professed to have discovered, northward of the Gila, large and populous cities, surpassing Mexico in size, splendor and wealth. He represented the people to be possessed of great abundance of gold, and that their commonest vessels, and the walls of their temples were covered with that precious metal. Upon the authority of "a man born in the principal city of Cibola"—the name given to the northern El Dorado—"the houses were built of lime and stone, the gates and small pillars of turquoises, and all the vessels and ornaments of the houses were made of gold." Other equally extravagant statements were obtained from other sources, as we perceive in the subjoined extracts, from a letter written by Coronado to the viceroy, Mendoza, bearing date March 8, 1539.

"In the province of *Topira* there are no great cities, but the houses are built of stone, and are very good; and within them the people have great stores of gold, which is, as it were, lost, because they know not what use to put it to. They wear emeralds and other precious jewels upon their breasts, are valiant, and have very strong armor made of silver, fashioned after the shapes of beasts. Beyond *Topira* there is still another country, the people whereof wear on their bodies gold, emeralds, and other precious stones, and are commonly served in gold and silver, wherewith they cover their houses; and the chief men wear great chains of gold, well wrought, about their necks, and are appareled with painted garments, and have a great store of wild kine."

At this time a sea expedition on the Pacific was undertaken by Ulloa, under the direction of Cortez, which had for its object not less the discovery of the golden region of the north, than the exploration of the coast. We have no room to trace its progress. Suffice to say, it returned with no tangible evidence of the wealth which it was expected to discover.

Cortez, who fancied he saw another Mexico in the golden country of the north, which was now the subject of conversation on every tongue, was eager to add its conquest to his already high renown. And when, in 1540, it was resolved to send northward a land expedition to explore the country, the right of command was contested between Cortez, as Captain-General of New Spain, and Mendoza, as Viceroy of Mexico. The latter was successful, and Cortez, disappointed and disgusted, returned to Spain.

The command of the expedition was given to Coronado, who set out, with a large party of armed followers, early in the year 1540. After a protracted journey he reached the Rio Gila, then called the *Nexpa*, and boldly ventured upon the rugged and broken country beyond it, toward the north. After many days' travel, in which he encountered innumerable obstacles and incredible hardships, he reached the valley of a stream flowing westward, and which recent discoveries have shown probably to have been the Rio Salinas, the principal northern tributary of the Gila. Here he found the cities of Cibola. The delusion was then dispelled. Instead of cities glittering with gold, he found a people living in considerable towns, cultivating the soil, and furnishing striking contrasts, in their simplicity, to the splendor which the conquerors had encountered in Mexico and Peru. They were not, however, ignorant of the precious metals; on the contrary, Coronado, whose ardor was already effectually cooled, expressly states that he "here found some quantity of gold and silver, which those skilled in minerals esteem to be very good. To this hour," he adds, with evident regret, "I can not learn of this people where they obtain it, and I see they refuse to tell me the truth, imagining that in a short time

I will depart hence. *I hope in God,*" concludes the devout commander, "*they shall no longer excuse themselves!*" The natives, nevertheless, succeeded in excusing themselves, and upon their representations Coronado was induced to cross the mountains to the eastward, into the valley of the Rio Grande, where he was further amused with accounts of a mysterious city called Quivera.* Here, it was said, ruled "a king whose name was *Tatratax*, with a long beard, hoary-headed, and rich, who worshiped a cross of gold, and the image of a woman, which was the queen of heaven." "This news," says Gomara, "did greatly rejoice and cheer up the army, although some thought it false, and the report of the friars." The golden Quivera, however, retreated like a phantom before the disappointed and impatient Spaniards. The natives, anxious only to rid themselves of the hated presence of the invaders, responded to every inquiry by pointing to the north-eastward, in which direction Coronado moved with his army. Instead of the long-sought Quivera, he found only the high, broad and desert plains of the great buffalo range, traversed by the roving Arapahoes and hostile Pawnees, and after wandering long in this inhospitable region, he returned completely dispirited to the Rio Grande, and speedily retraced his steps to Mexico.

It is worthy of mention that, while at Tucayan, a short distance to the northward of Cibola, the towns of which still exist, about one hundred and fifty miles to the westward of Santa Fé, on some of the northern tributaries of the Gila, he obtained an account of a great river to the north-west (undoubtedly the Colorado,) beyond which were mines of gold and great treasure. Thither he dispatched an officer, Lopez de Cardenas, with twelve men, who penetrated to the Colorado, but finding the country barren and uninviting, and the weather cold, he returned to Cibola without making any discoveries of interest.

The unfortunate results of Coronado's expedition had the effect to discourage all similar enterprises in the same quarter. Nevertheless, forty years thereafter, in 1586, Antonio de Espejo, animated by the accounts of a Franciscan monk named Ruiz, set out from the mines of San Barbara in

---

*** This fabulous city is not the "Gran Quivera" of the valley of the Pecos.**

Mexico, for the rich regions which he was assured existed far to the north-west. He went through the valley of the Rio Grande, where he found numerous traces of mineral wealth, and finally reached the towns of the Cibola. He here heard repeated the stories that had been told to Coronada, which, however, he relates in more distinct terms. He was told by the natives that "*sixty days' journey to the north-west* was a very mighty lake, upon the banks of which stood many great and good towns, and that the inhabitants of the same had plenty of gold," etc. He determined to proceed thither, but after going thirty leagues, he came to the towns of the Moqui, when, deserted by his followers, he was obliged to relinquish his design. He, nevertheless, "learned much of the great lake aforesaid," the reports agreeing fully with what he had before heard of the great abundance of gold in the vicinity of the lake.

It is eminently worthy of remark, that before returning, he visited "*certain very rich mines*" in the vicinity of the Moqui, (say two hundred and fifty miles west of Santa Fé) from which he assures us he took with his own hands, "*exceedingly rich metals holding great quantities of silver.*" These metals, he adds further, are found in broad and accessible veins.

It seems certain, both from the accounts of Coronado and Espejo, who alone have ever penetrated this northern country, that the natives had gold in their possession. It can not be supposed that it was obtained from so remote a deposit as that on the Sacramento; and the inference that it was found in their own vicinity, near the shores of the golden-sanded lake, to which their accounts refer, is sustained by the direct statements of Espejo, quoted above.

In this connection it may be mentioned, that immediately southward from the country of the Cabela, described by Coronado, and near the point where he probably crossed the Gila, the little river Prierte comes down from between the high mountains of the north. Concerning this stream, Col. Emory says, in his recent report of the march of the army of the west through the valley of the Gila—"As the story goes, the Prierte flows down from the mountains burnished with gold. Its sands are said to be full of the precious metal. A few adventurers, who ascended the river, hunting beaver, washed the sands at night, where they halted, and were richly rewarded for their trouble. Tempted by their success, they made a second trip, but were attacked and most of them killed by the Indians. My authority for this statement is Londeau, who, though illiterate, is truthful." It is well known that there are gold mines about one hundred and fifty miles to the eastward of this point, which have been, and still are, worked with considerable success.

The mention made by Espejo and other early writers, of mines and mineral wealth in the upper half of the valley of the Rio Grande, and probably in the valley of the Pecos river, has been confirmed by later authorities, whose accounts have superseded those of an earlier date. A number of mines are now worked in the valley, and from what is now known of the mineral productiveness of the Pacific slope, it is reasonable to conclude that the intervening country is equally rich in the precious metals. Indeed, from the geological features of the country, it can hardly be otherwise.*

The rapid sketches we have so far furnished, cover much of the earlier historical aspects of this period, drawn from strictly antiquarian researches; we will now proceed to give from more modern authorities, later views of our subject. Gregg, the intelligent and agreeable Santa Fé and New Mexican traveler, devotes an interesting chapter to this subject in his book "Commerce of America." He says:

"Tradition speaks of numerous and productive mines having been in operation in New Mexico before the expulsion of the Spaniards in 1680; but that the Indians, seeing that the cupidity of the conquerors had been the cause of their former cruel oppressions, determined to conceal all the mines by filling them up, and obliterating as much as possible every trace of them. This was done so effectually, as is told, that after the second conquest, (the Spaniards in the meantime not having turned their attention to mining pursuits for a series of years,) succeeding generations were never able to discover them again. Indeed, it is now generally credited by the Spanish population, that the Pueblo Indians, up to the present day, are acquainted with the *locales* of a great number of these wonderful mines, of which they most sedulously preserve

* The Author of Sam is indebted for much of the above narrative, to the researches of E. G. Squire, the antiquarian.

the secret. Rumor further asserts that the old men and sages of the Pueblos periodically lecture the youths on this subject, warning them against discovering the mines to the Spaniards, lest the cruelties of the original conquest be renewed toward them, and they be forced to toil and suffer in those mines as in days of yore. To the more effectual preservation of secrecy, it is also stated that they have called in the aid of superstition, by promulgating the belief that the Indian who reveals the location of these hidden treasures will surely perish by the wrath of their gods.

Playing upon the credulity of the people, it sometimes happens that a roguish Indian will amuse himself at the expense of his reputed superiors in intelligence, by proffering to disclose some of these concealed treasures. I once knew a waggish savage of this kind to propose to show a valley where virgin gold could be "scraped up by the basket-full." On a bright Sunday morning, the time appointed for the expedition, the chuckling Indian set out with a train of Mexicans at his heels, provided with mules and horses, and a large quantity of meal-bags to carry in the golden stores; but as the shades of evening were closing around the party, he discovered—that he couldn't find the place.

It is not at all probable, however, that the aborigines possess a tenth part of the knowledge of these ancient fountains of wealth, that is generally attributed to them; but that many valuable mines *were* once wrought in this province, not only tradition but authenticated records and existing relics sufficiently prove. In every quarter of the territory there are still to be seen vestiges of ancient excavations, and in some places, ruins of considerable towns evidently reared for mining purposes.

Among these ancient ruins the most remarkable are those of La Gran Quivira, about one hundred miles southward of Santa Fé. This appears to have been a considerable city, larger and richer by far than the present capital of New Mexico has ever been. Many walls, particularly those of churches, still stand erect amid the desolation that surrounds them, as if their sacredness had been a shield against which Time dealt his blows in vain. The style of architecture is altogether superior to anything at present to be found north of Chihuahua—being of hewn stone, a building material wholly unused in New Mexico. What is more extraordinary still, is, that there is no water within less than some ten miles of the ruins; yet we find several stone cisterns, and remains of aqueducts eight or ten miles in length, leading from the neighboring mountains, from whence water was no doubt conveyed. And, as there seem to be no indications whatever of the inhabitants ever having been engaged in agricultural pursuits, what could have induced the rearing of a city in such an arid, woodless plain as this, except the proximity of some valuable mine, it is difficult to imagine. From the peculiar character of the place and the remains of the cisterns still existing, the object of pursuit in this case would seem to have been a *placer*, a name applied to mines of gold-dust intermixed with the earth. However, other mines have no doubt been worked in the adjacent mountains, as many spacious pits are found, such as are usually dug in pursuit of ores of silver, etc.; and it is stated that in several places heaps of scoria are still to be seen.

By some persons these ruins have been supposed to be the remains of an ancient Pueblo or aboriginal city. That is not probable, however; for though the relics of aboriginal temples might possibly be mistaken for those of Catholic churches, yet it is not to be presumed that the Spanish coat-of-arms would be found sculptured and painted upon their facades, as is the case in more than one instance. The most rational accounts represent this to have been a wealthy Spanish city before the general massacre of 1680, in which calamity the inhabitants perished—all except one, as the story goes; and that their immense treasures were buried in the ruins. Some credulous adventurers have lately visited the spot in search of these long-lost coffers, but as yet none have been found.*

The mines of Cerrillos, twenty miles southward of Santa Fé, although of undoubted antiquity, have, to all appearance, been worked to some extent within the present century; indeed, they have been reopened within the recollection of the present generation; but the enterprise having been attended with little success, it was again abandoned. Among numerous pits still to be seen at this place, there is one of immense

* In the same vicinity there are some other ruins of a similar character, though less extensive; the principal of which are those of Abó, Tagique, Chililí. The last of these is now being resettled by the Mexicans.

depth cut through solid rock, which, it is believed, could not have cost less than $100,000. In the mountains of Sandia, Abiquiú, and more particularly in those of Picuris and Embudo, there are also numerous excavations of considerable depth. A few years ago, an enterprising American undertook to reopen one of those near Picuris; but after having penetrated to the depth of more than a hundred feet, without reaching the bottom of the original excavation, (which had probably been filling up for the last hundred and fifty years,) he gave it up for want of means. Other attempts have since been made, but with as little success. Whether these failures have been caused by want of capital and energy, or whether the veins of ore were exhausted by the original miners, remains for future enterprise to determine.

I should premise, before further reference to authorities, that the ruins of the *three* cities, so evidently built by the Indians, under the direction of the Spaniards, or rather of Spanish priests, are all met with in the valley of the Pecos, at no very great distance apart. They are Abio, Quarra, and Quivira. It is the ruins of Quarra which Major Abert, of the United States Commission Survey, was, at the time of this report we proceed to quote, now visiting. He says:

I now bade adieu to my generous entertainers, and with thousands of extravagant compliments from the kind people, I set out to overtake the party. After traveling southeast for six miles, I reached the ancient village of 'Quarra.' Here there is yet standing the walls of a time-worn cathedral; it is composed entirely of stone—red sandstone; the pieces are not more than two inches thick. The walls are two feet wide, and the outer face dressed off to a perfectly plain surface. The ground-plan presents the form of a cross, with rectangular projections in each of the angles. The short arm of the cross is thirty-three feet two inches wide; the long arm is eighteen feet nine inches wide; their axes are, respectively, fifty feet and one hundred and twelve feet long, and their intersection is thirty feet from the head of the cross. The rectangular projections, that partly fill the angles formed by the arms, are six feet square. At the foot of the cross are rectangular projections, that measure ten feet in the direction of the long axis, and six feet in the other direction.

Around the church are the less conspicuous remains of numerous houses that had been built of the same material, and the surfaces of the walls finished with tools; but these houses are almost level with the earth, while the walls of the ancient church rise to a hight of sixty feet.

While making my measurements, assisted by one of the men who had remained with me, a Mexican came up to me and said, in the most mysterious way, 'I know something of great moment, and want to speak to you—to you alone; no one must be near; come with me to my house.' I went; but when we arrived there, we found an old ruin fitted up with such modern additions as was necessary to render it habitable. Here were several women. I sat some time, talking of indifferent matters, waiting anxiously the important secret; but my friend did not like the presence of the women, and would not tell me then; so I got ready to re-commence my journey, while he endeavored, in a thousand ways to detain me. I asked him some questions about the geography of the country, and about the famous place called 'Gran Quivera.' He told me that it was exactly like the buildings of Quarra, thus confirming exactly what I had learned at Manzano.

I now signified my determination to proceed, when this man seemed extremely anxious about my going, and at last told me that he would meet me in a cedar grove, some distance in my route. In a little while I reached the grove, and saw him there. He then told me that he had discovered the greatest mine in the country, where there was an abundance of gold and silver. I asked him why he did not go and get it? 'O,' said he, 'you can not have been long in this country not to know that we poor people can keep nothing; the Ricos would seize all; but with your protection I would be secure in my labors.' Then he added, 'I 'll give you my name, write it down, it is José Lucero, of Quarra; you can inquire in the villages through which you pass, they will tell you that I am honest.' I took down José Lucero's name, and proceeded on in my journey, so that if any one wishes, they can go and seek the gold of Quarra.

It is the impression of all intelligent explorers, who have seen any one of the ruins mentioned, that from the geological character of the country surrounding them, their existence can only be accounted for, upon the supposition that they were built for mining purposes, and that since the entire extermination of their Spanish tyrants and taskmasters by the Indians in the first great rising of 1680—they have kept the secret of these mines concealed for the reasons given by Gregg, and frequently repeated by myself. The significant question:—"Why these long aqueducts, bringing water from great distances to cities in the midst of arid plains, when but a short distance south-east, or west, would have given the city-builders, pleasant, beautiful, and well-watered sites?"—has no other reasonable answer that I can perceive. The ignorant frontiers-men and savages of Texas had never heard the names of Quarra or Quivira, yet they clearly pointed them out, in connection with this very neighborhood of rich mines.

Dr. Wislizenus, in his report, says: Not far from these salinas the ruins of an old city are found, the fabulous '*la Gran Quivira.*' The common report in relation to this place is, that a very large and wealthy city was once here situated, with very rich mines, the produce of which was once or twice a year sent to Spain. At one season, when they were making extraordinary preparations for the transporting the precious metals, the Indians attacked them, whereupon the miners buried their treasures, worth fifty millions, and left the city together; but they were all killed except two, who went to Mexico, giving the particulars of the affair and soliciting aid to return. But the distance being so great and the Indians so numerous, nobody would advance, and the thing was dropped. One of the two went to New Orleans, then under the dominion of Spain, raised five hundred men, and started by way of the Sabine, but was never heard of afterward. So far the report. Within the last few years, several Americans and Frenchmen have visited the place; and, although they have not found the treasure, they certify at least to the existence of an aqueduct, about ten miles in length, to the still standing walls of several churches, the sculptures of the Spanish coat of arms, and to many spacious pits, supposed to be silver-mines. It was, no doubt, a Spanish mining town, and it is not unlikely that it was destroyed in 1680, in the general successful insurrection of the Indians in New Mexico against the Spaniards. Dr. Samuel G. Morton, in a late pamphlet, suggests the probability that it was originally an old Indian city, into which the Spaniards, as in several other instances, had intruded themselves, and subsequently abandoned it. Further investigation, it is to be hoped, will clear up this point.

Here are decidedly too many coincidences to be purely accidental and meaningless! Prescott mentions the fact that the quantities of gold found in the possession of the Mexicans by Cortez, are by no means accounted for, in the probable or even possible productiveness of any of the known mines of Mexico at the present day. How, then, *is* this great wealth to be accounted for? We think we have shown. It came, mostly, from New Mexico and the mysterious regions of the Gila and Colorado; and since this massacre of the Spaniards by the first, and the utter baffling of their search by the latter, these mines have been as a sealed book. But it will no longer continue to be sealed, when American enterprise shall have passed over these buried treasures.

But hear what is said by yet other historians, of the seemingly incalculable quantities of gold obtained by the Spanish conquest of Old and New Mexico, and no reader can be at a loss to account for the European prosperity and predominating insolence of the Catholic Church of this period, any more than he will find the insatiable cravings of the earlier Jesuit missionaries on the north, a difficult riddle to solve.

We shall merely quote a single passage from Prescott, the historian of the Conquest, in confirmation of the above, and conclude this branch of our subject.

In a few weeks most of them returned, bringing back large quantities of gold and silver plate, rich stuffs, and the various commodities in which the taxes were usually paid.

To this store Montezuma added, on his own account, the treasure of Axayacatl, previously noticed, some parts of which had been already given to the Spaniards. It was the fruit of long and careful hoarding—of extortion, it may be—by a prince who little dreamed of its final destination. When brought into the quarters, the gold alone was sufficient to make three heaps. It consisted partly of native grains; part had been melted into bars; but the greatest portion was in utensils, and various kinds of ornaments and curious toys, together with imitations of birds, insects, or flowers, executed with uncommon truth and delicacy. There were, also, quantities of collars, bracelets, wands, fans, and other trinkets, in which the gold and feather-work were richly powdered with pearls and precious stones. Many of the articles were even more admirable for the workmanship than for the value of the materials; such, indeed—if we may take the report of Cortez to one who would himself have soon an opportunity to judge of its veracity, and whom it would not be safe to trifle with—as no monarch in Europe could boast in his dominions!

"Magnificent as it was, Montezuma expressed his regret that the treasure was no larger. But he had diminished it, he said, by his former gifts to the white men. 'Take it,' he added, 'Malinche, and let it be recorded in your annals, that Montezuma sent this present to your master.'"

CHAPTER XXVIII.

Alas Poor Mexico!—Marquette and Joliet—La Salle—His pretended retirement from the Order of Jesus—His Fur Monopoly—He Descends the Mississippi to its mouth—His Death—Remarks—Commencement of the Second Intercolonial War.

POOR Mexico! delivered over to the tender mercies of Catholic "Missionary effort," how hast thou thriven? how grown apace in godliness and gold—in temporal and spiritual prosperity? Whither fled the god-born line of Moteuczoma, the far descended from the imperial loins of the Child of the Sun—Acamapitzin (he who has reeds in his fist), the first king of the rush-floated colony who had founded the empire of Mexico? Whither vanished the splendors of that haughty line? where those floating gardens, concerning the boundless magnificence and extent of which Cortez writes to Charles V, his master, that not all the royal gardens of Europe can afford a comparison of their grandeur? Where the huge temples to the God of Fire, with their myriad simple votaries to a strange but bloody creed? their splendid festivals of flowers, and dance, and feast, which made the round of the abundant year? Where the innumerable cities, hewn from huge blocks of stone, or piled as solidly from the imperishable sun-burnt bricks? Where the prodigious aqueducts and endless causeways which far surpassed the glories of old Rome? Where the mighty treasures of gold and silver — of priceless gems and arts as priceless? Where the pictured histories which, preserving the ancient story of a New World in graphic forms, was the rightful property of mankind?

"Where are these archives?" thunders "Sam." "Where are these treasures? Where these precious gems and more precious arts? Where the mighty "Ways"—these fast-built cities — these simple and happy millions, making merry amid peaceful abundance? Where the lost architecture? Where the ghosts of my majestic brothers, the Moteuczoma?"

"Sent to Purgatory, because they have not paid for masses enough yet to buy their way out," echoes a sepulchral answer from the tumbled ruins of fallen, desolate and ravished empire! Mexico is no more; she is but a myth, a fragment of the past; she has been "conserved" and converted by the Catholic Church! What more can be said? Amen. But to return to our proposed survey of the movements of the French Jesuits toward the South, of which La Salle is the principal hero.

The Jesuit Marquette had previously explored, in company with Joliet, a French trader, through the Wisconsin river, the upper waters of the Mississippi, as far as the mouth of the Arkansas, but were turned back from that point by the reports of dangerous and hostile tribes below. The discoveries of Marquette amounted to little more than convicting the heretofore entertained theory that the Mississippi discharged itself into the Chesapeake Bay instead of the Gulf of Mexico.

Among other adventurers who had passed over to New France since its transfer to the French West India Company, was the young La Salle, a native of Rouen, educated as a Jesuit, but who went to Canada to seek his fortune by discovering an over-land passage to China and Japan. After giving proofs of sagacious activity by explorations in Lakes Ontario and Erie, he had returned to France, and had obtained there from the king, to whom Canada had reverted since the recent dissolution of the West India Company, the grant of Fort Frontenac, a post at the outlet of Ontario, on the spot where Kingston now stands, built three years before by the Count de Frontenac, who had succeeded at that time to the office of Governor-General. On condition of keeping up that post, La Salle received the grant of a wide circuit of the neighboring country, and an exclusive right of trade with the Iroquois, as a check upon whom the fort had been built. But his ardent and restless disposition was not thus to be satisfied. Fired by reports of the recently discovered great river of the West, while Virginia was distracted by Bacon's insurrection, and New England yet smarting under the effects of Philip's war, La Salle left his fur trade, his fields, his cattle, his vessels and his Indian dependents at Fort Frontenac, and, repairing to France a second time, obtained a royal commission for perfecting the discovery of the Mississippi, and, at the same time, a monopoly of the trade in buffalo skins, which seemed likely to prove the chief staple of that region.

Thus successful in his mission, La Salle returned to Fort Frontenac with men and stores to prosecute his enterprise, accompanied by the Chevalier Tonti, an Italian soldier, who acted as his lieutenant. Before winter, he ascended Lake Ontario, entered the Niagara, and passing round the falls, selected a spot at the foot of Lake Erie, not far from the present site of Buffalo, where he commenced building the "Griffin," a bark of sixty tons. This bark, in the course of the next summer, was equipped with sails and cordage brought from Fort Frontenac, and in the autumn, first of civilized vessels, she plowed her way up Lake Erie, bearing La Salle, Tonti, the Fleming Hennepin, and several other friars of the Recollect order. Sixty sailors, boatmen, hunters and soldiers made up the company. Having entered Detroit, "the strait" or river at the head of Lake Erie, they passed through it into that limpid sheet of water, to which La Salle gave the characteristic name of St. Clair. Hence they ascended by a second strait into Lake Huron, and through the length of that great lake, by the Straits of Mackinaw, into Lake Michigan, whence they passed into Green Bay, and, after a voyage of twenty days, cast anchor at its head, thus first tracing a passage now fast becoming one of the great highways of commerce.

The Griffin was sent back with a rich lading of furs, under orders to return with provisions and supplies, to be conveyed to the head of Lake Michigan; but, unfortunately, she was shipwrecked on her homeward passage. La Salle and his company proceeded, meanwhile, in birch-bark canoes, up Lake Michigan, to the mouth of the St. Joseph's, where already there was a Jesuit mission. Here they built a fort called the Post of the Miamis, the name by which the river was then known. La Salle, with most of his people, presently crossed to a branch of the Illinois, down which they descended into the main stream, on whose banks, below

Peoria, they built a second fort, called *Crevecœur* (Heartbreak), to signify their disappointment at the non-arrival of the Griffin, of which nothing had yet been heard.

To hasten or replace the necessary supplies, the ardent and determined La Salle set off on foot, with only three attendants, and, following the dividing ridge which separates the tributaries of the lakes from those of the Ohio, he made his way back again to Fort Frontenac, where he found his affairs in the greatest confusion, himself reported dead, and his property seized by his creditors. But, by the Governor's aid, he made arrangements which enabled him to continue the prosecution of his enterprise.

During La Salle's absence, in obedience to orders previously given, Dacan and Hennepin descended the Illinois to the Mississippi, and, turning northward, explored that river as high up as the Falls of St. Anthony. On their way back they entered the Wisconsin, and, by the Fox river, passed to Green Bay; whence Hennepin returned to Quebec and to France, where he wrote and published an account of his travels.

Tonti, meanwhile, attacked by the Iroquois, who had made a sudden onslaught on the Illinois villages, fled also to Green Bay; and, when La Salle returned the next autumn with recruits and supplies, he found Forts Miami and Crevecœur deserted. Having built a new fort in the country of the Illinois, which he called St. Louis, with indefatigable energy he returned again to Frontenac, encountering Tonti on his way; and, having collected a new company, came back the same year to the Illinois, and during the winter built and rigged a small barge, in which, at length, he descended to the gulf. Formal possession of the mouth of the river was ceremoniously taken for the King of France. The country on the banks of the Mississippi received the name of LOUISIANA, in honor of Louis XIV, then at the hight of his power and reputation; but the attempt to fix upon the river itself the name of Colbert did not succeed.

Having made his way back to Quebec, leaving Tonti in command at Fort St. Louis, La Salle returned a third time to France, whither the news of his discovery had preceded him, and had excited great expectations. In spite of representations from Canada by his enemies, of whom his harsh and overbearing temper made him many, he was presently furnished with a frigate and three other ships, on board of which embarked five priests, twelve gentlemen, fifty soldiers, a number of hired mechanics, and a small body of volunteer agricultural emigrants, well furnished with tools and provisions; in all two hundred and eighty persons, designed to plant a colony at the mouth of the Mississippi.

Informed of this intended enterprise, Tonti, with twenty Canadians and thirty Indians, descended from Fort St. Louis to meet his old commander. But La Salle's vessels missed the entrance to the Mississippi, passed to the westward, and after a vain search for the river's mouth, landed their feeble and dispirited company at some undetermined spot on the coast of Texas. A fort was built and named St. Louis. La Salle, with characteristic activity, in the vain hope of finding the Mississippi, penetrated and explored the surrounding country. No succors came from France; the only vessel left with the colonists was wrecked; victims to the climate, to home-sickness, and despair, they were presently reduced to thirty-six persons. In this extremity, La Salle set off with sixteen men, determined to reach Canada by land; but, after three months' wanderings, he was murdered by two mutinous companions. The murderers were themselves murdered; some of the men joined the Indians; finally, five of them reached a point at the mouth of the Arkansas, where Tonti, returning disappointed from the gulf, had established a little post. With the Indians nearest the mouth of the Mississippi Tonti left a letter to La Salle, which they faithfully preserved for fourteen years, and delivered to the first Frenchmen who made their appearance.

The twenty men left by La Salle at Fort St. Louis obscurely perished, and even the site of the fort passed into oblivion. Yet France in after times claimed the region thus transiently occupied as a part of Louisiana. The same claim was revived more than a century afterward on behalf of the United States, to which Louisiana had been transferred by purchase.

This is Hildreth's account of La Salle and his career. But it may be as well to specify, in commenting upon this narrative, that Bancroft takes good care to mention that "La Salle being of a good family, he *had renounced* his inheritance by entering the seminary of the Jesuits. After profiting by the discipline of their schools, and obtaining their praise for purity and diligence, he had *taken his discharge from the fraternity;* and, with no companions but *poverty* and a boundless spirit of enterprise, about the year 1667, when the attention of all France was directed toward Canada, the young adventurer embarked for fame and fortune in New France." Now any one, who has carefully read our exposition of the principles of the organization of Loyola's Order, will understand how much this "taken his discharge" amounts to in reality. It means nothing more than that La Salle, at the urgency of his own adventurous spirit and probable request, had been transferred to some one of the many secret grades of the Order, which included not only women and Knights, but men of all ranks and occupations; he became, in a word, one of the "silent members," who, released from all ecclesiastical functions, outwardly constituted the most formidable agents of the Order. No better evidence of this could be offered than that his first effort was to obtain, in his own name, the coveted monopoly of the Fur Trade, which the missionaries proper have yet been unable wholly to absorb. But who can doubt that La Salle was virtually as good a Jesuit still—with that irrevocable vow of poverty upon his soul—as the saintly Marquette, or any avowed dignitary of the Order? La Salle still loved adventure much—but, as in duty bound—the Order more. It must be remembered that this vow of poverty, once taken, was retrospective, and as well forever, prospective, so that little good must his Fur Trade monopoly have ever done the poor adventurer—so soon as substantiated, it must have gone into the hands of the Order, whose agent in trust he was.

But thus it has ever been with those historical oracles whose brains and sympathies are so magnificently capacious that, to be merely Protestant, and tell a straight-forward truth plainly about a Body so revered for learning as this of the Jesuits, seems simply plebeian! Faugh! the contrast of the cool manner in which Hildreth disposes of this question may be remembered in the quotation given above. But this exploration of La Salle, though not immediately successful, constituted the future basis of French Imperial claims and Jesuit encroachments on the South; and we shall see too, even so early as during the progress of the third intercolonial war, they began to make themselves felt through their savage allies in that quarter. Hildreth thus relates the opening of this new war between the bloody partisans of Jesuitism and the Protestant colonies:

At the close of the late war, there had remained in the whole of Maine and Sagadahoc only four inhabited towns. Others had been reoccupied, and industry was resuming its course, when the breaking out of the new war with France excited new apprehensions. Earnest efforts were made to keep the Eastern Indians quiet. Dudley undertook a progress as far east as Pemaquid to renew the treaties. But a band of unprincipled colonists presently attacked and plundered the half-breed son of the Baron Castin, who dwelt on the Penobscot, and had succeeded there to some share of his father's influence. In consequence of this outrage, before long hostilities were renewed. (1703.)

The broken remnants of those Eastern tribes, whose vicinity to the English had exposed them most, were collected by the French, and established in two villages, Becancour and St. Francis, on two rivers of the same names, flowing from the south into the St. Lawrence. Here they had chapels and priests. Religious zeal and the remembrance of exile inflamed their natural aptitude for war. They were always ready for expeditions against the frontiers of New England, against which, in consequence of the truce with the Five Nations, the whole force of Canada was now directed. (1704.)

With two hundred Canadians and a hundred and fifty Indians, Hertelle de Rouville, descending along the Connecticut, approached Deerfield, then the northwestern frontier town of New England. Like the other frontier villages, it was inclosed by a palisade; but the sentinels slept, and high snow-drifts piled against the inclosure made entrance easy. Why repeat a story of monotonous horrors? The village was burned; forty-seven of the inhabitants were slain; the minister and his family, with upward of a hundred others, were carried into captivity. Dread and terror seized the inhabitants of Massachusetts. The whole of their extended northern frontier was liable to similar attacks. They were exposed alone to the whole brunt of the war. A reward of $66 was offered for Indian prisoners under ten years of age, and twice as much for older prisoners, or for scalps—premiums afterward variously modified and considerably increased. Thus stimulated, the colonial rangers were soon able to rival, and presently to surpass, the Indians in the endurance of cold and fatigue, and to follow up a trail with equal sagacity. Yet so shy and scattered were these lurking enemies, and so skilled in all the arts of that skulking warfare which they practiced, that each Indian scalp taken during this war was estimated to have cost the colony upward of £1000, $3333. The barbarizing influence of such a struggle was even more to be deprecated than its cost and its miseries. Some of the Connecticut Indians were employed as auxiliaries, but they seemed to have lost their warlike spirit.

The veteran Church, so soon as he heard of the burning of Deerfield, mounted his horse and rode seventy miles to offer his services to Governor Dudley.

Next year the Indian ravages became more alarming than ever. The very neighborhood of Boston was threatened. Hertelle de Rouville, again descended from Canada, this time by the valley of the Merrimac, attacked Haverhill, the frontier town on that river, scarcely yet recovered from the ravages of the former war. Having piously prayed together, De Rouville and his Indians rushed into the town about an hour before sunrise. The houses were plundered and set on fire; forty or fifty of the inhabitants were slain, some of them perishing in the flames of the houses; as many more, taken prisoners, were carried off to Canada. Hotly pursued from the neighboring towns, the assailants were obliged to fight shortly after leaving Haverhill, yet, with the loss of some of their prisoners, they succeeded in making good their retreat.

Alarmed at this new specimen of French and Indian enterprise, the General Court of Massachusetts called the queen's attention to the "consuming war" in which they had been engaged, now little short of twenty years. They begged her commands to the Mohawks to fall upon the French, and her assistance to conquer Canada and Acadie.

Vetch, a Boston merchant, one of the late commissioners to Quebec to treat for the exchange of prisoners, who had taken that opportunity to make soundings of the channel of the St. Lawrence, was sent to England to press this request. He came back with the promise of a fleet and army, news which, in spite of the opposition of the traders of Albany, who carried on a gainful commerce with Canada, excited in New York as well as New England, the greatest enthusiasm. Ingolsby, lieutenant-governor of New York, took care to keep the Assembly in good humor by resigning into their hands the appointment of officers, and the regulation, by a committee, of the commissary department. Five hundred men were raised; provisions were promised for the troops of the other colonies expected to co-operate; and bills of credit, for the first time in New York, were issued to pay the expense. To provide means for equipping their quotas, Connecticut and New Jersey, equally zealous, now also issued their first paper money.

This enthusiasm did not extend to Pennsylvania. Called upon by Governor Gookin to contribute a hundred and fifty soldiers, the Quaker Legislature protested, "with all humility," that "they could not, in conscience, provide money to hire men to kill each other." Out of their dutiful attachment to the queen, in spite of their scruples, they tendered her a present of £500; but this pittance Gookin refused to accept.

The plan of campaign devised twenty years before by Leisler and Phipps was now again revived. The four eastern clans of the Iroquois had been persuaded to raise the hatchet. The quotas of Connecticut, New York, and New Jersey, with four independent companies of a hundred men each, the regular garrison of New York, amounting in the whole to one thousand five hundred men, were assembled at Wood Creek, near the head of Lake Champlain, for an attack on Montreal. The command of these troops was given by the contributing Assemblies to Nicholson, bred an army officer, an old official, a man of very active disposition, whom we have seen successively governor of New York, of Maryland, and of Virginia, and whose former zeal in urging a grant by Virginia for the defense of New York was now gratefully remembered.

Another army of twelve hundred men, the quotas of Massachusetts, New Hampshire, and Rhode Island, destined to operate against Quebec, anxiously awaited at Boston the arrival of the promised British fleet. But new disasters in Spain again diverted this expected aid; and all these expensive preparations, by far the greatest yet made in the British colonies, fell fruitless to the ground.

The governors of the colonies concerned in this enterprise, met at Boston, and Nicholson and Vetch carried to England their solicitations and complaints. Schuyler, of Albany, who exercised a great influence over the Mohawks, imitated the policy of the governor of Canada, by taking with him to England five Mohawk warriors. Tricked out in scarlet cloaks, borrowed from the wardrobe of a London theater, these savages attracted a large share of public attention. The "Tatler" and "Spectator," then in the course of publication, make several allusions to them.

Nicholson and Vetch returned the next summer with two ships of war and five hundred marines. Connecticut and New Hampshire each raised a regiment; two regiments were contributed by Massachusetts; and Nicholson and Vetch, with twenty New England transports, sailed to attack Port Royal. The French garrison, feeble and mutinous, surrendered as soon as the siege was formed. By the terms of the capitulation, the inhabitants within a circuit of three miles, upon taking an oath of allegiance to England, were to be protected for two years, and were to have that period to dispose of their property. The miserable inhabitants of the other districts in vain solicited the same terms. They were treated as prisoners at discretion; their property was plundered; it was even proposed to drive them from their homes, "unless they would turn Protestants." A message was sent to the governor of Canada, that if he did not put a stop to the Indian parties against the frontiers of New England, any cruelties which they might inflict, should be retorted on the unhappy Acadians. Such conduct was little calculated to secure quiet possession of the province; and Vetch, left at Port Royal with four hundred men, soon found himself invested by the Acadians and the Indians.

Aid from England having been solicited by the colonies in this war, that which the Whigs consistently refused, had been, to the sudden surprise of the petitioners, granted by the new Tory administration. A large fleet and army was dispatched against Canada, under the command of General Hill and Sir Hovenden Walker. Hildreth says:

Within a fortnight after Nicholson had given the first notice of what was intended, a fleet of fifteen ships of war, with forty transports, bringing five veteran regiments of Marlborough's army, arrived at Boston. Here they were detained upward of a month, waiting for provisions and the colonial auxiliaries. The want of notice caused some inevitable delay; but the northern colonies exerted themselves with remarkable promptitude and vigor. The credit of the English treasury, broken down by a long and expensive war, was so low at Boston, that nobody would purchase bills upon it without an indorsement, which Massachusetts furnished in the shape of bills of credit to the amount of £40,000, advanced to the merchants who supplied provisions to the fleet. After a delay, of which the officers loudly complained, the ships sailed at last with seven thousand men on board, half regulars and half provincials.

New York issued £10,000 in bills of credit to pay the expense of her share of the enterprise, taking care, however, to deposit the money in the hands of special commissioners. Pennsylvania, under the name of a present to the queen, contributed £2,000, but none of the colonies further south seemed to have taken any interest in the matter. Some fifteen hundred troops, the quotas of Connecticut, New York, and New Jersey, again placed under the command of Nicholson, assembled at Albany, for an attack on Montreal simultaneously with that on Quebec, and Nicholson's camp was presently joined by eight hundred warriors of the Five Nations. But the advance was cut short by news of the failure of the expedition by sea.

As the fleet was proceeding up the St. Lawrence during a dark and stormy night, through the obstinacy and negligence of Admiral Walker, eight transports were wrecked, and near a thousand men perished. Discouraged at this disaster, the Admiral turned about, and, sending home the colonial transports, sailed direct for England, not even stopping by the way, as his instructions had indicated, to attack the French posts in Newfoundland. The British officers concerned in the expedition, attempted to shift off on the colonists the blame of this failure. They alleged 'the interestedness, the ill-nature, and sourness of these people, whose hypocrisy and canting are insupportable.' The indignant colonists, suspicious of the Tory ministry, believed that the whole enterprise was a scheme meant to fail, and specially designed for their disgrace and impoverishment. Harley, having quarreled with his colleagues, denounced it to the House of Commons as a job intended to put £20,000 into the pockets of St. John and Harcourt. Nowhere was the failure of this enterprise more felt than in New York. A war with the Five Nations was even apprehended. That confederacy showed a strong disposition to go over to the French."

That "the blood of the martyrs is the seed of the faith" worked well now. The Jesuits had at last obtained a hold upon the nations composing the League of the Iroquois, which had, as yet, proved the sole protectors of the early colonists on the lakes. There was an incidental war with the Tuscaroras in the meantime, against the German emigrants of North Carolina principally. Hear Hildreth's account:

The expedition against Norridgewock, which the Governor had delayed, but afterward, on the remonstrance of the court, had sent forward, was not successful in seizing Rasles; but his papers, which fell into the hands of the assailants, who pillaged the church and the missionary's house, strengthened suspicions that the Indians were encouraged by Canadian support. The Indians retorted the attack on Norridgewock by burning Brunswick, a new village recently established on the Androscoggin. The tribes of Nova Scotia, also, joined in the war. At the Gut of Canso they seized seventeen fishing vessels belonging to Massachusetts, several of which, however, were presently recovered, with severe loss to the Indian captors.

When the General Court came together, new disputes arose between the governor and the House as to the conduct of the war, of which the representatives sought to engross the entire management. Disgusted by the opposition of an Assembly "more fit," as he thought, "for the affairs of farming than for the duty of legislators," Shute had secretly obtained leave to return home; and, without giving any intimation of his purposes, he suddenly left the province. The administration, by his departure, passed into the hands of Dummer, the lieutenant-governor, who remained at the head of affairs for the next six years.

The General Court soon accommodated with Dummer the quarrel which Shute had left on his hands. He yielded to some of their demands, and they abandoned others. The Indian war proved expensive and annoying, and large issues of paper money became necessary to carry it on.

Connecticut, applied to for aid against the Indians, professed scruples as to the justice of the war, and begged Massachusetts to take care lest innocent blood were shed. These scruples were presently quieted, and Connecticut furnished the quota asked for. Attempts repeatedly made to engage the assistance of the Mohawks were less successful. They not only refused to take up the hatchet, but, what was still more unpalatable, they advised Massachusetts, as a sure means of peace, to restore the Indian lands and prisoners.

The attacks of the Indians extended along the whole northern frontier as far west as Connecticut river. To cover the towns in that valley, Fort Dummer was presently erected, on the site of what is now *Brattleborough*, the oldest English settlement within the limits of the present State of Vermont.

Having seized an armed schooner in one of the eastern harbors, a party of Indians cruised along the coast, and captured no less than seven vessels. It was deemed necessary to strike some decisive blow. Norridgewock was surprised by a second expedition; Rasles was slain, with some thirty of his Indian disciples; the sacred vessels and "the adorable body of Jesus Christ" were scoffingly profaned; the chapel was pillaged and burned, and the village broken up.

The premium on scalps was raised to £100, payable, however, in the depreciated currency. Lovewell, a noted partisan, surprised, near the head of Salmon Falls river, ten Indians asleep round a fire. He killed them all, and marched in triumph to Dover, with their scalps hooped and elevated on poles. In a second expedition he was less successful. Near the head of the Saco, on the margin of a pond, he fell into an Indian ambush, and was slain at the first fire, with eight of his men. The rest defended themselves bravely through a whole day's fight, repulsed the Indians, and made good their retreat.

Embassadors, meanwhile, were sent to Canada to remonstrate against the countenance given there to the hostile Indians; and an application was made to the king, to compel the neighboring colonies and the Mohawks to join in the war. The Board of Trade inclined to favor this request; but, already, the Penobscots had proposed a peace, which the colonists were very glad to accept; and the Norridgewocks presently came into it. Judicious measures were taken to protect the Indians against the extortion and villainy of private traders, by the establishment of public trading-houses to supply them with goods at cost. By this means, peace was preserved for many years, and the settlements in Maine and New Hampshire extended without interruption.

The complicated designs of the French Jesuits assume an aspect of mystery and entanglement, which it does not comport with our present purpose to unravel. We will let the plain historic character of the period tell for itself in the language of Hildreth. He says:

Though the progress of New France, as compared with that of the British colonies, was but slow and inconsiderable, the French still entertained the grand project of appropriating the whole of that vast western valley from the great lakes to the Gulf of Mexico. The Iroquois were no longer hostile; and, if the missionary spirit was dying out, it had been succeeded by a mercantile spirit hardly less energetic and determined. The French fur traders ranged the whole west; the Foxes, the only hostile tribe on the upper lakes, had been chastised and driven from Green Bay. By the treaty of Utrecht, the traffic with the western Indians was equally open to the English traders; but it still remained, for the most part, in the hands of the French, constituting, indeed, almost the sole resource of Canada. The lands along the banks of the St. Lawrence had been granted in seigniories, much like the patroonships of New Netherland. The tenants who cultivated them, known as *habitans*, produced little more than was necessary for the local consumption. They were often, however, better off than the *seigneurs*, or feudal lords, whose rents and feudal rights amounted to little. They looked chiefly to public offices or commissions in the army and navy as a means of support, and to them, therefore, peace was always distasteful. By an edict of Louis XIV, the nobles of Canada had been authorized to engage in commerce without any prejudice to their nobility. The fur trade, however, was principally in the hands of the bourgeoisie of Quebec and Montreal. The attempts to establish fisheries on the shores of the St. Lawrence had failed. Of the vessels that took cargoes to New France, some carried coal from Cape Breton to Martinique, to be used in boiling sugar; others bought fish in Newfoundland; but many returned in ballast. Notwithstanding objections in France, leave had been granted to establish linen manufactures in Canada, and coarse linens were now produced sufficient for the local demand. (1728.)

The administration of Canadian affairs was vested in the governor-general, the intendant, and a supreme council. The bishop named all the curates. The custom of Paris, the law of New France, under the conservative hands of the English, has preserved, like the Roman-Dutch code in British Guiana, authority in America long after having lost it in Europe. The population of Canada numbered at this time about thirty thousand. Quebec was a city of five thousand inhabitants. Many of the principal officers of the government were established there, and it could boast, in consequence, a more agreeable society than any other American town.

The "Creoles of Canada," natives, that is, of European descent, are described by Charlevoix as "well made, large, strong, robust, vigorous, enterprising, brave and indefatigable, but unpolished, presumptuous, self-reliant, esteeming themselves above all the nations of the earth, and somewhat lacking in filial veneration"—a portrait, not of the Canadian Creoles merely, but of the whole Creole-American race. The Canadians, true to their French origin, though inferior in industry, and much less wealthy, understood better than the Anglo-Americans the art of making themselves happy.

In Louisiana the French had secured the friendship of the Choctaws, a numerous confederacy inhabiting the region from the Lower Mississippi eastward to the Alabama, where they bordered on the Creeks. (1728.) Surrounded by the Choctaws, and dwelling mostly in a single village in the close vicinity of Fort Rosalie, where the Natchez, limited in numbers and extent of territory, but remarkable for a peculiar language and their singular religious and social institutions, which resembled, in several points, those of the Peruvians of

South America. Like the Peruvians, they worshiped the sun, from whom, also, their great chief claimed to be descended. In the great wigwam dedicated to their god, an undying fire was kept burning. Beside their principal chief, the "Great Sun," object of their highest reverence, there was a race of inferior chiefs or "suns," quite distinct from the common people. The hierarchical system was complete; but the small number of the Natchez did not allow of any of those striking results of combined labor, extorted by religious reverence, so remarkable among the Mexicans and Peruvians. The Natchez hardly differed in externals from the other tribes about them.

Alarmed at the encroachments of the French at Fort Rosalie, by whom their very village was demanded as a site for plantations, the Natchez presently began to grow hostile—a feeling stimulated by the Chickasaws, who dwelt northwardly up the east bank of the Mississippi, toward the mouth of the Ohio, and whose country extended eastward to the lands of the Cherokees.

Thus encouraged, the Natchez fell unexpectedly on the French settlement at Fort Rosalie, massacred the men to the number of two hundred, and made the women and children prisoners. (Nov. 1729.) The negro slaves were not harmed, and they presently joined the Indians. The settlers in the vicinity of New Orleans amounted, by this time, to near six thousand. But a third of that number were slaves, and dread of insurrection added to the terrors of Indian war.

While the people of New Orleans mustered their forces and fortified the city, Le Sueur, with a body of seven hundred Choctaw warriors, surprised the Natchez feasting over their victory, and liberated a part of the prisoners. Forces which presently arrived from New Orleans completed the success. Some of the discomfited Natchez fled to the Chickasaws, others crossed the Mississippi. But they were pursued, and only a few made good their escape. The great chief and four hundred others, prisoners in the hands of the French, were sent to St. Domingo and sold as slaves. (Jan. Feb. 1730.)

The English government, anxious to confirm their influence over the Cherokees, sent Sir Alexander Cumming to Carolina, specially authorized to renew the treaties with that powerful confederacy. Cumming held several councils in the Cherokee country; and seven of the principal chiefs were persuaded to accompany him to England on a visit to their "great father," the king. These chiefs signed a treaty with the Board of Trade, by which they promised the return of all runaway slaves, and were made to acknowledge themselves the subjects of Great Britain. Hence, in the subsequent controversy with the French, a pretense on the part of Great Britain, as in the case of the Six Nations, to sovereignty all over the Cherokee territory.

While these events transpired at the south, the Canadian authorities excited apprehensions, by sending a party from Montreal up Lake Champlain, to occupy Crown Point, within a hundred miles of Albany. The Assembly of New York resolved that "this encroachment, if not prevented," would prove of "the most pernicious consequence to this and other colonies;" and they sent notice to Massachusetts, Connecticut, and Pennsylvania, and applied to England for aid. Massachusetts entered warmly into their feelings. The Board of Trade supported their complaints; but the judicious policy of Walpole was peace. The experience of the last two wars, which had saddled England, to so little purpose, with a debt of two hundred and fifty millions of dollars, was not yet forgotten, and in spite of the remonstrances of New York and New England, the French were allowed quietly to occupy the shores of a lake, which, more than a century previous, they had been the first to explore.

Only at this single point, did the French yet approach the settlements of the English. There was a short and easy communication from Lake Erie with the upper waters of the Ohio; but no attempt was made by the French to occupy those waters, of which, indeed, they seem as yet to have known but little. The communication between Canada and Louisiana was carried on by the distant routes of Green Bay and the Wisconsin, Lake Michigan and the Illinois, and, presently, by the Maumee and the Wabash, which latter river was regarded by the French as the main stream, to which the Ohio was but a tributary. Low down the Wabash the post of St. Vincent's was presently established. The Blue Ridge bounded as yet the back settlements of Pennsylvania and Virginia. Unknown mountains and unthreaded forests separated, for a few years longer, the rival claimants of a continent.

Yet already the communication between Canada and Louisiana was exposed to obstructions. English traders from Carolina, penetrating through the country of the Cherokees, reached the distant Chickasaws, by whom, as enemies of the French, they were kindly received. These traders, in their turn, stimulated the hostility of the Chickasaws, whose canoes, filled with warriors, attacked the French boats navigating backward and forward from the Illinois to New Orleans. The Chickasaws even attempted, in conjunction with the English traders, to detach the tribes of the northwest from the French interest.

Puritan courage and enterprise seem to have been everywhere sufficient for the heading and counterbalancing all that corpse-like submission and fanaticism of the Jesuit could achieve. Protestantism had managed to make good friends in advance, as we have seen, of the Cherokees and Chickasaws, and opposed this alliance as a barrier upon the south nearly equal, in efficiency, to that of the Iroquois on the north. But hear further the narrative of the historian, upon whose careful labors the biographer of "Sam" has found that no one at this day can so far improve upon. He continues:

The Mississippi Company, utterly disappointed in its expectations of profit, and alarmed at the expense of the war with the Natchez, resigned Louisiana to the crown, and the Canadian Bienville, who had shared the fatigues and anxieties of the first settlement, was again commissioned as royal Governor; but the system of administration remained in most respects as before. The hostility of the Chickasaws seeming to threaten, in the south-west, an obstacle to the French dominion similar to that which the Iroquois had formerly presented to the north, it was resolved to attempt the conquest of that haughty nation, by a simultaneous attack from opposite directions.

Proceeding from New Orleans to Mobile with a fleet of sixty boats and canoes, Bienville ascended the Tombigbee to a fort or trading-house, lately established, two hundred and fifty miles up that river. There he was joined by twelve hundred Choctaws. The combined force having paddled up the Tombigbee to the head of navigation, marched from the landing now known as Cotton Gin Port against a stronghold of the Chickasaws, situated about twenty miles west of it. Aware, however, of the approach of their enemies, and encouraged by some English traders, the Chickasaws repulsed the attack, and compelled the French and their allies to an inglorious retreat.

D'Artaguette, who simultaneously descended from the Illinois with fifty Frenchmen and a thousand Indians, had been still more unlucky. Not hearing anything of the other expedition, he too had ventured a separate attack on a more northerly fort of the Chickasaws, in which he fell, severely wounded. His forces were repulsed and hotly pursued. Himself and several others, taken prisoners, were burned at the stake. In consequence, no doubt, of the expense of this war, the "card money" system which prevailed in Canada was introduced in Louisiana also.

Three years after, the whole strength of New France was again exerted for the conquest of the Chickasaws. At a post established within their country, at that bluff on the Mississippi now the site of the city of Memphis, twelve hundred French soldiers were assembled, with twice as many Indians and negroes. But the ranks were soon thinned by sickness, and the French were glad to purchase peace by withdrawing their forces, leaving the Chickasaws still independent and indomitable.

The process for vacating the charter of Carolina had been delayed by the privilege of peerage, enjoyed by several of the proprietaries. To bring this to a conclusion, it was proposed to buy the province, and the bargain for that purpose was presently confirmed by act of Parliament. Seven of the eight proprietaries relinquished to the crown all their interest for the sum of £17,500, to which were added £5000 more for arrears of quit-rents, claimed to the amount of £9000. Lord Carteret, the eighth proprietor, surrendered his rights of jurisdiction, but chose to retain his interest in the soil, his share of which, in the territory north of the Savannah, was specially set off to him next to the Virginia line, which had been lately run, and marked as far westward as the Blue Ridge.

Louisburg, on which the French had spent much money, was by far the strongest fort north of the Gulf of Mexico. But the prisoners of Canso, carried thither, and afterward dismissed on parole, reported the garrison to be weak, and the works out of repair. So long as the French held this fortress, it was sure to be a source of annoyance to New England, but to wait for British aid to capture it would be tedious and unçertain, public attention in Great Britain being much engrossed by a threatened invasion. Under these circumstances, Shirley proposed to the General Court of Massachusetts the bold enterprise of a colonial expedition, of which Louisburg should be the object. After six days' deliberation and two additional messages from the governor, this proposal was adopted by a majority of one vote. A circular letter, asking aid and co-operation, was sent to all the colonies as far south as Pennsylvania. In answer to this application, urged by a special messenger from Massachusetts, the Pennsylvania Assembly, still engaged in a warm controversy with Governor Thomas, voted £4000 of their currency to purchase provisions. The New Jersey Assembly, engaged, like that of Pennsylvania, in a violent quarrel with their governor, had refused to organize the militia or to vote supplies, unless Morris would first consent to all their measures, including a new issue of paper money. They furnished, however, £2000 toward the Louisburg expedition, but declined to raise any men. The New York Assembly, after a long debate, voted £3000 of their currency; but this seemed to Clinton a niggardly grant, and he sent, beside, a quantity of provisions purchased by private subscription, and ten eighteen-pounders from the King's magazine. Connecticut voted five hundred men, led by Roger Wolcott, afterward governor, and appointed, by stipulation of the Connecticut Assembly, second in command of the expedition. Rhode Island and New Hampshire each raised a regiment of three hundred men; but the Rhode Island troops did not arrive till after Louisburg was taken. The chief burden of the enterprise, as was to be expected, fell on Massachusetts. In seven weeks an army of three thousand two hundred and fifty men was enlisted, transports were pressed, and bills of credit were profusely issued to pay the expense. Ten armed vessels were provided by Massachusetts, and one by each of the other New England colonies. The command in chief was given to William Pepperill, a native of Maine, a wealthy merchant, who had inherited and augmented a large fortune acquired by his father in the fisheries; a popular, enterprising, sagacious man, noted for his universal good fortune, but unacquainted with military affairs, except as a militia officer. Whitfield, then preaching on his third tour throughout the colonies, gave his influence in favor of the expedition by suggesting, as a motto for the flag of the New Hampshire regiment, "*Nil desperandum Christo duce*"—"Nothing is to be despaired of with Christ for a leader." The enterprise, under such auspices, assumed something of the character of an anti-Catholic crusade. One of the chaplains, a disciple of Whitfield, carried a hatchet, specially provided to hew down the images in the French churches.

Eleven days after embarking at Boston, the Massachusetts armament assembled at Casco, to wait there the arrival of the Connecticut and Rhode Island quotas, and the melting of the ice by which Cape Breton was environed. The New Hampshire troops were already there; those from Connecticut came a few days after. Notice having been sent to England and the West Indies of the intended expedition, Captain Warren presently arrived with four ships of war, and, cruising before Louisburg, captured several vessels bound thither with supplies. Already, before his arrival, the New England cruisers had prevented the entry of a French thirty-gun ship. As soon as the ice permitted, the troops landed and commenced the siege, but not with much skill, for they had no engineers. The artillery was commanded by Gridley, who served thirty years after in the same capacity in the first Massachusetts revolutionary army. Cannon and provisions had to be drawn on sledges, by human strength, over morasses and rocky hills. Five unsuccessful attacks were made, one after another, upon an island battery which protected the harbor. In that cold, foggy climate, the troops, very imperfectly provided with tents, suffered severely from sickness, and more than a third were unfit for duty. But the French garrison was feeble and mutinous, and when the commander found that his supplies had been captured, he relieved the embarrassment of the besiegers by offering to capitulate. The capitulation included six hundred and fifty regular soldiers, and near thirteen hundred effective inhabitants of the town, all of whom were to be shipped to France. The Island of St. John's presently submitted on the same terms. The loss during the siege was less than a hundred and fifty, but among those reluctantly detained to garrison the conquered fortress ten times as many perished afterward by sickness. In the expedition of Vernon and this against Louisburg, perished a large number of the remaining Indians of New England, persuaded to enlist as soldiers in the colonial regiments.

Some dispute arose as to the relative merits of the land and the naval forces, which had been joined during the siege by additional ships from England. Pepperell, however, was made a baronet, and both he and Shirley were commissioned as colonels in the British army. Warren was promoted to the rank of rear admiral. The capture of this strong fortress, effected in the face of many strong obstacles, shed, indeed, a momentary luster over one of the most unsuccessful wars in which Britain was ever engaged. It attracted, also, special attention to the growing strength and enterprise of the people of New England, represented by Warren, in his communications to the ministry, as having "the highest notions of the rights and liberties of Englishmen; and, indeed, as almost Levelers."

The French, on their side, were not idle. The garrison of Crown Point sent out a detachment, which took the Massachusetts fort at Hoosick, now Williamstown, and presently surprised and ravaged the settlement recently established at Saratoga. Even the counties of Ulster and Orange, on the lower Hudson, struck with panic, expected the speedy arrival of Canadian and Indian invaders.

The easy conquest of Louisburg revived the often disappointed hope of the conquest of Canada. Shirley submitted to Newcastle a plan for a colonial army to undertake this enterprise. But the Duke of Bedford, then at the head of the British marine, took alarm at the idea of "the independence it might create in those provinces, when they shall see within themselves so great an army, possessed of so great a country by right of conquest." The old plan was therefore preferred, of sending a fleet and army from England to capture Quebec, to be joined at Louisburg by the New England levies, while the forces of other colonies operated in the rear, against Montreal.

Orders were accordingly sent to the colonies to raise troops, which the king would pay. Hardly were these orders across the Atlantic, when the ministers changed their mind; but, before the countermand arrived, the colonial levies were already on foot. In spite of the mortality at Louisburg, Massachusetts raised three thousand five hundred men, Connecticut raised a thousand, New Hampshire five hundred, Rhode Island three hundred. The province of New York voted sixteen hundred men, New Jersey five hundred, Maryland three hundred, Virginia one hundred. Money was voted by the Pennsylvania Assembly for enlisting four hundred men. The troops from the southern colonies, and those also from Connecticut, assembled at Albany. The command, declined by Governor Gouch, of Virginia, was assumed by Clinton, of New York. Not only was Clinton involved in a violent controversy with the Assembly, but a majority of the Council, headed by Delancey, the Chief Justice, continued to sit at New York during the Governor's absence at Albany, and to dispute with him the administration of the province. His military command was not less embarrassing. The corporation of Albany refused to provide quarters for the soldiers; the bills drawn by Clinton on the British treasury failed to purchase provisions; impressment was resorted to, but it was not without difficulty that the troops were subsisted.

The office of agent for the Five Nations, hitherto held by Major Shuyler's son, had been taken from him by Clinton and given to William Johnston, who led a party of Mohawks, destined to act in front of the main army. Of Scotch-Irish descent, Johnston had established himself some ten or twelve years previously on the Mohawk river, thirty miles west of Albany, at the head of a new frontier settlement, undertaken on behalf of his uncle, Admiral Warren, who had married in New York, and had thus been led to engage in colonial land speculations. A man of coarse but vigorous mind, and great bodily strength, Johnston carefully cultivated the good will of the Mohawks, with whom he carried on a lucrative traffic. He had an Indian wife, or mistress, sister of the afterward celebrated Brant; he acknowledged as his own, several half-breed children; and already had attained, by conformity to their customs and by natural aptitude, the same influence over the Mohawks possessed in the previous generation by Major Schuyler.

As the British fleet did not make its appearance, fifteen hundred of the Massachusetts troops were marched to Albany to join Clinton. But attention was soon drawn to matters nearer home. Instead of the expected English squadron, a French fleet of forty ships of war, with three thousand veteran troops on board, had sailed for the American coast, exciting a greater alarm throughout New England than had been felt since the threatened invasion of 1697. This alarm, the non-appearance of the British fleet, and the various difficulties encountered on the march, put a stop to the advance on Montreal. A body of troops from Canada appeared at the head of the Bay of Fundy, and, being joined by the French inhabitants there, threatened an attack on Annapolis. Boston was thought to be the great object of the enemy. To defend it, some ten thousand militia were collected, and such addditions were made to the fort, on Castle Island, as to render it the strongest British fortress in America. The French fleet, shattered by storms and decimated by a pestilential fever, effected nothing beyond alarm. The admiral died, the vice-admiral committed suicide. The command then devolved on La Jonquiere, appointed Governor-General of New France as successor to Beauharnois, who had held that office for the last twenty years. A second storm dispersed the ships, which returned singly to France. After the capture of Jonquiere in a second attempt to reach Canada, the office of Governor-General devolved on La Galissionniere.

Parliament subsequently reimbursed to the colonies the expenses of their futile preparations against Canada, amounting to £235,000, or upward of a million of dollars.

Indian parties from Canada severely harassed the frontier of New England. Even the presence of a British squadron on the coast was not without embarrassments. Commodore Knowles, while lying in Boston harbor, finding himself short of men, sent a press-gang one morning, into the town, which seized and carried off several of the inhabitants. As soon as this violence became known, an infuriated mob assembled, and, finding several officers of the squadron on shore, seized them as hostages for their imprisoned fellow-townsmen. Surrounding the town-house, where the General Court was in session, they demanded redress. After a vain attempt to appease the tumult, Shirley called out the militia; but they were very slow to obey. Doubtful of his own safety, he retired to the castle, whence he wrote to Knowles, representing the confusion he had caused, and urging the discharge of the persons he had impressed. Knowles offered a body of marines to sustain the governor's authority, and threatened to bombard the town unless his officers were released. The mob, on the other hand, began to question whether the governor's retirement to the castle did not amount to an abdication. Matters assumed a very serious aspect; and those influential persons who had countenanced the tumult, now thought it time to interfere for its suppression. The House of Representatives resolved to stand by the governor "with their lives and fortunes." The council ordered the release of the officers. The inhabitants of Boston, at a town meeting, shifted off the credit of the riot upon "negroes and persons of vile condition." The governor was escorted back by the militia; Knowles discharged the greater part of the impressed men, and presently departed with his squadron. No allusion was made, in the course of this affair, to the statute of Anne, prohibiting impressments in America. That act, indeed, according to the opinion of several English crown lawyers, had expired with Queen Anne's war. Shirley, in his letters to the Board of Trade, on the subject of this "rebellious insurrection," ascribes "the mobbish turn of a town of twenty thousand persons" to its constitution, which devolved the management of its affairs on "the populace, assembled in town meetings." Boston had already attained an amount of population at which it remained stationary for the next fifty years. (1747.)

The towns of Suffield, Somers, Enfield, and Woodstock, originally settled under Massachusetts grants, and assigned to that province in 1713, by the boundary convention with Connecticut, finding the rate of taxation in Massachussetts enhanced by the late military expenses, applied to Connecticut to take them into her jurisdiction. They claimed to be within the Connecticut charter. They alleged that the former agreement had never been ratified by the crown, and that Connecticut had received no equivalent for her surrender of jurisdiction. This application was listened to with favor. Some show, indeed, was made of asking the consent of Massachusetts; but, when that consent was refused, the towns were received by Connecticut without it, and to that province they have ever since belonged. Massachusetts threatened an appeal to the king in council, but hesitated to prosecute it, lest she might lose, as in her former controversy with New Hampshire, not only the towns in dispute, but other territory also.

Some liberated prisoners from Martinique, a great resort for French cruisers, brought a report to Philadelphia that a fleet of privateers, knowing the unfortified state of that city, and trusting that the Quakers would not fight, intended to make a combined expedition up the Delaware. In consequence of this alarm, fortifications were erected and a military organization adopted in Pennsylvania. The Assembly still refused to do anything; but an associated volunteer militia, ten thousand strong, was organized and equipped. Money was also raised by lottery to erect batteries for the defense of the Delaware, toward which the proprietaries contributed twelve pieces of cannon. "Plain Truth," a little pamphlet written by Franklin, greatly contributed to these movements. By twenty years of diligent labor as a printer, newspaper publisher and editor, Franklin had acquired a handsome property; and, at the age of forty, he now began to take an active part in the political affairs of the province, being chosen a member of the Assembly, of which, for ten years previous, he had acted as clerk.

A portion of the Quakers were inclined to justify defensive war. Chew, chief justice of Delaware, had been disowned by the yearly meeting for avowing that opinion, but it still continued to gain ground. The now venerable Logan, who, indeed, had never been much of a Quaker, entertained the same views; but increased age and infirmities had withdrawn him, for some time, from active participation in affairs.

The war so inconsiderately begun, through the resolution of the British merchants to force a trade with Spanish America, after spreading, first to Europe and then to India, and adding $144,000,000, (£30,000,000,) to the British national debt, was at last brought to a close by the peace of Aix la Chapelle. (Oct. 8, 1748.) Notwithstanding a former emphatic declaration of the British government, that peace never should be made unless the right to navigate the Spanish-American seas free from search were conceded, that claim, the original pretense for the war, was not even alluded to in the treaty. The St. Mary's was fixed as the boundary of Florida. Much to the mortification of the people of New England, Cape Breton and the conquered fortress of Louisburg were restored to the French, who obtained, in addition, the little islands of St. Pierre and Miquelon, on the south coast of Newfoundland, as stations for their fishermen. A new commission was also agreed to for the settlement of French and English boundaries in America—a matter left unsettled since the treaty of Ryswick.

CHAPTER XXIX.

Commencement of the final struggle between the French and English for the country on the great Lakes and the Mississippi—Fourth Intercolonial War.

WE come now to the fourth intercolonial war, in which Washington, the first incarnation of Sam in moderate earthly mould, makes his appearance upon a stage, the drama of which is to fill the eye of the world—a drama, of which he is to be the central figure.

We must again own our obligation to our admirable *American* historian for the narrative of this war.

Dr. Thomas Walker, of the council of Virginia, penetrating through the mountainous south-eastern regions of that province, had reached and crossed the ridge which separates the valley of the Tennessee from the head waters of the more northerly tributaries of the Ohio. To that ridge he gave the name of *Cumberland Mountains*, after the Duke of Cumberland, of the English blood royal, just then very famous by his victory over the Pretender, at Culloden. The name of Cumberland was also given to one of the rivers flowing down the western slope of that ridge. A more northerly stream, called by Walker the Louisa, still preserves its aboriginal appellation of *Kentucky*, not, however, without conformity to the English idiom in a retraction of the accent from the last to the second syllable. The region entered by Walker, full of abrupt and barren mountains, attracted little attention. The country about the head of the Ohio seemed much more inviting.

An association of London merchants and Virginia land speculators, known as the Ohio Company, obtained in England, shortly after the peace, a grant of six hundred thousand acres of land on the east bank of that river, with exclusive privileges of Indian traffic—a grant esteemed an encroachment by the French, who claimed as theirs, by right of discovery and occupation, the whole region watered by the tributaries of the Mississippi. (1749.) A counter claim, indeed, was set up by the English, in the name of the Six Nations, recognized by the treaties of Utrecht and Aix la Chapelle as under British protection, whose empire, it was pretended, had formerly been carried by conquest over the whole eastern portion of the Mississippi Valley, and the basin, also, of the lower lakes. In maintenance of these pretensions, Colden's "History of the Five Nations" had recently been published. The French, in reply, pointed to their posts, many of them of considerable antiquity, more than sixty in number, along the great lakes and the waters of the Mississippi. The missions had declined, but the Indian trade continued to flourish. At the principal posts were regular garrisons, relieved once in six years. Such of the disbanded soldiers as chose to remain, beside a grant of land, received a cow and a calf, a cock and five hens, an ax, a hoe, a gun, with powder and shot, grain for seed, and rations for three years. Wives were sent out to them from France, or they intermarried with the Indians. The boats from the Illinois country, descending annually to New Orleans, carried flour, Indian corn, bacon, both of hog and bear, beef and pork, buffalo robes, hides and tallow. The downward voyage was made in December; in February the boat returned with European goods for consumption and Indian traffic. The Indians north west of the Ohio, including the remains of the tribes whom the Iroquois had formerly driven from their homes on the Ottawa, the Hurons or Wyandots, the Miamies, the Illinois, all rejoiced in the alliance, or recognized the authority of the French. As respected the country on the upper lakes, the Mississipi, the Illinois, and the Wabash, the French title, according to European usage, was complete.

The country immediately south of Lake Erie, covered with dense forests, and with few Indian inhabitants, had hitherto, in a great measure, been neglected. But the Count de la Galissonniere, shortly after assuming office as governor-general, had sent De Celeron, with three hundred men, to traverse the country from Detroit east to the mountains, to bury, at the most important points, leaden plates with the arms of France engraved, to take possession with a formal process verbal, and to warn the English traders out of the country.

To secure Nova Scotia, to guard the commerce and fisheries of New England, and to offset the restored fortress of Louisburg, the British government hastened to establish at Chebucto the military colony and fort of Halifax, so called after the president of the Board of Trade, who took a great interest in its establishment. During the next twenty-five years this fortress cost Great Britain not less than three millions of dollars—a striking instance of the expenses of modern warlike preparations, equivalent, in fact, to a perpetual war.

Admiral De la Jonquiere having entered upon the government of New France, his predecessor, De la Galissonniere, proceeded to Paris as one of the boundary commissioners under the late treaty. In two thick quarto volumes of protocols, these commissioners vainly attempted to settle what had been meant in the treaty of Utrecht by the "ancient limits" of Acadie. The English claimed under that appellation both shores of the Bay of Fundy—indeed, the whole region east of the Penobscot. The French, on the other hand, sought to restrict the cession of Acadie to the peninsula to which the name of Nova Scotia is at present confined, claiming the north shore of the Bay of Fundy as a part of Canada. Nor did they satisfy themselves with protocols only. Troops from Canada established the posts of Gaspareau and Beau Sejour, at the narrowest part of the isthmus, between the waters of the Bay of Fundy and those of the Gulf of St. Lawrence—a vicinity in which was planted a considerable body of ancient French colonists still warmly attached to the French interest. Cornwallis, governor of Nova Scotia, wrote pressingly to Massachusetts for aid. Not strong enough to dislodge these intruders, he caused two opposing forts to be built at Beau Bassin and Minas. A third post was also established by the French near the mouth of the St. John. (1749.)

Determined also to strengthen their hold on the disputed western region, the French enlarged and strengthened their post at Niagara. (1750.) They even obtained leave to build a fort and trading house on the borders of the Mohawk country. Alarmed for the fidelity of the Six Nations, who never had recognized the claim of English dominion, Clinton, governor of New York, proposed a new treaty, in which he invited all the colonies to participate. (1751.) Only Massachusetts, Connecticut, and South Carolina chose to incur the expense. The French built vessels of unusual force at Fort Frontenac. They entered into friendly relations with those bands of Delawares and Shawanese whom the pressure of new settlements in Pennsylvania had lately driven from the Susquehanna toward the Ohio, and to whom the operations of the Ohio Company, in the establishment of a post and trading house at Redstone, now Brownsville, on the Monongahela, had given great offense. The Marquis Du Quesne, Jonquiere's successor as governor-general, followed up the same policy. A band of the Miamies, or Twigties, as the English called them, settled at Sandusky, having refused to remove to Detroit, and persisting in trade with the English, their village was burned. The English traders were seized, and their merchandise confiscated. Early the next year, twelve hundred men from Montreal built a fort at Presque Isle, now Erie, on the southern shore of the lake of that name. Crossing thence to the waters flowing south, they established posts at La Bœuf and Venango, the one on French Creek, the other on the main stream of the Allegany, which meets the Monongahela flowing north, and unites with it to form the Ohio. (1753.)

The Board of Trade reported to the king that, "as the French had not the least pretense of right to the territory on the Ohio, an important river rising in Pennsylvania and running through Virginia, it was matter of wonder what such a strange expedition, in time of peace, could mean, unless to complete the object so long in view, of conjoining the St. Lawrence with the Mississippi." Lord Holderness, successor to the Duke of Bedford, as Secretary of State, dispatched orders to the governors of Pennsylvania and Virginia, to repel force by force, "whenever the French were found within the undoubted limits of their provinces." (1749.) After remaining for three years in the hands of Thomas Lee and Lewis Burwell, successive presidents of the council, the government of Virginia had passed to Robert Dinwiddie, as lieutenant-governor, a Scotsman of ability, surveyor-general of the colonial customs, and previously a counselor, but not possessed of that suavity of manners for which Gouch, his predecessor, had been distinguished. Observing with anxiety and alarm the movements of the French, Dinwiddie held a treaty with the Indian bands on the Monongahela, from whom he purchased permission to build a fort at the junction of that river with the Alleghany. He resolved, also to send a message to the nearest French post, to demand explanations, and the release and indemnification of the captured traders. As bearer of this message he selected George Washington, a native of Westmoreland county, on the Potomac, where his ancestors had been planters for three generations. The paternal inheritance, by the law of primogeniture, having passed to his eldest brother, the young Washington, a major in the militia, followed the lucrative but laborious profession of a land surveyor in the Northern Neck, now the property of Lord Fairfax. Though not yet twenty-two, already he gave evidence of that rarest of combinations, a sound judgment, with courage, enterprise, and capacity for action.

After a dangerous winter's journey of four hundred miles, with only four or five attendants, the greater part of the way through uninhabited forests, Washington reached the French post at Venango, where he was received with characteristic politeness. Joncaire, the commander, promised to transmit Dinwiddie's message to his superiors in Canada, under whose orders he acted; but the French officers, over their cups, made no secret to Washington of the intention entertained by the French government permanently to occupy all that country. (1753.)

During Washington's absence, Dinwiddie applied to the Assembly for funds; but he found that Body in a very bad humor. With the consent of the Board of Trade, a fee had recently been imposed on the issue of patents for lands—a practice long established in other colonies, but hitherto unknown in Virginia. The House of Burgesses paid no attention to Dinwiddie's complaint of French encroachments and call for money. Wholly engrossed by the affair of the obnoxious fee, they resolved that whosoever paid it, ought to be regarded as betraying the rights of the people; and they sent to England, as bearer of their complaints, Peyton Randolph, attorney-general of the province, twenty years after president of the Continental Congress, to whom they voted a salary of £2,000, out of the provincial funds in the hands of the speaker.

Notwithstanding this disappointment, Dinwiddie enlisted a captain's command, and sent them to build a fort at the junction of the Alleghany and the Monongahela. The western boundary of Pennsylvania was not yet run. It was uncertain whether the head of the Ohio fell within that province; if not, it was claimed as appertaining to Virginia.

As soldiers could not be supported without money, Dinwiddie called on the neighboring colonies for aid, and presently again summoned the Virginia Assembly. Washington had now returned. The designs of the French were obvious, and the Assembly granted £10,000 toward the defense of the frontiers. A committee of the burgesses was appointed to act in concert with the governor in the expenditure of this money—an "encroachment on the prerogative," to which, from necessity, Dinwiddie reluctantly submitted.

Urged by Governor Hamilton to take measures to withstand the intrusions of the French, the Assembly of Pennsylvania offered supplies in paper money. But to this, Hamilton, by his instructions, could not assent, at least not without a suspending clause of reference to England, to which the Assembly would not agree. (1754.)

Again urged to co-operate with Virginia, the Assembly passed a new bill for paper money supplies, which the governor again rejected. Some members of the Assembly—and the same was presently the case in New York—expressed doubts if the crown actually had any claim to the territory on which the French were said to be encroaching. Governor Glen, of South Carolina, doubted too. But any such doubts were regarded by the zealous Dinwiddie as little short of treason. In New York also, as well as in Virginia and Pennsylvania, internal disputes distracted attention from the designs of the French. Clinton had resigned, wearied out by ineffectual struggles against Delancey, who had been joined, also, by Colden, and whom the united influence of Alexander, Smith, and Johnson, lately raised to the council, was not sufficient to overmatch. His successor, Sir Danvers

Osborne, came from England charged to rebuke the Assembly, and to re-establish the executive authority. His friends had obtained for him this appointment, hoping that business and a change of scene might enable him to throw off a fit of melancholy under which he was laboring. But the hopelessness of the task he had assumed so aggravated his disorder, that, within five days after his arrival, he committed suicide.

It fell to Delancey, as lieutenant-governor, to which dignity he had just been raised, to lay Osborne's instructions before the Assembly. An address to the king and a representation to the Board of Trade, indignantly denied the imputations of turbulence and disloyalty; but all the arts of Delancey were exhausted in vain, to move the Assembly from their policy of annual votes. The most he could obtain was, that money once voted, should be drawn out of the treasury on the order of the governor and council, and a promise not to interfere with executive matters.

The government of Maryland had recently been conferred on Horatio Sharpe, a military officer; but a quarrel about supplies, similar to that in Pennsylvania, prevented the aid which Dinwiddie had asked.

North Carolina alone, of all the colonies applied to, responded promptly, by voting a regiment of four hundred and fifty men. The temporary administration of that province was held by Michael Rowan, as president of the council, who availed himself of this opportunity to consent to a new issue of paper money. But these North Carolina troops proved of little use. By the time they reached Winchester, in Virginia, the greater part had disbanded on some doubts as to their pay, the appropriation for that purpose being already exhausted.

A regiment of six hundred men had been enlisted in Virginia, of which Frye was appointed Colonel, and Washington lieutenant-colonel. To encourage enlistment, Dinwiddie promised two hundred thousand acres of land to be divided among the officers and soldiers. Two independent companies from New York, and another from South Carolina were ordered to Virginia to assist in the operations against the French.

The Virginia troops, on their march to the frontier, encountered abundance of difficulties. Very little disposition was shown to facilitate their progress. It was only by impressment that means could be obtained to transport the baggage and stores. By slow and toilsome steps, the troops made their way to Will's Creek, on the Potomac, where they were met by alarming intelligence. The French, under Contrecœur, had descended in force from Venango, and, having sent off Dinwiddie's soldiers, who were building a fort at the head of the Ohio, they had themselves seized that important spot and commenced a fort, which they called Du Quesne, after the Governor-General.

A detachment under Washington hastily sent forward to reconnoiter, just before reaching Redstone, at a place called the Great Meadows, encountered a French party, which Washington attacked by surprise, and whose commander, Jumonville, was killed — the first blood shed in this war.

By Frye's death, the chief command devolved on Washington. He was soon joined by the rest of the troops, and, having erected a stockade at the Great Meadows, called Fort Necessity, pushed on toward Du Quesne. The approach of a much superior force under M. de Villier, brother of Jumonville, obliged him to fall back to Fort Necessity. His troops were fatigued, discouraged, and short of provisions; and, after a day's fighting, he agreed to give up the fort, and to retire with his arms and baggage. Washington did not know French; his interpreter, a Dutchman, was ignorant or treacherous, and the articles of capitulation were made to contain an express acknowledgment of the "assassination" of Jumonville. Having retired to Will's Creek, Washington's troops assisted in the erection of *Fort Cumberland*, which now became the westernmost English post.

At the same time, with his orders to Virginia and Pennsylvania, Holderness had addressed a circular letter to all the colonies, proposing a convention at Albany of committees from the several colonial Assemblies, to renew the treaty with the Six Nations, whose friendship at this crisis, was of great importance. Agreeably to his recommendation, New York, Pennsylvania, Maryland, and the four New England colonies, appointed committees. While Washington was operating toward the Monongahela, this convention met, and after carefully settling the question of precedence, organized itself, with Delancey, of New York, as presiding officer. The ill feeling between the Governor and the Assembly of Virginia, prevented any representation from that colony.

Having returned from his unavailing mission to Paris, Shirley had resumed the government of Massachusetts. But, what greatly damaged his popularity among a people so hostile to the French, and to all popish connections, he brought with him from Paris a young wife, a French woman and a Catholic. Perceiving a war to be approaching, he summoned the Eastern Indians to renew their treaties. But they eagerly availed themselves of this new opportunity to raise the hatchet. For the sixth time within eighty years, luckily destined to be the last, the frontiers of New England again suffered. The General Court readily voted money to repel these hostilities; and, as an offset to a reported French fort near the head of the Chaudiére—while Washington was fortifying at Will's Creek—Shirley built Fort Halifax, high up the Kennebec. Hardly had the Governor returned from the eastward, when Hoosick and Stockbridge, on the western frontier, were assailed by an Indian war party. These assailants belonged to a tribe largely composed of descendants of refugees driven from Massachusetts in the time of Philip's war. As a protection to that frontier, the Stockbridge tribe was taken into pay.

Maryland and New York voted in aid of Virginia, the one £6000, the other £5000; £10,000 were also received from England, whence came a commission to Sharpe, governor of Maryland, as Commander-in-Chief of the forces to be employed against the French. Warm disputes about rank and precedence had already arisen between the Virgina regimental officers and the captains of the independent companies. To stop this dispute, Dinwiddie had dispensed with field officers, and broken the Virginia regiment into separate companies—an arrangement which had driven Washington from the service.

The pending territorial disputes led about this time to the publication of the maps of Evans and Mitchell, the first embracing the middle colonies, the other the whole of North America. The first edition of Mitchell's map had appeared in 1749; but a new edition was now published, with improvements. The British North American colonies stretched a thousand miles along the Atlantic, but their extent inland was very limited. According to a return made to the Board of Trade, the population amounted to—

Whites,	1,192,896
Blacks,	292,738
Total	1,485,634

New France, on the other hand, had scarcely a hundred thousand people, scattered over a vastly wider space, from Cape Breton to the mouth of the Mississippi, but mainly collected on the St. Lawrence, betweeen Quebec and Montreal. The remote situation of their settlements, separated from the English by uninhabited forests and unexplored mountains, the very dispersion of their force over so vast a space, gave the French a certain security, while the whole western frontier of the English, from Maine to Georgia, lay exposed to attack by the Indian tribes, disgusted by constant encroachments on their hunting-grounds, and ripe and ready for a troublesome and cruel warfare. There were kept in Canada, for the defense of the province, thirty-three companies of regular troops, of about fifty men each.

The loud complaints of the English embassador at Paris were met by protestations esteemed unmeaning or insincere. A struggle was evidently impending in America, greater than had yet been known. In anticipation of approaching hostilities, a general order gave to all officers commissioned by the king or the commander-in-chief, precedence over such as had only colonial commissions—an order which created great disgust and occasioned much trouble in America. New clauses introduced into the annnal Mutiny Act, subjected the colonial soldiers, when acting in conjunction with regular troops, to the rigid rules of the regular service, and required the colonial Assemblies to provide quarters and certain enumerated supplies for the regular troops within their jurisdiction. General Braddock, appointed commander-in-chief, was dispatched to the Chesapeake with two British regiments. Two regiments of a thousand men each, to be paid by the crown, one Pepperell's, the other Shirley's, were ordered to be raised and officered in New England. The colonies were also to be called upon for their respective quotas of colonial levies. As the Quaker Legislature of Pennsylvania had scruples about raising troops, three thousand men were to be enlisted in that province by authority of the crown.

At Alexandria, on the Potomac, Braddock met a convention of colonial governors, with whom he settled the plan of the campaign. He undertook to march in person against Fort Du Quesne, and to expel the French from the Ohio. Shirley, lately promoted to the rank of major-general, was to march against Niagara. The capture of Crown Point, already planned by Shirley, and resolved upon by Massachusetts, was intrusted to Johnson, whose ascendency over the Six Nations had lately procured for him a royal appointment as general superintendent of Indian affairs, with the sole power of making treaties. There was already on foot a fourth expedition, concerted by Shirley and Lawrence, governor of Nova Scotia, for the capture of the French posts near the head of the Bay of Fundy, and the expulsion of the French from that province.

In anticipation of Braddock's arrival, application for troops had already been made by the several governors. Massachusetts responded with zeal, and a levy was ordered of three thousand two hundred men. The exportation of provisions, except to other British colonies, and any correspondence with the French were prohibited; but it required a pretty watchful eye to put a stop to this commerce. The treasurer was authorized to borrow £50,000, ($166,666,) on the credit of taxes to produce that sum within two years. This method of providing funds proved successful, and was adhered to during the war.

The Assembly of New York voted £45,000 in paper bills, for erecting fortifications and enlisting eight hundred men. They ordered barracks to be built; and though they made no appropriation for supplying the other articles required by the Mutiny Act, their unexpected promptitude and liberality were highly applauded by the Board of Trade. The New Jersey Assembly, beside providing for the subsistence of the king's troops, as the Mutiny Act required, ordered five hundred men to be raised, and to pay the expense, they raised £70,000 of new paper.

If the zeal and energy of the six northern colonies surpassed the expectations of the Board of Trade, the aid furnished by the more southern provinces was comparatively trifling. (1754.)

The Assembly of Maryland voted toward Braddock's expedition £10,000 in paper, to be redeemed out of fines and forfeitures. But the fines and forfeitures were claimed as a part of the personal revenue of the proprietary; the council non-concurred, and the appropriation thus fell to the ground.

After a hearing in England, the Virginia dispute about fees for land patents had been compromised, and, "because the times required harmony and confidence," Dinwiddie had been directed to restore Randolph to his former office of attorney-general. But feeling on this subject did not immediately subside, a dispute being still kept up about Randolph's payment as agent. The Assembly voted, however, £20,000 toward the support of the colonial levies; and, in anticipation of the taxes imposed to meet it, authorized the issue of treasury notes—the first paper money of Virginia.

As further aid toward "repelling the encroachments of the French," North Carolina voted £8,000. The government of that province had recently been given to Arthur Dobbs; and, thankful for the appointment of a ruler of "known abilities and good character"—for so the Assembly described him—they promised to "forget former contests." But the new governor, anxious to enhance his authority, soon became involved in disputes with the Assembly, whose speaker, Starkie, he stigmatized "as a Republican of puritanic humility, but unbounded ambition." Starkie was treasurer as well as speaker. He could lend money to the delegates; and his influence far exceeded that of a governor "who had not the power of rewarding his friends." (1755.)

A French squadron destined for America, was known to be fitting out at Brest, on board of which Dieskau presently embarked with four thousand troops. To intercept this squadron, Boscawen was sent with a British fleet to cruise on the banks of Newfoundland. Suspecting some such scheme, most of the French ships entered the Gulf of St. Lawrence by the Straits of Belle Isle, whence they proceeded to Quebec. Others passing Boscawen in the fog, landed a thousand men at

Louisburg. Two only of the French transports, with eight companies on board, fell into the hands of the English.

In consequence of this attack, the French embassador was recalled from London. The English ministry retorted by issuing letters of marque and reprisal, under which a great number of valuable merchant vessels and not less than seven thousand French seamen were seized. The French complained loudly as well of these aggressions as of Washington's attack on Jumonville. The English, in excuse, charged the French with invading Virginia and Nova Scotia. Hostilities were already flagrant, but neither party issued as yet a declaration of war.

While Boscawen was still cruising off Newfoundland, watching for the French fleet, three thousand men embarked at Boston for the Bay of Fundy. These troops, forming a regiment of two battalions, were led by John Winslow, a great grand-son of Edward Winslow, one of the patriarchs of Plymouth colony, and grandson of the commander of the New England forces at the great swamp fight in Philip's war; himself, during the previous war, a captain in Vernon's West India expedition. It was principally through his popularity and influence that the enlistments had been procured. He was a major-general in the Massachusetts militia, but was persuaded on this occasion to accept a commission as lieutenant-colonel. Arrived at Chignecto, at the head of the bay, Winslow's forces were joined by Colonel Moncton, with three hundred British regulars, the garrison of the British posts in that neighborhood, to whom also, Shirley had given a Massachusetts commission, with a rank higher than Winslow's. Under his command, they marched against the French forts recently established on the two shores of the isthmus at Beau Sejour and Gaspareau. Taken by surprise, these forts made but a trifling resistance. The fort at the mouth of the St. John's, on the approach of an English detachment, was abandoned and burned. The expulsion of the French troops from the Bay of Fundy had been accomplished without difficulty. But what was to be done with the French colonists, amounting now to some twelve or fifteen thousand, settled principally in three detached bodies about Beau Bassin, "the beautiful basin" of Chignecto, on the no less beautiful basin of Minas—the two divisions into which the upper Bay of Fundy divides—and on the fertile banks of the basin or river of Annapolis?

It was thirty years since Nova Scotia had become a British province; but these settlers, who had more than doubled their number in the interval, continued still French, not in language, religion and manners only, but also in attachments, receiving their priests from Canada, and always ready to favor any movement that tended to restore them to their ancient allegiance. By the terms granted when the British authorities took possession of the province, they were excused from any obligation to bear arms against France, and were thence known as "French neutrals." But they did not act up even to that character. Three hundred of their young men had been taken in arms at the surrender of Beau Sejour, and one of their priests had been actively employed as a French agent. To curb these hostile people would require several expensive garrisons. If ordered to quit the country, and allowed to go where they pleased, they would retire to Canada and Cape Breton, and strengthen the enemy there. To devise some scheme adequate to this emergency, Lawrence, lieutenant-governor of Nova Scotia, consulted with Boscawen and Mostyn, commanders of the British fleet, which had just arrived on the coast after its cruise to intercept Dieskau. These military men took counsel with Belcher, chief justice of the province, a son of the former governor of Massachusetts. The result was, notwithstanding an express provision in the capitulation of Beau Sejour that the neighboring inhabitants should not be disturbed, a plan for treacherously kidnapping the Acadiens, and transporting them to the various British provinces. The capitulation of Beau Sejour did not apply to the settlements of Minas and Annapolis; but the people there strenuously denied any complicity with the French invaders, which seems, indeed, in their case, to have been rather suspected than proved. (1755.)

The Acadiens had preserved all the gay simplicity of ancient French rural manners. Never was there a people more attached to their homes, or who had more reasons for being so. They lived in rustic plenty, surrounded by herds of cattle and sheep, and drawing abundant crops from the rich levels, fine sediment deposited by the tides on the borders of the basins, and which their industry had diked in from the sea. Knowing how much was to be dreaded from despair, the ruthless design against them was kept a profound secret. Assembled under various false pretenses at their parish churches, they were surrounded with troops, made prisoners, and hurried on board the ships assigned for their transportation! Wives separated from their husbands in the confusion of embarking, and children from their parents, were carried off to distant colonies, never again to see each other! Their lands, crops, cattle, everything except household furniture, which they could not carry away, and money, of which they had little or none, were declared forfeit to the crown; and, to insure the starvation of such as fled to the woods, and so to compel their surrender, the growing crops were destroyed, and the barns and houses burned, with all their contents!

More than a thousand of these unfortunate exiles, carried to Massachusetts, long remained a burden on the public, too broken-hearted and disconsolate to do much for themselves. Their misery excited pity, in spite of the angry feeling created by protracted hostilities; but such was still, in New England, the horror of Popery, that they were not allowed to console themselves by the celebration of the mass.

To every British North American colony was sent a quota of these miserable people, a burden on the public charity, for which the Assemblies were called on to provide. It was an object to get rid of them as speedily as possible. Some made their way to France, others to Canada, St. Domingo, and Louisiana, the expenses of their transport being paid in many instances by the colonial Assemblies. To such of these fugitives as escaped to Louisiana, lands were assigned in that district, above New Orleans, still known as the Acadien coast. The four hundred sent to Georgia, built rude boats, and coasted northward, hoping to reach the Bay of Fundy. Few, however, were so lucky as to regain a French home and the ministrations of the Catholic faith. The greater part, spiritless, careless, and helpless, died in exile, victims of disappointment and despair. Such was the result of that rivalry of a century and a half between the English of New England and the French of Acadie. Such is religious and national antipathy. May we not hope that hatreds so atrocious are fast dying out?

The authors of this cruel scheme had been confirmed in their purpose by a repulse which the English had, meanwhile, sustained in the attempt to drive the French from the Ohio. Braddock's regulars had been landed at Alexandria, a small town lately sprung up near the head of ship navigation on the Potomac. But great difficulties were encountered in obtaining provisions and means of transportation. The contractors perpetually failed in their engagements, and Braddock and his quarter-master, both men of violent tempers, gave vent, with very little reserve, to expressions of disgust and contempt for the colonists. With great difficulty the troops reached Cumberland, where they came to a full stop. Franklin, in his character of deputy postmaster, having visited the camp to arrange a post communication with Philadelphia, by assuming responsibilities on his own credit, which left him, in the end, a considerable loser, obtained wagons and horses among the Pennsylvania farmers, which enabled the army once more to move forward. The regulars had been joined by the detached companies of the Virginia levies, and the whole force now amounted to twenty-two hundred men. Washington had been invited by Braddock to attend him as an aid-de-camp.

From Cumberland to Redstone was a distance of fifty miles,, over several steep and rough ridges of the Alleghany Mountains. Only Indian paths yet traversed this difficult and uninhabited country, through which the troops had to cut a road for the wagons and artillery. Vexed at this delay, Braddock left Colonel Dunbar to bring up the heavy baggage, and pushed on in advance, at the head of thirteen hundred picked men. He was warned of the danger to which the nature of the country and the character of the enemy exposed him, and was advised to place the provincials in his front, to scour the woods. But he held both the enemy and the provincials in too much contempt to give attention to this advice. He had gained forty miles on Dunbar, and was now within five miles of Fort Du Quesne, when, about noon, just after fording the Monongahela a second time, his van, while ascending the rising bank of the river, was fired upon by an invisible enemy. The assailants, some two hundred French and six hundred Indians, with only thirteen French officers, and none above the rank of captain, were posted in an open wood, in some shallow undulations just deep enough to conceal them as they lay flat on the ground among the high grass. Braddock's main body hastened up with the artillery, but the unseen enemy continued to pour in a deadly fire; and the British troops, seized with sudden panic, were thrown at once into hopeless confusion. In vain the general exerted himself to restore order. He had five horses shot under him, and soon fell mortally wounded. Not less than sixty officers, chosen marks for the enemy's bullets, were killed or disabled; among the latter, Horatio Gates, captain of one of the independent companies, and twenty years afterward a general in the revolutionary army. The provincials, acquainted with the Indian method of fighting, alone made any effectual resistance. Washington, still weak from the effects of a recent fever, put himself at their head. They were the last to leave the field, and partially covered the flight of the discomfited regulars. Delay was thus given for bringing off the wounded, but the baggage and artillery were abandoned to the enemy. The English lost, in killed and disabled, some seven hundred men, or more than half their force engaged. The loss of the French and Indians did not exceed sixty. The victors, intent on the spoils of the field, pursued only a few miles, but the flying troops did not rally till they reached the camp of Dunbar, who abandoned the expedition, and, having destroyed all the stores not needed for immediate use, retired first to Cumberland and then to Philadelphia.

Shirley meanwhile, with his own and Pepperell's regiment, lately enlisted in New England, and some irrregulars and Indians drawn from New York, was on the march from Albany to Oswego, where he proposed to embark for Niagara. He had rivers to clear, boats to build, roads to cut, and provisions and munitions to transport through the wilderness. The army reached Oswego at last, but seriously disabled by sickness, and discouraged by the news of Braddock's defeat, whose death raised Shirley to the command-in-chief, in which he was presently confirmed by an appointment from England. Two strong forts were built at Oswego, vessels were prepared, and great preparations were made for proceeding against Niagara.

The Assembly of New York had already voted £8000 toward the enlistment, in Connecticut, of two thousand additional men, for the Niagara and Crown Point expeditions. After hearing of Braddock's defeat, they raised four hundred men of their own, in addition to the eight hundred already in the field. Delancey, though presently superceded in the government by Sir Charles Hardy, a Naval officer, still retained a principal influence in the administration.

The troops destined for the Crown Point expedition, some six thousand men, drawn from New England, New Jersey, and New York, advancing under General Lyman, of Connecticut, to the head of boat navigation on the Hudson, built there Fort Lyman, called afterward Fort Edward. Johnson joined them with the stores and artillery, assumed the command, and advanced to Lake George. Dieskau, meanwhile, had ascended Lake Champlain with two thousand men from Montreal, had landed at South Bay, the southern extremity of that lake, and had pushed on toward Fort Lyman. When quite near it, dreading its artillery, or for some other cause, he suddenly changed his plan, and marched to attack Johnson. Informed of his approach, Johnson sent forward Colonel Williams with a thousand Massachusetts troops, and a body of Mohawk Indians under Hendrick, a famous chief. In a narrow and rugged defile, about three miles from the camp, this detachment encountered the whole of Dieskau's army. Williams and Hendrick were slain, and their force driven back in confusion. Williams had secured himself a better monument than any victory could give. While passing through Albany he had made his will, leaving certain property to found a free school for Western Massachusetts, since grown into "Williams' College."

Following up the defeated troops, Dieskau assaulted Johnson's camp. It was protected on both sides by impassable swamps, and in front by a breastwork of fallen trees. Some cannon just brought up from Fort Edward, opened an unexpected fire, and the assailants were presently driven back in confusion. Dieskau, mortally wounded, was taken prisoner. The remains of his army fled to Crown Point. The French loss was estimated at a thousand men, the English at three hundred.

A party of New Hampshire troops on their way from Fort Lyman, encountered the baggage of Dieskau's army, which they captured after overpowering the guard. These three actions, fought the same day, and known as the battle of Lake George, were proclaimed through the colonies as a great victory, for which Johnson was rewarded with the honors of knighthood, and a parliamentary grant of £5,000. As Johnson had been wounded early in the action, the Connecticut troops claimed the honor of the victory for General Lyman, second in command.

One of the Massachusetts regiments distinguished in this action was commanded by Timothy Ruggles, afterward president of the Stamp Act Congress. The personal history of Ruggles serves to illustrate the simple manner of those times. Son of a minister, he had been educated at Cambridge, had studied law, and commenced the practice of it in Plymouth and Barnstable, with good success. Marrying the widow of a rich inn-keeper, he added tavern-keeping to his business as a lawyer. When the war broke out, he entered into the military line, and being a man of energy and sense, he served with distinction for the next five years. Israel Putnam, afterward a revolutionary major-general, now a captain in one of the Connecticut regiments, had already distinguished himself as a partisan officer, in which capacity he served during the war.

Though re-enforced from Massachusetts, which colony, on hearing of Braddock's defeat, had voted two thousand additional troops, Johnson made no attempt on Crown Point. He even allowed the French to establish and fortify themselves at Ticonderoga. Under the superintendence of Gridley, who acted as engineer, Fort William Henry was built, near the late field of battle, at the head of Lake George. The New Englanders accused Johnson of incapacity; but he alleged the want of provisions and means of transportation sufficient to justify active operations.

After having made great preparations at Oswego, heavy rains delayed Shirley's embarkation; and finally, owing to the approach of winter and the scanty supply of provisions, the enterprise against Niagara was given over for the season. Shirley left seven hundred men in garrison at Oswego; but all the colonial levies, except six hundred men to garrison

Fort William Henry, and such troops as Massachusetts kept up at the eastward for frontier defense, were marched home and disbanded.

The frontiers of Pennsylvania, Maryland, and Virginia, uncovered by Dunbar's precipitate retreat, were exposed to war-parties of Indians in the French interest. The discontented Delawarès on the northern borders of Pennsylvania, and the Shawanese in the interior, availed themselves of this crisis to commence hostilities. Governor Morris called loudly for men and money to defend the frontiers. The inhabitants of Philadelphia, in an address to the Assembly, urged a liberal grant. Dropping their favorite paper money project, the Assembly voted a tax of £50,000, to be levied on real and personal estates, "not excepting those of the proprietaries"—a clause, as they well knew, as contrary as the paper money, to the governor's instructions. If that clause might be omitted, some gentlemen of Philadelphia, in the proprietary interest, offered to contribute £5,000, the estimated amount of the tax on the proprietary estates. But the Assembly wishing to improve this emergency to establish a precedent, dexterously evaded the offer; the governor stood out, and the bill fell to the ground. Dunbar's regulars advancing from Philadelphia toward the frontier, afforded a temporary protection.

To furnish funds for defending their frontiers, the Assembly of Virginia voted £40,000 in taxes, in anticipation of which a new batch of treasury notes was issued. To Washington, for his gallant behavior at Braddock's defeat, £300 were voted, with lesser gratuities to several of the officers, and £5 to each of the surviving Virginia privates who remained in the service. Among the officers thus distinguished were Captain Adam Stephen, and Surgeon Hector Craig, the one afterward a major-general, the other at the head of the medical department of the revolutionary army. The Virginia regiment was reorganized, and Washington again placed at its head, with Stephen for lieutenant-colonel, undertook the difficult task of repelling the Indians, whose ravages now extended as far as Winchester. The Assembly of Maryland granted £6,000 for the defense of the province, and an additional sum was raised by voluntary subscription. A body of militia presently took the field under Governor Sharpe.

A violent dispute arose between Sharpe and Dinwidie, as to the command of Fort Cumberland. The pretensions of Dagworthy, in the Maryland service, who had formerly borne a royal commission, and who claimed precedence on that account over all officers with merely colonial commissions, was another source of trouble ; and Washington presently found himself obliged to make a winter's visit to Boston, to obtain from Shirley definite orders on that point.

The Quakers were still a majority in the Pennsylvania Assembly, but they could no longer resist the loud cry to arms, raised in Philadelphia and re-echoed from the frontiers, occasioned by Indian inroads on the Juniata settlements. The proprietary party made every effort, and not without success, to stir up the public discontent. After a sharp struggle with the governor, in consideration of a voluntary contribution by the proprietaries of £5,000, the Assembly consented to levy a tax of £55,000, from which the proprietary estates were exempted. The expenditure of this money was specially intrusted to a joint committee of seven, of whom a majority were members of Assembly, which committee became the chief managers of the war now formally declared against the Delawares and Shawanese. Thus driven, for the first time, to open participation in war, some of the Quaker members resigned their seats in the Assembly. Others declined a re-election. The rule of the Quakers came to an end. But this change, contrary to the hopes and expectations of the proprietaries, did not reconcile the quarrel between them and the Assembly. That body insisted as strenuously as ever on their right to tax the proprietary estates.

Toward the close of the year, Shirley met a convention of provincial governors at New York, to arrange plans for the next campaign. Expeditions against Fort Du Quesne, Niagara, and Crown Point were agreed upon, for which twenty thousand men would be necessary. New York voted seventeen hundred men as her quota, and issued £40,000 in paper, to support them. But the New England colonies, exhausted by their late efforts, and disgusted by their ill-success, did not respond to the expectations of Shirley. Feebly supported in his own province, the commander-in-chief was fiercely assailed by Johnson and Delancey, who ascribed to his alleged want of military experience, the ill success of the late expeditions against Niagara and Crown Point, and whose intrigues presently procured his recall.

Acts were passed in Pennsylvania for enrolling a volunteer militia and for raising rangers by enlistment. Having been very active in procuring these enactments, Franklin undertook the military command of the frontier, with the rank of colonel, and, under his directions, along the base of the Kittaniny Mountains, from the Delaware to the Maryland line, a chain of forts and block-houses was erected, commanding the most important passes, and inclosing the greater part of the settlements. This volunteer militia, however, was far from satisfactory to the proprietary party, who sought by every means to obstruct it, and the act, at the request of the proprietaries, was presently set aside by a royal veto. On the other hand, some of the sturdier Quakers protested against a tax for war purposes, and advised a passive resistance to its collection. William Denny, a military officer, was sent out to supersede Morris, as deputy-governor. (1756.)

The proprietary of Maryland having relinquished his claim to the fines and forfeitures, the Assembly granted £40,000, principally in paper money. A provision that papists should pay double taxes toward the redemption of this paper, evinced the still existing force of sectarian hostility. The lands and manors of the proprietary were also included among the articles taxed. Fort Cumberland was too far in advance to be of any use, and a new fort, called Frederick, was built at that bend of the Potomac which approaches nearest the Pennsylvania line.

Fifteen hundred volunteers and drafted militia, commanded by Washington, and scattered in forts, afforded but an imperfect defense to the suffering inhabitants of the Virginia Valley, many of whom abandoned their farms. In apology for the small number of these forces, Dinwiddie wrote to the Board of Trade, "We dare not part with any of our white men to any distance, as we must have a watchful eye over our negro slaves." Dumas, the conqueror of Braddock, in command at Fort Du Quesne, and De Celeron at Detroit, were constantly stimulating the Indians. Du Quesne having returned to the marine service, the Marquis de Vaudreuil de

Cavagnal had been appointed to succeed him as governor of New France.

The French had all along offered to treat; but they demanded, as a preliminary, the restoration of the merchant ships seized by the English—an act which they complained of as piratical. When this was refused, they commissioned privateers, and threatened to invade England with a fleet and army collected at Brest. To guard against this threatened invasion, a body of Hessian and Hanoverian troops was received into England. To excite the colonists to fresh efforts, £115,000 were voted as a reimbursement to the provinces concerned in Dieskau's defeat. Provision was also made for enlisting a royal American regiment, to be composed of four battalions of a thousand men each. A clause, afterward somewhat modified, authorizing the appointment of seventy officers in this regiment, from among the foreign Protestants settled and naturalized in America, gave great offense in the colonies, as did another clause, for the enlistment of indented servants, upon a compensation to be paid to their masters out of the colony funds. All hopes of reconciliation being now over, England formally declared war against France, to which the French court presently responded.

Vigorous measures were, meanwhile, in progress for the supply and re-enforcement of Oswego. Bradstreet, of New York, appointed commissary-general, employed in this service forty companies of boatmen, each of fifty men. Under him, Philip Schuyler took his first lessons in the art of war. William Alexander, another native of New York, known afterward in the revolutionary armies as Lord Sterling, acted as Shirley's military secretary. By promises of parliamentary reimbursements, and the advance to Massachusetts of £30,000 out of the king's money, in his hands, Shirley assembled at Albany seven thousand provincials, chiefly of New England, under the command of General Winslow. The remains of Braddock's regiments, ordered on the same service, were presently joined by two new regiments from England, under General Abercrombie, who outranked and superseded Shirley. But the Earl of Loudon, selected by the British war office as commander-in-chief, being daily expected, Abercrombie declined the responsibility of any forward movement.

Loudon gave an early specimen of his habitual procrastination, by not arriving till late in the summer. (July 27, 1756.) It was then determined to proceed with the bulk of the army against Ticonderoga and Crown Point, while one of the regular regiments marched under General Webb, to re-enforce Oswego—a movement made to late.

While the English army lay idle at Albany, short of provisions, and suffering from the small-pox, Montcalm, Dieskau's successor, lately arrived from France with a re-enforcement of troops, had ascended the St. Lawrence, had crossed Lake Ontario, had landed near Oswego with a force of five thousand men, regulars, Canadian militia and Indians, and had laid siege to the forts. One of them was abandoned as untenable. Colonel Mercer, the commanding officer, was killed. The dispirited troops, after a short bombardment, surrendered as prisoners of war. Upward of a thousand men, a hundred and thirty-five pieces of artillery, a great quantity of stores and provisions, and a fleet of boats and small vessels, built the year before for the Niagara expedition, fell into the hands of Montcalm.

To please the Six Nations, who had never been well satisfied at the existence of this post in the center of their territory, the French commander, with great policy, destroyed the forts, and by this concession induced the Indians to take a position of neutrality. The fall of Oswego occasioned almost as much alarm as the defeat of Braddock the year before. The British troops, on the march under Webb, fell back with terror and precipitation to Albany. Orders were sent to give over the march on Ticonderoga, and to devote the efforts of that army to strengthen Forts Edward and William Henry.

As the season advanced and their term of service expired, the provincials were disbanded. The loss by sickness had been very severe, and many died after their return. The regulars, except small garrisons at Forts Edward and William Henry, went into winter quarters at New York and Albany—not, however, till they had first been employed in keeping the peace between Massachusetts and New York. As the settlements approached each other, the boundary dispute between those two provinces had reached the extremity of riot and bloodshed. Loudon's demand at New York for gratuitous quarters for his officers involved him in a violent quarrel with the citizens, whom he frightened, at last, into obedience.

More money being absolutely necessary for the defense of the frontiers, by a sort of compromise between the governor and the Assembly of Pennsylvania, £30,000 were voted, to be issued in paper, and redeemed by a ten years' continuance of the lately-expired excise, to be appropriated toward the support of twenty-five companies of rangers. Franklin having retired from the military service, John Armstrong—afterward a general in the revolutionary army—was commissioned as colonel, and soon distinguished himself by a successful expedition against a hostile Indian town on the Alleghany. Charles Mercer, a Scotch physician—afterward also a revolutionary general—served in the same expedition as captain. The hostile Indians, thus attacked in their own villages, retired further to the west; yet scalping parties occasionally penetrated within thirty miles of Philadelphia. Large premiums were offered by the Assembly for Indian prisoners and Indian scalps. The feeling on the frontier against the Indians was very bitter. The Moravian missionaries, some of whose Indian converts had been seduced to join the hostile parties, became objects of suspicion. There were those, however, among the Quakers, still true to their pacific principles, who insisted, and not entirely without reason, that the Delawares, so long friendly to Pennsylvania, had not been driven into hostilities except by wrongs and intrusions that ought to be redressed. They formed an association, contributed money, and opened a communication with the Indians for the purpose of bringing about a peace. (1756.) Two conferences, not altogether unsuccessful, were held with this intent at Easton. Sir William Johnson complained, indeed, that the Quakers had intruded upon his office of Indian agent and sole negotiator. Others alleged that by this interference claims were suggested which, otherwise, the Indians never would have thought of. It was considered a great innovation upon the usual course of Indian treaties when Tedyuscung, the Delaware chief, in the second conference at Easton, had for his secretary, Charles Thompson, master of the Quaker academy at Philadelphia, afterward secretary to the Continental Congress. In spite of obloquy heaped upon them, in spite of accusations of partiality to the Indians and treachery to the white race, the Quakers persevered; and a third treaty, held the next year at Lancaster, at which delegates from the Six Nations were also present, afforded a partial relief to the frontier of Pennsylvania.

The Carolinas, thus far, had escaped the ravages of war; but serious apprehensions began to be felt lest the Cherokees might be seduced from their allegiance. Though very ill armed, they could muster three or four thousand warriors. In a treaty held with them early in the war, Governor Glen had obtained an extensive cession in the middle and upper part of South Carolina; and presently, in accordance, as it is said, with long-repeated solicitations on the part of the Indians, he built Fort Prince George, on one of the head streams of the Savannah, within gunshot of Kee-o-wee, the principal village of the Lower Cherokees. Another fort, in the country of the Upper Cherokees, on the head waters of the Tennessee River, near the south-western boundary of Virginia, was erected by a party from that province, and named Fort Loudon, after the commander-in-chief, who had also a commission as governor of Virginia.

In consequence of a violent dispute with the Assembly, in which Glen and his council had involved themselves, no military supplies had hitherto been granted by South Carolina. This quarrel abated on the arrival of a new governor, William H. Littleton, a cadet of the noble family of that name. He obtained a grant of £4000 toward enlisting two companies, to which a third was presently added, as garrisons for the forts. But the slave population of South Carolina was still more preponderant than in Virginia. It was no easy matter to enlist men, and the province presently received as welcome guests half a battalion of the Royal Americans, with three hundred colonial levies from North Carolina, and others from Virginia. (1757.)

The plan for the next campaign, proposed by Loudon at the annual military council, held this year at Boston, was limited to the defense of the frontiers and an expedition against Louisburg. To serve as garrisons for Forts William Henry and Edward, Loudon called on New England for four thousand, and on New York and New Jersey for two thousand men. Governor Hardy being appointed to a naval command, Lieutenant-governor Delancey reassumed the administration of New York. The Assembly of New Jersey took advantage of this occasion to put out a new issue of paper money. New Jersey, as well as Pennsylvania, suffered from the incursions of the Delawares, against whom it continued necessary to guard.

To aid in the defense of Pennsylvania, Colonel Stanwix was stationed in the interior, with five companies of the Royal Americans; but this was only granted on condition that two hundred recruits should be enlisted for that regiment, to serve in South Carolina. The Pennsylvania Assembly, again yielding, had voted a levy of £100,000, without insisting on their claim to tax the proprietary estates. But they protested that they did it through compulsion, and they sent Franklin as their agent to England to urge their complaints. The charter authorized the proprietaries, their deputies, and lieutenants, to make laws "according to their best discretion," by and with the advice and consent of the freemen. The Assembly took the ground that the proprietary instructions to the deputy governors, being a restraint upon their discretion, were therefore illegal and void.

Washington, with the Virginia levies, continued to watch the frontiers of that province. But no scheme of defense could answer much purpose, so long as the French held Fort Du Quesne. The defense of the frontiers thus provided for, Loudon sailed from New York with six thousand regulars, including late re-inforcements from England. At Halifax he was joined by the English fleet of eleven sail of the line, under Admiral Holborne, with six thousand additional soldiers on board. But Louisburg was discovered to have a larger garrison than had been supposed; and while Loudon lingered with characteristic indecision, seventeen French ships of the line anchored in the harbor, and made attack wholly out of the question. Loudon then re-embarked his forces and returned to New York.

Not only had Shirley lost his military command; the machinations of his enemies had deprived him of his government also. It was given to Thomas Pownall, whose brother was secretary to the Board of Trade. Pownall had first come to America with the unfortunate Sir Danvers Osborne. Holding a commission as lieutenant governor of New Jersey, he had been present at the Albany Congress, and afterward at the military convention at Alexandria. Though he had received some favors from Shirley, he joined the party against him, and, having gone to England, had obtained there the government of Massachusetts. Pownall had hardly reached the province, the administration of which for four months past had been in the hands of the council, by the death of Lieutenant-governor Phipps, when an express arrived from Fort Edward with alarming news of a French invasion.

The British army drawn aside for the futile attack on Louisburg, Montcalm, with eight thousand men, including the garrisons of Crown Point and Ticonderoga, ascended Lake George, landed at its southern extremity, and laid siege to Fort William Henry. Colonel Monroe, the English officer in command, had a garrison of two thousand men. General Webb lay at Fort Edward, only fourteen miles distant, with four thousand troops. Montcalm pressed the attack with vigor. No movement was made from Fort Edward for Monroe's relief. His ammunition was exhausted; and, after a six days' siege, he found himself obliged to capitulate. The garrison were to march out with the honors of war, and were to be protected, with their baggage, as far as Fort Edward. Montcalm's Indian allies, dissatisfied with these terms, and greedy for plunder, fell upon the retreating and disarmed troops. Monroe, with the greater part of the men, fell back to the French camp to demand protection. About six hundred fled into the woods, and the first who reached Fort Edward reported the massacre of the others. Some few were killed or never heard of; the rest came in one after another, many having lost their way and suffered extreme hardships. Frye, the commander of the Massachusetts forces, after wandering about some days, reached Fort Edward with no clothes but his shirt.

The fall of Fort William Henry occasioned even greater alarm than the loss of Oswego the year before. Pownall appointed Sir William Pepperell lieutenant general of Massachusetts. Orders were issued for calling out the militia, and twenty thousand men were assembled in arms. Satisfied with having caused so much terror and expense, Montcalm, without attempting any thing further, retired again to Canada.

The arrival of Pownall made a considerable change in the politics of Massachusetts. By taking Otis, of Barnstable, speaker of the House, and other opponents of Shirley, into favor, according to Hutchinson, who was presently appointed lieutenant governor, he disgusted the old friends of government, and greatly weakened the government party. Otis was promised a seat on the bench of the Supreme Court; his son, a young lawyer of shining abilities, was appointed advocate of the Admiralty. Though Pownall's habits were rather freer than suited the New England standard, these concessions to the opposition, his frank manners, and liberal political views, served to make him very popular.

On the death of the aged Belcher, Pownall went to New Jersey to assume authority as lieutenant governor. But he found it impracticable to govern both provinces at the same time. The government of New Jersey, after remaining some months in the hands of the president and council, was transferred to Francis Bernard, a practitioner in the English ecclesiastical courts.

The Massachusetts General Court had provided barracks at the castle, for such British troops as might be sent to the province. But some officers on the recruiting service, finding the distance inconvenient, demanded to be quartered in the town. They insisted on the provisions of the Mutiny Act; but the magistrates to whom they applied denied that act to be in force in the colonies. Loudon warmly espoused the cause of his officers; he declared "that in time of war the rules and customs of war must govern," and threatened to send troops to Boston to enforce the demand, if not granted within forty-eight hours. To avoid this extremity, the General Court passed a law of their own, enacting some of the principal provisions of the Mutiny Act; and Loudon, through Pownall's persuasions, reluctantly consented to accept this partial concession. The General Court did not deny the power of Parliament to quarter troops in America. Their ground was, that the act, in its terms, did not extend to the colonies. A similar dispute occurred in South Carolina, where great difficulty was encountered in finding winter quarters for the Royal Americans.

The first royal governor of Georgia, and his secretary, William Little, having involved themselves in a violent controversy with the Assembly, Reynolds had been superseded by Henry Ellis, a protégé of the Earl of Halifax, the head of an expedition, some nine years before, for the discovery of a northwest passage. The population of Georgia now amounted to six thousand. On the breaking out of the war, Reynolds had enlisted twenty rangers, but the quarrel with the Assembly prevented any provision for paying them. After Ellis's arrival, the Assembly voted money for erecting log forts at Savannah, Augusta, Ogeechee, Midway, and New Inverness. Ellis applied himself to the preservation of a good understanding with the neighboring Creeks and the Spanish governor of Florida. The rangers were taken into the king's pay, and Ellis obtained from Colonel Bouquet, commanding in South Carolina, a hundred provincial troops of Virginia, to be quartered in Savannah. A solemn council was presently held with the Creeks, and a new treaty of peace entered into with that powerful confederacy. A long dispute had been pending, in which the Creeks took a deep interest, growing out of the claims of Mary, the Indian interpreter, of whose services Oglethorpe had availed himself on his first arrival in Savannah. After the death of her first husband, she had married a second white man, and upon his death, a third—no less a person than Thomas Bosomworth, who had first been Oglethorpe's agent for Indian affairs, but afterward had gone to England, had obtained holy orders, and returned to Georgia as the successor of the Wesleys and Whitfield. The Creeks had made a conveyance to Mary, of their reservation of the islands on the coast, and the tract just above Savannah. She also claimed a large amount as arrears of her salary, as colonial interpreter. After a twelve years' controversy, which at times had threatened an Indian war, the matter was finally settled by a compromise, securing to Mary and her husband the title to the island of St. Catharine's and the payment of £2000 arrears, out of the sales of the other reserved lands. Another thing accomplished by Ellis was the division of the colony into eight parishes, and the establishment of the Church of England by law, with a salary of £25 to each parish minister. (1658.)

To the war in America, and the simultaneous contest between the English and French East India Companies on the other side of the globe, had been added a military struggle the greatest the world had yet seen, carried on in the heart of Europe. France and Austria, forgetting their ancient rivalries, and supported by Russia and most of the Germanic States, had united against Prussia and Hanover. The Hanoverian army had submitted to the disgraceful capitulation of Closter-Seven; that principality had been occupied by the French; and it required all the energy and military genius of Frederic of Prussia, to save him from a similar fate.

In America, after three campaigns, and extraordinary efforts on the part of the English, the French still held possession of almost all the territory in dispute. They had been expelled, indeed, from the Bay of Fundy; but Louisburg, commanding the entrance of the St. Lawrence, Crown Point and Ticonderoga on Lake Champlain, Frontenac and Niagara on Lake Ontario, Presque Isle on Lake Erie, and the chain of posts thence to the head of the Ohio, were still in their hands. They had expelled the English from their ancient post of Oswego, had driven them from Lake George, and had compelled the Six Nations to a treaty of neutrality. A devastating Indian war was raging along the whole northwestern frontier of the British colonies. A line from the mouth of the Kennebec, across the Merrimac and Connecticut to Fort Edward on the Hudson, and thence across the Mohawk, the Delaware, and the Susquehanna, to Fort Frederic on the Potomac, marked the exterior limit of the settlements; but Indian scalping parties penetrated into the very center of Massachusetts, approached within a short distance of Philadelphia, and kept Maryland and Virginia in constant alarm.

CHAPTER XXX.

Hildreth's account of the Progress and Conclusion of the Fourth Intercolonial War—Accession of George III—The English masters of the continent, north of the Gulf of Mexico, and east of the Mississippi.

WILLIAM PITT,' afterward Earl of Chatham, took adroit advantage of the popular discontent at the ill success of the war, to force himself to a chief seat in the British cabinet—a station which he owed more to his energy and eloquence than to court favor, or to the influence of family or party connections, hitherto, in England, the chief avenues to power. Leaving to Newcastle, who still acted as nominal head of the ministry, the details of the domestic administration, Pitt, as secretary of state, with the cipher, Holderness, as his colleague in that department, assumed to himself the control of foreign and colonial affairs, and the entire management of the war. (1757.)

Determined on a vigorous campaign in America, he addressed a circular to the colonies, in which he called for twenty thousand men, and as many more as could be furnished. The crown would provide arms, ammunition, tents, and provisions; the colonies were to raise, clothe, and pay the levies; but for all these expenses, Pitt promised a parliamentary reimbursement—a promise which acted like magic. Massachusetts voted seven thousand men, beside six hundred maintained for frontier defense. To fill up this quota, soldiers were drafted from the militia and obliged to serve. The advances of Massachusetts during the year, were not less than a million of dollars. Individual Boston merchants paid taxes to the amount of $2,000. The tax on real estate amounted to two-thirds the income. The insolvencies occasioned by the pressure of the war, gave rise to a bankrupt act, but this was disallowed in England. Connecticut voted five thousand men. New Hampshire and Rhode Island furnished each a regiment of five hundred men. The New York quota of one thousand seven hundred men was raised to two thousand six hundred and eighty. The New Jersey regiment was enlarged to a thousand. The Assembly of Pennsylvania appropriated £100,000 toward bringing two thousand seven hundred men into the field. Virginia raised two thousand men. (1758.)

To co-operate with these colonial levies, the Royal Americans were recalled from Carolina. Large re-enforcements of regulars were also sent from England, made disposable by a plan which Pitt had adopted for intrusting the local defense of Great Britain, to an organized and active body of militia. By means of these various arrangements, Abercrombie, appointed commander-in-chief, found fifty thousand men at his disposal—a greater number than the whole male population of New France. Of this army, twenty-two thousand were regulars, including the Royal Americans; the rest were provincials. The total number of the inhabitants of Canada able to bear arms, did not exceed twenty thousand; the regular troops were from four to five thousand. As the people had been so constantly called off to bear arms, cultivation had been neglected, and Canada suffered almost a famine.

Shirley's schemes of conquest were now renewed. Louisburg, Ticonderoga, and Fort Du Quesne were all to be struck at once. The first blow fell on Louisburg. Boscawen appeared before that fortress with thirty-eight ships of war, convoying from Halifax an army of fourteen thousand men, chiefly regulars, under General Amherst, but including, also, a strong detachment of New England troops. Louisburg was held by a garrison of three thousand men; eleven ships of war lay in the harbor. But the works were too much out of repair to withstand the operations of a regular siege; and the garrison, after suffering severe loss, found themselves obliged to capitulate. This capitulation included not Louisburg only, but the islands of Cape Breton, St. John's, (now Prince Edward's,) and their dependencies. The garrison became prisoners of war; the inhabitants, many of them refugees from Acadie, were shipped to France. Such was the end of the French attempts at colonization, in the Gulf of St. Lawrence, which now passed into exclusive English occupation. Amherst sailed with his army for Boston, and thence marched to the western frontier.

While the siege of Louisburg was going on, Abercrombie, with sixteen thousand men, embarked at Fort William Henry in flat boats prepared for the purpose, and, passing down Lake George, landed near its outlet. The van, advancing in some confusion through the woods, encountered a French scouting party, which had also lost its way, and a skirmish ensued, in which fell Lord Howe, a young officer who had made himself very popular with the provincials, and to whose memory, Massachusetts erected a monument in Westminster Abbey.

Ticonderoga was held by some two thousand French soldiers. As reinforcements were said to be approaching, Abercrombie, without waiting for his artillery, rashly ordered an assault. The rear and sides of the fort were covered by water, and the front by a morass. The storming party were ordered to rush swiftly through the enemy's fire, reserving their own till they had passed the breastwork. But that breastwork was nine feet high, much stronger than was expected, and guarded, in addition, by trees felled, with their branches sharpened, and pointing outward like so many lances against the assailants. After a four hours' struggle, and the loss in killed and wounded of two thousand men, Abercrombie abandoned the attack, and the next day made a precipitate and disorderly retreat to Fort William Henry. Among the wounded was Charles Lee, then a captain in the British service, afterward first major-general of the revolutionary army. In consequence of this defeat, Abercrombie was superseded, and the command-in-chief given to Amherst.

Though no further attempt was made on Ticonderoga, Abercrombie's forces were not wholly idle. With a detachment of three thousand men, chiefly provincials of New York and New England, Bradstreet marched to Oswego, embarked there in vessels already provided, and, having ascended the lake, landed at Fort Frontenac. That place was untenable. The feeble garrison, taken entirely by surprise, speedily surrendered. Nine armed vessels were captured; and the fort, with a large store of provisions, was destroyed. Bradstreet's loss by the enemy was inconsiderable; but not less than five hundred men perished by sickness. These troops, on their return, assisted in building Fort Stanwix, intermediate between Oswego and Albany, on the site now occupied by the flourishing village of Rome. Among the officers under Bradstreet were Woodhull, who fell nineteen years afterward on Long Island, and Van Schaick, afterward a colonel in the New York revolutionary line.

The expedition against Fort Du Quesne had been committed to General Forbes, with an army of seven thousand men, including the Pennsylvania and Virginia levies, the Royal Americans recalled from South Carolina, and an auxiliary force of Cherokee Indians. The Virginia troops were concentrated at Cumberland, and those of Pennsylvania at Raystown, on the south branch of the Juniata. Washington advised to march from Cumberland, along the road cut by Braddock's army; but, under the advice of some Pennsylvania land speculators, Forbes ordered a new road to be opened from Raystown. With a division of two thousand five hundred men, Bouquet, who commanded the advance, presently reached Loyal Hanna, on the Kiskiminitas, the south branch of the Alleghany. Major Grant, with eight hundred men, sent forward from Loyal Hanna to reconnoiter, was surprised and driven back, with the loss of three hundred men, being himself taken prisoner. The enemy presently attacked Bouquet in his camp, but were repulsed by the artillery. The obstacles along the new route proved very serious; and the Virginia Assembly, in a state of discouragement, resolved to withdraw a part of their troops. Forbes at last joined Bouquet with the main body and the heavy baggage. But the army, weakened by desertion and dispirited by sickness, was still fifty miles from Fort Du Quesne, and separated from it by an immense forest, without a road. Winter also was close at hand. A council of war advised the abandonment of the enterprise; but, before any retrograde motion was made, three prisoners, accidentally taken, revealed the feebleness of the enemy. The blow struck by Bradstreet at Fort Frontenac had been felt on the Ohio in the failure of expected supplies, and the French, in consequence, had been deserted by the greater part of their Indian allies. Inspired

22

with fresh ardor, and leaving baggage and artillery behind, the troops, in spite of obstacles, pushed forward, at a rate, however, of less than ten miles a day. The day before they reached the fort, the French garrison, reduced to less than five hundred men, set fire to the works, and retired down the river. A detachment of four hundred and fifty men was left to hold this important post, for the possession of which the war had commenced, and which was now named Fort Pitt by the captors. The rest of the army hastened to return, before the setting in of winter. Fruits of this conquest were speedily realized in the inclination of the neighboring Indians for peace. Virginia and Maryland were now relieved from Indian incursions. Already a treaty had been held at Easton, with the Six Nations and their dependent tribes, the Delawares and others, by which all existing difficulties had been finally settled, and peace once more restored to the frontiers of Pennsylvania.

Only the Eastern Indians still remained hostile. To hold them in check, and to cut off their communication with Canada, Fort Pownall was presently built on the Penobscot, the first permanent English occupation of that region.

The perseverance of the Pennsylvania Assembly triumphed at last. Tired of struggling on unpaid—for they resolutely refused to vote him any salary unless he would come to their terms—Governor Denny consented to a tax act in which the proprietary estates were included. The Assembly had indemnified him against the forfeiture of the bond by which he had bound himself to obey his instructions, and they rewarded this and other compliances by liberal grants of salary. But this violation of his instructions very soon cost Denny his office. (1759.)

Seconded by an eager Parliament, Pitt resolved to follow up the successes of the late campaign by an attack on Canada—an intention communicated, under an oath of secrecy, to the colonial Assemblies. Stimulated by the prompt reimbursement of their last year's expenses to the amount of near a million of dollars, the Assemblies acted with promptitude and energy. With the opening of the spring, twenty thousand colonial soldiers were again in the field, and to enable the commissariat department, which found it difficult to sell bills on the British treasury, to provide provisions for the troops, the Assemblies of New York and Pennsylvania advanced a large sum in paper money.

The plan now adopted for the conquest of Canada, was not materially different from that which Phipps and Warren had successively failed to execute. Amherst advanced by way of Lake Champlain with twelve thousand regulars and provincials; Wolfe, a young general who had distinguished himself at the siege of Louisburg, having sailed early in the spring from England, escorted by a powerful fleet, made his appearance in the St. Lawrence with an army of eight thousand regular troops, in three brigades, commanded by Moncton, Townshend, and Murray. The danger of Quebec caused the withdrawal of the garrisons of Ticonderoga and Crown Point, and both these places soon, without any serious struggle, passed into Amherst's hands.

According to the scheme of operations, Amherst should have proceeded down Lake Champlain to join Wolfe before Quebec, or, at least, to effect a diversion by attacking Montreal; but the want of vessels rendered this movement impossible. With Amherst was a body of New Hampshire Rangers, under Major Rogers, distinguished as a partisan officer, in whose corps served as captain, John Stark, a brigadier afterward in the revolutionary army. Two hundred of these rangers were detached from Crown Point, against the Indian village of St. Francis, whose inhabitants had long been the terror of the New England frontier. Enriched by plunder and the ransom of their captives, these Indians had a handsome Catholic chapel, with plate and ornaments. Their village was adorned by numerous scalps, trophies of victory, stretched on hoops, and elevated on poles. The rangers accomplished their march through the woods, and took the village entirely by surprise. A large part of the warriors were slain; the village—as had happened so often in New England—was first plundered, and then burned. Their object thus accomplished, fearing lest their trail from Crown Point might be watched, the victors attempted to return by way of Lake Memphremagog and the Connecticut. But their provisions fell short; some perished for want of food; some were killed by the pursuing Indians. The greater part, however, reached, at last, the uppermost settlements on the Connecticut, just below Bellows Falls, and thence made good their retreat to Crown Point.

In pursuance of the original plan of campaign, a third army, composed principally of provincials, and commanded by General Prideaux, had been collected at Oswego, for an attack on Niagara. Notwithstanding the late treaty of neutrality, the influence of Sir William Johnson had induced a large body of warriors of the Six Nations to join this army. After a prosperous voyage from Oswego, Prideaux landed at Niagara and opened his batteries, but was soon killed by the bursting of a gun, when Johnson succeeded to the chief command. Twelve hundred French regulars, drawn from the western posts, and followed by an equal force of Indian auxiliaries, advanced to raise the siege. Aware of their approach, Johnson took an advantageous position in advance of the fort. The relieving force was totally routed, and a large part taken prisoners. The fort surrendered the next day, and six hundred men with it. According to the plan of operations, Johnson should have descended Lake Ontario to co-operate on the St. Lawrence with Amherst and Wolfe; but the want of proper shipping, the small supply of provisions, and the incumbrance of the French prisoners, prevented him from doing so.

Deprived thus of all co-operation, Wolfe was left to besiege Quebec alone. Occupying a point of land on the north shore of the St. Lawrence, protected on the south by that river, and on the north by the tributary stream of the St. Charles, Quebec consisted then, as now, of an upper and a lower town, both regularly fortified. The lower town was built on a narrow beach at the water's edge, above which rose the Heights of Abraham, an almost perpendicular range of lofty rocks, forming the river banks. On the level of these heights stretched a wide plain, on which the upper town was built. Overhanging the St. Lawrence, and extending for a great distance above the town, the heights seemed to afford on that side, an almost impregnable defense. Several floating batteries and armed vessels were moored in the St. Charles, and beyond it, in a camp strongly intrenched, and covered by the Montmorency, another and larger river, which enters the St. Lawrence a short distance below Quebec, lay Montcalm's army, almost equal in numbers to that of Wolfe, but composed largely of Canadians and Indians. Every exertion had been made for the defense of the city, but the supply of provisions was very limited.

Wolfe had landed on the fertile island of Orleans, just below the city. His naval superiority gave him full command of the river. After a slight skirmish, he gained possession of Point Levi, held by a body of French troops, on the south bank of the St. Lawrence, opposite Quebec, where he erected batteries, which set fire to and destroyed the Cathedral and many houses, but the distance was too great for any effect on the fortifications. Wolfe then landed on the opposite bank, below the town, intending to force the passage of the Montmorency, and to bring Montcalm to an action. The French were very strongly posted, and the impetuosity of Wolfe's advanced party, which rushed to the attack before support was ready, obliged him to retire with a loss of five hundred men.

An attempt was then made to destroy the French shipping, and to alarm and draw out the garrison by descents above the town. One valuable magazine was destroyed, a great many houses were burned, much plunder was made, but it was impossible to cut out the French ships. To guard against future attacks, Montcalm sent De Bougainville up the river with fifteen hundred men.

The prospect was very discouraging. The season for action was fast passing. Nothing had been heard of the forces designed to co-operate from the side of New York, except reports from the enemy, of the retreat of Amherst. Though suffering from severe illness, instead of despairing, Wolfe embraced the bold proposal of his principal officers, to scale the Hights of Abraham, and thus to approach the city on the side where its defenses were feeblest. Above Quebec there was a narrow beach sufficient to afford a practicable landing place; but it might easily be missed in the dark; and the hights rose so steep above it, that even by daylight and unopposed, the ascent was a matter of hazard and difficulty. Should the French be on their guard, repulse was inevitable. (1759.)

The army, placed on ship-board, moved up the river, several miles beyond the proposed landing-place. To distract attention and conceal the real design, a show was made of disembarking at several points. When night had set in, flat-bottomed boats, with the soldiers on board, fell down the river with the tide, and, carefully avoiding the French sentinels, succeeded in finding the beach. The light troops were led by Colonel Howe, afterward Sir William, and commander-in-chief of the British armies in America. Assisted by the rugged projections of the rocks and the branches of trees, they made their way up the hights, and, having dispersed a small force stationed there, covered the ascent of the main body. Early in the morning, the whole British army appeared drawn up on the Plains of Abraham. To meet this unexpected movement, Montcalm put his troops in motion. Nothing now but a victory could prevent a siege and save the city. He advanced, accordingly, in order of battle. Bodies of Indians and Canadians in his front, kept up an irregular but galling fire. Wolfe gave orders to disregard these skirmishers, and to await the approach of the main body. The French had arrived within forty yards of the English, when their advance was checked by a heavy fire of musketry and grape. Eight or ten six-pounders, dragged up the hights by the seamen, were brought into line after the action began. The French appear to have had but two small field-pieces. The battle raged fiercest on the right of the English and the left of the French, where the two generals were respectively stationed opposite each other. Though already twice wounded, Wolfe gave orders for the charge. He fell, wounded a third time, and mortally; but the grenadiers still advanced. The French, close pressed by the English bayonets and the broadswords of the Scotch Highland regiments, began to give way. To complete their confusion, Montcalm fell with a mortal wound. The whole French line was soon in disorder. Five hundred Frenchmen were killed; a thousand, including the wounded, were taken prisoners. The English loss amounted to six hundred killed and wounded. A part of the dispersed army escaped into the town, but the bulk of the fugitives retired across the St. Charles. Hardly was the battle over, when De Bougainville made his appearance, marching hastily down the river. An hour or two sooner, and he might have changed the fortune of the day. As it was, after collecting the fugitives from behind the St. Charles, he retired again up the St. Lawrence.

Preparations for besieging the city were commenced by Townshend, whom Wolfe's death and Moncton's severe wound had made commander-in-chief, but through lack of provisions it surrendered on capitulation, five days after the battle—the regulars to be sent to France, the inhabitants to be guaranteed their property and religion. General Murray, with five thousand men, was left in garrison. The fleet, with the sick and the French prisoners, hastened to anticipate the approaching frost by retiring to Halifax, where the ships were to winter.

The Cherokees, who had accompanied Forbes in his expedition against Fort Du Quesne, returning home along the mountains, had involved themselves in quarrels with the back settlers of Virginia and the Carolinas, in which several, both Indians and white men, had been killed. Some chiefs, who had proceeded to Charleston to arrange this dispute, were received by Governor Littleton in very haughty style, and he presently marched into the Cherokee country at the head of fifteen hundred men, contributed by Virginia and the Carolinas, demanding the surrender of the murderers of the English. He was soon glad, however, of any apology for retiring. His troops proved very insubordinate; the smallpox broke out among them; and, having accepted twenty-two Indian hostages as security for peace and the future delivery of the murderers, he broke up his camp, and fell back in haste and confusion. (Jan. 1760.)

The hostages, including several principal chiefs and warriors, were placed for safe keeping in Fort Prince George, at the head of the Savannah. No sooner was Littleton's army gone, than the Cherokees attempted to entrap into their power the commander of that post, and, apprehensive of some plan for the rescue of the hostages, he gave orders to put them in irons. They resisted; and a soldier having been wounded in the struggle, his infuriated companions fell upon the prisoners and put them all to death. Indignant at this outrage, the Cherokees beleaguered the fort, and sent out war parties in every direction, to attack the frontiers. The Assembly of South Carolina, in great alarm, voted a thousand men, and offered a premium of £25 for every Indian scalp. North Carolina offered a similar premium, and authorized, in addition, the holding of Indian captives as slaves. An express, asking assistance, was sent to General Amherst, who detached twelve hundred men, under Colonel Montgomery, chiefly Scotch Highlanders, lately stationed on the western frontier, with orders to make a dash at the Cherokees, but to return in season for the next campaign against Canada.

Promoted to the government of Jamaica, Littleton had resigned the administration of South Carolina to William Bull, the lieutenant-governor, a native of the province, whose father, of the same name, had formerly administered the government, as president of the council. Bull, a man of talents and character, had received at Leyden a medical degree—the first, or one of the first, ever obtained by a native Anglo-American. With some short intervals, during which Thomas Boone, Lord Charles Montague, and Lord William Campbell acted as governors, he continued, as lieutenant-governor, at the head of affairs, till South Carolina ceased to be a British province.

Joining his forces with the provincial levies, Montgomery entered the Cherokee country, raised the blockade of Fort Prince George, and ravaged the neighboring district. Marching then upon Etchoe, the chief village of the Middle Cherokees, within five miles of that place he encountered a large body of Indians, strongly posted in a difficult defile, from which they were only driven after a very severe struggle; or, according to other accounts, Montgomery was himself repulsed. At all events, he retired to Charleston, and, in obedience to his orders, prepared to embark for service at the north. When this determination became known, the province was thrown into the utmost consternation. The Assembly declared themselves unable to raise men to protect the frontiers; and a detachment of four hundred regulars was presently conceded to Bull's earnest solicitations.

During the pressure of the war with the Western Indians, as one means of raising supplies, the Assembly of Virginia, by two or three successive acts, had carried the five per cent. standing duty on imported slaves as high as twenty per cent. This duty having "been found very burdensome to the fair purchaser, a great disadvantage to the settlement and improvement of the lands in the colony, introductive of many frauds, and not to answer the end thereby intended, inasmuch as the same prevents the importation of slaves, and thereby lessens the fund arising from the duty," it was now reduced to ten per cent—a positive and distinct legislative assertion, notwithstanding what Jefferson has represented to the contrary, that Virginia duty on slaves was imposed for revenue only.

The proprietaries of Pennsylvania, disgusted at Denny's faithlessness, had prevailed upon Hamilton to accept again the office of deputy-governor. But, to obtain means for furnishing the quota of that province toward the approaching campaign, he was obliged, like his predecessor, to consent to a tax on the proprietary estates. Bound by the consent of their deputy, though given against their instruction—for such was the constitutional doctrine established in Pennsylvania—the Penns petitioned for the royal veto on eleven acts which Denny had passed, including the tax act above referred to. Franklin, as an agent for the Assembly on the one hand, and the proprietaries on the other, were heard by their counsel before the Board of Trade. In giving their decision, the Lords of Trade commented in very severe terms on the collusion between the Assembly and Denny, evinced by a grant to the governor of a distinct sum of money for consenting to each of these eleven obnoxious acts. The other acts were disallowed; but, on the great point of the right to tax the proprietary estates, the Assembly triumphed. The Board of Trade required, indeed, certain modifications of the act, to which Franklin readily assented on behalf of the province. The Assembly gave him a vote of thanks; but they hesitated in fulfilling the agreement he had made; nor was it long before the dispute with the proprietaries broke out with more violence than ever.

After the fall of Quebec, Vaudreuil, the governor general of Canada, had concentrated all his forces at Montreal, and, during the winter, had made every possible preparation for attempting the recovery of the capital before the garrison could be relieved. As soon as the melting of the ice would permit, M. De Levi advanced for that purpose with ten thousand men. The English garrison had suffered during the winter for want of fresh provisions. A thousand soldiers had died of the scurvy. Murray could hardly muster three thousand men fit for duty. Anxious, however, to avoid a siege, and trusting to his superior discipline, he marched out, and gave battle at Sillery. He was beaten, however, with the loss of all his artillery and a thousand men, was driven back to Quebec, and besieged there. Some ships, dispatched from England very early in the season, presently arrived with supplies, anticipating not only the French fleet, but the English squadron also which had wintered at Halifax. Alarmed at their appearance, and supposing that the whole English fleet had arrived, M. De Levi gave over the siege, and retired precipitately to Montreal. Against this last stronghold of the enemy all efforts were now directed. Anxious to complete the conquest of Canada, the Northern colonies zealously contributed.

Three armies were soon in motion. Amherst, at the head of ten thousand men, beside a thousand Indians of the Six Nations, led by Johnson, embarked at Oswego, and sailed down the lake and the St. Lawrence to Montreal, where he was met by Murray with four thousand men from Quebec. Haviland arrived the next day, with a third army of three thousand five hundred men, by way of Lake Champlain. The force thus assembled was quite overwhelming. Resistance was not to be thought of. The French governor signed a capitulation, by which he gave up not only Montreal, but Presque Isle, Detroit, Mackinaw, and all the other posts of Western Canada. The regular troops, about four thousand men, were to be sent to France. The Canadians were guaranteed their property and worship.

Nowhere was the general joy of the colonies at the conquest of Canada more enthusiastically felt than in New York, of which the northern and western limits had so long been in dispute with the French. New York had indeed, in those directions, no definite boundary, though the Assembly had been accustomed to claim, by virtue of alleged cessions from the Six Nations, as far north as the outlet of Lake Champlain, and the whole peninsula between Lakes Ontario and Huron—pretensions extended, indeed, even to the peninsula of Michigan, and beyond it.

By the sudden death of Delancey, the administration of New York had devolved on Cadwallader Colden, who was presently appointed lieutenant-governor. Though now upward of seventy years of age, Colden continued in that office for sixteen years; and, in consequence of the frequent absence of the governors, was repeatedly at the head of affairs.

Great, too, was the exultation in New England, whose eastern and northern frontiers were now finally delivered from that scourge of Indian warfare by which they had been visited six times within the preceding eighty-five years. The Indians themselves, by these successive contests, had been almost annihilated. Most of the hostile tribes had emigrated to Canada, or else were extinct. There remained only a small band of Penobscots, on whom was bestowed a limited reservation, still possessed by their degenerate descendants.

While the northern colonies exulted in safety, the Cherokee war still kept the frontiers of Carolina in alarm. Left to themselves by the withdrawal of Montgomery, the Upper Cherokees had beleaguered Fort Loudon. After living for some time on horse-flesh, the garrison, under a promise of safe-conduct to the settlements, had been induced to surrender. But this promise was broken; attacked on the way, a part were killed, and the rest detained as prisoners; after which, the Indians directed all their fury against the frontiers. On a new application, presently made to Amherst, for assistance, the Highland regiment, now commanded by Grant, was ordered back to Carolina. (1761.)

New levies were also made in the province, and Grant presently marched into the Cherokee country with two thousand six hundred men. In a second battle, near the same spot with the fight of the previous year, the Indians were driven back with loss. Etchoe, with the other villages of the Middle Cherokees, was plundered and burned, and all the growing corn destroyed. The Indians took refuge in the defiles of the mountains, and, subdued and humbled, sued for peace. As the condition on which alone it would be granted, they were required to deliver up four warriors, to be shot at the head of the army, or to furnish four green Indian scalps within twenty days. A personal application to Governor Bull, by an old chief, long known for his attachment to the English, procured a relinquishment of this brutal demand, and peace was presently made, without any further effusion of blood.

The English arms were thus everywhere triumphant; but as the French might attempt the re-conquest of Canada, the colonies were still required to keep up their quotas at two-thirds of the former amount. The French officers in Canada, in the course of the war, had been guilty of immense peculations. There was outstanding, in unpaid bills on France, and in card or paper money, more than twenty millions of dollars, a large portion of it, as the French court contended, fraudulently issued. But a very small indemnity was ever obtained by the holders of this paper, the payment of which had been suspended immediately after the capture of Quebec.

Having obtained an appointment as governor of South Carolina, on which, however, he never entered, after a very popular administration, Pownall had been succeeded as governor of Massachusetts, by Francis Bernard, late governor of New Jersey, where Thomas Boone, and, on his speedy removal to South Carolina, Josiah Hardy supplied his place.

The British merchants loudly complained of a trade carried on by the northern colonies, not only with the neutral ports of St. Thomas and Eustatius, but directly with the French islands, under flags of truce granted by the colonial governors nominally for an exchange of prisoners, but intended, in fact, as mere covers for a commerce, whereby the French fleets, garrisons, and islands in the West Indies were supplied with provisions and other necessaries. Pitt had issued strict orders to put a stop to this trade; but it was too profitable to be easily suppressed. The colonists, indeed, maintained that it was policy to make as much money out of the enemy as possible, and they cited the example of the Dutch, who had fought with the Spaniards and traded with them at the same time.

Bernard, a great stickler for the authority of the mother country, found an able coadjutor in Thomas Hutchinson, late speaker of the House of Representatives, and now a counselor, whose zeal for the crown and appetite for emolument, had been rewarded by the office of judge of probate for Suffolk county, and, on Phipps's death, by the post of lieutenant-governor, to which was now added the place of chief justice, much to the disappointment of Otis, Hutchinson's successor as speaker, to whom Pownall had promised a seat on the bench. The strict enforcement of the acts of trade, attempted by Bernard, had provoked a strenuous opposition, and the custom-house officers had applied to the Superior

Court to grant them writs of assistance, according to the English Exchequer practice—warrants, that is, to search, when and where they pleased, for smuggled goods, and to call in the aid of others to assist them. To oppose the issue of these writs, the merchants retained Oxenbridge Thatcher and James Otis. Thatcher was a leading practitioner in Boston. Otis, son of the speaker, a young lawyer of brilliant talents and ardent temperament, was advocate of the Admiralty, and in that capacity bound to argue for the issue of the writs. But he resigned his office, and accepted the retainer of the merchants. Not content with Thatcher's merely legal and technical objections, Otis took high ground as to the rights of the colonies. He assailed the acts of trade as oppressive in some instances and unconstitutional in others, and by his vehement eloquence gave a tone to public sentiment, not without serious influence on subsequent events. The writs were granted, but they were so excessively unpopular as to be seldom used. Elected a representative from Boston, Otis became a leading member of the House, and a warm opponent of Hutchinson, whom he endeavored to exclude from the council by a bill declaring the places of chief justice and counselor incompatible with each other. But Hutchinson's influence was considerable, enough to defeat this bill. Another, which passed, requiring the oath of a custom-house officer to justify the issue of a writ of assistance, was rejected by the governor.

The accession of the young king, George III, though it introduced some new members into the cabinet, had made no immediate change of policy. (1760.) Canada conquered, the British arms had been turned against the French islands in the West Indies. Guadaloupe had been already captured. (1761.) General Moncton, after producing to the council of New York his commission as governor, sailed from that port with two line-of-battle ships, a hundred transports, and twelve thousand regular and colonial troops. Gates went out with him as aid-de-camp, and carried to England the news of the capture of Martinique. Montgomery, afterward, as well as Gates—a general of the revolutionary army—held in this expedition the rank of captain. The colonial troops were led by General Lyman. The successes of Moncton were not limited to Martinique. Grenada, St. Lucie, and

St. Vincent's—every island, in fact, which the French possessed in the Caribbee group, fell into the hands of the British.

The French fleet was ruined. French merchantmen were driven from the seas. British vessels, including many from New York and New England, acquired the carrying trade, not of the conquered islands only, but, under safe-conducts and flags of truce, of the larger and more wealthy colony of St. Domingo. This lucrative commerce, with the profits of privateering and of supplying provisions for the British fleets and armies, made the war very popular in America, and Pitt an idol; but that "great Commoner," as he delighted to be called, had ceased to be minister.

Charles III., on whom the crown of Spain had lately devolved, had never forgotten nor forgiven a threat of bombardment by a British admiral, to which, at a former period, when King of Naples, he had been obliged to yield. As King of Spain, he had signed with France a treaty known as the Family Compact, amounting substantially to an alliance offensive and defensive. Pitt had secret information of this treaty, and wished at once to declare war against Spain. But Pitt was an object of jealousy and dislike to the young king, desirous to secure for himself a more active participation in affairs than had been enjoyed by his two predecessors. The ministry split on this point, Pitt retired from office, and the king hastened to raise to the head of the administration the Marquis of Bute, his late preceptor. Yet, scarcely had Pitt left the ministry, when hostilities commenced on the part of Spain—a step which cost that declining monarchy dear. The Spanish colonial commerce was cut off by cruisers, and presently Havana, the key of the Gulf of Mexico, was taken by a British armament.

The present contest for territorial and commercial supremacy had extended even to the East Indies, thus, as it were, encircling the globe. A twenty years' struggle in Hindostan, between the French and English East India Companies, had ended in the complete triumph of the English, securing to them the dominion of the Carnatic and Bengal—the beginning of that career of territorial aggrandizement in India, since so remarkably carried out.

With finances almost ruined, powerless to struggle any longer against such a succession of losses, the French court was obliged to abandon the contest, and with it all claim to territorial possessions on the North American continent. The island and city of New Orleans, with all of Louisiana west of the Mississippi, were ceded to Spain, in consideration of her losses in the war. Louisiana, thus given to the Spaniards, contained about ten thousand inhabitants. The transfer was very disagreeable to them, and six years elapsed before the Spanish actually took possession.

By the treaty of Fontainebleau, all the vast region east of Mississippi, the island of New Orleans excepted, was yielded up to the British. Spain also ceded Florida in exchange for Havana. Thus was vested in the British crown, so far as the consent of rival European claimants could give it, the sovereignty of the whole eastern half of North America, from the Gulf of Mexico to Hudson's Bay and the Polar Ocean, including hundreds of thousands of square miles upon which the foot of the white man had never yet trod. By the terms of the treaty, the navigation of the Mississippi, from its source to its mouth, was to be free to both parties, without liability to stoppage, search, or duty.

Martinique, Guadaloupe, and St. Lucie, islands of the Carribee group, which some politicians wished Great Britain to retain instead of Canada, were restored to France; also her former rights in the Newfoundland fishery. Beside Canada and its appurtenances, Great Britain received also St. Vincent's, Dominica, and Tobago, islands hitherto called neutral, and the two former still possessed by the native Indian inhabitants—the French and English not having hitherto been able to agree which should be allowed to take possession of them. These islands were erected, by proclamation, into the government of Grenada. (1763.)

The same proclamation erected on the continent the three new British provinces of East Florida, West Florida, and Quebec. East Florida was bounded on the north by the St. Mary's, the intervening region thence to the Altamaha being annexed to Georgia. The boundaries of West Florida were the Appalachicola, the Gulf of Mexico, the Misssissippi, Lakes Ponchartrain and Maurepas; and on the north, the thirty-first degree of north latitude, for which, however, was substituted, the next year, a line due east from the mouth of the Yazoo, so as to include the French settlements about Natchez. The boundary assigned to the province of Quebec corresponded with the claims of New York and Massachusetts, being a line from the southern end of Lake Nepissing, striking the St. Lawrence at the forty-fifth degree of north latitude, and following that parallel across the foot of Lake Champlain to the sources of the Connecticut, and thence along the highlands which separate the waters flowing into the St. Lawrence from those which fall into the sea.

By the same proclamation, grants of land were authorised to the reduced officers and discharged soldiers who had served during the war—five thousand acres each to field officers, three thousand to captains, two thousand to subalterns and staff officers, two hundred to non-commissioned officers, and fifty to privates. To prevent the mischiefs and disputes which had grown out of the purchase of Indian lands by private individuals, all such purchases within the crown colonies were in future to be made only by public treaty, and for the use of the crown; nor, except in Quebec and West Florida, were any lands to be taken up beyond the heads of the rivers flowing into the Atlantic. These provisions were designed to restrain the backwoodsmen, and to prevent Indian hostilities; but already, before the proclamation had been issued, a new and alarming Indian war had broken out.

Since the capture of Fort Du Quesne, settlers from Pennsylvania, Maryland, and Virginia had poured over the mountains, very little scrupulous in their conduct toward the Indians, who began to see and feel the danger of being soon driven to new migrations. Perhaps, too, their prejudices were influenced—so at least the colonists thought—by the arts of French fur traders, who dreaded the competition of English rivals. The Delawares and the Shawnese, who had lately migrated from Pennsylvania, and who now occupied the banks of the Muskingum, Scioto, and Miami, seem to have taken the lead in a widespread confederacy, of which Pontiac, a Shawnese chief, is represented to have been the moving spirit. It included not only the tribes lately the allies of the French, but the Senecas also, the most western clan of the Six Nations. The other five clans, though not without much difficulty, were kept quiet by Sir William Johnson.

A simultaneous attack was unexpectedly made along the whole frontier of Pennsylvania and Virginia. The English traders scattered through the region beyond the mountains, were plundered and slain. The posts between the Ohio and Lake Erie were surprised and taken—indeed, all the posts in the western country, except Niagara, Detroit, and Fort Pitt. The two latter were closely blockaded; and the troops which Amherst hastily sent forward to relieve them, did not reach their destination without some very hard fighting.

This sudden onslaught, falling heaviest on Pennsylvania, excited the ferocity of the back settlers, chiefly Presbyterians of Scotch and Irish descent, having very little in common with the mild spirit of the Quakers. Well versed in the Old Testament, the same notion had obtained among them current in early times of New England and Virginia, that as the Israelites exterminated the Canaanites, so they ought to exterminate the bloody, heathen Indians, stigmatized as the children of Ham. Under this impression, and imagining them to be in correspondence with the hostile Indians, some settlers of Paxton township attacked the remnant of a friendly tribe, who were living quietly under the guidance of Moravian missionaries at Conestoga, on the Susquehanna. All who fell into their hands, men, women, and children, were ruthlessly murdered. Those who escaped by being absent, fled for refuge to Lancaster, and were placed for security in the work-house there. The "Paxton Boys," as they called themselves, rushed into Lancaster, broke open the doors of the work-house, and perpetrated a new massacre. It was in vain that Franklin, lately returned from Europe, denounced these murders in an eloquent and indignant pamphlet. Such was the fury of the mob, including many persons of respectable character and standing, that they even marched in arms to Philadelphia, for the destruction of some other friendly Indians who had taken refuge in that city. Thus beset, these unhappy fugitives attempted to escape to New York, to put themselves under the protection of Sir William Johnson, the Indian agent; but Lieutenant-governor Colden refused to allow them to enter that province.

John Penn, son and presumptive heir of Richard Penn, one of the joint proprietors, had lately arrived in Pennsylvania, to take Hamilton's place as governor. Politics still ran very high; but, in this emergency, the aid and advice of Franklin, the head of the opposition, and speaker of the Assembly, were eagerly sought. Owing to the royal veto on the late act for a volunteer militia, and the repeated refusals of the Assembly to establish a compulsive one, there was no organized military force in the province, except a few regular troops in the barracks at Philadelphia. By Franklin's aid, a strong body of volunteers, for the defense of the city, was speedily enrolled. When the insurgents approached, Franklin went out to meet them; and, after a long negociation, and agreeing to allow them to appoint two delegates to lay their grievances before the Assembly, they were persuaded to disperse without further bloodshed. So ended this most disgraceful affair. There was no power in the province adequate to punish these outrages. The Christian Indians presently re-established themselves high up the eastern branch of the Susquehanna. Five or six years after, destined yet to suffer further outrages, they migrated to the country northwest of the Ohio, and settled, with their missionaries, in three villages on the Muskingum.

General Gage, successor to Amherst as commander-in-chief of the British forces in America, had called upon the colonies for troops to assist in subduing the Indians. So extensive was the combination, that Major Loftus, while attempting to ascend the Mississippi with four hundred men, to take possessisn of the Illinois country, was attacked near the present site of Fort Adams, and obliged to give over the enterprise. New England, remote from the seat of danger, answered Gage's call scantily and reluctantly. Virginia furnished seven hundred men, and Pennsylvania one thousand. A pack of blood-hounds was sent out from England. Two expeditions were presently organized and sent into the Indian country, one under Bouquet, by way of Pittsburg, the other, under Bradstreet, along the lakes. The Indians, finding themselves thus vigorously attacked, consented to a treaty, by which they agreed to give up all prisoners, and to relinquish all claim to lands within gun-shot of any fort, of which, the British were authorized to build as many as they chose. Indians committing murders on white men were to be given up, to be tried by a jury, half Indians and half colonists. (1764.)

CHAPTER XXXI.

Condition of the Colonies at the conclusion of the Fourth Intercolonial War—Theory of the English Parliament—Grenville's Scheme of Colonial Taxation—Passage and Repeal of the Stamp Act.

THAT war by which the possession of North America had been confirmed to the English crown, had not been carried on without great efforts and sacrifices on the part of the colonists. By disease or the sword, thirty thousand colonial soldiers had fallen in the struggle. An expense had been incurred of upward of sixteen millions of dollars, of which only about five millions had been reimbursed by Parliament. Massachusetts alone had kept from four to seven thousand men in the field, beside garrisons, and recruits to the regular regiments. These men, it is true, served but a few months in the year. At the approach of winter they were generally disbanded, and for every campaign a new army had to be raised. They were fed at British cost; yet in the course of the war the expenses of Massachusetts, exclusive of all parliamentary reimbursements, had amounted to two millions and a half of dollars, all of which had been raised without resort to paper money, though not without incurring a heavy debt in addition to severe taxation. Connecticut, in the same period, expended not less than two million dollars. The outstanding debt of New York was near a million. If the expenditures of the southern colonies had been less profuse, they had far exceeded all former experience. Virginia, at the close of the war, had a debt of eight hundred thousand dollars. (1763.)

The New England clergy complained that the morals of their parishioners had been corrupted by service in the armies; and more disinterested observers might be willing to admit that the reverential simplicity of rural life, however tinged by superstition, was ill exchanged for any liberality of opinions or polish of manners to be acquired in a camp. Yet the intermixture of troops from various colonies, must have tended to enlarge the circle of ideas, and partially to do away with local prejudices; while co-operation in a common object, had impressed upon the colonial mind the idea of union and a common interest.

The royal and proprietary governors, to obtain the necessary supplies, had been obliged to yield to perpetual encroachments. The expenditure of the great sums voted by the Assemblies had been kept, for the most part, in their own hands, or those of their specially appointed agents; and, contrary to what usually happens, executive influence had been weakened instead of strengthened by the war, or rather, had been transferred from the governors to the colonial Assemblies.

In the prosecution of hostilities, much of the hardest and most dangerous service had fallen to the share of the colonial levies, employed especially as scouts and light troops. Though exceedingly disgusted by the superiority always assumed by the British regular officers, and allowed them by the rules of the service, the long continuance and splendid successes of the war, had filled the colonies with a martial spirit, and the idea of martial force had grown familiar, as a method, at once expedient and glorious, of settling disputed points of authority and right.

With colonies thus taught their strength and resources, full of trained soldiers, accustomed to extraordinary efforts and partial co-operation, the British ministry now entered on a new struggle—one, of which all like former contests, were but as faint types and forerunners. It was proposed to maintain in America ten thousand troops as a peace establishment, nominally for the defense of the colonies; perhaps also, in fact, as a support to that superintending metropolitan authority, of which the weakness had been sensibly felt on various occasions during the war. The outbreak of the western Indians served, however, to show that some sort of a peace establishment was really necessary.

Four great wars within seventy years, had overwhelmed Great Britain with heavy debts and excessive taxation. Her recent conquests, so far from relieving her embarrassments, had greatly increased that debt, which now amounted to £140,000,000, near $700,000,000. Even in the midst of the late struggle, in the success of which they had so direct an interest, the military contributions of the colonial Assemblies had been sometimes reluctant and capricious, and always irregular and unequal. They might, perhaps, refuse to contribute at all toward a standing army in time of peace, of which they would naturally soon come to be jealous. It seemed necessary, therefore, by some exertion of metropolitan authority, to extract from the colonies, for this purpose, a regular and certain revenue.

At the very commencement of the late war, the Board of Trade had proposed a scheme of parliamentary taxation for the colonies. In the course of the war, Pitt had intimated to more than one colonial governor, that, when it was over, the authority of Parliament would be exerted to draw from America the means for its own defense. Peace was no sooner established, than Pitt's successors in the ministry hastened to carry out the scheme thus foreshadowed.

That Parliament possessed a certain authority over the colonies, in some respects super-eminent, was admitted by all; but the exact limits of that authority had never been very accurately settled. As against the royal prerogative, the colonists had been eager to claim the benefits of English law; not the common law only, but all statutes, such as the Habeas Corpus Act, of a remedial and popular character. There were other statutes, however, the Mutiny Act, for instance, from which they sought to escape on the ground of non-extension to America. Against the interference of Parliament in matters of trade, most of the colonies, especially those of New England, had carried on a pertinacious struggle. In spite, however, of opposition, that interference had been extended from the trade of the colonies with foreign nations and each other, to many other matters but remotely connected with it. By the English post-office system, introduced into America, the transportation of mails and the rates of postage had been regulated. Parliament had interfered with the colonial currency, establishing the standard in coin, and restricting the issue of paper notes. Joint-stock companies, with more than a certain number of partners, had been prohibited. The collection of debts had been regulated. A uniform law of naturalization had been established. Parliament had prohibited or restricted certain trades and manufactures, and had even assumed to legislate respecting the administration of oaths. All or most of these exertions of authority had been protested against at the time; but the colonists had yielded at last, and the power of regulating colonial trade for the exclusive benefit of the mother country, exercised for two or three generations, and sustained by a system of custom-house officers and Admiralty courts, had acquired, in spite of unpopularity and a systematic evasion still extensively practiced, the character and attributes of a legal vested right. (1763.)

The super-eminent power of all, that of levying taxes for revenue, Parliament had never exercised. The rates of postage, of which the payment was voluntary, might be considered not so much a tax as an equivalent for services rendered. The intercolonial duties on "enumerated articles," producing little more than sufficient to pay the expenses of the custom-houses, had for their professed object, not revenue, but the regulation of trade. The trifling surplus paid into the British treasury was but a mere incident to that regulation. Yet the colonial custom-houses, though hitherto maintained with no intention of collecting taxes, might easily be adapted to that purpose; and, as the colonists were already accustomed to the payment of parliamentary duties, they might not readily distinguish between duties for regulation and duties for revenue.

A part of the new scheme, as suggested to Parliament by Lord Grenville, Bute's chancellor of the Exchequer, appears to have proceeded on this idea. In spite of recent vigilance in the enforcement of the acts of trade, the Molasses Act was still extensively evaded. By reducing the duties exacted under that act, now about to expire, Grenville proposed to diminish the temptation to smuggle; and, while seeming thus to confer a boon on the colonies, by opening to them, under moderated duties, the trade with the foreign sugar islands, by the same process, to convert the Molasses Act from a mere regulation of trade, into a source of revenue, to be enhanced by duties on other foreign products. Had the proposition stopped here, there might have been some chance of gradually forcing on the colonies the practice of parliamentary taxation. But the amount which could thus be raised would not suffice for the object in view, and Grenville proposed, in addition, a stamp tax—an impost, in several respects, much like those of the custom-house, and very like them in facility of collection. All bills, bonds, notes, leases, policies of insurance, papers used in legal proceedings, and a great many other documents, in order to be held valid in courts of law, were to be written on stamped paper, sold by public officers appointed for that purpose, at prices which levied a stated tax on every such document. Stamp duties, said to be an invention of the Dutch, though long familiar in England, were as yet almost unknown in America, where only one or two colonies had made some slight trial of them.

Shortly after the final treaty of peace, Grenville laid this plan before Parliament, not for immediate action, but by way of information and notice. The colonial agents, or some of them, wrote to America for instructions, but the public mind was engrossed by the sudden renewal of the war on the western frontier, and Grenville's proposition hardly attracted so much attention as might have been expected. The Assembly of Pennsylvania was content with simply stating a willingness "to aid the crown according to their ability, whenever required in the usual constitutional manner." They even proposed to forward a plan by which all the colonies might be made to contribute fairly and equitably to the public defense; but that idea they soon abandoned.

Bollan, so long the agent of Massachusetts, had been lately dismissed, and the place given to Jasper Manduit, whose letters, containing an account of Grenville's proposals, were laid before the General Court at an adjourned session. There seems at this moment to have been a lull in the politics of that province. The excitement growing out of the question of writs of assistance had subsided. Hutchinson, who still sat in the council, in spite of Otis's attempt to exclude him, had a principal hand in drawing up the instructions to the agent. They suggested, indeed, the right of the colonists to tax themselves, but in a very moderate tone. It was even voted to send Hutchinson as a special agent to England; but this was prevented by Governor Bernard, who thought it irregular for the lieutenant-governor to be absent from the province.

At the next session of Parliament, Grenville, now prime minister, brought forward his scheme of taxation in a more formal shape. After a debate which excited very little interest or attention, the House of Commons resolved, without a division, " that Parliament had a right to tax the colonies," and they recommended such a stamp act as the minister had proposed.

Further action as to this stamp tax was, however, delayed, to give the colonists an opportunity for suggesting, if they chose, some more satisfactory means for raising the half million of dollars which the minister required. The other part of the ministerial scheme was at once carried out by a law known as the " Sugar Act," reducing by one half, the duties imposed by the old Molasses Act on foreign sugar and molasses imported into the colonies ; levying duties on coffee, pimento, French and East India goods, and wines from Madeira and the Azores, which hitherto had been free ; and adding iron and lumber to the list of " enumerated articles," which could not be exported, except to England. Openly avowing in its preamble the purpose of " raising a revenue for defraying the expenses of defending, protecting, and securing his majesty's dominions in America," this act gave increased jurisdiction to the colonial Admiralty courts, and provided new and more efficient means for enforcing the collection of the revenue.

Partial accounts of these proceedings having reached Massachusetts previous to the annual election, the town of Boston took occasion to instruct its newly-chosen representatives to use all their efforts against the pending plan of parliament taxation, and for the repeal of any such acts already passed. These instructions, drafted by Samuel Adams, contained the first decided protest against Grenville's scheme. Among other things, they suggested the expediency of a combination of all the colonies for the defense of their common interests.

At the session which speedily followed, the House of Representatives resolved, " that the imposition of duties and taxes by the Parliament of Great Britain, upon a people not represented in the House of Commons, is absolutely irreconcilable with their rights." A pamphlet, lately published by Otis, " The Rights of the British Colonies asserted," was read and approved. A copy was transmitted to the agent in England, and along with it an energetic letter. " The silence of the province," said this letter, alluding to a suggestion of the agent, that he had taken silence for consent, "should have been imputed to any cause—even to despair—rather than be construed into a tacit cession of their rights, or the acknowledgment of a right in the Parliament of Great Britain to impose duties and taxes on a people who are not represented in the House of Commons." "If we are not represented, we are slaves!"

Following up the suggestions of the Boston instructions, a committee was appointed to correspond, during the recess, with the Assemblies of the other colonies.

These energetic measures, warmly supported by Thatcher and Otis, were adopted just at the close of the session, and in Hutchinson's absence. The concurrence of the council was not asked. Not that any open advocates for parliamentary taxation were to be found in that body; even Governor Bernard avowed his opposition, at least, to the proposed Stamp Act; but the council, for years past very much under Hutchinson's influence, was composed of wealthy and moderate men, who might not choose to venture on so vigorous a remonstrance.

Otis's pamphlet on colonial rights conceded to Parliament a superintending power to enact laws and regulations for the public good—a power limited, however, by the "natural rights of man," and "the constitutional rights of British subjects," claimed as the birthright of all born in the colonies. It was maintained as one of these rights, that taxes could not be levied on the people, "but by their consent in person or by deputation." The distinction was scouted between external and internal taxes, meaning in the one case, taxes on trade, and in the other, taxes on land and personal property. If trade might be taxed without the consent of the colonists, so might land and houses. Taxes of either kind were pronounced "absolutely irreconcilable with the rights of the colonists as British subjects and as men." Yet nothing like forcible resistance was hinted at. "There would be an end to all governments, if one, or a number of subjects or subordinate provinces, should take upon them so far to judge of the justice of an act of Parliament, as to refuse obedience to it." "Forcibly resisting the Parliament and the king's laws is high treason." "Therefore let the

Parliament lay what burdens they please on us, we must, it is our duty to submit, and patiently bear them till they will be pleased to relieve us." Such, at this moment, were the public professions, and most probably the private opinions of the strongest advocates of the rights of the colonists—at least of those who had been bred, like Otis, to the profession of the law. But this doctrine of patient submission to injustice, was not of a sort to go down in America.

Thatcher also published a tract against the scheme of parliamentary taxation, and similar tracts were put forth in Rhode Island "by authority;" in Maryland by Dulany, secretary of the province; and in Virginia by Bland, a leading member of the House of Burgesses.

The opposition of Massachusetts to the new "Sugar Act," was presently re-echoed from Pennsylvania, and strong instructions to oppose the whole scheme of taxation were given to Franklin, about to depart for England as the agent for the colony, to solicit the overthrow of the proprietary government.

At the adjourned session of the Massachusetts General Court, the powerful influence of Hutchinson again became obvious. The House adopted a strong petition to Parliament, drawn by a committee of which Otis was chairman. The council refused to concur. A joint committee then appointed, reported a petition to the House of Commons, drafted by Hutchinson, and not at all to the taste of the more ardent patriots. Yet, after some alterations, it was adopted by the Court. A letter to the agent, in a somewhat more decided tone, spoke of self-taxation as the right of the colony, not as a mere usage and favor, in which light the petition seemed to regard it.

Connecticut, following in the steps of Massachusetts, adopted the same moderate tone. The Assembly of New York agreed to a petition much more strongly expressed—so strongly, that no member of Parliament could be found to present it. This petition, adopted and re-echoed by Rhode Island, made the Massachusetts leaders still more dissatisfied with the tameness of theirs.

In the Virginia House of Burgesses, Peyton Randolph, the attorney-general, conspicuous formerly in the controversy with Dinwiddie, Richard Henry Lee, son of a former president of the council, George Wythe, and Edmund Pendleton, all distinguished lawyers and leaders of the colonial aristocracy, were appointed a committee to draw up a petition to the king, a memorial to the House of Lords, and a remonstrance to the Commons. These papers claimed for the colony, the privilege of self-taxation; but their tone was very moderate. Instead of relying on the matter of right, they dwelt at length on the embarassments and poverty of the province, encumbered by the late war with a heavy debt.

These faint protestations produced no effect on the made up minds of the British ministers. In spite of remonstrances addressed to Grenville by Franklin, Jackson, the newly-appointed agent of Massachusetts, Ingersoll, the agent for Connecticut, and other gentlemen interested in the colonies, a bill for collecting a stamp tax in America was presently brought in. The London merchants concerned in the American trade petitioned against it; but a convenient rule not to receive petitions against money bills, excluded this as well as those from the colonial Assemblies. In reply to Colonel Barre, who had served in America, and who made a speech against the bill, Townshend, one of the ministers, spoke of the colonists as "children, planted by our care, nourished by our indulgence, and protected by our arms." Barre's indignant retort produced a great sensation in the House. "They planted by your care? No; your oppressions planted them in America." "They nourished by your indulgence? They grew up by your neglect of them." "They protected by your arms? Those sons of liberty have nobly taken up arms in your defense. I claim to know more of America than most of you, having been resident in that country. The people, I believe, are as truly loyal subjects as the king has, but a people jealous of their liberties, and who will vindicate them, should they ever be violated. But the subject is too delicate; I will say no more." Barre placed his opposition on the ground of expediency; General Conway, and Alderman Beckford, one of the London members, denounced the bill as unjust. It passed, however, in the Commons, five to one; in the Lords there was no division nor the slightest opposition. (1765.)

A clause inserted into the annual Mutiny Act, carried out another part of the ministerial scheme, by authorizing as many troops to be sent to America as the ministers saw fit. For these troops, by a special enactment, known as "the Quartering Act," the colonies in which they might be stationed, were required to find quarters, fire-wood, bedding, drink, soap, and candles.

News of the passage of these acts, reached Virginia while the Assembly was sitting. The aristocratic leaders in that body hesitated. The session approached its close, and not one word seemed likely to be said. But the rights of the colonies did not fail of an advocate. Patrick Henry had already attracted the attention of the House, by his successful opposition to Robinson's proposed paper money loan, as mentioned in the previous chapter. Finding the older and more weighty members unlikely to move, he assumed the responsibility of introducing a series of resolutions, which claimed for the inhabitants of Virginia all the rights of born British subjects; denied any authority anywhere, except in the provincial Assembly, to impose taxes upon them; and denounced the attempt to vest that authority elsewhere, as inconsistent with the ancient Constitution, and subversive of British as well as of American liberty. Upon the introduction of these resolutions, a hot debate ensued. "Cæsar had his Brutus," said Henry, "Charles I. his Cromwell, and George III.—" "Treason! treason!" shouted the speaker, and the cry was re-echoed from the House. "George III.," said Henry, firmly, "may profit by their example. If that be treason, make the most of it!" In spite of the opposition of all the old leaders, the resolutions passed, the fifth and most emphatic, by a majority of only one vote. The next day, in Henry's absence, the resolutions were reconsidered, softened, and the fifth struck out. But a manuscript copy had already been sent to Philadelphia; and, circulating through the colonies in their original form, these resolutions gave everywhere a strong impulse to the popular feeling.

Before these Virginia resolutions reached Massachusetts, the General Court had met, at its annual session. Considering "the many difficulties to which the colonies are, and must be reduced by the operation of some late acts of Parliament," the House of Representatives appointed a committee of nine, to consider what steps the emergency demanded. That committee recommended a convention or congress, to be composed of "committees from the Houses of Representatives or Burgesses in the several colonies," to meet at New York on the first Tuesday of October following, there to consult "on the difficulties in which the colonies were, and must be placed by the late acts of Parliament levying duties and taxes upon them;" and, further, "to consider of a general and humble address to his majesty and the Parliament, to implore relief." Even the partisans of Bernard judged it best to concur in the adoption of this report; and they congratulated themselves that Ruggles and Partridge, two of the committee appointed to represent Massachusetts at the congress, were "prudent and discreet men, fast friends of government." The third was James Otis. A circular letter, addressed to all the other colonies, recommended similar appointments. Governor Fitch and a majority of the Connecticut assistants, seemed inclined to submit to the Stamp Act, but Trumbull and others loudly protested against it, and the popular feeling was all on their side.

The stamps were to be prepared in Great Britain, and sent to officers in the colonies, appointed to sell them. Anxious to make this unpopular measure as palatable as possible, the colonial agents were consulted as to the persons fit to be appointed. So little did even Franklin foresee the result, that he procured that office at Philadelphia for one of his particular friends and supporters. He also advised Ingersoll, the Connecticut agent, to accept that appointment for his own colony.

Before the stamps reached America, symptoms of a violent ferment appeared. A great elm in Boston, at the corner of the present Washington and Essex Streets, under which the opponents of the Stamp Act were accustomed to assemble, soon became famous as "liberty tree." Those persons supposed to favor the ministry were hung in effigy on the branches of this elm. A mob attacked the house of Oliver, secretary of the colony, who had been appointed stamp distributor for Massachusetts, broke his windows, destroyed his furniture, pulled down a small building, supposed to be intended for a stamp office, and frightened Oliver into a resignation. Jonathan Mayhew, the able minister of the West Church, in Boston—distinguished by some recent controversial tracts, in which he had severely criticised the conduct of the Society for the Propagation of the Gospel, in maintaining Episcopal missionaries in New England—preached a warm sermon against the Stamp Act, taking for his text, "I would they were even cut off which trouble you!" The Monday evening after this sermon the riots were renewed. The mob attacked the house of Story, registrar of the Admiralty, and destroyed not only the public files and records, but his private papers also. Next they entered and plundered the house of the controller of customs; and, maddened with liquor and excitement, proceeded to the mansion of Hutchinson, in North Square. The lieutenant-governor and his family fled for their lives. The house was completely gutted, and the contents burned in bonfires, kindled in the square. Along with Hutchinson's furniture and private papers, perished many invaluable manuscripts relating to the history of the province, which Hutchinson had been thirty years in collecting, and which it was impossible to replace.

As commonly happens on such occasions, the immediate actors in these scenes were persons of no note, the dregs of the population. Mayhew sent the next day a special apology and disclaimer to Hutchinson. The inhabitants of Boston, at a town meeting, unanimously expressed their "abhorrence" of these proceedings; and a "civic guard" was organized to prevent their repetition. Yet the rioters, though well known, went unpunished—a sure sign of the secret concurrence and good-will of the mass of the community. It is only in reliance on such encouragement, that mobs ever venture to commit deeds of violence. Those now committed were revolutionary acts, designed to intimidate—melancholy forerunners of civil war.

Throughout the northern colonies, associations on the basis of forcible resistance to the Stamp Act, under the name of "Sons of Liberty"—a title borrowed from Barre's famous speech—sprung suddenly into existence. Persons of influence and consideration, though they might favor the object, kept aloof, however, from so dangerous a combination, which consisted of the young, the ardent, those who loved excitement, and had nothing to lose. The history of these "Sons of Liberty" is very obscure; but they seem to have spread rapidly from Connecticut and New York into Massachusetts, Pennsylvania, and New Jersey, and to have taken up, as their special business, the intimidation of the stamp officers. In all the colonies, those officers were persuaded or compelled to resign; and such stamps as arrived either remained unpacked, or else were seized and burned. The Assembly of Pennsylvania unanimously adopted a series of resolutions, denouncing the Stamp Act as "unconstitutional, and subversive of their dearest rights." Public meetings to protest against it, were held throughout the colonies. The holding of such meetings was quite a new incident, and formed a new era in colonial history.

In the midst of this universal excitement, at the day appointed by Massachusetts, committees from nine colonies met in New York. The Assemblies of Virginia and North Carolina not having been in session since the issue of the Massachusetts circular, no opportunity had occurred of appointing committees. New York was in the same predicament; but a committee of correspondence, appointed at a previous session, saw fit to attend. In Georgia, Governor Wright refused to call the Assembly together; but the speaker of the House of Representatives, after consulting with a majority of the members, sent a letter to New York approving the proposed congress, and promising to support its measures. The New Hampshire House of Representatives gave their sanction to the congress, and offered to join in any suitable memorial; but, "owing to the particular state of their affairs" by which may be understood the predominant influence of Governor Wentworth, they sent no delegates. Dr. Franklin, about the close of his first agency in England, had obtained the post of Governor of New Jersey, vacated by Hardy, for his natural and only son, William Franklin. The new governor, who inherited all the prudence, with none of the patriotic ardor of his father, had prevailed upon the Assembly of that province to return a negative answer to the Massachusetts letter; but this proved so unsatisfactory to the people, that the speaker called the members together by circular, and delegates were appointed.

The Congress was organized by the appointment of Ruggles as president. There were present, among other members, beside Otis, of Massachusetts, William Johnson, of Connecticut; Philip Livingston, of New York; John Dickinson, of Pennsylvania; Thomas M'Kean, of Delaware, and

Christopher Gadsden and John Rutledge, of South Carolina, all subsequently distinguished in the history of the Revolution. A rule was adopted, giving to each colony represented, one vote.

In the course of a three weeks' session, a Declaration of the Rights and Grievances of the Colonies was agreed to. All the privileges of Englishmen were claimed by this declation, as the birthright of the colonists—among the rest, the right of being taxed only by their own consent. Since distance and local circumstances made a representation in the British Parliament impossible, these representatives, it was maintained, could be no other than the several colonial Legislatures. Thus was given a flat negative to a scheme lately broached in England by Pownall and others, for allowing to the colonies a representation in Parliament, a project to which both Otis and Franklin seem at first to have leaned.

A petition to the king, and memorials to each House of Parliament were also prepared, in which the cause of the colonies was eloquently pleaded. Ruggles refused to sign these papers, on the ground that they ought first to be approved by the several Assemblies, and should be forwarded to England as their acts. Ogden, one of the New Jersey delegates, withheld his signature on the same plea. The delegates from New York did not sign because they had no special authority for their attendance; nor did those of Connecticut or South Carolina, their commission restricting them to a report to their respective Assemblies. The petition and memorials, signed by the other delegates, were transmitted to England for presentation.

The several colonial Assemblies, at their earliest sessions, gave to the proceedings a cordial approval. The conduct of Ruggles, in refusing his-signature, was severely censured by the Massachusetts representatives. Ogden was burned in effigy by the people of New Jersey.

The first day of November, appointed for the Stamp act to go into operation, came and went, but not a stamp was anywhere to be seen. Two companies of rioters paraded that evening the streets of New York, demanding the delivery of the stamps, which Colden, on the resignation of the stamp distributor, and his refusal to receive them, had taken into the fort. Colden was hung in effigy. His carriage was seized, and made a bonfire of, under the muzzles of the guns; after which the mob proceeded to a house in the outskirts, then occupied by Major James, of the Royal artillery, who had made himself obnoxious by his free comments on the conduct of the colonists. James' furniture and property were destroyed, as Hutchinson's had been. General Gage, the commander-in-chief of the British forces in America, was at New York, but the regular garrison in the fort was very small. Alarmed for the safety of the city, and not willing to take any responsibility, as Sir Henry Moore, the recently appointed governor, was every day expected, Colden agreed by Gage's advice, the captain of a British ship of war in the harbor having refused to receive them, to give up the stamps to the mayor and corporation. They were accordingly deposited in the City Hall, under a receipt given by the Mayor.

These proceedings had been under the control of the inferior class of people, of whom Isaac Sears, formerly a shipmaster, and now inspector of potashes, was a conspicuous leader. The next day a meeting was called of the wealthier inhabitants, and a committee was appointed, of which Sears was a member, with four colleagues, to correspond with the other colonies. This committee soon brought forward an agreement to import no more goods from Great Britain till the Stamp Act was repealed—the commencement of a system of retaliation on the mother country repeatedly resorted to in the course of the struggle. This non-importation agreement, to which a non-consumption agreement was presently added, beside being extensively signed in New York, was adopted also in Philadelphia and Boston. At the same time, and as part of the same plan, a combination was entered into for the support of American manufactures, the wearing of American cloths, and the increase of sheep, by ceasing to eat lamb or mutton.

Business, suspended for a while, was presently resumed. Stamped papers were required in judicial proceedings, but by continuing the cases before them, or going on without notice of the deficiency, even the judges, after some hesitation, concurred in nullifying the act.

A change in the English ministry, which took place in July, and the news of which reached America in September, encouraged the colonists in the stand they had taken. This change originated in domestic reasons, wholly unconnected with colonial polity; it was regarded, however, as favorable to the general cause of freedom. The old Whig aristocracy, which had governed the kingdom since the accession of the house of Hanover, had split up, of late, into several bitter and hostile factions, chiefly founded on mere personal considerations. Pitt's repeated attacks on former ministries, and, at last, his forcing himself into power, had contributed not a little to this result. The accession of George III, had given rise to a new party, by which Pitt himself had been superseded—a party which called themselves "king's friends," composed partly of political adventurers from among the Whigs, such as Grenville, the late minister, but partly also of the representatives of the old Tory families, for half a century previous excluded by the Whigs from office. These "king's friends" were regarded as hostile to popular rights, and were looked upon by the great body of the middle class with very jealous eyes. It was their distinguishing doctrine, that the authority of the king had been usurped and encroached upon by the House of Commons. The Marquis of Rockingham, the new minister, leader of one of the fragments of the old Whig party, was liberally disposed; but as yet, there hardly existed in England a popular party, in our American sense. The interests of trade and manufactures were not, indeed, without their representatives, chosen from some of the large towns, but a great part of the boroughs were "rotten"—the property, that is, of one or more individuals, who, in fact, named the representatives; while money, in the shape of bribes, decided the choice in many of the rest. The House of Commons represented a narrow aristocracy, the majority of the members being substantially nominated by the great landholders. The House, thus chosen, debated with closed doors, only a few spectators being admitted, as a special favor. To publish an account of their proceedings was a breach of privilege, and only brief and imperfect sketches, even of the principal debates, found their way into print. Faint signs were but just beginning to appear, of that social revolution which has created the modern popular party of Great Britain and Europe, giving complete publicity to legislative proceedings, and organizing public opinion as a regular and powerful check upon authority.

In the address from the throne, at the opening of the session, the new ministry brought the state of colonial affairs before Parliament. They produced the correspondence of the colonial governors, and other papers relating to the late disturbance. Numerous petitions from British merchants, for the repeal of the Stamp Act, were also presented to the two Houses. (1766.)

Pitt, for some time past withdrawn by sickness from public affairs, was unconnected, at this moment, with either Grenville's or Rockingham's party. He now appeared in his place in the House of Commons, and delivered his opinion, "that the kingdom had no right to levy a tax on the colonies." "The Commons in America, represented in their several assemblies, have invariably exercised the constitutional right of giving and granting their own money; they would have been slaves if they had not; at the same time, this kingdom has ever possessed the power of legislative and commercial control. The colonies acknowledge your authority in all things, with the sole exception that you shall not take their money out of their pockets without their consent."

This decided avowal by Pitt, made a profound impression on the House. After a long pause, Grenville rose to vindicate the Stamp Act. The tumults in America bordered, he averred, on open rebellion; but if the doctrines now promulgated were upheld, they would soon lose that name, and become a revolution. Taxation was a branch of the sovereign power, constantly exercised by Parliament, over the unrepresented. Resorting, then, to a method of intimidation common with politicians, "the seditious spirit of the colonies," he said, "owes its birth to the faction in this House." This invidious assault was met by Pitt with characteristic intrepidity. "A charge is brought against gentlemen sitting in this House, of giving birth to sedition in America. The freedom with which they have spoken their sentiments against this unhappy act, is imputed to them as a crime. But the imputation shall not discourage me." "We are told America is obstinate—America is almost in open rebellion. Sir, I rejoice that America has resisted. Three millions of people so dead to all the feelings of liberty as voluntarily to submit to be slaves, would have been fit instruments to make slaves of all the rest." "The Americans have been wronged! They have been driven to madness by injustice! Will you punish them for the madness you have occasioned? No! Let this country be the first to resume its prudence and temper; I will pledge myself for the colonies, that on their part, animosity and resentment will cease."

The new ministry were under no obligation to support the policy of their predecessors. Anxious to escape the difficulty by the readiest means, they brought in a bill for repealing the Stamp Act. Franklin, summoned to the bar of the House as a witness, testified that the act could never be enforced. His prompt and pointed answers gained him great credit for information, acuteness, and presence of mind. In favor of repeal, Burke, introduced into Parliament by Rockingham, to whom he had been private secretary, and for one of whose rotten boroughs he sat, gave his eloquent support. In spite of a very strenuous opposition on the part of the supporters of the late ministry, the bill of repeal was carried in the House of Commons, by a vote of two hundred and seventy-five to one hundred and sixty-seven.

But the ministers by no means went the length of Pitt. They placed the repeal on the ground of expediency merely, and they softened the opposition by another bill, previously passed, which asserted the power and right of Parliament "to bind the colonies in all cases whatsoever." Lord Camden, formerly Chief-justice Pratt, made a vigorous opposition to this bill, in the House of Lords. "My position is this—I repeat it—I will maintain it to the last hour—taxation and representation are inseparable. The position is founded in the law of nature. It is more: it is itself an eternal law of nature." Lord Mansfield, on the other hand, maintained the sovereign power of Parliament as including the right to tax; an idea quite too flattering to the pride of authority to be easily relinquished.

CHAPTER XXXII.

Dawn of the Revolutionary Period—Humorous "History of John Bull's Children"—Contrast between causes which led to the Revolution of 1688, in England, and those which led to the American Revolution; from Judge Drayton's Charge, in 1776.

We now come to a new era of struggle, in the history of "Sam," by, and through which, his youthful prowess, thus continually exercised, as we have witnessed, becomes meet for successful collison with the uttermost force which is likely to array itself against his future. He has one more covert foe, with whom it is necessary that he should be finally "at quits," and who, (though not necessarily an internal one as are the Jesuits!) is yet, through his machinations, as dangerous, and even more important.

As usual, with the most serious affairs of the kind—it is a family quarrel, in which his elder first cousin, John Bull, assumes a domineering and pugilistic attitude, to the great tribulation of Sam—who, for the very reason that he was born of nothing but a cloud, was particularly sensitive about the matter of descent, primogeniture, reversions, titles, etc. Now all this may seem to have been very inconsistent on his part, but a slight sketch of his family history about those times, will illustrate these traits of Sam sufficiently.

"THE HISTORY OF JOHN BULL'S CHILDREN."

We find the following in the "*Maryland Gazette*" of August, 1776, into which it was copied from the "*London Chronicle.*"

I, Sir Humphrey Polesworth, who formerly gave the world a true and faithful account of John Bull, and of his mother, and his sister, and wives, and his servants, now write the history of his children, and how they were got, and how they were educated, and what befell them. Courteous reader, if thou hast any curiosity to know these things, read the following chapters, and learn.

CHAPTER I.—Of seven natural children, which John Bull had in his younger days by Doll Secretary, his mother's maid; namely, three boys, John, junior, or master Jacky, Yorky, and Jerry: four girls, Penelope, Mary, Virgy, and Caroline. How the old lady would suffer no bastards in her family; and how the poor infants were turned adrift on the fish-ponds as soon as born; how they landed on the western shore, and were there nursed by a wild bear, all under the green wood tree.

CHAPTER II.—How John disowned them, and left them to get over the children's disorders the best way they could, without paying a farthing for nurses, or apothecary's bills; and how, as soon as they had cut their eye-teeth, and were able to walk alone, John claimed them for his own.

CHAPTER III.—How Master Jacky turned fisherman and ship-carpenter. Yorky and Jerry drove a great trade; Miss Penny dealt in flour, called the Maid of the Mill, and never courtesied to anybody. How Mary and Virgy set up a snuff-shop; and Caroline turned dry salter, and sold indigo; and how they all flourished exceedingly, and laid out every penny they earned, in their father's warehouse.

CHAPTER IV.—Of two children more, that John had afterward, in lawful wedlock (viz: a boy whom he called Georgy, after his great patron, and a girl, whom he called Peg, after his sister Margaret); how he crammed them with sugar-plums, and how they remain sickly, rickety brats to this day.

CHAPTER V.—How young Master Baboon, old Louis' only son, fell in love with Miss Virgy, and how he came behind with intent to ravish her; how she squealed, and alarmed her dad.

CHAPTER VI.—How John called for his stick and his barge, and crossed the pond to save his daughter's virtue; how young Louis gave him a confounded rap on his fingers and drove him back; then at his daughter again.

CHAPTER VII.—How her brother Jack came to her assistance, and threw young Louis on his back; how old Louis

Baboon flew to help his son, and carried Lord Strutt along with him; how John Bull returned and mustered all his children at his back, and to it they went.

CHAPTER VIII.—How they had a long tussle; how John's children saved their old dad from a broken head, and helped to seize young Louis and tie him; how the old folks agreed to leave young Louis in custody, and drink friends themselves; and how John made his children pay a share of the reckoning, without giving them any of the drink.

CHAPTER IX.—How John, in his cups, bragged of his exploits, and said he had done all himself, and his children nothing; how he made choice of fair George, the gentle shepherd, for his house-steward, and because he could tell, without the book, that two and three make five, and had the multiplication table by heart.

CHAPTER X.—The whole stewardship of fair George—how he neglected to protest Louis Baboon's note of hand on the day of payment, and released Lord Strutt from a mortgage on his manor of Eastland; how he took an aversion to cider, and would allow none to be drunk in his family; how he rummaged every man's chest for pen, ink, and paper, and obliged those he caught writing, to stand atop of the table, with a wooden neckcloth under their chin, while he counted sixty times sixty; and how this is called the gentle shepherd's benefit of the clergy, unto this day.

CHAPTER XI.—How fair George took an antipathy to John's children, because he said they put nothing into the box at Christmas; and when they came to pay their shop accounts, they brought in their money at the back door; how he advised John to brand them on the far buttock, as they do stray cattle, that he might know them as his own.

CHAPTER XII.—How John's children rode restive, and swore they would not have the broad R. stamped on their b—k-s—des; how John, in heating the irons, burnt his own fingers, most d—ly; how all his neighbors laughed, and fair George could not find him a plaster.

CHAPTER XIII.—How John, in a passion, kicked fair George down stairs, and rung up other servants; how they advised him to consult his wife; and how Mrs. Bull advised him to let his children alone; that, though they were born in sin, they were his own flesh and blood, and needed no stamp to show it; how John took her advice, and let the irons cool again; and how some suspected if John's fingers had not smarted he would not have complied so soon.

CHAPTER XIV.—A dialogue on education, between fair George and lame Will. How Will proved it to be both cruel and impolitic to pinch children till they cried, and then pinch them for crying; and how George answered and said nothing.

CHAPTER XV.—How John, by means of his new servants, became beloved of his children, and respected by his neighbors; how he obliged Louis Baboon to beat down the walls of Ecclesdown castle, because it overlooked his pond, and harbored seagulls, to gobble up his fish. How he made him also pay up his note of hand; and how Lord Strutt ——.

What Lord Strutt did, does not appear, but this veracious narrator of the olden time, has furnished us with a genealogical treatise, invaluable in itself, and highly illustrative of many striking peculiarities, which we find to be even at this day, the distinctive family traits of "Sam," who has clearly inherited many of the good as well as bad qualities complained of, and portrayed above in the character of his ancestor, John Bull. Though Sam is in this instance the rather graphic complainant, yet we have endeavored to show, that in many instances since, his own conduct would have been no discredit to the attributes of the venerable elder John, himself!

But that "Sam" now began to have real causes of complaint, we shall perceive by the following "catalogue of oppressions, and contrast of the causes which led to the revolution which deposed James II., and those which led to the American Revolution." This valuable document is from

JUDGE DRAYTON'S CHARGE,

At an adjournment of the Court of GENERAL SESSIONS OF THE PEACE, OYER AND TERMINER, ASSIZE, AND GENERAL GAOL DELIVERY, held at *Charleston*, for the District of Charleston, on Tuesday, the 23d day of April, 1776, before the HON. WILLIAM HENRY DRAYTON, Esq., Chief-justice, and his Associates, justices of the colony of *South Carolina*.

Even the famous revolution in England, in the year 1688, is much inferior. However, we need no better authority than that illustrious precedent, and I will therefore compare the causes of, and the law upon the two events.

On the 7th of February, 1688, the Lords and Commons of England, in convention, completed the following resolutions:

"Resolved, That King James II., having endeavored to subvert the constitution of the kingdom, by breaking the original contract between king and people; and, by the advice of Jesuits and other wicked persons, having violated the fundamental laws, and having withdrawn himself out of this kingdom; has abdicated the government, and that the throne is thereby vacant."

That famous resolution deprived James of his crown, and became the foundation on which the throne of the present king of Great Britain is built; it also supports the edifice of government which we have erected.

In that resolve, there are but three facts stated to have been done by James. I will point them out, and examine whether those facts will apply to the present king of Great Britain, with regard to the operations of government, by him or his representative immediately, or by consequence, affecting this colony.

The first fact is, the having endeavored to subvert the constitution of the kingdom, by weakening the original contract.

The violation of the fundamental laws is the second fact; and in support of these two charges, the Lords spiritual and temporal, and Commons, assembled at Westminister, on the 12th day of February, 1688, declared James was guilty:

"By assuming and exercising a power of dispensing with, and suspending of laws, and the execution of laws, without consent of Parliament;

"By committing and prosecuting divers worthy prelates, for humbly petitioning to be excused from concurring to the said assumed power;

"By issuing and causing to be executed a commission, under the great seal, for erecting a court, called the Court of Commissioners for Ecclesiastical Causes;

"By levying money for, and to the use of the crown, by pretense of prerogative, for other time, and in other manner, than the same was granted by Parliament;

"By raising and keeping a standing army within this kingdom in time of peace, without consent of Parliament; and quartering soldiers contrary to law;

"By causing several good subjects, being Protestants, to be disarmed, at the same time when papists were both armed and employed, contrary to law;

"By violating the freedom of election of members to serve in Parliament;

"By prosecuting in the Court of King's Bench, for matters and causes cognizable only in Parliament; and by divers other arbitrary and illegal courses."

This declaration, thus contains two points of criminality—breach of the original contract, and violation of fundamental law.

The catalogue of our oppressions, continental and local, is enormous. Of such oppressions, I will mention only some of the most weighty:

Under color of law, the King and Parliament of Great Britain, have made the most arbitrary attempts to enslave America:

By claiming a right TO BIND THE COLONIES IN ALL CASES WHATSOEVER;

By laying duties, at their mere will and pleasure, upon all the colonies;

By suspending the Legislature of New York;

By rendering the American charters of no validity, having annulled the most material parts of the charter of Massachusetts Bay;

By divesting multitudes of the colonists of their property without legal accusation or trial;

By depriving whole colonies of the bounty of Providence on their own proper coasts, in order to coerce them by famine;

By restricting the trade and commerce of America;

By sending to, and continuing in America, in time of peace, an armed force, without and against the consent of the people;

By granting impunity to a soldiery instigated to murder the Americans;

By declaring, that the people of Massachusetts Bay are liable for offences, or *pretended* offences, done in that colony, to be sent to, and tried for the same in ENGLAND; or in any *colony where they can not have the benefit of a jury of the vicinage.*

By establishing, in Quebec, the Roman Catholic religion, and an arbitrary government; instead of the Protestant religion and a free government.

And thus America saw it demonstrated, that no faith ought to be put in a royal proclamation; for I must observe to you that, in the year 1763, by such a proclamation, people were invited to settle in Canada, and were assured of a legislative representation, the benefit of the common law of England, and a free government. It is a misfortune to the public, that this is not the only instance of the inefficiency of a royal proclamation. However, having given you one instance of a failure of royal faith in the northern extremity of this abused continent, let it suffice, that I direct your attention to southern extremity, respecting which, the same particulars, were, in the same manner promised, but the deceived inhabitants of St. Augustine are left by their grand jury, in vain to complain and lament to the world, and yet scarcely permitted to exercise even that privilege distinguishing the miserable distinction that royal faith is not kept with them.

Let us contrast the causes which led to the Revolution which deposed James II, with those which led to the American Revolution:

In the first place then, it is laid down in the best law authorities, that protection and subjection are reciprocal; and that these reciprocal duties form the original contract between king and people. It therefore follows, that the original contract was broken by James' conduct, as above stated, which amounted to a not affording due protection to his people. And it is clear that he violated the fundamental laws, by the suspending of laws, and the execution of laws; by levying money; by violating the freedom of election of members to serve in parliament; by keeping a standing army in time of peace; and by quartering soldiers contrary to law, and without consent of parliament—which is as much as to say, that he did those things without consent of *the legislative Assembly* chosen by the PERSONAL ELECTION *of that people,* over whom such doings were exercised.

These points, reasonings and conclusions, being settled in, deduced from, and established upon parliamentary proceedings and the best law authorities, must ever remain unshaken. I am now to undertake the disagreeable task of examining whether they will apply to the violences which have lighted up, and now feed the flames of civil war in America.

James II. suspended the operations of laws—George III. caused the charter of the Massachusetts-Bay to be, in effect, annihilated; he suspended the operation of the law which formed a legislature in New York, vesting it with adequate powers; and thereby he caused the very ability of making laws in that colony to be suspended.

King James levied money without the consent of the representatives of the people, called upon to pay it—King George has levied money upon America, not only without, but expressly *against* the consent of the representatives of the people in America.

King James violated the freedom of election of members to serve in parliament—King George, by his representative, Lord William Campbell, acting for him and on his behalf, broke through a fundamental law of this country, for the certain holding of general assemblies; and, thereby, as far as in him lay, not only violated, but annihilated the very ability of holding a general assembly.

King James, in time of peace, kept a standing army in England, without consent of the representatives of the people, among whom that army was kept—King George hath, in time of peace, invaded this continent with a large standing army, without the consent, and he hath kept it within this continent expressly against the consent of the representatives of the people, among whom that army is posted.

All which doings by King George III., respecting America, are as much contrary to our interests and welfare, as much against law, and tend as much, at least, to subvert and extirpate the liberties of this colony, and of America, as the similar proceedings, by James II., operated respecting the people of England. For the same principle of law, touching the premises, equally applies to the people of England in the one case, and to the people of America in the other. And this is the great principle. Certain acts done, over, and affecting a people, against and *without* THEIR CONSENT, *expressed by themselves, or by* REPRESENTATIVES *of their* OWN ELECTION. Upon this *only* principle was grounded the complaints of the people of England—upon the *same* is grounded the complaints of the people of America. And hence it clearly follows, that if James II. violated the fundamental laws of England, George III. hath also violated the fundamental laws of America.

Again:—King James broke the original contract by not affording due protection to his subjects, although he was not charged with having seized their towns, or with having held them against the people—or, with having laid them in ruins, by his arms—or, with having seized their vessels—or, with having pursued the people with fire and sword—or, with having declared them rebels for resisting his arms, levelled to destroy their lives, liberties, and properties. But George III. hath done all these things against America; and, it is, therefore, undeniable that he hath not afforded due protection to the people. Wherefore, if James II. broke the original contract, it is undeniable that George III. has also broken the original contract between king and people; and that he made use of the most violent measures by which it could be done—violences of which James *was* GUILTLESS—measures carrying conflagrations, massacre and open war amidst a people whose subjection to the king of Great Britain the law holds to be due *only* as a return for protection. And so tenacious and clear is the law upon this very principle, that it is laid down, subjection is not due even to a king, *de jure*, or of right, unless he be also king *de facto*, or in possession of the executive powers dispensing protection.

Again, the third fact charged against James is, that he withdrew himself out of the kingdom—and we know that the people of this country have declared, that Lord William Campbell, the king of Great Britain's representative, "having used his utmost efforts to destroy the lives, liberties, and property of the good people here, whom by the duty of his station he was bound to protect, withdrew himself out of the colony." Hence it will appear, that George III. hath withdrawn himself out of this colony, provided it be established that exactly the same natural consequence resulted from the withdrawal in each case respectively—King James personally out of England, and King George out of Carolina, by the agency of his substitute and representative, Lord William Campbell.

By King James' withdrawing, the executive magistrate was gone; thereby, in the eye of the law, the executive magistrate was dead, and of consequence, royal government actually ceased in England:—so by King George's representative withdrawing, the executive magistrate was gone; the death, in law, became apparent, and of consequence royal government actually ceased in this colony. Lord William withdrew as the king's representative, carrying off the great seal and royal instructions to governors; and acting for, and on the part of his principal, by every construction of law, that conduct became the conduct of his principal; and thus, James II. withdrew out of England, and George III. withdrew out of South Carolina; and by such a conduct, respectively, the people in each country were exactly in the same degree injured.

The three facts against King James being thus stated, and compared with similar proceedings by King George, we are now to ascertain the result of the injuries done by the first, and the law upon that point—which being ascertained, must naturally constitute the judgement in law, upon the result of the similar injuries done by the last; and I am happy that I can give you the best authority upon this important point.

Treating upon this great precedent in constitutional law, the learned Judge Blackstone declares, that the result of the facts "amounted to an abdication of the government, which abdication did not affect only the person of the king himself, but also, *all his heirs;* and rendered the throne absolutely and completely vacant." Thus it clearly appears that the government was not abdicated, and the throne vacated by the resolution of the Lords and Commons, but that the resolution was only declaratory of the law of Nature and reason, upon the result of the injuries proceeding from the three combined facts of mal-administration. And thus, as I have on the foot of the best authorities made it evident, that George III., king of Great Britain, has endeavored to subvert the constitution of this country, by breaking the original contract between king and country; by the advice of wicked persons, has violated the fundamental laws, and has withdrawn himself, by withdrawing the constitutional benefits of the kingly office, and his protection out of this country; from such a result of injuries, from such a conjunction of circumstances, the law of the land authorizes me to declare, and it is my duty boldly to declare the law, that George III., king of Great Britain, has abdicated the government, and that the throne is thereby vacant—that is, *he has no authority over us*, and *we owe no obedience to him*. The British ministers already have presented a charge of mine to the notice of the Lords and Commons, in Parliament; and I am nothing loth that they take equal resentment against this charge. For, supported by the fundamental laws of the constitution, and engaged as I am in the cause of virtue, I fear no consequences from their machinations.

Thus having stated the principal causes of our *last* revolution, it is clear as the sun in meridian, that George III. injured the Americans, at least as grievously as James II. injured the people of England; but that James did not oppress these in so *criminal* a manner as George has oppressed the Americans.

CHAPTER XXXIII.

Townshend's scheme of Colonial Taxation—Repeal of the new taxes, except that on Tea—Local Affairs—Trade of the Colonies—Attempt to collect the Tax on Tea—Reminiscences of the Position of the Tea Ships at Boston—Destruction of the Tea in Boston Harbor.

In spite of the Parliamentary claim, of power to bind the colonies in all cases whatsoever, the repeal of the Stamp Act produced throughout America a great burst of loyalty and gratitude. Virginia voted a statue to the king. New York voted statues to the king and to Pitt, both of which were presently erected. Maryland voted a statue to Pitt, and a portrait of Lord Camden. Faneuil Hall was adorned with full-length pictures of Barre and Conway. Pitt became more than ever a popular idol. Resolutions of thanks to him and others were agreed to by most of the colonial Assemblies.

A resolution of the House of Commons had demanded indemnity from the colonies for such crown officers as had suffered losses in the late Stamp Act riots. New York promptly complied. After much urging by the governor, Massachusetts passed a similar act; but a free pardon to the rioters, inserted in it, betrayed the state of public feeling, and gave great offense in England.

As the first burst of exultation died away, new discontents began to spring up. The Stamp Act was repealed, but the "Sugar Act" remained in force, and, though modified by a still further reduction of the duties on molasses, to one penny per gallon, it continued to give great dissatisfaction, especially in the northern colonies. Another modification of that act prohibited all direct trade with France. But iron and lumber, lately placed in the list of "enumerated articles," were allowed to be exported to European ports south of Cape Finisterre.

The opponents of the Stamp Act, or some of them, especially Pitt, had taken a distinction between a direct tax levied on the colonies, and commercial imposts which might be supposed to fall under the admitted parliamentary right of regulating trade. Of this distinction Townshend took advantage in framing his new project—but in one respect his bill violated the established policy of the mother country. The royal negative had been repeatedly placed on colonial acts levying imposts on British goods. But this bill, along with tea, included paints, paper, glass, and lead—articles of British produce—as objects of custom-house taxation in the colonies. The exportation of tea to America was encouraged by another act, allowing for five years a drawback of the whole duty payable on the importation.

The impossibility of enforcing the Stamp Act, not any sense of right or justice, had produced its repeal. This new act of Townshend's, the immediate cause of all the subsequent troubles, was supposed to be of easier execution, and passed with very little opposition. By another act, reorganizing the colonial custom-house system, a Board of Revenue Commissioners for America was established, to have its seat at Boston. (June, 1767.)

The Massachusetts House of Representatives consisted at this time of upward of a hundred members, by far the most numerous Assembly in America. Its debates had begun to attract attention, and a gallery had lately been erected for the accommodation of spectators. The council, purged by dropping Hutchinson and several other officials, was now chiefly influenced by James Bowdoin. His grandfather, a French Huguenot, had migrated to New England shortly after the revocation of the Edict of Nantes. His father, from very small beginnings, had acquired the largest fortune in Boston, all of which, being an only child, Bowdoin had inherited at the age of twenty-one. In the prime of life, of elevated character and a studious turn of mind, for several years past a member of the council, he acted in close concert with Adams, to whose impetuous ardor and restless activity his less excitable but not less firm temper served as a useful counterpoise. (1768.)

Meanwhile the merchants had been greatly irritated by new strictness in the collection of duties, and by suits even for past breaches of the revenue laws. Shortly after the meeting of the new General Court, the seizure of the sloop Liberty, belonging to Hancock, on the charge of having smuggled on shore a cargo of wine from Madeira, occasioned a great riot. The newly-appointed revenue commissioners fled for their lives, first on board a ship-of-war in the harbor, and then to the barracks on Castle Island, where a company of British artillery was stationed. A town meeting, held in Faneuil Hall, petitioned the governor to remove the ship-of-war from the harbor. The council passed resolutions strongly condemning the rioters, but would not advise that the commissioners might safely return to the town, nor could the governor induce them to take any decided step of any sort. The House took no notice at all of the matter. An attempt to prosecute those engaged in the riot failed for want of witnesses, and even the proceedings against the vessel had to be given up for the same cause.

Before news had reached England, of the late riot in Boston, two regiments from Halifax had been ordered thither. When news of that riot arrived, two additional regiments were ordered from Ireland. The arrival of an officer, sent by Gage from New York, to provide quarters for these troops, occasioned a town meeting in Boston, by which the governor was requested to summon a new General Court, which he peremptorily refused to do. The meeting then recommended a convention of delegates from all the towns in the province, to assemble at Boston in ten days; "in consequence of prevailing apprehensions of a war with France"—such was the pretense—they advised all persons not already provided with fire-arms to procure them at once; they also appointed a day of fasting and prayer, to be observed by all the Congregational societies. Delegates from more than a hundred towns met accordingly at the day appointed, chose Cushing, speaker of the late House, as their chairman, and petitioned Bernard to summon a General Court. The governor not only refused to receive their petition, but denounced the meeting as treasonable. In view of this charge, the proceedings were exceedingly cautious and moderate. All pretensions to political authority were expressly disclaimed. In the course of a four days' session, a petition to the king was agreed to, and a letter to the agent, De Berdt, of which the chief burden was to defend the province against the charge of a rebellious spirit. Such was the first of those popular conventions, destined within a few years to assume the whole political authority of the colonies.

The day after the adjournment, the troops from Halifax arrived. There was room in the barracks at the castle, but Gage, alarmed at the accounts from Massachusetts, had sent orders from New York to have the two regiments quartered in the town. The council were called upon to find quarters, but by the very terms of the Quartering Act, as they alleged, till the barracks were full there was no necessity to provide quarters elsewhere. Bernard insisted that the barracks had been reserved for the two regiments expected from Ireland, and must, therefore, be considered as already full. The council replied, that, even allowing that to be the case, by the terms of the act, the provision of quarters belonged not to them, but to the local magistrates. There was a large building in Boston belonging to the province, known as the "Manufactory House," and occupied by a number of poor families. Bernard pressed the council to advise that this building be cleared, and prepared for the reception of the troops; but they utterly refused. The governor then undertook to do it on his own authority. The troops had already landed, under cover of the ships of war, to the number of a thousand men. Some of them appeared, to demand an entrance into the Manufactory House; but the tenants were encouraged to keep possession; nor did the governor venture to use force. One of the regiments encamped on the Common; for a part of the other regiment, which had no tents, the temporary use of Faneuil Hall was reluctantly yielded; to the rest of it, the Town House, used also as a State House, all except the council chamber, was thrown open by the governor's order. It was Sunday. The Town House was directly opposite the meeting-house of the First Church. Cannon were planted in front of it; sentinels were stationed in the streets; the inhabitants were challenged as they passed. The devout were greatly aggravated and annoyed by the beating of drums, and the marching of the troops.

Presently Gage came to Boston to urge the provision of quarters. The council directed his attention to the terms of the act, and referred him to the selectmen. As the act spoke only of justices of the peace, the selectmen declined to take any steps in the matter. Bernard then constituted what he called a Board of Justices, and required them to find quarters; but they did not choose to exercise a doubtful and unpopular authority. Gage was finally obliged to quarter the troops in houses which he hired for that purpose, and to procure out of his own military chest the firing, bedding, and other articles mentioned in the Quartering Act, the council having declined to order any expenditure for those purposes, on the ground that the appropriation of money belonged exclusively to the General Court.

The seventeen months during which the British troops had been stationed in Boston, even the agreement of the commanding officer to use only a single drum and fife on Sundays, had by no means reconciled the townspeople to their presence. A weekly paper, the "Journal of the Times," was filled with all sorts of stories, some true, but the greater part false or exaggerated, on purpose to keep up prejudice against the soldiers. A mob of men and boys, encouraged by the sympathy of the mass of the inhabitants, made it a constant practice to insult and provoke them. The result to be expected soon followed. After numerous fights with straggling soldiers, a serious collision at length took place. A picket guard of eight men, provoked beyond endurance by words and blows, fired into a crowd, killed three persons, and dangerously wounded five others. The bells were rung; a cry spread through the town—"the soldiers are rising." It was late at night; but the population poured into the streets; nor was it without difficulty that a general combat was prevented. The next morning, at an early hour, Faneuil Hall was filled with an excited and indignant assembly. At a town meeting, legally warned, held that afternoon in the old South Meeting-house, the largest building in the town, it was voted "that nothing could be expected to restore peace, and prevent blood and carnage, but the immediate removal of the troops." A committee was appointed, with Samuel Adams as chairman, to carry this vote to the lieutenant governor and council. Adams entered the council chamber at the head of his committee, and delivered his message. Colonel Dalrymple, the commander of the troops, was present, as was the commander of the ships of war in the harbor. Hutchinson disclaimed any authority over the soldiers. Adams answered by a reference to that clause in the charter which declared the governor, or, in his absence, the lieutenant governor, commander-in-chief of all the military and naval forces in the province. After a consultation with Dalrymple, Hutchinson replied that the colonel was willing to remove one of the regiments to the castle, if that would satisfy the people. "Sir," said Adams, "if the lieutenant governor, or Colonel Dalrymple, or both together, have authority to remove one regiment, they have authority to remove two; and nothing short of the departure of both regiments will satisfy the public mind, or preserve the peace of the province." The town meeting, after the return of their committee, voted the lieutenant governor's offer unsatisfactory. Hutchinson and Dalrymple seem to have been mutually anxious to shift upon each other the responsibility of yielding to the popular demand. Finally, upon the unanimous advice of the council, it was agreed that all the troops should be removed, the colonel pledging his honor that mean while not a single soldier should be seen in the streets after dark. The funeral of the slain, attended by a vast concourse of people, was celebrated with all possible pomp. The story of the "Boston Massacre," for so it was called, exaggerated into a ferocious and unprovoked assault by brutal soldiers on a defenseless people, produced every where intense excitement. The officer and soldiers of the picket guard were indicted and tried for murder. They were defended, however, by John Adams and Josiah Quincy, two young lawyers, among the most zealous of the popular leaders; and so clear a case was made out in their behalf, that they were all acquitted except two, who were found guilty of manslaughter, and slightly punished.

The British cabinet, after great struggles, had been quite sifted of its Whig members. The "king's friends" section of it had expelled all their opponents, and Francis North, eldest son of the Earl of Guilford, by courtesy Lord North, as the leader of that section, had risen to the head of the ministry. As it happened, on the very day of the Boston massacre Lord North brought forward the promised motion to repeal the whole of Townshend's act except the duty on tea. That act, he observed, had been the occasion of most dangerous, violent, and illegal combinations in America against the importation and use of British manufactures. The British merchants had petitioned against it. As to articles of British produce, ever to have taxed them was indeed an absurd violation of established policy. The tax on tea stood on a different ground. When that tax was imposed, a drawback had been allowed on the exportation of tea to America; and as the colonists were thus relieved of a duty amounting, on an average, to a shilling a pound, they had no right to complain of a tax of threepence, since they gained, in fact, ninepence the pound by the change. He could have wished to repeal the whole act, could that have been done without giving up the right of taxing the colonies—a right he would contend for to the last hour of his life. The proposed repeal, without any relaxation of authority, was intended as a persuasive to bring the colonists back to their duty. The existing combinations in the colonies, against the use of British manufactures, he thought, would soon come to an end.

Pownall moved to include tea in the repeal, supporting this amendment rather on grounds of expediency and commercial policy than as a matter of colonial right. He was seconded by Conway and Barre. Grenville declared that when he laid the stamp tax, he had the best information that it would be submitted to. In laying that tax he had acted systematically, to make every portion of the king's dominions bear a part of the public burdens. When that act raised troubles in America, the ministers who succeeded him acted systematically too. Theirs, perhaps, was the next best system to his own. They took the Americans by the hand, and restored things to the state they were in before the passing of the Stamp Act. In this statement, however, Grenville overlooked the Sugar Act, which the Rockingham ministry had left in full force; but that he probably regarded as a mere modification of the old Molasses Act, though essentially different from it in principle, involving the claim of parliamentary taxation hardly less than the Stamp Act itself. "Since that time," said Grenville, "no minister had acted with common sense. The next ministry laid a tax diametrically repugnant to commercial principles, bringing in no money, and throwing North America into ten times greater flame than before." He was in favor of easing the Americans; but the ministers had no plan. The partial repeal which they proposed would do no good; and the proposed amendment was so very little better, that he did not think it worth while to force it upon a reluctant ministry. He, therefore, should not vote upon the question. The amendment was defeated, two hundred and four to one hundred and forty-two; and, on a subsequent day, Lord North's bill of repeal became law. The obnoxious Quartering Act, limited by its terms to three years, was suffered silently to expire. But the Sugar Act, and especially the tax on tea, as they involved the whole principle of parliamentary taxation, were quite sufficient to keep up the discontent of the colonies.

Lord North's act, in one respect, accomplished its object, in furnishing an excuse for abandoning the non-importation and non-consumption agreements, which soon became limited to the article of tea. Those agreements, though only partially observed, and that not without great jealousies and heart-burnings, were not, however, without permanent consequences. The discontinuance of that pomp of mourning and funeral expenses, for excess in which the colonists had been hitherto distinguished, takes its date from this occasion. The infant manufactures of America received, too, from these agreements, a strong impulse. Home-made became all the fashion. The graduating class at Cambridge took their degrees this year in homespun suits.

The trade between Great Britain and the colonies is stated for the year 1770, as follows, and the average of the last ten years, allowing for a moderate increase, had not been materially different:

Exports to Great Britain.

New England	£148,011	$657,168
New York	69,882	310,276
Pennsylvania	28,109	124,803
Virginia and Maryland	435,094	1,931,801
Carolinas	278,097	1,234,750
Georgia	55,532	234,352
	£1,014,725	$4,493,150

Imports from Great Britain.

New England	£394,451	$1,751,362
New York	475,991	2,113,400
Pennsylvania	134,881	599,093
Virginia and Maryland	717,782	3,186,952
Carolinas	146,272	649,446
Georgia	56,193	249,496
	£1,925,570	$8,549,749

The surplus of imports was paid for by the profits of the trade with Spain, Portugal, and the West Indies.

The taxation dispute, after a ten years' growth, was now fast coming to a head. The ministers saw with no little vexation, that the tax on tea, retained for the express purpose of vindicating the authority of Parliament, was substantially nullified, partly by smuggling, and partly by the non-importation and non-consumption agreements, observed as yet with considerable fidelity, especially in the middle and southern colonies. Perhaps it would have been the more politic course, to have given time for these combinations to die away, leaving the gradual introduction of the use of duty-paid tea to the vigilance of the customhouse officers, to appetite, and commercial cupidity and rivalry. Instead of adopting that temporizing policy, the impatient ministers resolved to force at once upon the reluctant colonies a large quantity of the obnoxious article; well satisfied that, if landed and offered for sale, it would easily find its way into consumption. (1773.)

By an act of the preceding session, the allowance of drawback on teas exported, had been reduced to three-fifths of the duty. So far as America was concerned, a drawback of the whole duty was now revived. The existing restraints upon the East India Company, to export teas on their own account, were also repealed, and arrangements were presently entered into with that Company, for the consignment of several cargoes of teas to the principal American ports.

No sooner did this project become known in America, than steps were taken to counterwork it. A public meeting of the people of Philadelphia protested, in eight resolutions, against taxation by Parliament; and denounced as an enemy to his country," "whosoever shall aid or abet in unloading, receiving, or vending the tea." In accordance with one of the resolutions, a committee was appointed to wait on the reputed consignees in that city, "to request them, from a regard to their own characters, and the public peace and good order of the city and province, immediately to resign their apppointments." The Messrs. Wharton gave a satisfactory answer, which was received with shouts of applause. Groans and hisses greeted the refusal of another firm to commit themselves till the tea arrived.

The names of three well-known firms in Boston, presently began to be noised about as the intended consignees of the East India Company's tea. An anonymous notice was sent to these reputed consignees to be present at noon on a certain day, under Liberty Tree, to resign their appointments, for which day and hour an anonymous hand-bill called a public meeting to hear their resignations. Several hundred persons assembled accordingly; the consignees not appearing, a committee was sent to wait upon them; but this committee they treated with contempt.

Two days after, by a call of the selectmen, a legal town meeting was held, at which Hancock presided. After a preamble of their own, this meeting adopted the eight Philadelphia resolutions, with a supplement, acknowledging some remissness hitherto, in the matter of the agreement not to import or consume tea, but insisting for the future upon strict observance. A committee, appointed in the terms of one of the resolutions, waited upon the consignees to request them to resign. After some little delay and evasion, they replied that, being as yet without any definite advices from England, they could give no decisive answer—a reply, voted by the meeting, "unsatisfactory" and "daringly affrontive."

News presently arriving that the tea ships had sailed, and might be daily expected, another town meeting was summoned for the next day, to consult "what further application shall be made to the consignees, or otherwise to act as the town shall think fit at the present dangerous crisis." In the evening, the house of Clarke, one of the consignees, was surrounded by a crowd, making many offensive noises, and a pistol having been fired at them, they retorted by smashing in the windows.

The town meeting, the next day, sent a committee to the the consignees, to inquire definitely, whether or not they intended to resign. Upon receipt of an answer in the negative, the meeting dissolved without a word. This evidence of a determination to act instead of resolving, struck terror into the consignees. They presented a petition the next day, to the governor and council, asking to resign themselves and the property committed to their care, into the hands "of his excellency and their honors," and praying them to take measures for landing and securing the teas. The council, led by Bowdoin, were very little inclined to interfere. They deprecated the late riot at Clarke's house, at least in words, and advised that the rioters be prosecuted; but they asked further time to consider the petition. Several adjournments accordingly took place, and before any decision was reached, one of the tea ships arrived. The council having met next day, presented a paper to the governor, declining to become parties to an unconstitutional attempt to levy taxes, against which the General Court had so repeatedly protested, or to make themselves chargeable for the tea, by interfering to receive it. Meetings in all the neighboring towns had resolved to sustain Boston; and while the council was thus declining to intermeddle with the matter, a mass meeting, or "body," as they called themselves, of the people of Boston and the neighboring towns, assembled in Faneuil Hall, sent for the owner of the tea ship, ordered her to be moored at a certain wharf, and appointed a watch of twenty-five volunteers to watch her. It was resolved to send her back with her cargo, and the master and the owner were charged not to attempt, at their peril, to unlade her. The consignees, among whom were two of the governor's sons, frightened at these demonstrations, took refuge at the castle, where was a regiment of British regulars. The "body" having met again the next day, the governor sent the sheriff of the county with a proclamation, declaring the meeting illegal, and ordering the people to disperse. They heard the message, hissed it, and voted unanimously not to regard it. The governor was powerless. He had ordered the Cadets, his guard of honor, to be in readiness; but what could he expect of a company commanded by Hancock? The troops at the castle, and the ships of war in the harbor, had no warrant to interfere in a purely municipal matter; nor was there any ground for the governor to call upon them, till something in the nature of riot, if not rebellion, had actually occurred. The consignees offered, if the tea might be landed, to keep it in store till orders came from England; but this was rejected, and the master and the owner of the vessel, were both constrained to promise to carry it back. The owners of two other vessels on the way, were required to make a similar promise. Tea was denounced as a "pernicious weed," and all persons who might henceforward be concerned in its importation, were declared enemies of their country. After a resolution to carry the matter through, at the risk of their lives and property, the "body" dissolved, leaving matters in the hands of a committee.

The owner of the vessel was very little disposed to carry out the agreement extorted from him. The governor was resolved that no clearance should be granted till the cargo was landed. At the end of thirty days from her arrival, the vessel would be liable to seizure, for non-payment of duties. Two other tea ships presently arrived, and were placed in custody like the other. Provoked and alarmed at the non-departure of the first vessel, the "body" re-assembled. The owner was sent for, and a committee was appointed to go with him to demand a clearance, which the collector, after taking time to consider, refused to give till the cargo was landed. The owner was then sent anew to the governor, at his country-house at Milton, to request a permit, without which the vessel could not pass the fort and the ships-of-war in the harbor. He returned late in the afternoon, and announced the governor's refusal; he had no power, he said, to grant the permit till a clearance was first exhibited. This had been anticipated and prepared for. A band of some fifty men, "very dark-complexioned persons, dressed like Mohawks, of very grotesque appearance," so says the Massachusetts Gazette of that day, "approached the hall with an imitation of the war-whoop, and, while Josiah Quincy harangued the people on the necessity of adhering to their resolutions, whatever might be the consequences, the pretended Mohawks proceeded to the wharf, and boarded the tea vessels. It was now six oclock; the evening dusk had set in; the 'body' was dissolved, and the people, hastening to the wharf, looked on in silent anxiety, while in the course of two hours, three hundred and forty-two chests of tea were drawn up from the holds of the vessels and emptied into the water."

There have been some doubts concerning the destruction of the tea, on the 16th of December, 1773. The number of the ships, and the place where they were situated, is not quite certain. One gentleman, now living, over seventy years of age, thinks they were at Hubbard's Wharf, as it was then called, about half way between Griffin's (now Liverpool) and Foster's Wharf, and that the number of ships were four or five. Another gentleman, who is seventy-five years of age, and who was one of the guard detached from the new grenadier company, says that he spent the night, but one, before the destruction of the tea, in company with General Knox, then a private in that company, on board one of the tea ships; that this ship lay on the south side of Russell's Wharf; and and that there were two more on the north side of the same wharf, and he thinks one or two at Griffin's Wharf. A gentleman now living, who came from England in one of the tea ships, thinks there were but two, but is uncertain where they lay. A song, written soon after the time, tells of "Three ill-fated ships at Griffin's wharf." The whole evidence seems to result in this: there were *three* ships—but whether at Russell's or Griffin's wharf, or one or more at each, is not certain. The number of chests destroyed was, according to the newspapers of the times, 342. There was a "body-meeting" on the 16th of December, 1773. This matter of the tea was the occasion of the meeting. The meeting began at Fanueil Hall, but that place not being large enough, it was adjourned to the Old South, and even that place could not contain all who came.

Jonathan Williams was moderator. Among the spectators was John Rowe, who lived in Pond street, where Mr. Prescott now lives; among other things, he said: "Who knows how tea will mingle with salt water?" and this suggestion was received with great applause. Governor Hutchinson was at this time at the house on Milton Hill, where Barney Smith, Esq., lives. A committee was sent from the meeting to request him to order the ships to depart. While they were gone, speeches were made, for the purpose of keeping the people together. The committee returned about sunset, with his answer, that he could not interfere. At this moment the Indian yell was heard from the street. Mr. Samuel Adams cried out that it was a trick of their enemies to disturb the meeting, and requested the people to keep their places—but the people rushed out, and accompanied the Indians to the ships. The number of persons disguised as Indians is variously stated—none put it lower than sixty, none higher than eighty. It is said by persons who were present, that nothing was destroyed but the tea—and this was not done with noise and tumult, little or nothing being said either by the agents or the multitude who looked on. The impression was that of solemnity rather than that of riot and confusion. The destruction was effected by the disguised persons, and some young men who volunteered; one of the latter collected the tea which fell into the shoes of himself and companions, and put it into a vial and sealed it up—which vial is now in his possession, containing the same tea.

The contrivers of this measure, and those who carried it into effect, will never be known; some few persons have been mentioned as being among the disguised, but there are many and obvious reasons why secresy then, and concealment since, were necessary. None of the persons who were confidently said to have been of the party (except some who were then minors or very young men) have ever admitted that they were so. The person who appeared to know more than any one I ever spoke with, refused to mention names. Mr. Samuel Adams is thought to have been in the counseling of this exploit, and many other men, who were leaders in the political affairs of the times; and the hall of council is said to have been in the back-room of Edes & Gill's printing-office, at the corner of the alley leading to Battle street church, from Court street. There are very few alive now who helped to empty the chests of tea, and these few will probably be as prudent as those who have gone before them.

At length, after great delays, the New York tea ship arrived at Sandy Hook. The pilots, under instructions from the city committee, refused to bring her up, and a "Committee of Vigilance" soon took possession of her. Brought to town, the captain was informed by a deputation from the city committee that he must take back ship and cargo. He desired to see the consignee, and was escorted to him; but the consignee declined to give any orders. Meanwhile, another ship, commanded by a New York Captain, arrived at the Hook, and, on assurance that she had no tea on board, was allowed to come to town. But a report to the contrary soon spread, and the captain was obliged to acknowledge that he had eighteen chests, not belonging to the East India Company, but a private adventure. The indignant populace seized the tea and emptied it into the river. A day or two after, with great parade, headed by a band playing, "God save the King," the bells ringing, and colors flying from the liberty pole and the shipping, the captain of the East India tea ship was escorted from the custom-house to a pilot boat, which took him to the Hook, where, under directions of the Committee of Vigilance, the anchors were weighed, and the vessel started on her homeward voyage.

The Charleston tea ship reached that city the same day that the New York tea ship reached the Hook. The teas were landed, but were stored in damp cellars, where they soon became worthless. We give here a very rare copy of the resolutions entered upon, at a great meeting of the citizens of Philadelphia, commending the course of the Boston tea rioters.

A public meeting of the inhabitants was held at the State House, on the 18th of October, at which great numbers attended, and the sense of the city was expressed in the following resolutions:—

1. That the disposal of their own property is the inherent right of freemen; that there can be no property in that which another can, of right, take from us without our consent; that the claim of Parliament to tax America, is, in other words, a claim of right to levy contributions on us at pleasure.

2. That the duty imposed by Parliament upon tea landed in America, is a tax on the Americans, or levying contributions on them without their consent.

3. That the express purpose for which the tax is levied on the Americans, namely, for the support of government, administration of justice, and defense of his Majesty's dominions in America, has a direct tendency to render Assemblies useless, and to introduce arbitrary government and slavery.

4. That a virtuous and steady opposition to this ministerial plan of governing America, is absolutely necessary to preserve even the shadow of liberty, and it is a duty which every freeman in America owes to his country, to himself, and posterity.

5. That the resolution lately entered into by the East India Company, to send out their tea to America, subject to the payment of duties on its being landed here, is an open attempt to enforce the ministerial plan, and a violent attack upon the liberties of America.

6. That it is the duty of every American to oppose this attempt.

7. That whoever shall directly or indirectly countenance this attempt, or in anywise aid or abet in unloading, receiving, or vending the tea sent, or to be sent out by the East India Company, while it remains subject to the payment of a duty here, is an enemy to his country.

8. That a committee be immediately chosen to wait on those gentlemen who, it is reported, are appointed by the East India Company, to receive and sell the said tea, and request them, from a regard to their own character, and the peace and good order of the city and province, immediately to resign their appointment.

Upon an hour's notice, on Monday morning, a public meeting was called, and the State House not being sufficient to hold the numbers assembled, they adjourned into the Square. This meeting is allowed by all to be the most respectable, both in the numbers and rank of those who attended it, that has been known in this city. After a short introduction, the following resolutions were not only agreed to, but the public approbation testified in the warmest manner.

1. That the tea, on board the ship Polly, Captain Ayres, shall not be landed.

2. That Captain Ayres shall neither enter nor report his vessel at the custom-house.

3. That Captain Ayres shall carry back the tea immediately.

4. That Captain Ayres shall immediately send a pilot on board his vessel, to take charge of her, and proceed to Reedy Island, next high water.

5. That the captain shall be allowed to stay in town till to-morrow, to provide necessaries for his voyage.

6. That he shall then be obliged to leave the town and proceed to his vessel, and make the best of his way out of our river and bay.

7. That a committee of four gentlemen be appointed to see these resolves carried into execution.

The Assembly was then informed of the spirit and resolution of New York, and Charleston, S. C., and the conduct of the people of Boston, whereupon it was unanimously resolved—

That this assembly highly approve the conduct and spirit of the people of New York, Charleston, and Boston, and return their hearty thanks to the people of Boston for their resolution in destroying the tea, rather than suffering it to be landed.

CHAPTER XXXIV.

The troubles thicken—Gage re-inforced—Assembly of the first Continental Congress at Philadelphia.

The unscrupulous and brutal Gage had now resumed command of the British forces, as well as entered upon his appointment as governor of Massachusetts. Boston Neck had been fortified by him, and seven regiments been added to his command. The "non-importation and consumption bill," recommended by the General Court, had been agreed to by many of the colonies, and the general aspect of affairs became threatening for the young Sam.

The Congress, which had now assembled, by agreement, to consider the affairs of the country, commenced their session at Philadelphia, in defiance of the strenuous opposition of Gage. This Congress consisted of fifty-three delegates, the leading men of twelve provinces, Georgia, alone, of the originally British colonies, being unrepresented. Beside others of less note, there were present in this assembly the two Adamses, of Massachusetts; Sherman and Deane, of Connecticut; Philip Livingston, Jay, and Duane, of New York; William Livingston, of New Jersey; Galloway, of Pennsylvania; Rodney, Read, and M'Kean, of Delaware; Chase, of Maryland; Randolph, Richard Henry Lee, Washington, and Henry, of Virginia; the two Rutledges, and Gadsden, of South Carolina. The post of honor was freely conceded to Virginia, by the choice of the now aged Peyton Randolph as president. Charles Thompson, late master of the Quaker academy at Philadelphia, was chosen secretary. Samuel Adams, himself a stiff Congregationalist, moved the appointment of an Episcopal chaplain, and Jacob Duchè, a popular preacher of Philadelphia, was accordingly appointed. As no means were at hand to estimate the relative importance of the colonies, it was agreed that each province should have a single vote. All proceedings were to be with closed doors, and nothing was to be published except by order.

A committee of two from each province reported, in the form of a series of resolves, accepted and adopted by the Congress, a "Declaration of Colonial Rights." The enjoyment of life, liberty, and property were claimed in this Declaration as natural rights. The privilege of being bound by no law, to which they had not consented by their representatives, was claimed for the colonists in their character of British subjects. The sole and exclusive power of legislation for the colonies was declared to reside in their respective Assemblies, reserving to Parliament the enactment of such laws only as might be essential to the *bona fide* regulation of trade, but excluding all taxation, internal or external. The common law of England was claimed as the birthright of the colonists, including the right of trial by a jury of the vicinage, the right of public meetings, and of petition. A protest was made against standing armies maintained in the colonies without their consent; and a similar protest against legislation by councils dependent on the crown—this last in allusion to the Quebec Act. All immunities hitherto enjoyed in the colonies, whether by charter or custom, were claimed as established rights, beyond the power of the mother country to abrogate. Eleven acts of Parliament, passed since the accession of George III.—the Sugar Act, the Stamp Act, the two Quartering Acts, the Tea Act, the Act Suspending the New York Legislature, the two Acts for the Trial in Great Britain for offenses committed in America, the Boston Port Bill, the Act for Regulating the Government of Massachusetts, and the Quebec Act—were enumerated, in conclusion, as having been passed in derogation of the rights of the colonies. (1774.)

As means for enforcing this claim of rights, fourteen articles were agreed to, as the basis of an "American Association," pledging the associators to an entire commercial non-intercourse with Great Britain, Ireland, and the West Indies, and the non-consumption of tea and British goods: this non-intercourse to be extended to such provinces of North

America as should decline to come into the Association, and to last till the obnoxious acts of Parliament were repealed. The non-importation clauses were to commence in December, but the non-exportation clauses were postponed for nine months longer. The slave trade was specially denounced, and entire abstinence from it, and from any trade with those concerned with it, formed a part of the Association. The associators were also pledged to encourage the breeding of sheep, and the disuse of mourning. Traders were not to be allowed to enhance the price of goods in consequence of this agreement. Committees were to be appointed in every county, city, and town, to detect and to publish the names of all violators of it; and all dealings with such "enemies of American liberty" were to be immediately broken off.

Patrick Henry, who had electrified the Congress by his eloquence, was selected by the committee, to which that business was intrusted, to draft the petition to the king. But this draft, when received, did not give satisfaction. Dickinson, lately added to the Pennsylvania delegation, was added also to the committee, and a new draft was prepared by him, which the Congress approved.

While the Continental Congress was still in session, matters in Massachusetts were fast verging to a crisis. Gage had summoned a House of Representatives to meet him at Salem, to proceed to business under the late act of Parliament; but the spirit evinced in the resolutions of the town meetings and county conventions induced him to issue a proclamation countermanding the Assembly. It was denied, however, that the Governor could prorogue the Court till it had first met; and, notwithstanding the countermand, most of the members elect assembled at Salem on the day appointed. As nobody appeared to open the session and administer the oaths, they adopted the advice already given by the Essex county Convention, resolved themselves into a Provincial Congress, adjourned to Concord, and there organized by choosing John Hancock as president, and for secretary Benjamin Lincoln, a farmer of Hingham, afterward a major-general in the revolutionary army. A large committee, appointed to consider the state of the province, reported an address to Gage, which the Congress adopted; after which they adjourned to Cambridge, whence a committee was sent to present the address to the governor. The Congress, in this address, protested their attachment to Great Britain, their loyalty to the king, and their love of peace and order, but complained of the recent acts of Paliament, the employment of the powers of government to harass and enslave them, the military force concentrated in Boston, and the fortifications erecting there. The people, they declared, would never be satisfied till these military preparations were discontinued and those fortifications demolished.

Gage replied that his military preparations were only in self-defense, and justified by threats everywhere uttered. He disavowed, on behalf of Great Britain, any design to harass or enslave; expressed a wish for harmony; begged them to consider, while complaining of violations of their charter, whether their present assembly was not a violation of it; and required them, in conclusion, to desist from their illegal proceedings.

So far from desisting, the Congress appointed a Committee of Safety, at the head of which was John Hancock, with power to call out the militia. A committee was also raised to take measures for the defense of the province, and another to procure military stores and provisions, towards which the sum of £20,000, $66,666, was appropriated. Constables and other collectors of taxes were ordered to pay no more money to the late Treasurer of the province, but to hand over all future collections to a new Treasurer appointed by the Congress. Preble, of Falmouth, an old militia officer, Artemus Ward, a colleague of Ruggles on the bench of the Worcester Common Pleas, and Pomeroy, who led a regiment at the battle of Lake George, were commissioned as generals. The militia were called upon to choose company and regimental officers of their own, and to perfect themselves in military discipline. The Congress disavowed any intention to attack the British troops; but, as their Capital was occupied by a large force, as the military stores of the province had been seized, and as there was too much reason to apprehend a still more direct invasion of their rights, they declared these measures necessary for defense. Gage issued a proclamation denouncing their proceedings, to which no attention was paid, while the recommendations of the Provincial Congress had all the force of law. Gage had no support except in his troops and a few trembling officials, while the zealous co-operation of an intelligent, firm, energetic, and overwhelming majority of the people gave to the Congress all the strength of an established government.

While the colonies were thus busy in defense of their rights, the frontiers of Pennsylvania and Virginia had been again visited by Indian war. Surveyors, sent under the royal authority, at the request of the Assembly of Virginia, to extend the western limits of that province, had pushed their explorations to a great distance westward. Some of these surveyors had descended the Ohio as far as the Falls, and had traced up the Kentucky a considerable distance from its mouth. Collisions took place between these explorers and the Indians on the Ohio. Under the impulse of a false rumor of previous hostilities on the part of the Indians, nine persons, the family of Logan, a chief distinguished for friendship to the whites, were murdered in cold blood. This and other similar attrocities excited the Indians to revenge. The jurisdiction of the region about Pittsburgh was still disputed between Virginia and Pennsylvania. St. Clair and others, who recognized the authority of Pennsylvania, endeavored to conciliate matters, and an appeal was made to Sir William Johnson, by the Pennsylvania authorities, to induce the Six Nations to act as mediators. Just at this time Sir William died, but the business was undertaken by his son-in-law, Guy Johnson, soon appointed his successor as superintendent of the Northern Indians. While these efforts for peace were made by Pennsylvania, Conolly and others in the Virginia interest were bent on war, in which they were fully supported by Governor Dunmore. Daniel Boone was sent to guide back by land the surveyors employed on the Lower Ohio; after which he was placed in command of a frontier fort. Volunteers to march against the Indians were easily obtained. Major M'Donald, with four hundred men, having assembled at Fish Creek, on the Ohio, just below Wheeling, marched against and destroyed the Shawanese village on the Muskingum, some fifteen miles below the present Coshocton; but the Indians made their escape. Dunmore himself, with fifteen hundred men, presently moved against the Indian villages on the Scioto, while Colonel Lewis, with another division of twelve hundred men, descended the Kanawha. Near the mouth of that river, Lewis found the Indians in force, under Logan, Cornstalk, and other chiefs. A very hard-fought battle ensued; the Virginians finally carried the day, but not without the loss of sixty or seventy killed, and a large number wounded. Shelby, afterwards first governor of Kentucky, led a company in this battle.

Alarmed at Dunmore's approach toward their villages, the Indians had already entered into negotiations, and Dunmore sent word to Lewis to put a stop to hostilities—orders which the backwoodsmen were somewhat reluctant to obey. Logan was not present at the treaty, but he sent the following speech: "I appeal to any white man to say if ever he entered Logan's cabin hungry, and he gave him not meat; if ever he came cold and naked, and he clothed him not. During the last long and bloody war, Logan remained idle in his cabin, an advocate for peace. Such was my love for the whites, that my countrymen pointed as they passed, and said, 'Logan is the friend of white men!' I had even thought to have lived with you, but for the injuries of one man. Colonel Cresap, the last spring, in cold blood, and unprovoked, murdered all the relatives of Logan, not even sparing women and children. There runs not a drop of my blood in the veins of any living creature. This called on me for revenge! I have sought it; I have killed many; I have fully glutted my vengeance! For my people, I rejoice at the beams of peace; but do not harbor a thought that mine is the joy of fear. Logan never felt fear. He will not turn on his heel to save his life! Who is there to mourn for Logan? Not one!"

At Fort Gower, at the junction of the Hocking with the Ohio, the officers of Dunmore's army, on their homeward march, held a meeting, at which they complimented the governor, and resolved to bear faithful allegiance to the king, but also to maintain the just rights of America, by every means in their power.

At the same time with these difficulties on the Virginia frontier, some collisions took place in Georgia, between the settlers on the recently ceded lands, and the Creeks and Cherokees, who seemed disposed to support each other in case of hostilities. But, instead of having recourse to arms, Governor Wright proclaimed a suspension of trade. The

Indians, by this means, were soon brougnt to terms, and a new treaty of peace was arranged.

Two successive cargoes of tea which arrived at Portsmouth, had been reshipped. A quantity brought to Annapolis was burned, and the ship with it; the owner himself, to soothe the excitement, setting fire to it with his own hand. The Assembly of Connecticut gave orders to the towns to lay in a double supply of ammunition. They directed the cannon at New London to be mounted, and the militia to be frequently trained. The proceedings of the Continental Congress were approved, and the same delegates were re-appointed.

Measures, meanwhile, were everywhere on foot, by the appointment of committees of inspection, to enforce the American Association. Philadelphia set the example. New York followed, by appointing a city committee of sixty, with full powers for that purpose. At a third session of the Massachusetts Congress, held after a short adjournment, the delegates to the late Continental Congress made a report of the doings of that body, all of which were fully approved. It was voted to enroll twelve thousand "minute men"—volunteers, that is, from among the militia, pledged to be ready for service at a minute's notice; and negotiations were ordered with the other New England colonies, to make up this force to twenty thousand. John Thomas, of Plymouth county, who had led a regiment in the late war, and William Heath, a Roxbury farmer, were commissioned as generals. Domestic manufactures were strongly urged upon the attention of the people. The same delegates as before were appointed to the Continental Congress, to be held in the Spring. Directions were also issued for the election of a new Provincial Congress, to meet early in the year, at which time, the members of the last elected Council were requested to be present. The Congress then adjourned, to attend the annual thanksgiving, of which they had assumed the appointment. Their authority was zealously seconded in every town, by a Committee of Safety, vested with general executive powers, a Committee of Correspondence, and a Committee of Inspection, appointed to look after the observance of the American Association.

In the absence of the ships-of-war, usually stationed in Narraganset Bay, forty-four pieces of cannon were taken from the batteries at Newport, and conveyed to Providence. When called upon by the British naval commander for an explanation, Governor Wanton bluntly avowed that these cannon had been taken away to prevent their falling into his hands, and were intended for use against any power that might offer to molest the colony. This movement in Rhode Island, was induced by a royal proclamation prohibiting the export of military stores to America. It was soon followed up in New Hampshire. Instigated by Paul Revere, from Boston, and led by John Sullivan, a leading lawyer, late a delegate to the Continental Congress, and by John Langdon, a principal merchant of Portsmouth, a large party entered the fort at that place, which was only guarded by four or five men, and carried off a hundred barrels of powder, some cannon and small arms.

The doings of the Continental Congress were approved by a Convention in Maryland, and the several counties took measures for enforcing the Association. The Convention of Maryland assumed, in fact, the powers of government; they ordered the militia to be enrolled, and voted £10,000 to purchase arms. The Assembly of Pennsylvania also approved the doings of Congress, and appointed delegates to the new one. In South Carolina, delegates to the new Congress, and Committees of Inspection to enforce the Association, were appointed by a Provincial Convention, of which Charles Pinckney was president, called together by the committee of ninety-nine. (1775.)

A general election had recently taken place in Great Britain, but the result boded no good to the colonies. Parties in the new House of Commons stood very much as before. Lord North, and his colleagues in the ministry, had an overwhelming majority. Ministers not only were sure of support from Parliament, and from the personal feelings of the king, strongly bent upon bringing the colonies to unconditional submission: they were also sustained by the general sentiment of the British people, by whom the stigma of rebellion was already affixed to the conduct of the colonists.

Yet there was not wanting, both in and out of Parliament, a very respectable minority, opposed to subduing the colonists by force, and anxious to promote an amicable adjustment. The merchants trading to America, were very averse that any occasion should be given to their debtors for postponing or refusing the payment of their debts, or that actual war should put a final stop to a profitable trade, already so seriously threatened by the American Association, compared with which, all former non-importation agreements had been limited and inefficient. The English Dissenters were inclined by religious sympathies to favor the colonists. Such fragments of the old Whig party as had not coalesced with the "king's friends," headed by the Marquis of Rockingham and the Earl of Chatham, supported by the colonial experience of Pownall and Johnstone, and sustained by the eloquence of Burke, Barre, Dunning, and the youthful Fox, few, but able, maintained with zeal those principles of liberty, which had descended to them from the times of the English civil wars, and which the threatened civil war in America seemed now again to arouse to new life.

After a long absence, Chatham re-appeared in the House of Lords, and proposed an address to the king, advising the recall of the troops from Boston; but this motion, though supported by Lord Camden, after a warm debate, was rejected by a very decisive majority. In the Commons, the papers relating to America were referred to a committee of the whole. The petitions for conciliation, which flowed in from all the great trading and manufacturing towns of the kingdom, ought properly to have gone to the same committee; but the ministers procured their reference to another committee for a subsequent day, which the opposition derided as a "committee of oblivion." Among the papers laid before Parliament, was the petition from the Continental Congress to the king. Three of the colonial agents, Franklin, Bollan, and Arthur Lee, to whose care this petition had been intrusted, asked to be heard upon it by counsel, at the bar of the House. But their request was refused, on the ground that the Congress was an illegal assembly, and the alleged grievances only pretended.

Still persevering in his schemes for conciliation, Chatham brought forward, in the Lords, a bill for settling the troubles in America. It required a full acknowledgement on the part of the colonists, of the supremacy and superintending power of Parliament, but provided that no tax should ever be levied, except by colonial Assemblies. It contained, also, a provision for a Congress of the colonies to make the required acknowledgement, and to vote, at the same time, a free grant to the king of a certain perpetual revenue, to be placed at the disposal of Parliament. Chatham exerted himself, on this occasion, with renewed and remarkable vigor; but, in spite of all his efforts, after a warm and very pointed debate, his bill was refused the courtesy of lying on the table, and, contrary to the usual course, was rejected by a vote of two to one, at the first reading.

Agreeably to the scheme foreshadowed in his speech on the address, Lord North, in the House of Commons, brought in a bill for cutting off the trade of New England elsewhere than to Great Britain, Ireland, and the British West Indies—intended as an offset to the American Association—and suspending the prosecution from those colonies of the Newfoundland fishery, a principal branch at that time of their trade and industry. An address to the throne, proposed by the ministers, and carried after great debates, declared that a rebellion already existed in Massachusetts, countenanced and fomented by unlawful combinations in other colonies. Effectual measures were recommended for suppressing this rebellion; and the support of Parliament was pledged to the king, in the maintenance of the just authority of the crown and the nation.

Burke, as representative of the Rockingham section of the opposition, brought forward a series of resolutions proposing the abandonment of all attempts at parliamentary taxation, and a return to the old method of raising American supplies by the free grant of the colonial Assemblies. He supported these resolutions in an elaborate speech; but his motion was voted down, as was a similar one, introduced a few days after, by David Hartley, on behalf of the Chatham section of the opposition.

We give here the most important portions of this famous speech of Burke, which, from the direct light it sheds upon questions at issue, between Sam and the old country, is of great importance.

The Speech of Edmund Burke, Esq., on moving his resolutions for conciliation with the colonies, March 22, 1775.

"I have in my hand two accounts; one a comparative statement of the export trade of England to its colonies, as it stood in the year 1704, and as it stood in the year 1772. The other, a statement of the export trade of this country to its colonies alone, as it stood in 1772, compared with the whole trade of England to all parts of the world (the colonies included,) in the year 1704. They are from good vouchers: the latter period, from the accounts on your table; the earlier, from an original manuscript of Davenant, who first established the inspector general's office, which has been, ever since his time, so abundant a source of Parliamentary information.

The export trade to the colonies consists of three great branches. The African, which, terminating almost wholly in the colonies, must be put to the account of their commerce, the West Indies and the North American. All these are so interwoven, that the attempt to separate them would tear to pieces the contexture of the whole; and, if not entirely destroy, would very much depreciate the value of all the parts. I therefore consider these three denominations to be, what in effect they are, one trade.

The trade to the colonies, taken on the export side, at the beginning of this century, that is, in the year 1704, stood thus:

Exports to North America and the West Indies,	£483,265
To Africa..................................	86,665
	£569,930

In the year 1772, which I take as a middle year between the highest and and the lowest of those lately laid on your table, the accounts were as follows:

To North America and the West Indies......	£4,791,734
To Africa...............................	866,398
To which, if you add the export trade to and from Scotland, which had, in 1704, no existence	364,000
	£6,022,132

From five hundred and odd thousands, it has grown to six million; it has increased no less than twelve-fold. This is the state of the colony trade as compared with itself at these two periods, within this century: and this is matter for meditation. But this is not all. Examine my second account. See how the export trade to the colonies alone, in 1772, stood in the other point of view, that is, as compared with the whole trade of England, in 1704:—The whole export trade of England, including that to the colonies, in 1704, was £6,509,000; the exports to the colonies alone, in 1772, amounted to £6,024,000.

Thus the trade with America alone is now within less than £500,000 of being equal to what this great commercial nation, England, carried on at the beginning of this century with the whole world! If I had taken the largest year of those on your table, it would rather have exceeded. But it will be said, is not this American trade an unnatural protuberance, that has drawn the juices from the rest of the body? The reverse; it is the very food that has nourished every other part into its present magnitude. Our general trade has been greatly augmented; and augmented more or less in almost every part to which it ever extended; but with this material difference, that of the six millions, which, in the beginning of the century, constituted the whole mass of our export commerce, the colony trade was but one-twelfth part; it is now (as a part of seventeen million) considerably more than a third of the whole.

This is the relative proportion of the importance of the colonies at these two periods; and all reason concerning our mode of treating them, must have this proportion as its basis, or it is a reasoning, weak, rotten, and sophistical.

Mr. Speaker, I can not prevail upon myself to hurry over this great consideration. It is good for us to be here. We stand where we have an immense view of what is, and what is past. Clouds indeed, and darkness rest upon the future. Let us, however, before we descend from this noble eminence, reflect that this growth of our national prosperity, has happened within the short period of the life of man—it has happened within sixty-eight years. There are those alive, whose memory might touch the two extremities! For instance, my Lord Bathurst, might remember all the stages of the progress. He was, in 1704, of age at least be made to comprehend such things; he was then old enough, *acta parentum jam legere, et quæ sit proterit cognoscere virtus.* Suppose, sir, that the angel of this auspicious youth, foreseeing the many virtues, which made him one of the most amiable, as he is one of the most fortunate men of his age, had opened to him in vision that when, in the fourth generation, the third prince of the house of Brunswick had sat twelve years on the throne of that nation which (by the happy issue of moderate and healing councils) was to be made Great Britain, he should see his son, Lord Chancellor of England, turn back the current of hereditary dignity to its fountain, and raise him to a higher rank of peerage, while we enriched the family with a new one; if, amid these bright and happy scenes of domestic honor and prosperity, that angel should have drawn up the curtain, and unfolded the rising glories of his country, and while he was gazing with admiration on the then commercial grandeur of England, the genius should point out to him a little speck, scarce visible in the mass of the national interest, a small seminal principle, rather than a formed body, and should tell him—"Young man, there is America, which at this day serves for little more than to amuse you with stories of savage men, and uncouth manners; yet shall, before you taste death, show itself equal to the whole of that commerce which now attracts the envy of the world. Whatever England has been growing to by a progressive increase of improvements, brought in by variety of people, by successsion of civilizing conquests and civilizing settlements, in a series of seventeen hundred years, you shall see as much added to her by America, in the course of a single life." If this state of his country had been foretold to him, would it not require all the sanguine credulity of youth, and all the fervid glow of enthusiasm, to make him believe it? Fortunate man, he has lived to see it! Fortunate indeed, if he lives to see nothing that shall vary the prospect, and cloud the setting of his day!

This noble effort at conciliation, seems, however, to have fallen upon deaf ears.

The new provincial Congress of Massachusetts, consisting of upward of three hundred members, having met at Cambridge, Elbridge Gerry, a merchant of Marblehead, for two or three years past prominent in the General Court, was placed at the head of the Committee of Supplies. Active measures were taken for arming and drilling the militia, and especially for procuring powder; and magazines of provisions and military stores began to be laid up at Concord, Worcester, and other places. An appeal to the people was put forth, and a day of fasting and prayer appointed; after which the Congress took a short adjournment.

Aware of what was going on, Gage sent a detachment to Salem, whence the British troops had been withdrawn for concentration at Boston, to seize some cannon said to be deposited there. A hundred and fifty regulars, sent from Boston by water, landed at Salem on this business. Not finding the cannon there, they marched in search of them toward the adjoining town of Danvers. At a bridge between the towns they encountered a party of militia, under Colonel Pickering, who claimed the bridge as private property, and proposed to dispute the passage. It was Sunday; one of the Salem ministers interfered, and, taking advantage of reverence for the day, with much difficulty prevented a collision. The soldiers were allowed to pass the bridge, but soon returned without finding the cannon. About the same time, two officers were sent in disguise to examine the country and the roads towards Worcester.

The Connecticut Assembly, in a special session, though they declined to take immediate steps for enlisting troops, yet commissioned David Wooster as major-general, and Joseph Spencer and Israel Putnam as brigadiers. The Massachusetts Congress shortly after voted to raise an army for the defense of the province. They sent committees to the other New England colonies to solicit their aid and concurrence, and meanwhile took another recess.

Gage's force at this time amounted to twenty-eight hundred and fifty men. As the spring opened, he determined by active movements to nip these rebellious preparations in the bud. Two officers, sent from Boston to make a reconnoissance, reported that some cannon and a quantity of provisions and military stores had been collected at Concord, an interior town, about twenty miles from Boston. To destroy these stores, eight hundred British troops, light infantry and grenadiers, left Boston, under Colonel Smith, with great secresy, shortly after midnight, and reached Lexington, within six miles of Concord, before sunrise. But the alarm had been given—it was supposed their object might be to arrest Hancock and Samuel Adams, who were lodging at Lexington—and the minute men of the neighborhood, about a hundred in number, had assembled on the green in front of the meeting-house. The head of the British column came suddenly upon them, led by two or three officers, who called upon the minute men to throw down their arms and disperse. When these orders were not instantly obeyed, a volley was fired, by which eight of the minute men were killed, and several wounded. The British alleged, however, that the minute men fired first. The survivors scattered at once, and the regulars marched on to Concord. As they approached that village, another body of minute men was seen assembled on a hill in front of the meeting-house; but, as the regulars advanced, they retired across a bridge to another hill back of the town. The bridge was taken possession of by the regulars, a guard of three companies was stationed at it, and three other companies were sent across to destroy some stores at a distance. The main body halted near the meeting-house, and commenced destroying the stores found there. The minute men on the hill, increased by constant accessions, presently advanced toward the bridge. The guard of regulars having retired across it, began to take up the planks, and, as the minute men continued to approach, they fired. The fire was returned, and several regulars were killed; yet such was the hesitation at this first shedding of blood, that the three British companies beyond the bridge were suffered to re-cross without molestation. They fell back to the village, and the whole detachment commenced a speedy retreat. It was time. The alarm had spread; the country was up. The minute men, hurrying in from every side, threatened the rear, the flanks, the front of the retreating column, and from behind trees, fences and stone walls, poured in an irregular but galling and fatal fire. The British suffered very severely; the commanding officer was wounded; the retreat was fast turning into a rout; the whole party would have fallen into the hands of the provincials but for seasonable aid found at Lexington, whither Gage, with wise caution, had dispatched Lord Percy, with a supporting column of nine hundred men and two pieces of cannon. The artillery kept the minute men at bay; Percy's men received their exhausted companions within a hollow square, and the retreat, after a short halt, was again re-commenced. By throwing out strong flanking parties, Percy covered his main body, and by sunset the regulars reached Charlestown, worn out with fatigue, and with a loss in killed and wounded of near three hundred men. The provincial loss was about eighty-five. The exhausted regulars encamped on Bunker Hill, under cover of the ships of war in the river. The next day they crossed the ferry to Boston.

From all parts of New England volunteers marched at once, and within a day or two after the fight, Boston was beleaguered by a considerable but irregular army. The news, forwarded by express, spread fast through the colonies. Yet, with the hottest haste which could then be made, it took twenty days to reach Charleston, in South Carolina.

The re-assembled Congress of Massachusetts voted to raise thirteen thousand six hundred men, arranged presently into twenty-seven regiments. The other New England colonies were called upon to make up the army to thirty thousand men. Ward was appointed captain general, Thomas lieutenant general. A regiment of artillery was authorized, the command being given to Gridley, appointed also chief engineer. A captain's commission was promised to any person who would enlist fifty-nine men; any person who could procure the enlistment of ten companies was to be made a colonel. This method facilitated raising the men, but brought many incompetent officers into the service.

The issue of paper money, one of the greatest miseries of war, disused in Massachusetts for the last quarter of a century, was now revived. Provincial notes were issued to the amount of £100,000, $333,333, in sums small enough to circulate as a currency.

Depositions to show that the regulars had fired first at Lexington, without provocation, were dispatched to England by a special packet, with a short but energetic address to the inhabitants of Great Britain, expressing the resolution "to die or be free." Franklin, to whom this address and the depositions were inclosed, was requested to have them printed and distributed, and to communicate them especially to the city of London. But Franklin had sailed for America, leaving the Massachusetts agency in the hands of Arthur Lee.

The appeal to the other New England colonies was not made in vain. The Rhode Island Assembly voted an army of observation of fifteen hundred men—a measure opposed, however, by Governor Wanton and two or three of the assistants, who entered a protest against it as dangerous to their charter privileges, likely to involve the colony in a war, and contrary to their oath of allegiance. Stephen Hopkins and Samuel Ward, former governors and political rivals, were re-appointed delegates to the Continental Congress. Wanton was re-chosen governor at the election shortly after; but, as he did not appear to take the oaths, the Assembly directed that the duties of the office should be performed by Deputy Governor Cooke, who continued for the next three years at the head of affairs. A body of Rhode Island volunteers had appeared before Boston, led by Nathaniel Greene, a young iron-master, educated a Quaker, but now disowned by that communion on account of his military propensities. He was appointed by the Assembly commander-in-chief of the army of observation, with the rank of brigadier.

The Connecticut Assembly voted to raise six regiments of a thousand men each, four of them to serve with the army before Boston. Wooster, Spencer, and Putnam, already commissioned as generals, were each to have a regiment; the other three were to be commanded by Hinman, Waterbury, and Parsons. Putnam was already in the camp before Boston. Old man of sixty, as he was, on hearing the news of the battle of Lexington, he had left his plow in the furrow to put himself at the head of the Connecticut volunteers.

A special convention of delegates from the nearest towns, called together by the New Hampshire Committee of Safety, on hearing the news of the battle of Lexington, did not think it best to anticipate the action of a Provincial Congress, already summoned for the seventeenth of May, by taking steps for organizing an army; but the several towns were requested to forward supplies to the volunteers who had followed Stark to Boston. Meanwhile, the Massachusetts Congress directed enlistments among the New Hampshire soldiers in camp. As the new regiments began to be formed, the volunteers returned home. For some weeks, the force before Boston was very small, amounting to only two or three thousand men.

In hopes that matters might possibly be reconciled, Governor Trumbull and the Connecticut Assembly sent a deputation to Gage, to act as mediators—a step which excited much alarm in Massachusetts. The Provincial Congress remonstrated against any separate negotiations; and they voted Gage a public enemy, an instrument in the hands of tyrants, whom there was no further obligation to obey. Some correspondence took place between Gage and Trumbull, but nothing came of the Connecticut mediation.

The Assembly of New York having refused to appoint delegates to the new Continental Congress; an ardent struggle had taken place in the city, not altogether unaccompanied with violence, on the question of electing members to a Provincial Convention, for the purpose of choosing such delegates. The popular party carried the day; and by the Convention presently held, twelve delegates were appointed, any five of whom were authorized to represent the province in the Congress.

The Corresponding Committee of New York, on receiving news of the battle of Lexington, drew up an Association for the Defense of Colonial Rights, which everybody was called upon to sign—an expedient presently adopted in several other of the colonies, those especially, in which considerable differences of opinion existed. The same committee also issued a circular to the several county committees, recommending the speedy meeting of a Provincial Congress, "to deliberate on, and direct such measures as may be expedient for our common safety."

News having arrived of the fight at Lexington, a great public meeting was held in Philadelphia, at which measures were taken for entering into a volunteer military association, which soon pervaded the whole province. In spite of the admonitions of their elders, many of the young Quakers took a part in this organization. Mifflin was the moving spirit of the whole. John Dickinson accepted the command of a regiment, as did Thomas M'Kean and James Wilson, leading lawyers in the city. M'Kean was a native of Pennsylvania, of Scotch-Irish descent; Wilson was born in Scotland, but he had studied law, and for the last eight years had been a resident in Philadelphia, where his talents had raised him to conspicuous notice. The Assembly, which met shortly after, appropriated £1,800 toward the expenses of the volunteers. They also appointed a Committee of Safety, of which Franklin, just returned from England, was made chairman. This committee took measures for the defense of Philadelphia, and in a short time assumed the whole executive authortity. Franklin, Wilson, and Willing were added to the congressional delegation; Galloway, at his own earnest request, was excused from serving. Governor Penn laid Lord North's conciliatory proposition before the Assembly, but it did not meet with much favor.

The Delaware Assembly had already approved the doings of the late Continental Congress, and had appointed delegates to the new one, in which they were presently imitated by the Assembly of Maryland.

The Virginia Convention, which met at Richmond to appoint delegates to the new Continental Congress, had been persuaded, by the energy and eloquence of Patrick Henry, to take measures for enrolling a company of volunteers in each county. Before news had arrived of the battle of Lexington, Governor Dunmore had ordered the powder belonging to the province, to be taken from the public store at Williamsburg, and placed on board an armed vessel in the river. This proceeding caused a great excitement, increased by news of the Lexington fight. Having collected some companies of the new volunteers, Henry marched toward Williamsburg, and compelled the king's receiver to give bills for the value of the powder taken away. Dunmore sent his family on board a ship in the river, fortified his palace, and issued a proclamation declaring Henry and his coadjutors guilty of rebellion; but their conduct was sustained and approved by numerous county conventions.

In spite of all Martin's efforts to prevent it, a Provincial Congress met in North Carolina, simultaneously with the Assembly, and, for the most part, composed of the same members. Both bodies concurred in approving the proceedings of the late Continental Congress, and in appointing delegates to the new one. News arriving of the battle of Lexington, an Association was entered into by the friends of colonial rights, pledging the associators to defend those rights by force, if necessary. The citizens of Mechlenburg county carried their zeal so far, as to resolve, at a public meeting, to throw off the British connection, and they framed a formal Declaration of Independence. We append here, an authentic copy of these famous Mechlenburg Resolutions, which should be sacredly preserved in any record of the early acts of Sam.

MECHLENBURG RESOLUTIONS.

The citizens of Mechlenburg county, in this State, made a declaration of independence more than a year before Congress made theirs.

NORTH CAROLINA,
Mechlenburg County, May 20, 1775.

In the spring of 1775, the leading characters of Mechlenburg county, stimulated by the enthusiastic patriotism which elevates the mind above considerations of individual aggrandizement, and scorning to shelter themselves from the impending storm by submission to lawless power, etc., held several detached meetings, in each of which the individual sentiments were "that the cause of Boston was the cause of all; that their destinies were undoubtedly connected with those of their Eastern fellow-citizens—and that they must either submit to all the impositions which an unprincipled, and to them an unrepresented Parliament might impose—or support their brethren who were doomed to sustain the first shock of that power which, if successful there, would ultimately overwhelm all in the common calamity. Conformably to these principles, Col. Adam Alexander, through solicitations, issued an order to each captain's company in the county of Mechlenburg (then comprising the present county of Cabanus), directing each militia company to elect two persons, and delegate to them ample power to devise ways and means to aid and assist their suffering brethren in Boston, and also generally to adopt measures to extricate themselves from the impending storm, and to secure, unimpaired, their inalienable rights, privileges and liberties, from the dominant grasp of British imposition and tyranny.

In conforming to said order, on the 19th of May, 1775, the said delegation met in Charlotte, vested with unlimited powers; at which time official news, by express, arrived of the battle of Lexington on that day of the preceding month. Every delegate felt the value and importance of the prize, and the awful and solemn crisis which had arrived—every bosom swelled with indignation at the malice, inveteracy, and insatiable revenge developed in the late attack upon Lexington. The universal sentiment was—let us not flatter ourselves that popular harangues, or resolves—that popular vapor will avert the storm, or vanquish our common enemy—let us deliberate, let us calculate the issue—the probable results, and then let us act with energy, as brethren leagued to preserve our property, our lives—and what is still more endearing—the liberties of America. ADAM ALEXANDER was then elected chairman, and JOHN MCKNITT ALEXANDER, clerk. After a free and full discussion of the various objects for which the delegation had been convened, it was unanimously ordained—

1. That whoever directly or indirectly abetted, or in any way, form, or manner, countenanced the unchartered and dangerous invasion of our rights, as claimed by Great Britain, is an enemy to this country—to America—and to the inherent and inalienable rights of man.

2. That we, the citizens of Mechlenburg county, do hereby dissolve the political bands which have connected us to the mother country, and hereby absolve ourselves from allegiance to the British crown, and abjure all political connection, contract, association, with that nation, which has wantonly trampled on our rights and liberties—and inhumanly shed the innocent blood of American patriots at Lexington.

3. That we do hereby declare ourselves a free and independent people, which is, and of right ought to be, a sovereign and self-governing association, under the control of no power other than that of our God, and the general government of the Congress—to the maintenance of which independence, we solemnly pledge to each other our mutual co-operation, our lives, our fortunes, and our most sacred honor.

4. That, as we now acknowledge the existence and control of no law, or legal office, civil or military, within this county, we do hereby ordain and adopt, as a rule of life, all, each, and every of our former laws—wherein, nevertheless, the crown of Great Britain never can be considered as holding rights, privileges, immunities, or authorities.

5. That it is also further decreed, that all, each, and every military officer in this county, is hereby reinstitated to his former command and authority, he acting conformably to these regulations. And that every member present of this delegation, shall henceforth be a civil officer—viz: a justice of the peace, in the character of a "Committee man," to

issue process, hear and determine all matters of controversy, according to said adopted laws, and to preserve peace, and union, and harmony in said county, and to use every exertion to spread the love of country and fire of freedom, throughout America, until a more general and organized government be established in this province.

A number of bylaws were also added, merely to protect the Association from confusion, and to regulate their general conduct as citizens. After sitting in the Court-house all night, neither sleepy, hungry, nor fatigued, and after discussing every paragraph, they were all passed, sanctioned, and decreed, *unanimously*, about 2 o'clock, A. M., May 20. In a few days, a deputation of said delegation convened, when Captain James Jack, of Charlotte, was deputed as express to the Congress at Philadelphia, with a copy of said resolves and proceedings, together with a letter addressed to our three representatives, viz.: Richard Caswell, Wm. Hooper, and Joseph Hughes, under express injunction, personally, and through the State representation, to use all possible means to have said proceedings sanctioned and approved by the General Congress. On the return of Captain Jack, the delegation learned that their proceedings were individually approved by the members of Congress, but that it was deemed premature to lay them before the House. A joint letter from said three members of Congress was also received, of the zeal in the common cause, and recommending perseverance, order, and energy.

The subsequent harmony, unanimity, and exertion in the cause of liberty and independence, evidently resulting from these regulations, and the continued exertion of said delegation, apparently tranquilized this section of the State, and met with the concurrence and high approbation of the Council of Safety, who held their sessions at Newbern and Wilmington, alternately, and who confirmed the nomination and acts of the delegation in their official capacity.

From this delegation originated the Court of Enquiry of this county, who constituted and held their first session in Charlotte; they then held their meetings regularly at Charlotte, at Colonel James Harris', and at Colonel Phifer's, alternately, one week at each place. It was a civil court, founded on military process. Before this judicature all suspicious persons were made to appear, who were formally tried, and banished, or continued under guard. Its jurisdiction was as unlimited as toryism, and its decrees as final as the confidence and patriotism of the country. Several were arrested and brought before them from Lincoln, Rowan, and the adjacent counties.

In addition to this instrument, is another, claimed to be even of prior date; in which it will be seen that the form which the final Declaration assumed under the hand of Jefferson, was very clearly sketched out for him by the sagacious brain of George Mason. It is the only copy of this singular and valuable document which we have seen, and we shall, therefore, lay it before the readers of Sam without hesitation, as it at least demonstrates, in connection with the Mechlenburgh Resolutions, how general and spontaneous were the sentiments of the final Declaration. That Jefferson had this document before him, there can be no shadow of doubt:

DECLARATION OF RIGHTS.

(*Copy of the first Draught, by George Mason.*)

A declaration of rights, made by the representatives of the good people of Virginia, assembled in full and free convention; which rights do pertain to them and to their posterity, as the basis and foundation of government.

1. That all men are *created* equally free and independent, and have certain inherent *natural* rights, of which they can not, by any compact, deprive or divest their posterity.* *Among which are* the enjoyment of life and liberty, with the means of acquiring and possessing property, and pursuing and obtaining happiness and safety.

2. That all power is, *by God and nature,* vested in, and consequently derived from the people; that magistrates are their trustees and servants, and at all times amenable to them.

3. That government is, or ought to be, instituted for the common benefit, protection and security of the people, nation or community. Of all the various modes and forms of

government, that is best which is capable of producing the greatest degree of happiness and safety, and is most effectually secured against the danger of mal-administration; and that whenever any government shall be found inadequate or contrary to these purposes, a majority of the community hath an indubitable, unalienable, and indefeasible right to reform, alter, or abolish it, in such manner as shall be judged most conducive to the public weal.

4. That no man, or set of men, are entitled to exclusive or separate emoluments or privileges from the community, but in consideration of public services; which not being descendible, neither ought the offices of magistrate, legislator, or judge to be hereditary.

5. That the legislative and executive powers of the State should be separate and distinct from the *judicial;* and, that the members of the two first may be restrained from oppression, by feeling and participating in the burthens of the people, they should, at fixed periods, be reduced to a private station, and return unto that body from which they were originally taken, and the vacancies be supplied by frequent, certain, and regular elections.

6. That elections of members to serve as representatives of the people in the *legislature*, ought to be free, and that all men having sufficient evidence of permanent common interest with, and attachment to the community, have the right of suffrage, and cannot be taxed, or deprived of their property for public uses, without their own consent, or that of their representatives so elected, nor bound by any law to which they have not, in like manner, assented for the *common* good.

7. That all power of suspending laws, or the execution of laws, by any authority, without consent of the representatives of the people, is injurious to their rights, and ought not to be exercised.

8. That in all capital or criminal prosecutions, a man hath a right to demand the cause and nature of his accusation, to be confronted with the accusers and witnesses, to call for evidence in his favor, and to a speedy trial by an impartial jury of his vicinage, without whose unanimous consent

he can not be found guilty, nor can he be compelled to give evidence against himself; *and*, that no man be deprived of his liberty, except by the law of the land, or the judgment of his peers.

9. That excessive bail ought not to be required, nor excessive fines imposed, nor cruel and unusual punishments inflicted.

10. (This article was inserted by the Convention.)

11. That in controversies respecting property, and in suits between man and man, the ancient trial by jury is preferable to any other, and ought to be held sacred.

12. That the freedom of the press is one of the great bulwarks of liberty, and can never be restrained but by despotic governments.

13. That a well-regulated militia, composed of the body of the people trained to arms, is the proper, natural, and safe defense of a free State; that standing armies in time of peace, should be avoided, as dangerous to liberty; and that, in all cases, the military should be under strict subordination to, and governed by the civil power.

14. (This article was also inserted by the Convention.)

15. That no free government, or the blessing of liberty, can be preserved to any people, but by a firm adherence to justice, moderation, temperance, frugality and virtue, and by frequent recurrence to fundamental principles.

16. That religion, or the duty which we owe to our Creator, and the manner of discharging it, can be directed only by reason and conviction, not by force or violence, and therefore, *that* all men *should enjoy the fullest toleration in the exercises of religion, according to the dictates of conscience, unpunished and unrestrained by the magistrate; unless, under cover of religion, any man disturb the peace, the happiness, or the safety of society.* And *that* it is the mutual duty of all, to practice Christian forbearance, love, and charity, toward each other.

This Declaration of Rights was the first in America; it received a few alterations or additions in the Virginia Convention, (some of them not for the better,) and was afterward closely imitated by the other United States.

The foregoing was copied verbatim, from the original, in the hand-writing of the author, Col. George Mason, of Virginia, left in the possession of his son, Gen. John Mason, of Georgetown. In order to facilitate the comparison of it, with that which was adopted by the Convention, and is still in force, it has been thought proper to number the articles as in the adopted Declaration, omitting the tenth and fourteenth, which were inserted entire by the Convention, and to place those words in italics which were either expunged or altered, and put an asterisk where others were added.

CHAPTER XXXV.

Arnold's Defeat before Ticonderoga and Crown Point—Gage's Proclamation exempting from pardon John Hancock and Adams—Battle of Bunker Hill.

Previous to the battle of Lexington, the expediency of seizing Ticonderoga and Crown Point had been suggested to the Massachusetts Committee of Safety. Their attention was now re-called to the subject by Benedict Arnold, a New Haven trader and shipmaster, who commanded a company of volunteers in the camp before Boston. Arnold received a commission as colonel, with authority to raise men in Vermont to attempt the surprise of these fortresses. The attention of Connecticut had been called to the same subject, and, about the time of Arnold's departure, some persons deputed for that purpose had induced Ethan Allen and Seth Warner, the two most active leaders among the Green Mountain Boys, to raise a force for the same enterprise. Arnold, as yet without men, joined Allen's party and claimed the command, but, being refused, agreed to serve as a volunteer. Allen approached Ticonderoga with eighty men, penetrated undiscovered into the center of the fort, surprised the commanding officer in his bed, and summoned him to surrender "in the name of the great Jehovah and the Continental Congress!" Crown Point was taken by Warner with equal ease. The total garrisons of both points were only sixty men. Upward of two hundred pieces of artillery, and a large and precious supply of powder, of which there was a great scarcity in the camp before Boston, fell into the hands of the captors. Arnold was presently joined by some fifty recruits, who had seized a schooner, and taken several prisoners and some pieces of cannon, at Skenesborough, a new settlement, (now Whitehall, at the head of Lake Champlain,) founded by Colonel Skene, a British officer, who had gone to England to solicit an appointment as Governor of Ticonderoga. In this captured vessel Arnold proceeded down the lake, entered the Sorel, surprised the post of St. John's, where the navigation terminates, captured an armed vessel there, and carried off some valuable stores. Allen proposed to hold St. John's, but was obliged to retire by a superior force from Montreal. Arnold, with his vessels, returned to Crown Point.

The Continental Congress proceeded, meanwhile, to the delicate task of appointing a commander-in-chief. Unanimity on this important occasion was much promoted by John Adams, very anxious to conciliate the good-will and support of the southern colonies. George Washington, present as a member of Congress from Virginia, was nominated by Johnson, of Maryland, and unanimously chosen. It has been freely insinuated that "Sam" *im*-personally had a *hand* in this nomination, which took every body by surprise, as the accomplished soldier of fortune Lee, or the English renegade Gates, had been more generally looked to as the nominee. See our plate on next page for explanation. He accepted the appointment in a modest speech, in which he declined any compensation beyond payment of expenses. Artemas Ward, Charles Lee, Phillip Schuyler, and Israel Putnam, were chosen major generals; Horatio Gates, adjutant general, with the rank of brigadier. Ward and Putnam were already in the camp before Boston, the one as captain general, under a Massachusetts commission, the other as a Connecticut brigadier. Schuyler had been recommended as a major general by the New York Provincial Congress. Gates, an Englishman by birth, formerly a captain in the British service, had recently sold out his commission and settled in Virginia. Lee was a person of very eccentric habits, a mere soldier of fortune, but possessing a high reputation for military experience and science, having served with distinction both in Europe and America. He held, at the time of his election, a lieutenant colonel's commission in the British service. During the last eighteen months he had been traveling through America, and had recently been induced by Gates to purchase lands in Virginia. For some unknown private cause, he was bitterly hostile to the British ministry. Congress undertook to indemnify him for any pecuniary loss he might sustain by entering into their service, and subsequently advanced him $30,000 for that purpose. Before accepting this American appointment, he resigned his British commission in a formal letter to the Secretary of War. A strenuous opposition was made in Congress to the appointment of both Lee and Gates. Washington urged it on account of their military knowledge and experience, but they both occasioned him afterward a great deal of trouble.

Pomeroy, Heath, and Thomas, of Massachusetts; Wooster and Spencer, of Connecticut; and Greene, of Rhode Island, already holding colony commissions as general officers, were commissioned as brigadiers. To these were added Sullivan, a member of Congress from New Hampshire, and Montgomery, of New York, a native of the north of Ireland. Though bred a lawyer, and without military experience, Sullivan soon proved himself an able officer. Montgomery had served with credit in a subaltern rank at the siege of Louisburg, and under Wolfe at Quebec. Within two or three years past he had disposed of his commission, had married into the Livingston family, and settled in New York, and, along with Schuyler, had been recommended for military rank by the New York Provincial Congress, of which he was a member. The colonels and other inferior officers in the camp before Boston were confirmed in their commands, and presently received continental commissions. The selection of general officers by Congress occasioned a good deal of heart-burning, particularly the Connecticut appointments. Wooster and Spencer, who had led regiments in the last French war, complained loudly at being superseded by Putnam, who had not risen in that service beyond the rank of a lieutenant colonel. A representation on this subject was made to Congress by the Connecticut officers and the Connecticut Assembly. Pomeroy, from some disgust, had already retired, nor did he accept his continental commission.

Before these new arrangements were completed, an important battle had been already fought. Largely reinforced by the arrival of additional troops, under Generals Howe, Burgoyne, and Clinton, distinguished and accomplished officers, the British Army in Boston had been increased to twenty regular regiments, amounting to upward of ten thousand men. Thus strengthened, Gage had issued a proclamation of martial law, offering pardon, however, to all who would forthwith return to their allegiance, John Hancock and Samuel Adams excepted, whose guilt was too flagitious to be overlooked.

We here insert a copy of this famous Proclamation of the English Gates, who was no renegade:—

The minds of men having been gradually prepared for the worst extremities, a number of armed persons, to the amount of many thousands, assembled on the 19th of April last, and from behind walls and lurking holes, attacked a detachment of the king's troops, who, not expecting so consummate an act of frenzy, unprepared for vengeance, and willing to decline, made use of their arms only in their own defense. Since that period the rebels, deriving confidence from impunity, have added insult to outrage; have repeatedly fired upon the king's ships and subjects, with cannon and small arms; have possessed the roads and other communications by which the town of Boston was supplied with provisions; and, with a preposterous parade of military arrangement they affect to hold the army besieged; while part of their body make daily and indiscriminate invasions upon private property, and with a wantonness of cruelty ever incident to lawless tumult, carry depredation and distress wherever they turn their steps. The actions of the 19th of April are of such notoriety, as must baffle all attempts to contradict them, and the flames of buildings and other property, from the islands, and adjacent country, for some weeks past, spread a melancholy comfirmation of the subsequent assertions.

In this exigency of complicated calamities, I avail myself of the last effort within the bounds of my duty to spare the effusion of blood; to offer, and I do hereby in his Majesty's name, offer and promise his most gracious pardon, to all persons who shall forthwith lay down their arms, and return to the duties of peaceable subjects, excepting only from the benefits of such pardon, SAMUEL ADAMS and JOHN HANCOCK, whose offenses are of too flagitious a nature to admit of any other consideration than that of condign punishment.

And to the end that no person within the limits of this proffered mercy may plead ignorance of the consequences of refusing it, I, by these presents proclaim, not only the persons above named and excepted—but also all their adherents, associates and abettors—meaning to comprehend in those terms, all and every person, and persons, of what class, denomination or description, soever, who have appeared in arms against the king's government, and shall not lay down the same as afore mentioned; and likewise all such as shall so take up arms after the date hereof, or who shall in anywise protect or conceal such offenders, or assist them with money, provision, cattle, arms, ammunition, carriages, or any other necessary for subsistence or offense, or shall hold secret correspondence with them by letter, message, signal, or otherwise, to be rebels and traitors, and as such to be treated.

And whereas, during the continuance of the present unnatural rebellion, justice can not be administered by the common law of the land, the course whereof has, for a long time past, been violently impeded, and wholly interrupted, from whence results a necessity for using and exercising the law martial; I have therefore thought fit, by the authority vested in me, by the royal charter to this province, to publish, and I do hereby publish, and proclaim, and order the use and exercise of the law martial, within and throughout this province, for so long time as the present unhappy occasion shall necessarily require; whereof all persons are hereby required to take notice, and govern themselves as well to maintain order and regularity among the peaceable inhabitants of the province, as to resist, encounter, and subdue the rebels and traitors above described, by such as shall be called upon for those purposes.

The New England army, before Boston, sixteen thousand strong, consisted of thirty-six regiments, twenty-seven from Massachusetts, and three from each of the other colonies. John Whitcombe, who had led a regiment in the French war, and Dr. Joseph Warren, president of the Congress, and chairman of the Committee of Safety, had been appointed first and second major-generals of the Massachusetts forces.

To make the blockade of Boston more complete, by order of the Committee of Safety, Colonel Prescott, with about a thousand men, including a company of artillery, with two field-pieces, marched at nightfall to take possession of Bunker Hill, a considerable eminence just within the peninsula of Charlestown, and commanding the great northern road to Boston. By some mistake, Prescott passed Bunker Hill and advanced to Breed's Hill, at the southern end of the peninsula, and much nearer Boston. Before morning the troops had thrown up a considerable redoubt, greatly to the surprise of the British, who opened immediately a fire upon them, from the ships in the harbor and the batteries in Boston. Under the direction of Gridley and of Knox, late commander of a Boston artillery militia company, the provincials labored on, undisturbed by the fire. By noon they had thrown up a breastwork extending from the redoubt down the northern slope of the hill, toward the water. Cannon mounted in the redoubt would command the harbor, and might make Boston itself untenable. To avert this threatened danger, three thousand men, picked corps of the British army, led by Generals Howe and Pigot, embarked in boats from the wharves in Boston, and landed at the eastern foot of Breed's Hill. Such was the want of order and system in the provincial camp, and so little was the apprehension of immediate attack, that the same troops who had been working all night, still occupied the intrenchments. General Putnam was on the field, but he appears to have had no troops, and no command. The same was the case with General Warren, whom the rumor of attack had drawn from Cambridge. Two New Hampshire regiments, under Stark, arrived on the ground just before the action began, and took up a position on the left of the unfinished breastwork, but some two hundred yards in the rear, under an imperfect cover, made by pulling up the rail fences, placing them in parallel lines a few feet apart, and filling the intervening space with the new-mown hay which lay scattered on the hill. Other troops had been ordered to Charlestown; but, owing to some misapprehension, they did not arrive in season to take part in the battle. The supply of ammunition was very short.

Here is Washington Irving's description of this important battle, contained in his new "Life of Washington." He here takes up the word from Hildreth.

THE BATTLE OF BUNKER HILL.

The sound of drum and trumpet, the clatter of hoofs, the rattling of gun carriages, and all the other military din and bustle in the streets of Boston, soon apprised the Americans, on their rudely fortified hight, of an impending attack. They were ill-fitted to withstand it, being jaded by the night's labor and want of sleep, hungry and thirsty, having brought but scanty supplies, and oppressed by the heat of the weather. Prescott sent repeated messages to General Ward, asking reinforcements and provisions. Putnam seconded the request in person, urging the exigencies of the case.

Ward hesitated. He feared to weaken his main body at Cambridge, as his military stores were deposited there, and it might have to sustain the principal attack. At length, having taken advice of the Council of Safety, he issued orders to Colonels Stark and Read, then at Medford, to march to the relief of Prescott, with their New Hampshire regiments. The order reached Medford about eleven o'clock. Ammunition was distributed in all haste—two flints, a gill of powder, and fifteen balls to each man. The balls had to be suited to the different calibres of the guns; the powder to be carried in powder-horns, or loose in the pocket, for there were no cartridges prepared. It was the rude turn-out of yeoman soldiery, destitute of regular accoutrements.

In the meanwhile, the Americans on Breed's Hill were sustaining the fire from the ships and from the battery on Copp's Hill, which opened upon them about ten o'clock. They returned an occasional shot from one corner of the redoubt, without much harm to the enemy, and continued strengthening their position until about eleven o'clock, when they ceased to work, piled up their intrenching tools in the rear, and looked out anxiously and impatiently for the anticipated reinforcements and supplies.

About this time, General Putnam, who had been to headquarters, arrived at the redoubt, on horseback. Some words passed between him and Prescott with regard to the intrenching tools, which have been variously reported.

The most probable version is, that he urged to have them taken from their present place, where they might fall into the hands of the enemy, and be carried to Bunker Hill, to be employed in throwing up a redoubt, which was part of the original plan, and which would be very important, should the troops be obliged to retreat from Breed's Hill. To this, Prescott demurred that those employed to convey them, and who were already jaded with toil, might not return to his redoubt. A large part of the tools were ultimately carried to Bunker Hill, and a breastwork commenced, by order of General Putnam. The importance of such a work was afterward made apparent.

About noon, the Americans descried twenty-eight barges crossing from Boston in parallel lines. They contained a large detachment of grenadiers, rangers and light infantry, admirably equipped, and commanded by Major General Howe. They made a splendid and formidable appearance with their scarlet uniforms, and the sun flashing upon muskets and bayonets, and brass field pieces. A heavy fire from the ships and batteries covered their advance, but no attempt was made to oppose them, and they landed about one o'clock at Moulton's point, a little to the north of Breed's Hill.

Here General Howe made a pause. On reconnoitering the works from this point, the Americans appeared to be much more strongly posted than he had imagined. He descried the troops also hastening to their assistance. These were the New Hampshire troops, led on by Stark. Howe immediately sent over to General Gage for more forces and a supply of cannon-balls, those brought by him being found, through some egregious oversight, too large for the ordnance. While awaiting their arrival, refreshments were served out to the troops, with "grog" by the bucketful; and tantalizing it was to the hungry and thirsty Provincials to look down from their ramparts of earth and see their invaders seated in groups upon the grass, eating and drinking, and preparing themselves by a hearty meal for the coming encounter.

The only consolation was to take advantage of the delay, while the enemy were carousing, to strengthen their position. The breastwork on the left of the position extended to what was called the Slough, but beyond this, the ridge of the hill and the slope toward the Mystic River, were undefended, leaving a pass by which the enemy might turn the left flank of the position, and seize upon Bunker Hill. Putnam ordered his chosen officer, Captain Knowlton, to cover this pass with the Connecticut troops under his command. A novel kind of rampart, savoring of rural device, was suggested by the rustic General.

About six hundred feet in the rear of the redoubt, and about one hundred feet to the left of the breastwork, was a post-and-rail fence, set in a low foot-wall of stone, and extending down to Mystic River. The posts and rails of another fence were hastily pulled up and set a few feet in behind this, and the intermediate space was filled up with new-mown hay, from the adjacent meadows. The double fence, it will be found, proved an important protection to the redoubt, although there still remained an unprotected interval of about seven hundred feet.

While Knowlton and his men were putting up this fence, Putnam proceeded with other of his troops to throw up the works on Bunker Hill, dispatching his son, Captain Putnam, on horseback, to hurry up the remainder of his men from Cambridge. By this time, his compeer in French and Indian warfare, the veteran Stark, made his appearance with the New Hampshire troops, five hundred strong. He had grown cool and wary with age, and his march from Medford, a distance of five or six miles, had been in character. He led his men at a moderate pace, to bring them into action fresh and vigorous. In crossing the Neck, which was enfiladed by the enemy's ships and batteries, Captain Dearborn, who was by his side, suggested a quick step. The veteran shook his head. "One fresh man in action is worth ten tired ones," replied he, and marched steadily on.

Putnam detained some of Stark's men, to aid in throwing up the works on Bunker Hill, and directed him to reinforce Knowlton with the rest.

Stark made a short speech to his men, now that they were likely to have warm work. He then pushed on, and did good service that day at the rustic bulwark.

About two o'clock, Warren arrived on the hights, ready to engage in their perilous defense, although he had opposed the scheme of their occupation. He had recently been elected a Major General, but had not received his commission; like Pomeroy, he came to serve in the ranks, with a musket on his shoulder.

Putnam offered him the command at the fence; he declined it, and merely asked where he could be of most service as a volunteer. Putnam pointed to the redoubt, observing that he would be under cover. "Don't think I seek a place of safety," replied Warren quickly; "where will the attack be hottest?" Putnam still pointed to the redoubt. "That is the enemy's object; if that can be maintained, the day is ours." Warren was cheered by the troops as he entered the redoubt. Colonel Prescott tendered him the command. He again declined. "I have come to serve only as a volunteer, and shall be happy to learn from a soldier of your experience." Such were the spirits assembled on these perilous hights.

The British now prepared for a general assault. An easy victory was anticipated; the main thought was, how to make it most effectual. The left wing, commanded by General Pigot, was to mount the hill and force the redoubt, while General Howe, with the right wing, was to push on between the fort and Mystic River, turn the left flank of the Americans, and cut off their retreat.

General Pigot accordingly advanced up the hill, under cover of a fire from field-pieces and howitzers, planted on a small hight, near the landing-place on Moulton's Point. His troops commenced a discharge of musketry, while yet at a long distance from the redoubts.

The Americans within the works, obedient to strict command, retained their fire until the enemy were within thirty or forty paces, when they opened upon them with a tremendous volley. Being all marksmen, accustomed to take deliberate aim, the slaughter was immense, and especially fatal to officers. The assailants fell back in some confusion, but, rallied on by their officers, advanced within pistol-shot. Another volley, more effective than the first, made them again recoil. To add to their confusion, they were galled by a flanking fire from the handful of Provincials posted in Charlestown. Shocked at the carnage, and seeing the confusion of his troops, General Pigot was urged to give the word for a retreat.

In the meanwhile, General Howe, with the left wing, advanced along the Mystic River, toward the fence where Stark, Read, and Knowlton were stationed, thinking to carry this slight breastwork with ease, and so get in the rear of the fortress. His artillery proved of little avail, being stopped by a swampy piece of ground, while his columns suffered from two or three field-pieces, with which Putnam had fortified the fence. Howe's men kept up a fire of musketry as they advanced; but not taking aim, their shot passed over the heads of the Americans. The latter had received the same orders with those in the redoubt—not to fire until the enemy should be within thirty paces. Some few transgressed the command. Putnam rode up, and swore he would cut down the next man that fired contrary to orders.

When the British arrived within the stated distance, a sheeted fire opened upon them from rifles, muskets, and fowling-pieces, all leveled with deadly aim. The carnage, as in the other instance, was horrible. The British were thrown into confusion, and fell back; some even retreated to the boats.

There was a general pause on the part of the British. The American officers availed themselves of it, to prepare for another attack, which must soon be made. Prescott mingled among his men in the redoubt, who were all in high spirits at the severe check they had given the "regulars." He praised them for their steadfastness in maintaining their post, and their good conduct in reserving their fire until the word of command, and exhorted them to do the same in the next attack.

Putnam rode about Bunker Hill and its skirts, to rally and bring on reinforcements, which had been checked or scattered in crossing Charlestown Neck, by the raking fire from the ships and batteries. Before many could be brought to the scene of action, the British had commenced their second attack. They again ascended the hill to storm the redoubt; their advance was covered, as before, by discharges of artillery. Charlestown, which had annoyed them on the first attack by a flanking fire, was in flames by shells thrown from Copp's Hill, and by marines from the ships. Being built of wood, the place was soon wrapped in a general conflagration.

The thunder of artillery from the batteries and ships, the bursting of bombshells, the sharp discharges of musketry, the shouts and yells of the combatants, the crash of burning buildings, and the dense volumes of smoke which obscured the summer sun, all formed a tremendous spectacle. "Sure I am," said Burgoyne, in one of his letters—"Sure I am, nothing ever has or ever can be more dreadfully terrible than what was to be seen or heard at this time. The most incessant discharge of guns that ever was heard by mortal ears."

The American troops, though unused to war, stood undismayed amidst a scene where it was bursting upon them with all its horrors. Reserving their fire as before, until the enemy was close at hand, they again poured forth repeated volleys, with the fatal aim of sharpshooters. The British stood the first shock, and continued to advance; but the incessant stream of fire staggered them. Their officers remonstrated, threatened, and even attempted to goad them on with their swords; but the havoc was too deadly; whole ranks were mowed down; many of the officers were either slain or wounded, and among them several of the staff of General Howe. The troops again gave way, and retreated down the hill.

All this passed under the eyes of thousands of spectators of both sexes and all ages, watching from afar, every turn of the battle in which the lives of those most dear to them, were at hazard. The British soldiery in Boston, gazed with astonishment and incredulity at the resolute and protracted stand of the raw militia, whom they had been taught to despise, and at the havoc made among their own veteran troops. Every convoy of wounded brought over to the town, increased their consternation; and General Clinton, who had watched the action from Copp's Hill, embarking in a boat, hurried over as a volunteer, taking with him reinforcements.

A third attack was now determined on, though some of Howe's officers remonstrated, declaring it would be downright butchery. A different plan was adopted. Instead of advancing in front of the redoubt, it was to be taken in flank on the left, where the open space between the breastwork and the fortified fence, presented a weak point. It having been accidentally discovered that the ammunition of the Americans was nearly expended, preparations were made to carry the works at the point of the bayonet; and the soldiery threw off their knapsacks, and some even their coats, to be more light for action.

General Howe, with the main body, now made a feint attack on the fortified fence; but while a part of his force was thus engaged, the rest brought some field-pieces to enfilade the breastwork on the left of the redoubt. A raking fire soon drove the Americans out of this exposed place into the inclosure. Much damage, too, was done in the latter by balls which entered the sallyport.

The troops were now led on to assail the works; those who flinched, were, as before, goaded on by the swords of the officers. The Americans again reserved their fire until their assailants were close at hand, then made a murderous volley, by which several officers were laid low, and General Howe himself was wounded in the foot.

The British soldiery this time likewise reserved their fire, and rushed on with fixed bayonets. Clinton and Pigot had reached the southern and eastern sides of the redoubt, and it was now assailed on three sides at once. Prescott ordered those who had no bayonets, to retire to the back part of the redoubt, and fire on the enemy as they showed themselves on the parapet. The first who mounted, exclaimed in triumph, "The day is ours!"

He was instantly shot down, and so were several others who mounted about the same time. The Americans, however, had fired their last round, their ammunition was exhausted; and now succeeded a desperate and deadly struggle, hand to hand, with bayonets, stones, and the stocks of their muskets.

At length, as the British continued to pour in, Prescott gave the order to retreat. His men had to cut their way through two divisions of the enemy, who were getting in the rear of the redoubt, and they received a destructive volley from those who had formed on the captured works. By that volley fell the patriot Warren, who had distinguished himself throughout the action. He was among the last to leave the redoubt, and had scarce done so, when he was shot through the head with a musket ball, and fell dead on the ground.

While the Americans were thus slowly dislodged from the redoubt, Stark, Read, and Knowlton maintained their ground at the fortified fence, which indeed, had been nobly defended throughout the action. Pomeroy distinguished himself here by his sharpshooting, until his musket was shattered by a ball. The resistance at this hastily constructed work, was kept up after the troops in the redoubt had given way, and until Colonel Prescott had left the hill, thus defeating General Howe's design of cutting off the retreat of the main body, which would have produced a scene of direful confusion and slaughter. Having effected their purpose, the brave associates of the fence abandoned their weak outpost, retiring slowly, and disputing the ground inch by inch, with a regularity remarkable in troops, many of whom had never before been in action.

The main retreat was across Bunker Hill, where Putnam had endeavored to throw up a breastwork. The veteran, sword in hand, rode to the rear of the retreating troops, regardless of the balls whistling about him. His only thought was to rally them at the unfinished works. "Halt! make a stand here!" cried he, "we can check them yet. In God's name, form, and give them one shot more."

Pomeroy, wielding his shattered musket as a truncheon, seconded him in his efforts to stay the torrent. It was impossible, however, to bring the troops to a stand. They continued on down the hill to the Neck, and across to Cambridge, exposed to a raking fire from the ships and batteries, and only protected by a single piece of ordnance. The British were too exhausted to pursue them; they contented themselves with taking possession of Bunker Hill, were reinforced from Boston, and threw up additional works during the night.

The provincials might consider such a defeat as little less than victory. Out of three thousand British troops engaged, over one thousand were killed or wounded—a loss, such as few battles can show. The ministry were so little satisfied with the accounts sent them of this transaction, that Gage was superseded in command. The provincial loss was four hundred and fifty; but among the slain was General Warren. Ardent, sincere, disinterested, and indefatigable, his death was deeply deplored. He left an infant family with small means of support; for whom, by the zeal and perseverance of Arnold, the Continental Congress was at last pushed to make some provision. The battle of Bunker Hill, figures in history, as having tested the ability of the provincials to meet a British army in the field. That, however, was a point, on which the provincials themselves never had any doubts, and the battle, at the moment, was less thought of than now. Nor were the men engaged in it, all heroes. The conduct of several officers on that day, was investigated by court-martial, and one, at least, was cashiered for cowardice.

In contrast with the dastardly conduct of a few animals known as men, at the battle of Bunker Hill, we give the following letter from one of the daughters of "Sam," written about this period, which exhibits the true sentiment of that momentous time, and coming even from the hearts of the Women of America.

From the *Richmond Enquirer.*

FEMALE PATRIOTISM.

The manuscript of the following interesting letter was politely forwarded to us by a gentleman of Baltimore, and was found among some old papers of a distinguished lady of Philadelphia. It is a copy of a letter from a lady of Philadelphia to a British officer at Boston, written immediately after the battle of Lexington, and previous to the declaration of Independence. It fully exhibits the feelings of those times. A finer spirit never animated the breasts of the Roman matrons, than the following letter breathes:

SIR: We received a letter from you wherein you let Mr. S. know that you had written directly after the battle of Lexington, particularly to me, knowing my martial spirit, and that I would delight to read the exploits of heroes. Surely, my friend, you must mean the New England heroes, as they alone performed exploits worthy of fame—while the regulars, vastly superior in numbers, were obliged to retreat with a rapidity unequalled except by the French at the battle of Minden. Indeed, General Gage gives them their due credit, in his letter home, where he says Lord Percy was remarkable for his activity. You will not, I hope, take offense at any expression that, in the warmth of my heart, shall escape me, when I assure you that, though we consider you a public enemy, we regard you as a private friend; and while we detest the cause you are fighting for, we wish well to your own personal interest and safety. Thus far by way of apology. As to the martial spirit you suppose me to possess, you are greatly mistaken. I tremble at the thought of war, and of all wars, a civil one; our all is at stake, and we are called upon by every tie that is dear and sacred, to exert the spirit that Heaven has given to us in this righteous struggle for liberty.

I will tell you what I have done. My only brother I have sent to the camp, with my prayers and blessings; I hope he will not disgrace me; I am confident he will behave with honor, and emulate the great examples he has before him; and had I twenty sons and brothers, they should go. I have retrenched every superfluous expense in my table and family; tea I have not drank since last Christmas, nor bought a new cap or gown since your defeat at Lexington; and, what I never did before, have learned to knit, and am now making stockings of American wool for my servants, and this way do I throw in my mite for the public good. I know this, that as free I can die but once, but as a slave I shall not be worthy of life. I have the pleasure to assure you that these are the sentiments of all my sister Americans. They have sacrificed both assemblies, parties of pleasure, tea drinking, and finery, to that great spirit of patriotism that actuates all ranks and degrees of people throughout this extensive continent. If these are the sentiments of females, what must glow in the breasts of our husbands, brothers and sons? They are, as with one heart, determined to die or be free. It is not a quibble in politics, a science which few understand, which we are contending for; it is this plain truth, which the most ignorant peasant knows, and is clear to the weakest capacity, that no man has a right to take their money without their consent. The supposition is ridiculous and absurd, as none but highwaymen and robbers attempt it. Can you, my friend, reconcile it with your own good sense, that a body of men in Great Britain, who have little intercourse with America, and, of course, know nothing of us, nor are supposed to see or feel the misery they would inflict upon us, shall invest themselves with a power to command our lives and properties, at all times and in all cases whatsoever? You say you are no politician. Oh, sir, it requires no Machiavelian head to develope this, and to discover this tyranny and oppression. It is written with a sunbeam. Every one will see and know it, because it will make them feel, and we shall be unworthy of the blessing of Heaven if we ever submit to it.

All ranks of men among us are in arms. Nothing is heard now in our streets but the trumpet and the drum; and the universal cry is "Americans to arms." All your friends are officers; there are Captain S. B., Lieutenant B., and Captain J. S. We have five regiments in the city and county of Philadelphia, complete in arms and uniform, and very expert in their military manœuvres. We have companies of light horse, light infantry, grenadiers, riflemen, and Indians, several companies of artillery, and some excellent brass cannon and field pieces. Add to this, that every county in Pennsylvania, and the Delaware government, can send two thousand men to the field. Heaven seems to smile on us, for in the memory of man never were known such quantities of flax, and sheep without number. We are making powder fast, and do not want for ammunition. In short, we want for nothing but ships of war to defend us, which we could procure by making alliances; but such is our attachment to Great Britain, that we sincerely wish for reconciliation, and cannot bear the thought of throwing off all dependence upon her, which such a step would assuredly lead to. The God of Mercy will, I hope, open the eyes of our king, that he may see that in seeking our destruction, he will go near to complete his own. It is my ardent prayer that the effusion of blood may be stopped. We hope yet to see you in this city, a friend to the liberties of America, which will give infinite satisfaction to Your sincere friend, C. L.

To CAPTAIN S., *in Boston.*

But here is a still more touching incident, which, though at first glance Amazonian in aspect, reveals truthfully the true sentiment of the mothers of the heroes of an heroic period:

From the *Dedham* (Mass.) *Register*, of December, 1820.

FEMALE PERSEVERANCE.

We were much gratified to learn that during the sitting of the Court in this town, the last week, Mrs. Gannett, of

Sharon, in this county, presented for renewal, her claims for services rendered her country, as a *soldier* in the revolutionary army. The following brief sketch, it is presumed, will not be uninteresting:

This extraordinary woman is now in the sixty-second year of her age. She possesses a clear understanding, and a general knowledge of passing events—fluent in speech, and delivers her sentiments in correct language, with deliberate and measured accents—easy in her deportment, affable in her manners, robust and masculine in her appearance. She was about eighteen years of age when our revolutionary struggle commenced. The patriotic sentiments which inspired the heroes of those days, and urged them to battle, found their way to a female bosom. The news of the carnage which had taken place on the plains of Lexington, had reached her dwelling—the sound of the cannon at Bunker Hill had vibrated on her ears—yet, instead of diminishing her ardor, it only served to increase her enthusiasm in the sacred cause of liberty, in which cause she beheld her country engaged. She privately quitted her peaceful home, and the habiliments of her sex, and appeared at the headquarters of the American army as a young man, anxious to join his efforts to those of his countrymen, in their endeavors to oppose the inroads and encroachments of the common enemy. She was received and enrolled in the army by the name of *Robert Shurtliffe.* For the space of *three years* she performed the duties, and endured the hardships and fatigues, of a soldier, during which time she gained the confidence of her officers by her expertness and precision in the manual exercise, and by her exemplary conduct. She was a volunteer in several hazardous enterprises, and was twice wounded by musket balls. So well did she contrive to conceal her sex, that her companions in arms had not the least suspicion that this "blooming soldier" fighting by their sides was a female, till at length, a severe wound which she had received in battle, and which had well nigh closed her earthly campaign, occasioned the discovery. On her discovery, she quitted the army, and became intimate in the families of General Washington and other distinguished officers of the revolution. A few years afterward she was married to her present husband, and is now the mother of several children. Of these facts there can be no doubt. There are many living witnesses in this county, who recognized her on her appearance at the court, and were ready to attest to her services. We often hear of such heroines in other countries, but this is an instance in our own country, and within the circle of our acquaintance.

Heath was appointed major-general in Warren's place, and a similar commission was given to Frye, both colonels in the Masachusetts army, and Frye, commander-in-chief of the Massachusetts forces at the unfortunate capture of Fort William Henry. But these commissions, and the other previous ones, were soon superseded by the new continental appointments. About a fortnight after the battle of Bunker Hill, Washington, attended by several ardent young men from the southern provinces, arrived in the camp, and assumed the command. He found there, excellent materials for an army, but great deficiencies of arms and ammunition, and some great defects of discipline and organization. To prevent the British, not greatly inferior in numbers, and perfectly armed, equipped, and disciplined, from penetrating into the country, it was necessary to guard a circuit of eight or nine miles. Washington established his head-quarters at Cambridge. Ward, in command of the right wing, was stationed at Roxbury; and Lee, with the left, on Prospect Hill. Joseph Trumbull, a son of the governor of Connecticut, and commissary for the troops of that province, was appointed commissary-general of the consolidated army. The post of quartermaster-general was given by Washington, under authority from Congress, to Mifflin, who had followed him from Philadelphia as an aid-de-camp. The post of secretary to the commander-in-chief was bestowed on Joseph Reed, another Philadelphian; but, on Reed's return to Philadelphia a few months afterward, Washington selected for that important and confidential duty, Robert H. Harrison, a lawyer of Maryland, with whom he had formerly had business relations, and who continued for several years to discharge its responsible duties, very much to the general's satisfaction. Edmund Randolph, a nephew of Peyton Randolph, but whose father, the attorney-general of Virginia, was a decided Royalist, had accompanied the commander-in-chief to Boston, and acted for a while as aid-de-camp. But he was presently recalled to Virginia by his uncle's sudden death.

The camp was soon joined by some companies of riflemen from Maryland, Virginia, and Western Pennsylvania, enlisted under the orders of Congress. One of the Virginia companies was led by Daniel Morgan, formerly a wagoner, in which capacity he had been wounded at Braddock's defeat. A man of Herculean frame and indomitable energy, his qualities as a partisan soon made him distinguished.

CHAPTER XXXVI.

The first Sea Fight—and origin of the U. S. Navy—Ethan Allen taken captive and sent to England—Capture of St. Johns and Montreal—The expedition against Quebec—Reorganization of the Army—Lord Howe in Boston—Movements of the British in Virginia.

THE Gaspé, an armed schooner in the revenue service, had given great and often unnecessary annoyance to the shipping employed in Narraganset Bay. A plan, in consequence, had been formed for her destruction. Enticed into shoal water by a schooner, to which she had been induced to give chase, she grounded, and was boarded and burned by a party from Providence. In consequence of this daring outrage, an act of Parliament had passed for sending to England for trial all persons concerned in the colonies in burning or destroying his Majesty's ships, dock-yards, or military stores. A reward of £600 sterling, and a free pardon to any accomplice, was offered for the discovery of the destroyers of the Gaspé; and a board was constituted to examine into the matter, composed of the governor of Rhode Island, the chief justices of Massachusetts, New York, and New Jersey, and the judge of the Admiralty for the Northern District. But, though the perpetrators were well known, no legal evidence could be obtained against them.

Hildreth speaks of this as the *first* sea fight, from which statement, however, the old records vary somewhat, as the following narrative will show:—

THE FIRST SEA FIGHT.

The late Rev. Dr. Bentley, of Salem, Massachusetts, whose decease was equally deplored by the friends of religion, patriotism, and literature—who for many years enriched the columns of the "*Essex Register*" with his remarks, when speaking of the revolutionary pension law, seized the opportunity to give the following interesting scrap of history:—

"The following history may discover how a man may engage in the public service, and yet not be qualified according to law, for the bounty of a term short of one year's service. Joshua Ward, who belonged to Salem, but who lived many years at Marblehead, a painter, marched on the 19th of April to Charlestown Neck, as a fifer of the first company in Colonel Timothy Pickering's regiment of militia, commanded by Captain William Pickman, and soon after entered the army under Captain Thomas Barnes. From Cambridge, he was ordered to Watertown to guard the public stores, and remained at this station till the battle of Bunker Hill. He then joined the regiment under Colonel Mansfield, on Prospect Hill, in Charlestown, in the Massachusetts line, and acted as fife-major till he joined General Sullivan's brigade, on Winter Hill, when he was promoted to fife-major-general. He continued in the service till the first day of January, 1776, when he was discharged—having continued the time of his enlistment. He then entered Captain Benjamin Ward's company and performed garrison duty at Fort William and Mary, now Fort Pickering, till the 19th of June following. He then volunteered with the first Lieutenant Haraden, a well-known, brave and able officer, with others of his companions, on board the Tyrannicide, a public armed brig of fourteen guns and seventy-five men, commanded by Captain John Fiske, afterward a major-general in Massachusetts, and eminent by his public services. He was in this brig during three cruises, and was at the taking of eight prizes, the first of which was the king's armed schooner Dispatch, belonging to Lord Howe's fleet, then on their passage to New York, it being the 10th July. In the engagement one man was killed in the Tyrannicide, three wounded, and one died of his wounds. He continued in the vessel till the 14th of February, 1777, when he returned from a four and a half month's cruise in the West Indies, and all were discharged. He is now 72 years of age. In the action with the Dispatch, which lasted seven glasses, her commander, John Goodrich, 2d lieutenant of the Renown, of fifty guns, then in the fleet, was killed, and several men. Mr. Moore sailing master, was wounded, and his limb amputated. Mr. Collingsin, midshipman, had his limb amputated, but he died. The Dispatch was so disabled that they were obliged to take her in tow, and they brought her into Salem, after being out seventeen days. The Dispatch had eight carriage guns, twelve swivels, and a complement of forty-one picked men from different ships in the fleet. *This was the first sea fight.* The Tyrannicide was the first vessel that was built for the public service, and her commission was signed by John Hancock. The Dispatch was no prize to the crew, excepting a small bounty on her guns. And yet this worthy man in his poverty comes not within the letter of the law, and instead of his bounty, must accept a hearty recommendation to the generous care of his fellow-citizens.

Our narrative carries us on to the period when the downfall of British authority in the colonies has become a fixed fact in history, and the United Thirteen Colonies a firm-rooted empire on the face of the New World! "Sam," as we have now perceived, is stretching his huge arm toward the sea.

A constant alarm was kept up by British cruisers, which hovered on the coast of New England, and landed occasionally to obtain supplies. Lieutenant Mowatt, who commanded one of these cruisers, chased a vessel from the West Indies into Gloucester harbor. The boats sent to take her being repulsed by the townspeople, Mowatt fired upon the town, and attempted to land. But he was again repulsed, with the loss of his boats, and thirty-five men taken prisoners. Narraganset Bay was much annoyed by a squadron of British cruisers, and Bristol was bombarded to frighten the inhabitants into furnishing a supply of provisions. Mowatt was presently sent to Falmouth, (now Portland,) where, a few months before, the loading of a royal mast ship had been obstructed and Mowatt himself arrested and treated with some rudeness. On the refusal of the inhabitants to give up their arms, after allowing two hours for the removal of the women and children, a bombardment was commenced, and that rising town of five hundred houses was presently in flames. The townspeople, not to be so frightened, stood to their arms, and defeated Mowatt's attempt to land. Such outrages did but exasperate feelings already sufficiently inflamed.

It was not long before the colonists tried their hands also at maritime warfare. Rhode Island, Massachusetts, and Connecticut equipped each an armed vessel or two. In Massachusetts a law was passed to authorize and encourage the fitting out of privateers, and a court was established for the trial and condemnation of prizes. Maryland, Virginia, and South Carolina each had their navy boards and armed vessels, and so did Pennsylvania for the defense of the Delaware. Five or six armed vessels, fitted out by Washington, cruised to intercept the supplies received at Boston by sea. Most of the officers of these vessels proved incompetent, and the men mutinous; but Captain Manly, of the schooner Lee, furnished a brilliant exception. In the midst of storms he kept the hazardous station of Massachusetts Bay, and, among other prizes, captured an ordnance brig, laden with heavy guns, mortars, and working tools—a most acceptable supply to the continental army.

Under instructions from the Assembly of Rhode Island, the delegates of that colony called the attention of the Continental Congress to the subject of a navy. A Marine Committee was appointed, and four armed vessels were ordered to be fitted out at continental expense. All ships of war employed in harassing the colonies, and all vessels bringing supplies to the British forces, were declared lawful prize. Privateering was authorized, and the colonies were requested to establish courts for the trial of captures, reserving an appeal to Congress. Rules and regulations for the navy were adopted; and the Naval Committee were presently authorized to fit out thirteen frigates, of from twenty-four to thirty-two guns.

The clergy and the seigneurs of Canada, well satisfied with the late Quebec Act, were inclined to sustain the British authority; but some partisans of the American cause were hoped for among the cultivators and citizens, as well as among the immigrants since the conquest. The body of the Canadian people, notwithstanding a proclamation of martial law, paid very little attention to Governor Carleton's loud calls upon them to arm for the defense of the province. Hinman's Connecticut regiment, stationed at Ticonderoga, at the head of which Schuyler placed himself, descended the lake in boats, entered the Sorel, and occupied the Isle Aux

Noix. After an unsuccessful attempt on St. John's, where was a garrison of five or six hundred British troops, the principal regular force in Canada, leaving the command to Montgomery, Schuyler returned to the rear to hasten forward men and supplies. The equipment of the New York regiments was greatly delayed by the difficulty of finding arms, and Wooster was ordered from Albany, to join Montgomery.

Meanwhile Ethan Allen, with a small party, principally Canadians, was taken prisoner in a wild attempt, without orders, to surprise Montreal. Contrary to Carleton's usual conduct, Allen experienced very hard usage, being sent in irons to England, and treated rather as a leader of banditti than as a prisoner of war.

Joined by Wooster and some Canadians, Montgomery renewed the siege of St. John's. By the surprise and capture of Chambly, lower down the Sorel, against which he sent a detachment, he obtained a seasonable supply of ammunition, which enabled him to press the siege of St. John's with vigor. For the relief of that important post, Governor Carleton exerted himself to raise the Canadian militia; but, in attempting to cross from the island of Montreal to the south bank of the St. Lawrence, he was repulsed by an advanced division of Montgomery's army. Another party of Canadian militia, from the neighborhood of Quebec, advancing up the Sorel, was driven down that river to its junction with the St. Lawrence, at which point the Americans established a post and erected batteries. Relief thus cut off, the garrison of St. John's presently surrendered as prisoners of war; after which Montgomery pushed forward to Montreal, a town at that time of but two or three thousand inhabitants, open, and without fortifications. Carleton passed down the river in a fast-sailing boat, and escaped to Quebec. General Prescott, with the feeble garrison, attempted to escape the same way, but was interrupted by the batteries at the Sorel, and taken prisoner.

With the woolens found at Montreal the American general was enabled to clothe his troops, of which they stood in great need. A regiment of Canadians was organized under Colonel Livingston; but Montgomery encountered great discouragements in the lateness of the season and the insubordination of his soldiers, of whom many, disgusted with the hardships of the service, deserted and returned home. Still he pushed on for Quebec, in expectation of meeting there a co-operating force.

When obliged to give up the command of Ticonderoga to Hinman, Arnold had behaved with a good deal of insubordination; had disbanded his men, and returned in disgust to the camp before Boston. There, however, he presently obtained employment in an enterprise suggested some time before by Brewer, colonel of one of the Massachusetts regiments. Detached with eleven hundred men, including a company of artillery and Morgan's Virginia riflemen, to co-operate with the northern army, against Quebec, Arnold ascended in boats to the head of the Kennebec, and, guided in part by the journal of a British officer who had passed over that route some fifteen years before, struck across the wilderness to the head streams of the Chaudière, down which he descended toward the capital of Canada. In crossing these uninhabited wilds, the troop suffered severely, and the rear division, discouraged and short of provisions, turned about and gave over the enterprise. With the other divisions Arnold persevered; and, after a six weeks' struggle, a few days before Montgomery entered Montreal, he reached the south bank of the St. Lawrence, opposite Quebec. He was kindly received by the Canadian peasantry, and his sudden appearance caused the greatest alarm. Quebec had but two hundred regular troops; there was a good deal of discontent among the inhabitants. Could Arnold have crossed at once, he might, perhaps, in the absence of Carleton, have got possession of the city. But, on some intimation of his approach, the boats had all been removed or destroyed, and some days elapsed before he could collect birch-bark canoes in which to cross. Meanwhile Carleton made his appearance, having escaped down the river from Montreal. He sent all the non-combatants out of the city; organized the traders and others into military companies, landed the sailors; and, with his force thus increased to near twelve hundred men, put the town into a complete state of defense. Two armed vessels were stationed in the river to intercept Arnold; but he crossed in the night; and, ascending the same rugged precipices which Wolfe had climbed before him, drew up his forces on the Plains of Abraham. His little army, hardly five hundred and fifty effective men, approached the city; but the garrison did not come out to meet him; and, as he had no means to undertake a siege, he retired some twenty miles up the river to wait for Montgomery, of whose approach he had notice.

Leaving Wooster in command at Montreal, Montgomery advanced down the river; but all his Connecticut troops became entitled to their discharge on the tenth of December, and his ranks were so thinned by desertions and the detachments he was obliged to leave behind him, that, when he joined Arnold, their united force did not exceed a thousand men. They returned, however, to Quebec, and opened batteries against it; but their artillery, only a few field pieces, was too light to take any effect. The works were extensive; some weak point might perhaps be found; an assault was resolved upon, as the last desperate chance. While a snowstorm was waited for, to cover the movement, deserters carried into the town information of what was intended. To distract the enemy's attention, two feints were made against the upper town. It was against two opposite sides of the lower town that the real attacks were directed; the one led by Montgomery, the other by Arnold. Some rockets, thrown up as a signal, being seen by the enemy, they took the alarm and hastened to the ramparts. Montgomery, with the New York troops, approached the first barrier, on the south side of the lower town. The enemy fled; not, however, without discharging a piece of artillecy, by which Montgomery and his two aids were slain. Discouraged by the loss of their leader, this division abandoned the attack. Arnold, on his side, pushed through the northern suburb, and approached a a two-gun battery, the advanced post of the enemy in that direction. While cheering on his men, the bone of his leg was shattered by a musket ball. He was borne from the field; but Morgan, at the head of his riflemen, made a rush at the battery, carried it, and took the guard prisoners. Morgan had no guide; the morning was dark; totally ignorant of the situation of the town, he came to a halt. He was joined by some fragments of other companies, and, when the day dawned, found himself at the head of some two hundred men, who eagerly demanded to be led against the second barrier, a few paces in front, but concealed from sight by a turn in the street.

Morgan gave the order, and his men advanced and planted their ladders; but those who mounted saw on the other side a double hedge of bayonets ready to receive them, while a fire, at the same time, was opened by parties of the enemy relieved from duty elsewhere by the failure of the other attack, and sent out of the gates to take them in the rear. Exposed in a narrow street to an incessant fire, Morgan's ranks were soon thinned. His men threw themselves into the store-houses on each side of the street; but, overpowered by numbers, benumbed with cold, their muskets rendered unserviceable by the snow, they were obliged to surrender. Not less than four hundred men were lost in this unlucky assault, of whom three hundred became prisoners. Arnold retired with the remnant of his troops three miles up the river, and, covering his camp with ramparts of frozen snow, kept up the blockade of Quebec through the winter.

While these operations were carried on in Canada, the term of service of the troops before Boston was rapidly approaching its termination. The time of the Connecticut and Rhode Island regiments expired early in December. None of the troops were engaged for a longer period than the first of April.

A committee from Philadelphia had visited the camp, and, in consultation with Washington, and with committees from the New England colonies, had agreed upon a plan, presently sanctioned by Congress, for the reorganization of the besieging army. It was to consist, according to this plan, of twenty-six regiments, beside riflemen and artillery: Massachusetts to furnish sixteen, Connecticut five, New Hampshire three, and Rhode Island two—in all, about twenty thousand men; the officers to be selected by Washington, out of those already in service, willing and qualified to act. But this was a business much easier to plan than to execute. The selection of officers was a most delicate and embarrassing matter, in which, not qualifications only, but provincial and personal prejudices had to be consulted, for not a man would enlist till he knew the officers under whom he was to serve. Even then, enlistments, though only for a year, were obtained with difficulty. The first effervescence of patriotism was over. The barracks were cold and comfortless, and the supply of fuel scanty. A short experience of military life had damped the ardor of many. All the new recruits required a furlough to visit their families. Those who did not re-enlist refused to serve a moment beyond their time. One or two of the Connecticut regiments marched off some days beforehand. The camp was in danger of being left bare, and, to supply the deficiency in the Continental regiments, five thousand militia had to be called in, who answered much better than Washington had feared.

Surrounded with difficulties, the commander-in-chief exhibited a fortitude, assiduity, discrimination, and patience absolutely essential for the station which he held, and amply vindicating the judgment of Congress. In his private correspondence he could not wholly suppress his feelings. He complained bitterly of "an egregious want of public spirit," and of "fertility in all the low arts of obtaining advantage."

Here is one precious example which we have to offer, of the metal and character of the foe with whom "Sam" in these early times was compelled, against his will, to contend, in the first agonies of separation from the Primal Stock. We have other instances of the sort in reservation.

Parliament promptly voted twenty-five thousand men to be employed in America. As it was difficult to obtain enlistments in Great Britain, Hanoverian troops were hired to garrison the fortresses in the Mediterranean, in order to set free an equivalent number of British soldiers, for service in America. This employment of foreign mercenaries was very much stigmatized by the Opposition; but the same policy was presently carried much further. In the course of the session, treaties were laid before Parliament, by which the Duke of Brunswick, and the Landgrave of Hesse-Cassel agreed to hire out seventeen thousand of their subjects to serve as mercenaries in America. The employment of German troops had been suggested by Lord Howe, who expressed, in his correspondence with the ministry, a great dislike of Irish Catholic soldiers, as not at all to be depended on. These treaties, after violent debates, were sanctioned by Parliament, and the necessary funds were voted. The forces to be employed in America were thus raised to upward of forty thousand men.

General Howe, who had now replaced Gage in the command of the British army, was well satisfied that Boston was not a point from which military operations could be advantageously carried on, and, but for the deficiency of shipping, would have evacuated that place before the setting in of winter. Abundant supplies were sent from England at very great expense, but many ships were wrecked, and others were captured; and the British troops felt the want, during the winter, of fuel and fresh provisions. Fuel was supplied by pulling down houses. To diminish the consumption of provisions, numbers of the poorer people were sent out of the town. The troops on Bunker Hill remained under canvas the whole winter, and suffered severely from the cold. The British officers amused themselves as they could. They got up balls and a theater. The Old South, the largest meeting-house in the town, was turned into a riding-school.

Lord Dunmore, after his departure from Williamsburg, being joined by several British armed vessels in the Chesapeake, began to threaten Lower Virginia. The settlers west of the Laurel Ridge had met at Pittsburg, had agreed to support the American Association, and had chosen delegates to the Virginia Convention. Dunmore, however, not without hopes of making some impression in that quarter, gave to Conolly, formerly his agent in that region, a lieutenant-colonel's commission, and sent him to visit Gage at Boston. After his return, Conolly proceeded up the Chesapeake, landed near its head, and set off with several companions on his way across the mountains, in hopes, by his personal influence with the western settlers, to raise a regiment, and, in conjunction with some regulars from Detroit, to operate against the back part of Virginia. It was even said to be a part of his plan to stimulate the Indians to hostilities. But the whole scheme was cut short by Conolly's arrest at Fredericton, in Maryland, whence he and his companions were sent prisoners to Philadelphia.

Meanwhile Dunmore landed at Norfolk, and seized and carried off a printing-press, on which he printed a proclamation, which he dispersed abroad, declaring martial law, calling upon all persons able to bear arms, to join him, and offering freedom to all slaves and indented servants of rebels, who would enlist under his banner. We furnish a copy of this **infamous Proclamation:—**

Since the 19th of May last I have not received a single line from any one in administration, though I have written volumes to them, in each of which I have prayed to be instructed, but to no purpose. I am therefore determined to go on, doing the best of my power for his Majesty's service. I have accordingly ordered a regiment, called the Queen's own royal regiment, of five hundred men, to be raised immediately, consisting of a lieutenant-colonel, commandant, a major, and ten companies, each of which is to consist of one captain, two lieutenants, one ensign, and fifty privates, with non-commissioned officers in proportion. You may observe by my proclamation, *that I offer freedom to the blacks of all rebels, that join me*, in consequence of which there are between two and three hundred already come in, and those I form into a corps, as fast as they come in, giving them white officers and non-commissioners in proportion—and from these two plans, I make no doubt of getting men enough to reduce this colony to a proper sense of their duty. My next distress will be the want of arms, accoutrements and money, all of which you may be able to relieve me from. The latter I am sure you can, as there are many merchants here who are ready to supply me, on my giving them bills on you, which you will have to withdraw, and give your own in their room. I hope this mode will be agreeable to you; it is the same that General Gage proposed.

Having drawn together a considerable force, Dunmore ascended Elizabeth river to the Great Bridge, the only pass by which Norfolk can be approached from the land side; dispersed some North Carolina militia collected there; made several prisoners; and then, descending the river, took possession of Norfolk. The rise of that town had been very rapid. Within a short time past it had become the principal shipping port of Virginia. Its population amounted to several thousands, among whom were many Scotch traders, not well disposed to the American cause.

Fugitive slaves and others began now to flock to Dunmore's standard. A movement was now made in his favor on the east shore of Maryland, which it required a thousand militia to suppress. The Convention of Virginia, not a little alarmed, voted four additional regiments, afterward increased to seven, all of which were presently taken into continental pay. Among the colonels of the new regiments, were Mercer, Stephen, and Muhlenberg, the latter a clergyman, who laid aside the surplice to put on a uniform. The Committee of Safety were authorized to imprison all persons guilty of taking up arms against the colony, and to appropriate the produce of their estates to the public service. Woodford, with the second Virginia regiment, took possession of the causeway leading to the Great Bridge, which was still held by Dunmore's troops. An attempt to dislodge the Virginians having failed, with loss, Dunmore abandoned the bridge and the town, and again embarked. Norfolk was immediately occupied by Woodford, who was promptly joined by Howe's regiment from North Carolina.

After a descent on the eastern shore of Virginia, to whose aid marched two companies of Maryland minute men, being reinforced by the arrival of a British frigate, Dunmore bombarded Norfolk. A party landed and set it on fire. The town was mostly built of wood, and that part of it nearest the water was rapidly consumed. The part which escaped, was presently burned by the provincials, to prevent it from becoming a shelter to the enemy. Thus perished, a prey to civil war, the largest and richest of the rising towns of Virginia. Dunmore continued, during the whole summer, a predatory warfare along the rivers, of which his naval superiority gave him the command, burning houses and plundering plantations, from which he carried off upward of a thousand slaves. He was constantly changing his place to elude attack; but watched, pursued, and harassed, he finally found it necessary to retire to St. Augustine with his adherents and his plunder. (1776.)

The draft of a Declaration, prepared by Jefferson, and reported by the Committee, was then taken up. Not to offend the friends of America in Great Britain, it was agreed to strike out several paragraphs especially severe upon the British government. An emphatic denunciation of the slave trade, and a charge against the king, of having prostituted his negative for the defeat of all legislative attempts to prohibit or restrain "that execrable traffic," was also omitted. It would have been going too far to ask Georgia to vote for that clause. Thus amended, the Declaration was adopted, and signed by most of the members present.

The new Provincial Congress of New York, which met a few days after, at White Plains, with authority to form a government, gave their sanction to the Declaration, which thus became the unanimous act of the Thirteen UNITED STATES. It was presently ordered to be engrossed on parchment, and was subsequently signed by all the delegates then present, including several who were not members at the time of its adoption.

The proclamation of Independence was signalized at New York, by destroying a picture of the king, which had decorated the City Hall. The king's leaden statue, which stood in the Bowling Green, was also thrown down and run into bullets. This feeling of exultation was, however, far from unanimous. A large number of the wealthier citizens looked on with distrust; and the Episcopal clergy showed their dissatisfaction by shutting up the churches.

Meanwhile, by reinforcements from Europe, including a part of the German mercenaries, to whom were added the forces lately employed against Charleston, and some regiments from Florida and the West Indies, Howe's army, encamped on Staten Island, was raised to twenty-four thousand men.

The obstructions placed by General Putnam, with vast labor and expense, in the Hudson and East Rivers, were not found to answer the purpose intended. In spite of the artillery of Forts Washington and Lee, several British vessels ascended the Hudson. An attempt was made to burn them with fire ships; but, having reconnoitered and taken soundings, they descended again without material injury.

It was, however, by way of Long Island, that Howe proposed to approach the city. Washington had expected as much; and a corps of the American army, nine thousand strong, lay at Brooklyn, opposite New York, behind intrenchments thrown up under the direction of Greene. Between this camp and the bay at the southwest corner of Long Island, where the British army presently landed, there stretched a range of thickly-wooded hills, crossed by two roads; a third road followed the shore round the western base of these hills; a fourth, penetrating inland, turned them on the east. Intrenchments had been thrown up to guard the passes over these hills and around their western base, and troops had been detailed for that service. A severe attack of sickness had obliged Greene to give up the command; Putnam, from his recent transfer to it, was yet imperfectly acquainted with the situation of the works and passes in front of the camp; and in the confusion and want of discipline which prevailed, the orders to watch and guard those passes were imperfectly obeyed.

Two British columns advancing by night, one by the shore road and the other over the hills, captured or evaded the patrols, forced the defiles without difficulty, and early the next morning came in contact with two American corps, one under Sterling, sent forward by Putnam, on news of the approach of the British, to guard the shore road, the other under Sullivan, who advanced hastily, with such troops as he could collect, to prevent the passage over the hills. Meanwhile, a third British column, led by Clinton, proceeded along the eastern road, which had been left unguarded, turned the hills, and pushed in between Sullivan's corps and the American camp. Driven backward and forward between a double fire, a few of that corps took advantage of the broken and wooded ground to escape; but the greater part were taken prisoners, and Sullivan along with them.

The corps under Sterling made a steady resistance to the troops in their front, and when Clinton threatened to gain their rear, by great exertions they got back to the camp, not, however, without losing their commander, who was taken prisoner while covering the retreat. For this important victory, in which he lost less than four hundred men, Howe was rewarded by the Order of the Bath. The American loss was never very accurately ascertained; but, beside several hundreds killed or missing, about a thousand remained prisoners in the hands of the enemy. Some five thousand men had been engaged in the battle, principally from New Jersey, Pennsylvania, Delaware, and Maryland. Smallwood's Maryland regiment, forming a part of Sterling's division, behaved with great gallantry, and suffered very severely.

The victorious forces, fifteen thousand strong, encamped directly in front of the American lines, which a vigorous assault might probably have carried. But, with the caution fashionable at that day in military operations, and not diminished by the experiment at Bunker Hill, preparations were made for regular approaches. The camp at Brooklyn had been re-enforced; but Washington would not risk the loss of so considerable a part of his army; and, after holding a council of war, he determined to withdraw the troops. The command of the boats was given to Colonel Glover, of Massachusetts, and they were manned with the men of his regiment, mostly fishermen of Marblehead. M'Dougall, who was not without some experience in marine affairs, superintended the embarkation, and, in the course of the night, favored by a thick fog, a masterly retreat was effected across the East River. As a consequence of this movement, the whole of Long Island fell into the hands of the British. Woodhull, late president of the Provincial Congress, employed on Long Island, with a small body of militia, in driving off cattle, was surprised the day after the battle by a party of light horse, under Oliver Delancey, wounded after his capture, and treated with such cruel neglect that his wounds mortified, and he died in consequence. The Long Island Tories, who had experienced considerable harshess, had now an opportunity to retort on their opponents.

Washington left a considerable force in the city, but his main body was encamped on Harlem Hights, very strong ground toward the northern end of York Island. That all things might be ready for instant retreat, the surplus stores and baggage were sent across Harlem River, on the east side of which, at Morrisania, Washington's head quarters were established.

It was very desirable, at this moment, to obtain correct information of the force and position of the British troops at Brooklyn; and, at Washington's desire, and the request of Colonel Knowlton, Nathan Hale, a captain in one of the Connecticut regiments, a young man of education and enthusiasm, volunteered on that hazardous service. He crossed to Brooklyn, obtained the necessary information, and was about to return, when he was arrested on some suspicion, and being betrayed by his embarrassment, was carried before General Howe, tried and convicted as a spy, and hanged the next morning. (1776.)

Washington's army, by this time, was greatly reduced. The term of service of the militia was fast expiring. The whole flying camp soon claimed their discharge; and no inducements could procure a moment's delay. Some of the New York militia refused to do duty. Howe, they said, offered "peace, liberty, and safety"—so they understood his proclamation—and what more could they ask? The Continentals were enlisted only for a year, and their term of service was fast drawing to a close; nor did they always wait to complete it, desertions being very numerous. Exclusive of Heath's division in the Highlands, and the corps under Lee, on the east side of the Hudson, Washington's army did exceed four thousand men. The ground which he occupied was a level plain between the Hackensack and the Passaic; the army had no intrenching tools; and a British Column, led by Cornwallis, was rapidly approaching.

Obliged to retreat, but anxious not to be cut off from Philadelphia, Washington crossed the Passaic to Newark, his troops exposed to all the severity of approaching winter, without tents, badly supplied with blankets, and very imperfectly clad. The British, well furnished with every necessary, pressed upon him with a much superior force; and Washington again retired, first across the Raritan to Brunswick, and thence to Princeton, where a corps was left, under Stirling, to check the enemy's advance, while Washington continued his retreat to Trenton, where he transported his remaining stores and baggage across the Delaware.

The news of Washington's retreat produced the greatest commotion in Philadelphia; fears on one side, and hopes on the other. Putnam had been sent to take the command in that city. Mifflin was also there, endeavoring to raise the spirits of the people. Some fifteen hundred city militia, sent forward through the active agency of Mifflin, joined Washington at Trenton, and he advanced again upon Princeton. But Cornwallis approached with a superior force, and the American army was obliged to cross the Delaware. As the rear guard left the Jersey shore, the advance of the British came in sight; indeed, during the whole course of the retreat, the American rear guard, employed in pulling up bridges, was constantly within sight and shot of the British pioneers sent forward to rebuild them. Washington had secured all the boats on the Delaware, and he placed his forces so as to guard the principal fords. The enemy, finding no means to cross, occupied the eastern bank, above and below Trenton.

A body of fifteen hundred Hessians, stationed at Trenton, was selected by Washington as the object of attack. On the evening of Christmas, with two thousand five hundred men and six pieces of artillery, including the New York company under Alexander Hamilton, he commenced crossing the Delaware about nine miles above Trenton. Two corps of militia, one opposite Trenton, the other lower down, at Bristol, under General Cadwallader, were to have crossed at the same time; but the quantity of floating ice made the passage impossible. It was only with great difficulty, and after struggling all night, that Washington's troops got over at last. About four o'clock in the morning, in the midst of a snow-storm, they commenced their march for Trenton, in two columns, one led by Greene, the other by Sullivan, Stark's New Hampshire regiment heading Sullivan's advance. The two columns took different roads—Sullivan along the bank of the river, the other some distance inland. It was eight o'clock before they reached the town; but the Hessians, sleepy with the night's debauch, were completely surprised. Some little resistance was made by the guard of the artillery, but they were soon overpowered, and the pieces taken. Washington's artillery was planted to sweep the streets of the town. The Hessian commander, while attempting to form his troops, was mortally wounded. The light horse and a portion of the infantry, who fled on the first alarm, escaped to Bordentown. The main body attempted to retreat by the Princeton road, but found it already occupied by Colonel Hand and his regiment of Pennsylvania riflemen. Thus cut off, ignorant of the force opposed to them, and without enthusiasm for the cause, they threw down their arms and surrendered. About a thousand prisoners were taken, and six cannon. The Americans had two frozen to death, two killed, and a few wounded in assaulting the artillery, among them James Monroe, then a lieutenant, afterward President of the United States. Had the milita, lower down, been able to cross the success might have been still more complete.

Washington re-crossed the Delaware with his prisoners, who were sent to Philadelphia, and paraded through the streets in a sort of triumph. The British, astonished at such a stroke from an enemy whom they reckoned already subdued, broke up their encampments along the Delaware, and retired to Princeton. Washington thereupon re-occupied Trenton, where he was speedily joined by three thousand six hundred Pennsylvania militia, relieved, by the withdrawal of the enemy, from their late duty of guarding the Delaware. At this moment the term of service of the New England regiments expired; but the persuasions of their officers, and a bounty of ten dollars, induced them to remain for six weeks longer.

Alarmed by the surprise at Trenton, and the signs of new activity in the American army, Howe detained Cornwallis, then just on the point of embarking for England, and sent him to take the command at Princeton. Re-enforcements now came up from Brunswick, and Cornwallis advanced in force upon Trenton. Washington occupied the high ground on the eastern bank of a small river which enters the Delaware at that town. The bridge and the ford above it were guarded by artillery. After a sharp cannonade, the British kindled their fires and encamped for the night. (1777.)

Washington was now in a dangerous predicament. He had about five thousand men, half of them militia, but a few days in camp. Could such an army stand the attack of British regulars, equal in numbers, and far superior in discipline and equipments? To attempt to cross the Delaware in the face of the enemy would be more hazardous than a battle. Washington, according to his custom, called a council of war. The large force which Cornwallis evidently had with him led to the inference that the corps in the rear could not be very strong. The bold plan was adopted of gaining that rear, beating up the enemy's quarters at Princeton, and, if fortune favored, falling on his stores and baggage at Brunswick. In execution of this plan, the American baggage was silently sent off down the river to Burlington; and, after replenishing the camp fires, and leaving small parties to throw up intrenchments within hearing of the enemy's sentinels, the army marched off about midnight, by a circuitous route toward

Princeton. Three British regiments had spent the night in that town; and by sunrise, when the Americans entered it, two of them were already on their march for Trenton. The leading regiment was attacked and broken; but it presently rallied, regained the Trenton road, and continued its march to join Lord Cornwallis. General Mercer, who had led this attack with a column of militia, was not very well supported; he fell mortally wounded while attempting to bring his men up to the charge, and was taken prisoner. The marching regiment in the rear, after a sharp action, gave way and fled toward Brunswick. The regiment in the town occupied the college, and made some show of resistance; but some pieces of artillery being brought to bear upon them, they soon surrendered. Three hundred prisoners fell into the hands of the Americans, besides a severe loss to the enemy in killed and wounded. The American loss was about a hundred, including several valuable officers.

When Cornwallis heard the roar of the cannon at Princeton, he penetrated at once the whole of Washington's plan. Alarmed for his magazines at Brunswick, he hastily put his troops in motion, and by the time the Americans were ready to leave Princeton, he was again close upon them. Again Washington was in great danger. His troops were exhausted; all had been one night without sleep, and some of them longer; many had no blankets; others were barefoot; all were very thinly clad. It was necessary to give over the attack upon Brunswick, and to occupy some more defensible ground, where the troops could be put under cover. At Morristown, on the American right, were the skeletons of three regiments, detached, as already mentioned, from the northern army; also the troops sent forward by Heath, but stopped on the reception of Washington's countermand. Some militia had also joined them. The high ground in that vicinity offered many strong positions. As Cornwallis would hardly venture to cross the Delaware with an enemy in his rear, Washington concluded to march for Morristown, where he intrenched himself.

Not anxious to continue this winter campaign, Cornwallis retired to New Brunswick. The parties sent out by Washington to assail and harass the British quarters, were eagerly joined by the inhabitants, incensed by the plunder and ravage of the British and Hessians, against whom, even Howe's protections had proved a very uncertain defense. Plundering, into which soldiers very easily fall, was by no means confined to the British. Washington was again obliged to issue stern orders against "the infamous practice of plundering the inhabitants, under pretense that they are Tories."

Another proclamation was presently issued, requiring all those who had taken British protections, either to remove within the enemy's lines, or else to repair to the nearest general officer, give up their protections, and take an oath of allegiance to the United States. Objections were made to this proclamation, and one of the New Jersey delegates in Congress, raised some question about it, on the ground that it was an interference with State rights, allegiance being due to the State, and not to the confederacy; but Congress sustained Washington in the course he had taken.

Huts were erected at Morristown, and there the main body of the American army remained during the winter. The right was at Princeton, under Putnam; the left in the Highlands, under Heath; cantonments were established at various places along this extended line. Skirmishes occasionally took place between advanced parties, but for six months, no important movement was made upon either side. Washington, busy in organizing the new army, was, in fact, very weak. Recruits came in but slowly; and detachments of militia, principally from the eastern States, had to be called out for temporary service. These were judiciously posted, so as to make the best possible show; but, for several months, there was little more than the shadow of an army. The enemy, made cautious by their losses, fortunately were ignorant of Washington's real situation. The strong ground occupied by the Americans, and the winter, which had now fairly set in, seemed to forbid the hope of successful attack. In skirmishes, the Americans were generally successful; the British quarters were straitened, their supplies were cut off, and they were reduced to great distress for forage and fresh provisions.

The recovery of the Jerseys by the fragments of a defeated army, which had seemed just before on the point of dissolution, gained Washington a high reputation, not at home only, but in Europe also, where the progress of the campaign had been watched with great interest,, and where the disastrous loss of New York, and the retreat through the Jerseys, had given a general impression that the Americans would not be able to maintain their Independence. The recovery of the Jerseys produced a reaction. The American general was extolled as a Fabius, whose prudence availed his country not less than his valor. At home, also, these successes had the best effect. The recruiting service, which before had been almost at a stand, began now to revive, and considerable progress was presently made in organizing the new army.

The extensive powers which Congress had intrusted to Washington, were exercised energetically indeed, but with the greatest circumspection, and a single eye to the public good. The State appointments of officers for the new army, too often the result of favoritism, were rectified, so far as prudence would justify; and, by commissions in the sixteen additional battalions, Washington was enabled to provide for such meritorious officers as had been overlooked in the new appointments.

We give here a history of cotemporary events, by a cotemporary, which conveys to us much of the realities of this period of trial, which nothing of the diction of the Eclectic historians of the events which now followed in such rapid succession, will ever be able to impress upon the genuine children of "Sam." It is a tedious history, compressed in a few paragraphs, by one of those truly patriotic souls, which were fired by the imminence of the events which they witnessed.

THE POLITICAL PART OF THE CHARGE OF HIS HONOR, CHIEF JUSTICE WILLIAM HENRY DRAYTON, OF SOUTH CAROLINA.

At a Court of GENERAL SESSIONS OF THE PEACE, OYER AND TERMINER, ASSIZE, AND GENERAL GOAL DELIVERY, begun and holden at CHARLESTON, for the district of CHARLESTON, *the* 21*st October*, 1777, before the Hon. WILLIAM HENRY DRAYTON, Esq., chief justice, and his Associates, justices of said court.

Human policy at best is but short-sighted; nor is it to be wondered at, that the original formation of the continental army was upon an erroneous principle. The people of America are a people of property; almost every man is a freeholder. Their superior rulers thought such men, living at ease on their farms, would not become soldiers, under long enlistments; nor, as all that was then aimed at was redress of grievances, did they think there would be occasion for their military services, but for a few months. Hence the continental army was formed upon short enlistments—a policy that unexpectedly dragged America back to the door of slavery. As the time of enlistments expired the last year, the American army decreased in power, till it possessed scarce anything but its appellation. And Washington, a name which needs no title to adorn it, a freeman above all praise, having evacuated Long Island and New York to a far superior force, having repeatedly baffled the enemy at the White Plains, they, quitting that scene of action, suddenly took Fort Washington (Nov. 16), and bending their course to Philadelphia, he, with but a handful of men, boldly threw himself in their front, and opposed their progress. With a chosen body of veterans, who have no near prospect of discharge, it is a difficult operation to make an orderly, leisurely, and effectual retreat before a superior enemy; but with Washington's little army, not exceeding four thousand men, raw troops, who had but a few weeks to serve, to make such a retreat, for eighty miles, and through a populous country, without being joined by a single neighbor—a most discouraging circumstance—nothing in the whole science of war could be more difficult; yet it was most completely performed. Washington caused the Delaware to bound the enemy's advance. He summoned General Lee with the corps under his command, to join him. That veteran, disobeying his repeated orders, for which I presume rigid inquisition is yet to be made, loitering where he should have bounded forward, allowed himself to be surprised and made a prisoner (Dec. 13), at a distance from his troops. Washington in the abyss of distress, seemed to be abandoned by the officer next in command—by the Americans themselves, who seemed appalled by the rapid progress of the enemy. Rape and massacre, ruin and devastation indiscriminately overwhelmed whigs and tories, and marked the advance of the British forces. The enemy being but a day's march from Philadelphia, the Quakers of that city, by a public instrument, dated the 20th of December, declared their attachment to the British domination—a general defection was feared—the Congress removed to Baltimore—American liberty evidently appeared as in the last convulsion !

Washington was now at the head of about two thousand five hundred men ; their time of service was to expire in a few days, nor was there any prospect that they could be induced to stay longer. 'This, such as it was, appeared the only force that could be opposed to the British, which seemed to halt only to give time to the American vigor to dissolve of itself, and display us to the world as an inconstant people, noisy, void of public virtue, and even shame. But it was in this extremity of affairs, when no human resource appeared in their favor, that the Almighty chose to manifest his power, to show the Americans that he had not forsaken them ; and to convince the States that it was by him alone they were to be maintained in their Independence, if they deserved to possess it.

Like Henry IV. of France, one of the greatest men who ever lived, Washington, laying aside the generalissimo, assumed the partisan. He had but a choice of difficulties. He was even in a more desperate situation than that in which the king of Prussia was before the battle of Torgau ; when there was no step which rashness dictated, but prudence advised him to attempt. The enemy was now in full possession of the Jerseys. A principal body of them were posted at Trenton, on the Delaware. Washington occupied the opposite bank. His army, our only apparent hope, now somewhat short of two thousand five hundred men, was to be disbanded in a very few days ; he resolved to lead it to battle before that fatal period, and at least afford it an opportunity of separating with honor. He prepared to attack the enemy at the dawn of day, on the 26th of December. The weather was severe. The ice on the river prevented the passage of a part even of his small force. But with those (one thousand five hundred men) that he transported across the river, through a violent storm of snow and hail, he marched against the enemy. The unavoidable difficulties in passing the river, delayed his arrival at their advanced posts, till eight in the morning. The conflict was short. About thirty of the British troops were killed. Six hundred fled. Nine hundred and nine officers and privates surrendered themselves prisoners, with six pieces of brass artillery, and four pair of colors.

This brilliant success was obtained at a very small price—only two officers and one or two privates wounded. In a word, the victory in effect re-established the *American* affairs. The consent of the victors to continue six weeks longer under their leader, and the elevation of the spirits of the people, were its immediate consequences—most important acquisitions at that crisis. The enemy roused from their inactivity, and with the view of allowing Washington as little time as possible to reap other advantages, they, in a hurry, collected in force and marched against him. He was posted at Trenton. On the second of January, in the afternoon, the front appeared; they halted, with design to make an attack in the morning, and in the meantime a cannonade was begun, and continued by both parties till dark. Sanpinck creek, which runs through Trenton, parted the two armies. Our forces occupied the south bank, and at night fires were lighted on both sides. At twelve, Washington having renewed his fires, and leaving guards on the passages over the creek, and about five hundred men to amuse the enemy, with the remainder of his army, about one in the morning, marched to Princeton to cut off a re-inforcement that was advancing. He arrived at his destination by sunrise, and dislodged them; they left upward of one hundred men dead on the spot, and near three hundred more as prisoners to the victors.

It was by such decisive conduct that the King of Prussia avoided being overwhelmed by a combined attack upon his camp at Lignitz, on the morning of the 15th of August, 1760, by three armies led by Dann, Londohn, and Czernicheue, who were advancing against him from different quarters. In the night the king marched, and in the morning, by the time Dann arrived at his empty camp, he had defeated Londohn in his advance. So the Roman consul, C. Claudius Nero, dreading the junction of Hannibal and his brother Asdrubal, who was in full march to him with a powerful re-inforcement, left his camp before Hannibal, with such an appearance as to persuade him he was present, and with the nerves and sinews of his army privately quitting it, he rapidly marched almost the whole length of Italy, while

Rome trembled at his steps, and, joining the other consul, he defeated Asdrubal, who, had he with his forces joined his brother, had made them in all probability an over match for the Roman. Thus equal geniuses prove their equality by wisely adapting their conduct to their circumstances.

The action at Trenton was as the making of the flood. From that period success rolled in upon us with a spring tide. That victory gave us an army; the affair of Princeton procured us a force and the re-possession of all the Jerseys but Brunswick and Amboy—for the enemy, astonished at Washington's vivacity, dreaded the loss of those posts, in which they had deposited their stores, and ran back to hide themselves behind the works they had thrown up around them. Washington pursued, and by the fifth of January those forces which, but a few days before, were in full possession of the Jerseys, he had closely confined to the environs of Brunswick and Amboy. In this situation both armies continued until the 13th of June last, when General Howe made an attempt to proceed to Philadelphia; but, being baffled, he suddenly abandoned Brunswick, (June 22d,) and in a day or two after, Amboy, and retired to Staten Island.

In the meantime General Burgoyne was advancing from Canada against Ticonderoga. He appeared before the place on the 28th of June—*a day glorious to this country*—and General St. Clair, who commanded in that important post, without waiting till the enemy had completed their works, or given an assault, to sustain which, without doubt, he had been sent there, suddenly abandoned the fortress and its stores to the enemy, (July 6th.) The public have loudly condemned this evacuation, and the Congress have ordered strict inquiry to be made into the cause of it.

General Burgoyne having thus easily possessed himself of Ticonderoga, immediately began to measure the distance to New York. But being destitute of horses for his dragoons, wagons for the conveyance of his baggage, and in urgent want of provisions, he halted near Saratoga, to give time for the operation of the proclamation he had issued (June 23d) to assure the inhabitants of security, and to induce them to continue at home with their effects. But, regardless of public engagements, (August 9th,) he suddenly detached lieutenant colonel Baum with fifteen hundred men, and private instructions to strip the people of their horses, wagons, and provisions; and gave "stretch" to his Indians to scalp those whom he had exhorted to "REMAIN QUIETLY AT THEIR HOUSES!"

Things now wore a dreadful aspect in that part of America, but General Stark soon changed the countenance of affairs. With a body of two thousand men, principally militia, he attacked (August 16th) Lieutenant Colonel Baum, at Bennington, stormed his works, killed about two hundred of his men, took six hundred and fifty-six prisoners, together with four brass field pieces and a considerable quantity of baggage, losing only about thirty men killed and fifty wounded. This successful attack at once rescued the country from massacre and ruin, and deprived General Burgoyne of those supplies which alone could enable him to advance; nor was it less important in respect to the time at which it was made. For at this juncture, Fort Stanwix was hard pressed by General St. Ledger, who, having advanced from Lake Ontario, had laid siege to it on the 2d of August. General Arnold had been preparing to march to its relief, and he had now full liberty to continue his route. His near approach compelled the enemy with precipitation to raise the siege, (August 22,) leaving their tents, and a large part of their ammunition, stores, provisions and baggage, nor did he lose any time in setting out in pursuit of them.

Such unexpected strokes utterly discouraged General Burgoyne. Our militia began to assemble in considerable numbers. He now anxiously cast his eyes behind to Ticonderoga, and wished to trace back his steps; but, while General Gates was advancing against his front, at Stillwater, with considerable force, the front of Bennington and Stanwix, a part of the American troops had occupied posts in his rear, and even penetrated to Ticonderoga. In their advance they took two hundred batteaux and two hundred and ninety-three prisoners; and having seized the old French lines near that fortress, on the 18th of September they summoned the place to surrender. Later advices, which, though not indisputable, yet well authenticated, say General Burgoyne is totally defeated and taken prisoner, and that Ticonderoga, with all its stores, is in our possession. Indeed, from *the events we already know*, we have every reason to believe that the American arms are decisively triumphant in that quarter.

As to General Howe, at the head of the grand British army, even when the campaign was far advanced, he had not done anything in aid of his master's promise, in June last, to his Parliament, that his forces would "effectually crush" America in the course of "the present campaign." Driven from the Jerseys, and having embarked his troops, on the 23d of July, he put to sea from Sandy Hook, with two hundred and twenty-six sail, and having entered the Chesapeake, he landed his army (about twelve thousand strong) the 30th of August, on Turkey Point, at the head of the bay. Skirmishing with the American light troops, he pushed on to Brandywine Creek, behind which Washington was posted to obstruct his passage. By a double onset, on the 11th of September, at Chad's Ford and Jones', six miles above, when, because of uncertain and contradictory intelligence, Washington had not made a disposition, adequate to the force with which the enemy attacked, they crossed, first at Jones' and then at Chad's. The engagement was long and obstinate. The highest account does not make our whole loss exceed one thousand men and nine field-pieces; the lowest statement of the enemy is not so low as one thousand killed—a slaughter, from which we may form some idea of the proportion of their wounded. Not having made good the defense of the Brandywine, the American army fell back twenty-six miles, to the Schuylkill; nor did General Howe derive any advantage from the possession of the field of battle. This is the fortieth day since the engagement, and we have heard from Philadelphia, in less than half the time, circumstances furnishing reasonable ground to conclude, that for at least three weeks after his victory, General Howe made no impression upon the army of the United States; and that he purchased his passage of the Brandywine at no small price. He carried Bunker Hill; but he lost Boston. I trust he has passed the Brandywine but to sacrifice his army as it were, in presence of our illustrious Congress, as an atonement for his ravages and conflagrations in America.

Having thus taken a general and concise view of the progress of the war in the north, let us now turn our attention to our situation at home. In respect of our government, it is affectionately obeyed. With regard to cannon, arms and ammunition, we are in a truly respectable condition. As to trade, we are the grand emporium for the continent. Oh! that I could but give as good an account of the *public vigor of the people.*

Alas! it seems to have been exported in the same bottoms with the growth of their lands. What? are we sensible that we are yet at war with Great Britain? We proceed as if we had totally vanquished the enemy. Are we aware, that to continue such a conduct is to allure them to enact in this State, that tragedy they performed the last winter in the Jerseys? Do we intend to acquire an experimental knowledge of the horrors of war? Do we desire to be driven from this beautiful town—to be dispossessed of this valuable seat of trade—to see ourselves flying we know not whither—our heirs uselessly sacrificed in our sight, and their bodies mangled with repeated stabs of bayonets? Tell me, do you mean that your ears shall be pierced with the unavailing shrieks of your wives, and the agonizing screams of your daughters, under the brutal violence of British or Brunswick ruffians? Rouse, rouse yourselves into an activity capable of securing you against such horrors. In every quarter the enemy are vanquished or baffled. They are at a stand. Cease, my beloved countrymen, cease, by your languor in public defense, and your ardor after private gain, to invite them to turn their steps this way and seize your country as a rich and easy prey. The States of America are attacked by Britain. They ought to consider themselves as an army drawn up to receive the shock of assault, and from the nature of their ground, occupying thirteen towns and villages in the extent of their line. Common prudence dictates that the several corps, in their respective stations, during the whole time they are in battalia, should use the utmost vigilance and diligence in being on their guard, and in adding strength to strength for their security. We are in the right wing of the American line, and at a distance from the main body—are we doing our duty? No, we have in a manner laid up our arms—nay, even prizes are prepared for the horse-race! We can spare no laborers to the public, because we are employing them to collect, on all sides, articles of private emolument. We amuse ourselves with enquiries into the conduct of those who permitted the loss of Ticonderoga, nor do we appear to have an idea that others will, in their turn, scrutinize our conduct at this juncture—a crisis when we know that the enemy have collected their force, and are actually advanced against the main battle of the Americans; where, if they find they can make no impression—and we have now a flattering prospect that they will find their efforts abortive—it is but reasonable to imagine they will recoil upon upon our post. They will *sail* faster against, than aid can be *marched* to us. Their arrival will be sudden—*shall they find us shamefully occupied in the amusements and business of peace?* Why has the Almighty endowed us with a recollection of events, but that we may be enabled to prepare against dangers, by avoiding the errors and follies, the negligence and supineness by which others have been ruined. If a sense of our duty to our country, or of safety to posterity, is too weak to rouse us to action, if the noble passions of the mind have not force to elevate us to glory—the meaner ones, perhaps, may drive us into a state of security. The miser, amidst all his anxiety to add to his heap, is yet careful to provide a strong box for its safety. Shall we neglect such an example of prudence? Pride raised Cassius' dagger against Cæsar, and procured for him the glorious title of *the last of the Romans.* We were the first in America who publicly pronounced Lord North's famous conciliatory motion inadmissible—we raised the first regular forces upon the continent, and for a term of three years—we first declared the causes of taking up arms—we originated councils of safety—we were among the first who led the way to Independence, by establishing a constitution of government—we were the first who made a law authorizing the capture of British vessels, without distinction—we alone *have defeated a British fleet*—we alone have *victoriously pierced through, and reduced* a powerful nation of Indians, who, urged by Britain, had attacked the United States. But such brilliant proceedings, unless supported with propriety, will cover us with infamy. They will appear as the productions of faction, folly and temerity, not of patriotism, wisdom and valor. What a contrast! how humiliating the one—how glorious the other! Will not pride spur us on to add to the catalogue? Will you not strive to rival the *vigor of the North?* Do we admire the great names of antiquity? Do we wish for an opportunity to be equally celebrated by posterity?

Then the present—there never was a more inviting or certain opportunity of acquiring an immortal name. A world to be converted into an Empire, is the work now in hand—a work wherein the names of the workmen will be engraved in indelible characters. Shall we not exert ourselves to be ranked in this most illustrious list? Nor is it so difficult a thing to acquire place in it as may be imagined; it is in every man's power to exert himself with vigor and constancy.

My dear countrymen, trifle not with an opportunity unexampled, and not to be recalled—it is passing with rapidity. Let us put our hands to our breasts, and examine what we have done in forwarding this imperial structure. How many must say, I have youth, strength, activity, an abundant fortune, learning, sense—or some of these blessings; but—I have shown my attachment to America, only by a momentary vigor, to mark my inconstancy—scrutinizing the conduct of others—good wishes—and inquiring the news of the day. Such men must be sensible of a *disgraceful* inferiority, when they hear those *American* names, which the trumpet of fame now sounds through the world—a blast that will reach the ears of the latest posterity.

Surely, such men may have a desire to be relieved from so oppressive a sensation? The remedy is within their own power; and if they will use it, while it throws off their disgrace, it will operate for the benefit of their country. Let them inquire of the President, WHAT SERVICE THEY CAN RENDER THE STATE? To a rich planter he would say, if you will send twenty, thirty, or forty laborers to the public works, and *for whom you shall be paid*, you will do an essential service in a critical time. To another, if you will diligently overlook, and push on the construction of such a battery, or line, you will merit the thanks of your fellow-citizens. To a third, if instead of hunting, you will ride about your neighborhood, or a little beyond, and endeavor to instruct those who are ignorant, of the importance of the public contest—reclaim the deluded—animate the timid—rouse the languid—and raise a spirit of emulation as to who shall exert himself most in the cause of freedom and America, you will deserve the applause of the continent. How many opportu nities are there for a man to distinguish himself, and to be beneficial to his country!

CHAPTER XXXVII.

The Settlements in the West—Biography of Boone, by Himself—Biography of Simon Kenton.

Since the peace with the Indians on the western frontier, various projects had been started for settlements beyond the mountains. In a treaty held at Fort Stanwix, the Six Nations, in consideration of the payment of £10,460, had ceded to the crown all the country south of the Ohio, as far as the Cherokee or Tennessee river. So much of this region as lay south of the Great Kanawha was claimed, however, by the Cherokees as a part of their hunting-grounds. The banks of the Kanawha, or New river, flowing north into the Ohio, across the foot of the great central Allegheny ridge, already began to be occupied by individual settlers. Application was soon made to the British government, by a company —of which Franklin, Sir William Johnson, Walpole, a wealthy London banker, and others, were members—for that part of this newly-ceded territory north of the Kanawha, and thence to the Upper Ohio. They offered to refund the whole amount paid to the Indians, and proposed to establish on the ceded lands a new and separate colony. This grant, though opposed by Lord Hillsborough, was finally agreed to by the ministry; but the increasing troubles between the colonies and the mother country prevented its final completion. Other grants solicited and ceded north of the Ohio were defeated by the same cause. Such was the origin of the Walpole or Ohio Company, the Vandalia Company, the Indiana Company—founded on a cession said to have been made to certain traders at the treaty of Fort Stanwix—and other land companies, not without a marked influence on the politics of a future period. Even the distant regions on the shores of Lake Superior attracted the attention of some adventurous speculators, by whom attempts were made to work the mines; but the expenses attendant upon so remote an undertaking, caused it to be speedily abandoned.

The first settlement within the limits of the present State of Tennessee was made by emigrants from North Carolina, under the leadership of James Robinson, who settled on the Wataga, one of the head streams of the Tennessee river, on lands of the Cherokees, from whom, however, these settlers presently obtained an eight years' lease. As in the early settlements of New England, these emigrants organized themselves into a body politic. A code of laws was assented to, and signed by each individual of the colony. Others who joined them soon extended the settlement down the Valley of the Houlston, and, crossing the intervening ridges, occupied the banks of the Nolichucky and Clinch rivers, while others yet passed into Powell's Valley, the south-western corner of the present State of Virginia.

John Finley, an Indian trader, returning to North Carolina from the still more distant regions beyond the westernmost mountains, brought back glowing accounts of that fertile country. He persuaded Daniel Boone, a native of Maryland, and four other settlers on the Yadkin, to go with him to explore it. Having reached the head waters of the Kentucky, these adventurers saw from the hills fertile plains stretching toward the Ohio, covered with magnificent forests, ranged over by numerous herds of buffalo, and abounding with other game. They had several encounters with Indians. But we furnish here an account of Boone's own life, taken down from his own lips, by a cotemporary:

ADVENTURES OF CAPTAIN DANIEL BOONE.

Comprising an Account of the Wars with the Indians on the Ohio, from 1769 *to* 1782.

WRITTEN BY HIMSELF.

It was on the 1st of May, 1769, that I resigned my domestic happiness, and left my family and peaceable habitation on the Yadkin river, in North Carolina, to wander through the wilderness of America, in quest of the country of Kentucky, in company with John Finley, John Stuart, Joseph Holden, James Monay, and William Cool.

On the 7th of June, after travelling in a western direction, we found ourselves on Red river, where John Finley had formerly been trading with the Indians, and from the top of an eminence saw with pleasure the beautiful level of Kentucky. For some time we had experienced the most uncomfortable weather. We now encamped, made a shelter to defend us from the inclement season, and began to hunt, and reconnoiter the country. We found abundance of wild beasts in this vast forest. The buffaloes were more numerous than cattle in the settlements, browsing on the leaves of the cane, or cropping the herbage on these extensive plains. We saw hundreds in a drove, and the numbers about the salt-springs were amazing. In this forest, the habitation of beasts of every American kind, we hunted with great success until December.

On the 22d of December, John Stuart and I had a pleasing ramble; but fortune changed the day at the close of it. We passed through a great forest, in which stood myriads of trees, some gay with blossoms, others rich with fruits. Nature was here a series of wonders and a fund of delight. Here she displayed her ingenuity and industry in a variety of flowers and fruits, beautifully colored, elegantly shaped, and charmingly flavored; and we were favored with numberless animals presenting themselves perpetually to our view. In the decline of the day, near Kentucky river, as we ascended the brow of a small hill, a number of Indians rushed out of a canebreak and made us prisoners. The Indians plundered us, and kept us in confinement seven days. During this time, we discovered no uneasiness or desire to escape, which made them less suspicious; but in the dead of night, as we lay by a large fire in a thick canebrake, when sleep had locked up their senses, my situation not disposing me to rest, I gently awoke my companion. We seized this favorable opportunity and departed, directing our course toward the old camp, but found it plundered, and our company destroyed cr dispersed.

About this time, my brother with another adventurer, who came to explore the country shortly after us, were wandering through the forest, and accidentally came upon our camp.

SAM'S INDIAN HUNTER, DANIEL BOONE, SURVEYING HIS FUTURE POSSESSIONS. (SEE CHAP. XXVI.)

Notwithstanding our unfortunate circumstances, and our dangerous situation, surrounded with hostile savages, our meeting fortunately in the wilderness gave us the most sensible satisfaction.

Soon after this my companion in captivity, John Stuart, was killed by the savages, and the man who came with my brother, while on a private excursion was soon after attacked and killed by the wolves. We were now in a dangerous and helpless situation, exposed daily to perils and death, among savages and wild beasts, not a white man in the country but ourselves.

Although many hundred miles from our families, in the howling wilderness, we did not continue in a state of indolence, but hunted every day, and prepared a little cottage to defend us from the winter. On the 1st of May, 1770, my brother returned home for a new recruit of horses and ammunition, leaving me alone, without bread, salt, or sugar, or even a horse or a dog. I passed a few days uncomfortably. The idea of a beloved wife and family, and their anxiety on my account, would have disposed me to melancholy if I had further indulged the thought.

One day I undertook a tour through the country, when the diversities and beauties of nature I met with in this charming season expelled every gloomy thought. Just at the close of the day, the gentle gales ceased; a profound calm ensued; not a breath shook the tremulous leaf. I had gained the summit of a commanding ridge, and looking around with astonishing delight, beheld the ample plains and beauteous tracts below. On one hand, I surveyed the famous Ohio rolling in silent dignity, and marking the western boundary of Kentucky with inconceivable grandeur. At a vast distance, I beheld the mountains lift their venerable brows and penetrate the clouds. All things were still. I kindled a fire near a fountain of sweet water, and feasted on the loin of a buck which I had killed a few hours before. The shades of night soon overspread the hemisphere, and the earth seemed to gasp after the hovering moisture. At a distance I frequently heard the hideous yells of savages. My excursion had fatigued my body and amused my mind. I laid me down to sleep, and awoke not until the sun had chased away the night. I continued this tour, and in a few days explored a considerable part of the country, each day equally pleasing as the first; after which I returned to my old camp, which had not been disturbed in my absence. I could not confine my lodging to it, but often reposed in thick canebrakes to avoid the savages, who I believe frequently visited my camp, but, fortunately for me, in my absence. No populous city, with all its varieties of commerce and stately structures, could afford such pleasure to my mind, as the beauties of nature I found in this country.

Until the 27th of July, I spent my time in an uninterrupted scene of sylvan pleasures, when my brother, to my great felicity, met me according to appointment, at our old camp. Soon after, we left the place, and proceeded to Cumberland river, reconnoitering that part of the country, and giving names to the different rivers.

In March, 1771, I returned home to my family, being determined to bring them as soon as possible, at the risk of my life and fortune, to reside in Kentucky, which I esteemed a second Paradise.

On my return, I found my family in happy circumstances. I sold my farm on the Yadkin, and what goods we could not carry with us, and on the 25th of September, 1773, we took leave of our friends and proceeded on our journey to Kentucky, in company with five more families, and forty men that joined us in Powell's Valley, which is one hundred and fifty miles from the new settled parts of Kentucky. But this promising beginning was soon overcast with a cloud of adversity.

On the 10th of October the rear of our company was attacked by a party of Indians, who killed six, and wounded one man. Of these my oldest son was one that fell in the action. Though we repulsed the enemy, yet this unhappy affair scattered our cattle and brought us into extreme difficulty. We returned forty miles, to the settlement on Clench river. We had passed over two mountains, Powell and Walden's, and were approaching Cumberland mountain, when this adverse fortune overtook us. These mountains are in the wilderness, in passing from the old settlement in Virginia to Kentucky; they range in a southwest and northeast direction; are of great length and breadth, and not far distant from each other. Over them Nature has formed passes less difficult than might be expected from the view of such huge piles. The aspect of these cliffs is so wild and horrid, that it is impossible to behold them without horror.

Until the 6th of June, 1774, I remained with my family on the Clench, when myself and another person were solicited by Governor Dunmore, of Virginia, to conduct a number of surveyors to the falls of Ohio. This was a tour of eight hundred miles, and took sixty-two days.

On my return, Gov. Dunmore gave me the command of three garrisons during the campaign against the Shawnese. In March, 1765, at the solicitation of a number of gentlemen of North Carolina, I attended their treaty at Wataga with the Cherokee Indians, to purchase the lands on the south side of Kentucky river. After this, I undertook to mark out a road in the best passage from the settlements through the wilderness to Kentucky.

Having collected a number of enterprising men, well armed, I soon began this work. We proceeded until we came within fifteen miles of where Boonsborough now stands, where the Indians attacked us, and killed two, and wounded two more of our party. This was on the 22d of March, 1775. Two days after we were again attacked by them, when we had two more killed, and three wounded. After this, we proceeded on to Kentucky river without opposition.

On the 1st of April, we began to erect the fort of Boonsborough, at a salt lick sixty yards from the river, on the south side. On the 4th the Indians killed one of our men. On the 14th of June, having completed the fort, I returned to my family on the Clench, and whom I soon afterward removed to the fort. My wife and daughter were supposed to be the first white women that ever stood on the banks of Kentucky river.

On the 24th of December, the Indians killed one of our men, and wounded another; and on the 15th of July, 1776, they took my daughter prisoner. I immediately pursued them with eight men, and on the 16th overtook and engaged them. I killed two of them and recovered my daughter.

The Indians, having divided themselves into several parties, attacked in one day all our infant settlements and forts, doing a great deal of damage. The husbandmen were ambushed and unexpectedly attacked while toiling in the field. They continued this kind of warfare until the 15th of April, 1777, when nearly one hundred of them attacked the village of Boonsborough, and killed a number of its inhabitants. On the 16th Colonel Logan's fort was attacked by two hundred Indians. There were only thirteen men in the fort, of whom the enemy killed two, and wounded one.

On the 20th of August, Colonel Bowman arrived with one hundred men from Virginia, with which additional force we had almost daily skirmishes with the Indians, who began now to learn the superiority of the "long knife," as they termed the Virginians; being out-generalled in almost every action. Our affairs began now to wear a better aspect; the Indians no longer daring to face us in open field, but sought private opportunities to destroy us.

On the 7th of February, 1778, while on a hunting excursion alone, I met a party of one hundred and two Indians, and two Frenchmen, marching to attack Boonsborough. They pursued and took me prisoner, and conveyed me to Old Chilicothe, the principal Indian town on Little Miami, where we arrived on the 18th of February, after an uncomfortable journey. On the 10th of March I was conducted to Detroit, and while there, was treated with great humanity by Gov. Hamilton, the British commmander at that port, and Intendant for Indian affairs.

The Indians had such an affection for me, that they refused one hundred pounds sterling, offered them by the Governor, if they would consent to leave me with him, that he might be enabled to liberate me on my parole. Several English gentlemen then at Detroit, sensible of my adverse fortune, and touched with sympathy, generously offered to supply my wants, which I declined with many thanks, adding that I never expected it would be in my power to recompense such unmerited generosity.

On the 10th of April, the Indians returned with me to Old Chilicothe, where we arrived on the 25th. This was a long and fatiguing march, although through an exceeding fertile country, remarkable for springs and streams of water. At Chilicothe I spent my time as comfortably as I could expect; was adopted, according to their custom, into a family where I became a son, and had a great share in the affection of my new parents, brothers, sisters, and friends. I was exceedingly familiar and friendly with them, always appearing as cheerful and contented as possible, and they put great confidence in me. I often went a hunting with them, and frequently gained the applause for my activity at our shooting matches. I was careful not to exceed many of them in shooting, for no people are more envious than they in this sport. I could observe in their countenances and gestures the greatest expressions of joy when they exceeded me, and when the reverse happened, of envy. The Shawanese king took great notice of me, and treated me with profound respect, and entire friendship, often intrusting me to hunt at my liberty. I frequently returned with the spoils of the woods, and as often presented some of what I had taken to him, expressive of duty to my sovereign. My food and lodging were in common with them; not so good, indeed, as I could desire, but necessity made everything acceptable.

I now began to meditate an escape, and carefully avoided giving suspicion. I continued at Chilicothe until the 1st day of June, when I was taken to the salt springs on Sciotha, and there employed ten days in the manufacturing of salt. During this time, I hunted with my Indian masters, and found the land, for a great extent about this river, to exceed the soil of Kentucky.

On my return to Chilicothe, one hundred and fifty of the choicest Indian warriors were ready to march against Boonsborough. They were painted and armed in a frightful manner. This alarmed me, and I determined to escape.

On the 26th of June, before sunrise, I went off secretly, and reached Boonsborough on the 30th, a journey of one hundred and sixty miles, during which I had only one meal. I found our fortress in a bad state, but we immediately repaired our flanks, gates, posterns, and formed double bastions, which we completed in ten days. One of my fellow-prisoners escaped after me, and brought advice, that on account of my flight, the Indians had put off their expedition for three weeks.

About the 1st of August, I set out with nineteen men, to surprise Point Creek-town, on Sciotha, within four miles of which we fell in with forty Indians going against Boonsborough. We attacked them, and they soon gave way, without any loss on our part.

The enemy had one killed and two wounded. We took three horses and all their baggage. The Indians having evacuated their town, and gone altogether against Boonsborough, we returned, passed them on the 6th, and on the 7th, arrived safe at Boonsborough.

On the 9th, the Indian army, consisting of four hundred and forty-four men, under the command of Captain Duquesne, and eleven other Frenchmen, and their chiefs, arrived and summoned the fort to surrender. I requested two days' consideration, which was granted. During this we brought in through the posterns all the horses and other cattle we could collect.

On the 9th, in the evening, I informed their commander, that we were determined to defend the fort while a man was living. They then proposed a treaty: they would withdraw. The treaty was held within sixty yards of the fort, as we suspected the savages. The articles were agreed to and signed, when the Indians told us, as it was their custom for two Indians to shake hands with every white man in the treaty, as an evidence of friendship. We agreed to this also. They immediately grappled us to take us prisoners, but we cleared ourselves of them, though surrounded by hundreds, and gained the fort safe, except one man, who was wounded by a heavy fire from the enemy.

The savages now began to undermine the fort, beginning at the watermark of Kentucky river, which is sixty yards from the fort; this we discovered by the water being made muddy by the clay. We countermined them by cutting a trench across their subterraneous passage. The enemy discovering this by the clay we threw out of the fort, desisted. On the 20th of August, they raised the siege, during which we had two men killed, and four wounded. We lost a number of cattle. The loss of the enemy was thirty-seven killed, and a much larger number wounded. We picked up one hundred and twenty-five pounds of their bullets, beside what stuck in the logs of the fort.

In July, 1779, during my absence, Colonel Bowman, with one hundred and sixty men, went against the Shawanese of Old Chilicothe. He arrived undiscovered. A battle ensued, which lasted until ten in the morning, when Colonel Bowman retreated thirty miles. The Indians collected all their strength and pursued him, when another engagement ensued for two hours, not to Colonel Bowman's advantage. Colonel Harrod proposed to mount a number of horses, and break the enemy's line, who at this time fought with remarkable fury. This desperate measure had a happy effect, and the savages fled on all sides. In these two engagements we had nine men killed and one wounded. Enemy's loss uncertain. Only two scalps were taken.

June 23d, 1780, five hundred Indians and Canadians under Colonel Bird, attacked Riddle and Martain's station, and the forks of Licking River, with six pieces of artillery. They took all the inhabitants captive, and killed one man and two women, loading the others with the heavy baggage, and such as failed in the journey were tomahawked.

The hostile disposition of the savages caused General Clarke, the commandant at the falls of Ohio, to march with his regiment and the armed force of the country against Peccaway, the principal town of the Shawanese, on a branch the Great Miami, which he attacked with great success, took seventy scalps, and reduced the town to ashes, with the loss of seventeen men.

About this time, I returned to Kentucky with my family; for during my captivity, my wife, thinking me killed by the Indians, had transported my family and goods, on horses, through the wilderness, amidst great dangers, to her father's house in North Carolina.

On the 6th of October, 1780, soon after my settling again at Boonesborough, I went with my brother to the Blue Licks, and on our return, he was shot by a party of Indians, who followed me by the scent of a dog, which I shot and escaped. The severity of the winter caused great distress in Kentucky, the enemy, during the summer, having destroyed most of the corn. The inhabitants lived chiefly on buffalo's flesh.

In the spring of 1702, the Indians harassed us. In May, they ravished, killed, and scalped a woman and her two daughters, near Ashton's station, and took a negro prisoner. Captain Ashton pursued them with twenty-five men, and in an engagement which lasted two hours, his party were obliged to retreat, having eight killed, and four mortally wounded. Their brave commander fell in the action.

On August 18th, two boys were carried off from Major

Hoy's station. Captain Holder pursued the enemy with seventeen men, who were also defeated, with the loss of seven killed and two wounded. Our affairs became more and more alarming. The savages infested the country, and destroyed the whites as opportunity presented. In a field *near* Lexington, an Indian shot a man, and running to scalp him, was himself shot from the fort, and fell dead upon the ground. All the Indian nations were now united against us.

On August 15th, five hundred Indians and Canadians came against Briat's station, five miles from Lexington. They assaulted the fort, and killed all the cattle round it; but being repulsed, they retired the third day, having about eighty killed; their wounded uncertain. The garrison had four killed, and nine wounded.

On August 10th, Colonels Todd and Trigg, Major Harland and myself, speedily collected one hundred and seventy-six men, well-armed, and pursued the savages. They had marched beyond the Blue Licks, to a remarkable bend of the main fork of the Licking River, about forty-three miles from Lexington, where we overtook them on the 19th. The savages observing us, gave way, and we, ignorant of their numbers, passed the river. When they saw our proceedings, having greatly the advantage in situation, they formed their line of battle from one end of the Licking to the other, about a mile from the Blue Licks. The engagement was close and warm for about fifteen minutes, when we, being overpowered by numbers, were obliged to retreat, with a loss of sixty-seven men, seven of whom were taken prisoners. The brave and much lamented colonels, Todd and Trigg, Major Harland, and my second son, were among the dead. We were afterward informed that the Indians, on numbering their dead, finding that they had four more killed than we, four of our people they had taken, were given up to their young warriors, to be put to death after their barbarous manner.

On our retreat, we were met by Colonel Logan, who was hastening to join us with a number of well-armed men. This powerful assistance we wanted on the day of the battle. The enemy said, one more fire from us would have made them give way.

I can not reflect upon this dreadful scene, without great sorrow. A zeal for the defense of their country, led these heroes to the scene of action, though with few men, to attack a powerful army of experienced warriors. When we gave way, they pursued us with the utmost eagerness, and in every quarter spread destruction. The river was difficult to cross, and many were killed in the fight, some just entering the river, some in the water, others after crossing, in ascending the cliffs. Some escaped on horseback, a few on foot; and being dispersed everywhere, in a few hours brought the melancholy news of this unfortunate battle to Lexington. Many widows were now made. The reader may guess what sorrow filled the hearts of the inhabitants, exceeding any thing that I am able to describe. Being reinforced, we returned to bury the dead, and found their bodies strewed everywhere, cut and mangled in a dreadful manner. This mournful scene exhibited a horror almost unparalleled; some torn and eaten by wild beasts; those in the river by fishes; all in such a putrid condition that one could not be distinguished from another.

When General Clarke, at the falls of the Ohio, heard of our disaster, he ordered an expedition to pursue the savages. We overtook them within two miles of their town, and we should have obtained a great victory, had not some of them met us when about two hundred poles from their camp. The savages fled in the utmost disorder, and evacuated all their towns. We burned to ashes Old Chilicothe, Peccaway, New Chilicothe, and Willstown; entirely destroyed their corn and other fruits, and spread desolation through their country. We took seven prisoners and fifteen scalps, and lost only four men, two of whom were accidentally killed by ourselves. This campaign damped the enemy, yet they made secret incursions.

In October, a party attacked Crab Orchard, and one of them, being a good way before the others, boldly entered a house, in which were only a woman and her children, and a negro man. The savage used no violence, but attempted to carry off the negro, who happily proved too strong for him, and threw him on the ground, and in the struggle, the woman cut off his head with an ax, while her little daughter shut the door. The savages instantly came up, and applied their tomahawks to the door, when the mother putting an old rusty gun barrel through the crevice, the savages immediately went off.

From that time till the happy return of peace between the United States and Great Britain, the Indians did us no mischief. Soon after this, the Indians desired peace.

Two darling sons and a brother, I have lost by savage hands, which have also taken from me forty valuable horses, and abundance of cattle. Many dark and sleepless nights have I spent, separated from the cheerful society of men, scorched by the summer's sun, and pinched by the winter's cold, an instrument ordained to settle the wilderness.

DANIEL BOONE.

Fayette County, Kentucky.

We will, while upon this subject, furnish also a biographical sketch of Simon Kenton, the heroic cotemporary of Daniel Boone, and which is attributed to his own rude pen. Taking the two sketches together, they comprise a graphic summary of Indian history in the West, at this period of the life of "Sam."

Simon Kenton was a Virginian by birth, and emigrated to the wilds of the West in the year 1771. He was born, (according to a manuscript which he dictated to a gentleman of Kentucky, several years since,) in Fauquier county, on the 15th of May, 1755, of poor parents. His early life was passed principally on a farm. At the age of sixteen, having a quarrel with a rival in a love-affair, he left his antagonist upon the ground for dead, and made quick steps for the wilderness. In the course of a few days, wandering to and fro, he arrived at a small settlement on Cheat Creek, one of the forks of the Monongahela, where he called himself Butler. Here, according to Mr. M'Clung, whose interesting account of Kenton, in the "Sketches of Western Adventure," we are following, he attached himself to a small company headed by John Mahon and Jacob Greathouse, which was about starting farther west, on an exploring expedition. He was soon induced, however, by a young adventurer of the name of Yager, who had been taken by the western Indians when a child, and spent many years among them, to detach himself from the company, and go with him to a land which the

Indians called Kan-tuc-kee, and which he represented as being a perfect elysium. Accompanied by another young man, named Strader, they set off for the backwoods paradise in high spirits: Kenton not doubting that he should find a country flowing with milk and honey, where he would have little to do but to eat, drink, and be merry. Such, however, was not his luck. They continued wandering through the wilderness for some weeks, without finding the "promised land," and then retraced their steps, and successively explored the land about Salt-Lick, Little and Big Sandy, and Guyandotte. At length, being totally wearied out, they turned their attention entirely to hunting and trapping, and thus spent nearly two years. Being discovered by the Indians, and losing one of his companions, (Strader,) Kenton was compelled to abandon his trapping-waters, and hunting-grounds. After divers hardships, he succeeded in reaching the mouth of the Little Kenhawa, with his remaining companion, where he found and attached himself to another exploring party. This, however, was attacked by the Indians, soon after commencing the descent of the Ohio, compelled to abandon its canoes, and strike diagonally through the woods for Greenbriar county. Its members suffered much in accomplishing this journey, from fatigue, sickness and famine; and on reaching the settlements, separated.

Kenton's rival of the love-affair had long since recovered from the castigation which he had given him. But of this, the young hero had not heard. He therefore did not think proper to venture home; but, instead, built a canoe on the Monongahela, and once more sought the mouth of the Great Kenhawa, where he hunted till the spring of 1774. This year, he descended the Ohio as far as the mouth of Big Bone creek, and was engaged in various explorations till 1778, when he joined Daniel Boone in his expedition against the Indian town on Paint creek. Immediately on his return from this, he was despatched by Colonel Bowman, with two companions, to make observations upon the Indian towns on Little Miami, against which the colonel meditated an expedition. He reached the towns in safety, and made the necessary surveys without being observed by the Indians; and the expedition might have terminated much to his credit, and been very useful to the settlers in Kentucky, had he not, before leaving the towns, stolen a number of the Indians' horses. The animals were missed early on the following morning, the trail of the marauders was discovered, and pursuit instantly commenced. Kenton and his companions soon heard cries in their rear, knew that they had been discovered, and saw the necessity of riding for their lives. They therefore dashed through the woods at a furious rate, with the hue and cry after them, until their course was suddenly interrupted by an impenetrable swamp. Here they from necessity, paused for a few moments, and listened attentively. Hearing no sounds of pursuit, they resumed their course—and skirting the swamp for some distance, in the vain hope of crossing it, they dashed off in a straight line for the Ohio. They continued their furious speed for forty-eight hours, halting but once or twice for a few minutes to take some refreshment, and reached the Ohio in safety. The river was high and rough, and they found it impossible to urge the jaded horses over. Various efforts were made, but all failed. Kenton was never remarkable for prudence; and on this occasion, his better reason seems to have deserted him entirely. By abandoning the animals, he might yet have escaped, though several hours had been lost in endeavoring to get them over. But this he could not make up his mind to do. He therefore called a council, when it was determined, as they felt satisfied they must be some twelve hours in advance of their pursuers, that they should conceal their horses in a neighboring ravine, and themselves take stations in an adjoining wood, in the hope that by sunset, the high wind would abate, and the state of the river be such as to permit their crossing with the booty. At the hour waited for, however, the wind was higher, and the water rougher than ever. Still, as if completely infatuated, they remained in their dangerous position through the night. The next morning was mild, the Indians had not yet been heard in pursuit, and Kenton again urged the horses over. But, recollecting the difficulties of the preceding day, the affrighted animals could not now be induced to enter the water at all. Each of the three men therefore mounted a horse, abandoning the rest, (they had stolen quite a drove,) and started down the river, with the intention of keeping the Ohio and Indiana side till they should arrive opposite

Louisville. But they were slow in making even this movement; and they had not ridden over a hundred yards when they heard a loud halloo, proceeding apparently from the spot which they had just left. They were soon surrounded by the pursuers. One of Kenton's companions effected his escape, the other was killed. Kenton was made prisoner—"falling a victim," says Mr. M'Clung, "to his excessive love of horseflesh."

After the Indians had scalped his dead companion, and kicked and cuffed Kenton to their hearts' content, they compelled him to lie down upon his back, and stretch out his arms to their full length. They then passed a stout stick at right angles across his breast, to each extremity of which, his wrists were fastened by thongs of buffalo-hide. Stakes were next driven into the earth near his feet, to which they were fastened in like manner. A halter was then tied round his neck, and fastened to a sapling which grew near. And finally, a strong rope was passed under his body, and wound several times round his arms at the elbows—thus lashing them to the stick which lay across his breast, and to which his wrists were fastened, in a manner peculiarly painful. He could move neither feet, arms, nor head; and was kept in this position till the next morning. The Indians then wishing to commence their return-journey, unpinioned Kenton, and lashed him by the feet, to a wild, unbroken colt, (one of the animals he had stolen from them,) with his hands tied behind him.

In this manner he was driven into a captivity, as cruel, singular, and remarkable in other respects, as any in the whole history of Indian warfare upon this continent. "A fatalist," says the author of the *Sketches of Western Adventure*, "would recognise the hand of destiny in every stage of its progress. In the infatuation with which Kenton refused to adopt proper measures for his safety, while such were practicable; in the persevering obstinacy with which he remained on the Ohio shore until flight became useless; and afterward, in that remarkable succession of accidents, by which, without the least exertion on his part, he was so often at one hour tantalized with a prospect of safety, and the next plunged into the deepest despair. He was eight times exposed to the gauntlet—three times tied to the stake—and as often thought himself upon the eve of a terrible death. All the sentences passed upon him, whether of mercy or condemnation, seem to have been pronounced in one council only to be reversed in another. Every friend that Providence raised up in his favor, was immediately followed by some enemy, who unexpectedly interposed, and turned his short glimpse of sunshine into deeper darkness than ever. For three weeks he was constantly see-sawing between life and death; and during the whole time, *he* was perfectly passive. No wisdom, or foresight, or exertion, could have saved him. Fortune fought his battle from first to last, and seemed determined to permit nothing else to interfere.

He was eventually liberated from the Indians, when about to be bound to the stake for the fourth time and burnt, by an Indian agent of the name of Drewyer, who was anxious to obtain intelligence for the British commander at Detroit, of the strength and condition of the settlements in Kentucky. He got nothing important out of Kenton; but the three weeks, Football of Fortune was sent to Detroit, from which place he effected his escape in about eight months, and returned to Kentucky. Fearless and active, he soon embarked in new enterprises; and was with George Rogers Clarke, in his celebrated expedition against Vincennes and Kaskaskia; with Edwards, in his abortive expedition to the Indian towns in 1785—and with Wayne, in his decisive campaign of 1794.

Simon Kenton, throughout the struggles of the pioneers, had the reputation of being a valuable scout, a hardy woodsman, and a brave Indian fighter; but in reviewing his eventful career, he appears to have greatly lacked discretion, and to have evinced frequently a want of energy. In his after life he was much respected, and he continued to the last fond of regaling listeners with stories of the early times. A friend of ours, who about three years ago made a visit to the abode of the venerable patriarch, describes in the following terms his appearance at that time: "Kenton's form, even under the weight of seventy-nine years, is striking, and must have been a model of manly strength and agility. His eye is blue, mild, and yet penetrating in its glance. The forehead projects very much at the eyebrows—which are well defined—and then recedes, and is neither very high nor very broad. His hair, which in active life was light, is now quite gray; his nose is straight; and his mouth, before he lost his teeth, must have been expressive and handsome. I observed that he had yet one tooth—which, in connection with his character and manner of conversation, was continually reminding me of Leatherstocking. The whole face is remarkably expressive, not of turbulence or excitement, but rather of rumination and self-possession. Simplicity, frankness, honesty, and a strict regard to truth, appeared to be the prominent traits of his character. In giving an answer to a question which my friend asked him, I was particularly struck with his truthfulness and simplicity. The question was, whether the account of his life, given in the *Sketches of Western Adventure*, was true or not. "Well, I'll tell you," said he; "not true. The book says that when Blackfish, the Injun warrior, asked me, when they had taken me prisoner, if Colonel Boone sent me to steal their horses, I said 'no, sir!' Here he looked indignant and rose from his chair. "I tell you I never said '*sir!*' to an Injun in my life; I scarcely ever say it to a white man." Here Mrs. Kenton, who was engaged in some domestic occupation at the table, turned round and remarked, that when they were last in Kentucky, some one gave her the book to read to her husband; and that when she came to that part, he would not let her read any further. "And I tell you," continued he, "I was never tied to a stake in my life to be burned. They had me painted black when I saw Girty, but not tied to a stake."

We are inclined to think, notwithstanding this, that the statement in the "Sketches," of his being three times tied to the stake, is correct; for the author of that interesting work had before him a manuscript account of the pioneer's life, which had been dictated by Mr. Kenton, to a gentleman of Kentucky, a number of years before, when he had no motive to exaggerate, and his memory was comparatively unimpaired. But he is now beyond the reach of earthly toil, or trouble, or suffering. His old age was as exemplary as his youth and manhood had been active and useful. And though his last years were clouded by poverty, and his eyes closed in a miserable cabin to the light of life, yet shall he occupy a bright page in our border history, and his name soon open to the light of fame.

CHAPTER XXXVIII.

Interesting Sketch of the life of General Stark, the hero of Bennington—The Battle of Bennington—Boston a century ago—Captain William Cunningham.

OUR history, which must necessarily be somewhat episodical in its character, since we could hardly pretend to give in a single volume, a detailed history of Sam, must now return to the more northern arena of his struggles with the great foe whom he has so daringly defied, and with whom he so pertinaciously struggles. We shall give only rapid sketches of the concluding scenes of the Revolution, with some characteristic specimens of the indomitable humor with which the "giant youngling" met all the difficulties of his new position of contention with the foremost Powers of all the world. The battle of Bennington, which has been referred to in a graphic summary of the events of this period, in a previous chapter, and taken principally from Judge Drayton's charge, has found a worthy historian in Richard Everett, the brother of Edward, and we do not conceive, that the transfer of this noble sketch of the bluff and hardy hero, Stark, to our pages, does any discredit to the true history of "Sam" and his children.

THE BATTLE OF BENNINGTON.

BY RICHARD EVERETT.

"When Yankees skilled in martial rule,
First put the British troops to school;
Instructed them in warlike trade,
And new maneuvers of parade,
The true war dance of Yankee reels,
And manual exercise of heels;
Made them give up like saints complete,
The arm of flesh, and trust the feet,
And work like Christians undissembling,
Salvation out with fear and trembling."

John Stark, the hero of Bennington, was a native of New Hampshire. At an early age he enlisted in a company of rangers, participated in several conflicts with the savages, and at last fell into their hands, a prisoner of war. Redeemed by his friends for one hundred and three dollars, he joined Rogers' rangers, and served with distinction through the French and Indian difficulty. When the news came to his quiet home, that American blood had been spilt upon the green at Lexington, he rallied his countrymen, and hurried on to Boston with eight hundred brave mountaineers. He presented himself before the American commander on the eve of the battle of Bunker Hill, and receiving a colonel's commission, instantly hurried to the intrenchments.

Throughout the battle of Bunker Hill, Stark and his New Hampshire men nobly sustained the honor of the patriot cause, and no troops exceeded in bravery the militia regiment of Colonel John Stark. In the spring of 1776, he went to Canada, and at the battle of Trenton he commanded the right wing of Washington's army. He was at Princeton, Bennington, and several other severe battles, always sustaining his reputation, as a brave, honorable, sterling patriot, and an able general. He was a great favorite of General Washington, and very popular in the army. On the 8th of May, 1822, aged ninety-three years, he "was gathered to his fathers," and his remains repose upon the banks of the beautiful Merrimac, beneath a monument of granite, which bears the inscription—"MAJOR-GENERAL STARK."

Having given a very brief sketch of the celebrated officer who led our patriot militia upon the field of Bennington, we will proceed with the account of that battle.

The magnificent army of General Burgoyne, which invaded the States in 1777, having become straightened for provisions and stores, the royal commander ordered a halt, and sent Colonel Baume, a Hessian officer, to scour the country for supplies. Baume took a strong force of British infantry, two pieces of artillery, and a squadron of heavy German dragoons. A great body of Indians, hired and armed by the British, followed his force, or acted as scouts and flanking parties.

Stark, on the intelligence of Burgoyne's invasion, was offered the command of one of two regiments of troops which were raised in New Hampshire, through the exertions, chiefly, of John Langdon, Speaker of the General Assembly. Stark had served for a long period as General, but at that time was at home, a private citizen. But at the call of his countrymen he again took the field. The two regiments were soon raised, and with them, as senior officer, Stark hastened to oppose the British army. At that time the Vermont militia were enrolled into an organization, called the "Berkshire Regiment," under Colonel Warner.

On arriving near Bennington, Stark sent forward Colonel Gregg, with a small force to reconnoiter, but that officer soon returned with information that a strong force of British, Hessians, and Indians was rapidly approaching. Upon this intelligence, Stark resolved to stand his ground and give battle. Messengers were sent at once to the Berkshire militia to hurry on, and the patriots were directed to see that their weapons were in good order. This was on the 14th of August, 1777. During the day, Baume and his army appeared, and learning that the militia were collecting in front of his route, the commander ordered his army to halt, and throw up intrenchments. An express was also sent to General Burgoyne, for reinforcements.

The 15th was dull and rainy. Both armies continued their preparations, while waiting for reinforcements. Skirmishing was kept up all day and night, between the militia and the Indians, and the latter suffered so severely, that a great portion of the savage force left the field, saying that "the woods were full of Yankees." About 12 o'clock on the night of the 15th, a party of Berkshire militia came into the American camp. At the head of one company, was the Reverend Mr. Allen, of Pittsfield, and that worthy gentleman appeared full of zeal to meet the enemy. Sometime before daylight, he called on General Stark, and said: "General, the people of Berkshire county have often been called out, without being allowed to fight, and if you don't give them a chance, they have resolved never to turn out again." "Very well," replied Stark, "do you want to go at it now, while it is dark and rainy?" "No, not just at this moment," said the warlike minister. "Then," said the General, "if the Lord shall once more give us sunshine, and I do not give you fighting enough, I'll never ask you to come out again!" This satisfied the preacher, and he went out to cheer up his flock with the good news.

Day dawned, bright and warm, on the 16th. All nature, invigorated by the mild August rain, glared with beauty and freshness. Before sunrise, the Americans were in motion, while from the British intrenchments, the sound of bugles and the roll of drums, told that Baume's forces were ready for action. Stark early arranged his plan of attack. Colonel Nichols, with three hundred men, was sent out to attack the British rear; Colonel Herrick, with three hundred men, marched against the right flank, but was ordered to join Nichols before making his assault general. With about three hundred men, Colonels Hubbard and Stickney were sent against the entrenched front, while Stark, with a small reserve, waited to operate whenever occasion offered. It must be remembered that the American forces were *militia*, while Baume's army was made up of well-disciplined, well-armed, and experienced soldiers. Many of the patriots were armed with fowling-pieces, and there were whole companies without a bayonet. They had no artillery.

General Stark waited impatiently until the roar of musketry proclaimed that the different detachments had commenced their attack, and then forming his small battalion, he made his memorable speech: "*Boys! there's the enemy, and we must beat them, or Molly Stark sleeps a widow to-night*—Forward!" His soldiers, with enthusiastic shouts, rushed forward upon the Hessian defenses, and the battle became general. The Hessian dragoons, dismounted, met the Americans with stern bravery. The two cannons, loaded with grape and cannister, swept the hill-side with dreadful effect.

Stark's white horse fell in less than ten minutes after his gallant rider came under fire, but on foot, with his hat in one hand, and his saber in the other, he kept at the head of his men, who, without flinching a single foot, urged their way up the little hill. Brave Parson Allen, with a clubbed musket, was seen amid the smoke, fighting in the front platoon of his company. The whole field was a volcano of fire. Stark, in his official report, says that the two forces were within a few yards of each other, and "the roaring of their guns was like a continuous clap of thunder!" The

Hessian and British regulars, accustomed to hard-fought fields, held their ground stubbornly and bravely. For more than two hours the battle hung in even scale. At length, Baume ordered a charge; at that instant he fell, mortally wounded, and his men charging forward, broke their ranks in such a manner, that the Americans succeeded, after a fierce hand to hand fight, in entering the intrenchments.

Stark shouted to his men, "Forward, boys, charge them home!" and his troops, maddened by the conflict, swept the hill with irresistible valor. They pushed forward without discipline or order, seized the artillery, and gave chase to the flying enemy. The field being won, plunder became the object of the militia.

The guns, sabres, stores and equipments of the defeated foe were being gathered up, when Col. Breyman, with five hundred men, suddenly appeared upon the field. He had been sent by Burgoyne to re-inforce Baume, but the heavy rain had prevented his men from marching at a rapid rate. The flying troops instantly rallied and joined the new array, which speedily assumed an order of battle, and began to press the scattered forces of the patriots. This was a critical period. Stark put forth every effort to rally his men, but they were exhausted, scattered, and nearly out of ammunition. It seemed as if the fortune of the day was in the royal hands, when from the edge of a strip of forest, half a mile off, came a loud and genuine American cheer. Stark turned, and beheld emerging from the wood, the Berkshire regiment, under Colonel Warner. This body of men, also delayed by the rain, after a forced march, had just reached the battle field, panting for a share in the affray. General Stark hastened to the captain of the foremost company, and ordered him to lead his men to the charge at once. But the captain cooly asked, "Where's the colonel? I want to see Colonel Warner before I move." The colonel was sent for, and the redoubtable captain, drawing himself up, said, with the nasal twang peculiar to the puritans of old, "Naow, Kernal, what d'ye want me tu dew?" "Drive those red-coats from the hill yonder," was the answer. "Wall, it shall be done," said the captain, and issuing the necessary orders, he led his men to the charge without a moment's hesitation.

Said an eye-witness, afterwards, "The last we saw of Warner's regiment for half an hour, was when they entered the smoke and fire about half way up the hill." Stark with a portion of his rallied troops supported the Berkshire men, and the royal forces were defeated, after a close contest. A portion of them escaped, but seven hundred men and officers were taken prisoners, among the latter Colonel Baume, who soon died of his wound.

The British lost two hundred and seven men killed, and a large number wounded. Of the Americans, about one hundred were killed and the same number wounded The spoils consisted of four pieces of cannon, several hundred stand of excellent muskets, two hundred and fifty dragoon swords, eight brass drums, and four wagons laden with stores, clothing and ammunition.

This victory severely crippled Burgoyne, and discouraged his army, while it enlivened the Americans from one extent of the country to the other. It taught the British troops to respect the American militia, and it was a brilliant precursor to the victories of Saratoga and Bemis' Hights.

Congress voted thanks to General Stark and his brave troops for their great victory, and took measures to push on the war with renewed energy and hope.

But the joke of "or Molly Stark's a widow," is not the only fun indulged in at this period, by "Sam," and at the expense too of "the magnificent army of Burgoyne." This pompous and important person had just before issued the following conciliatory document:

PROCLAMATION.

By John Burgoyne, Esq., Lieutenant General of His Majesty's armies in America, Colonel of the Queen's regiment of Light Dragoons, Governor of Fort William, in North Britain, one of the Representatives of the Commons of Great Britain, and commanding an army and fleet employed on an Expedition from Canada, etc., etc., etc.

The forces entrusted to my command are designed to act in concert, and upon a common principle, with the numerous armies and fleets which already display in every quarter of

America the power, the justice, and, when properly sought, the mercy of the king.

The cause in which the British army is thus exerted, applies to the most affecting interests of the human heart; and the military servants of the crown, at first called forth for the sole purpose of restoring the rights of the constitution, now combine with love of their country and duty to their sovereign, the other extensive incitements, which form a due sense of the general privileges of mankind. To the eyes and ears of the temperate part of the public, and the breasts of suffering thousands in the provinces, be the melancholy appeal, whether the present unnatural rebellion has not been made a foundation for the completest system of tyranny that ever God, in his displeasure, suffered for a time to be exercised over a stubborn and froward generation.

Arbitrary imprisonment, confiscation of property, persecution and torture, unprecedented in the inquisition of the Romish church, are among the palpable enormities that verify the affirmative. These are inflicted by assemblies and committees who dare to profess themselves friends to liberty, upon the most quiet subjects, without distinction of age or sex, for the sole crime, often for the sole suspicion, of having adhered in principle to the government under which they were born, and to which, by every tie, divine and human, they owe allegiance. To consummate these shocking proceedings, the profanation of religion is added to the most profligate prostitution of common reason—the consciences of men are set at naught, and multitudes are not only compelled to bear arms, but also to swear subjection to a usurpation they abhor.

Animated by these considerations—at the head of troops in the full powers of health, discipline and valor—determined to strike where necessary, and anxious to spare where possible—I, by these presents, invite and exhort all persons, in all places whither the progress of this army may point—and, by the blessing of God, I will extend it far—to maintain such a conduct as may justify me in protecting their lands, habitations and families. The intention of this address is to hold forth security, not degradation, to the country. To those whom spirit and principle may indue to partake the glorious task of redeeming their countrymen from dangers, and re-establishing the blessings of legal government, I offer encouragement and employment; and upon the first intelligence of their association, I will find means to assist their undertakings. The domestic, the industrious, the infirm, and even the timid inhabitants, I am desirous to protect, provided they remain quietly at their houses—that they do not suffer their cattle to be removed, nor their corn or forage to be secreted or destroyed—that they do not break up their bridges or roads, nor by any other act, directly or indirectly, endeavor to obstruct the operations of the king's troops, or supply or assist those of the enemy.

Every species of provisions brought to my camp will be paid for at an equitable rate, and in solid coin.

In consciousness of Christianity, my royal master's clemency, and the honor of soldiership, I have dwelt upon this invitation, and wished for more persuasive terms to give it impression. And let not people be led to disregard it by considering their distance from the immediate situation of my camp. I have but to give stretch to the Indian forces under my direction—and they amount to thousands—to overtake the hardened enemies of Great Britain and America. I consider them the same wherever they may lurk.

If, notwithstanding these endeavors and sincere inclinations to effect them, the frenzy of hostility should remain, I trust I shall stand acquitted in the eyes of God and men, in denouncing and executing the vengeance of the State against the willful outcasts. The messengers of justice and of wrath await them in the field; and devastation, famine, and every concommitant horror that a reluctant but indispensable prosecution of military duty must occasion, will bar the way to their return.

JOHN BURGOYNE.

Camp at Ticonderoga, July 2, 1777.

By order of his excellency, the Lieutenant General:

ROBERT KINGSTON, *Secretary*.

Now hear "Sam's" answer through one of his chosen sons, to this facetious pronunciamento! It is a veritable document of the "olden time," which the children of "Sam," during this or the last generation, have had no opportunity of perusing:

To John Burgoyne, Esq., Lieutenant General of his Majesty's armies, in America, Colonel of the Queen's regiment of light dragoons, Governor of Fort William in North Britain, one of the Representatives of the Commons of Great Britain, and commanding an army and fleet employed on an Expedition from Canada, etc., etc. etc.

MOST HIGH, MOST MIGHTY, MOST PUISSANT, AND MOST SUBLIME GENERAL:—When the forces under your command arrived at Quebec, in order to act in concert, and upon a common principle, with the numerous fleets and armies which already display in every quarter of America, the justice and mercy of your king, we, the reptiles of America, were struck with unusual trepidation and astonishment. But what words can express the plentitude of our horror, when the Colonel of the Queen's regiment of light dragoons advanced toward Ticonderoga. The mountains shook before thee, and the trees of the forest bowed their lofty heads—the vast lakes of the north were chilled at thy presence, and the mighty cataracts stopped their tremendous career, and were suspended in awe at thy approach. Judge, then, Oh! Ineffable Governor of Fort William, in North Britain, what must have been the terror, dismay, and despair that overspread this paltry continent of America, and us, its wretched inhabitants. Dark and dreary, indeed, was the prospect before us, till, like the sun in the horizon, your most gracious, sublime, and irresistible proclamation, opened the doors of mercy, and snatched us, as it were, from the jaws of annihilation.

We foolishly thought, blind as we were, that your gracious master's fleets and armies were come to destroy us and our liberties; but we are happy in hearing from you (and who can doubt what you assert?) that they were called forth for the sole purpose of restoring the rights of the Constitution to a froward and stubborn generation.

And is it for this, O! Sublime Lieutenant-General, that you have given yourself the trouble to cross the wide Atlantic, and with incredible fatigue traverse uncultivated wilds? And we ungratefully refuse the proffered blessing? To restore the rights of the Constitution, you have called together an amiable host of savages, and turned them loose to scalp our women and children, and lay our country waste—

this they have performed with their usual skill and clemency, and yet we remain insensible of the benefit, and unthankful for so much goodness.

Our Congress has declared Independence, and our Assemblies, as your Highness justly observes, have most wickedly imprisoned the avowed friends of that power with which they are at war, and most profanely compelled those whose consciences will not permit them to fight, to pay some small part toward the expenses their country is at, in supporting what is called a necessary defensive war. If we go on thus in our obstinacy and ingratitude, what can we expect, but that you should, in your anger, give a stretch to the Indian forces under your direction, amounting to thousands, to overtake and destroy us? or, which is ten times worse, that you should withdraw your fleets and armies, and leave us to our misery, without completing the benevolent task you have begun, of restoring to us the rights of the Constitution?

We submit—we submit—Most Puissant Colonel of the Queen's regiment of light dragoons, and Governor of Fort William, in North Britain. We offer our heads to the scalping-knife, and our bellies to the bayonet. Who can resist the force of your eloquence? Who can withstand the terror of your arms? The invitation you have made in the consciousness of Christianity, your royal master's clemency, and the horror of soldiership, we thankfully accept. The blood of the slain, the cries of injured virgins and innocent children, and the never-ceasing sighs and groans of starving wretches, now languishing in the jails and prison-ships of New York, call on us in vain, while your sublime proclamation is sounded in our ears. Forgive us, O! our country! Forgive us, dear posterity! Forgive us, all ye foreign powers, who are anxiously watching our conduct in this important struggle, if we yield implicitly to the persuasive tongue of the most elegant Colonel of her Majesty's regiment of light dragoons.

Forbear, then, thou magnanimous Lieutenant-General! Forbear to denounce vengeance against us. Forbear to give a stretch to those restorers of Constitutional rights, the Indian forces under your direction. Let not the messenger of justice and wrath await us in the field, and devastation, and every concomitant horror, bar our return to the allegiance of a prince, who, by his royal will, would deprive us of every blessing of life, with all possible clemency.

We are domestic, we are industrious, we are infirm and timid; we shall remain quietly at home, and not remove our cattle, our corn, our forage, in hope that you will come, at the head of your troops, in the full powers of health, discipline, and valor, and take charge of them yourselves. Behold our wives and daughters, our flocks and herds, our goods and chattels, are they not at the mercy of our Lord the King, and of his Lieutenant-General, member of the House of Commons, and Governor of Fort William, in North Britain?

A. B.
C. D.
E. F., ETC., ETC., ETC.

Saratoga, 10th July, 1777.

" Sam" makes condescenaing proposals for a compromise with his haughty master, General Burgoyne, and asks him in philanthropical spirit, to be "as mild as he can!"

Proposal for an exchange of General Burgoyne. Ascribed to his Excellency William Livingston, Esq., Governor of the State of New Jersey.

Should the report of General Burgoyne having infringed the capitulation, between Major General Gates and himself, prove to be true, our superiors will doubtless take proper care to prevent his reaping any benefit from it; and should he be detained as a prisoner, for his infraction of any of the articles, I would humbly propose to exchange him, in such a manner as will, at the same time, flatter his vanity and redound to the greatest emolument to America. To evince the reasonableness of my proposal, I would observe, that by the same parity of reason that a general is exchanged for a general, a colonel for a colonel, and so on with respect to other officers, mutually of equal rank, we ought to have for one and the same gentleman who shall happen to hold both these offices, both a general and a colonel. This will appear evident from the consideration that those exchanges are never regulated by viewing the persons exchanged in the light of *men*, but as *officers;* since otherwise, a colonel might as well be exchanged for a sergeant as for an officer of his own rank; a sergeant being, undoubtedly, equally a *man*, and, as the case sometimes happens, *more of a man too.* One prisoner, therefore, having twenty different offices, ought to redeem from captivity twenty prisoners, aggregately holding the same offices; or such greater or less number as shall, with respect to rank, be equal to his twenty offices. This being admitted, I think General Burgoyne is the most profitable prisoner we could have taken, having more offices, or, (what amounts to the same thing in Old England,) more titles, than any gentleman on this side the *Ganges.* And as his *impetuous Excellency* certainly meant to avail himself of his titles, by their pompous display in his proclamation, had he proved conqueror, it is but reasonable that we should avail ourselves of them, now he is conquered; and, till I meet with a better project for that purpose, I persuade myself that the following proposal will appropriate them to a better use than they were ever applied to before.

The exchange I propose is as follows:

I. For John Burgoyne, Esquire.

Some worthy justice of the peace, *magnanimously stolen out of his bed,* or taken from his farm by a band of ruffians in the uniform of British soldiery, and now probably perishing with hunger and cold in a loathsome jail in New York.

II. For John Burgoyne, *Lieutenant General of His Majesty's armies in America.*

Two Majors General.

III. For John Burgoyne, *Colonel of the Queen's regiment of Light Dragoons.*

As the British troops naturally prize everything in proportion as it partakes of *royalty*, and undervalue whatever originates from a *Republican government,* I suppose a colonel of *Her Majesty's own* regiment will procure at least *three Continental Colonels of horse.*

IV. For John Burgoyne, Governor of Fort William, in North Britain.

Here I would demand one governor of one of the United States, as his *multitulary excellence* is governor of a *fort*, and two more, as that *fort* is in *North Britain,* which his Brittanic majesty may be presumed to value in that proportion; but considering that the said fort is called *William,* which may excite in his majesty's mind the *rebellious* idea of liberty,

I deduct one on that account, and, rather than puzzle the cartel with any perplexity, I am content with *two governors.*

V. For John Burgoyne, one of the Representatives of Great Britain.

The first member of Congress who may fall into the enemy's hands.

VI. For John Burgoyne, *Commander of a fleet employed in an expedition from Canada.*

The Admiral of our navy.

VII. For John Burgoyne, *Commander of an army employed in an expedition from Canada.*

One Commander-in-Chief in any of our departments.

VIII. For John Burgoyne, *etc., etc., etc.*

Some connoisseurs in hieroglyphics imagine that these three et ceteras are emblematical of three certain *occult* qualities of the general, which he never intends to exhibit in more legible characters, viz: *prudence, modesty,* and *humanity.* Others suppose that they stand for *king of* America, and that, had he proved successful, he would have fallen upon General Howe, and afterwards have set up for himself. Be this as it may, (which it, however, behooves a certain gentleman on the other side the water seriously to consider,) I insist upon it, that as all dark and cabalistical characters are suspicious, these *incognoscible enigmas* may portend much more than is generally apprehended. At all events, General Burgoyne has availed himself of their importance, and I doubt not they excited *as much* terror in his proclamation as any of his more *luminous* titles. As his person, therefore, is by the capture, become the property of the Congress, all his titles, (which some suppose to constitute his very essence,) whether more splendid or opaque, latent or visible, are become, *ipso facto,* the lawful goods and chattels of the Continent, and ought not to be restored without a considerable equivalent. If we should happen to overrate them, it is his own fault, it being in his power to ascertain their intrinsic value, and it is a rule in law, that when a man is possessed of evidence to disprove what is alleged against him, and refuses to produce it, the presumption raised against him is to be taken for granted. Certain it is, that these three et ceteras must stand for three *somethings,* and as these three somethings must, at least, be equal to three somethings without rank or title, I had some thoughts of setting them down for *three privates;* but then, as they are three somethings in General Burgoyne, which must be of twice the value of *three anythings* in *any three privates,* I shall only double them, and demand in exchange for these three problematical, enigmatical, hieroglyphical, mystic, necromantical, cabalistical, and portentious et ceteras, *six privates.*

So that, according to my plan, we ought to detain this *ideal* conquerer of the North, now a *real* prisoner in the East, till we have got in exchange for him, one esquire, two majors-general, three colonels of light horse, two governors, one member of Congress, the admiral of one navy, one commander-in-chief in a separate department, and six privates; which is probably more than this extraordinary hero would fetch in any part of Great Britain, were he exposed at public auction for a year and a day. All which is nevertheless, humbly submitted to the consideration of the honorable, the Congress, and his excellency, General Washington.

Princeton, December 8th, 1777.

In order that good jokes may not go abroad without company we append the following, which are quite equally expressive of the spirit of the times of which we treat:

REMINISCENCES.

BOSTON LESS THAN A CENTURY AGO.

Dress, etc.—Seventy years ago cocked hats, wigs, and red cloaks, were the usual dress of gentlemen—boots were rarely seen, except among military men. Shoe-strings were worn only by those who could not afford to buy buckles. In winter, round coats were used, made stiff with buckram—they came down to the knees in front.

Before the Revolution, boys wore wigs and cocked hats; and boys of genteel families wore cocked hats till within the last thirty years.

Ball-dress for gentlemen was silk coat, and breeches of the same, and embroidered waistcoats—sometimes white satin breeches. Buckles were fashionable till within the last fifteen or twenty years, and a man could not have remained in a ball-room with shoe-strings. It was usual for the bridegroom and maids, and men attending, to go to church together three successive Sundays after the wedding, with a change of dress each day. A gentleman who deceased not long since, appeared the first Sunday in white broadcloth, the second in blue and gold, the third in peach bloom, pearl buttons. It was a custom to hang the escutcheon of a deceased head of a family out of a window over the front door, from the time of his decease until after his funeral. The last instance which is remembered of this, was in the case of Gov. Hancock's uncle, 1764. Copies of the escutcheon, painted on black silk, were more anciently distributed among the pall-bearers, rings afterward—and, until within a few years, gloves. Dr. A. Elliott had a mug full of rings which were presented to him at funerals. Till within twenty years, gentlemen wore powder, and many of them sat from thirty to forty minutes under the barber's hand, to have their hair cropped; suffering no inconsiderable pain from hair-pulling, and sometimes from hot tongs. Crape cushions and hoops were indispensable in full dress, until within thirty years. Sometimes ladies were dressed the day before the party and slept in easy chairs, to keep their hair in fit condition for the following night. Most ladies went to parties on foot, if they could not get a cast in a friend's carriage or chaise. Gentlemen rarely had a chance to ride.

The latest dinner hour was two o'clock; some officers of the colonial government dined later occasionally. In genteel families, ladies went to drink tea about four o'clock, and rarely stayed after candle-light in summer. It was the fashion for ladies to propose to visit—not to be sent for. The drinking of punch in the forenoon, in public houses, was a common practice with the most respectable men, till about five and twenty years; and evening clubs were very common. The latter, it is said, were more common formerly, as this afforded the means of communion on the state of the country. Dinner parties were very rare. Wine was very little in use; convivial parties drank punch or toddy. Half boots came into use about thirty years ago. The first pair that appeared in Boston were worn by a young gentleman, who came here from New York, and who was more remarkable for his boots than anything else. Within twenty years, gentlemen wore scarlet coats, with black velvet collars and very costly buttons, of mock pearl, cut steel, or painted glass—and neckcloths edged with lace, and laced ruffles over the hands. Before the Revolution, from five to six hundred pounds was the utmost of annual expenditure in those families where carriages, and corresponding domestics were kept. There were only two or three carriages, that is chariots or coaches, in 1750. Chaises on four wheels, not phætons, were in use in families of distinction.

The history of the *Liberty-Tree* is said to be this: That a certain Capt. McIntosh illuminated the tree, and hung upon it effigies of obnoxious characters, and that these were taken down by the liberty boys and burnt, and the tree thus got its name.

The Popes.—A stage was erected on wheels—on this stage was placed a figure in the chair, called the pope; behind him, a female figure, in the attitude of dancing, whom they called Nancy Dawson; behind her Admiral Byng, hanging on a gallows; and behind him the devil. A similar composition was made at the South-end, called South-end pope. In the daytime the processions, each drawing with them their popes and their attendants, met and passed each other, on the mill or draw-bridge, very civilly; but in the evening, they met at the same point, and a battle ensued with fists, sticks and stones; and one or the other of the popes was captured. The North-end pope was never taken but once, and then the captain had been early wounded and taken from the field. The pope conflicts were held in memory of the powder-plot of Nov. 5, and were some sort of imitation of what was done in England on the same anniversary.

A man used to ride on an ass, with immense jackboots, and his face covered with a horrible mask, and was called, Joyce Jr. His office was to assemble men and boys, in mob style, and ride in the middle of them, and in such company to terrify the adherents to the royal government, before the Revolution. The tumult which resulted in the massacre of 1770, was excited by such means. Joyce, junior, was said to have a particular whistle, which brought his adherents, etc., whenever they were wanted.

About 1730 to 1740, there was no meat market; there were only three or four shops in which fresh meat was sold—one of them was the corner of State street and Cornhill, where Mr. Hartshorn now keeps. Gentlemen used to go the day before, and have their names put down for what they wanted. Outside of this shop was a large hook, on which carcasses used to hang. A little man, who was a justice of the peace, came one day for meat, but came too late. He was disappointed, and asked to whom such and such pieces were to go? One of them was to go to a *tradesman;* (it was not a common thing in those days, for tradesmen to eat fresh meat,) the justice went out, saying he would send the tradesman a salad for his lamb. He sent an overdue and unpaid tax-bill. Soon after, the tradesman met the justice near this place, and told him he would repay his kindness; which he did, by hanging the justice up by the waistband of his breeches to the butcher's hook, and leaving him to get down as he could.

TARRING AND FEATHERING ORIGINALLY A YANKEE TRICK.

From the *American Mercury.*

This appears from the speech of McFingal, the Tory Sagamore, to the Yankee mob:

"Was there a *Yankee trick* ye knew,
They did not play as well as you?
Did they not lay their heads together,
And gain *your* art to tar and feather?"

TARRING AND FEATHERING LAWFUL!

This appears, by the authority of the sentence which was pronounced on McFingal. This sentence, be it remembered, though seemingly an order and decree of a committee, in fact, had its origin in the brain of a man who was a judge of the Supreme Court of the State of Connecticut. Whether appointed judge from this specimen of his *judicial knowledge,* or not, is not now in question; but let us hear the sentence on McFingal, king of the Tories.

"Meanwhile, beside the pole, the guard
A bench of justice had prepared,
Where, sitting round in awful sort,
The grand committee hold the Court;
While all the crew in silent awe,
Wait from their lips the lore of *law.*
Few moments with deliberation,
They hold the solemn consultation,

When soon in judgment all agree,
And clerk declares the dread decree
"That Squire McFingal, having grown,
The vilest Tory in the town,
And now, on full examination,
Convicted by his own confession,
Finding no token of repentance,
This Court proceed to render sentence:
That first, the mob, a slip-knot single,
Tie round the neck of said McFingal;
And in due form do tar him next,
And feather, as the *law directs:*
Then through the town attendant ride him
In cart, with constable beside him,
And having held him up to shame,
Bring to the pole, from whence he came."

Vision and prediction of McFingal, king of the Tories, when in coat of tar and feathers:

"Tar, yet in embryo in pine,
Shall run, on Tories' back to shine;
Trees rooted fair in groves of fallows,
Are growing for our future gallows;
And geese unhatched, when plucked in fray,
Shall rue the feathering of that day."

In order to show that there may be two sides to every question, we give also, the confession of a rank Tory of this period, which goes far to exhibit the origin of the Lynch law, in a somewhat palliative light. "Sam," it will be perceived, has never licensed Lynch law, from the beginning: but that its possibility constitutes one of the facetiæ of his moods, the detail of provocations in this extract will clearly show.

CAPTAIN WILLIAM CUNNINGHAM.

The following is copied from the *American Apollo*, No. 7, Vol. 1, Friday, February 17, 1792, printed at Boston, by Belknap & Young, State street, (a weekly paper, in the form of a pamphlet,):

The Life, Confession, and last Dying Words of Captain William Cunningham, formerly British Provost Marshal in the city of New York, who was executed in London, the 10th of August, 1791.

I, William Cunningham, was born in Dublin Barracks, in the year 1738. My father was trumpeter to the Blue Dragoons, and at the age of eight I was placed with an officer as his servant, in which station I continued until I was sixteen, and, being a great proficient in horsemanship, was taken as an assistant to the riding-master of the troops, and in the year 1761, was made sergeant of dragoons; but the peace coming the year after, I was disbanded. Being bred to no profession, I took up with a woman who kept a gin-shop in a blind alley, near the Coal Quay; but the house being searched for stolen goods, and my dosy taken to Newgate, I thought it most prudent to decamp. Accordingly I set off for the North, and arrived at Drogheda, where, in a few months after, I married the daughter of an exciseman, by whom I had three sons.

About the year 1772, we removed to Newry, where I commenced the profession of a scow-banker, which is that of enticing the mechanics and country people to ship themselves for America; they are sold or obliged to serve a term of years for their passage. I embarked at Newry in the ship Needham, for New York, and arrived at that port the 4th day of August, 1774, with some indented servants I kidnapped in Ireland; but these were liberated in New York on account of the bad usage they received from me during the passage. In that city I followed the profession of breaking horses, and teaching ladies and gentlemen to ride, but rendering myself obnoxious to the citizens in their infant struggle for freedom, I was obliged to fly on board the Asia man-of-war, and from thence to Boston, where my own opposition to the measures pursued by the Americans in support of their rights, was the first thing that recommended me to the notice of General Gage, and when the war commenced I was appointed Provost Marshal to the royal army, which placed me in a situation to wreak my vengeance on the Americans. I shudder to think of the murders I have been accessory to, *both with and without orders from Government*, especially while in New York—during which time there were more than two thousand prisoners starved in the different churches, by stopping their rations, which I sold.

There were also two hundred and seventy-five American prisoners and obnoxious persons executed, out of all which number there were only about one dozen public executions, which chiefly consisted of British and Hessian deserters. The mode for private executions was thus conducted: A guard was despatched from the provost, about half-past twelve at night, to the barracks street, and the neighborhood of the upper barracks, to order the people to shut their window shutters and to put out their lights, forbidding them, at the same time, to presume to look out of their windows and doors, on pain of death; after which, the unfortunate prisoners were conducted, gagged, just behind the upper barracks, and hung without ceremony, and then buried by the black pioneer of the provost.

At the end of the war, I returned to England with the army, and settled in Wales, as being a cheaper place of living than in any of the populous cities, but being at length persuaded to go to London, I entered so warmly into the dissipations of that capital, that I soon found my circumstances much embarrassed. To relieve which I mortgaged my half pay to an army agent, but that being soon expended, I forged a draft for three hundred pounds sterling, on the Board of Ordnance, but being detected in presenting it for acceptance, I was apprehended, tried, and convicted—and for that offense am here to suffer an ignominious death.

I beg the pardon of all good Christians, and also pardon and forgiveness of God, for the many horrid murders I have been accessory to.

WILLIAM CUNNINGHAM.

The disastrous defeat of Burgoyne, with the details and consequences of which our readers are already sufficiently familiar, had been immediately preceded by a regular influx of foreign adventurers, comprising every stamp of the true Condittori, which at that time swarmed throughout the countries of Europe. They came here like the plagues of Egypt, with insolent buzzings around the doors of Congress, instigated by the too easy promises of Deane, and gave occasion, finally, to one of the most bitter letters ever written by Washington, who, goaded, like some noble animal by gad-flies, besought Congress to rid him of these endless swarms. De Kalb, Pulaski, Steuben, and the enthusiastic Lafayette, were of course exceptions. Enthusiasm and the accident of birth, which gave him court influence at Paris, seem always to have been more the merit of the last, than talent—much as he has been lauded and almost deified. Nevertheless, Washington—the then representative of "Sam"—saw his uses, and loved him as an excellent man, as he undoubtedly was. He proved of great use through his disinterested interest in our cause, in conciliating toward us and bringing about our treaty with France—which, by the way, it was not a whit more to our interest than than it should never have been formed.

At the commencement of the war, the aid of foreign officers had been thought highly desirable, especially in the departments of artillery and engineering, in which there was a great deficiency of native skill and science. It was one part of Deane's commission to engage a few officers of this description, a matter in which he had gone a good deal beyond his instructions. Beset with endless solicitations, to which the fear of giving offense, and the hope of securing influence, induced him too often to yield, he had sent out not less than fifty officers of all ranks, to whom he had made extravagant promises of promotion, which occasioned great discontent among the native officers, and no little embarrassment to Congress. Greene, Sullivan, and Knox, in a joint letter, a few weeks before Washington's visit to Congress, had threatened to resign if a certain M. Du Coudray were promoted to the command of the artillery, with the rank of major general, agreeably to a contract which Deane had signed with him, in consideration of certain supplies which he had furnished. Congress, with a just sense of its dignity, voted this letter of the generals "an attempt to influence their decision, an invasion of the liberties of the people, and indicating a want of confidence in the justice of Congress," for which the writers were required to make an apology. Having consented to serve for the present as a volunteer, with a merely nominal rank, Du Coudray was drowned shortly after in crossing the Schuylkill.

There was, indeed, among the American officers excessive jealousy and great heart-burnings on the subject of rank, precedence and command, not only as to foreigners, but as to each other. Congress professed to be governed in its promotions by the complex considerations of former rank, meritorious service, and the number of troops raised by the States to which the officers respectively belonged. But the officers imagined, and not always without reason, that intrigue and personal favor had quite as much influence.

Among the contracts made by Deane was one with Du Portail, La Radière, and Du Govion, three engineer officers of merit, recommended by the French court, who were now placed at the head of the engineer department, thus completing the organization of the new army. Kosciusko, whose entry of the service has been already mentioned, was appointed engineer for the northern department.

The Count Pulaski, who had already gained distinction in Europe by his attempts to resist the first partition of Poland, had just arrived in America, and had offered his services to Congress.

The foreign officers above named were persons of merit; but too large a proportion of those who came to seek commissions in America, whether sent by Deane, or adventurers on their own account, even some who brought high recommendations, were remarkable for nothing but extravagant self-conceit, and boundless demands for rank, command, and pay.

Of a very different character was the Marquis de Lafayette, a youth of nineteen, belonging to one of the most illustrious families of France, who had just arrived in America, and whom General Washington now met at Philadelphia for the first time. Like all other French nobles of that day, he had received a military education, and held a commission in the French army. In garrison at Metz, he had been present at an entertainment given by the governor of that city to the Duke of Gloucester, brother of the British king, and on that occasion, from the duke's lips, he first heard the story of the American rebellion. His youthful fancy was fired by the idea of this transatlantic struggle for liberty, and, though master of an ample fortune, and married to a wife whom he tenderly loved, he resolved at once to adventure in it. For that purpose he opened a communication with Deane. His intention becoming known, the French court, which still kept up the forms of neutrality, forbade him to go. But he secretly purchased a ship, which Deane loaded with military stores, and set sail at a moment when the news of the loss of New York and the retreat through the Jerseys made most foreigners despair of the American cause. The French court sent orders to the West Indies to intercept him; but he sailed directly for the United States, arrived in safety, presented himself to Congress, and offered to serve as a volunteer, without pay. Admiring his disinterestedness not less than his zeal, and not uninfluenced by his rank and connections, Congress gave him the commission of major general, which Dean had promised; but, for the present, content with the rank without any command, he entered the military family of Washington, for whom he soon contracted a warm and lasting friendship, which Washington as warmly returned. La Fayette brought with him eleven other officers; among them the Baron De Kalb, a German veteran, presently commissioned as major general.

The unsuccessful battles of Brandywine and Germantown, which soon followed, brought into rather singular contrast, the military reputations of Washington and the English renegade, Gates, who commanded at the surrender of Burgoyne. The terrible winter of 1777, had been passed by Washington's miserable army, at Valley Forge, amidst the extremes of suffering, from privations of every kind, when there at once appears to be a formidable cabal on hand, for supplanting him, in favor of the mediocre adventurer, Gates. Here is Hildreth's account of this infamous cabal.

While Washington was exerting himself to the utmost, to preserve the army from total disorganization, a project was on foot to remove him from the chief command. Several persons, conspicuous in Congress and the army, were more or less concerned in this movement; but most of the information respecting it, has been carefully suppressed, and its history is involved in some obscurity. Every biographer has been very anxious to shield his special hero, from the charge of participation in this affair, indignantly stigmatized, by most writers, as a base intrigue. Yet doubts, at that time, as to Washington's fitness for the chief command, though they might evince prejudice or a lack of sound judgment, do not necessarily imply either selfish ends or a malicious disposition. The Washington of that day was not Washington as we know him, tried and proved by twenty years of the most disinterested and most successful public services. As yet, he had been in command but little more than two years, during which, he had suffered, with some slight exceptions, a continued series of losses and defeats. He had recovered Boston, to be sure, but had lost New York, Newport, and Philadelphia. He had been completely successful at Trenton, and partially so at Princeton, but had been beaten, with heavy loss, on Long Island and at Fort Washington, and lately, in two pitched battles, on ground of his own choosing, at Brandywine and Germantown. What a contrast to the battles of Behmis' Hights, and the capture of Burgoyne's whole army! Want of success, and sectional and personal prejudices, had created a party in Congress against Schuyler and against Sullivan. Could Washington escape the common fate of those who lose? Richard Henry Lee and Samuel Adams seem to have been the leaders of a party gradually formed in Congress, and for some time strong enough to exercise a material influence on its action, which ascribed to the commander-in-chief a lack of vigor and energy, and a system of favoritism deleterious to the public service. The Pennsylvanians were much annoyed at the loss of Philadelphia; and several leading persons in that State, seem to have co-operated with this party, especially Mifflin—a plausible, judicious, energetic, ambitious man, very popular and very influential, but of whose recent management of the quarter-master's department, Washington had loudly complained. Nor were other malcontents wanting in the army. The marked confidence which Washington reposed in Greene, gave offense to some; others had purposes of their own to serve. Conway aspired to the office of inspector-general, the establishment of which he had suggested; and, not finding his pretensions favored by Washington, he indulged in very free criticisms on the state of the troops, and the incapacity of the commander-in-chief. Gates, who might aspire, since his sucesses at the north, to the most elevated station, should the post of commander-in-chief become vacant, had lately behaved toward Washington with marked coldness and neglect. A correspondence, highly derogatory to Washington's military character, was carried on between Gates, Mifflin, and Conway. By the indiscretion of the youthful Wilkinson, who talked rather too freely over his cups, at Sterling's quarters, when on his way to Congress with the news of Burgoyne's surrender, a pointed sentence from one of Conway's letters to Gates leaked out, and was communicated by Sterling to Washington, who inclosed it in a note to Conway. Suspecting that Hamilton, during his visit to Albany, had, as he expressed it, "stealingly copied" Conway's letter, Gates demanded to know, in very high terms, by what breach of confidence Washington had become possessed of the extract. When Wilkinson was given as the authority, he changed his ground, and, in an elaborate letter, alleged that the pretended extract was a forgery, and that Conway had written nothing of the sort. Conway's letter, however, was not produced; and to Washington's sarcastic allusion to that fact, and to the manifest discrepancy between his first and second letters, Gates, anxious to hush up the matter, made a very tame and submissive answer.

In the composition of the new Board of war, the influence of the party opposed to Washington became very apparent. Gates was made president of it, and Mifflin a member. The other members were Pickering, who resigned for that purpose his office of adjutant-general, Joseph Trumbull, the late commissary-general, and Richard Peters, secretary of the old Board. Harrison, Washington's secretary, was elected, but declined. In spite of Washington's earnest remonstrances, Conway, promoted over the heads of all the brigadiers to the rank of major-general, was made inspector of the armies of the United States. An attempt was also made, but without success, to gain over La Fayette, by offering him the command of an expedition against Canada. Beside these open measures, calculated to disgust Washington, and to cause him to resign, secret intrigues were resorted to, of a very disreputable character. Anonymous letters, criticising Washington's conduct of the war, were addressed to Patrick Henry, governor of Virginia, and to Laurens, president of Congress; but these gentlemen, in the true spirit of honorable candor, at once inclosed these letters to Washington. One of them, Washington ascribed to Dr. Rush.

When these intrigues became known in the army, they produced among the officers a great burst of indignation. Nor did the idea of a new commander-in-chief find any support in the State Legislatures or the public mind. In spite of losses, the inevitable result of insufficient means, Washington was firmly rooted in the respect and affection of the soldiers and the people, who had not failed to perceive and to appreciate his incomparable qualifications for the station which he held. Seeing how strongly the country and the army were against them, most of the parties concerned in the late project for a new commander-in-chief denied or concealed as much as possible, their participation in it; and the result served at once to evince and to strengthen the hold of Washington on the general confidence. (1778.)

Being presently ordered to the northern department, Conway sent a letter to Congress, in which he complained of ill-treatment in being thus banished from the scene of action, and offered to resign. Very contrary to his intention, he was taken at his word. All his attempts to get the vote reconsidered were in vain. He was wounded soon after in a duel with General Cadwallader, who had accused him of cowardice at the battle of Brandywine; and, supposing himself near his end, he sent a humble apology to Washington. On his recovery he returned to France.

Gates was sent to the Highlands to superintend the new fortifications to be erected there. Both he and Mifflin ceased to act as members of the Board of War, and their place on it was ultimately supplied by two members of Congress, appointed to serve for short periods.

Mifflin obtained leave to join the army again; but the other officers, not liking this intrusion on the part of one who had never held any command in the line, got up a charge against him, which was referred to a court of inquiry, of having mismanaged the quarter-master's department. The accounts and business of that department had been left in a good deal of confusion; but there seems to have been no serious ground of charge against Mifflin. Finding himself so unpopular with the officers, he presently resigned his commission of major-general; but he continued to take an active and leading part in affairs, being presently appointed a member of Congress from Pennsylvania.

The more Congress reflected on the terms of Burgoyne's capitulation, the less satisfactory those terms appeared. The troops of that army, transported to England, and placed in garrison there, would relieve just as many other men for service in America. Some cavils had begun to be raised about an alleged deficiency of cartouch-boxes surrendered, when an impatient letter from Burgoyne furnished a much more plausible pretext. The British general complained that proper accommodations had not been furnished to his officers, and, in the vexation of the moment, incautiously alleged that the Americans had broken the convention. Catching eagerly at this hasty expression, which Congress chose to construe into a repudialion of the treaty by the very officer who had made it, it was resolved to suspend the embarkation of the troops "till a distinct and explicit ratification of the convention of Saratoga shall be properly notified by the court of Great Britain." Nor could any remonstrances or explanations on the part of Burgoyne, obtain any change or modification in a policy founded, indeed, more on considerations of interest than of honor, and for which Burgoyne's letter had but served as a pretext. The transports which had arrived at Boston were ordered to depart. Burgoyne only, with one or two attendants, was suffered to go to England, on parole.

Such was the end of this famous triumph, the capture of Burgoyne, and of the cabal to which it gave a head, which, had it proved successful, would have caused the first important triumph of "Sam" to have been the ruin of his people. Throwing their destinies into the hands of two military adventurers, as it would have done, it requires no prophet to foresee what disastrous consequences must have followed. Even so late as this year, 1778, we find the following significant letter from Washington, which affords a clear glimpse of the trials through which this heroic man was compelled to pass, in keeping together our unfortunate army:—

Extract of a letter from General Washington, to Congress, dated Head Quarters, Springfield, 20th June, 1780.

"The honorable the committee will have informed Congress, from time to time, of the measures which have been judged essential to be adopted for co-operating with the armament expected from France, and of their requisitions to to the States in consequence. What the result of these has been I cannot determine, to my great anxiety, as no answers on the subject of them have been yet received. The period is come when we have every reason to expect the fleet will arrive—and yet, for want of this point of primary consequence, it is impossible for me to form or fix on a system of co-operation—I have no basis to act upon—and, of course, were this generous succour of our ally to arrive, I should find myself in the most awkward, embarrassing and painful situation. The general and the admiral, from the relation in which I stand, as soon as they approach our coast, will require of me a plan of the measures to be pursued; and these ought, of right, to be prepared; but circumstanced as I am, I cannot give them conjectures. From these considerations, I have suggested to the committee, by a letter I had the honor of addressing them yesterday, the indispensable necessity of their writing again to the States, urging them to give immediate and precise information of the measures they have taken and of the result. The interest of the States, the honor and reputation of our councils, the justice and gratitude due our allies, a regard to myself—all require that I should, without delay, be enabled to ascertain and inform them what we can, or cannot undertake. There is a point which ought now to be determined, on which the success of all our future operations may depend, which for want of knowing our prospects, I am altogether at a loss what to do in. For fear of involving the fleet and army of our allies in circumstances which, if not seconded by us, would expose them to material inconvenience and hazard, I shall be compelled to suspend it, and the delay may be fatal to our hopes.

Beside the embarrassments I have mentioned above, and on former occasions, there is another of a very painful and humiliating nature. We have no shirts, from the best inquiry I can make, to distribute to the troops, when the whole are in great want, and when a great part of them are absolutely destitute of any at all. Their situation too with respect to summer overalls, I fear, is not likely to be much better. There are a great many on hand, it is said, in Springfield, but so indifferent in their quality as to be scarcely worth the expense of transportation and delivery. For the troops to be without clothing at any time, is highly injurious to the service and distressing to our feelings; but the want will be more peculiarly mortifying when they come to act with those of our allies. If it is possible, I have no doubt immediate measures will be taken to relieve their distress. It is also most sincerely to be wished that there could be some supplies of clothing furnished for the officers.

There are a great many whose condition is really miserable still, and in some instances it is the case with almost whole State lines. It would be well for their own sakes, and for the public good, if they could be furnished. When our friends come to co-operate with us, they will not be able to go on the common routine of duty, and if they should, they must be held, from their appearance, in low estimation.

What a commentary does this manly letter furnish upon the petty and venal injustice of his cotemporary foes, toward one of the greatest of all the characters of history!

CHAPTER XXXIX.

Sketch of Colonel Daniel Morgan--The Non-resistant Principles of the Quakers—Its consequences about these times.

It is impossible for us to continue a detailed account of the succeeding Revolutionary events. These are too familiar to the general reader, to render their relation necessary, even if our space admitted of such dilation. Our object has been, to reproduce such characteristic memorials of the prominent events in the history of "Sam," as—being likely, from their antiquity, to be lost—renew also, by their cotemporary freshness, our memory of the true spirit of that early time, which is likely to prove so necessary to this degenerate period. The following sketch of that noble old patriarch of *American* heroes, Daniel Morgan, has an unction in it, which might serve to regenerate a thousand modern Tories.

DANIEL MORGAN.

From the "Custis Recollections and Private Memoirs of the Life and Character of Washington."

The outposts of the two armies were very near to each other, when the American commander, desirous of obtaining particular information respecting the positions of his adversary, summoned the famed leader of the riflemen, Colonel Daniel Morgan, to headquarters.

It was night, and the chief was alone. After his usual polite, yet reserved and dignified salutation, Washington remarked: "I have sent for you, Colonel Morgan, to intrust to your courage and sagacity, a reconnoiter of the enemy's lines, with a view to your ascertaining correctly, the position of their newly-constructed redoubts; also of the encampments of the British troops that have lately arrived, and those of their Hessian auxiliaries. Select, sir, an officer, a non-commissioned officer, and about twenty picked men, and, under cover of the night, proceed, but with all possible caution, get as near as you can, and learn all you can, and by day dawn retire, and make your report to headquarters. But mark me, Colonel Morgan, mark me well, on no account whatever, are you to bring on any skirmishing with the enemy; if discovered, make a speedy retreat; let nothing induce you to fire a single shot; I repeat, sir, that no force of circumstances will excuse the discharge of a single rifle on your part, and for the extreme preciseness of these orders, permit me to say, that I have my reasons." Filling two glasses with wine, the general continued: "And now, Colonel Morgan, we will drink a good night, and success to your enterprise." Morgan quaffed the wine, smacked his lips, and assuring his excellency that his orders should be punctually obeyed, left the tent of the commander-in-chief.

Charmed at being chosen as the executive officer of a daring enterprise, the leader of the woodsmen repaired to his quarters, and calling for Gabriel Long, his favorite captain, ordered him to detach a sergeant and twenty prime fellows, who being mustered, and ordered to lay on their arms, ready at a moment's warning, Morgan and Long stretched their manly forms before the watch-fire, to await the going down of the moon, the signal for departure.

A little after midnight, and while the rays of the setting moon still faintly glimmered in the western horizon, "Up, sergeant," cried Long, "stir up your men," and twenty athletic figures were upon their feet in a moment. "Indian file, march," and away all sprung, with the quick, yet light and stealthy step of the woodsmen. They reached the enemy's lines, crawled up so close to the pickets of the Hessians, as to inhale the odor of their pipes, discovered, by the newly turned-up earth, the positions of the redoubts, and by the numerous tents that dotted the field for "many a rood around," and shone dimly amid the night haze, the encampments of the British and German reinforcements, and, in short, performed their perilous duty without the slightest discovery; and pleased, prepared to retire, just as chanticleer, from a neighboring farmhouse, was "bidding salutation to the morn."

The adventurous party reached a small eminence, at some distance from the British camp, and commanding an extensive prospect over the adjoining country. Here Morgan halted, to give his men a little rest, before taking up his line of march for the American outposts. Scarcely had they thrown themselves on the grass, when they perceived, issuing from the enemy's advanced pickets, a body of horse, commanded by an officer, and proceeding along the road that led directly by the spot where the riflemen had halted. No spot could be better chosen for an ambuscade, for there were rocks and ravines, and also scrubby oaks, that grew thickly on the eminence by which the road we have just mentioned, passed, at not exceeding a hundred yards.

"Down, boys, down," cried Morgan, as the horse approached, nor did the clansmen of the Black Rhoderick, disappear more promptly amid their native heather, than did Morgan's woodsmen in the present instance, each to his tree or rock. "Lie close there, my lads, till we see what these fellows are about."

Meantime, the horsemen had gained the hight, and the officer, dropping the rein on his charger's neck, with a spy-glass reconnoitered the American lines. The troops closed up their files, and were either cherishing the noble animals they rode, adjusting their equipments, or gazing upon the surrounding scenery, now fast brightening in the beams of a rising sun.

Morgan looked at Long, and Long upon his superior, while the riflemen, with panting chests and sparkling eyes, were only awaiting the signal from their officers, "to let the ruin fly."

At length, the martial ardor of Morgan overcame his prudence and sense of military subordination. Forgetful of consequences, reckless of everything but his enemy, now within his grasp, he waved his hand, and loud and sharp rang the report of the rifles amid the surrounding echoes. At pointblank distance, the certain and deadly aim of the Hunting Shirts of the revolutionary army is too well known to history to need remark at this time of day. In this instance we have to record, the effects of the fire of the riflemen were tremendous. Of the horsemen, some had fallen to rise no more, while their liberated chargers rushed wildly over the adjoining plain; others wounded, but entangled with their stirrups, were dragged by the furious animals expiringly along; while the very few who were unscathed, spurred hard to regain the shelter of the British lines.

While the smoke yet canopied the scene of slaughter, and the picturesque forms of the woodsmen appeared among the foliage, as they were reloading their pieces, the colossal figure of Morgan stood apart. He seemed the very genius of war, as gloomily he contemplated the havoc his order had made. He spoke not, he moved not, but looked as one absorbed in an intensity of thought. The martial shout, with which he was wont to cheer his comrades in the hour of combat, was hushed, the shell* from which he had blown full many a note of battle and of triumph, on the fields of Saratoga, hung idly by his side; no order was given to spoil the slain; the arms and equipments for which there was always a bounty from Congress, the shirts, for which there was so much need in that, the sorest period of our country's privation, all, all were abandoned, as with an abstracted air, and a voice struggling for utterance, Morgan suddenly turning to his captain, exclaimed: "Long, to the camp, march." The favorite captain obeyed, the riflemen with trailed arms fell into file, and Long and his party soon disappeared, but not before the hardy fellows had exchanged opinions on the strange termination of the late affair. And they agreed, *nem. con.*, that their colonel was tricked, (conjured,) or assuredly, after such a fire as they had just given the enemy, such an emptying of saddles, and such a squandering of the troopers, he would not have ordered his poor rifle boys from the field, without so much as a few shirts or pairs of stockings

---

* Morgan's riflemen were generally in the advance, skirmishing with the light troops of the enemy, or annoying his flanks; the regiment was thus much divided into detachments, and dispersed over a very wide field of action. Morgan was in the habit of using a conch-shell frequently, during the heat of the battle, with which he would blow a loud and war-like blast. This, he said, was to inform his boys that he was still alive, and from many parts of the field was beholding their prowess; and like the celebrated sea-warrior of another hemisphere's last signal, was expecting that "every man would do his duty."

being divided among them. "Yes," said a tall, lean, and swarthy-looking fellow, an Indian hunter, from the frontier, as he carefully placed his moccasined feet in the footprints of his file leader, "Yes, my lads, it stands to reason, our colonel is tricked."

Morgan followed slowly on the trail of his men. The full force of his military guilt had rushed upon his mind, even before the reports of his rifles had ceased to echo in the neighboring forests. He became more and more convinced of the enormity of his offense, as with dull and measured strides, he pursued his solitary way, and thus he soliloquized:

"Well, Daniel Morgan, you have done for yourself. Broke, sir, broke to a certainty. You may go home, sir, to the plow; your sword will be of no further use to you. Broke, sir, nothing can save you; and there is an end of Colonel Morgan. Fool, fool—by a single act of madness, thus to destroy the earnings of so many toils, and many a hard-fought battle. You are broke, sir, and there is an end of Colonel Morgan."

To disturb this reverie, there suddenly appeared at full speed, the aid-de-camp, the Mercury of the field, who, reining up, accosted the colonel with, "I am ordered, Colonel Morgan, to ascertain whether the firing just now heard, proceeded from your detachment." "It did sir," replied Morgan, sourly. "Then, colonel," continued the aid, "I am further ordered to require your immediate attendance upon his excellency, who is approaching." Morgan bowed, and the aid, wheeling his charger, galloped back to rejoin his chief.

The gleams of the morning sun upon the sabres of the horse guard, announced the arrival of the dreaded commander—that being who inspired with a degree of awe, every one who approached him. With a stern, yet dignified composure, Washington addressed the military culprit: "Can it be possible, Colonel Morgan, that my aid-de-camp has informed me aright? Can it be possible, after the orders you received last evening, that the firing we have heard proceeded from your detachment? Surely, sir, my orders were so explicit as not to be easily misunderstood." Morgan was brave, but it has been often, and justly too, observed, that the man never was born of a woman, who could approach the great Washington, and not feel a degree of awe and veneration for his presence. Morgan quailed for a moment before the stern, yet just displeasure of his chief, till arousing all his energies to the effort, he uncovered and replied: "Your excellency's orders were perfectly well understood, and agreeably to the same, I proceeded with a select party to reconnoiter the enemy's lines by night. We succeeded even beyond our expectations, and I was returning to headquarters to make my report, when, having halted a few minutes to rest the men, we discovered a party of horse coming out from the enemy's lines. They came up immediately to the spot where we lay concealed in the brushwood. There they halted, and gathered up together like a flock of partridges, affording me so tempting an opportunity of annoying my enemy, that, may it please your excellency, flesh and blood could not refrain."

On this rough, yet frank, bold, and manly explanation, a smile was observed to pass over the countenances of several of the general's suite. The chief remained unmoved, when, waving his hand, he continued: "Colonel Morgan, you will retire to your quarters, there to await further orders." Morgan bowed, and the military cortege rode on to the inspection of the outposts.

Arrived at his quarters, Morgan threw himself upon his hard couch, and gave himself up to reflections upon the events which had so lately and so rapidly succeeded each other. He was aware that he had sinned past all hopes of forgiveness. Within twenty-four hours he had fallen from the command of a regiment, and being an especial favorite with the general, to be, what?—a disgraced and broken soldier. Condemned to retire from scenes of glory, the darling passions of his heart—forever to abandon the "fair fields of fighting men," and in obscurity to drag out the remnant of a wretched existence, neglected and forgotten. And then his rank, so hardly, so nobly won, with all his "blushing honors," acquired in the march across the frozen wilderness of the Kennebec, the storming of the lower town, and the gallant and glorious combats of Saratoga.

The hours dragged gloomily away; night came, but with it no rest for the troubled spirit of poor Morgan. The drums and fifes merrily sounded the soldier's dawn, and the sun arose, giving "promise of a good day." And to many within the circuit of that widely-extended camp, did its genial beams give hope, and joy, and gladness, while it cheered not with a single ray the despairing leader of the woodsmen.

About ten o'clock, the orderly on duty reported the arrival of an officer of the staff, from headquarters, and Lieutenant Colonel Hamilton, the favorite aid of the commander-in-chief, entered the markee. "Be seated," said Morgan; "I know your errand, so be short, my dear fellow, and put me out of my misery at once. I know that I am arrested; 'tis a matter of course. Well, there is my sword; but surely, his excellency honors me, indeed, in these last moments of my military existence, when he sends for my sword by his favorite aid, and my most esteemed friend. Ah, my dear Hamilton, if you knew what I had suffered since the cursed horse came out to tempt me to ruin."

Hamilton, about whose strikingly-intelligent countenance there always lurked a playful smile, now observed: "Colonel Morgan, his excellency has ordered me to—" "I knew it," interrupted Morgan, "to bid me prepare for trial! Guilty, sir, guilty past all doubt. But then, (recollecting himself,) perhaps my services might plead—nonsense; against the disobedience of a positive order? no, no, it is all over with me; Hamilton, there is an end of your old friend and of Colonel Morgan." The agonized spirit of our hero then mounted a pitch of enthusiasm, as he exclaimed: "But my country will remember my services, and the British and Hessians will remember me too, for though I may be far away, my brave comrades will do their duty, and Morgan's riflemen be, as they always have been, a terror to the enemy."

The noble, the generous-souled Hamilton could no longer bear to witness the struggles of the brave unfortunate; he called out: "Hear me, my dear colonel, only promise to hear me for one moment, and I will tell you all." "Go on, sir," replied Morgan, despairingly, "go on." "Then," continued the aid-de-camp, "you must know that the commanders of regiments dine with his excellency to-day." "What of that?" again interrupted Morgan; "what has that to do with me, a prisoner, and—" "No, no," exclaimed Hamilton, "no prisoner; a once offending, but now forgiven soldier; my orders are to invite you to dine with his excellency to-day at three o'clock, precisely. Yes, my brave and good friend, Colonel Morgan, you still are, and likely long to be, the valued and famed commander of the rifle regiment."

Morgan sprang from the camp-bed on which he was sitting, and seized the hand of the little great man in his giant grasp, wrung and wrung until the aid-de-camp literally struggled to get free, then exclaimed, "Am I in my senses? but I know you, Hamilton—you are too noble a fellow to sport with the feelings of an old soldier." Hamilton assured his friend that all was true, and, kissing his hand as he mounted his horse, bade the now delighted colonel remember three o'clock, and to be careful not to disobey a second time, galloped to the headquarters.

Morgan entered the pavilion of the commander in chief as it was fast filling with officers, all of whom, after paying their respects to the general, filed off to give a cordial squeeze of the hand to the commander of the rifle regiment, and to whisper in his ear words of congratulation. The cloth removed, Washington bade his guests fill their glasses, and gave his only, his unvarying toast—the toast of the days of trial, the toast of the evening of his "time-honored" life, amid the shades of Mount Vernon—"All our friends." Then, with his usual old-fashioned politeness, he drank to each guest by name. When he came to "Colonel Morgan, your good health, sir," a thrill ran through the manly frame of the gratified and again favorite soldier, while every eye in the pavilion was turned upon him. At an early hour the company broke up, and Morgan had a perfect escort of officers to accompany him to his quarters, all anxious to congratulate him upon his happy restoration to rank and favor, all pleased to assure him of their esteem for his person and services.

And often in his after-life did Morgan reason upon the events which we have transmitted to Americans and their posterity, and he would say, "What could the unusual clemency of the commander-in-chief towards so insubordinate a soldier as I was, mean? Was it that my attacking my enemy wherever I could find him, and the attack being crowned with success, should plead in bar of the disobedience of a positive order? Certainly not. Was it that Washington well knew I loved, nay, adored him above all human beings? That knowledge would not have weighed a feather in the scale of his military justice. In short, the whole affair is explained in five words: It was my first offense."

The clemency of Washington to the first offense, preserved to the army of the revolution one of its most valued and effective soldiers, and had its reward in little more than two years from the date of our narrative, when Brigadier General Morgan consummated his own fame, and shed an undying lustre on the arms of his country, by the glorious and ever-memorable victory of the Cowpens.

Nearly twenty years more had rolled away, and our hero, like most of his companions, had beaten his sword into a plowshare, and was enjoying, in the midst of a domestic circle, the evening of a varied and eventful life. When advanced in years, and infirm, Major General Morgan was called to the supreme legislature of his country, as a representative from the State of Virginia. It was at this period that the author of these memoirs had the honor and happiness of an interview with the old general, which lasted for several days. And the veteran was most kind and communicative to one, who, hailing from the immediate family of the venerated chief, found a ready and warm welcome to the heart of Morgan. And many and most touching reminiscences of the days of trial were related by the once famed leader of the woodsmen, which were eagerly devoured and carefully treasured by their youthful and delighted listener, in a memory of no ordinary power.

And it was there the unlettered Morgan, a man bred amid the scenes of danger and hardihood that distinguished the frontier warfare, with little book knowledge, but gifted by nature with a strong and discriminating mind, paid to the fame and memory of the father of our country, a more just, more magnificent tribute than, in our humble judgment, has emanated from the thousand and one efforts of the best and brightest geniuses of the age. General Morgan spoke of the necessity of Washington to the army of the revolution, and the success of the struggle for independence. He said, "We had officers of great military talents, as, for instance, Greene and others; we had officers of the most consummate courage and enterprising spirit, as, for instance, Wayne and others. One was yet necessary, to guide, direct, and animate the whole, and it pleased Almighty God to send that one in the person of GEORGE WASHINGTON."

The modern tories, to whom we alluded in introducing this fine sketch, will find something also, in the subjoined papers to freshen their memories, in regard to who were most justly regarded as tories of the olden time:—

BRITISH IN PHILADELPHIA.

A much-valued friend has placed in the hands of the editor, a large volume of papers, containing the correspondence of Brigadier-General Lacey, of Pennsylvania, who commanded the Militia stationed on the east bank of the Schuylkill, to watch the motions of the enemy, and prevent his obtaining supplies.

General Lacey's orders to his scouting parties, March 9, 1778:—"If your parties should meet with any people going to market, or any persons whatever going to the city, and they endeavor to make their escape, you will order your men to fire upon the villains. You will leave such on the roads—their bodies and their marketing lying together. This I wish you to execute on the first offenders you meet, that they may be a warning to others."

General Washington to General Lacey, dated at Valley Forge, 20th March, 1778:—Sunday next being the time on which the Quakers hold one of their general meetings, a number of that society will probably be attempting to go into Philadelphia. This is an intercourse that we should by all means endeavor to interrupt, as the plans settled at these meetings are of the most pernicious tendency.* I would

* I was in great doubt—whether I ought to publish or suppress this letter—but, on reflection, have thought best to insert it. It must be admitted that a great majority of the Quakers in Pennsylvania, were "well inclined" to the British, and some of them went great lengths out of the rules of their profession, to aid and comfort the enemy of their country; others by adhering to those rules and refusing to take any part in the contest, even by the payment of taxes, were improperly suspected of disaffection, when in fact they were only neutral, refusing to have anything to do with the war; a few, however, laid aside their testimony against fighting, and contended gallantly for freedom. Persons of this religious persuasion in some other States, were sincerely attached to the cause of Independence, and

therefore have you dispose of your parties in such a manner as will most probably fall in with these people, and if you should, and any of them should be mounted on horses fit for draught, or the service of light dragoons, I desire they may be taken from them, and sent over to the quarter-master-general. Any such are not to be considered as the property of the parties who may seize them, as in other cases. Communicate the above orders to any of the officers who may command scouting parties on your side of the Schuylkill."

[General Lacey, in reply, says he had ordered out his horse to stop the Quakers, with orders, "if they refuse to stop when hailed, to fire into them, and leave their bodies lying in the road."]

This is the commentary of Niles, of the old *Register*, who published this correspondence nearly thirty-five years ago, and for the first time, but we would beg leave to add, as a comment upon his apology, the following extract from the speech of a prominent Revolutionary leader, upon the floor of the Continental Congress. It is taken from his own columns:—

I have excluded those from the privileges of free white inhabitants in the several States, who refuse to take up arms in defense of the confederacy—a measure, in my opinion, perfectly just. It is said, example before precept. Let the Quakers take shelter under any text in Scripture they please—the best they can find is but a far-fetched implication in their favor. However, had their precept been in more positive terms, I think I have an example at hand, capable of driving them from such a cover. We read that "Jesus went into the temple of God, and cast out all them that sold and bought in the temple, and overturned the tables of the money-changers." Here we see the arm of the flesh raised up, and a degree of hostile violence exercised, sufficient to the end in view. And shall it be said, violence is not justifiable? Did not God command Moses to number "all that were able to go forth in war, in Israel?"

---

did all they consistently could do to assist the whigs. A stoppage of the intercourse with Philadelphia, at the time, was indubitably necessary and proper—but General Washington was misinformed, I apprehend, when he spoke of the "plans" settled at the "meetings" of the Quakers—whatever they may have done as *individuals*, their "*meetings*" must have passed without the adoption of any plans of a political nature—for such things are not suffered to be mentioned in them.

Did not Moses, by the Divine order, send twelve thousand men to cut off the Midianites. And, although "they slew all the males," were they not reprehended for having "saved all the women alive?" Did not the Almighty command the children of Israel, that when they had passed into Canaan "then they should drive out all the inhabitants of the land from before them?" Did not Moses direct that when the people were "come nigh unto the battle," the priests should encourage them, declaring that the Lord their God was with them "to *fight* for them against their enemies?" And yet the Quakers have sagaciously found out a few words which, by implication, they contend restrain from doing *now*, what God *then* commanded as just. *The grand principles of moral rectitude are eternal.* Dare the Quakers contend that the myriads who have drawn the sword since the commencement of the Christian era, are damned for having done so? And unless they maintain this position, they seem to have no reasonable excuse for their creed and conduct. They seem to have forgot that it is written "how hardly shall they that have riches enter into kingdom of God!" Are there any people on the face of the earth more diligent after riches than the Quakers? We, in this time of calamity, know it to our cost. Without doubt, there are many valuable men of that sect; men of that persuasion are very good citizens in time of peace, but it is their principle in time of war I condemn. Is there a Quaker who will not bring his action for trespass? Is not this an opposition to force? Have they forgot their principles of meekness and non-resistance? The great Lord Lyttleton, in his *Dialogues of the Dead,* tells us "it is blasphemy to say that any folly could come from the fountain of wisdom. Whatever is inconsistent with the great laws of nature, and with the necessary state of human society, cannot be inspired by the Divinity. Self-defense is as necessary to nations as to men. And shall men particularly have a right which nations have not? True religion is the perfection of reason. Fanaticism is the disgrace, the destruction of reason." Than all this, nothing could be more just, certain, and evident. Can those men reasonably claim an equal participation in civil rights, who, under any pretence whatsoever, will not assist in defending them? Shall there be a people maintained in the possession of their riches by the blood and labor of other men? Are not the Quakers, some few excepted, the most inveterate enemies to the independence of America? Have they not openly taken part with those in arms against us? I consider them not only as a dead weight upon our hands, but as a dangerous body in our bosom, and I would, therefore, gladly be rid of them. I almost wish to "drive out all such inhabitants of the land from before us." The Canaanites knew not God. But the Quakers say they know him; and yet, according to the idea of Lord Lyttleton, would have gross folly and injustice to proceed from the fountain of wisdom and equity. I entertain these sentiments with a conscience perfectly at ease on this point. If such treatment shall be termed persecution, the conscientious Quakers can never take it amiss, when they recollect it is "blessed are they that are persecuted for Christ's sake." I do not consider this as such a persecution. But if they should, can they be displeased at being placed in a situation to be blessed? And I would lay it down as a truth, that whoever of that sect should be offended at such treatment, would deserve to be expelled from our society, as the buyers, sellers, and money-changers were cast out of the temple. I am not afraid of any resentment, when it is my duty to act in behalf of the rights and interests of America. I trust I fully demonstrated this resolution when, on the 25th of April, 1776, I had the honor, in the supreme seat of justice, to make the first public declaration in America, that my countrymen owed no allegiance to the king of Great Britain.

CHAPTER XL.

The Treaty with France—The progress of the War, North and South—The Cowpens—Yorktown—Surrender of Cornwallis—Letter from General Washington.

We will now proceed with a rapid summary of the concluding events of the great war.

The important treaties with France, of commerce and defensive alliance, which had been so long and eagerly sought for, were the first events of consequence which now ensued. The importance of these treaties, however, except so far as they finally served to strengthen our now rapidly declining financial credit, the historian of "Sam" thinks to have been habitually overrated by local and provincial historians; seeing that the very basis of their formation was plainly avowed to rest upon the fact, that he had already exhibited his full ability to take care of himself. That he had already demonstrated himself, by virtue of his mighty thews and sinews, to be the master of his own destiny, afforded, no doubt, to Johnny Crapeaud, a mighty opportunity for a grand display of magnanimity, in helping him to a place of national recognition, in which no leaven of ancient animosity was, of course, mingled, to disflavor the generosity of the patronage!

That France had hated England from the beginning, was necessarily, to the modern foes of "Sam," no reason why France loved America less! Her disinterestedness in sending us the cast-of military adventurers of Europe, who crowded her capital, and of whom she was only too happy to be rid, and who only managed to annoy Congress and Washington, with endless importunities for their precious services, which were never rendered, except in second rate skirmishes, although they had unanimously consented to fight his battles for him, in the subordinate positions of prepaid and overpaid Generals, Brigadiers, etc!

Be this as it may, for these evidences of disinterestedness, "Sam" has, however, for seventy-nine years since, shown himself duly or unduly, so scrupulously grateful, as to have allowed to all foreigners greater franchises than he has ever permitted even to his own children. He has given them most of his offices, set them to teaching most of his schools, with professorships and gratuities of every imaginable grade and class, and all because he had three or four honorable and upright servitors among them, during the dark hours of his tribulation.

But it unluckily appears, that this excessive gratitude on the part of "Sam," instead of covering them with humility, and rendering them grateful for largess bestowed with a magnanimous hand, has filled them with the insolence which has always accompanied the reaction of servility, and caused them to assume the airs of masters, and even sovereign dictators.

But "Sam" has lost patience at last, and his mighty arm is now raised over them in wrath, and with one haughty finger pointing at the pillory, he brandishes aloft the whips of his electric threatenings above their cowering backs, and gives them to understand, in a voice that shakes the continent, "hence, to your kennels, hounds! I am master here! disorganizers, tories, insolent and ungrateful presumers upon a precious magnanimity, which you were too much born-serfs in your own pageant-saddled and king-ridden lands to comprehend, learn to respect my own born children, and know your places! Know that ye are but fugitive-slaves, among a people of sovereign freemen, and only tolerated on good behavior, until a sufficient period of probation has shown you to be worthy the privileges of citizenship!" Yes, the time has come for the peremptory rebuke of this presuming arrogance, against the annoyance of which, even during this early period of the Revolution, the lofty and patient Washington found it necessary to write several complaining letters to the Continental Congress, beseeching them to cease giving any further encouragements to these clamorous and greedy cormorants, who incessantly beset his marquee, and worried him with their unheard of demands!

So great had this evil at this time become, that Congress thought it necessary to recall their foolish and imprudent agent at Paris, Dean, and force him to give a stern account of his conduct, for having sent over such a swarm of impudent beggars, to assail every department of the Goverment with their importunate clamors. And the example of such beggar lazzaroni as they then complained of, has been very successfully followed up to the present day.

But it is time for us to return to our proposed hasty outline. The French fleet, under D'Estaing, had now arrived. The British found it necessary to withdraw from Philadelphia. When the evacuation became known to the American army, Washington determined upon immediate pursuit; and every one will remember the indecisive battle of Monmouth which followed, and the either treacherous or dastardly conduct on the field, of Lee, whom Washington, in his irritation, impetuously denounced as a coward, when he met him in full retreat, with the whole American advance.

The conduct of Lee has been much discussed, *pro* and *con*, but we think that no one who will take the trouble to remember his precedents, will for a moment delude himself with the supposition that Lee's conduct was the result of cowardice. Yet we have always thought he ought to have been court-martialed and cashiered on the spot, or else strung as high as Arnold would have been hung, had he been caught; for his conduct was clearly the result of personal jealousy of Washington, and a desire to defeat a movement which he had opposed in a council of war, which preceded the pursuit.

Had he succeeded in effecting this "masterly inactive" policy of his, and the British army been permitted to escape without harrassment or loss, it would, in the then existing conditions of bitter jealousy and intrigue against Washington, have greatly shocked the as yet unshaken confidence of the sagacious Congress, which carefully overlooked, with penetrating vision, the whole field of operations in their favorite servant and general, Washington; in which event, Master Lee, who was second in command, might have naturally looked forward to the eagle plume of chieftainship.

This Congress affords, perhaps, the only instance in which a legislative body has, with just discrimination, supervised the operations of a long and perilous war, without rashly entrusting too great powers to its generals, or embarrassing them with impertinent interference. Such bodies usually fail in one extreme or the other.

But the hand of " Sam," under God, was over this body, than whom, a wiser and nobler assemblage history does not record to have ever assembled before, for executive purposes.

The Indian wars, which now ravaged the Western and Northern Frontiers, now resulted in the savage massacre of Wyoming, which was promptly followed by a proportionate retribution against our quondam friends, the Six Nations, and the prompt return of several tribes to their ancient allegiance. The war, then transferred to the South, was attended with serious calamities to our cause. Savannah taken, and Georgia subdued, North and South Carolina were reduced to extremities.

In the meantime, King's Ferry, on the Hudson, was occupied by the British; Stoney Point surprised; and Spain takes a hand against America in the war—and John Paul Jones, the Americanized Scotchman, performed Herculean prodigies of valor on the sea. Charleston soon after capitulated, and with it came the submission of the State to British rule.

A savage partisan warfare now arose, and the gallants Marion and Sumpter, began to be heard of, through the indomitable prowess of their surprising feats. The disastrous rout at Camden, and the treachery of Arnold, with the trial and execution of André, followed in close succession. The gallant Greene, appointed to the command in the south, to take the place of the renegade Gates, soon caused a change in the aspect of affairs in this direction.

The sharp and close fighting of our backwoods' men at the battle of King's Mountain, somewhat revived the spirits of the South. A quarrel between Great Britain and Holland, which occurred about this time, tended somewhat to the embarrassment of the former.

The financial embarrassments and depreciation of Continental currency, had now about reached its climax, and the disaffection of the army, and the difficulty of keeping it together, became every day more great. Several regiments rebelled, and many left the field entirely, for want of pay.

The battle of the "Cowpens," on the borders of the Carolinas, in which the redoubtable conch-shell of the burley Morgan, carried terror to the craven heart of the bloody Tarleton, and set the lordly Cornwallis on his "pegs," into the hasty trot of retreat, at the cost of a great loss of stores and baggage—roused up the ever-vigilant Greene; and although Cornwallis had been discreetly compelled to reduce his whole army to the condition of a light infantry corps, for the purpose of pursuing the discreet retreat of the victorious Morgan, Greene was enabled to effect an immediate junction with Morgan, who had managed to effect his escape, owing to the sudden rise of waters which prevented the pursuit of his enemies.

The battle of Gilford Court-house, which now follows, and may be called a drawn battle, (though attended with great loss to the British, and compelling Cornwallis to retire,) was very inspiriting to our cause.

Green was everywhere successful. The petulant and irritable D'Estaing had in the meantime returned with his fleet from the West Indies. Cornwallis, who had finally reached Virginia on his fourth retreat, found himself rapidly involved in the inextricable meshes, from which he never finally escaped.

The details of the subsequent movements of Washington and Greene, one moving suddenly from the north and the other from the south, are too well known to require any greater detail here. It is sufficient that now came the great climax of our struggle. Washington, Greene, and the Count De Grasse, who had now assumed the command of the French force, by a long concerted movement, as we shall proceed to show, now unexpectedly closed upon the army of the British lord, who found himself, to his great dismay, beleaguered from all sides, in the paltry village of Yorktown.

As our purpose has been to add new light to old and well-known facts, rather than to follow slavishly old records of familiar details, we append the following ancient and authentic documents concerning this great event. We give first the following document, containing a private letter written by Washington in 1778.

☞ *It has been controverted, whether the capture of General Cornwallis was the result of a plan preconcerted between General Washington and Count De Grasse: or rather, whether the arrival of the Count in the Chesapeake, was predetermined and expected by General Washington, and consequently all the preparations to attack New York, a mere finesse to deceive the enemy: or whether the real intention was against New York, and the siege of Yorktown planned upon the unexpected arrival of the French fleet, in the Bay. The following letter will set the matter in its true light.*—[Carey's Museum.

MOUNT VERNON, *July* 31, 1788.

SIR—I duly received your letter of the 14th inst., and can only answer you briefly, and generally from memory—that a combined operation of the land and naval forces of France, in America, for the year 1781, was preconcerted the year before; that the point of attack was not absolutely agreed upon,* because it could not be foreknown where the enemy would be most susceptible of impression; and because we (having the command of the water, with sufficient means of conveyance) could transport ourselves to any spot with the greatest celerity; that it was determined by me, nearly twelve months beforehand, at all hazards, to give out, and cause it to be believed, by the highest military, as well as civil officers, that New York was the destined place of attack, for the important purpose of inducing the Eastern and Middle States to make greater exertions in furnishing specific supplies, than they otherwise would have done, as well as for the interesting purpose of rendering the enemy less prepared elsewhere; that, by these means, and these alone, artillery, boats, stores, and provisions, were in seasonable preparation to move with the utmost rapidity to any part of the continent; for the difficulty consisted more in providing, than knowing how to apply the military apparatus. That, before the arrival of the Count De Grasse, it was the fixed determination *to strike the enemy in the most vulnerable quarter*, so as to insure success with moral certainty, as our affairs were then in the most ominous train imaginable; that New York was

* Because it would be easy for Count De Grasse in good time before his departure from the West Indies, to give notice, by express, at what place he could most conveniently first touch, to receive advice.

thought to be beyond our efforts, and consequently, that the only hesitation that remained, was between an attack upon the British army in Virginia, and that in Charleston; and finally, that, by the intervention of several communications, and some incidents which can not be detailed in a letter, the hostile post in Virginia, from being a *provisional and strongly expected*, became the *definitive and certain object* of the campaign.

I only add, that it never was in contemplation to attack New York, unless the garrison should first have been so far degarnished, to carry on the Southern operations, as to render our success in the siege of that place, as infallible as any future military event can ever be. For I repeat it, and dwell upon it again, some splendid advantage (whether upon a larger or smaller scale was almost immaterial) was so essentially necessary, to revive the expiring hope and languid exertions of the country, at the crisis in question, that I never would have consented to embark in any enterprise, wherein, from the most rational plan and accurate calculation, the favorable issue should not have appeared to my view as a ray of light. The failure of an attempt against the posts of the enemy, could, in no other possible situation during the war, have been so fatal to our cause.

That much trouble was taken, and finesse used, to misguide and bewilder Sir Henry Clinton, in regard to the real object, by fictitious communications, as well as by making a deceptive provision of ovens, forage, and boats in the neighborhood, is certain; nor were less pains taken to deceive our own army; for I always conceived where the imposition does not completely take place at home, it would never sufficiently succeed abroad.

Your desire of obtaining truth is very laudable; I wish I had more leisure to gratify it, as I am equally solicitous the undisguised verity should be known. Many circumstances will unavoidably be misconceived and misrepresented. Notwithstanding most of the papers which may properly be deemed official, are preserved, yet the knowledge of innumerable things of a more delicate and secret nature, is confined to the perishable remembrance of some few of the present generation.

With esteem, I am, sir, your most obedient humble servant,

GEORGE WASHINGTON.

We will now give a graphic account of the ceremonies attending the surrender of Yorktown.

THE SURRENDER AT YORKTOWN.

From the *Richmond Compiler*, of April 10, 1818.

As every incident connected with our Revolutionary history, is interesting to the great mass of the people, I shall solicit a niche in your paper, to answer an inquiry in a late *Compiler*, concerning the surrender of the British army, at Yorktown, Virginia; and hope that your readers will experience the same pleasure in reading the account, that I enjoy in the narration.

"At two o'clock in the evening, October 19th, 1781, the British army, led by General O'Hara, marched out of its lines, with colors cased, and drums beating a British march.

"It will be seen in the sequel, that O'Hara, and *not* Cornwallis, surrendered the British army to the allied forces of France and America. In this affair, Lord Cornwallis seemed to have lost all his former magnanimity and firmness of character—he sunk beneath the pressure of his misfortunes, and, for a moment, gave his soul up to chagrin and sorrow.

"The road through which they marched, was lined with spectators, French and Americans. On one side, the commander-in-chief, surrounded by his suite and the American staffs, took his station; on the other side, opposite to him, was the Count de Rochambeau, in like manner attended. The captive army approached, moving slowly in column, with grace and precision.

"Universal silence was observed amidst the vast concourse, and the utmost decency prevailed, exhibiting in demeanor, an awful sense of the vicissitudes of human life, mingled with commiseration for the unhappy. The head of the column approached the commander-in-chief; O'Hara, mistaking the circle, turned to that on his left, for the purpose of paying his respects to the commander-in-chief, and requesting further orders; when quickly discovering his error, with embarrassment in his countenance, he flew across the road, and advanced up to Washington, asked pardon for his mistake, apologized for the *absence of Lord Cornwallis*, and begged to know his further pleasure.

"The General, feeling his embarrassment, relieved it by referring him, with much politeness, to General Lincoln for his government. Returning to the head of the column, it again moved, under the guidance of Lincoln, to the field selected for the conclusion of the ceremony.

"Every eye was turned, searching for the British commander-in-chief, anxious to look at a man, heretofore so much their dread. All were disappointed.

"Cornwallis held himself *back* from the humiliating scene; obeying sensations which his great character ought to have stifled. He had been unfortunate, not from any false step, or deficiency of exertion on his part, but from the infatuated policy of his superior, and the united power of his enemy brought to bear upon him alone. There was nothing with which he could reproach himself; there was nothing with which he could reproach his brave and faithful army; why not then *appear* at its head in the day of misfortune, as he had always done in the day of triumph?

"The British general in this instance, deviated from his usual line of conduct, dimming the splendor of his long and brilliant career.

"Thus ended the important co-operation of the allied forces. Great was the joy diffused throughout our infant empire."

I can not end this interesting detail, as recorded by Henry Lee, without giving you his panegyric on the father of our country:

"This wide acclaim of joy and of confidence, as rare as sincere, sprung not only from the conviction that our signal success would bring in its train the blessings of peace, so wanted by our wasted country, and from the splendor with which it encircled our national name, but from the endearing reflection that the mighty exploit had been achieved by our faithful, beloved Washington. We had seen him struggling throughout the war, with inferior force, against the best troops of England, assisted by her powerful navy; surrounded by difficulties, oppressed by want, never dismayed, never appalled, *never despairing* of the commonwealth.

"We have seen him renouncing his fame as a soldier, his safety as a man, in his unalloyed love of country; weakening his own immediate force to strengthen that of his lieutenants; submitting with equanimity to his own subsequent inability to act, and rejoicing in their triumphs, because best calculated to uphold the great cause entrusted to his care; at length, by one great and final exploit, under the benign influence of Providence, lifted to the pinnacle of glory, the reward of his toil, his sufferings, his patience, his heroism, and his virtue. Wonderful man! rendering it difficult by his conduct throughout life, to decide whether he most excelled in goodness or in greatness."

Here also is a curious paper which illustrates the effect of the surrender of Cornwallis, given in the words of an eyewitness, a candid Englishman, who was an habitué of the British Court at the time of the arrival of the news:

SURRENDER OF LORD CORNWALLIS.

From Sir N. W. Wraxall's "Memoirs of his Own Time."

NOVEMBER, 1781. During the whole month of November the concurring accounts transmitted to government, enumerating Lord Cornwallis' embarrassments and the positions taken by the enemy, augmented the anxiety of the Cabinet. Lord George Germain, in particular, conscious that on the prosperous or adverse termination of that expedition, must hinge the fate of the American contest, his own stay in office, as well as probably the duration of the ministry itself, felt, and even expressed to his friends, the strongest uneasiness on the subject. The meeting of Parliament, meanwhile, stood fixed for the 27th of November. On Sunday, the 25th, about noon, official intelligence of the surrender of the British forces at Yorktown, arrived from Falmouth, at Lord Germain's house in Pall Mall. Lord Walsingham, who, previous to his father, Sir William de Gray's elevation to the peerage, had been under secretary of state in that department, and who was selected to second the address in the House of Peers on the subsequent Tuesday, happened to be there when the messenger brought the news. Without communicating it to any person, Lord George, for the purpose of despatch, immediately got with him into a hackney-coach and drove to

Lord Stormount's residence in Portland Place. Having imparted to him the disastrous information, and taken him into the carriage, they instantly proceeded to the Chancellor's house, in Great Russel Street, Bloomsbury, whom they found at home; when, after a short consultation, they determined to lay it themselves, in person, before Lord North. He had not received any intimation of the event when they arrived at his door, in Downing Street, between one and two o'clock. The first minister's firmness, and even his presence of mind, gave way for a short time, under this awful disaster. I asked Lord George afterwards, how he took the communication when made to him? "As I would have taken a ball in my breast," replied Lord George. "For he opened his arms, exclaiming wildly, as he paced up and down the apartment during several minutes, 'O! God! it is all over!' Words which he repeated many times, under emotions of the deepest agitation and distress."

When the first agitation of their minds had subsided, the four ministers discussed the question, whether or not it might be expedient to prorogue Parliament for a few days; but, as scarcely an interval of forty-eight hours remained before the appointed time of assembling, and, as many members of both houses were already either arrived in London, or on the road, that proposition was abandoned. It became, however, indispensable to alter, and almost to model anew the king's speech, which had already been drawn up, and completely prepared for delivery from the throne. This alteration was, therefore, made without delay; and at the same time, Lord George Germain, as secretary for the American department, sent off a despatch to his majesty, who was then at Kew, acquainting him with the melancholy termination of Lord Cornwallis' expedition. Some hours having elapsed before these different, but necessary acts of business could take place, the ministers separated, and Lord George Germain repaired to his office in Whitehall. There he found a confirmation of the intelligence, which arrived about two hours after the first communication; having been transmitted from Dover, from which place it was forwarded to Calais with the French account of the same event.

I dined on that day at Lord George's; and though the information which had reached London in the course of the morning, from two different quarters, was of a nature not to admit of long concealment, yet it had not been communicated to me, nor to any individual of the company, as it might naturally have been, through the channel of common report, when I got to Pall Mall, between five and six o'clock. Lord Walsingham, who likewise dined there, was the only person present, except Lord George, who was acquainted with the fact. The party, nine in number, sat down to table. I thought the master of the house appeared serious, though he manifested no discomposure. Before the dinner was finished, one of his servants delivered him a letter, brought back from the messenger who had been despatched to the king. Lord George opened and perused it; then looking at Lord Walsingham, to whom he exclusively directed his observation, "The king writes," said he, "just as he always does, except that I observe he has omitted to mark the hour and the minute of his writing, with his usual precision." This remark, though calculated to awaken some interest, excited no comment; and while the ladies, Lord George's three daughters, remained in the room, we repressed our curiosity. But they had no sooner withdrawn, than Lord George, having acquainted us that from Paris information had just arrived of the old Count de Maurepas, first minister, lying at the point of death: "It would grieve me," said I "to finish my career, however far advanced in years, were I first minister of France, before I had witnessed the termination of this great contest between England and America." "He has survived to see that event," replied Lord George, with some agitation. Utterly unsuspicious of the fact which had happened beyond the Atlantic, I conceived him to allude to the indecisive naval action fought at the mouth of the Chesapeake, early in the preceding month of September, between Admiral Graves and Count de Grasse; which, in its results, might prove most injurious to Lord Cornwallis. Under this impression, "my meaning," said I, "is that if I were the Count de Maurepas, I should wish to live long enough to behold the final issue of the war in Virginia." "He has survived to witness it completely," answered Lord George, "the army has surrendered, and you may peruse the particulars of the capitulation in that paper," taking at the same time one from his pocket, which he delivered into my hand, not without visible emotion. By his permission, I read it aloud, while the company listened in profound silence. We then discussed its contents, as it effected the ministry, the country and the war. It must be confessed that they were calculated to diffuse a gloom over the most convivial society, and that they opened a wide field for practical speculation.

After perusing the account of Lord Cornwallis's surrender at Yorktown, it was impossible for all present not to feel a lively curiosity to know how the king had received the intelligence, as well as how he expressed himself in his note to Lord George Germain, on the first communication of so painful an event. He gratified our wish by reading it to us, observing at the same time, that it did the highest honor to his Majesty's fortitude, firmness, and consistency of character. The words made an impression on my memory which the lapse of more than thirty years has not erased; and I shall here communicate its tenor, as serving to show how that prince felt and wrote, under one of the most afflicting, as well as humiliating occurrences of his reign. The billet ran nearly to this effect: "I have received, with sentiments of the deepest concern, the communication which Lord George Germain has made me, of the unfortunate result of the operations in Virginia. I particularly lament it, on account of the consequences connected with it, and the difficulties which it may produce in carrying on the public business, or in repairing such a misfortune. But I trust that neither Lord George Germain, nor any member of the cabinet, will suppose that it makes any alteration in those principles of my conduct which have directed me in past times, and which will always continue to animate me under every event, in the prosecution of the present contest." Not a sentiment of despondency or despair was to be found in the letter; the very handwriting of which indicated composure of mind. Whatever opinion we may entertain relative to the practicability of reducing America, to obedience, by force of arms, at the end of 1781, we must admit that no sovereign could manifest more calmness, dignity, or self-command than George III. displayed in this reply.

Severely as the general effect of the blow received in Virginia was felt throughout the nation, yet no immediate symptoms of ministerial dissolution, or even of Parliamentary defection became visible in either House. All the animated invectives of Fox, aided by the contumelious irony of Burke, and sustained by the dignified denunciations of Pitt, enlisted on the same side, made little apparent impression on their hearers, who seemed stupefied by the disastrous intelligence. Yet never, probably, at any period of our history, was more indignant language used by the opposition, or supported by administration. In the ardor of his feelings at the recent calamity beyond the Atlantic, Fox not only accused ministers of being virtually in the pay of France, but menaced them in the name of an undone people, who would speedily compel them to expiate their crimes on the public scaffold. Burke, with inconceivable warmth of coloring, depicted the folly and impracticability of taxing America by force, or, as he described it, "shearing the wolf." The metaphor was wonderfully appropriate, and scarcely admitted of denial. Pitt leveled his observations principally against the cabinet, whom he represented as destitute of principle, wisdom, or union of design. All three were sustained, and I had almost said, outdone, by Mr. Thomas Pitt, who, in terms of gloomy despondency, seemed to regard the situation of the country as scarcely admitting of a remedy, under such a Parliament, such ministers, and such a sovereign. Lord North, in this moment of general depression, found resources within himself—he scornfully repelled the insinuations of Fox, as deserving only contempt; justified the principles of the war, which did not originate in a despotic wish to tyrannize over America, but from the desire of maintaining the constitutional authority of Parliament over the colonies; deplored in common with the opposition, the misfortunes which had marked the progress of the contest; defied the threat of punishment; and finally adjured the House not to aggravate the present calamity by dejection or despair, but by united exertion, to secure our national extrication.

Such a picture of the consternation of the British Court, on hearing this disastrous news of the ignominious wreck of a second army in America, has never before been furnished to the public eye; and significantly suggests how the stentorian words of "Sam," "I am master here!" rung portentously even at that early period, in the ears of the hoary and feeble despotisms of the Old World.

"Sam" was now a freeman; and "youngling" as he was, the weight of his ponderous limbs had, even through the storm and crash of battle, made verge and room enough whereon to stretch themselves at ease on their "old couch of space."

CHAPTER XLI.

Trouble with the Indians—Tecumseh's League—General Harrison—Battles with the Indians—The British treat with them—Death of Tecumseh.

JOHN Bull seems to have had enough of "Sam," after the surrender of Cornwallis, to stay his stomach for the present. That portly gentleman would appear now to have come to the conclusion, that he had counted rather much upon the respect due to age, plethora, and gout, and to have become rapidly more philosophical, and more reasonable in his views, as to his own, and the rights of others. The future conqueror of Napoleon had been soundly thrashed by a big baby, to be sure, but what of that?—many a kind, but uxorious father had been conquered by big babies before, through the excess of his parental feeling—and where was the shame? It was all human nature, to say the most of it. Babies will be fractious, and fathers will be fond. And the more John reasoned, and philosophised, the more reasonable and philosophical he became, of course—until finally the bright idea illuminated his brain, through the fumy fog of after-dinner Port, and cigar, that it might be well to let the poor "youngling" up, since he had beaten him with sufficient severity for this, his first fall, and hoped, in the gracious serenity of his more contemplative and propitious mood, that the rude, but willful, though not contumacious boy, might still have some elements of submission and reformation in him. And John grinned with a grim smile, as he hitched up the already nearly bursting waistband, which heaved with the throes of beef, plum-pudding, and paternal sentiment. Ha! ha! ha! the wild, young dog! I'll let him up now, but may be the next time, I have occasion to lay my hand upon him, his mother won't know him, when I'm done with him!

But as Mrs. Bull was not present, to say whether she thought it likely she would, this important historical problem must remain through all time a solemn mystery, to be solved by some transcendental historian of the Bancroft order, in some remote era of the "spiritual" regime, which is now so rapidly approaching.

Certainly John Bull proved himself in earnest in the apostolic threat of the "laying on of hands," some short time afterward—as we shall see—and we shall see, too, the result.

But "Sam," fortunately, was of the philosophic temperament too,—by inheritance, no doubt—and remained very meekly contented with the drubbing he had received, and a little unimportant concession of liberty to do as he pleased hereafter. To be sure he found himself with an empty treasury, a plundered, ravaged continent, a half-rebellious people at his disposal, but managed with a remarkable placidity, through the easy temperament for which he is noted, to reconcile himself—with what John Bull would have called a vainglorious contemplation of the manifold trophies of two entire captured armies, and the paltry pittance, for which he was obviously indebted to paternal magnanimity, of a perpetual fief to lands, demense rents, etc., to which he naturally considered himself, in all humility, somewhat entitled, by virtue of "Squatter Sovereignty." To be sure, "Sam" had never been a tailor, except in the Eve and Adam sense, or the "Rough and Ready"—and therefore, could not be strictly considered a "squatter." As it was, we proceeded very meekly to organize a government, and weld a constitution, the iron hinges of which have as yet successfully resisted the shock of all elemental forces, which have been brought combined against it.

This achievement, though, no doubt, owing to the inspiration of filial gratitude, solely, and the sentiment of thankfulness for his full release, through the gracious and benign magnanimity of his new-found and portly sire—for we had thought "Sam" the child of the elements solely—nevertheless placed him in a position among the nations of the earth, which caused Old Empire to verily stare at the Young Monstrosity.

The Federal Constitution organized, America an independdent nation of the earth, and Washington inaugurated as president, we must leave the intervening period to other histories, and make a long stride to that of the war of 1812 with Tecumseh.

The pressure of Bonaparte's commercial system, not confined to the civilized world, was felt even by the wild tribes of the North American forests. The price of furs, in consequence of their exclusion from the Continent of Europe, their chief market, had sunk so low that the Indian hunters found their means of purchase from the traders greatly curtailed. The rapid extension of settlements north of the Ohio had not only occasioned an alarming diminution of game, but, in the facilities afforded for the introduction of whisky, had inflicted a still greater evil on the Indians. Among those tribes, Delawares, Shawanese, Wyandots, Miamis, and, further to the northwest, Ottowas, Potawatomies, Kickapoos, Winnebagoes, and Chippewas, a remarkable influence had of late been established by two twin brothers of the Shawanese tribe, who possessed between them all the qualities held in greatest esteem by the Indians. Tecumseh was an orator and a warrior, active, intrepid, crafty, and unscrupulous. His brother, commonly known as The Prophet, was not only an orator, but a "medicine man" of the highest pretensions, claiming to hold direct intercourse with the Great Spirit, and to possess miraculous powers. He announced himself as specially sent, and instructed to require of the red men, as a first step toward a return to their ancient prosperity, to renounce all those innovations borrowed from the whites, more especially the use of whisky, which had made them the slaves of the traders. But these denunciations were not limited to the vices borrowed from the white men; they were equally levelled at those approaches to civilization, and those new religious opinions, which the agents of the government on the one hand, and a few missionaries on the other, had been laboring to introduce.

Separating himself from his own tribe, which was slow, at first, in recognizing his mission, the Prophet had established (1806) a village of his own at Greenville, near the western border of Ohio, on lands already ceded to the United States. Meanwhile Tecumseh traveled from tribe to tribe, spreading everywhere his brother's fame. While the Prophet's immediate followers, engrossed in their religious exercises, were often on the verge of starvation, it was reported, and believed at a distance, that he could make pumpkins as big as a wigwam spring out of the ground at a single word, along with stalks of corn, of which a single ear would suffice to feed a dozen men. Denounced by the chiefs of their own and the neighboring tribes as impostors, they retorted by charges of subserviency to the whites, and even of witchcraft, a very terrible accusation among the Indians, under which they procured the death of two or three hostile Delaware Chiefs. It was, however, among the more remote tribes that the greater part of their convicts were obtained; and this, perhaps, was one reason why the Prophet, in the summer of 1808, removed his village to the Tippecanoe, a northern branch of the Upper Wabash, a spot belonging to the Miamis and Delawares, but which he occupied in spite of their opposition. At this new village, disciples and spectators flocking in from all sides, the Prophet continued to celebrate his appointed seasons of fasting and exhortations: religious exercises, which were intermingled with or followed by warlike sports, such as shooting with bows, by which the rifle was to be superseded, and wielding the stone tomahawk or war-club, ancient Indian weapons, before the hatchet was known.

These military exercises, and an alleged secret intercourse with the British traders and agents, had drawn upon the Prophet and his brother the suspicions of Harrison, governor of the Indiana Territory, and superintendent of Indian affairs; but these suspicions were, in a great measure, dispelled by a visit which the Prophet paid to Vincennes, in which he assumed the character of a warm friend of peace, his sole object being, as he declared, to reform the Indians, and especially to put a stop to the use of whisky. Not long after this visit, Harrison held a treaty at Fort Wayne with the Delawares, Potawatomies, Miamis, Kickapoos, Weas, and Eel River Indians, at which, in consideration of annuities amounting to $2350, and of presents in hand to the value of $8200, he obtained a cession of lands extending up the Wabash above Terre Haute, and including the middle waters of White river. Neither the Prophet nor the tribe to which he belonged had any claim to these lands, except, indeed, under a doctrine which he had lately set up, that all the Indian lands belonged to all the tribes in common, and that none could be sold without the consent of all. On this ground the Prophet and his brother denounced the late treaty as void, and they threatened to kill all the chiefs concerned in making it—a threat the more formidable, in consequence of the accession to the Prophet's party, at this moment, of the Wyandots, a tribe on Lake Erie, not numerous, but famous warriors, and regarded with great respect by all the northwestern tribes, who called them uncles.

In consequence of new reports of intended hostilities, Harrison invited the Prophet and his brother to a new interview, which took place in a field just outside the village of Vincennes. Though requested not to bring more than thirty followers, Tecumseh came attended by some four hundred warriors. The governor, surrounded by several hundred of the unarmed townspeople, was seated in a chair, attended by the jduges of the Territory. by several officers of the army, and by Winnemack, a friendly Potawatomie chief, who had on this, as on other occasions, given notice of Tecumseh's designs. Under some trees on the border of the field were placed a sergeant and twelve men from the fort. The Indians, who sat in a semicircle on the grass, had left their rifles at their camp, but they had their tomahawks by them.

Tecumseh, in his opening speech, fully avowed the design of himself and his brother to establish, by a combination among the tribes, the principle of no more cessions of Indian lands except by general consent. He admitted a determination to kill all the chiefs concerned in the late treaty, but disavowed any intention to make war upon the whites, and denounced those who had accused him of it as liars. This was aimed at Winnemack, whom Tecumseh overwhelmed with a torrent of reproaches, and who, as he sat on the ground, near Harrison's chair, secretly charged a pistol, and held it concealed, ready for use.

Harrison, in reply, ridiculed Tecumseh's assertions that the Great Spirit had intended the Indians to be one people; for, if so, why had he put different tongues into their heads?

Why had he not given them one language, which all might understand? The land in dispute had been bought of the Miamis, whose fathers had owned it while the Shawanese lived in Georgia; and the sale had been consented to by all the tribes who by occupancy had any claim. They had seen fit to sell the land, and what business had the Shawanese to interpose? Here the governor paused for the interpreter to repeat to the Indians what he had said, in the midst of which Tecumseh broke in, declaring, with violent gesticulations, that the governor's statements were false, and that he and the United States had cheated and imposed upon the Indians. As he went on with increased vehemence, his warriors sprang upon their feet and began to brandish their tomahawks. Harrison started from his chair and drew his sword, as did the officers who stood by; Winnemack cocked his pistol; and the unarmed citizens caught up such missiles as came to hand, principally brickbats from an ancient kiln. The guard of soldiers came running up, and were about to fire, but were checked by the governor, who asked the interpreters what was the matter. Being told what Tecumseh had said, Harrison pronounced him a bad man, with whom he would hold no further conference. As he had come under the protection of the council fire, he might depart in safety, but he must instantly leave the neighborhood. Thereupon the council broke up, and Tecumseh retired to his camp.

The people of Vincennes stood to their arms, expecting an attack that night. But, changing his tactics, Tecumseh the next morning expressed the greatest regret at the violence into which he had been betrayed, and requested and obtained another interview. This time his deportment was dignified and collected. He denied any intention of using force, ascribing the demonstration of the day before to the advice of white men—and Harrison had enemies in the Territory, who had accused him of having cheated the Indians—by whom he had been told that, if he made a vigorous opposition to the treaty, the governor would be recalled, and the land given up. But, though he disclaimed any hostile intentions, upon being asked whether he meant to interfere with the survey of the land, he significantly replied that he should adhere to the old boundary. He was followed by a Wyandot, a

Potawåtomie, an Ottawa, a Kickapoo, and a Winnebago, all of whom declared their adherence, and that of their tribes, to the new confederacy.

Anxious to ascertain Tecumseh's real feelings and intentions, Harrison paid him a visit in his camp. He expressed, on this occasion, great reluctance to go to war with the Americans, and promised, if the recent cessions were given up, and the principle adopted of taking no more land from the Indians without the consent of all the tribes, to be a faithful ally, and to assist the Americans in any war with the British; otherwise, though well aware that the pretended friendship of the British was all for their own purposes, he should be obliged to join them. Harrison, though he held out no hope of success, promised to lay the matter before the President.

Numerous complaints, some months after, from the frontier, of horses stolen, houses plundered, and even alleged murders, caused Harrison to send word to Tecumseh that, if he did not put a stop to these outrages, he might expect to be attacked. Tecumseh replied by a personal visit, but with no satisfactory result. Shortly after, he started on a journey to the South, in hope to bring the Creeks, Choctaws, and Chickasaws into his confederacy. Among the Creeks especially he might hope for some influence, as his mother had belonged to that tribe.

Harrison had suggested to the administration the establishment of a post high up the Wabash, and they had proposed the seizing of Tecumseh and his brother as hostages for peace. Boyd's regiment of regular infantry had been for some time stationed at Pittsburgh, with a view to possible operations in the West. Fresh complaints coming from the Illinois Territory, Boyd was directed to place himself under Harrison's command. Harrison was authorized, should the Prophet commence or threaten hostilities, to attack him, and to call out militia for that purpose; but considering the threatening state of relations with Great Britain, much anxiety was at the same time expressed for the preservation of peace. The people of Vincennes and its neighborhood, dreaded being suddenly attacked at any time. They were eager to strike a decisive blow; and, though somewhat embarrassed by his orders, Harrison thought that policy the best. With Boyd's regiment, about three hundred strong, and some five hundred militia, partly from Kentucky, including two or three mounted companies, advancing some sixty miles up the Wabash to Terre Haute, he established a post there, named after himself; and thence he dispatched some Delaware chiefs, that tribe still remaining friendly, on a mission to the Prophet. These messengers were very ill received, and were dismissed with insults and contempt. The troops then advanced, and, after eight days' cautious march, encamped within ten miles of the Prophet's town. The march being resumed the next day, small parties of Indians began to appear, with whom it was in vain attempted to communicate; but within three miles of the town, some chiefs came forward, who asked the meaning of this hostile movement; urged the Prophet's desire for peace; and obtained a halt, and the appointment of a council for the morrow. The army encamped in a hollow square, surrounded by a chain of sentinels, the troops sleeping on their arms, with orders, if attacked, to maintain their position at all hazards. Just before daybreak—the light of the moon, then in its third quarter, obscured by clouds, with an occasional drizzle of rain—an alarm was given by the discharge of a gun by one of the sentinels, followed by the Indian yell, and a desperate rush and heavy fire upon the left rear angle of the camp. The Indians had crept close to the sentinels, designing to overpower them by surprise. The men stood at once to their arms. All the camp-fires were immediately extinguished, lest they might serve to guide the aim of the Indians. The attack soon extended to almost the whole square, the Indians advancing and retiring at a signal made by the rattling of deer's hoofs. Not being able to break the square, and being charged, soon after daylight, by the mounted men, they presently disappeared, carrying off their wounded, but leaving forty dead on the field. This battle, for the present, ended the war with the Indians, until Tecumseh, after the declaration of the war of 1812, formed an alliance with the English, when it was resumed with all its terror. The final death of Tecumseh, which occurred soon after, at the battle of the Thames, broke up the formidable alliance among ten Indian tribes, of which he was the head, and defeated, finally, his grand and masterly scheme,

BATTLE WITH THE INDIANS — DEATH OF TECUMSEH. (SEE CHAP. XLI.)

of annihilating the entire western settlements, by a combination of all the savage tribes of the West and North.

The death of Tecumseh, in this battle, was in reality one of the great events of western history. The circumstances of his fall, of which so great use has been made for paltry political ends, which attributed it to the prowess of Colonel Richard M. Johnson, that Ethiop-loving demagogue of the democracy, have been, for the first time, properly delineated in our cut. He was undoubtedly slain by Colonel Whitley, of the Kentucky mounted men, in a single-hand conflict, and we have furnished a correct portrait of the noble horse which he rode on the occasion, and which, wounded by the last shot from the pistol of Tecumseh, survived, and finally came into the possession of the father of the present narrator. This event virtually ended the war, in this direction.

This expedition gave rise to abundant discussions. Harrison's consenting to suspend his march; his selection of a camp so near the Indians; his omission to fortify it, for which the want of axes was pleaded in excuse; and his conduct also during the battle, were all very closely canvassed. A dispute also arose, as to whether the merits of the repulse belonged to him or to Boyd. Harrison, however, was sustained, and his conduct approved by the President, and by resolutions of the Legislatures of Kentucky and Indiana; and such was the general impression throughout the West, as to give him a decided military reputation.

The question of war with Great Britain, which it is well remembered turned solely upon the question of embargo, and the right of impressment, which Johnny Bull, with the full recollection of his reserved, apostolic right of the "laying on of hands," claimed that he possessed the power of enforcing, to the virtual ruin of our national commerce and navy, caused immense discussion, in which the most brilliant of the children of "Sam" developed their finest powers of oratory and invective, pro and con.

Randolph, with his fierce wit and demoniac satire, stood like the incarnate ghost of famine, in the halls of our Congress, hurling savage epithets at the heads of the promoters of the war; shaking his spectral finger, with terrible denunciations, at the eloquent and subtle Clay, whose clarion voice, the very music of war, had roused our people to battle against the predominating insolence of British naval ascendancy. But Randolph squeaked his dire epithets in vain—a stronger spell than he could wake was upon the hearts of the people—and, in spite of Tories, Jesuits, and Quakers, the nation rose up as one man, and drove the vaunted tyrant of the seas from our waters, more humiliated than ever.

This time pursy John Bull did "give up the ship; "Sam" had thrashed him on the land before, and now it became necessary to thrash him on the sea, which, in the glorious battles of the Constitution and the Guerriere, the United States and the Macedonian, the Wasp and the Hornet, he quickly demonstrated, that on whatever element he chose to carry his arms and his commerce, they should be respected. Nor did he find it necessary to bombard any Greytowns, at that, or perform any other such superlative heroics.

Now, too, culminated the reputations of Jackson, Harrison, and Scott—stalwart men, all, and good generals. The first, the greatest, and strongest since Washington, the man of iron will and lofty aim, the rude, unlettered hero of the savage West! the gaunt Titan of modern pigmies of democracy! Who can forget his long career of opposition and dauntless conquest against aggressions of all kinds, whether military, political, or social?

It would be impossible for us, within our narrow limits, to follow up, in detail, the incidents of this important war. We can do nothing more than glance at some of its important events. We will only mention, that throughout its entire course, the whole conduct of John Bull exhibited a most unrelenting determination to consummate the purposes of his avowed vengeance.

In doing this, he scrupled at no intrigue, however infamous, no strategy, however brutal, and no affiliation, however debasing. He, without hesitation, sought the aid of the French Jesuits, whom he hated and feared more than any other power, except that of the recreant "Sam," upon whom he was sworn to be avenged; and, through their agency, he formed treaties with the savage tribes of the continent, over whom they had now obtained ascendancy, north and south, made them the medium of his revengeful largess in arms, ammunition, and money, and thus turned them loose from every "Reduction"—the cordon of which had now been completed by the intrigues of these holy fathers, who gladly availed themselves of such temporary alliance with their old foes, to wreak their own hoarded vengeance against the Protestant cause.

Thus inflamed, the sanguinary savages of the entire continent were turned loose upon the women and children of our vast and defenseless borders, and the war assumed many aspects of tomahawk and scalping-knife horror, which had remained, until now, to assume their full sanguinary coloring.

The battle in which Perry so singularly defeated the entire naval force of John Bull, upon the Northern Lakes, was the first and most important check which his hired brigands received during the war. Jackson's operations consummated, by the battle of the Great Horse-shoe Bend, and the submission of the Creeks inforced a peace with the Southern Indians.

Brown's invasion of Canada, and the battle of Chippewa, in which the young Scott distinguished himself, and the battle of Bridgewater, and the siege of Fort Erie, followed in rapid succession. The march on Washington, the battle of Bladensburg, and the attack and defense of Baltimore, which rapidly succeeded the capture of the capital, were soon followed by the advance on and the battle of Plattsburg, and the retreat of the British, which virtually ended the war in the North.

Then came the battle of New Orleans, of which we shall give some more detailed account.

Previous to Jackson's arrival at New Orleans, everything had remained there, intervening dilapidations excepted, in the same condition in which Wilkinson had left it, a stop having been put, immediately after his departure, to every measure of defense which he had commenced. The total population of Louisiana did not exceed one hundred thousand, of whom half were slaves or free people of color. New Orleans had about twenty thousand, of whom less than half were whites. Of these whites a large portion were French creoles, while there were also many adventurers of foreign birth, whose attachment to the United States was not implicitly relied upon. The adjoining districts of Mississippi contained not above forty thousand inhabitants, of whom half were slaves. In consequence of communications sent by General Jackson from Mobile, Governor Claiborne had ordered all the militia of Louisiana to hold themselves in resdiness for instant service, those of the city to exercise twice a week, and those of the country half as often. A public meeting was soon after called in New Orleans and a committee of defense organized, of which Edward Livingston was appointed chairman. Having recovered possession at last of his batture, Livingston had begun to rise above the wave of obloquy with which he had been so long overwhelmed; but he was still so unpopular, and such were the local jealousies and quarrels, that another and rival committee of defense was presently organized. Determined to avail himself of every means of defense, Jackson issued from Mobile an affectionate address to "the noble-hearted, generous, free men of color." Repudiating the mistaken policy which had hitherto excluded them from the military service, he called on them to enroll themselves in a distinct corps—a call to which they quickly responded, under an act of the Louisiana legislature, called together in special session, and by which a joint committee of defense was appointed, apparently, however, with very little hopes that any very serious attack could be withstood.

The arrival of Jackson, who was soon followed by a few regulars from Mobile, served to give some encouragement. But he saw at once that he must rely for defense mainly on exterior resources; nor were there any to which he could look except Coffee's brigade, which, after the expulsion of the British from Pensacola, he had ordered to march for the Mississippi, and other detachments of militia from Kentucky and Tennessee, called for some time before, and expected down the river, but which, as yet, had scarcely set out. Such, in fact, was the poverty and disorganization of the quartermaster's department in the West, that the Kentucky troops had only been enabled to embark, by the credit of individnal citizens pledged for the necessary supplies. Intent to augment his forces by all means, Jackson accepted the aid of Lafitte and a portion of the Baratarian buccaneers, who again tendered their services on condition of pardon. The convicts, also, in the prison, were released and embodied.

A flat-bottomed frigate, commenced by Wilkinson, and

which would have been invaluable at the present moment, lay unfinished on the shores of Lake Pontchartrain. The only naval force on that lake and Lake Borgne, was five gunboats and a small schooner; these, with a few other gun-boats and barges in the Mississippi, the schooner Carolina of fourteen guns, and the ship Louisiana of sixteen, the latter just taken into service, constituted the whole naval means of defending the water approaches. While Jackson was inspecting the forts St. Philip and Leon, which guarded the ascent of the river, news reached New Orleans that the expected British fleet had anchored at Cat Island, off the entrance of Lake Borgne. The force on board, without counting four thousand sailors and marines, amounted, as it afterward appeared, to twelve thousand men, commanded by Packingham, Keene, Lambert, and Gibbs, able and experienced generals of Wellington's late Peninsular army, whence, also, the troops had mostly been drawn. Some forty or fifty British barges succeeded after a hard fight, in capturing the American flotilla on Lake Borgne, thus laying open the passage to New Orleans; and about the same time, the post called the Balize, at the entrance of the river, with all the pilots stationed there, fell into the enemy's hands.

The Louisiana militia were at once called into the field; but a serious difficulty arose from the want of arms. Jackson, some months before, had called for a supply from the arsenal at Pittsburg; but, from an unwillingness to pay the freight demanded by the only steamer which then navigated the Mississippi, these necessary means of defense had been shipped in keel boats, nor did they arrive till the fate of the city had been decided. Even the muskets on hand would have been useless, but for a supply of flints furnished by Lafitte, the Baratarian pirate. The Legislature passed an act extending for four months the payment of all bills and notes; but they hesitated to suspend the habeas corpus act: whereupon Jackson, under whose command Governor Claiborne had placed himself and the militia, took the responsibility of proclaiming martial law.

Expresses had already been sent up the river, to get news, if possible, of Coffee's brigade, and of the militia expected from Tennessee and Kentucky. Coffee, after encountering great hardships from excessive rains and short supplies, had reached the neighborhood of Baton Rouge about the time that the British appeared off Cat Island. On receiving Jackson's orders, he had marched with one thousand three hundred and fifty men, leaving three hundred sick behind, and pushing forward himself with eight hundred of the best mounted, he accomplished the distance of one hundred and fifty miles in two days, encamping on the third within four miles of the city. A body of Mississippi dragoons, which had marched from Mobile about the same time, arrived shortly after. On news of Carroll's approach with the additional Tennessee militia, the steamboat which had just arrived from Pittsburg had been sent to bring them down; and Jackson thus found himself at the head of five thousand men, of whom somewhat less than a thousand were regulars.

Meanwhile the British Army, advancing in their light transports to the head of Lake Borgne, under the pilotage of some Italian fishermen who dwelt in that neighborhood, found a water passage by the Bayou Bienvenu, to within a short distance of the Mississippi, of which the left bank, about fifteen miles below New Orleans, was gained by General Keene with an advanced party of two thousand light troops. This approach from the front was a fortunate circumstance; had the British advanced by Lake Pontchartrain, thus cutting off the communication of New Orleans with the country above, the result might have been very different.

As soon as Jackson was informed of this lodgment, leaving Carroll and the Louisiana country militia to cover the city, he marched to meet the enemy, taking with him the regulars, the city militia, Coffee's brigade dismounted, and the Mississippi dragoons. The British left rested on the river, exposed to the fire of the schooner Carolina. Coffee was detached to gain their right, while Jackson, with the rest of the troops, and two pieces of artillery, advanced on their front. It was dark before the action began, a circumstance favorable in some respects to the raw American troops, but preventing co-operation, and producing some confusion. The attack was made with vigor. The British, greatly annoyed by the fire of the schooner, were driven to take several new positions; but at last they got into a very strong one, between an old levee, which covered them from the schooner, and a new one, raised within, which guarded their right; and finding that this position could not be forced, Jackson retired with a loss of two hundred and twenty-three in killed, wounded, and prisoners. The enemy's loss was rather greater. The next day Jackson took up a position behind a deep trench, running from the river to the swamp, at a point where the solid land between was less than a mile in breadth, a position naturally strong, and which every effort was made to strengthen. Just as the late action closed, the British had been joined by a new division from their ships; but, alarmed at the warm reception they had met, and ignorant of Jackson's force, which the American prisoners greatly exaggerated, instead of pressing forward at once, which would have been their best chance, they waited to bring up reinforcements and artillery. This interval was diligently employed by Jackson in strengthening his position, bales of cotton being used to form a rampart, which, as well as the ditch in front of it, was extended into the swamp. A British battery, established on the levee, succeded in destroying the Carolina by hot shot, but the Louisiana was saved, and towed out of reach. The next day the enemy advanced in force, driving in Jackson's outposts, and having approached within a half a mile of his lines, they opened upon them with artillery, bombs, and Congreve rockets. Jackson had five pieces of heavy artillery already mounted, and served by the crew of the Carolina. These guns, aided by the raking fire of the Louisiana, checked the enemy's advance, and after a seven hours' cannonade, he retired with considerable loss.

As matters thus approached a crisis, Jackson and Claiborne were not a little troubled at the apprehension of treachery within the city. Fulwar Skipworth, who, from having been governor of the late insurgent republic of West Florida, was now speaker of the Louisiana Senate, had made some inquiries of Major Butler, left in command at New Orleans, as to the truth of a rumor, that, rather than surrender, Jackson would destroy the city and retire up the river, from which, and other circumstances, it was conjectured that the Legislature might intend to save the city by offering to capitulate. Jackson directed Clairborne, in case any move was made in that direction, to arrrest the members of the Legislature; an order to which Claiborne gave such an interpretation, contrary, it was afterward said, to Jackson's intentions, that, without waiting to see whether there were any grounds for his suspicions, he placed a military guard at the door of the hall, and broke up the legislative session. Jackson also authorized a general search of houses and stores for arms, and, to prevent any skulking from militia duty, he directed a registration of all the male inhabitants.

With the commencement of the new year, the enemy renewed his attack with more and heavier artillery; but, in the interval, the works had been much strengthened; and, after a heavy cannonade, the British guns were dismounted and silenced. Jackson's preparations for defense were not confined to the left bank of the river. By the Bay of Barataria and the inlets connected with it, the bank opposite the city might be approached, without passing the forts on the river; and to guard against attack from that quarter, General Morgan had been sent across, with orders to throw up defenses like those on the eastern side. At last the long expected Kentuckians arrived—2250 men, led by General Adair, that old friend of Burr's—but half of them were without arms, which Jackson could not furnish. Detachments of these Kentuckians and of the Louisiana militia were sent to join Morgan, whose force was thus raised to 1500 men, stationed behind an intrenchment, defended by several brass twelves and by a battery of twenty four-pounders, commanded by Commodore Patterson. The men without arms were employed by Jackson upon a second line of intrenchments, as a place of rally should he be driven from his first line.

Preparations had meanwhile been made by the British for a grand attack. Boats having been drawn, with great labor, from the bayou into the river, Colonel Thornton was sent across in the night, with a British detachment, to assault Morgan. At the same time, under the fire of a battery of six eighteen pounders, erected also during the night, the main body, led by Packenham in person, advanced to storm Jackson's position. "Booty and beauty," such was the watchword; comment enough on British military morals. One column marched by the river, and, without much difficulty, carried an advanced redoubt, by the guns of which the approach to the American line was raked through its whole extent. The other and main column, led by Gibbs and Keene, approached that part of the American line nearest to the fatal fire of the Tennessee sharp-shooters, and of nine pieces of heavy artillery, was speedily thrown into confusion. Packingham, in attempting to restore order, was killed; the other two generals were wounded, Gibbs mortally; and after an hour's struggle, and two unsuccessful advances, Lambert, who succeeded to the command, was obliged to withdraw, at the same time abandoning the redoubt on the river, which the other column had carried. Thornton, on the opposite bank, notwithstanding some delay in his advance, had proved entirely successful, and the position he had gained would have given great advantage for renewing the attack. But the British army had lost two thousand men in killed and wounded; and Lambert, dreading still further disasters, hastened to withdraw Thornton's troops, and to abandon the whole enterprise. Having taken all proper precautions to cover his retreat, he first fell back to the original landing place on Lake Borgne, from which point the army was presently re-embarked. Jackson's loss was but trifling, only seventy-one on both sides of the river, while his total loss in the campaign had been but three hundred and thirty-three. But with his raw troops, whose flight before Thornton had shown how little they could be depended on, he did not choose to risk anything in attempting to intercept the enemy's retreat, who, retiring first to Cat Island, proceeded thence, as if not to fail entirely, to the attack and capture of Fort Bowyer. About the same time the enemy withdrew from the coast of Georgia; but not until they had caused a proclamation of martial law, and had thrown that State, and South Carolina also, into a paroxysm of alarm.

Rumors of Jackson's successes beginning to arrive at Washington, successes which the administration, so far as anything had been done by them, had very little right to expect, came like an exhilarating cordial to the baffled and mortified war party. Confirmations, with additional particulars, continued to arrive, and to be welcomed with the loudest exultations; but, before the whole story was known, the public attention was drawn off to a fresh piece of news, of even greater interest and importance.

The British sloop of war Favorite, arriving at New York under a flag of truce, brought two messengers, one British, the other American, bearers of an unexpected treaty of peace, already ratified by the British government. It was late of a Saturday night; but no sooner was the joyful word PEACE circulated through the city—and it spread like electricity—than, without stopping to inquire or to think about the terms, the whole active population, of all parties, rushed into the streets in a perfect ecstasy of delight; and, amid shouts, illuminations, and a perfect uproar of joy, expresses were sent off, north and south, with the news. In thirty-two hours (thought to be a great effort of speed) the announcement reached Boston, where it was received on Monday morning with the most clamorous rejoicings. All the bells were at once set to ringing; messengers were despatched in every direction to spread the delightful intelligence; the schools received a holyday; the whole population, quitting their employments, hastened to congratulate each other at this relief, not only from foreign war, but from the still more dreadful impending cloud of internal and civil struggle. The blockaded shipping, rotting forlorn at the wharves, got out all their flags and streamers, and, before night, once more the hum of commerce sounded, ship-carpenters and riggers were busy at work, cargoes were being shipped, and crews engaged. The joy was the same along the whole maritime frontier; nor, however they might strive to conceal their emotions, was it less among the politicians at Washington, including those most forward to precipitate their country into a struggle so unequal and disastrous. At the same time they made a very dexterous use of the sudden halo of glory diffused by Jackson's victory, to conceal from themselves, as well as from the people, the desperate point to which affairs had been reduced. Troup had the audacity to congratulate the House even before the contents of the treaty were known, it having but just been laid before the Senate, on the glorious termination of the most glorious war ever waged by any people—provided, as he cautiously added, that the treaty should prove an honorable one!

The weakness of the British possessions in North America; the necessity of some barrier against that ambitious spirit admirals and vice-admirals failed, as the same proposal has often done since, but an important change was made in of annexation exhibited in the acquisition of Louisiana, the threatened conquest of Canada, and the constant curtailment of the Indian territory, these had been stated by the British commissioners, at the opening of the negotiation, as grounds of their claim for an assignment to the British Indian allies, of a permanent neutral territory, with a prohibition to the United States to establish fortresses or keep ships on the great lakes. The American commissioners had protested, in reply, against this attempted interference with the Indians, as a thing which the policy of Great Britain had never permitted in her own case, and as contrary to the assurances originally given of a disposition to treat on terms of perfect reciprocity. They denied, with emphasis, that the conquest of Canada had ever been a *declared* object of the war; and they dwelt on the humane disposition of their government toward the Indians, protesting, also, against the British employment of Indian auxiliaries. Finally, after some pretty sharp controversy, the British commissioners had agreed to be content with a mutual stipulation for peace with the Indians, the tribes still actively engaged in hostilities at the close of the war, to be restored to the same position in which they had stood at its commencement. This question disposed of by the provisional assent of the American commissioners, the next related to boundaries. The false idea that the Mississippi had its source north of the forty-ninth degree of latitude, had rendered nugatory the provision of the treaty of 1783 as to the northern boundary of the United States, west of the Lake of the Woods. That boundary, indeed, since the acquisition of Louisiana, remained to be extended far to the west, the United States claiming, under that cession, even to the Pacific Ocean. The provision for a boundary on the northeast, so far as related to the territory between the head of the St. Croix and the head of the Connecticut, had likewise failed, so the British commissioners contended, from similar geographical ignorance; and, as the basis of a new arrangement, they had suggested that each party should retain what he held at the signing of the treaty. To this the American commissioners had refused to agree. So the negotiation had stood at the latest accounts previous to the arrival of the treaty of peace.

The treaty, as signed, provided for the mutual restoration

of all conquered territory, and for the appointment of three commissions: one to settle the title to the islands in Passamaquoddy Bay; another to mark out the northeastern boundary as far as the St. Lawrence; and a third to run the line through the St. Lawrence and the lakes, to the Lake of the Woods. In case of disagreement in either commission, the point in dispute was to be referred to some friendly Power. No provision was made as to the boundary west of the Lake of the Woods, nor as to the fishery on the shores of British America. The British commissioners refused to accept, in return for this right of fishing, a modified renewal of the article for the navigation of the Mississippi, which, in their view, was also terminated by the war. The result, therefore, was, that, instead of leaving the parties where they began, the war took away from Great Britain a nominal right, never used, of navigating the Mississippi, and from the New England fishermen a valuable right, hitherto used from the earliest times, of catching and curing fish on the shores of the Gulf of St. Lawrence, the loss of which long continued to be felt. Hostilities on land were to terminate with the ratification of the treaty, and on the ocean in certain specified periods, according to distances, of which the longest was four months. By some adroit management, the English commissioners were induced to admit into the treaty a clause copied from that of 1783, with the history of which probably they were not familiar, against carrying away "any negroes or other property." The only remaining article related to the slave trade, for the suppression of which, as irreconcilable with the principles of humanity and justice, both parties promised to use their best endeavors.

The treaty, having been unanimously ratified and formally promulgated, was celebrated everywhere throughout the country with the loudest rejoicings. The Federalists, and all the more sensible Republicans, considered the country lucky in the peace, such as it was. The violent war men, greatly cooled by this time, concealed their mortification behind the smoke of Jackson's victory, and vague declamations about the national rights vindicated, the national character exalted, and the military and naval glory of the war. Considering the new demands of Great Britain, put forward at Ghent, they seemed to esteem it a triumph to be allowed to stop where they began, leaving the whole question of impressments and neutral rights, the sole ostensible occasion of the war, without a word said on the subject, to be settled at some convenient opportunity: a common termination of wars, even for the most powerful and belligerent nations, and of which Great Britain herself has given more than one instance.

The war thus happily ended, Dallas's bank scheme, which had been again revived and carried through the Senate, was indefinitely postponed in the House by a majority of one vote. Instead of the scheme of finance which he had proposed, a loan of $18,400,000 was authorized, being the amount of treasury notes outstanding; and, as immediate means to go on with, new treasury notes to the amount of twenty-five millions. A part of these notes, to be issued in sums under a hundred dollars, payable to the bearer, and without interest, were intended to serve as a currency. Those over a hundred dollars were to bear an interest of five and two-fifths per cent.,—a cent and a half a day for every hundred dollars. Both kinds were to be receivable for all public dues, and fundable at the pleasure of the holder—those bearing interest, in six per cent. stock, and those without interest in seven per cent. stock.

Haste was made to repeal, in favor of all reciprocating nations, the act imposing discriminating duties on foreign vessels, and all remnants and remainders, if any there were, of the old non-intercourse and non-importation acts; also an act passed only a few days before, containing many strong provisions, some of them of very questionable constitutionality, for the extinguishment of trade and intercourse with Great Britain. The commissioners at Ghent, before terminating their mission, signed a commercial convention for four years, copied substantially from Jay's treaty, but with an additional proviso for absolute reciprocity in the direct trade, by the abolition, on both sides, of all discriminations.

Appropriations were made for rebuilding the public edifices lately burned by the British; not, however, without a good deal of opposition. Rhea proposed to encircle the ruins of the Capitol with an iron balustrade, to let the ivy grow over them, and to place on their front, in letters of brass, this inscription: "Americans! This is the effect of British barbarism! Let us swear eternal hatred to England!" Many of the Southern members were quite electrified by this burst of patriotic indignation; but the effect passed rapidly away, as it occurred to them that Rhea was a Pennsylvanian, anxious to have the seat of government removed to Philadelphia or Lancaster.

Jefferson had offered a library of some seven thousand volumes, which he had been all his life collecting, to supply the place of that burned by the British; but the appropriation for this purpose did not pass without violent opposition. It was proposed to pay for these books about thirty thousand dollars—more, no doubt, than they would have sold for, though probably not much more than they had cost. But this act of mutual accommodation—for Jefferson needed the money—was violently denounced by many of the Federalists as an approach to a system of pensions. The same objection defeated a bill to pay to the destitute family of Vice President Gerry, who had died during the session, his salary for the remainder of the year. A vast deal of Federal spleen was vented in the not very creditable debates on these two bills. The Democrats fully retorted in the discussion of a bill, which also failed to pass, to repay to Massachusetts and Connecticut their advances for local defense during the war—advances of which a large amount, amid millions squandered on more favored States, remains unpaid to this day.

The President recommended a peace establishment of 20,000 men. The House wished to reduce it to 6000; the Senate preferred 15,000; 10,000 was finally agreed to as a compromise. Two major generals, four brigadiers, and the necessary number of staff, regimental, and company officers, were to be selected by the President from those in service. The supernumerary officers and men, according to the original terms of enlistment, were to be discharged with three months' extra pay. An additional bounty in land was also proposed, but not carried.

The flotilla act was repealed, and the remaining gun-boats ordered to be sold. The naval establishment was left as it stood, with an additional appropriation of $200,000 annually, for three years, for its gradual increase. A bill for appointing the swamp, occupied by Carroll's division. The ditch in front was very deep and broad; and the storming column, exposed the naval administration, by creating a board of three naval officers, to exercise, under the Secretary of the Navy, the general superintendence of that department.

The three national ships at sea when peace was concluded did not return without additional laurels. Off Lisbon, the Constitution engaged in a moonlight action two British sloops of war, the Cyane, of twenty-four guns, and the Levant, of eighteen. Keeping the wind, and taking a distance favorable to her long twenty-fours, but too great for the carronades, the enemy's principal armament, herself, as it were, in the apex, and the two hostile ships at the opposite angles of a nearly equilateral triangle, the Constitution compelled first the Cyane and then the Levant to strike, with a lose to herself of only three killed and twelve wounded, and no essential damage to the vessel. She then proceeded with her prizes to Porto Praya, in the Cape de Verd Islands, whence she barely escaped, in a fog, from a squadron of heavy British vessels, by which the Levant was recaptured.

The rendezvous appointed for the Hornet and Peacock, on getting out of New York, was Tristran d'Acunha, off the Cape of Good Hope. Shortly before arriving there, the Hornet, Captain Biddle, encountered and captured the brig-of-war Penguin, of eighteen guns, just about her match. The Penguin suffered very severely, with loss of foremast and bowsprit, so that it became necessary to destroy her. The Peacock appeared the next day, when both vessels proceeded together to the Indian Ocean. As they entered that sea they were chased by a seventy-four, from which the Hornet escaped with difficulty, being obliged to throw overboard almost everything moveable, and returning to New York without boat, anchor, or cable, and with but one gun. The Peacock, Captain Warrington, kept on her cruise, and in the Straits of Sunda, captured the Nautilus, an East India cruiser, of fourteen guns. Though told that peace had been made, Warrington insisted that the Nautilus should strike to him, and he compelled her to do so by a broadside, which killed six men and wounded eight others. But the next day she was given up, and so ended the naval hostilities.

The whole number of British vessels captured during the war, on the lakes and on the ocean, as well by privateers (of which there remained some forty or fifty at sea when peace was concluded) as by national vessels, omitting those recaptured, was reckoned at seventeen hundred and fifty. According to an official British return, there had been captured or destroyed by ships of the royal navy, forty-two American national vessels, including twenty-two gun-boats, two hundred and thirty-three privateers, and fourteen hundred and thirty-seven merchant vessels—sixteen hundred and eighty-three in all, manned by upward of eighteen thousand seamen. The captures by British privateers were not numerous.

Owing to the early disasters by land, the balance of prisoners had been all along against the Americans. Horrid, indeed, were the tales brought back, equal to those of the Jersey prison-ship, from Dartmoor and other British depots for prisoners, where war had been seen stripped of all its gilding, and felt in all its grim horrors. Much feeling was also occasioned by an unlucky disturbance which occurred at Dartmoor after the peace was known, the guard firing on the prisoners and killing several.

As to the maritime results of the war, the British remained very sore. A party, with the *London Times* at its head, bitterly complained that any peace should have been assented to before stripping the upstart and insolent Yankees of their naval laurels. Madison, on the other hand, exhibited his anxiety to avoid the impressment question for the future by recommending the passage of an act excluding foreign seamen from American ships.

The Algerine war which now broke out, although it contributed to the making of a naval hero of Decatur, being of minor importance, in comparison with the great events which we are commemorating, Hildreth disposes of very summarily.

Just as the late war with Great Britain had broken out, the Dey of Algiers, taking offense at not having received from America the precise articles in the way of tribute, demanded, had unceremoniously dismissed Lear, the consul, had declared war, and had since captured an American vessel, and reduced her crew to slavery. Immediately after the ratification of the treaty with England, this declaration of war had been reciprocated. Efforts had been at once made to fit out ships, new and old, including several small ones lately purchased for the proposed squadrons of Porter and Perry, and before many weeks Decatur sailed from New

York with the Guerriere, Macedonian, and Constellation frigates, the Ontario, new sloop-of-war, four brigs, and two schooners. Two days after passing Gibraltar, he fell in with and captured an Algerine frigate of forty-four guns, the largest ship in the Algerine navy, which struck to the Guerriere after a running fight of twenty-five minutes. A day or two after, an Algerine brig was chased into shoal water on the Spanish coast, and captured by the smaller vessels. Decatur having appeared off Algiers, the terrified Dey at once consented to a treaty, which he submitted to sign on Decatur's quarter-deck, surrendering all prisoners on hand, making certain pecuniary indemnities, renouncing all future claim to any American tribute or presents, and the practice, also, of reducing prisoners of war to slavery. Decatur then proceeded to Tunis and Tripoli, and obtained from both indemnity for American vessels captured under the guns of their forts by British cruisers during the late war. The Bey of Tripoli being short of cash, Decatur agreed to accept in part payment the restoration to liberty of eight Danes and two Neapolitans, held as slaves.

Later in the season, Bainbridge sailed from Boston with the Independence, seventy-four, the Erie sloop-of-war, and two smaller vessels. Being joined by the Congress frigate, which had carried Eustis to Holland, and by Decatur's squadron, and finding every thing settled, he had nothing to do but to display his force in the ports of the Mediterranean, where the eclat of the American naval victories over the British caused him to be received with marked respect. A little incident which occurred at Malaga deserves notice, as showing how natural is the insolence of power, and how readily our navy officers could fall into the very practices of which we had complained so loudly in the British. A deserter from the Independence, being seized in the streets of Malaga by one of her officers, was discharged by the civil authority on the claim which he set up of being a Spanish citizen. Bainbridge, however, still demanded him, threatening, if he were not given up, to land and take him by force, and, if resistance were made, to fire upon the town—threats to which the authorities yielded.

The return of Bonaparte to France excited a momentary alarm, lest the unsettled questions of impressment and neutral rights might again come up; but his speedy downfall destroyed these apprehensions, and with them the hopes, also, of a new harvest to be reaped by neutral commerce.

The posts of Prarie du Chien and Michilimackinac having been re-occupied, steps were taken for the complete pacification of all the northwestern tribes. At a council held at Detroit, at which were represented the Senecas, Delawares, Shawanese, Wyandots, Potawatomies of Lake Michigan, Ottawas, and Chippewas, with some bands, also, of the Winnebagoes and Sauks, and at which the famous Prophet, the brother of Tecumseh, was present, the hatchet was formally buried as between all these tribes and as between them and the United States. Other treaties soon followed, with the Potawatomies of Illinois, the Piankeshaws, Osages, Iowas, Kansas, Foxes, Kickapoos, and various bands of the great Sioux confederacy, with several of which formal relations were now first established.

CHAPTER XLII.

Causes of the War — Debates in Congress — Extracts from Mr. Clay's Speeches on the different phases of the War Question.

THE causes of this war of 1812, which was now brought to an almost immediate conclusion, by the treaty of Ghent, and which have been much debated, are best illustrated by the speeches of Mr. Clay, its great champion, as well as the universal champion of human rights and freedom everywhere. Mr. Clay, in his urgency for this war, won for himself the most enduring basis of that singular personal popularity, which has since marked his reputation, as the noblest of the sons of "Sam" since his first representative, Washington.

It is remarkable, that the two great nations of western Europe, Great Britain and France, while at war with each other, should have presumed, that they could do any amount of injury to the rights and commercial interests of the United States with impunity. The British blockade of 1806 was followed by the Berlin edicts, and the British orders in council by the edicts of Milan, and these belligerent powers made war on the commerce of a friend, the better to carry on war between themselves. The United States were made the victim of their rapacity. From February 28, to May 20, 1811, less than three months, twenty-seven American merchant-vessels were sent into British ports, prizes to British cruisers, for violation of the orders in council, and the British admiralty courts were constantly occupied in adjudicating on American property, thus brought under their jurisdiction, little of which escaped forfeiture for the crime of a neutral commerce, and for attempting to enter ports which had no other blockade than parchment orders. At the same time that these outrages were committed on American commerce, swelling up to millions annually, British manufactures were allowed and encouraged to enter, in neutral bottoms, the very ports from which American vessels, laden with American produce, were excluded, and for having papers of that destination, were captured!

But Great Britain, having command of the seas, asserted another offensive power, in relation to the United States, to maintain her maritime ascendancy, by seizing American seamen, on board American merchantmen, and forcing them into the British navy, under the pretense of searching for British subjects, and claiming their services, while all parties knew the wrong that was done. The seizure of the property of a neutral power, as a belligerent right, and claiming it as forfeited, though sufficiently atrocious, was a much less exasperating offense, than that of forcing neutrals to fight the battles of a belligerent. France was wreng; Great Britain was more so. The former had some magnanimity, when it was convenient to exercise it; while the latter seemed bent on wrong for the love of it. It is true, that Great Britain pretended to be fighting for existence, and her own vindicators asserted the law of necessity: but that was neither consolation, nor relief, to those whose rights she violated.

The truth undoubtedly was, that the United States had fallen into contempt, and the time had arrived when it was necessary to vindicate their rights. The mission of John Henry, into New England, in 1809, acting under the instructions of Sir James Craig, governor of Canada, with designs against the Union, as proved by Mr. Madison's communications to Congress, March 9, 1812, is sufficient evidence, that something more than contempt actuated the British government in the repeated and aggravated insults and injuries done to the government and people of the United States, for a series of years, naught abated by time and remonstrance, but ever on the increase. The conclusion seemed to have been adopted in Europe, that, though the United States had fought once, and gained their independence, there was no great danger of their fighting again, though insulted and wronged; that they might be injured to any extent with impunity. What else could account for the treatment received from France and

Great Britain, especially the latter? Such was the state of things which led to the war of 1812.

Congress was convoked a month before the regular time, in the fall of 1811, and the message of President Madison was decidedly in the war tone. The winter was spent in notes of preparation, and by the 20th of March, Congress had passed, and the President approved, bills of the following titles: To fill up the ranks and prolong the enlistment of the army; to raise an additional regular force of twenty-five thousand men; to raise six companies of mounted rangers for the defense of the western frontier; to arm the militia; to authorize detachments of militia to fortify the maritime frontier; to repair and fit the entire naval force; to procure camp-equipage, baggage-wagons, etc.; to purchase ordnance and military stores; to obtain supplies of sulphur and salt-peter; to make further provisions for the corps of engineers; to establish a quartermaster's department, and create commissary-generals; to provide for the support of the army and navy; and to authorize a loan of eleven millions.

In the meantime, there had been a vigorous opposition to these measures; but when, on the 1st of April, Mr. Madison sent in his special message, with the documents respecting Henry's mission, there was a burst of indignant feeling from Congress, and from the whole nation, well calculated to unite the country in hostile measures. From this time till the declaration of war, on the 19th of June, the utmost spirit of preparation was manifested in the legislative and executive branches of the government, to begin the contest.

The well-known moderation of President Madison's character demanded powerful influences, to bring him up to the required temper for the responsibilities of this new position, as the head of the government; and there was probably but one man who was capable, by his extraordinary power over others, of imparting to him the spirit that was needed for the time. It hardly need be said, that HE was the speaker of the House of Representatives—Mr. Clay. By the same cause, Congress was ready for the war before the president was. He was still laboring in vain at the oar of negotiation, with Mr. Foster, the British minister, when an informal deputation from the other branch of the government waited upon him, with Mr. Clay at their head, and before they retired the die was cast. Nothing remained but the formal act of declaration.

It may be remarked, that Mr. Clay's feelings in relation to the insults and wrongs suffered by the country from Great Britain, had been for several years maturing for that course of action which he pursued after the struggle commenced, and were on various occasions, and in sundry forms, publicly expressed—often incidentally. In a speech in the Senate, December 25, 1810, in vindication of President Madison's occupation of the territory in dispute between the United States and Spain, eastward from the Mississippi to the line of the Perdido, he said—

"The gentleman [Mr. Horsey, of Delaware] reminds us, that Great Britain, the ally of Spain, may be obliged, by her connection with that country, to take part with her against us, and to consider this measure of the president as justifying an appeal to arms. Sir, is the time never to arrive, when we may manage our own affairs, without the fear of insulting his Britannic majesty? Is the rod of British power to be forever suspended over our heads?—Does Congress put on an embargo to shelter our rightful commerce against the piratical depredations committed upon it on the ocean? We are immediately warned of the indignation of offended England. Is a law of non-intercourse proposed? The whole navy of the haughty mistress of the seas is made to thunder in our ears. Does the president refuse to continue a correspondence with a minister, who violates the decorum belonging to his diplomatic character by giving and deliberately repeating an affront to the whole nation? We are instantly menaced with the chastisement which English pride will not fail to inflict. Whether we assert our rights by sea, or attempt their maintenance by land—whithersoever we turn ourselves, this phantom incessantly pursues us. Already has it had too much influence on the councils of the nation. It contributed to the repeal of the embargo—that dishonorable repeal, which has so much tarnished the character of our government. Mr. President, I have before said on this floor, and now take occasion to remark, that I most sincerely desire peace and amity with England; that I even prefer an adjustment of all differences with her, before one with any other nation. But if she persists in a denial of justice to us, or if she avails herself of the occupation of West Florida, to commence war upon us, I trust and hope that all hearts will unite, in a bold and vigorous vindication of our rights."

Mr. Clay, foreseeing that war with Great Britain was inevitable, had declined going into the Senate again, and in 1811 was elected to the House of Representatives, as the more important branch of the public service for the occasion. Having made up his mind, that war was the only course to vindicate the national honor and rights, all his efforts were directed to bring about the final measure, from which there could be no retreat, till those rights should be acknowledged and respected. Though Speaker of the House, opportunities were afforded him, in committee of the whole on the state of the Union, to express his sentiments; and it was in this field that he wielded a paramount influence. His addresses in the secret sessions, while the question of war was pending, which, as represented, were most animating and stirring, are of course lost; and but a few of those delivered in public debate, are extant. While the bill to raise an additional regular force of twenty-five thousand men, was pending, Mr. Clay addressed the House, in committee, on the 31st of December, 1811. The following are extracts from this speech:

"Mr. Clay [the Speaker] said, that when the subject of this bill was before the House in the abstract form of a resolution, proposed by the committee of foreign relations, it was the pleasure of the House to discuss it while he was in the chair. He did not complain of this course of proceeding; for he did not at any time wish the House, from considerations personal to him, to depart from that mode of transacting the public business which they thought best. He merely adverted to the circumstance, as an apology for the trouble he was about to give the committee. He was at all times disposed to take his share of responsibility, and under this impression, he felt that he owed it to his constituents and to himself, before the committee rose, to submit to their attention a few observations. * * *

"The difference between those who were for fifteen thousand, and those who were for twenty-five thousand men, appeared to him to resolve itself into the question, merely, of a short or protracted war; a war of vigor, or a war of languor and imbecility. If a competent force be raised in the first instance, the war on the continent will be speedily terminated. He was aware that it might still rage on the ocean. But where the nation could act with unquestionable success, he was in favor of the display of an energy correspondent to the feelings and spirit of the country. Suppose one-third of the force he had mentioned (twenty-five thousand men) could reduce the country, say in three years, and that the whole could accomplish the same object in one year; taking into view the greater hazard of the repulsion and defeat of the small force, and every other consideration, do not wisdom and true economy equally decide in favor of the larger force, and thus prevent failure in consequence of inadequate means? He begged gentlemen to recollect the immense extent of the United States: our vast maritime frontier, vulnerable in almost all its parts to predatory incursions, and he was persuaded, they would see that a regular force of twenty-five thousand men was not much too great during a period of war, if all designs of invading the provinces of the enemy were abandoned. * * *

"The object of the force, he understood distinctly to be war, and war with Great Britain. It had been supposed by some gentlemen, improper to discuss publicly so delicate a question. He did not feel the impropriety. It was a subject in its nature incapable of concealment. Even in countries where the powers of government were conducted by a single ruler, it was almost impossible for that ruler to conceal his intentions when he meditates war. The assembling of armies, the strengthening of posts—all the movements preparatory to war, and which it is impossible to disguise, unfolded the intentions of the sovereign. Does Russia or France intend war: the intention is almost invariably known before the war is commenced. If Congress were to pass a law, with closed doors, for raising an army for the purpose of war, its enlistment and organization, which could not be done in secret, would indicate the use to which it was to be applied; and we could not suppose England would be so blind, as not to see that she was aimed at. Nor could she, did she apprehend, injure us more by thus knowing our purposes, than if she were kept in ignorance of them. She may, indeed, anticipate us, and commence the war. But that is what she is in fact doing, and she can add but little to the injury which she is inflicting. If she choose to declare war in form, let her do so—the responsibility will be with her."

The purpose of this measure having been avowed, all the questions of expediency in the nation's taking so momentous a step, of course came up for consideration, and were required to be solved—of which that of the public finances was not among the least. Was the nation prepared for the cost? As a matter of fact, the foreign commerce of the country, and as a consequence the public revenue, were almost entirely ruined by the belligerents. The revenue had fallen from sixteen millions to six, and it was scarcely possible to be worse. The wrongs inflicted on the country by the operation of the British orders in council and the French decrees, were not only disastrous to the public revenue, but equally so to the interests of private individuals, by the seizure, adjudication, and forfeiture of their property afloat on the high seas, under plea of a violation of those orders and decrees. The business of the country, and the wheels of the government, were both in a fair way of being stopped. Things, indeed, had come to such a pass, by the operation of these causes, that apart from peril of life, and injury to public morals, and as a simple question of finance, it was scarcely possible that war should not make business, and pay for itself, so far as it respected the nation at large, though it should run the government in debt. In such a state of things it could not be worse.

There was national character, too; honor, a nation's best treasure, trampled under foot, and kicked about Europe as a despicable thing. There were thousands of American sailors, forced into the British navy, and compelled to fight the battles of the British sovereign, without remedy, without hope. To the ruin of American commerce were added indignity to the nation, by disregarding its remonstrances, and the violation of the personal rights of American citizens, by depriving them of freedom, and forcing them into a service where they owed no allegiance, to the peril of their lives, and the destruction of their fortunes—holding them in captivity from country, home, and friends. And when the French decrees were revoked, as respected American commerce, the British government held the American government responsible for their revocation as respected all other nations, before they would repeal the orders in council! In view of this state of things, Mr. Clay said:

"England is said to be fighting for the world, and shall we, it is asked, attempt to weaken her exertions? If, indeed, the aim of the French emperor be universal dominion (and he was willing to allow it to the argument), how much nobler a cause is presented to British valor! But how is her philanthropic purpose to be achieved? By a scrupulous observance of the rights of others; by respecting that code of public law which she professes to vindicate; and by abstaining from self-aggrandizement. Then would she command the sympathies of the world. What are we required to do by those who would engage our feelings and wishes in her behalf? To bear the actual cuffs of her arrogance, that we may escape a chimerical French subjugation! We are invited, conjured, to to drink the potion of British poison, actually presented to our lips, that we may avoid the imperial dose prepared by perturbed imaginations. We are called upon to submit to debasement, dishonor, and disgraee; to bow the neck to royal insolence, as a course of preparation for manly resistance to Gallic invasion! What nation, what individual, was ever taught, in the schools of ignominious submission, these patriotic lessons of freedom and independence? Let those who contend for this humiliating doctrine, read its refutation in the history of the very man against whose insatiable thirst of dominion we are warned. The experience of desolated Spain, for the last fifteen years, is worth volumes. Did she find her repose and safety in subserviency to the will of that man? Had she boldly stood forth and repelled the first attempt to dictate to her councils, her monarch would not be now a miserable captive in Marseilles. Let us come home to our own history: it was not by submission that our fathers achieved our independence. The patriotic wisdom that placed you, Mr. Chairman, under that canopy, penetrated the designs of a corrupt ministry, and nobly fronted encroachment on its first appearance. It saw, beyond the petty taxes with which it commenced, a long train of oppressive measures, terminating in the total annihilation of liberty, and, contemptible as they were, it did not hesitate to resist them. Take the experience of the last four or five years, which he was sorry to say exhibited, in appearance at least, a different kind of spirit. He did not wish to view the past, further than to guide us for the future. We were but yesterday contending for the indirect trade—the right to export to Europe the coffee and sugar of the West Indies. To-day we are asserting our claim to the direct trade—the right to export our cotton, tobacco, and other domestic produce, to market. Yield this point, and to-morrow intercourse between New York and New Orleans, between the planters on James river and Richmond, will be interdicted. For, sir, the career of encroachment is never arrested by submission. It will advance while there remains a single privilege on which it can operate. Gentlemen say that this government is unfit for any war, but a war of invasion. What, is it not equivalent to invasion, if the mouths of our harbors and outlets are blocked up, and we are denied egress from our own waters? Or, when the burglar is at our door, shall we bravely sally forth and repel his felonious entrance, or meanly skulk within the cells of the castle? * * * * *

"He [Mr. Clay] was one, who was prepared (and he would not believe that he was more so than any other member of the committee) to march on in the road of his duty, at all hazards. What! shall it be said, that our *amor patriæ* is located at these desks; that we pusillanimously cling to our seats here, rather than boldly vindicate the most inestimable rights of the country? While the heroic Daviess, and his gallant associates, exposed to all the dangers of treacherous, savage warfare, are sacrificing themselves for the good of their country, shall we shrink from our duty?"

When the army-bill was disposed of, a navy-bill came up, which, among other objects, proposed to build a *blank* number of frigates. The most important question was the filling up of this blank. Mr. Cheves, of South Carolina, moved for the number of TEN. Mr. Rhea, of Tennessee, moved to strike out this section, which was negatived by a vote of 52 to 47—a test vote. It was during the pendency of Mr. Rhea's motion, that Mr. Clay addressed the committee against it, and in favor of the proposal of Mr. Cheves. Mr. Clay said:

"The attention of Congress has been invited to this subject by the president, in his message, delivered at the opening of the session. Indeed, had it been wholly neglected by the chief magistrate, from the critical situation of the country, and the nature of the rights proposed to be vindicated, it must have pressed itself upon our attention. But, said Mr. Clay, the president, in his message, observes: 'Your attention will, of course, be drawn to such provisions on the subject of our naval force, as may be required for the service to which it is best adapted. I submit to Congress the reasonableness, also, of an authority to augment the stock of such materials as are imperishable in their nature, or may not, at once, be attainable?' The president, by this recommendation, clearly intimates an opinion, that the naval force of this country is capable of producing effect; and the propriety of laying up imperishable materials was no doubt suggested for the purpose of making additions to the navy, as convenience and exigencies might direct.

"It appeared to Mr. Clay a little extraordinary, that so much, as it seemed to him, unreasonable jealousy, should exist against the naval establishment. If, said he, we look back to the period of the formation of the constitution, it will be found that no such jealousy was then excited. In placing the physical force of the nation at the disposal of Congress, the convention manifested much greater apprehension of abuse in the power given to raise armies, than in that to provide a navy. In reference to the navy, Congress is put under no restrictions; but with respect to the army, that description of force which has been so often employed to subvert the liberties of mankind, they are subjected to limitations designed to prevent the abuse of this dangerous power. But it was not his intention to detain the committee by a discussion on the comparative utility and safety of these two kinds of force. He would, however, be indulged in saying, that he thought gentlemen had wholly failed in maintaining the position they had assumed, that the fall of maritime powers was attributable to their navies. They have told you, indeed, that Carthage, Genoa, Venice, and other nations, had navies, and, notwithstanding, were finally destroyed. But have they shown, by a train of argument, that their overthrow was in any degree attributable to their maritime greatness? Have they attempted, even, to show that there exists in the nature of this power a necessary tendency to destroy the nation using it? Assertion is substituted for argument; inferences not authorized by historical facts are arbitrarily drawn; things wholly unconnected with each other are associated together; a very logical mode of reasoning, it must be admitted! In the same way he could demonstrate how idle and absurd our attachments are to freedom itself. He might say, for example, that Greece and Rome had forms of free government, and that they no longer exist; and, deducing their fall from their devotion to liberty, the conclusion, in favor of despotism, would very satisfactorily follow! He demanded what there is in the nature and construction of maritime power, to excite the fears that have been indulged? Do gentlemen really apprehend, that a body of seamen will abandon their proper element, and placing themselves under an aspiring chief, will erect a throne to his ambition? Will they deign to listen to the voice of history, and learn how chimerical are their apprehensions?

"But the source of alarm is in ourselves. Gentlemen fear, that if we provide a marine, it will produce collisions with foreign nations, plunge us into war, aud ultimately overturn the constitution of the country. Sir, if you wish to avoid foreign collision, you had better abandon the ocean surrender all your commerce; give up all your prosperity. It is the thing protected, not the instrument of protection, that involves you in war. Commerce engenders collision, collision war, and war, the argument supposes, leads to despotism. Would the counsels of that statesman be deemed wise, who would recommend that the nation should be unarmed; that the art of war, the martial spirit, and martial exercises, should be prohibited; who should declare, in the language of Othello, that the nation must bid farewell to the neighing steed, and the shrill trump, the spirit-stirring drum, the ear-piercing fife, and all the pride, pomp and circumstance of glorious war; and that the great body of the people should be taught, that national happiness was to be found in perpetual peace alone? No, sir. And yet, every argument in favor of a power of protection on land, applies in some degree to a power of protection on the sea. Undoubtedly, a commerce void of naval protection is more exposed to rapacity than a guarded commerce; and if we wish to invite the continuance of the old, or the enactment of new edicts, let us refrain from all exertion upon that element where we must operate, and where, in the end, they must be resisted."

It can not but be seen that this debate is greatly instructive, not alone as it shows the position occupied by Mr. Clay, but as it discloses the position of the country, at the time, the views of public policy entertained by existing parties, the untried condition and ability of the naval force, the want of faith in that arm of the public service, and the difficulties which were to be encountered in raising it from infancy to manhood, and sending it out boldly to assert the rights and exemplify the valor of the nation on the deep.

It is clear enough, that Mr. Clay, though speaker of the House of Representatives, and sufficiently tasked in that capacity, was also a leader in debates, and leader of the party disposed to stir up the nation to a trial of strength with at least one of the great transatlantic belligerents, both of which had done such wrongs, and offered such insults, to the people and government of the United States. The House was accustomed to go into committee—thus relieving Mr. Clay from the duties of speaker—for the purpose of giving him opportunities to express his views on any pending measures, and of availing itself of the benefit of his counsels, and of his stirring eloquence. Fresh from the bosom of the patriotic and gallant people of the west, himself not behind in these lofty sentiments, animated by the ardor and nerved with the vigor of a young statesman, endowed with such facilities of persuasion as few men ever possessed, sensitive, not less to public than to private honor, thoroughly informed in the foreign relations of the government and the capabilities of the United States, Mr. Clay viewed with mortification the position of the country. and looked with scorn and indignation at the wrongs and insults of Great Britain and France, which had placed it there Unused to arms since the national independence was acquired, and that great battle having been fought for freedom—for the "lives, fortunes, and sacred honor" of the people—it was a great problem what might be the result of a conflict waged on such grounds as were at this time presented, and a great responsibility in pushing the nation into it. But the alternatives were only two: commercial ruin and national debasement on the one hand, or bearding the British lion in his den, on the other. A young nation born into existence by agony from which there was no escape, was now to measure weapons with the oldest and most powerful empire on earth, in defence of its honor. The responsibility of a leader in such an enterprise was great.

Having just come out of the debate on a measure for raising a suitable land force, about which all reasonings could be based on some tangible probabilities, the navy was a subject which could not but be regarded with extreme concern, in a war with "the mistress of the seas." And yet it was a subject that must be approached, in a preparation for such a war; and it presented a question that must be disposed of. Should the sea be abandoned to the foe, and its road to national wealth and greatness be surrendered to the sole travel of an arrogant highwayman? Or should a young nation, reduced by a visionary policy to gun-boat tactics and garrison defenses, like a chicken on a dunghill defying the hawk that is sailing downward on his prey, go out in such a field against such odds? It is no wonder that discouragement, and a feeling like dismay, should have pervaded so many minds at the prospect. To begin to build a navy, at the moment of going into war with the greatest maritime power in the world, was indeed a bold proposal—apparently bordering on presumption. But it was a necessity, before the face of which patriotism could not flee—a doom which national gallantry was forced to encounter.

We come now to the discussions in regard to building the navy, with the view of chastising the insolence of John Bull upon the seas, to the sole dominion and undivided rights upon which he had chosen to assert his domineering sovreignty.

The following remarks of Mr. Clay, on the importance of foreign commerce to the people and government of the country, and on the intimate connection between a commercial and military marine, are not more forcibly stated than true:

"He considered the prosperity of foreign commerce indissolubly allied to the marine power. Neglect to provide the one, and you must abandon the other. Suppose the expected war with England is commenced, you enter and subjugate Canada, and she still refuses to do you justice; what other possible mode will remain to operate on the enemy, but upon that element where alone you can then come in contact with him? And if you do not prepare to protect there your own commerce, and to assail his, will he not sweep from the ocean every vessel bearing your flag, and destroy even the coasting trade? But, from the arguments of gentlemen, it would seem to be questioned, if foreign commerce is worth the kind of protection insisted upon. What is this foreign commerce, that has suddenly become so inconsiderable? It has, with very trifling aid from other sources, defrayed the expenses of government, ever since the adoption of the present constitution; maintained an expensive and successful war with the Indians; a war with the Barbary powers; a quasi war with France; sustained the charges of suppressing two insurrections, and extinguishing upward of forty-six millions of the public debt. In revenue, it has, since the year 1789, yielded one hundred and ninety-one millions of dollars. During the first four years after the commencement of the present government, the revenue averaged only about two millions annually; during a subsequent period of four years, it rose to an average of fifteen millions, annually, or became equivalent to a capital of two hundred and fifty millions of dollars, at an interest of six per centum per annum. And if our commerce be re-established, it will, in the course of time, net a sum for which we are scarcely furnished with figures, in arithmetic. Taking the average of the last nine years (comprehending, of course, the season of the embargo), our exports average upward of thirty-seven millions of dollars, which is equivalent to a capital of more than six hundred millions of dollars, at six per centum interest; all of which must be lost in the event of a destruction of foreign commerce. In the abandonment of that commerce, is also involved the sacrifice of our brave tars, who have engaged in the pursuit, from which they derive subsistence and support, under the confidence that government would afford them that just protection which is due to all. They will be driven into foreign employment, for it is vain to expect that they will renounce their habits of life.

"The spirit of commercial enterprise, so strongly depicted by the gentleman from New York [Mr. Mitchell], is diffused throughout the country. It is a passion, as unconquerable as any with which nature has endowed us. You may attempt, indeed, to regulate, but you can not destroy it. It exhibits itself as well on the waters of the western country, as on the waters and shores of the Atlantic. Mr. Clay had heard of a vessel, built at Pittsburg, having crossed the Atlantic and entered a European port (he believed that of Leghorn). The master of the vessel laid his papers before the proper customhouse officer, which, of course, stated the place of her departure. The officer boldly denied the existence of any such American port as Pittsburg, and threatened a seizure of the vessel, as being furnished with forged papers. The affrighted master procured a map of the United States, and pointing out the Gulf of Mexico, took the officer to the mouth of the Mississippi, traced the course of the Mississippi more than a thousand miles, to the mouth of the Ohio, and conducting him still a thousand miles higher, to the junction of the Alleghany and the Monongahela—'There,' he exclaimed, 'stands Pittsburg, the port from which I sailed!'"

The efforts of Mr. Clay in Congress, and in all his private relations, during this season of preparation for war, were unremitting, desiring to go into it with unanimity and vigor, that it might end with honor and the achievement of the objects of the conflict.

When war was declared, the manifest importance of having at the head of the army a man of talents, decision, energy, and weight of character, notwithstanding Mr. Clay had been trained exclusively in the civil service, suggested to the mind of President Madison, that he was THE MAN, and he had made up his mind to send in his name to the Senate for the office of major-general. Mr. Gallatin—though he and Mr. Clay have never been on the best of terms—is understood to have said, that he knew of no man so prompt and fruitful in expedients for an exigency, as Mr. Clay—a qualification, of all others, the most important for a military captain. This is the universal opinion of his character, and it has been sufficiently proved. Mr. Madison, doubtless, had made this discovery, and it is an interesting subject of hypothetical review, what would probably have been the result, if Mr. Clay had been put in this important position. None who know the man can doubt, that the utmost activity and energy would have been displayed in the military operations of the country, and that the war might have been brought to a close in half the time and at half the expense. What other consequences might have followed in Mr. Clay's civil history, after having worn an epaulet and sword, with credit to himself and benefit to his country, is matter of innocent conjecture. Mr. Madison, however, was dissuaded from his purpose, on the ground that Mr. Clay's services were indispensable in the national councils. The president tendered to him the mission to Russia, for important public purposes, after the war, and afterward one of the executive departments, both of which were declined—doubtless for the reasons which had induced him to decline the more elevated and dignified position of a senator, for the more useful one of a commoner. Mr. Monroe afterward offered Mr. Clay a secretaryship at home, and a *carte blanche* of all the foreign missions; but he preferred the House of Representatives.

It is well known, that the first year of the war was not very creditable to the American arms, and that it was disheartening to the spirit of the country. The opposition, in Congress, heaped upon the administration *reproachful* censure for having engaged in the war, which roused Mr. Clay, not only to its vindication, but to some vehement expressions of patriotic indignation. In January, 1813, a bill was before Congress, to increase the army by twenty additional regiments. On the 8th of this month, in committee of the whole, Mr. Clay noticed these attacks on the government, and replied to some invectives on the merits of the war.

In recording the services of a statesman, in peace or war, he is to be represented in the field which he occupies, or in which he enacts his part. The roar of artillery and the clash of steel are not in the senate of a nation; but there are battles even there. The statesman who sways the councils of his country, by his wisdom and eloquence, occupies a position more lofty and more commanding, than any other public agent. Armies are raised and moved, and fleets scour the seas, for pacific functions, or in search of the foe, under his orders. He is forced to look on all at home, and all abroad—to secure, protect, and vindicate domestic interests and rights, against foreign policies and foreign aggressions. His tent is the canopy of heaven, and his field the world. He fights in war, and fights in peace. There is no repose for him who guards with vigilance and fidelity the public weal.

The position which Mr. Clay occupied in the war of 1812, was eminent. That he had been eminently influential in its inception, and in committing the nation to the hazard, could not be unknown; and in view of the adverse events of its early history, the opponents of the war and of the administration, fell heavily upon him who had been so active in bringing it about. He thus replies:

"Sir, gentlemen appear to me to forget, that they stand on American soil; that they are not in the British House of Commons, but in the chamber of the House of Representatives of the United States; that we have nothing to do with the affairs of Europe, the partition of territory and sovereignty there, except so far as these things affect the interests of our own country. Gentlemen transform themselves into the Burkes, Chathams, and Pitts of another country, and forgetting, from honest zeal, the interests of America, engage with European sensibility in the discussion of European interests. If gentlemen ask me, whether I do not view with regret and horror the concentration of such vast power in the hands of Bonaparte, I reply, that I do. I regret to see the emperor of China holding such immense sway over the fortunes of millions of our species. I regret to see Great Britain possessing so uncontrolled a command over all the waters of our globe. If I had the ability to distribute among the nations of Europe their several portions of power and sovereignty, I would say that Holland should be resuscitated, and given the weight she enjoyed in the days of her De Witts. I would confine France within her natural boundaries, the Alps, Pyrenees, and the Rhine, and make her a secondary naval power only. I would abridge the British maritime power, raise Prussia and Austria to their original condition, and preserve the integrity of the empire of Russia. But these are speculations. I look at the political transactions of Europe, with the single exception of their possible bearing upon us, as I do at the history of other countries, or other times. I do not survey them with half the interest that I do the movements in South America. Our political relation with them is much less important than it is supposed to be. I have no fears of French or English subjugation. If we are united, we are too powerful for the mightiest nation in Europe, or all Europe combined. If we are separated and torn asunder, we shall become an easy prey to the weakest of them. In the latter dreadful contingency, our country will not be worth preserving.

"Next to the notice which the opposition has found itself called upon to bestow upon the French emperor, a distinguished citizen of Virginia, formerly president of the United States, has never for a moment failed to receive their kindest and and most respectful attention. An honorable gentleman from Massachusetts, [Mr. Quincy,] of whom I am sorry to say, it becomes necessary for me, in the course of my remarks, to take some notice, has alluded to him in a remarkable manner. Neither his retirement from public office, his eminent services, nor his advanced age, can exempt this patriot from the coarse assaults of party malevolence. No, sir. In 1801, he snatched from the rude hand of usurpation the violated constitution of his country, and *that* is his crime. He preserved that instrument, in form, and substance, and spirit, a precious inheritance for generations to come; and for *this* he can never be forgiven. How vain and impotent is party rage, directed against such a man! He is not more elevated by his lofty residence upon the summit of his own favorite mountain, than he is lifted, by the serenity of his mind, and the consciousness of a well-spent life, above the malignant passions and bitter feelings of the day. No! his own beloved Monticello is not less moved by the storms that beat against its sides, than is this illustrious man by the howlings of the whole British pack, set loose from the Essex kennel! When the gentleman to whom I have been compelled to allude, shall have mingled his dust with that of his abused ancestors, when he shall have been consigned to oblivion, or, if he lives at all, shall live only in the treasonable annals of a certain junto, the name of Jefferson will be hailed with gratitude, his memory honored and cherished as the second founder of the liberties of the people, and the period of his administration will be looked back to, as one of the happiest and brightest epochs of American history—an oasis in the midst of a sandy desert. But I beg the gentleman's pardon; he has indeed secured to himself a more imperishable fame than I had supposed: I think it was about four years ago that he submitted to the House of Representatives, an initiative proposition for the impeachment of

Mr. Jefferson. The House condescended to consider it. The gentleman debated it with his usual *temper*, *moderation*, and *urbanity*. The House decided upon it in the most solemn manner, and, although the gentleman had somehow obtained a second, the final vote stood, ONE for, *and one hundred and seventeen against*, the proposition! * * *

"But, sir, I must speak of another subject, which I never think of but with feelings of the deepest awe. The gentleman from Massachusetts, in imitation of some of his predecessors of 1799, has entertained us with a picture of cabinet plots, presidential plots, and all sorts of plots, which have been engendered by the diseased state of the gentleman's imagination. I wish, sir, that another plot, of a much more serious and alarming character—a plot that aims at the dismemberment of our Union—had only the same imaginary existence. But no man who has paid any attention to the tone of certain prints, and to transactions in a particular quarter of the Union, for several years past, can doubt the existence of such a plot. It was far, very far, from my intention to charge the opposition with such a design. No, I believe them generally incapable of it. But I cannot say as much for some, who have been unworthily associated with them, in the quarter of the Union to which I have referred. The gentleman can not have forgotten his own sentiment, uttered even on the floor of this House, 'Peaceably if we can, *forcibly* if we must,' nearly at the very time Henry's mission to Boston was undertaken. The flagitiousness of that embassy had been attempted to be concealed, by directing the public attention to the price which, the gentleman says, was given for the disclosure. As if any price could change the atrociousness of the attempt on the part of Great Britain, or could extenuate, in the slightest degree, the offense of those citizens who entertained and deliberated upon a proposition so infamous and unnatural! There was a most remarkable coincidence between some of the things which that man states, and certain events in the quarter alluded to. In the contingency of war with Great Britain, it will be recollected, that the neutrality and eventual separation of that section of the Union was to be brought about. How, sir, has it happened, since the declaration of war, that British officers in Canada have asserted to American officers, that this very neutrality would take place? That they have so asserted can be established beyond controversy. The project is not brought forward openly, with a direct avowal of the intention. No, the stock of good sense and patriotism in that portion of the country is too great to be undisguisedly encountered. It is assailed from the masked batteries of friendship, of peace and commerce, on the one side, and by the groundless imputation of opposite propensities on the other. The affections of the people there are to be gradually undermined. The project is suggested or withdrawn; the diabolical *dramatis personæ*, in this criminal tragedy, make their appearance or exit, as the audience to whom they address themselves, applaud or condemn. I was astonished, sir, in reading lately, a letter, or pretended letter, published in a prominent print in that quarter, and written, not in the fervor of party zeal, but coolly and dispassionately, to find that the writer affected to reason about a separation, and attempted to demonstrate its advantages to the different portions of the Union—deploring the existence now of what he terms prejudices against it, but hoping for the arrival of the period when they shall be eradicated. But, sir, I will quit this unpleasant subject.

* * * * * * *

"The war was declared because Great Britain arrogated to herself the pretension of regulating our foreign trade, under the delusive name of retaliatory orders in council—a pretension by which she undertook to proclaim to American enterprise, 'Thus far shalt thou go, and no further'—orders which she refused to revoke, after the alleged cause of their enactment had ceased; because she persisted in the practice of impressing American seamen; because she had instigated the Indians to commit hostilities against us; and because she refused indemnity for her past injuries upon our commerce. I throw out of the question other wrongs. The war, in fact, was announced, on our part, to meet the war which she was waging on her part. So undeniable were the causes of the war, so powerfully did they address themselves to the feelings of the whole American people, that when the bill was pending before this House, gentlemen in the opposition, although provoked to debate, would not, or could not, utter one syllable against it. It is true, they wrapped themselves up in sullen silence, pretending they did not choose to debate such a question in secret session. While speaking of the proceedings on that occasion, I beg to be admitted to advert to another fact which transpired—an important fact, material for the nation to know, and which I have often regretted had not been spread upon our journals. My honorable colleague [Mr. McKee] moved, in committee of the whole, to comprehend France in the war; and when the question was taken upon the proposition, there appeared but ten votes in support of it, of whom seven belonged to this side of the house, and three only to the other! It is said that we were inveigled into the war by the perfidy of France; and that, had she furnished the document in time, which was first published in England, in May last, it would have been prevented. I will concede to gentlemen everything they ask about the injustice of France toward this country. I wish to God that our ability was equal to our disposition to make her feel the sense that we entertain of that injustice. The manner of the publication of the paper in question, was, undoubtedly, extremely exceptionable. But I maintain, that, had it made its appearance earlier, it would not have had the effect supposed; and the proof lies in the unequivocal declarations of the British government. I will trouble you, sir, with going no further back than to the letters of the British minister, addressed to the Secretary of State, just before the expiration of his diplomatic functions. It will be recollected by the committee, that he exhibited to this government a dispatch from Lord Castlereagh, in which the principle was distinctly avowed that, to produce the effect of a repeal of the orders in council, the French decrees must be absolutely and entirely revoked as to all the world, and not as to America alone. A copy of that despatch was demanded of him, and he very awkwardly evaded it. But on the 10th of June, after the bill declaring war had actually passed this House, and was pending before the Senate, (and which, I have no doubt, was known to him,) in a letter to Mr. Munroe, he says: 'I have no hesitation in saying, sir, that Great Britain, as the case has hitherto stood, never did, and never *could*, engage, without the greatest injustice to herself and her allies, as well as to other neutral nations, to repeal her orders, as affecting America alone, leaving them in force against other states, upon condition that France would except, singly and specially, America from the operation of her decrees.' On the 14th of the same month, the bill still pending before the Senate, he repeats: 'I will now say, that I feel entirely authorized to assure you, that if you can, at any time, produce a *full and unconditional* repeal of the French decrees, as you have a right to demand it, in your character of a neutral nation, and that it be disengaged from any question concerning our maritime rights, we shall be ready to meet you with a revocation of the orders in council. Previously to your producing *such* an instrument, which I am sorry to see you regard as unnecessary, you can not expect of us to give up our orders in council.' Thus, sir, you see that the British government would not be content with a repeal of the French decrees as to us only. But the French paper in question was such a repeal. It could not, therefore, satisfy the British government. It could not, therefore, have induced that government, had it been earlier promulgated, to repeal the orders in council. It could not, therefcre, have averted the war. The withholding of it did not occasion the war, and the promulgation of it would not have prevented the war. But gentlemen have contended, that, in point of fact, it did produce a repeal of the orders in council. This I deny. After it made its appearance in England, it was declared by one of the British ministry, in Parliament, not to be satisfactory. And all the world knows that the repeal of the orders in council resulted from the inquiry, reluctantly acceded to by the ministry, into the effect upon their manufacturing establishments, of our non-importation law, or to the warlike attitude assumed by this government, or to both. * * * * *

"It is not to the British principle [of allegiance], objectionable as it is, that we are alone to look; it is to her practice; no matter what guise she puts on. It is in vain to assert the inviolability of the obligation of allegiance. It is vain to set up the plea of necessity, and to allege that she cannot exist without the impressment of HER seamen. The naked truth is, she comes, by her press-gangs, on board of our vessels, seizes OUR native as well as naturalized seamen, and drags them into her service. It is the case, then, of the assertion of an erroneous principle, and of a practice not conformable to the asserted principle—a principle which, if it were theoretically right, must be forever practically wrong

—a practice which can obtain countenance from no principle whatever, and to submit to which, on our part, would betray the most abject degradation. We are told, by gentlemen in the opposition, that government has not done all that was incumbent on it to do, to avoid just cause of complaint on the part of Great Britain; that in particular the certificates of protection, authorized by the act of 1796, are fraudulently used. Sir, government has done too much, in granting those paper protections. I can never think of them without being shocked. They resemble the passes which the master grants to his negro slave: 'Let the bearer, Mungo, pass and repass without molestation.' What do they imply? That Great Britain has a right to seize all who are not provided with them. From their very nature, they must be liable to abuse on both sides. If Great Britain desires a mark by which she can know her own subjects, let her give them an ear mark. The colors that float from the mast-head should be the credentials of our seamen. There is no safety to us, and the gentlemen have shown it, but in the rule that all who sail under the flag (not being enemies) are protected by the flag. It is impossible that this country should ever abandon the gallant tars, who have won for us such splendid trophies. Let me suppose that the genius of Columbia should visit one of them in his oppressor's prison, and attempt to reconcile him to his forlorn and wretched condition. She would say to him, in the language of gentlemen on the other side: 'Great Britain intends you no harm; she did not mean to impress you, but one of her own subjects; having taken you by mistake, I will remonstrate, and try to prevail upon her, by peaceable means, to release you; but I can not, my son, fight for you.' If he did not consider this mere mockery, the poor tar would address her judgment, and say: 'You owe me, my country, protection; I owe you, in return, obedience. I am no British subject; I am a native of old Massachusetts, where lived my aged father, my wife, my children. I have faithfully discharged my duty. Will you refuse to do yours?' Appealing to her passions he would continue: 'I lost this eye in fighting under Truxton, with the Insurgente; I got this scar before Tripoli; I broke this leg on board the Constitution, when the Guerriere struck.' If she remained still unmoved, he would break out in the accents of mingled distress and despair,

'Hard, hard is my fate! once I freedom enjoyed,
Was as happy as happy could be!
Oh! how hard is my fate, how galling these chains!'

I will not imagine the dreadful catastrophe to which he would be driven by an abandonment of him to his oppressor. It will not be, it cannot be that his country will refuse him protection."

Having shown by documentary evidence that there was nothing in the alleged repeal of the British orders in council that could constitute a ground of pacification, Mr. Clay proceeded to the consideration of other points of attack from the opposition. The focus of the fires that were poured in, he sent back his scorching flames on the assailants of the administration. When they averred that those most interested in impressment were most opposed to the war, he taunted this lack of humanity, and pointed to the sympathy of the West, to shame them for such an avowal. He could not believe they would so libel themselves, or that they had done justice to their constituents. Did not the latter sympathise with their western brethren, exposed to the Indian tomahawk? No matter whether an American citizen seeks subsistence amid the dangers of the deep, or draws it from the bowels of the earth, or from agriculture, or from the humblest occupations of mechanic life—whatever be his vocation—the rights of American freemen are sacred, and when assailed, all hearts should unite, and every arm be braced, to vindicate his cause. But the rights of seamen, who brave the hardships and perils of the deep, in bold adventure for the common good as well as for their own personal advantage, are especially sacred.

Continuing in this sarcastic vein, well provoked, Mr. Clay said:—

"When the administration was striving, by the operation of peaceful measures, to bring Great Britain back to a sense of justice, they were for old-fashioned war. And now they have got old-fashioned war, their sensibilities are cruelly shocked and all their sympathies lavished upon the harmless inhabitants of the adjoining provinces. What does a state of war present? The united energies of one people arrayed against the combined energies of another; a conflict in which each party aims to inflict all the injury it can, by sea and land, upon the territories, property, and citizens of the other—subject only to the rules of mitigated war, practised by civilised nations. The gentlemen would not touch the continental provinces of the enemy, nor, I presume, for the same reason, her possessions in the West Indies. The same humane spirit would spare the seamen and soldiers of the enemy. The sacred person of his majesty must not be attacked; for the learned gentlemen, on the other side, are quite familiar with the maxim that the king can do no wrong. Indeed, sir, I know of no person on whom we may make war, upon the principles of the honorable gentleman, but Mr. Stephen, the celebrated author of the orders in council, or the board of admiralty, who authorize and regulate the practice of impressment!

"The disasters of the war admonish us, we are told, of the necessity of terminating the contest. If our achievements by land have been less splendid than those of our intrepid seamen by water, it is not because the American soldier is less brave. On the one element, organization, discipline, and a thorough knowledge of their duties, exist, on the part of the officers and their men. On the other, almost everything is yet to be acquired. We have, however, the consolation that our country abounds with the richest materials, and that in no instance, when engaged in action, have our arms been tarnished. At Brownstown and at Queenstown, the valor of veterans was displayed, and acts of the noblest heroism were performed. It is true, that the disgrace of Detroit remains to be wiped off. That is a subject on which I cannot trust my feelings; it is not fitting I should speak. But this much I will say, it was an event which no human foresight could have anticipated, and for which the administration cannot be justly censured. It was the parent of all the misfortunes we have experienced on land. But for it, the Indian war would have been, in a great measure, prevented or terminated, the ascendancy on Lake Erie acquired, and the war pushed on, perhaps to Montreal. With the exception of that event, the war, even upon the land, has been attended by a series of the most brilliant exploits."

Fortunately for the country, the labors of Mr. Clay and

his coadjutors were not in vain. The navy, on the Atlantic and on the lakes, earned for itself an imperishable fame, and demonstrated to the full conviction of the American people —a most desirable result—the vast importance of sustaining and rendering efficient this arm of the national strength. The army nobly retrieved its character, and the war was ended in the full blaze of the victory of New Orleans, January 8, 1815.

The long period of obscure political travail which now followed, while peace and prosperity blessed our flourishing land, is of too complex, and comparatively unimportant a character to require that we should dilate upon its events. It is sufficient to state, that so soon as peace was firmly established, political agitation took the place, amid the restless elements of organization in which we were yet involved, of military action. And we were soon complicated amid the stormy ferment of United States Bank and Tariff discussions, the organization and purchase of new territory, the intrigues of the Burr conspiracy, and then in rapid succession, secession, and French spoliations, under the iron rule of Jackson, the settlement of Texas, the Missouri question, the compromise of Clay, the revolution and annexation of Texas, and finally, the war with Mexico, of which the events are of too recent date, to require that we should dwell upon, as illustratory of the now established prowess of "Sam." We will therefore return, in the conclusion of our volume, to a consideration of the incendiary work of the Jesuits, concerning whom we have spoken so much, toward the observation of whom the attention of our people was now sufficiently turned inwardly, to be able to give some necessary regard. Their machinations, which during all this period of external distraction, had been unceasing, had now begun to assume a formidable front. Strong men rose up in every part of the land to battle with them, and to develop the dangerous tendency.

To say nothing of the famous destruction of the convents, by the indignant mob of Baltimore, and the incessant denunciations which were thundered from the Protestant pulpits, and the press, the incessant efforts to exclude the Bible from the public schools, which was the avowed and settled policy of the Catholic clergy, headed by the insolent and presumptuous Irishman, Bishop Hughes, of New York (or rather

Cardinal Hughes, as he is now)! their conduct as citizens had not ceased to provoke the profoundest indignation, of the true children of "Sam," who at length determined to rid themselves of internal foes, who had proved themselves so ominous and so dangerous. The attempts to control education, and thereby corrupt Protestant children, had become too notorious to be further submitted to. Open war was accordingly declared against them, and the vermin horde of serfs and ignorant followers, with which they yearly swarmed our shores, overrunning the land like the plagues of Egypt, it was found necessary to check, as well as their patient and continued aggressions upon freedom of conscience, and rights of individuals.

It became necessary for the American-born sons of "Sam" to assert their right to the soil upon which they moved and breathed and had a being! Their attempts at political interference had become an outrage which no reasonable stretch of patience could be expected further to endure.

We have before repeated all that is contained in the subjoined extract, but as it proceeds to more particulars than we have yet given, we furnish it, with the context, to our readers.

The Jesuits, in consequence of their political intrigues, and their immoral principles and practices, were expelled successively by all the governments of Europe. "Wearied at length," says Dr. Duff, "and worn out by their unscrupulous rapacity and all-grasping ambition—their treachery and stratagems—their seductions and briberies—their intrigues and cabals—their laxation of public morals, and disturbance of social order—their fomenting of seditions, disloyalties and rebellions—their instigating massacres, and parricidal cruelties, and royal assassinations—the monks and courtiers, judges and civil magistrates, churches and public schools, princes and emperors of all nations in Europe, Asia, Africa, and America—all, all, successively united their efforts in sweeping them clean away, and causing their Institute to perish from off this earth, and from under these heavens." Finally, Pope Clement XIV. was constrained to suppress the order in July 1773—an act which cost him his life! For in a short period he was poisoned by these his implacable enemies. But in 1814, Pius VII. reinstated this dangerous order in all its privileges, and now it is spreading its baleful influence over the whole world. Their repeated expulsions from Roman Catholic governments, and their suppression by the Pope, afford sufficient evidence of their dangerous character. But let us look at a few unexceptional testimonies concerning the moral principles of the order.

In 1642, an assembly of Romish clergy at Nantes denounced a work by the Jesuit Bauni, "as calculated to encourage licentiousness and the corruption of manners; as violating natural equity, and the rights of man, and tolerating blasphemy, usury, simony, and many other enormous crimes, as offenses of no magnitude." In 1643, the Romish university of Paris declared themselves ready to prove that there is no article in religion which the Jesuits have not corrupted, and do not daily corrupt, by erroneous novelties; that the scholastic theology has been depraved by the dangerous opinions of their writers, who have had the approbation, or at least the connivance of the whole society; that Christian morality had become a body of problematical opinions, since their society had undertaken, by a general understanding, to accommodate it to the luxury of the age; that the laws of God had been sophisticated by their unheard of subtleties; that there was no longer any difference between vice and virtue; that by a base indulgence, they promised impunity to the most flagrant crime; that there was no conscience, however erroneous, which might not obtain peace, if it would confide in them; and that, in short, their doctrines, inimical to all order, had equally resisted the power of kings and the authority of the hierarchy; that if the light which God had placed in all reasonable minds, in order to show the distinction between purity and equity, were so far extinguished that such a pernicious theology could be universally received—in that case deserts and forests would be preferable to cities; and society with wild beasts, who have only their natural arms, would be better than with men who, in addition to the violence of their passions, would be instructed by this *doctrine* of *devils* to dissimulate and feign, and to counterfeit the characters of intimate friends, in order to destroy others with the greater impunity." In 1762, the Parliament of Popish France gave the following decision: "The court has ordained that the passages extracted from the books of one hundred and forty-seven Jesuit authors having been verified, a collected copy shall be presented to his Majesty, that he may be made acquainted with the wickedness of the doctrine constantly held by the Jesuits, from the institution of their society to the present moment, together with the approbation of their theologians, the permission of superiors and generals, and the praise of other members of the said society—a doctine authorizing robbery, lying, perjury, impurity—all passions and all crimes; inculcating homicide, parricide, and regicide; overturning religion, in order to substitute in her stead, superstition; and thereby sanctioning magic, blasphemy, irreligion, and idolatry. And his majesty shall be most humbly entreated to consider what results from instruction so pernicious."

With regard to the facilities afforded by Jesuit morality for violating the *seventh* commandment, I will only quote the language of Dr. Duff: "Hitherto I have been enabled to proceed with separate quotations to show how every commandment of the Decalogue may be violated with impunity. But there is one, as to which I must beg to be excused for not entering on it at all. It is the *seventh*. How to violate it in its letter and spirit—in thought, word, and deed—in every imaginable, and, apart from Jesuit imaginations, every unimaginable form—is pointed out in their writings, with a minuteness, a loathsomeness, and a pruriency, compared with which the most filthy passages in the grossest of the heathen poets and satirists bear the stamp and impress of relative refinement. It is, in fact, a bottomless abyss of obscenities, nudities, criminal liberties, and defiling turpitudes—an abyss from which I most gladly hasten away, as from one whose very brink is thickly fringed all around with pollution."

The time would fail me to do anything like justice to this dark subject. Let me earnestly request those who are willing to know the true character of the morality of the Jesuits, to read Dr. Duff's little work on this subject, and especially the Provincial Letters of Blaise Pascal, who was a Papist of the Jansenist order, and an elegant writer. From this work, says Dugald Stuart, "Voltaire, notwithstanding his strong prejudices against the author, dates the *fixation* of the French language; of which the same excellent judge has said, 'Moliere's best comedies do not excel them in wit, nor the compositions of Bossuet in sublimity.'"

And are these the men to whom American and even Christian parents are willing to intrust the training of their children? Are such men to have a principal agency in fixing in their minds those principles of action by which they are to be governed through life? It is too true, that many, unacquainted certainly with their principles, have placed their children under their withering influence. Far better would it be to commit their education to men who denounce all religion, than to those who, in the name of Jesus, teach men how to perpetrate the worst crimes without suffering from the lashings of a guilty conscience. How can such men teach mental and moral science? It may be said, the Jesuits do not, in this country, avow the abominable sentiments attributed to their order. True, they are not likely to destroy their influence by an avowal of principles which are held in abhorrence in this Protestant country; but their concealment, and their pretended sanctity, only enable them the more easily to destroy the morals of the youth committed to them. It is impossible that the influence of such men shall be other than most mischievous. It has been so from the origin of the order, and it will be so, while it has an existence.

Roman institutions will never teach HISTORY correctly. For more than twelve centuries past, the Pope has been a temporal prince, and has used his spiritual power for the purposes of self-aggrandizement, and the extension of the power, wealth and influence of Rome. He has been quite as busily engaged as his cotemporaries in the intrigues, civil combinations and alliances that form a considerable part of the history of the ages preceding the Reformation. The persecutions of the Pope and his clergy, too, constitute a prominent part of the history of the past. Who, for example, could write the history of Spain, of Portugal, and of Italy, without giving prominence to the horrid Inquisition, its officers, its dungeons, its tortures, and its *autos da fe?* Or who could write the history of that wonderful people, the Waldenses, without telling of the long-continued, exterminating persecutions of them, set on foot and kept up by the Popes and general councils? Or who will ever be able to write the history of our world in the sixteenth century, without making the Reformation a most prominent theme,

RESULT OF THE VIRGINIA ELECTION IN SPRING OF 1855—SAM BADLY BEATEN—HE LIVES TO CHASTIZE THEM.

and showing how the Pope and his clergy labored to crush the spirit of liberty which began then to manifest itself, and to claim the right to think and investigate, without being trammeled by the decrees of Popes and Councils of the dark ages? Who can write the history of England, without recording the persecutions of "Bloody Mary?"

And is it to be expected that the Roman clergy will allow these things to be presented in their true light, before the minds of the youth committed to their charge? Why, the history of the past must be, in the view of every man, an unanswerable refutation of Rome's pretended infallibility. No man can believe the claim well founded, who, before his prejudices are excited, reads the history of the doings of Rome.

It may be said, Protestants, too, may have reason for concealment; because the churches to which they severally belong have not always done right. I answer, Protestants do not claim infallibility for their churches. They may admit that they have erred, and they may record their errors as a lesson to the present, and to future generations. There is little or no temptation, therefore, to them to falsify history.

Roman schools will never teach the principles of civil and religious liberty, on which the free institutions of our country are founded. The fundamental principles of Popery, as I have proved in preceding lectures, are at war with liberty of conscience and the freedom of the press. Rome has ever been found the firm supporter of despotism, and the irreconcilable enemy of liberty. The Roman clergy of our country are, many of them, foreigners, who secured their education under the prevailing spirit of despotism; and those who have been educated in our own country have sat at the feet of foreigners, and imbibed their principles. They have certainly received the principles of Popery, and can not, therefore, hold the principles which are dear to every true American. In the organization of the Church of Rome there is nothing democratic; not one popular principle is admitted. In her legislation, and in the administration of her government, the voice of the people is never heard, directly or indirectly. The Pope is an absolute monarch, whose signature fixes upon the dogmas of the church the seal of infallibility; who dispenses those "heavenly treasures—Indulgences," to the people as to him seems good; and whose decisions are laws. The cardinals are his chosen counsellors, who aid him in carrying out the principles of despotism which characterize the system. The bishops of every grade are his lords, who meet in general council at his call, or who hold their provincial councils, and humbly submit their deliberations to be approved or condemned by "His Holiness." The priests are the humble servants of the Pope and his coadjutors, who move at his bidding. The inferior orders and the people hear the law, believe, and obey. How can persons, whose whole characters are molded under such despotism, teach the great principles of civil and religious liberty? How can it be expected that men who dare not say one word against the intolerance of Italy, Austria, Spain, Portugal, France, Mexico, and South America, will boldly and sincerely advocate the fundamental principles of our noble constitution, which guaranties to every American citizen the right to worship God according to the dictates of his own conscience? It would be just as reasonable to expect a true American to go to Austria, and, as a teacher of youth, to inculcate the despotic principles of that government; or to Spain, and to plead for the restoration of the Inquisition. Will individual priests and nuns fly in the face of their lord, Gregory XVI., and inculcate the principles of freedom of speech and of the press, denounced by him as contrary to the principles of the church, and ruinous in their consequences? Can men who, like Archbishop Eccleston, of Baltimore, denounce a convention, whose object is to promote the better observance of the Sabbath, as contrary to the Constitution of the United States, hold and teach the principles of that Constitution?

I have proved that the moral principles of Rome, and especially of the Jesuits, are rotten to the very core. Let me now say, that there exists not on earth a government so absolutely despotic as that of the order of Jesuits. "The grand principle," says Dr. Duff, "which pervades, animates, and cements into one firm and continuous chain the entire course of probationary exercises, is the reiterated, the incessant, the perpetual inculcation of a blind, implicit, unquestioning obedience to the monarchical general of the order, or to the superior acting in his stead or name. In every conceivable variety of shape and form his will is declared to be law, sole and supreme law—his will is virtually that of omnipotence. To him must the inclinations, the reason, and the conscience of every member be unconditionally surrendered." In the constitutions of the order, which, after being long concealed, were dragged to light in France, in 1761, the novice is exhorted to "devote himself to the service of God, leaving the care of all other things to his superior, *who doubtless holds the place of Christ our Lord.*" Again, novices are to "desire with perfect concurrence to be guided by them (their superiors), and not wishing to be led by their own judgment, except it agrees with that of those who are to them *instead of Christ our Lord.*" Again—"It is especially conducive to advancement, nay, even necessary, that all yield themselves to perfect obedience, regarding the superior as Christ the Lord, and submitting to him with inward reverence and affection. Let them obey, not only in the outward performance of what he enjoins, entirely, promptly, resolutely, and with all due humility, without excuses or murmurs, even though he order things hard to be done, and repugnant to their own sense; but let them also strive to acquire perfect resignation and denial of their own will and judgment to that which the superior wills and judges (where sin is not perceived)—the will and judgment of the superior being set before them as the rule of their will and judgment." Once more—"Let every one persuade himself that they who live under obedience should permit themselves to be moved and directed, under divine Providence, by their superiors, *just as if they were a corpse, which allows itself to be moved and handled in any way;* or as the staff of an old man, which serves him wherever or in whatever thing he who holds it in his hand pleases to use it"—"persuading themselves that everything is just, suppressing every repugnant thought and judgment of their own in a certain obedience," etc. And lest any one might suppose, says Dr. Duff, that the *formal* introduction of any apparently exceptionary clauses—non-obligation of committing sin by way of obedience—formed any real or substantial limitation, it is expressly added, by way of explanation, that the constitution of the society does not "involve an obligation to commit sin, mortal or venial, unless the superior command them in the name of the Lord Jesus Christ, or in virtue of holy obedience; which shall be done in those cases or persons, wherein it shall be judged that it shall greatly conduce to the particular good of each, or to the general advantage."

The Romish king of Portugal, in a manifesto addressed to his bishops in 1759, gives the following description of the principles of the Jesuits. "In order to form the union, the consistency, and the strength of the Society, there should be a government not only monarchical, but so sovereign, so absolute, so despotic, that even the Provincials themselves should not have it in their power, by any act of theirs, to resist or retard the execution of the orders of the General. By this legislative, inviolable, and despotic power—by the profound devotedness of the subjects of this Company to mysterious laws with which they are not themselves acquainted—by the blind and passive obedience by which they are compelled to execute, without hesitation or reply, whatever their superiors command—this Society is at once become the most consolidated and powerful body, and, at the same time, the greatest and most enormous of abuses, to which there is an urgent necessity that the Church and State should apply the most prompt and efficacious remedy."

Robertson gives the following account of the organization and principles of the Order. "But Loyola, full of the ideas of implicit obedience, which he had derived from his military profession, appointed that the government of his Order should be purely monarchical. A general, chosen for life by deputies from the several provinces, possessed power that was supreme and independent, extending to every person, and to every case. He, by his sole authority, nominated provincials, rectors, and every other officer employed in the government of the Society, and could remove them at pleasure. In him was vested the sovereign administration of the revenues and funds of the Order. Every member belonging to it was at his disposal; and by his uncontrolable mandate, he could impose on them any task, or employ them in what service soever he pleased. To his commands they were required not only to yield outward obedience, but to resign up to him the inclinations of their own wills, and the sentiments of their own understandings. They were to listen to his injunctions, as if they had been uttered by Christ himself. Under his direction they were to be mere passive instruments, like clay in the hands of the potter; or, like dead carcasses, incapable of resistance. Such a singular form of policy could not fail to impress its character on all the members of the Order, and to give a peculiar force to all its operations. *There is not in the annals of mankind, any example of such perfect despotism, exercised not only over monks shut up in the cells of a convent, but over men dispersed among all the nations of the earth.*"* Even Reeve, the Romish historian, while zealously defending the Jesuits, states that "their form of government was monarchical, vested in a general chosen by the Body, for life;" and that "prompt obedience, when there appeared no sin in the execution, *was their characteristic virtue.*"† We have already seen how easily they perform, and teach others to perform, the most atrocious acts, without regarding themselves as sinning.

Are these the men by whose instructions the characters of American youth are to be formed? Are they to inspire them with the spirit of liberty, and prepare them to be the worthy descendants of the patriots of '76? Will they teach them, while themselves under the most absolute of all despotism, to prize and preserve the free institutions of our happy country?

It is a fact—an important fact, that Roman schools are not designed to promote thorough education, but to make converts to popery, and to enrich the clergy and the Church. The Roman clergy are aware that their cause has nothing to gain by that free spirit of free inquiry generated by a thorough education. The man who has been accustomed to inquire into reasons and evidences on all other subjects, will not readily found his religious faith upon the *dicta* of the clergy. He will desire to be able to give a reason for the hope that is in him.

But if they are indeed the ardent friends of education, why do they, to so great an extent, neglect those countries where their faith is established? With great zeal, and at great expense, they are establishing in our country, colleges and schools of every grade, for the education of both males and females. Why is not equal zeal manifested in popular education in Italy, Spain, Portugal, Mexico, and South

* Charles V., Book vi, pp. 288, 289. † Hist. of Ch., vol. ii, p. 257.

America? It is a notorious fact, that in all these countries the masses of the people are uneducated and are grossly ignorant. We know that the people of Mexico, where popery has prevailed for ages past, are to this day semi-savages, possessing neither intelligence nor virtue sufficient to sustain a free government. There is not in Mexico one literary institution of a high character; and although it is very common to find the lower classes of the people able to read, there are no such institutions for general education as the Roman clergy are so zealous in establishing in our country. Waddy Thompson, Esq., says: "The only institution of any character in the city (of Mexico) is the Mineria—the College of Mines, as its name implies. * * * The professorships are very few, chiefly connected with physical science, and the chairs filled by persons of extremely moderate attainments. The philosophical apparatus is altogether contemptible. * * The University, which was founded in 1531, is in a declining condition, if indeed it is not already extinct. There are some other colleges as they are called, but they are scarcely respectable primary schools."* The same writer says, "There are scarcely any of those charitable institutions to which we are accustomed in all our principal cities. There are more of these, I have no doubt, in either of the cities of Boston or Philadelphia than in Mexico." How shall we account for the great zeal of the Roman clergy and of their allies in Europe, for establishing schools and benevolent institutions in this enlightened country, and their entire indifference to these same things in Mexico and other Romish countries? It would not even be necessary to send to Europe, as do the clergy of the United States, for funds; for the Roman clergy of Mexico possess a large proportion of all the wealth of that country. "I have heard intelligent men express the opinion," says Thompson, "that *one-fourth* of the property of the country is in the hands of the priesthood; and, instead of diminishing, is continually increasing." †

The truth is, it is not the zeal of the Roman clergy in the cause of general education, which causes them to establish in our country so many schools. But there is among us a public sentiment in favor of education. Parents will educate

---

* Recollections of Mexico, pp. 147, 148. † Ibid, p. 41.

their children, and if they be educated by Protestant teachers, few of them will ever embrace popery. This the clergy well understand. Moreover, the great principles of the Reformation are so generally received—it is so universally believed that the Scriptures are the only infallible guide in religious faith, that the clergy find it extremely difficult to make converts of adults, by preaching. Hence, their great anxiety to monopolize, as far as possible, the education of our youth.

I have said the design of Roman schools is not to give a thorough education. I have not had the opportunity of forming a judgment of those established in this city; but I had, during *nine* years, a fair opportunity of ascertaining the literary character of their most celebrated schools in Kentucky. I have repeatedly received pupils from their nunneries, while myself conducting a female institution; and in every instance their minds had been injured rather than improved. I have attended their examinations, and found them, notwithstanding the special previous preparation, very superficial. I have known young men who were impatient to finish their literary course, leave other colleges and go to St. Joseph's, at Bardstown, because they could graduate there at least twelve months sooner. Some years since, two young men, after taking the course, and one of them receiving his diploma at that institution, went to an eastern college; and the young graduate was not able to enter, without first studying for several months under a tutor! Another fact it may be worth while to record. Several years ago, I had occasion, as the editor of a weekly paper, to make some remarks not very favorable to the literary character of St. Joseph's college. Those remarks were brought before a literary society of that institution; whereupon several resolutions intended to be offensive were passed, and sent to me with a request to publish them. The document which was drawn up by a committee, one of whom had graduated, and others received their diplomas a few weeks afterward, was introduced, as a paper emanating from a literary society should be, with a Latin motto, which read as follows:

"Ii qui vivunt dominibus vitreis, caveunt quo modo lapides mittere."

To this Latin, which is not Latin, and to the resolutions

passed, which were equally defective, both in orthography and syntax, I referred the public, for evidence conclusive that I had not undervalued the literary merits of the college. The affair caused some amusement in the town and much excitement in the college.

The truth is, the Roman clergy of this country have, by much boasting, gained a reputation for learning, which generally they do not deserve. I know of no denomination of professing Christians, whose clergy are educated men, that does not possess a larger share both of talent and learning.

But whatever may be the defects of Roman institutions, they are certainly adapted admirably to accomplish one chief object for which they are established, viz: *to make converts to popery.* I have said that children and youth can never be very successfully taught by instructors who fail to secure their respect and affection. The great pretensions of Roman instructors to superior knowledge, is adapted to secure the former, and their special kindness to the children of Protestants, whose conversion they anxiously seek, is extremely likely to accomplish the latter. Young girls, far from their parents and friends, naturally become strongly attached to the nuns, who, never losing sight of the great object—their conversion—lavish kindness upon them; and youth of every class, inexperienced and unsuspecting, readily become strongly attached to their kind instructors. How natural for them to conclude that they are the best people in the world, and that their religion has made them so; and, of course, that their religion is the best in the world. How natural that they should set down all that is said against popery as misrepresentation and slander, and that they should feel indignant at those who oppose it, and who seem to them to persecute their respected and beloved teachers. In this state of mind, who does not see that they are already more than half converted?

And then there is in the priests and nuns such an appearance of sanctity. To those unacquainted with true religion there was something very imposing in the broad phylacteries of the ancient Pharisees, in their frequent fasts, their many ablutions, their tithing of mint, anise, and cummin, and the like. There is even a greater show of sanctity in our priests and nuns. Will your children see through all this show of piety, and reject it? If they do, as some more advanced in years may, is there no reason to fear that they will feel a contempt for all religion, and become confirmed infidels?

But the Romanists claim for their religion a venerable antiquity; and they have a thousand stories to tell of saints, and miracles, and the like, well adapted to excite the minds of youth, and make lasting impressions upon them. Why, you may tell your children stories of ghosts and apparitions, till they will be afraid to sleep alone in a dark room. There is something in human nature that lays strong hold of such things; and the impressions made by them are not readily eradicated. Then, at every turn, the images of those wonder-working saints are presented before the eyes of the pupils in Roman schools; and they see the devout priests and nuns, with awful solemnity, kneeling before them in prayer. Can all this, with all the pomp and show of Roman worship, be constantly witnessed by the susceptible minds of youth, without making a deep impression?

Another fact is worthy of special consideration, viz: the children and youth placed in Roman schools, are required to attend and assist at all the public religious exercises. In the prospectus of one of their female institutions, I find the following: "Pupils of every religious denomination are admitted into the institution. No improper influence is ever to be used to bias the religious principles of the young ladies, nor will any of the scholars be allowed to embrace the Catholic religion, without a written or verbal permission from their parents. *For the sake of order, all the boarders are required to observe the general regulations of exterior worship.*"* The reader will please mark the language here employed. The conductors of this institution do not say that they will exert *no influence* to bias the religious opinions of their pupils, but "NO IMPROPER influence" is to be used. What kind of influence do they regard as improper? On this point they are silent; and we may content ourselves with the assurance they have given, that they will use no influence for the conversion of Protestant children, which they regard as improper! But they assure the public that they will not allow any of their pupils to become Roman Catholics, without permission

* Catholic Almanac for 1846, p. 96.

from their parents. A poor consolation this, when they have filled the minds of children with their superstitions, and excited their strongest prejudices against the faith of their parents. Mark the fact, however, that "for the sake of order, all the boarders are required to observe the general regulations of exterior worship,"—to unite in their prayers and devotions.

In the prospectus of St. Gabriel's College, Vincennes, Ia., we find a similar regulation: "There is no interference whatever, with the religious belief of the pupils; but for the sake of order, they are expected to comply with the external forms of Catholic worship, which is the religion professed by the members of this college." In the prospectus of St. Mary's Female Academy, it is stated, that the "members of the Protestant denominations are only required to assist with propriety and respect at the public exercises of the Catholic religion."* Such are the regulations in all Roman schools, as far as my information extends. In view of these regulations I have two remarks to make:

1st. Every intelligent Protestant believes a considerable part of the religious worship of Roman Catholics to be unscriptural and idolatrous; for example, the worship of the consecrated wafer, the worship of saints and angels, praying before images, and the like. No enlightened and conscientious Protestant could be induced to participate in such worship, even externally. The three Hebrews preferred being thrown into the fiery furnace, to conforming externally to the worship ordained by Nebuchadnezzar. Primitive Christians preferred death to throwing a handful of incense on a pagan altar. What right, then, I emphatically ask, have Protestant parents to place their children where they are obliged, at least externally, to commit idolatry? What right have they to compel their children to do what they themselves could not, and would not do? What right have they to compel them to sin against God? Is this the way to train them up in the nurture and admonition of the Lord? I appeal to those parents who do not profess to be religious, but who do not believe the Roman worship to be Scriptural. Will they not admit, that if there is any one thing in which

* Catholic Almanac for 1846, p. 118–125.

sincerity should be preserved, and in which our external conduct should accord with the convictions of the mind, the worship of God is that thing? Why, then, will you compel your children to conform to religious worship which you feel constrained to tell them is not true, and not right? Can such a course be adopted without serious injury to the moral principles of children? Can parents who place their children under such influences, wonder if they become decided Papists?

2d. The children of Protestants are not only compelled to unite in religious worship which is unscriptural and idolatrous, but they are obliged to hear all that may be said against the religion of the Bible, and in favor of Romanism—all the gross misrepresentations of the Reformers and the Reformation, and all the wonderful stories about saints and ghosts, which may be introduced at the religious services they attend. Are their minds sufficiently stored with religious instruction to resist all this? Is there no danger that convictions will be fastened on their minds that can never be eradicated? The Sabbath, too, which their parents have taught them to remember to keep it holy, is now to be spent in idolatrous worship, and in hearing the worst religious errors plausibly set forth and defended. I know not how Protestant parents, who have any regard for their own religious obligations, or for the moral and religious training of their children, can place them in the midst of such influences. I can account for their conduct only by supposing them unacquainted with the real character of Roman institutions.

Another important fact which I must not omit to mention, is this: While every possible influence is thrown around the children of Protestants to convert them to Popery, they are as carefully guarded against every influence that might serve to strengthen early impressions in favor of the religion of their parents. They are, to a great extent, cut off from all intercourse with Protestants; and they are not permitted to have a single book which has not been approved by the president or superior. In the regulations of Georgetown College, District of Columbia, I find the following: "All books, of whatever kind, must, however, be submitted to the supervision of the prefect of the schools, without whose permission none will be allowed circulation in the college."* In Mount St. Mary's College, near Emmitsburg, "No books are allowed to circulate among the students which have not received the president's approval."† In the Academy of the Ursuline Nuns, the Prospectus says: "The scholars will not be permitted to bring any books, except such as are used in the school, and books of devotion."‡ Among the rules of St. John's college, I find the following: "No books will be allowed circulation among the students, which have not been previously submitted to the supervision and received the approval of either the president of the college, or the prefect of studies."§

The children of Protestants, you perceive, especially if they are boarders, are wholly under the influence of Romanism. Parents can not put in their hands such religious books as they desire them to read, such, for example, as Doddridge's Rise and Progress of Religion in the Soul, Baxter's Saint's Rest, D'Aubigne's History of the Reformation. Such books could never receive the approbation of presiding officers in those schools. And it is extremely questionable whether the Bible is not a prohibited book. Certainly the Protestant Bible is. Some years ago, Dr. Henry Riley, a most excellent man, with whom I am well acquainted, who had been a student in Georgetown College, published a particular account of his stay in that institution, and of his conversion to Popery. Among other things, he stated the following facts: "Previous to my leaving home, my mother (she was a Presbyterian) gave me a small Bible, with the hope that I would make good use of it. But her hopes were all in vain—for on reaching the college our trunks were sujected to rigid inspection, and everything removed beyond our control, except such books or things as they in their wisdom saw fit to entrust us with. Several of my books, I never afterward saw—what became of them is better known to others than to me. Fathers Grassie, Kohlman, McElroy, etc., can, no doubt, give some account of them. Restitution of *unlawfully borrowed* property is enjoined by these spiritual fathers, on those who in their confessions acknowledge the commission of such a crime. * * But it may be said, the books were of a demoralizing

* Catholic Almanac for 1846, p. 77. †Ibid., p. 78. ‡Ibid., p. 97. §Ibid., p. 111.

character. They were such as a solicitous parent had given me, and one was what God had given to a ruined world for its salvation. I occasionally saw one of these books in the hands of a novice (candidate for Holy orders, or rather for full admission into the society), and though I recognized it as mine, I dared not whisper that it was." Instead of the books which a pious mother had put in the hands of her son, he says, "prayer-books, catechisms, etc., were put into my hands; and it was but a short time before I avowed myself a decided, determined Catholic. Ere long, he tells us, he "had fully imbibed the sentiments which the officers of the college so industriously endeavored to impress on the minds of all, that out of the pale of the Catholic church, there is *no possible salvation*, and my purpose now was *fully* to become a priest—a thorough Jesuit." Dr. Riley was greatly troubled at the thought that his parents were Protestants; but so completely infatuated was he, that he felt confident of being able at once to convince them of the truth of his new creed, when he should return home. He says, "It was my purpose, however, notwithstanding any opposition I might meet with, to remain firm in my determination to live, to labor, and to die, a Jesuit, for I had been taught not to heed the admonitions and the opposition of parents and friends in the prosecution of so good a cause." He mentions several others, sons, of Protestants, who, like himself, soon became confirmed Papists.

The officers of Roman schools, it is possible, may sometimes deem it wise to allow the child of Protestant parents to retain a Bible; but are young persons likely to read that sacred book, when they know the opposition of their teachers, and that perseverance in such a course will necessarily expose them to ridicule and reproach, if not to unkind treatment?

To show what reliance is to be placed on the pledges of Roman institutions not to interfere with the religious opinions of Protestant children, I must state another fact. A Protestant lady who resided in one of the southern States, several years ago, sent her adopted son to St. Mary's college, in Kentucky, an institution under the care of the Jesuits. About twelve months after, she visited her son, and was surprised and exceedingly troubled when she ascertained that he had been already received into the Romish church. She immediately removed him from the college, and placed him under my care. I afterwards published the facts as she stated them to me. The President of St. Joseph's college, situated at Bardstown, made a publication in reply, in which he asserted that the boy's mother was a Roman Catholic, whose dying request to his adopted mother was to have him trained in that faith; that he had learned this from the adopted mother herself; and that her son, a gentleman of high standing, had so directed the professors of St. Mary's college; and he even obtained from one of those Jesuits a certificate to this effect. Providentially it so happened, that whilst the subject was exciting public attention, the gentleman who was said to have directed the boy to be taught in the Romish faith, reached the town, (Bardstown, Kentucky,) and immediately gave me a certificate that he had given no such direction; that the boy's mother was not known to have been a Roman Catholic, and had never made such a request as the President of St. Joseph's had pretended.* Thus did those Reverend gentlemen abuse the confidence placed in them, and then fabricate stories to shield themselves from merited reproach. Many similar facts might be stated, but it is unnecessary. It is a fact that the schools established in our country are regarded as a most important part of that machinery by which the Roman clergy hope to promote and establish their faith. Will they not, then, do their utmost to bring about the desired result? They may not, in all cases make direct efforts to convince the children of Protestants that the religion of their parents is heresy; for often they will see that indirect influences are likely to be the most effectual.

Some years ago, Bishop Flaget, of Bardstown, Kentucky, wrote to his friends in Europe, as follows: "Still, had I treasures at my disposal, I would multiply colleges and schools for girls and boys; I would consolidate all these establishments, by annexing to them lands or annual rents; I would build hospitals and public houses; in a word I would compel all my Kentuckians to admire and love a religion so

---

* These facts, and others connected with the case, were published in the *Western Protestant*, then edited by the author of these lectures, in Bardstown, Kentucky, in the summer of 1836. The *Protestant* was the first paper in the West, so far as the editor is informed, devoted to the Romish controversy.

benevolent and generous, *and perhaps I should finish by converting them.*" The editor of the Annals of the Association for the Propagation of the Faith, comments as follows on Bishop Flaget's communication: "Mgr. Flaget has established in his diocese many convents of nuns, devoted to the education of young females. These establishments do wonderful good. Catholics and Protestants are admitted indiscriminately. The latter, after having finished their education, return to the bosom of their families, full of esteem and veneration for their instructresses. They are ever ready to refute the calumnies which the jealousy of heretics loves to spread against the religious communities; *and often, when they have no longer the opposition of their relations to fear, they embrace the Catholic religion.*" In the publications made by the Roman clergy in this country, concerning these schools, Protestant parents are assured that no influence will be exerted on the minds of their children, to change their religious sentiments, or to convert them to Popery. But in their communications to their patrons in Europe, they boast of the number of Protestant children converted, who, so soon as they can do so, openly embrace the Romish faith. Representations so contradictory can never be reconciled with truth and candor; and none but a corrupt system of religion would seek to sustain itself by such means.

But even if the conductors of Roman schools should strictly regard their pledge not to interfere with the religious sentiments of Protestant children, it would still be most unsafe to commit to them their education. They can not give such an education as American parents should desire their children to have; and the various influences brought to bear upon them, directly or indirectly, would still secure the conversion of many of them to Popery. It will be found, on examination, that the large proportion of the youth educated in Roman schools, if they are not decided converts, are decidedly prejudiced in favor of their teachers and of their religious faith. There are in the minds of all of us, pleasing and hallowed recollections connected with our school-boy days; and it is most unwise in parents to allow those pleasing recollections to be associated with religious error and a loose morality.

The very best that Protestant parents hope for their children, when placed in Roman schools, is, that they will not be seriously injured as to their moral and religious principles. They do not expect them to receive correct religious instruction. But what right have parents to place their children beyond the reach of scriptural instruction and Christian influence, during that most interesting period of life when the deepest and most permanent impressions are made upon them? What right have they to expose them to dangers which more mature minds often fail to resist? When they pray for themselves, "Lead us not into temptation," what kind of a prayer do they offer for their children whom they have placed in Roman schools?

I can not close this lecture without saying something particularly concerning those *nunneries* in which so many Protestant children are educated. The nuns all take the vow of *poverty, chastity*, and *obedience.* However rich the institution with which they are connected, they possess nothing. Separated from friends and relatives, they must yield the most implicit obedience to their superiors. They are the best *slaves* in the world. Their vows are more potent than the legal claims of slaveholders; and, as they are taught to believe that sufferings endured in this life will shorten their stay in the fires of purgatory, they deny themselves the comforts of life, and endure the greatest hardships most willingly. Or, if they discover their error, and deplore the folly committed in taking such vows upon them, there is no escape from their gloomy prison. It is so disreputable in the view of Romanists to return to the world, that they prefer suffering even unto death, to such a course.

Nunneries are *money-making* establishments. Some of the nuns are employed as teachers; some are house and kitchen servants; and some labor in the fields! In Kentucky they have been seen in the harvest fields, driving the ox-cart, making a fire for the priest, saddling his horse, and the like. All their labors are performed, as already intimated, without hope of pecuniary compensation. There is a nunnery near Bardstown, Kentucky, located on a farm of several hundred acres, the number of whose female boarders has averaged from one hundred to one hundred and fifty. The charges for each, including *extras*, would not be less than one hundred and fifty dollars. The annual income of the institution is not less than *fifteen thousand dollars.* The outlay is not very considerable, since their provisions are mainly raised on the farm. If I were to set down the clear annual profit of the institution at *ten thousand dollars,* I should probably be below the mark. Almost the whole of this money is earned by the nuns; but no part of it goes to them. Their coarse fare and clothing is all they receive. The clergy are enriched by the degradation of these poor women, whom they have succeeded in deluding. I know not how others may feel, but it appears to me that every Christian and every American should set his face against those prisons, where females are incarcerated, and degraded from the sphere they are destined to fill.

But what is the real character of the nunneries of our country? Are they as pure in morals as they should be? Who knows? The nuns are unmarried females. Unmarried men have access to those establishments at all times; and the inmates are expected to confess all their sins to them. The affairs of the institution are concealed from the eye of the public. Most of the nuns are not known, perhaps, to a human being within hundreds of miles of them. Some may be removed to a distance, and others take their places, and the change may never be known to the community in which the nunnery is located. There is every possible facility for concealing vices which can scarcely be committed by others without detection. It is a fact, admitted even by Roman writers, that multitudes of the priests and bishops, and even some of the popes have disregarded their vow of chastity. It is admitted, as I proved in a preceding lecture, that many, very many priests, whilst hearing confessions, have fallen into gross vice and ruined their penitents. It is notorious, that in other countries, vice has found its way into nunneries; and they have become corrupt. What evidence, then, have we, that those secret establishments among us are what they should be? Suppose a number of unmarried Protestant ministers should conclude to establish institutions of a similar character, and should collect from all quarters unmarried females, secluded from public view; would they be tolerated in such a course? And suppose that some of those women should live in their houses with them, as they do in the houses of the Roman bishops—houses not by any means so public as those of other men, but removed from the street, and surrounded by a high wall—what would be thought of such men? And what right have the Roman clergy to claim public confidence, when pursuing a course that would be considered most disreputable in other men of equal claims to confidence?

I must here take leave to give you a very brief history of a case in point. Some twelve years ago, a nun, in Kentucky, left the institution with which she was connected, and returned to her father's house, alleging as her reason the improper conduct of the presiding priest toward her. Her father and relatives were ignorant and bigoted Papists. They regarded her as guilty of a horrid crime in preferring charges against one of the *holy priesthood;* and she was driven from home with threats of violence. She went to the house of a Baptist minister, a near neighbor, to whom she told her story. The report soon spread through the neighborhood, that this woman was charging the priest with immorality. A large proportion of the people were Papists, and, of course, there arose much excitement against her. She remained a short time in the neighborhood, and was suddenly missing; and from that day to this she has never been heard of!

The present speaker was then editing a paper in Bardstown, and he published the facts in the case. A suit for libel was instituted against him by the President of St. Joseph's College, in behalf of the priest implicated in the affair. The damages were laid at *ten thousand dollars.* The suit was pending twelve months. The Roman clergy of Kentucky fully identified themselves with the suit. The weight of all the nunneries in that region, of which there were several, was thrown into the scales. Eminent lawyers were employed on both sides. The priests had every motive to explain the mysterious absence of the nun, and to produce her before the public. The court decided that the defendant was bound to prove the actual guilt of the priest, and that the missing nun was the only competent witness in plea of justification. Much testimony was taken, and many facts not previously published were proved. The verdict of the jury gave the priest damages to the amount of ONE CENT! The character of the jurymen was assailed by some of the friends of the priests, or by the priests in disguise. In consequence of which, *nine* of them (two others resided at a distance) made a publication, from which I read the following: "He [the writer of the charges against them] again states that one of the most intelligent of the jury has stated publicly, since the trial, that he was for damages, or heavy damages. If there was any such juror on that jury, he kept his opinion to himself—he did not make it known to the other jurors, as he ought to have done. We do affirm that *one cent* was the highest damages named by any one on that jury in our hearing; and we further state, that every one of the jury, who was for finding a verdict for the plaintiff [the priest], did state that he would glory in making each one pay his own costs, if it were in his power to do so. And we also state, that under all the circumstances, but for the instructions of the court, we would have been compelled to find a verdict for the defendant" [Rice]. The testimony was taken down at the time, signed by the court, and filed among the records of the Nelson County Circuit Court. I immediately published in the *Western Protestant*, and afterwards in a small volume, a full account of the trial, with the testimony in the case. And it is a fact, that the priests, though they instituted suit professedly for the purpose of obtaining the testimony and laying it before the public, never have published one line of it, nor even the verdict rendered! The public would have remained ignorant of the verdict, but for the Protestant press.

I have given this brief history of the only law-suit in which I was ever involved, because it is the only suit of the kind which has occurred in our country; because it shows the estimation in which the character of a priest and his nunnery were held, where they were well known, where the legal testimony was fully heard, and where the most powerful influences were brought to bear by the bishop and his clergy to sustain the suit.

The fate of MILLY MCPHERSON, the lost nun, is still involved in profound mystery. Many believe, and will believe, that she was murdered to prevent further exposures of the priests and nunneries!

Prudent parents will pause and consider, before they place their daughters in Roman nunneries to be educated. It can not be, that nuns, the most superstitious of all people, who never think for themselves, are the persons to discipline the minds of female youth to vigorous and independent thinking. It will be found, I apprehend, that the education given in nunneries is far more ornamental than solid. But if they were what they are not, the best literary institutions in the land, they are not the places for the daughters of Protestant parents. I have in my possession other evidences most conclusive, that the nunneries of our country are not all pure. Some years ago, a Roman priest, who, in consequence of some difficulty with his bishop, had ceased to officiate, though not deposed, placed in my hands several letters of nuns, one addressed to himself, and the others to another priest, which leave no room to doubt that corruption had found its way into the nunnery with which they were connected. As this nunnery had connected with it a female school to which Protestant parents were sending their daughters, I deemed it my duty to publish them, which I did in the *Western Protestant.* The Roman clergy preserved a profound silence, never publishing one word by way of vindication.

In the letter addressed to the priest who placed it in my hands, the nun says: "I did not see F. David (the bishop) until the next Tuesday after we got home. I went then to speak to him. He told me he had received my letters in due time, but that I had not opened any secret to him whatever—that he knew these things long before, and that he was not at all astonished at anything that had happened, from the experience of former years. I do not mention these things to excuse my own faults; neither have I any reason to regret the manifestations I then made, though at the time so repugnant to my feelings. * * * Then let me entreat you, as a friend to virtue, not to let your mind be prejudiced by what is past with regard to the little community now under your pastoral care. [This priest had just taken charge of the nunnery.] If some have had the misfortune to be implicated by them, all have not, to my certain knowledge," etc. Another nun addresses her priest in the following style:—"Oh! do come and see your *poor sacred dog*—if only to spend a few hours with her. Pray much for your *poor sacred dog,* and favor her with a few lines." This same nun after her priest had turned with scorn and contempt from her, addressed him another letter, in which she says: "Since you have found out the unknown blessing of my being removed from this place, I shall not give way to excessive grief on the occasion. * * * I am very far from wishing to stay with a confessor, that avails himself of every provocation, real or imaginary, to express his aversion to my person, and his regret for my coming back. If I stay it will be through compulsion. * * * If I wished the appellation of *wife, sweetheart*, or *lovely dear*, as you told me I did, I certainly would take some means to gain them."

I take no pleasure in making such developments as these; but nunneries are public institutions, where Protestant parents are invited to educate their daughters; and it is the solemn duty of those who know something of their true character, to lift a warning voice. There may, possibly, be nunneries free from such scandals; but there is so much concealment about them, that it is impossible for the public to know them. And those who know any thing of human nature, we would think, would never confide in them.

In conclusion, I must express my deep conviction, that Protestant denominations have committed one capital error in the important matter of education. They have established and endowed colleges for boys and young men; *but they have left female education almost wholly dependent upon individual enterprise.* The consequence has been, and is, that their female schools have been generally short-lived. Teachers, generally, have not funds to erect suitable buildings, furnish apparatus, and place schools on a solid foundation. There have, therefore, been constant efforts and constant failures; and the public, losing confidence in Protestant schools, have turned to those permanently established by Papists.

And why should such a difference be made in providing for the education of the two sexes? Is female education less important, either to Church or State? It is not. The earliest and the deepest moral impressions ever made on the mind by human instrumentality are those made by mothers. If the mother of a family be an ignorant, sluttish woman, it matters not what is the character of the father, *the family is ruined.* If the mother be a Roman Catholic, the children will not probably be Protestants.

I should like to say much more on this important subject; but I have already occupied much of your time. Allow me to say, that the Roman clergy understand this subject. They have seen the error of Protestants; and they have multiplied female institutions in every part of the country. They are far more numerous than their colleges and schools for boys. I trust the day is at hand when Protestants generally, will awake to the incalculable importance of this subject, and will establish permanent female institutions of a proper character, and so endowed, as to place a good education within the reach of the poor as well as the rich. Then, and not until then, will Protestant American females be freed from the direful influence of Papacy.

But "Sam" is again awake; and the great God who has triumphantly guided his steps thus far, from infancy to manhood's prime, will, no doubt, continue to direct him in the future, and save our Union from the certain ruin and decay, inevitably consequent upon the sway and misrule of despotic Popery.

May God direct us, and save us from such a fate. AMEN.

www.ingramcontent.com/pod-product-compliance
Lightning Source LLC
LaVergne TN
LVHW021231110826
845150LV00002B/299